SIGNAL TO SYNTAX:
Bootstrapping From Speech to Grammar in Early Acquisition

SIGNAL TO SYNTAX:
Bootstrapping From Speech to Grammar in Early Acquisition

Edited by

James L. Morgan
Katherine Demuth
Brown University

 LAWRENCE ERLBAUM ASSOCIATES, PUBLISHERS

1996   Mahwah, NJ

Lawrence Erlbaum Associates
10 Industrial Avenue
Mahwah, NJ 07430

Library of Congress Cataloging-in-Publication Data

Signal to syntax : bootstrapping from speech to grammar in early
    acquisition / edited by James L. Morgan & Katherine Demuth.
        p. cm.
    Papers presented at a conference held Feb. 19–21, 1993, Brown
University, Providence, R.I.
    Includes bibliographical references and indexes.
    ISBN 0-8058-1265-2. — ISBN 0-8058-1266-0 (pbk.)
    1. Language acquisition—congresses. I. Morgan, James L. II.
Demuth, Katherine.
P118.S4574 1996
401'.93—dc20   95-40890
                                                             CIP

Books published by Lawrence Erlbaum Associates are printed on
acid-free paper, and their bindings are chosen for strength and durability.

Printed in the United States of America
10 9 8 7 6 5 4 3 2 1

Contents

PART V: SPEECH AND THE ACQUISITION OF LANGUAGE

First Authors

Richard Aslin
Department of Psychology
Meliora Hall
University of Rochester
Rochester, NY 14627
aslin@cvs.rochester.edu

Nan Bernstein Ratner
Dept. of Hearing & Speech Sci.
University of Maryland
College Park, MD 20742
nratner@bss1.umd.edu

Anne Cutler
Max-Planck-Institut für
   Psycholinguistik
Wundtlaan 1
6525 XD Nijmegen
The Netherlands
anne@mpi.nl

Katherine Demuth
Cognitive & Linguistic Sciences
Brown University
Box 1978
Providence, RI 02912
katherine_demuth@brown.edu

Elan Dresher
Department of Linguistics
University of Toronto
Toronto, Ontario
dresher@epas.utoronto.ca

Catharine Echols
Department of Psychology
University of Texas, Austin
Austin, TX 78712
echols@psyvax.psy.utexas.edu

Peter Eimas
Cognitive & Linguistic Sciences
Brown University
Box 1978
Providence, RI 02912
eimas@browncog.bitnet

Anne Fernald
Department of Psychology
Stanford University
Palo Alto, CA 94305
fernald@psych.stanford.edu

Cynthia Fisher
Department of Psychology
University of Illinois
603 E. Daniel
Champaign, IL 61820
cfisher@s.psych.uiuc.edu

LouAnn Gerken
Department of Linguistics
University of Arizona
Tucson, AZ 85721
gerken@ccit.arizona.edu

Katherine Hirsh-Pasek
Department of Psychology
Temple University
Philadelphia, PA 19122
v5080e@templevm.bitnet

Peter Jusczyk
Department of Psychology
SUNY-Buffalo
Buffalo, NY 14260
psypwj@ubvms.cc.buffalo.edu

Michael Kelly
Department of Psychology
University of Pennsylvania
3813 Walnut Street
Philadelphia, PA 19104
kelly@cattell.psych.upenn.edu

Larry Leonard
Audiology & Speech Science
Purdue University
Heavilon Hall
Lafayette, IN 47907
xdxl@purccvm.bitnet

Philip Lieberman
Cognitive & Linguistic Sciences
Brown University
Box 1978
Providence, RI 02912
lieberman@browncog.bitnet

Reiko Mazuka
Department of Psychology
Duke University
Durham, NC 27706
mazuka@psych.duke.edu

Jacques Mehler
Laboratoire de Sciences
    Cognitives et
    Psycholinguistique
CNRS-EHESS
54, Bd Raspail
75270 Paris Cedex 06
France
mehler@lscp.lab-cog-psy.fr

James Morgan
Cognitive & Linguistic Science
Brown University
Box 1978
Providence, RI 02912
james_morgan@brown.edu

Ann Peters
Department of Linguistics
University of Hawaii
Honolulu, HI 96882
ann@uhunix.bitnet

Patti Price
SRI International
EJ133
333 Ravenwood Ave.
Menlo Park, CA 94025
pprice@speech.sri.com

Elizabeth Selkirk
Department of Linguistics
Univ. of Massachusetts
Amherst, MA 01003
selkirk@coins.cs.umass.edu

Mark Steedman
Moore School of Engineering
University of Pennsylvania
Philadelphia, PA 19104
steedman@linc.cis.upenn.edu

Jennifer Venditti
Department of Linguistics
Ohio State University
204 Cunz Hall
Columbus, OH 43210
venditti@ling.ohio-state.edu

Janet Werker
Department of Psychology
Univ. of British Columbia
2509-2136 W. Mall
Vancouver, BC V6T 1W5
jwerker@cortex.psych.ubc.ca

Preface

The contents of this volume are based on the proceedings of a confer- ence held at Brown University, Providence, RI, February 19-21, 1993. The goal of the conference was to bring together scholars with a variety of disciplinary and philosophical backgrounds (including theoretical linguists, computer scientists, acousticians, and psychologists and cogni- tive scientists specializing in speech perception and language acquisi- tion) to discuss issues bearing on how children's perception and repre- sentation of the speech stream may contribute to acquisition of syntax.

Funding for the conference and preparation of this volume was pro- vided by the National Science Foundation (DBS-9209461), the Mellon Foundation, the Brown University Wayland Collegium, and the De- partment of Cognitive and Linguistic Sciences, Brown University.

We are indebted to several staff members and graduate students at Brown for their aid in planning and preparing for the conference, assist- ing during the conference, and preparing this volume: Monica Sylvester, Emily Pickett, Paul Allopenna, Amit Almor, Jean Andruski, Sam Bayer, Annette Burton, Gary Byma, Steve Finney, Rachel Kessinger, Eun-Joo Kwak, Thanassi Protopappas, Rushen Shi, Marty Smith, and Jennifer Utman.

Jim Morgan
Katherine Demuth

1 Signal to Syntax: An Overview

James L. Morgan and Katherine Demuth

Brown University

In setting forth the theoretical approach that has provided the most influential logical framework for the study of language acquisition, Chomsky (1965, p. 30) began by noting

> A child who is capable of learning language must have ...
> (i) a technique for representing input signals
> (ii) a way of representing structural information about these signals

Understanding the nature of input signals and of infants' and children's capacities for perceiving and representing such signals are important for formulating complete explanations of the acquisition of language. This is because, as Chomsky noted, no child can learn any particular language in the absence of exposure to, perception of, and representation of input (i.e., speech or signing) from that language. Languages vary in the sounds that they include, in the sequences in which these sounds can be arranged, in the mappings of such sequences onto concepts, in the manners in which meaningful elements may be concatenated to form word-level units, and in the possibilities for combining words to form phrases, clauses, and sentences. Language learners must have some means of determining which of the possible alternatives at each of these levels are manifest in the specific languages they are learning. This can only be provided by appropriate representation of examples drawn from those languages.

Accounts seeking to characterize or explain children's grammatical development, however, generally accord little weight to factors involving perception, representation, or production of speech. Most textbooks on language acquisition include only brief mention of basic results from infant speech perception research and little if any material on children's developing linguistic representations. The recently published *Handbook of Language Acquisition* (Fletcher & MacWhinney, 1995), whose advertising asserts that it is "the definitive encyclopedia of child language," includes no contributions from researchers studying development of speech perception. Whereas naive theories of language acquisition might accord significant explanatory force to children's representations of the speech that they hear, scientific theories, as they have been developed to date, for the most part do not.

The purpose of this volume, and the conference on which it was based, was to bring together an interdisciplinary group of scholars in order to encourage further consideration of the possibility that children's representation of speech may provide important clues to basic aspects of syntactic categories and configurations that assist children in establishing grammars. After all, children's perceptual analyses of speech *must precede* (both logically and developmentally) application of syntactic or semantic analyses to representations of input utterances. Thus, it is reasonable to inquire whether such perceptual analyses might themselves yield information about some basic properties of grammar.

The notion that clues to syntactic structure may be discovered in speech has come to be known as the "prosodic bootstrapping hypothesis." This term, introduced by Pinker (1984), is unfortunately something of a misnomer. What has been contemplated in earlier accounts advanced by Gleitman and Wanner (1982), Morgan (1986), and Jusczyk, Hirsh-Pasek, Kemler Nelson, Kennedy, Woodward, and Piwoz (1992), as well as newer accounts advanced in many of the chapters in this volume, is not that mature or complete syntactic structures can be read off perceptual representations of input utterances nor that there is a one-to-one correspondence between perceptual cues and grammatical constructs. Rather, these accounts propose that information available in speech may contain clues to certain fundamental syntactic distinctions, providing additional constraints on children's syntactic and semantic analyses, signaling the domains within which such analyses may be efficiently deployed, and helping to ensure that these analyses get started in the proper direction. Thus, the "bootstrapping" part of "prosodic bootstrapping" is accurate.

However, the "prosodic" part is overly confining and, hence, misleading. Many of these accounts do suggest that suprasegmental cues may contribute information useful for acquisition of grammar. The prosody of infant- and child-directed speech is clearly different from that of adult-directed speech (Fernald, Taeschner, Dunn, Papousek, de Boysson-Bardies, & Fukui, 1989; Garnica, 1977), and infants display early sensitivities to prosodic characteristics of speech (Cooper & Aslin, 1994; DeCasper & Fifer, 1980; Mehler, Jusczyk, Lambertz, Halsted, Bertoncini, & Amiel-Tison, 1988). Nevertheless, none of these accounts argues that *prosody* is unique in contributing information useful for acquisition. Rather, several forms of information are available in input speech—phonetic, phonotactic, prosodic, stochastic—and any or all of these could contribute to syntactically rich representations of input utterances. As a more appropriately general descriptor, we suggest the term *phonological bootstrapping* as a rubric for hypotheses that children can derive rudimentary grammatical information from their perceptual analyses of input speech.

Before proceeding to our overview of the chapters in this volume, we briefly discuss two overarching issues concerning hypotheses of Phonological Bootstrapping. First, why (other than for the sake of completeness) should such hypotheses be entertained? Second, how should such hypotheses be evaluated? We draw upon the formal work of Morgan (1986) to illustrate preliminary answers to these questions.

A compelling reason for considering hypotheses of Phonological Bootstrapping is that such hypotheses have the potential to significantly alter the dialectic of the debate over determinants of language acquisition. Inclusion of appropriately rich representations of input may entail modifications of theories of grammatical development, particularly with regard to theoretical characterization of the initial state. This has been formally demonstrated by Morgan (1986). Morgan investigated the learnability-theoretic consequences for induction of "standard" transformational grammars (Chomsky, 1965) of the assumption that children's representation of input utterances includes some surface phrase bracketing information. This theory of grammar was adopted because previous work by Wexler and Culicover (1980) on learnability of this type of grammar—from input explicitly assumed *not* to include any surface phrase bracketing information—was available to serve as a baseline for comparison. The assumption of richer syntactic representations had several consequences. First, learnability could be demonstrated on the basis of simpler data: Morgan's proof required only Degree 1 input (sentences containing, at most, one level of embedding), whereas Wexler and Culicover's proof required Degree 2 input. Requiring only Degree 1 input is a beneficial result because sentences with two or more levels of embedding appear in children's input only rarely (Morgan, 1986). Second, learnability could be demonstrated with many fewer required constraints on grammatical hypotheses, that is, with a simpler theory of Universal Grammar. In place of grammatical constraints that would otherwise be required, Morgan's proof substituted a set of perceptual mechanisms responsible for representation of phrase bracketing.

Although Morgan's learnability result establishes that syntactically rich representations could bear explanatory weight in accounts of acquisition of syntax, it does not bear on the plausibility of assuming such representations. Hypotheses of rich representations of language input must be evaluated with regard to both evidence concerning the nature of speech that infants hear—does such speech incorporate valid cues to aspects of syntactic structure?—and evidence concerning the nature of infants' perceptual abilities—do infants possess capacities for recognizing and exploiting such cues in appropriate fashion? These questions constitute central concerns of the chapters in this volume.

However, there is another factor that must be considered in evaluating hypotheses of Phonological Bootstrapping: The plausibility of any such hypothesis cannot be judged except with reference to a theory of the grammar that is being acquired. In the case of Morgan's (1986) learnability result, not all phrase bracketing needed to be represented. In that proof, the key contribution of representations of surface bracketing was to disambiguate the structural locations of permuted constituents. If the inventory of possible "landing sites" for moved constituents were constrained, then so too would be the amount of bracketing that would need to be represented in order for this information to make effective contributions to acquisition of grammar.[1]   More generally, the presence or absence of cues to particular syntactic distinctions may or may not be relevant given the nature of human grammars and how they are acquired.   For example, several chapters in this volume (Fernald & McRoberts, Fisher & Tokura, Gerken, and Jusczyk & Kemler Nelson) note that, in English, prosodic cues fail to indicate that pronominal subjects and verbs are elements of separate syntactic constituents.   However, the consequences of "misrepresentation" of the syntactic constituency of pronominal subjects are unknown; without such knowledge, it is impossible to judge how such evidence should be weighed in evaluating hypotheses of Phonological Bootstrapping.   An alternative view of such evidence is that the presence or absence of phonological cues to particular distinctions or the existence of particular perceptual capacities in infants may provide clues to the nature of grammar (cf. Steedman, this volume) or to aspects of grammar whose early acquisition is of prime importance (Mazuka, this volume).

We organized our overview of the chapters in this volume to address three issues that might account for the paucity of influence that work on infant perception and representation has had on language acquisition theorizing.   First, theoretical and methodological mismatches have tended to impede intellectual interactions among the diverse fields involved in studies of speech, perception, and language acquisition. The chapters in Part I ("The nature, perception, and representation of input speech") address issues relevant to bridging the disciplinary gaps between these fields.

Second, much of the work on the acquisition of syntax has been carried out with weak assumptions about the nature of input representations (typically that infants represent input utterances merely as strings of words or sometimes morphemes).   For the most part, these assumptions have been accepted without examination.   The chapters in Part II ("Speech and the acquisition of words") discuss aspects of early word-level speech segmentation.   These chapters explore the plausibility of the assumption that infants represent input utterances as strings of words, providing evidence on the perceptual and computational capacities entailed by this assumption.   Successful word-level segmentation requires sophisticated capacities on the part of language learners, no less sophisticated than those required for representation of additional grammatical properties of input.   The capacities for formulating richer representations of the sort contemplated under hypotheses of Phonologi-

---

[1] On independent grounds, Baltin (1982), working within Extended Standard Theory, proposed a constrained set of landing sites for moved constituents.   Several accounts within the Government and Binding tradition (e.g., Chomsky, 1986) have similarly proposed constraints on the output of 'Move α.'   It should also be noted that the relevant bracketing would not need to be represented for every sentence token.

cal Bootstrapping are thus likely to be in place by virtue of the need to perform word-level segmentation.

Third, current theories of language have inherited the tenet of structuralist linguistics that the syntactic systems of languages are independent of their sound systems. On this view there is scant reason to believe that children's analyses of speech (regardless of their sophistication) will provide information useful to acquisition of syntax. Chapters in Parts III and IV ("Speech and the acquisition of grammatical morphology and form classes," and "Speech and the acquisition of phrase structure") consider whether in fact children's analyses of speech might provide information useful to the acquisition of morpho-syntax, debating whether language input contains reliable and valid phonotactic, prosodic, and stochastic cues (or sets of cues) to syntactic categories and structures.

Finally, chapters in Part V ("Speech and the acquisition of language") consider bootstrapping in broader developmental perspective, conjecturing about how early advancements in cognition and speech perception may be related and how Phonological Bootstrapping may interact with, and ultimately give way to, more sophisticated syntactic and semantic analyses of language input.

PART I: THE NATURE, PERCEPTION, AND REPRESENTATION OF INPUT SPEECH

Serious consideration of the role of speech in early language acquisition requires examination of several types of evidence. These include results of distributional and phonetic analyses of speech that infants and children hear, findings bearing on infant's perceptual and representational capacities, data on the contributions of phonetic and prosodic factors in sentence processing, and linguistic descriptions of phonological and syntactic systems and their possible interrelations. Forging these diverse types of evidence into a coherent whole faces obstacles commonly encountered in efforts to foster interdisciplinary cooperation (Abrahamsen, 1987): Different disciplines employ different methods, value different types of data, and analyze problems at different levels of abstractness and generality. At the same time, different disciplines may sometimes adopt the same technical terms while assigning them different reference. Thus, disagreements that appear to be substantive may turn out to be largely terminological.

A brief comparison of the fields of infant speech perception and child language acquisition illustrates many of these points. Research in infant speech perception developed directly from the pioneering work on adult perception conducted at Haskins Laboratory (Liberman, Cooper, Shankweiler, & Studdert-Kennedy, 1967; Liberman, Delattre, & Cooper, 1952); its methodological lineage can be traced to the early psychophysical work of Helmholtz. In contrast, research in child language acquisition has its roots in diary and case studies by individuals such as Darwin (1877), Dewey (1894), Lewis (1936) and Velten (1943). Studies of speech perception are experimental; studies of language acquisition tend to be observational or formal. Historically, research in infant speech perception has focused more on infants' abilities for discriminating speech sounds than on any other single issue. While important in its own right, this issue is of little interest to acquisition of grammar, for which data on perception and representation of morphemes, words, phrases, and clauses would be of relevance. Both fields may have interest in *prosody*, but this term is used to refer to different phenomena: In studies of speech perception, as in analyses of speech, the term *prosody* applies to manipulations or measurements of duration, intensity, pitch, or pitch contour, characteristics of suprasegmental aspects of speech that might be considered to be acoustic or "phonetic." In contrast, in studies of language acquisition (particularly those that draw heavily on phonological theory), the term *prosody* applies to phenomena such as meter or stress, and to the word- or phrase-level domains in which these are realized. These phenomena are more "phonemic" in character, inasmuch as they are typically defined with reference to particular linguistic systems. One consequence of this terminological ambiguity is that the debate over the role of prosody in Phonological Bootstrapping is muddied: Accounts adopting more "phonetic" definitions of prosody tend to be more optimistic about the possibility that prosody may contribute to early acquisition of aspects of grammar, whereas accounts adopting more "phonemic" definitions of prosody tend to emphasize the prior learning required to deploy prosodic categories in representing input. This divergence in views is evident in several chapters in this volume.

Essential steps toward reconciling data and arguments from different disciplines include basic familiarity with these data and arguments, as well as understanding of the methodological foundations on which these are based. In this spirit, the chapters in Part I offer a series of brief tutorials on several fields bearing on the possibility of bootstrapping from speech to grammar in early language acquisition; each chapter contains pointers into the associated literature for interested readers to pursue. Eimas provides an overview of research in infant speech perception, summarizing evidence that has been amassed on infants' early processing capacities and on later changes to these capacities as effects of exposure to particular languages. Eimas also discusses the development of methods for assessing infants' linguistic representations, as the field of infant speech perception begins to move beyond issues concerning discrimination and categorization of speech segments. Dresher introduces prosodic theory, providing arguments and linguistic evidence for units in the *prosodic hierarchy*: the phonological word, the phonological phrase, the intonational phrase, and the phonological utterance. Dresher then sketches metrical theory, noting some of the parameters involved and suggesting how these parameters might be set. Lieberman sets the study of prosody in biological perspective, noting that all mammalian species, humans included, use prosody for a variety of nonlinguistic purposes. Price and Ostendorf outline the methods and goals of research in automatic speech recognition, an area whose precision, explicitness, and rigor might serve as a model for research in language acquisition (these desiderata are exemplified in recent work by Markey, 1994). Price and Ostendorf review results on analyses of prosody (ascertaining which components of prosody signal grammatical distinctions) and note that inclusion of prosodic information may enhance performance of statistical models of speech recognition, even when those models are provided with several other sources of knowledge. This work suggests that prosody and other phonological information may be especially useful to infants, who lack lexical and grammatical knowledge available to mature speakers.

PART II: SPEECH AND THE ACQUISITION OF WORDS

As noted earlier, theories of syntax acquisition commonly adopt the assumption that, prior to acquiring structural knowledge of their language, children can represent input utterances as strings of words. A few theorists have worried over how children might attain proper word-level representations (e.g., Brown, 1973; Peters, 1983). Most often, however, this assumption has been adopted uncritically.

In contrast, the problem of word-level speech segmentation has attracted considerable attention in the adult psycholinguistic literature. As Cutler notes in her chapter, many of these models argue that word segmentation occurs serendipitously, as a byproduct of word recognition. Such models appear to be inappropriate as descriptions of segmentation in acquisition, particularly in the earliest stages, for the simple reason that beginning language learners lack the very lexical knowledge that is required for "serendipitous segmentation." Rather, a bottom-up process exploiting one or more prelexical (or sublexical) units may be required for bootstrapping segmentation. Cutler argues for a "universal rhythmic segmentation hypothesis," according to which listeners adopt whichever unit constitutes the organizational basis for rhythmic structure in their primary language as a prelexical cue to word boundaries. In languages such as English, this unit is the stress foot; in languages such as French, the syllable; in languages such as Japanese, the mora; other units are possible in principle though they have not yet been attested. Cutler reviews evidence from studies of adult speech processing suggesting that English speakers do use the stress foot, French speakers the syllable, and Japanese speakers the mora as preferred units of initial segmentation. Studies by Jusczyk, Cutler, and Redanz (1993) and Morgan (in press) show that 9- and 10-month-old English-learning infants prefer to listen to and more coherently represent bisyllables manifesting the strong–weak rhythmic pattern that constitutes binary stress feet in English and predominates in the English lexicon, as Cutler's hypothesis suggests.

The available evidence is compatible with the possibility that infants exploit speech rhythm in discovering word-level units in fluent speech. However, several questions remain to be addressed. How do infants discover which rhythmic unit is appropriate for their language? How do infants discover the preferred internal rhythmic organization of this unit? How do infants identify the edges of basic rhythmic units? In languages in which words often comprise multiple basic rhythmic units (e.g., French or Japanese), how do infants locate word boundaries? Efficient application of the strategy Cutler suggests for English, the Metrical Segmentation Strategy, requires that listeners be able to discriminate between lexical words and function words. How can infants make such discriminations prior to locating word boundaries? Some of these questions are taken up in chapters in this volume; others remain for future research.

Mehler, Dupoux, Nazzi, and Dehaene-Lambertz address the question of how infants discover the rhythmic unit appropriate for their language. They review evidence showing that very young infants can discriminate stimuli varying in numbers of vowels and can discriminate languages differing in rhythmic structure, even when speech in those languages has been low-pass filtered. Because the information retained in low-pass filtered speech is concentrated in vocalic segments, Mehler et al. argue that vowels are highly salient for infants. Integrating these findings, Mehler et al. propose a model in which representation of the timing and intensity of vowels in utterances allows infants to classify languages into one of a small number of possible rhythmic classes. For example, utterances in which neither intervocalic intervals nor vowel amplitude display much variation might be classified as being drawn from a syllable-timed language such as French, whereas utterances in which high- and low-intensity vowels alternate and intervals between high-intensity vowels display little variation might be classified as being drawn from a stress-timed language such as English. It seems likely, however, that some utterances infants hear will fail to correspond closely to any one rhythmic template. Moreover, because utterances addressed to infants tend to be short (and hence contain small numbers of vowels), the statistical power for deciding whether the distribution of, say, intervocalic intervals observed in a given utterance fits one template or another may be limited. Evaluation of the computational feasibility of this model must await detailed measurements of infant-directed utterances drawn from languages with several different rhythmic structures. In the interim, however, the model that Mehler et al. offer as a first-order language classification device is psychologically appealing as it relies on well-attested perceptual capacities.

Edges of at least some word-level units may be identified by phonotactic patterns. In any language, certain (sequences of) consonants may occur in either syllable onsets or syllable codas; often, however, the edges of words may contain greater numbers or wider repertoires of possible consonants than the edges of word-internal syllables. In their chapter, Aslin, Woodward, LaMendola, and Bever investigate whether knowledge of phonotactic patterns—specifically, knowledge of those patterns that occur at the ends of utterances—may be sufficient to predict within-utterance word boundaries. Aslin et al. show that back-propagation neural networks trained on utterance-final phonotactic patterns can indeed identify utterance-internal word boundaries with high levels of accuracy. Presumably, infants must eventually integrate phonotactic and rhythmic information in segmenting and recognizing words in fluent speech. What the relative contributions of these and other potentially relevant types of information are, and how and when infants integrate them, are questions that must be answered by further research (see Werker, Lloyd, Pegg, & Polka, this volume, for additional discussion).

Beyond being able to carve up continuous input utterances into appropriate lexical units, infants must be able to recognize specific word tokens as exemplars of particular lexical types. This ability is prerequisite for use of any lexical information, such as using word meanings to infer form class membership or subcategorization frames to constrain hypotheses of sentence structure. In her chapter, Ratner suggests that this problem may be somewhat simplified for children in early stages of acquisition on two grounds. First, the fact that early lexicons are quite sparse entails that phonological neighborhoods will not be at all dense. Thus children may be able to more easily tolerate variability across tokens than are adults, whose lexical neighborhoods are more densely populated. Second, in certain respects, tokens may vary less in infant-directed than in adult-directed speech. For example, VOT ranges tend to be narrower and adults use several optional phonological rules less often in infant-directed speech. On the other hand, as Ratner acknowledges, young children do attend to fine-grained phonetics of input speech (and may be less certain of which phonetic variations fall within or cross phonemic boundaries). Moreover, although tokens may manifest less segmental variability in infant-directed speech, they are likely to manifest greater suprasegmental variability. Aslin et al. note that new words tend to be introduced in utterance-final position, where they tend to be loud, lengthened, and high-pitched (Fernald & Mazzie, 1991). When words later appear in utterance-medial positions, they will have none of these characteristics. At this point, it seems fair to say that neither the dimensions of the problem that infants face nor the processes by which infants solve the token–type problem are as yet well understood. Both of these issues are important topics for future research.

Analyses of input and research demonstrating that infants possess the component perceptual skills required for segmentation necessarily stop short of providing evidence on the nature and ontogenesis of infant segmentation itself. For this, measures of relevant aspects of infant perception and representation will be required, and these are only now beginning to be developed (see Jusczyk & Kemler Nelson, this volume and Werker et al., this volume). An alternative approach is to make inferences about infant segmentation through observations of children's productions (e.g., Peters, 1983). As Echols notes in her chapter, however, disentangling effects of perception, representation, and production factors is a subtle enterprise (see also Gerken, this volume). Echols' earlier analyses of children's productions suggested that children preferentially utter syllables that are either stressed or target-final, but what to attribute children's omissions of unstressed, nonfinal syllables to is unclear. Evidence from 2-year-olds' imitations of stimuli varying in both stress and articulatory difficulty suggests that, by that advanced age, children extract and represent both stressed and unstressed syllables, but, on Echols view, the representation of stress (or, more generally, salience) continues to play a pivotal role in children's choice of which syllables to utter. Echols suggests that this apparent limitation on production may recapitulate earlier limitations on perception and representation of input speech.

Demuth argues, however, that an adequate characterization of children's early words cannot be constructed by appealing to perceptual salience alone. Rather, Demuth contends that the varying shapes of children's early productions reflect sensitivity to the prosodic word structures of languages, conforming to linguistically specified notions of *minimal word*, which are defined in terms of the prosodic hierarchy (see Dresher, this volume). Minimal words comprise binary feet, but the constituency of binary feet varies across languages. The default shape (if neither stress nor syllable weight is specified) for binary feet is the trochaic bisyllable. As children begin to represent lexical stress and syllable weight (for languages whose phonological systems make use of these factors), binary feet can assume new forms, either trochaic or iambic, and either monosyllabic or bisyllabic, depending on the language. In languages with phonological systems in which neither lexical stress nor syllable weight figure, as in Sesotho, the minimal word will remain a trochaic bisyllable. Cross-linguistic evidence comports with these predictions. Demuth concludes that limitations of children's early word-shapes reflect neither perceptual nor representational deficiencies but rather systematic phonological constraints on output forms. One implication of this is that children achieve accurate representations of words in their languages very early in acquisition.

In sum, the chapters in Part II show that infants make substantial progress toward solving the word-level segmentation problem in the first year of life, perhaps completing this process before they begin to produce structured utterances. Thus, the assumption that syntactic analyses are based on representations of input utterances that encode linear orders of words appears to be tenable. Solving the segmentation problem, however, is by no means trivial. To do so, infants must at minimum be able to attend to, discriminate, represent, and integrate metrical, phonotactic, and distributional properties of input speech, all under the guidance of certain preprogrammed constraints on the characteristics of the linguistic unit being sought. In addition, solving the token–type problem will minimally require capabilities for normalizing across variation in both speaker characteristics and speech rate. An extensive set of perceptual and computational capacities is thus needed for word-level segmentation and lexical access. No evidence exists showing that infants possess such capacities solely for the purpose of discovering words. The chapters in Parts III and IV consider whether these capacities might also suffice to provide infants with representations of basic form classes and fundamental aspects of phrase structure.

PARTS III & IV: SPEECH AND THE ACQUISITION OF GRAMMATICAL MORPHOLOGY, FORM CLASSES, AND PHRASE STRUCTURE

A fundamental tenet of structuralist linguistics, the tradition from which transformational grammar and subsequent developments in contemporary theoretical linguistics emerged, is that grammars are composed of multiple systems that are not reducible to one another. Although in writing about "the arbitrariness of the sign," Saussure (1916/1959) focused primarily on the independence of the sound-shapes of words and their meanings, it is clear that he intended this notion to apply as well to the independence of the sound-shapes of words, their grammatical categories, and their proclivities for combining syntactically with other words. Hockett (1966) employed the term *duality of patterning* to refer specifically to the observed independence of phonology and syntax in human languages.

As Kelly (1992) noted, one legacy of the ascendance of these concepts has been an absence of consideration of possible contributions of phonological information to acquisition of aspects of syntax. Whereas the structuralist claims that, for example, form class is not reducible to phonology and phrase structure is not reducible to prosody may be correct, this does not preclude the possibility that correlations exist between these grammatical domains. What the nature of these correlations might be, how infants might discover them, and whether such correlations are exploited in the course of acquisition are the topics considered in chapters in Parts III and IV. To anticipate somewhat, it does not seem likely that mappings from phonology to form class or to phrase structure are either language-universal or transparent. This might be taken as *prima facie* evidence against the possibility of bootstrapping from speech to these aspects of syntactic structure. However, as we saw earlier, the phonological bases of word-level segmentation are neither language-universal nor transparent either. Infants nevertheless solve the segmentation problem, suggesting that they may possess the perceptual, representational, and computational capacities to exploit whatever phonology–form class or phonology–phrase structure mappings may exist in language input.

Scholars of language have long noted that words can be sorted into two superordinate grammatical categories. This distinction has been variously characterized as *content words* versus *function words, open class items* versus *closed class items,* or *referential morphemes* versus *inflectional morphemes.* Scholars of language acquisition have also long noted that children's early speech contains primarily open class lexical items, and that closed class grammatical function items take some time to appear consistently. Since Abney's (1987) formal syntactic characterization of *lexical* and *functional* categories, linguists have become increasingly concerned with the different grammatical roles played by these two grammatical classes. This concern has generated a rapid growth in studies that have begun to focus anew on the acquisition of grammatical function morphology and its implications for the development of syntactic structure (for example, see Radford, 1990, and chapters in Meisel, 1992, and Lust, Suñer, & Whitman, 1994). Systematically missing from most of these discussions, however, has been any awareness of the phonological differences between grammatical function morphology and lexical form classes, and how these might influence early stages of syntactic analysis or language production (though see Demuth, 1992, 1994). The chapters in Part III deal with these issues from perspectives of perception, representation, and production.

Selkirk provides a novel theoretical treatment of grammatical function morphology in terms of prosodic words. Drawing on previous work involving the prosodic hierarchy and data from English and Serbo-Croatian, she identifies four different ways in which grammatical function words can be prosodically realized. She shows how the surface realization of these four prosodic types of grammatical morphology can be affected by the different ordering, or ranking, of prosodic constraints, in accord with recent optimality theoretic proposals (McCarthy & Prince, in press; Prince & Smolensky, in press). Selkirk shows how the prosodic distinction between weak and strong forms of grammatical function words in English (e.g. auxiliaries, prepositions, object pronouns) can be handled be appealing to three different types of morphosyntactic input structures, all with the same ranking of prosodic constraints. She then demonstrates that different accentual phenomena in dialects of Serbo-Croatian involve the same morphosyntactic structure, but different rankings of prosodic constraints. This chapter therefore provides a detailed analysis of grammatical function words as part of larger prosodic word units. The acquisition of these prosodic structures is an interesting and important study in and of itself. However, there is much a child must learn about prosodic structure before the information discussed here can be used to inform the acquisition of syntactic structure itself.

An alternative possibility is that young children might exploit low-level phonetic and distributional properties of words and syllables in input speech to assign these elements to basic grammatical categories. Morgan, Shi, and Allopenna suggest that the statistical, syntactic and semantic characteristics of content words and function words universally tend to result in these words having constellations of distinctive phonological (and hence perceptual) characteristics. Arguing on the basis of measures of English and Mandarin infant-directed speech, Morgan et al. show that single measures fail to provide highly valid cues to superordinate form class membership. However, sets of measures considered ensemble are valid predictors, as results of simulations with self-organizing neural networks demonstrate. Noting evidence that, at some time between 6 and 12 months, infants have developed the more sophisticated perceptual and integrative abilities needed to use such higher-order information, Morgan et al. argue that it is possible that infants use cues provided in the input signal as a first pass toward grammatical categorization, even before gaining access to the semantics of words or mastering the phonology of the language being learned. Once rudimentary category membership has been determined, the identification of phrase boundaries and more fine-grained sets of form classes may be facilitated, providing the basis for acquisition of language-particular aspects of syntactic structure.

The arguments advanced by Selkirk and Morgan et al. concern how children might come to represent lexical and functional items as members of distinct grammatical classes. Neither chapter attempts to account for the appearance of functional items in children's productions. It has long been know, however, that functional items do not appear as a class in children's repertoires, but rather emerge one-by-one, in orders that vary across languages but that tend to be stable within languages (Brown, 1973; Slobin, 1982). Peters and Strömqvist propose that the tonal or intonational structure of a language may facilitate the production of grammatical morphology if those morphemes are prosodically salient in some way, where salient may be interpreted as "contrastive" or "different." To evaluate this hypothesis they examine early word productions in Swedish, focusing on interactions between the realization of inflectional morphology and (unmarked) acute versus (marked) grave pitch accent. They suggest that the marked grave accent (fall on stressed syllable, with post-stress rise) may be prosodically salient for children, helping to focus attention on inflectional morphology when producing early words. Examining the early speech of one child, they find that polysyllabic words are initially produced correctly with grave pitch accent and that, around 23 months, with a rise in MLU, the child begins to overgeneralize the unmarked acute accent. Peters and Strömqvist suggest that the grave pitch accent serves as a "spotlight" at the very early stages of acquisition, focusing the child's attention on the word-final grammatical morphology of polysyllabic words. They conclude by suggesting two areas of research needed to test their "spotlight" hypothesis. First, they recognize the need for perceptual studies that will complement the production study presented here. Second, they point to the importance of crosslinguistic studies of production, especially in closely related languages where prosodic phenomena such as stress-timing, syllable duration, vowel quality, and tonal pitch-accent may vary.

Leonard and Eyer address Peters and Strömqvist's second proposal by comparing SLI (specific language impairment) children's production of grammatical morphology in English, Italian, and Hebrew. Their thesis is that being able to identify and process grammatical morphology may facilitate the acquisition of syntax. However, it has been observed that children with specific language impairment have difficulties with grammatical morphology, as well as with various aspects of syntax. Leonard and Eyer review comparative studies of English, Italian, and Hebrew SLI populations and their MLU controls, showing that the SLI children generally perform worse on grammatical morphology when those forms are in syntactic positions where they are relatively short in duration. However, in cases where grammatical morphemes fall on stressed syllables, as is frequently the case in Hebrew, or in phrase-final lengthened positions, as is often the case in Italian, SLI children perform with increased accuracy. Leonard and Eyer therefore conclude that grammatical morphemes with relatively short durations pose problems for SLI children. Furthermore, they show that languages vary in the extent to which grammatical function morphology is realized by forms with short duration—English has many such forms, whereas Italian and Hebrew have fewer. (Interestingly, Morgan et al., this volume found that vowel duration was an important component of the sets of cues distinguishing content and function words in both English and Mandarin.) If duration is one of the major factors required for linguistic processing, English-speaking SLI children might be expected to omit more grammatical function morphemes than their Italian and Hebrew SLI counterparts, and this seems to be the case. Leonard and Eyer propose that this may then hinder accurate representation of the internal structure of phrases and clauses, thereby interfering with the development of higher level syntactic abilities.

Although the distinction between lexical and functional categories is arguably most basic, this is clearly not the only distinction among form classes that is important for acquisition of grammar. In his chapter, Kelly argues that nouns and verbs may also be differentiated on the basis of phonological cues such as duration of syllables, vowel quality, consonant quality, phoneme type, and number of syllables. Kelly demonstrates that regular phonological cues such as surface stress patterns (iambic vs. trochaic) and number of syllables serve as reliable indicators distinguishing English nouns and verbs, and that both adults and 3- to 4-year-olds have developed strategies for classifying novel words using these phonological cues. Classification in English is enhanced if phonological cues are combined with semantic information, but even in cases where semantics is not available, as in languages with abstract gender classes, use of phonological cues is also effective. Kelly concludes by arguing that phonological cues are both available and exploited by early language users, and that these cues facilitate the construction of grammatical classes.

In sum, the chapters in Part III point to the presence of phonological, acoustic and statistical/distributional differences between functional and lexical categories, as well as distinctions within the class of lexical items. These differences occur not only in English, but in other languages as well, perhaps universally. Furthermore, several of the chapters suggest that language learners may exploit these types of information from the earliest stages of acquisition, using them to form rudimentary grammatical categories—a necessary prerequisite for the construction of higher levels of syntactic structure. However, these chapters also point to the fact that much more research is needed to determine the relationship between children's early perceptual and production abilities with respect to different grammatical classes and to flesh out the implications this has for the course of language development in both normal and language-delayed populations.

Several early Phonological Bootstrapping proposals suggested that language learners might be able to retrieve information about phrase bracketing from analyses of input speech (e.g., Gleitman & Wanner, 1982; Morgan, 1986; Morgan & Newport, 1981). These proposals were inspired partly by linguistic evidence for links between phonology and syntax (especially at the level of prosodic structure—stress feet, prosodic words, pitch accent, tone, intonation—and its correlation with various syntactic boundaries; cf. Inkelas & Zec 1990), and partly by evidence of phonology–syntax relations from studies of adult-directed speech (e.g., Cooper & Paccia-Cooper, 1980) and adult sentence processing (e.g., Streeter, 1978). As Fernald and McRoberts note, analyses of adult-directed speech have typically proceeded by examining prosodic correlates of known aspects of sentence phrase structure. They point out that the conditional probability involved in such analyses is not the one of concern for language learners, whose task concerns instead attempting to induce sentence structure from observed prosodic phenomena. Thus, cue reliability is of import for learners. Fernald and McRoberts contend that prosodic phenomena are at best moderately reliable cues to phrase structure in adult-directed speech. Moreover, they note that studies of adult speech processing show that listeners assign more weight to syntactic cues than prosodic cues in inferring phrase structure.

The relevance of adult data to evaluation of Phonological Bootstrapping proposals, however, is unclear. Obvious differences exist between adult-directed and infant-directed speech (Fernald et al., 1989), and adult and infant sentence processing capabilities must also be different, by virtue of the vastly different stores of linguistic knowledge that infants and adults possess. Evidence from analyses of adult-directed speech and adult language processing is neither necessary nor sufficient for bootstrapping arguments. Such evidence has played a heuristic, rather than logical, role in motivating Phonological Bootstrapping proposals.

More to the point, Fernald and McRoberts observe that prosodically delimited stretches of infant-directed speech often fail to correspond to clauses. However, no Phonological Bootstrapping proposals have suggested that clauses are uniquely cued (note that proposals that "clauses are perceptual units" are not equivalent to proposals that "perceptual units are clauses"; cf. Hirsh-Pasek, Kemler Nelson, Jusczyk, Wright Cassidy, Druss, & Kennedy, 1987). The utility of such unique cueing would appear to be minimal, especially since, on all accounts, infants hear few multi-clause utterances. Rather, cueing of various types of phrase groupings, in combination with capacities for limited distributional analyses, is likely to be more informative for inferring the hierarchical organization of clause-level syntactic structure.

Whether prosodic cues in infant-directed speech in fact delimit phrases is subject to dispute. Fernald and McRoberts assert that a significant proportion of infant-directed utterances are sub-phrasal. In contrast, in earlier analyses of child-directed speech, Snow (1972) and Newport (1977) reported that the sentence fragments that occurred were overwhelmingly well-formed phrases. Clearly, the grammatical framework adopted is critical for determining what may and may not constitute phrases. In his chapter, Steedman demonstrates that putative prosody–syntax mismatches disappear given a Combinatory Categorial Grammar (CCG) account of syntax, which draws largely on semantic information from subcategorization frames and admits a wider variety of phrase types than other theories. From a CCG perspective, the child will need access to semantic interpretations, or at least an understanding of conceptual meaning and discourse context, in order to acquire syntactic competence. Of course, adoption of a Phonological Bootstrapping account does not preclude learners' use of semantic information (we return to this point in our discussion of Part V), but, as we noted earlier, children's perceptual analyses of speech must come before semantic analyses of representations of input utterances

A related issue concerns how the prosodic cues that serve to delimit stretches of speech differ across languages. Silence is likely a universal delimiter. Venditti, Jun, and Beckman show in addition how prosodic phenomena such as pitch-accent, boundary tones, intonational phrases, and downstep in Japanese, Korean, and English all bear on prosody–syntax mappings, but each in a distinct fashion. They suggest that general similarities in prosodic organization may reflect basic aspects of grouping and focus. Beyond this, however, prosodic structure and details of prosody–syntax mappings may vary somewhat arbitrarily across languages. Venditti et al.'s arguments are based on analyses of adult-directed utterances. To determine the utility of prosodic structure as a means for bootstrapping syntactic structure for young children, comparable analyses of corpora of infant-directed speech are required, for both qualitative and quantitative reasons. Qualitatively, as we have pointed out, adult- and infant-directed speech registers often exhibit strikingly different phonological characteristics. Quantitatively, it may be less important to know that particular pairings of prosodic and syntactic structures are possible than to know how often such pairings occur in infants' input.

Fisher and Tokura begin to provide such evidence, reporting on acoustic analyses of spontaneous maternal infant-directed speech in English and Japanese. They suggest that acoustic and distributional correlates of phrase boundaries and given–new information might provide language learners with means of accessing basic syntactic structure. In keeping with observations by Fernald and Mazzie (1991) and Aslin et al. (this volume), they note that new information tends to appear at the ends of utterances, where it is often marked with dramatic pitch changes—reminiscent of Peters and Strömqvist's (this volume) "spotlight" effect. In contrast, pronominal subjects, which are given information, take the form of phonologically reduced elements in English, and are missing altogether in languages like Japanese; hence, NP–VP boundaries are typically unmarked in infant-directed utterances, in which lexical subjects are infrequent. Fisher and Tokura conclude that spontaneous speech may provide infants with both direct and indirect acoustic support for both utterance-level and some aspects of clause-level syntactic structure.

Partial bracketings of phrases within larger utterances may be compatible with several different hierarchical geometries and thus may not provide sufficient bases for representation of sentence phrase structure. However, Mazuka suggests that certain basic configurational parameters can be set early in the acquisition process using suprasegmental prosodic cues. It has long been observed that children generally use correct word order from the onset of two-word utterances, evidence that the parameter governing Head Direction (the order of heads and their complements, such as verbs and their objects) is set from the onset of speech. To do this, the child must have segmented words and phrases, must have some access to semantics, and must have identified parts of speech. Mazuka argues that infants may use global prosodic cues to clauses in a small number of complex sentences to set the parameter governing Branching Direction (whether tree structures tend grow in depth to the left or to the right) prior to assigning a full semantics to their input. Thus, early sensitivity to larger, clause-level prosodic cues may provide infants with an initial pass at organizing complex sentences into hierarchical structures. Once the Branching Direction parameter is set, additional phonologically encoded information can be harnessed.

Jusczyk and Kemler Nelson note that, in addition to evidence for the existence of phonological correlates of syntactic structure in input, Phonological Bootstrapping accounts require evidence that infants can detect the relevant phonological properties and make use of these properties in organizing their representations of input. Jusczyk and Kemler

Nelson review results of preference studies showing that, beginning at $4^1/_2$ months, infants display sensitivity to the sets of prosodic cues that have been implicated in signaling clause- and utterance-final boundaries. By 9 months, infants are sensitive to the subtler prosodic cues that have been implicated in signaling phrase-final boundaries. Moreover, as early as 2 months, infants appear to exploit prosody in representing speech: 2-month-olds are more likely to detect segmental changes in strings of words spoken with sentential prosody than in identical strings spoken with list prosody. Nevertheless, echoing a view expressed in several other chapters, Jusczyk and Kemler Nelson caution against a naive version of Phonological Bootstrapping in which prosody transparently reveals syntactic structure. Rather, prosodic cues are only one of several types of probabilistic information in input speech that learners may use in beginning to unravel the syntactic structure of their language.

In sum, the chapters in Part IV point to the potential use of global prosodic cues to phrase structure as a first pass at organizing syntactic units. They also point to the necessity of including other types of acoustic, distributional, and segmental information for conducting utterance-internal analyses. On this view, analyses of phonology-syntax relations in infant-directed speech have not yet succeeded in capturing all of the information potentially available to language learners. First, cues to phrase groupings do not occur in isolation, but rather in correlation with one another. Most analyses to date have examined single cues, whereas the predictiveness of sets of cues may be substantially greater (see Morgan et al., this volume). Second, infants do not hear words in isolation, but rather in connected discourse. Most analyses to date have relied on absolute measures of phonological properties of words, but analyses that take into account effects of both segmental and suprasegmental context would be more likely to reflect the sorts of information on which infants must rely. Third, infants are not engaged in the single task of discovering phonology–phrase structure relations, but are rather engaged in analyses at a variety of linguistic levels. Tentative results of some of these other analyses (for example, identification of words as function words or content words) may help to inform infants' analyses of relations between phonology and syntax. The chapters in Part V consider how acquisition of words, grammatical categories, and phrases, and the uses of phonological, semantic, and syntactic sources of information, might be interrelated

PART V: SPEECH AND THE ACQUISITION OF LANGUAGE

Gerken discusses how learners come to be able to locate words and phrases in continuous speech, identify category memberships of words and phrases, and discover hierarchical structure of input utterances. She suggests that these processes exploit different forms of information: Segmentation of words and phrases makes particular use of prosody, labeling words as members of lexical categories depends on recognition of function morphemes, and hierarchical structuring of utterances requires attention to distributional patterns across sentences and sentence fragments. Gerken characterizes word- and phrase-level segmentation, acquisition of grammatical categories, and apprehension of clause-level syntactic structure as "potentially distinct problems" for language learners. Indeed, from an analytic perspective, it is probably useful to initially consider these problems independently.

Nevertheless, it seems likely that acquisition of these different levels of syntactic structure must be intertwined. Consider, for example, how speech rhythm may assist in word-level segmentation: For English in particular, as Cutler (this volume) has argued, strong–weak pairs of syllables are sequences likely to be words. However, this generalization holds only if the weak syllable is *not* a function word syllable. Strong monosyllabic content words are often followed by weak function words, and segmenting such sequences as words would be misleading at best. Hence, efficient application of metrical strategies in word-level segmentation requires some knowledge of category memberships of words. Conversely, one partial predictor of the category memberships of words is the number of syllables they contain (Kelly, this volume), so that assignment of words to grammatical categories is partly dependent on successful word-level segmentation. Knowledge of category membership may assist in bracketing input (Morgan et al., this volume), whereas knowledge that a phrase boundary occurs between a strong syllable and a weak one should inhibit consideration of this pair of syllables as a word. The manner in which acquisition of words, grammatical categories, and phrase structure interact with one another is an important topic for further research.

Gerken notes that early acquisition of syntax doubtless proceeds contemporaneous with acquisition of native language phonology (and may indeed inform acquisition of some aspects of phonology). As emphasized here, learners will not only need some knowledge of native language phonology but will also need to be able to integrate diverse forms of phonological and other linguistic information to bootstrap into grammar. In their chapter, Werker, Lloyd, Pegg, and Polka review findings on the attunement of infant speech perception capacities to properties of the native language. In accordance with the model proposed by Mehler et al. (this volume), these accommodations appear first in relation to gross prosodic properties and vocalic categories of the native language and later spread to consonantal categories. Werker et al. note that there are domain-general, age-related changes in infants' abilities for remembering and exploiting environmental regularities and propose that certain reorganizations in infant speech perception occur in concert with such domain-general changes. They note evidence that inhibition of discrimination for nonnative consonantal contrasts is correlated with ability to form visual categories based on arbitrarily correlated features; both changes occur around 10 months. In light of this and other evidence, Werker et al. urge that theories of early acquisition be cognizant of the changing cognitive nature of the language learner, putting the baby in the bootstraps, as it were.

The concluding chapter by Hirsh-Pasek, Tucker, and Golinkoff observes that infants are engaged in a variety of developmental tasks, linguistic and nonlinguistic, while immersed in an ocean of information available over a variety of channels. Noting that proposals for Phonological (or prosodic) Bootstrapping have intended to account for how infants formulate representations of input to which syntactic and semantic analyses can be suitably applied, Hirsh-Pasek et al. propose that phonological and other forms of information are used in combination across development. This view is elaborated from the perspective of dynamic systems theory. Hirsh-Pasek et al. suggest a non-linear model of language learning in which different forms of input information, rather than being cast in a rigid ranking of importance, assume differing weights as acquisition proceeds. They note that systems theory suggests a specific set of empirical approaches and provides a framework for integrating future research across disciplinary boundaries, research of the sort needed to explain the child's acquisition of language.

On our view, the contents of this volume offer an emerging picture of how and what infant's perception and representation of phonetic, phonotactic, prosodic, and stochastic patterns manifest in input speech contribute to the acquisition of language. Acquisition must begin with analysis of speech (or signing), for it is these *signals* that constitute the linguistic environment for the learner. Although analyses of speech will not carry acquisition to its completion, such analyses are essential. A Phonological Bootstrapping account of language development may be envisioned in which primitive linguistic representations based on perceptual analyses of input phonology suffice for making rudimentary syntactic inductions. The deductive consequences of these inductions allow infants to exploit new forms of information (semantic, syntactic, or pragmatic) for linguistic purposes and may also allow infants to use aspects of input phonology that were once indecipherable. Access to these new forms of information paves the way for the development of more detailed linguistic representations, which then serve as bases for making more complex linguistic inductions. In this upward spiraling of linguistic abilities, input phonology may assume a progressively less important role. At the root, however, it is the signal that conveys words, phrases, sentences, indeed grammars to each new generation.

REFERENCES

Abney, S. (1987). *The English noun phrase in its sentential aspect*. Unpublished doctoral dissertation, MIT, Cambridge, MA.

Abrahamsen, A. H. (1987). Bridging boundaries versus breaking boundaries: Psycholinguistics in perspective. *Synthese, 72*, 355–388.

Baltin, M. (1982). A landing site theory of movement rules. *Linguistic Inquiry, 13*, 1–38.

Brown, R. (1973). *A first language*. Cambridge, MA: Harvard University Press.

Chomsky, N. (1965). *Aspects of the theory of syntax*. Cambridge, MA: MIT Press.

Chomsky, N. (1986). *Barriers*. Cambridge, MA: MIT Press.

Cooper, R. P., & Aslin, R. N. (1994) Developmental differences in infant attention to the spectral properties of infant-directed speech. *Child Development, 65*, 1663–1677.

Cooper, W. E., & Paccia-Cooper, J. (1980). *Syntax and speech*. Cambridge, MA: Harvard University Press.

Darwin, C. (1877). A biographical sketch of an infant. *Mind, 2*, 285–294.

DeCasper, A. J., & Fifer, W. P. (1980). Of human bonding: Newborns prefer their mothers' voices. *Science, 208*, 1174–1176.

Demuth, K. (1992). Accessing functional categories in Sesotho: Interactions at the morpho-syntax interface. In J. Meisel (Ed.), *The acquisition of verb placement: Functional categories and V2 phenomena in language development* (pp. 83-107). Dordrecht: Kluwer Academic Publishers.

Demuth, K. (1994). On the 'underspecification' of functional categories in early grammars. In B. Lust, M. Suñer, & J. Whitman (Eds.), *Syntactic theory and first language acquisition: Cross-linguistic perspectives*. (pp. 119-134). Hillsdale, NJ: Lawrence Erlbaum Associates.

Dewey, J. (1894). The psychology of infant language. *Psychological Review, 1*, 63–66.

Fernald, A., & Mazzie, C. (1991). Prosody and focus in speech to infants and adults. *Developmental Psychology, 27*, 209-221.

Fernald, A., Taeschner, T., Dunn, J., Papousek, M., Boysson-Bardies, B., & Fukui, I. (1989). A cross-language study of prosodic modifications in mothers' and fathers' speech to preverbal infants. *Journal of Child Language, 16*, 477–501.

Fletcher, P., & MacWhinney, B. (1995). *Handbook of language acquisition*. Oxford: Blackwell.

Garnica, O. K. (1977). Some prosodic and paralinguistic features of speech to young children. In C. E. Snow and C. A. Ferguson (Eds.), *Talking to children* (pp. 63–88). Cambridge: Cambridge University Press.

Gleitman, L. R., & Wanner, E. (1982). Language acquisition: The state of the state of the art. In E. Wanner & L. R. Gleitman (Eds.), *Language acquisition: The state of the art* (pp. 3–48). Cambridge, England: Cambridge University Press.

Hirsh-Pasek, K., Kemler Nelson, D. G., Jusczyk, P. W., Wright Cassidy, K., Druss, B., & Kennedy, L. (1987). Clauses are perceptual units for young infants. *Cognition, 26*, 269-286.

Hockett, C. F. (1966). The problem of universals in language. In J. H. Greenberg (Ed.), *Universals of Language*, 2nd edition (pp. 1-29). Cambridge, MA: MIT Press.

Inkelas, S., & Zec, D. (Eds.) (1990). *The syntax/phonology connection*. Chicago: University of Chicago Press.

Jusczyk, P. W., Cutler, A., & Redanz, L. (1993). Infants' sensitivity to predominant stress patterns in English. *Child Development, 64*, 675–687.

Jusczyk, P. W., Hirsh-Pasek, K., Kemler Nelson, D. G., Kennedy, L. J., Woodward, A., & Piwoz, J. (1992). Perception of acoustic correlates of major phrasal units by young infants. *Cognitive Psychology, 24*, 252–293.

Kelly, M. H. (1992). Using sound to solve syntactic problems: The role of phonology in grammatical category assignments. *Psychological Review, 99*, 349–364.

Lewis, M. M. (1936). *Infant speech: A study of the beginnings of language*. New York: Harcourt Brace.

Liberman, A. M., Cooper, F. S., Shankweiler, D. P., & Studdert-Kennedy, M. (1967). Perception of the speech code. *Psychological Review, 74*, 431–461.

Liberman, A. M., Delattre, P. C., & Cooper, F. S. (1952). The role of selected stimulus variables in the perception of unvoiced stop consonants. *American Journal of Psychology, 65*, 497–516.

Lust, B., Suñer, M., & Whitman, J. (Eds.) (1994). *Syntactic theory and first language acquisition: Cross-linguistic perspectives.*. Hillsdale, NJ: Lawrence Erlbaum Associates.

Markey, K. L. (1994). *The sensorimotor foundations of phonology: A computational model of early childhood articulatory and phonetic development*. Unpublished doctoral dissertation, University of Colorado, Boulder.

McCarthy, J., & Prince, A. (in press). *Prosodic morphology: I. Constraint interaction & satisfaction*. Cambridge, MA: MIT Press.

Mehler, J., Jusczyk, P. W., Lambertz, G., Halsted, G., Bertoncini, J., & Amiel-Tison, C. (1988). A precursor of language acquisition in young infants. *Cognition, 29,* 143–178.

Meisel, J. (Ed.) (1992). *The acquisition of verb placement: Functional categories and V2 phenomena in language development* . Dordrecht: Kluwer Academic Publishers.

Morgan, J. L. (1986) *From simple input to complex grammar.* Cambridge, MA: MIT Press.

Morgan, J. L. (in press). A rhythmic bias in preverbal speech segmentation. *Journal of Memory and Language.*

Morgan, J. L., & Newport, E. L. (1981). The role of constituent structure in the induction of an artificial language. *Journal of Verbal Learning and Verbal Behavior, 20,* 67-85.

Newport, E. L. (1977). Motherese: The speech of mothers to young children. In N. Castellan, D. B. Pisoni, & G. Potts (Eds.), *Cognitive theory* (Vol. 2, pp. 177-217). Hillsdale, NJ: Lawrence Erlbaum Associates.

Peters, A. M. (1983). *The units of language acquisition.* New York: Cambridge University Press.

Pinker, S. (1984). *Language learnability and language development.* Cambridge, MA: Harvard University Press.

Prince, A., & Smolensky, P. (in press). *Optimality theory: Constraint interaction in generative grammar,* Cambridge, MA: MIT Press.

Saussure, F. de (1916/1959). *Course in general linguistics.* New York: Philosophical Library.

Slobin, D. I. (1982). Universal and particular in the acquisition of language. In E, Wanner & L. Gleitman (Eds.), *Language acquisition: The state of the art* (pp. 128-170). Cambridge: Cambridge University Press.

Snow, C. E. (1972). Mothers' speech to children learning language. *Child Development, 43,* 549-565.

Streeter, L. A. (1978). Acoustic determinants of phrase boundary perception. *Journal of the Acoustical Society of America, 64,* 1582-1592.

Velten, H. V. (1943). The growth of phonemic and lexical patterns in infant language. *Language, 19,* 281–292.

Wexler, K., & Culicover, P. W. (1980). *Formal principles of language acquisition.* Cambridge, MA: MIT Press.

PART I

THE NATURE, PERCEPTION, AND REPRESENTATION OF INPUT SPEECH

2 The Perception and Representation of Speech by Infants

Peter D. Eimas
Brown University

To begin to learn the phonology and syntax of the parental language requires at minimum that young infants segment and internally represent the stream of speech at phonetic and lexical levels of processing. Moreover, it is undoubtedly necessary for the acquisition of syntax that representations of greater complexity, for example, phrases and clauses, also become a part of the repertoire of the internal representations of speech during the first two to five years of life (e.g., Morgan, 1986; Pinker, 1984; Wexler & Culicover, 1980). Although there is not agreement as to which representations must be available and which rules or parameter settings are acquired or selected during the earliest phases of language acquisition, there is general agreement that the speech signal must be segmented and represented at different levels of processing if linguistic competence is to be attained.

Acquisition theorists assume representations of varying complexity in their attempts to describe the course of language acquisition, including the infant's earliest use of language. Confirmation of these theoretical efforts rests not only on their ability to accommodate the infant's very early production and comprehension of language, but also for some theorists on the theory's ability to lead smoothly to the hypothesized view of mature linguistic competence. Of course, even approximations to these criteria may be taken as evidence for the psychological reality of both the presumed representations and rule systems. There is, however, at least the appearance of circularity with regard to assuming theoretical constructs and linguistic representations in such an approach. Many different sets of representations will serve as the units over which rule structures will operate, provided suitable adjustments are made in the rule systems that are presumed to underlie the infant's competence and the theoretical smoothness that describes the infant's progression from one level of competence to another. Nevertheless this is not to argue against the current approach to determining the rules and representations that permit the acquisition of language. After all it has served us well for over 30 years. Rather, I suggest that theories of language acquisition not rest unquestionably on representations that may lack psychological reality. This is in effect a call for a programmatic search for the manner in which infants and young children represent the speech they hear—a strategy that assumes that this major component of theories of language acquisition should rest on independent, empirical evidence whenever possible (see Frazier, in press, who argues persuasively for the primary role of representation in linguistic theory).

The present chapter attempts first to provide an overview of the speech processing capacities of young infants. A brief review of the effects of experience with the parental language during the first year of life is also presented. These latter findings illustrate the young infant's keen sensitivity to properties in the speech signal that have linguistic significance during the first year of life and perhaps even earlier, that is, in utero, and in so doing lend credence to arguments that the linguistic representations of infants may undergo a number of reorganizations early in life. Finally, I consider the state of our knowledge regarding the infant's sensitivity to potential information in the signal for the segmentation and representation of speech and end by describing a means for investigating the representational units of speech in young infants.

As I hope to make apparent, we know much about the processes of perception, as well as about the effects of experiencing the parental language on these processes during the first year of life. However, we know very little about the segmentation of speech and the resulting representations that serve as the units over which the first rules of grammar are presumed to operate. This, I believe, is not solely a consequence of the fact that this is a very new domain of research (see Jusczyk & Kemler Nelson, this volume), but is also an inherent consequence of the study of the representations of speech (and other input modalities) in infants (and adults). Problems arise from difficulties in eliminating alternative formulations, although appropriate designs can markedly reduce the number of possibilities (see, for example, Eimas, Miller, & Jusczyk, 1987; Mehler, Dupoux, Nazzi, & Dehaene-Lambertz, this volume; Mehler, Dupoux, & Segui, 1990).

PROCESSES OF PERCEPTION

The comprehension of speech ultimately requires extracting the speaker's intended meaning from a nearly continuous acoustic signal that is not segmentable at all linguistically relevant levels of representation solely on the basis of the acoustic properties that comprise speech. It is of course how the listener derives the intended meaning of the speaker that we must ultimately understand and explain. From more than three decades of research with this goal in mind, we have witnessed the postulation of a large number of processing procedures and levels of representation that presumably operate and intervene between reception of the signal and the extraction of meaning. Indeed, even efforts to determine the representations suitable for lexical access and recognition and the processes by which they are derived from the speech signal are marked by numerous alternatives, often complex in nature and almost always controversial (e.g., Segui, Dupoux, & Mehler, 1990). It is at this prelexical level of processing, the traditional domain of speech perception, that I describe the basic characteristics of the perception of speech by infants.

What is for many most interesting about segmental and syllabic percepts in adult listeners, and of course necessary for communication, is their perceived constancy, or near constancy. This constancy obtains despite considerable variation in the spectral and temporal structure of speech from one articulation to the next both within and across speakers. The variations in articulation with their corresponding variations in the acoustic structure of speech have many sources, including the age, sex, and emotional state of the speaker as well as the rate of articulation and the phonetic environment that precedes and follows the segmental and syllabic units that are the percepts of interest.

The study of perceptual constancy involves understanding the means—the mechanisms and their processing characteristics—that extract a (nearly) phenomenally identical percept from physically differing signals. To be complete it also requires an understanding of when these mechanisms become functional and how they change, if indeed they do, during the course of ontogenesis. It is toward describing the earliest functioning—the earliest characteristics of the mechanisms of speech perception—that this discussion is directed. However, in that we are concerned with the processing characteristics of young infants, it is obvious that the results of experimental investigations into their phenomenal experiences cannot be reported. Measures necessary to infer the perceptual identity of two experiences simply do not exist for observers this young. What is possible to study with infant listeners, however, is the extent to which two physically different speech signals that are phenomenally the same for adult listeners yield equivalent responses. This is in effect to study the extent to which selected signals are perceived as belonging to the same category or as yielding a common representation which, although not a direct indicant of perceptual constancy, is certainly a necessary condition for constancy and for making communication in different contexts and among numerous individuals possible. The methods for such studies are quite varied. They often involve a habituation–release from habituation procedure that varies in its details with the age of the infant and "instincts" of the experimenter as well as conditioned head-turning procedures that rely on learned responses rather than unlearned habituation and dishabituation responses to indicate to the experiment whether an infant has perceived a difference among stimuli.

There is at this writing considerable evidence that infants as young as 1 month of age represent speech categorically, and do so in a manner that is apparently very similar to that which is evidenced in adult listeners (Eimas, Miller, & Jusczyk, 1987; Repp, 1983, for reviews). By categorical perception, I mean simply that many acoustic variants are mapped onto a single linguistically relevant category. Furthermore, as a consequence of this mapping two acoustically different exemplars of speech are either difficult or easy to discriminate. If two acoustically different exemplars of speech are mapped onto the same categorical representation, discrimination is typically difficult. However, if two exemplars distinguished by the same acoustic difference are mapped onto the different internal structures, discrimination is easy. The ease of discriminability may be viewed as a consequence of listeners finding it difficult to attend to the acoustic differences among exemplars mapped onto the same category and easy to attend to acoustic differences that are sufficient to signal different categories. Thus, for example, Eimas, Siqueland, Jusczyk, and Vigorito (1971) found that 1- and 4-month-old infants failed to discriminate small (20 ms) differences in voice onset time (VOT) that marked different exemplars drawn from within either of the two voicing categories of English (and many other languages) in syllable-initial position. However, when the same acoustic difference in VOT provided information sufficient to distinguish two syllable-initial stop consonants from different voicing categories—[b] and [pʰ] in this instance—the two speech sounds were reliably discriminated. Similar findings have been obtained for voicing information with infants about the same age being raised in other language communities, for acoustic information corresponding to differences in place and manner of articulation, and for vocalic distinctions provided the latter are sufficiently brief (Eimas et al., 1987, for a review).

Further evidence for the categorical nature of infant speech perception comes from a series of experiments by Kuhl (e.g., 1979, 1983) using a quite different experimental procedure and somewhat older infants. She has shown that infants, approximately 6 months of age, form equivalence classes for a number of consonantal and vocalic categories whose exemplars were selected so as to vary considerably in their acoustic properties and be readily discriminable. Thus, for example, 6-month-old infants showed the ability to perceive different instances of the vowels /a/ and /i/ as belonging to two separate categories, despite substantial acoustic differences among the exemplars of each category resulting from differences in speaker and intonation pattern. Moreover, given that categorization occurred on the first exposure to novel category exemplars, categorization would appear to be a biologically driven, natural consequence of the perception of speech by infants. This conclusion is further strengthened by the demonstration by Hillenbrand (1984) that infants formed equivalence classes based on manner of articulation for stop and nasal consonants that varied in place of articulation and speaker, but did not categorize the same segmental units when they were randomly assigned to categories—that is, when the categorical designations were arbitrary and not linguistically based.

Kuhl's findings are interestingly in marked contrast to findings with Japanese quail as subjects. Kluender, Diehl, and Killeen (1987) showed that Japanese quail took literally thousands of training trials before evidence of equivalence classes was available—a finding not surprising to those who hold to the view that (most of) the processes of communication among conspecifics, in being biologically important and undoubtedly a product of evolution, are necessarily species specific (e.g., Eimas & Miller, 1991, 1992; Liberman & Mattingly, 1985). What is natural and easy for one species with respect to perception of its communicative calls is unnatural and difficult for another species, even for relatively closely related species (Zoloth, Petersen, Beecher, Green, Marler, Moody, & Stebbins, 1979).

It is important to note that although both experimental approaches to the study of categorization in infants have shown the spontaneous categorical nature of speech perception, they do not provide independent evidence regarding the nature of the categorical representations. That is, studies of this nature with infant listeners do not inform us directly whether the categorical representation is linguistic and if so whether it is at the featural, segmental, or syllabic levels or even whether the signal, typically a monosyllabic unit, yields a coherent (organized) percept—a point to which I return later.

A categorization process, such as that which exists for the processing of speech, in effect maps a potentially indefinite number of signals onto a single representation that is phonetic in nature, as some believe to be the case even for infants (e.g., Eimas & Miller, 1991, 1992). What is particularly interesting is that this many-to-one mapping is itself not invariant. Studies with young infants, based on experiments performed originally with adult listeners, have shown that the boundary between categories can be altered as a consequence of systematically varying contextual factors. For example, Miller and Liberman (1979) found with adult listeners that the acoustic correlate of rate of articulation, syllable duration, can alter the boundary between [b] and [w] along a temporally based continuum—the duration of the formant transitions. When the exemplars to be identified represented rapidly articulated speech, the category boundary separating [b] from [w] was located at a smaller value of transition duration than when the exemplars represented slowly articulated speech. The same shift in the boundary has been found with 3- and 4-month-old infants (Eimas & Miller, 1980; Miller & Eimas, 1983). (That this process may be a consequence of a general auditory mechanism and not of a specialized module for the perception of speech is suggested by comparable findings with nonspeech acoustic signals in both infants and adults [Jusczyk, Pisoni, Reed, Fernald, & Myers, 1983; Pisoni, Carrell, & Gans, 1983].) Further evidence of an analogous nature has been presented by Carden, Levitt, Jusczyk, and Walley (1981). They found that the phonetic context can determine whether differences in the spectral properties of formant transitions in consonant-vowel contexts are discriminated by adults. Transitions were discriminated but only when they were preceded by a neutral (noninformative) fricative noise and heard by adults as [fa] and [θa]. When the noise was absent both sounds were heard as [ba] and were not discriminated. Levitt, Jusczyk, Murray, and Carden (1988) obtained the same results with regard to discrimination (but of course without measures of identification) in infants 6 to 12 weeks of age (see Eimas & Miller, 1991, for a similar effect of context, in this case, the duration of silence preceding formant transitions in medial-syllabic position).

In a similar vein, research with adults, and more recently with infants, has shown that the multiple acoustic properties that are sufficient and available to signal phonetic contrasts enter into perceptual trading relations. This is simply to say that the many properties that typically signal the same phonetic contrast have been shown to influence one another. More specifically, the value of one of these properties affects the range of stimuli varying along a second property that maps onto the phonetic categories in question. Evidence for this mutual influence has been obtained, for example, by Fitch, Halwes, Erikson, and Liberman (1980) with adults and by Miller and Eimas (1983) with infants 3 and 4 months of age. Moreover, the multiple cues for speech derive their perceptual effectiveness to a large extent from the manner in which they specify categorical (presumably phonetic) representations and not simply from their acoustic distinctiveness both in adults (Fitch et al., 1980) and infants (Eimas, 1985)—evidence in accord with the view that there exists a module or processes dedicated to the perception of speech (e.g., Liberman & Mattingly, 1985).

Finally, there is the matter of the organization of speech percepts (representations) in young infants. Obviously, in order for grammatical knowledge to be acquired, the perception of speech at levels from segments to clauses must be organized, reflecting the organization in the signal that instantiates language. This is simply to say that the initial percepts (representations) must at some point in development be coherent linguistic structures and not simply unstructured collections of auditory or phonetic features or unstructured collections of higher units, for example, an unordered listing of segments or syllables to represent a word or of words to represent a phrase.

Eimas and Miller (1992) showed that consonant-vowel syllables were perceived as organized entities by 3- and 4-month-old infants—a beginning into what is required for potentially meaningful linguistic representations of connected speech. Using a methodology designed for the study of duplex perception, they presented synthetic speech patterns dichotically such that one ear received only an isolated third-formant transition, appropriate for the syllable [da] or [ga]. The other ear received the remaining acoustic information necessary for perception of the two syllables—the base—which was identical for both syllables. In this situation, adults perceive a nonspeech-like chirp at the ear receiving the transition and the syllable [da] or [ga] located at the ear receiving the base—which syllable is heard depends on which isolated transition was presented. Infants discriminated the two patterns and, most importantly, did so even when the third-formant transitions were attenuated in intensity to the extent that infant listeners could not discriminate them when presented in isolation. Thus, discrimination could not be based solely on the isolated transitions. Presumably the two distinct sources (speech and nonspeech) and directions (left and right with reference to the listener) of acoustic information, the transition and the base, were integrated into a single organized percept, linguistic in nature, that made discrimination possible. Interestingly, a more recent study by Eimas and Miller (unpublished) showed that this integration did not occur when the transitions were attenuated and the base consisted only of the remaining portion of the third formant—evidence favoring the view that the organization that occurred in the original experiment provided a percept that was linguistic in nature. How the linguistic information is represented in this organized percept cannot be assessed on the basis of the results obtained by Eimas and Miller. We do not know whether undifferentiated syllables or sequentially ordered phonetic segments or even sequentially ordered lists of features form the organized percept.

EFFECTS OF THE PARENTAL LANGUAGE

There are a number of findings with young infants that show changes in processing speech at prelexical levels by 12 months of age. First, Kuhl and her associates (Grieser & Kuhl, 1989; Kuhl, 1991; Kuhl, Williams, Lacerda, Stevens, & Lindblom, 1992) showed that vocalic categories of 6-month-old infants and adults have a prototype structure. Of considerable importance for those holding to the view that speech is processed by a specialized, species-specific module, these same vocalic categories did not have a prototype structure for Japanese macaques. In addition, the prototype structure of the English vowel /i/ and Swedish vowel /y/ differs for infants raised in homes where American English is spoken as opposed to homes where Swedish is spoken. This is evidence for an effect of language on phonetic processing surprisingly early in life.

At the level of segments, Werker and Tees (1984) showed a marked decrease in the ability to discriminate segmental contrasts not in the parental language, but this decrement was not evidenced until the infants were 10 to 12 months of age. (For interesting differences in the effects of linguistic experience on different contrasts, see Werker, Lloyd, Pegg, & Polka, this volume, for work with vowels, and Best, McRoberts, & Sithole, 1988, who found that Zulu clicks were discriminated by native American English-speaking adults and infants raised in homes where American English was the spoken language. And see Eimas, 1990, for a discussion of the results of Best et al. based on assumptions from a modular view of speech perception.)

The processing of speech at a phonetic level shows additional effects of very early linguistic experience relevant to the acquisition of linguistic competence, namely, the role of phonotactic constraints found in the parental language (Jusczyk, Friederici, Wessels, Svenkerud, & Jusczyk, 1993). Nine-month-old but not 6-month-old infants raised in English-speaking homes preferred to listen to English words as opposed to Dutch words that contained segmental units and sequences that were not permissible in English. In a second study, in which the Dutch and English words contained the same segmental units but with some segmental sequences that were permissible in only one language, 9-month-old infants, but again not 6-month-old infants preferred listening to words from the parental language, be it Dutch or English. Obviously, infants, probably starting near the age of 6 months (cf. Kuhl et al., 1992), are beginning to record and represent not only which segments are occurring in the parental language, but also which sequences of these sounds are permissible and thus occur. Those that do occur become preferred. Further support for the hypothesis that it was phonetic information that was driving these preferences comes from the failure of Jusczyk et al. (1993) to find preferences for words from the native language when the materials were low pass filtered.

There are also early effects of the parental language on production in the first year and one half of life (e.g., Boysson-Bardies, Halle, Sagart, & Durand, 1989; Boysson-Bardies & Vihman, 1991). These researchers found that the production of vowels by 10-month-old infants during babbling reflected the distribution of vowels of the parental language as indicated by comparison of a number of summary measures of the acoustic structures of the vocalic productions of infants and adult members of the infants' linguistic community. In addition, they showed that the distribution of consonants in the babbling and first words of infants between 9 and 19 months of age reflected the distribution of consonants with respect to place and manner of articulation in the parental language. Taken together, these results strongly support the view that the production of speech is driven to a considerable degree by perceptual representations that have been acquired over the course of listening to the parental language during the first year or so. The processes of perception and production thus interact and a reasonable guess as to when this interaction begins is around 6 months of age (cf. Kuhl et al., 1992)—the earliest age to date at which phonetic categories have been shown to be influenced by linguistic experience.

TOWARD ESTABLISHING THE EXISTENCE OF LINGUISTIC REPRESENTATIONS

Determining units of representation for infants involves first discovering the sources of information in speech that are in principle sufficient (even if not available in all utterances) to signal beginnings and endings of linguistic structures or their approximation in the case of words and demonstrating that infants are in fact sensitive to this information. It likewise requires showing that the presumed segmented units are psychologically real and ultimately that they are available and used for language acquisition. A number of such (potential) sources of information are known to exist. There is evidence in English that the boundaries between clauses and phrases are marked by large alterations in fundamental frequency, final syllable lengthening, and relatively long pauses at least in the case of clauses (see Jusczyk, Hirsh-Pasek, Kemler Nelson, Kennedy, Woodward, & Piwoz, 1992, for a summary of supporting evidence). In addition, stress patterns, for example, the strong–weak pattern that is dominant in English, can convey information marking the locus, if not the edges, of (some) lexical units (Cutler & Norris, 1988).

What is important is that there is growing evidence that infants are sensitive to these and other prosodic properties of speech. For example, not only are infants sensitive to the highly inflected speech directed to infants and young children, but they prefer this form of speech to adult-directed speech (Fernald, 1984, 1985). Moreover, this preference would seem to be carried by low frequency prosodic information, for example, fundamental frequency and rhythm (Fernald & Kuhl, 1987) as would likewise seem to be the case for the preference of infants four days of age for the parental language (Mehler, Jusczyk, Lambertz, Halsted, Bertoncini, & Amiel-Tison, 1988). In addition, DeCasper and Fifer (1980) showed that infants three days of age and younger preferred their mother's voice to the voice of another female. Mehler, Bertoncini, Barriere, and Jassik-Gerschenfeld (1978) found the same preference in 1-month-old infants and that it was even evidenced with low pass filtered speech, that is, when only prosodic information was available. The origins of these preferences, based most likely on the infant's greater familiarity with fundamental frequency and its patterning across connected speech in the mother's voice, may well begin in the last trimester of gestation. This is possible inasmuch it is now known that the fetal environment passes low frequency information and that infants are sensitive to sound in the third trimester (e.g., Lecanuet, Busnel, DeCasper, Granier-Deferre, & Maugeais, 1986). A major function of these preferences may be to separate speech from other environmental sounds as well as direct attention to speech, thereby helping to provide an independent set of linguistic representations necessary for language acquisition.

As noted earlier, the approximate beginnings and endings of some words of English can be marked by the predominant strong–weak pattern of stress. Recently, Jusczyk, Cutler, and Redanz (1993) found that infants 6 months of age from American English–speaking homes listened equally to unfamiliar words with a strong–weak or a weak–strong stress pattern. At 9 months of age, however, a reliable preference was obtained for words with the predominant strong–weak pattern of stress as well as for the same materials when they were low pass filtered. As Jusczyk et al. (1993) noted, these results do not indicate that infants are actually segmenting and representing fluent speech as lexical-like units on the basis of the stress pattern. Such a demonstration awaits future research. Moreover, it remains to be shown whether infants are sensitive to language-specific stress patterns in fluent speech.

In two series of simple, but highly informative experiments, Hirsh-Pasek, Kemler Nelson, Jusczyk, Cassidy, Druss, and Kennedy (1987) and later Jusczyk et al. (1992) obtained evidence that infants are sensitive to information marking clausal and phrasal boundaries in connected discourse, respectively. In the first set of experiments, Hirsh-Pasek et al. inserted 1-s pauses either at the end of clauses, thereby in effect lengthening naturally occurring pauses and forming what they called natural versions of speech, or in the middle of the same clauses, thereby producing what they referred to as the unnatural versions. Infants 6 to 10 months old showed reliable preferences for the natural versions. In addition, Kemler Nelson, Hirsh-Pasek, Jusczyk, and Cassidy (1989) found that this preference was evidenced for child-directed but not adult-directed speech—a strong demonstration for one of many possible roles for child-directed speech in acquiring language.

Using the same methodology, Jusczyk et al. (1992) demonstrated a preference for samples of speech in which 1-s pauses were inserted at the major phrasal boundary (i.e., at the boundary between subject and predicate phrases) as opposed to locations within a phrase. It is worth noting that pronounced pauses typically do not occur at these syntactic junctures with natural speech, and thus in this series of experiments pausing is not a cue for syntactic structures *per se* but a means of highlighting other cues, for example, fundamental frequency declination and resetting. In these experiments the effect was again evidenced for child-directed speech but not for adult-directed speech (cf. Kemler Nelson et al., 1989) and there was now a developmental effect: Preferences were reliable for 9-month-old infants but not for 6-month-olds. Jusczyk et al. (1992) speculated that the developmental effect may reflect a need for greater familiarity with the parental language in order to determine how phrases are marked, perhaps because of the greater inconsistency in the information for phrases across languages. But this explanation appears to leave unanswered why 6-month-old infants from English-speaking families prefer speech with pauses after fundamental frequency resettings and syllable-final lengthenings when these acoustic properties mark clauses but not when they mark phrases—sources of information that Jusczyk et al. showed were available in their stimulus materials and the probable source of the preference of older infants.

The experiments by Hirsh-Pasek et al. (1987), Jusczyk et al. (1992), and Kemler Nelson et al. (1989) provide firm evidence for the sensitivity of infants to prosodic information that can assist the discovery of major syntactic units, phrases, and clauses in continuous speech (see also Jusczyk, 1993, in press, for additional evidence and discussion). In effect, bootstraps would appear not only to exist in the speech signal but to be available to young infants. The question remains whether these bootstraps are in fact used to segment speech into the linguistic units that theories of language acquisition require.

Showing experimentally that (some) linguistic units of whatever complexity are actually represented in the mental structures of infants is by no means a simple experimental task (see Jusczyk & Kemler Nelson, this volume; Morgan, 1994, for work on this problem). With respect to representations that are important for phonological theory, features, segments, and syllables, obtaining evidence as to whether these units are independently encoded in a hierarchical arrangement or whether features and segments are derived from the next higher representations is unlikely. We simply do not appear to have the methodology necessary to unequivocally separate these alternatives, whether in infant or adult listeners (but see Mehler et al., 1990; Segui et al., 1990). Nevertheless, further use of experimental designs with appropriate stimuli, which essentially involves finding linguistic bases for categorization and for the effects of attention on categorization (Bertoncini, Bijeljac-Babic, Kennedy, Jusczyk, & Mehler, 1988; Hillenbrand, 1983; Jusczyk, Bertoncini, Bijeljac-Babic, Kennedy, & Mehler, 1990), could provide additional evidence for the availability of representations for syllabic structures, segmental units, and perhaps even phonetic features.

With respect to representations for words (or word-like representations in the case of prelinguistic infants) or even representations that involve coherent sequences of such items, the methodology of Eimas and Miller (1992) can (in principle) be extended to help assess perceptual organization at these levels of representation. As will be recalled, Eimas and Miller (1992) found that infants 3 and 4 months of age formed a coherent percept when the third-formant transition and the remaining acoustic information for the syllable [da] or [ga] were presented dichotically. Moreover, they argued that the evidence supported the view that the processes of organization occur at a phonetic level and thus yield coherent representations that are linguistic in nature, a necessary requirement for lexical and grammatical acquisition (see Mehler et al., 1990, for a discussion of prerequisites for learning words).

Consider a means to demonstrate coherent representations for word and word-like units of varying numbers of connected syllables. I describe only some of the experimental conditions—those that are minimally necessary to convey the general idea of the logic of these experiments—and do so only for a bisyllabic stimulus, although stimulus patterns with any number of syllables can be used. Two groups of 3- and 4-month-old infants will be familiarized with the stimulus REBUT. The stimulus will be presented dichotically such that the second- and third-formant transitions for the phoneme /b/ will be presented to one ear and the remainder of the item—the base—to the other ear. Without presentation of the isolated transitions, the base would sound quite like REDUT to adult listeners. On meeting the familiarization criterion, one group of infants will then hear a complete REBUT (i.e., a speech pattern that will include the second- and third-formant transitions for /b/) and be presented monotically to the ear receiving the base during familiarization. The second group will hear a complete version of REDUT that will include the second- and third-formant transitions for /d/ and again be presented monotically. No sound will be presented to the other ear during the second part of the experiment.

Consider the predictions for the two groups if integration does *not* occur during familiarization. Infants receiving REDUT during the second phase of the experiment should not show recovery of looking time, the dependent measure to be used to reflect discrimination, having received more-or-less the same stimulus during familiarization. However, the infants receiving REBUT should increase their looking times, given the novelty of REBUT compared to the familiar REDUT. Consider now the expectations if integration *does* occur. Infants hearing REBUT would now not show recovery; the electronically and perceptually integrated versions of REBUT should be nearly identical experiences for infants as they are for adults (cf. Eimas & Miller, 1992). However, infants hearing the now novel REDUT during the second phase should show increased looking. Given the later pattern of outcomes, the reasonable inference is that integration had occurred and that an organized bisyllabic word-like representation had been formed, provided only that we also show that the initial syllable /ri/ is part of the percept. That is to say, the processes of integration, as described, lead to the presence of an organized syllable, /but/. However, whether this representation also includes the initial syllable /ri/ (which for now at least I assume to be coherent) needs to be determined experimentally by appropriate control conditions. For example, we need to determine whether infants would notice its absence or any changes in its segmental structure, and if such evidence is obtained we have evidence compatible with the idea that the syllable /ri/ was also represented. In effect, experiments of this nature attempt to determine first whether integration has occurred for a linguistic unit of varying duration or number of segments (integration may occur for units larger than a single segment [Eimas, unpublished data]) and second whether this representation includes other units of varying duration and number.

If this approach is successful with infants this age or infants closer to the age of lexical understanding, additional experiments are possible that vary, for example, the number of connected syllables in the target item and their stress pattern (cf. Cutler & Norris, 1988) together with the presence of a varying number of word-like structures that precede the target item with and without natural intonation. What might be sought in research of this nature is when word-like representations—the forerunners of true lexical representations—can be evidenced, how these representations change with the complexity and intonation pattern of the incoming signal, and when and under what conditions they begin to also include preceding and following word-like units—the forerunners, I would argue, of phrases and clauses. Experiments of this general nature can further seek to determine if and when fundamental frequency declinations and resettings as well as final syllable lengthenings influence the formation of representations for word-like signals and sequences of such items. Information of this nature should further illuminate the manner ın which speech is processed during the first year of life. Even more importantly it should provide a beginning toward anchoring the presumed linguistic representations of acquisition theorists in the psychological reality of infants.

ACKNOWLEDGMENTS

Preparation of this chapter was supported by Grant HD 05331 from the National Institute of Child Health and Human Development. I thank Joanne L. Miller for her critical comments on an earlier version.

REFERENCES

Bertoncini, J., Bijeljac-Babic, R., Kennedy, L., Jusczyk, P. W., & Mehler, J. (1988). An investigation of young infants' perceptual representations of speech sounds. *Journal of Experimental Psychology: General, 117*, 21-33.

Best, C. T., McRoberts, G. W., & Sithole, N. M. (1988). Examination of perceptual reorganization for nonnative speech contrast: Zulu click discrimination by English-speaking adults and infants. *Journal of Experimental Psychology: Human Perception and Performance, 14*, 345-360.

Boysson-Bardies, B. de, Halle, P., Sagart, L., & Durand, C., (1989). A crosslinguistic investigation of vowel formants in babbling. *Journal of Child Language, 16*, 1-17.

Boysson-Bardies, B. de, & Vihman, M. M. (1991). Adaptation to language evidence from babbling and first words in four languages. *Language, 67*, 297-319.

Carden, G., Levitt, A., Jusczyk, P. W., & Walley, A. (1981). Evidence for phonetic processing of cues to place of articulation: Perceived manner affects perceived place. *Perception & Psychophysics, 29*, 26-36.

Cutler, A., & Norris, D. G. (1988). The role of strong syllables in segmentation for lexical access. *Journal of Experimental Psychology: Human Perception and Performance, 14*, 113-121.

DeCasper, A. J., & Fifer, W. P. (1980). Of human bonding: Newborns prefer their mothers' voices. *Science, 208*, 1174-1176.

Eimas, P. D. (1985). The equivalence of cues in the perception of speech by infants. *Infant Behavior & Development, 8*, 125-138.

Eimas, P. D. (1990). Comment: Some effects of language acquisition on speech perception. In I. G. Mattingly & M. Studdert-Kennedy (Eds.), *Modularity and the motor theory of speech perception* (pp. 111-116). Hillsdale, NJ: Lawrence Erlbaum Associates.

Eimas, P. D., & Miller, J. L. (1980). Contextual effects in infant speech perception. *Science, 209*, 1140-1141.

Eimas, P. D., & Miller, J. L. (1991). A constraint on the perception of speech by young infants. *Language and Speech, 34*, 251-263.

Eimas, P. D., & Miller, J. L. (1992). Organization in the perception of speech by young infants. *Psychological Science, 3*, 340-345.

Eimas, P. D., Miller, J. L., & Jusczyk, P. W. (1987). On infant speech perception and the acquisition of language. In S. Harnad (Ed.), *Categorical perception: The groundwork of cognition* (pp. 161-195). New York: Cambridge University Press.

Eimas, P. D., Siqueland, E. R., Jusczyk, P., & Vigorito, J. (1971). Speech perception in infants. *Science, 171*, 303-306.

Fernald, A. (1984). The perceptual and affective salience of mothers' speech to infants. In L. Feagans, C. Garvey, & R. Golinkoff (Eds.), *The origins and growth of communication* (pp. 5-29). Norwood, NJ: Ablex.

Fernald, A. (1985). Four-month-old infants prefer to listen to motherese. *Infant Behavior and Development, 8,* 181-195.

Fernald, A., & Kuhl, P. (1987). Acoustic determinants of infant preference of motherese speech. *Infant Behavior & Development, 10,* 279-293.

Fitch, H. L., Halwes, T., Erikson, D. M., & Liberman, A. M. (1980). Perceptual equivalence of two acoustic cues for stop-consonant manner. *Perception & Psychophysics, 27,* 343-350.

Frazier, L. (in press). Issues of representation in psycholinguistics. In J. L. Miller & P. D. Eimas (Eds.), *Handbook of perception and cognition: Vol. 11. Speech, language, and communication.* Orlando, FL: Academic Press.

Grieser, D., & Kuhl, P. K. (1989). Categorization of speech by infants: Support for speech-sound prototypes. *Developmental Psychology, 25,* 577-588.

Hillenbrand, J. (1983). Perceptual organization of speech sounds by infants. *Journal of Speech and Hearing Research, 26,* 268-282.

Hirsh-Pasek, K., Kemler Nelson, D. G., Jusczyk, P. W., Cassidy, K. W., Druss, B., & Kennedy, L. (1987). Clauses are perceptual units for young infants. *Cognition, 26,* 269-286.

Jusczyk, P. W. (1993). From general language-specific capacities: The WRAPSA Model of how speech perception develops. *Journal of Phonetics, 21,* 3-28.

Jusczyk, P. W. (in press). Language acquisition: Speech sounds and the beginnings of phonology. In J. L. Miller & P. D. Eimas (Eds.), *Handbook of perception and cognition: Vol. 11. Speech, language, and communication.* Orlando, FL: Academic Press.

Jusczyk, P. W., Bertoncini, J., Bijeljac-Babic, R., Kennedy, L. J., & Mehler, J. (1990). The role of attention in speech perception by young infants. *Cognitive Development, 5,* 265-286.

Jusczyk, P. W., Cutler, A., & Redanz, N. (1993). Preference for predominant stress patterns of English words. *Child Development, 64,* 675-687.

Jusczyk, P. W., Friederici, A. D., Wessels, J., Svenkerud, V. Y., & Jusczyk, A. M. (1993). Infants' sensitivity to the sound patterns of native language words. *Journal of Memory and Language, 32,* 402-420.

Jusczyk, P. W., Hirsh-Pasek, K., Kemler Nelson, D. G., Kennedy, L. J., Woodward, A., & Piwoz, J. (1992). Perception of acoustic correlates of major phrasal units by young infants. *Cognitive Psychology, 24,* 252-293.

Jusczyk, P. W., Pisoni, D. B., Reed, M. A., Fernald, A., & Myers, M. (1983). Infants' discrimination in the duration of a rapid spectrum change in nonspeech signals. *Science, 222,* 175-177.

Kemler Nelson, D. G., Hirsh-Pasek, K., Jusczyk, P. W., & Cassidy, K. W. (1989). How the prosodic cues in motherese might assist language learning. *Journal of Child Language, 16,* 55-68.

Kluender, K. R., Diehl, R. L., & Killeen, P. R. (1987). Japanese quail can learn phonetic categories. *Science, 237,* 1195-1197.

Kuhl, P. K. (1979). Speech perception in early infancy: Perceptual constancy for spectrally dissimilar vowel categories. *Journal of the Acoustical Society of America, 66,* 1668-1679.

Kuhl, P. K. (1983). Perception of auditory equivalence classes for speech in early infancy. *Infant Behavior & Development, 6,* 263-285.

Kuhl, P. K. (1991). Human adults and human infants show a "perceptual magnet effect" for the prototypes of speech categories, monkeys do not. *Perception & Psychophysics, 50,* 93-107.

Kuhl, P. W., Williams, K. A., Lacerda, F., Stevens, K. N., & Lindblom, B. (1992). Linguistic experience alters phonetic perception in infants by 6 months of age. *Science, 255,* 606-608.

Lecanuet, J.-P., Busnel, M.-C., DeCasper, A. J., Granier-Deferre, C., & Maugeais, R. (1986, November). *Fetal perception and discrimination of speech stimuli.* Paper presented at the Meeting of the International Society for Developmental Psychobiology, Annapolis, Maryland.

Levitt, A., Jusczyk, P. W., Murray, J., & Carden, G. (1988). Context effects in two-month-old infants' perception of labiodental/interdental fricative contrasts. *Journal of Experimental Psychology: Human Perception and Performance, 14,* 361-368.

Liberman, A. M., & Mattingly, I. G. (1985). The motor theory of speech perception revised. *Cognition, 21*, 1-36.

Mehler, J., Bertoncini, J., Barriere, M., & Jassik-Gerschenfeld, D. (1978). Infant recognition of mother's voice. *Perception, 7*, 491-497.

Mehler, J., Dupoux, E., & Segui, J. (1990). Constraining models of lexical access: The onset of word recognition. In G. T. M. Altmann (Ed.), *Cognitive models of speech processing* (pp. 236-262). Cambridge, MA: MIT Press.

Mehler, J., Jusczyk, P., Lambertz, G., Halsted, N., Bertoncini, J., & Amiel-Tison, C. (1988). A precursor of language acquisition in young infants. *Cognition, 29*, 143-178.

Miller, J. L., & Liberman, A. M. (1979). Some effects of later-occurring information on the perception of stop consonant and semivowel. *Perception & Psychophysics, 25*, 457-465.

Miller, J. L., & Eimas, P. D. (1983). Studies on the categorization of speech by infants. *Cognition, 13*, 135-165.

Morgan, J. L. (1986). *From simple input to complex grammar.* Cambridge, MA: MIT Press.

Morgan, J. L. (1994). Converging measures of speech segmentation in prelingual infants. *Infant Behavior & Development, 17*, 389-403.

Pinker, S. (1984). *Language learnability and language development.* Cambridge, MA: Harvard University Press.

Pisoni, D. B., Carrell, T. D., & Gans, S. J. (1983). Perception of rapid spectrum changes in speech and nonspeech signals. *Perception & Psychophysics, 34*, 314-322.

Repp, R. (1983). Categorical perception: Issues, methods, findings. In N. J. Lass (Ed.), *Speech and language: Advances in basic research and practice* (Vol. 10, pp. 243-335). New York: Academic Press.

Segui, J., Dupoux, E., & Mehler, J. (1990). The role of the syllable in speech segmentation, phoneme identification, and lexical access. In G. T. M. Altmann (Ed.), *Cognitive models of speech processing* (pp. 263-280). Cambridge, MA: MIT Press.

Werker, J. F., & Tees, R. C. (1984). Cross-language speech perception: Evidence for perceptual reorganization during the first year of life. *Infant Behavior and Development, 7*, 49-63.

Wexler, K., & Culicover, P. (1980). *Formal principles of language acquisition.* Cambridge, MA: MIT Press.

Zoloth, S. R., Petersen, M. R., Beecher, M. D., Green, S., Marler, P., Moody, D. B., & Stebbins, W. (1979). Species-specific perceptual processing of vocal sounds by monkeys. *Science, 204*, 870-873.

3 Introduction to Metrical and Prosodic Phonology

B. Elan Dresher
University of Toronto

The purpose of this chapter is to serve as a brief introduction to prosodic and metrical phonology. Prosodic and metrical structure, related to phonetics and the acoustic signal on one side and to syntax and semantic interpretation on the other, play a central role in the issues raised in this volume. Because of their relevance to so many areas of language, they have been investigated from many different points of view, including phonetics, intonation, stress-focus relations, discourse, psycholinguistics, and other perspectives. For reasons of space and coherence, the following overview is limited to prosodic and metrical structure as they pertain to phonology. I sketch some major results that have emerged in the context of research in phonological theory and the relation between syntax and phonology.

PROSODIC THEORY

Chomsky and Halle (1968; henceforth *SPE*) observed that the input to the phonological component is not surface syntactic structure Σ, the output of the syntax, but a structure Σ', a reduced and adjusted version of Σ. They relate the existence of this adjusted structure to a hypothesis of Miller and Chomsky (1963) about processing. Miller and Chomsky assume a two-stage memory: The first stage is a short-term system, restricted in capacity and access and operating in real time, which recovers Σ' from the input signal; the second stage is a larger system that takes Σ' as input and derives full syntactic (Σ) and semantic representations.

Two related questions arise concerning this adjusted structure Σ', which we henceforth refer to as prosodic structure:

1. Issues in prosodic phonology
   a. What is the nature of prosodic structure Σ'?
   b. How is syntactic structure Σ mapped into prosodic structure Σ'?

SPE did not attempt to develop an elaborate theory of prosodic structure. It was assumed there that Σ' consists of a linear string of phonological feature matrices separated by boundaries. Therefore, the main operation in the mapping from syntax to prosodic structure involved trading in syntactic labeled brackets for phonological boundary symbols (see Selkirk, 1972).

The *SPE* boundary theory, however, does not offer an adequate account of prosodic structure. Chomsky and Halle noted that complex sentences are first analyzed into a sequence of phonological phrases. This reanalysis "depends on syntactic structure, but is not always syntactically motivated" (1968, 9-10, 371-2). A famous example is given in (2):

2. Mismatches between Σ and Σ'
   a. Σ: This is [$_{NP}$ the cat that caught [$_{NP}$ the rat that stole [$_{NP}$ the cheese]]]
   b. Σ': (This is the cat) (that caught the rat) (that stole the cheese)

Whereas the major syntactic breaks are as indicated in (2a), the actual phrasing is rather as in (2b), cutting across major syntactic divisions. The principles for achieving the required rebracketing of this sentence were left unformulated. More generally, the *SPE* boundary theory requires a too-radical reduction of structure, and is not rich enough to account for phonological phrasing.

The Prosodic Hierarchy

To remedy this problem, Selkirk (1978) proposed that Σ', like Σ, is a hierarchically organized structure: Rather than exchanging syntactic brackets for boundaries, she proposed that syntactic brackets are exchanged for prosodic ones. The constituents of prosodic structure are arranged in a prosodic hierarchy; Selkirk (1978) proposed the hierarchy shown in (3):

3. The prosodic hierarchy above the word
Phonological Utterance	U
Intonational Phrase	I
Phonological Phrase	P
Phonological Word	W

Though various proposals for modifying this inventory have been made, we assume it to be basically correct in the following review. We start at the top of the hierarchy with the phonological utterance, U.

The Phonological Utterance

There is no precise definition of what may constitute a single U and what may not; a number of conditions are suggested by Nespor and Vogel (1986). Most ordinary sentences, like (4a), can constitute a U, as can fragments of sentences (b), and even a sequence of separate sentences if they meet various pragmatic conditions, such as being logically connected (c, d):

4. Some utterances (Nespor & Vogel, 1986)
   a. John plays the trumpet, but Bill plays the clarinet.
   b. The third from the right.
   c. Turn up the heat. I'm freezing.
   d. That's a nice cat. Is it yours?

In prosodic phonology, the main evidence for a prosodic level is the existence of a phonological rule that applies in its domain. Nespor and Vogel, following Kahn (1980), observed that U is the domain of the (North American) English rule of *t*-flapping, whereby a *t* or *d* between vowels in certain contexts is pronounced as a quick "flap," [D], rather than as a stop. This rule applies inside words: Compare *heat*, with [t], with *heater*, where the *t* is pronounced [D], and *late* ([t]) with *latter* ([D], the same as in *ladder*). It also applies when some of its context is supplied by different words. The rule may apply in (4c, d) in the words *heat* (*hea[D] I'm*) and *cat* (*ca[D] Is*). By contrast, we do not expect flapping across two unrelated sentences like *Turn up the heat. I'm Frances*, which would not, under ordinary circumstances, be grouped together as a U. In practice, U is usually taken as a given in prosodic theory.

The Intonational Phrase

The intonational phrase I is commonly defined as the domain of an intonation contour; further, the ends of intonational phrases coincide with positions where pausing and lengthening may occur (Bierwisch, 1966; Bing, 1979; Downing, 1970; Selkirk, 1984). It has been noted that certain syntactic constructions usually form their own I-phrase. These include parenthetical expressions, as in (5a), nonrestrictive relative clauses (b), lists (c), and other such expressions (Nespor & Vogel, 1986; Selkirk, 1978, 1984, and the references therein):

5. Syntax and I-phrases (Nespor & Vogel, 1986)
   a. Parenthetical expressions
      ($_I$Lions) ($_I$as you know) ($_I$are dangerous)
   b. Nonrestrictive relative clauses
      ($_I$My brother) ($_I$who loves animals) ($_I$just bought a cat)
   c. Lists
      ($_I$ They brought milk) ($_I$eggs) ($_I$bread) ($_I$and cheese)

Since the parenthetical in (a) and the relative clause in (b) form I-phrases, the surrounding material must also be grouped into (at least) one I-phrase on each side.

I-phrase boundaries also tend to occur, though not obligatorily, after subject noun phrases and at clause divisions. Constituents that do not ordinarily delimit I-phrases when they are short tend to be broken up as their length increases. In addition to these general tendencies, I-phrases may be shorter or longer at the discretion of the speaker, depending on factors such as speech rate and register, degree of emphasis, and other rhetorical considerations.

The Phonological Phrase

Given the relative fluidity of these higher levels of prosodic structure, it is difficult to arrive at a mapping algorithm that will derive U- and I-phrases from syntactic structure, beyond the general guidelines mentioned earlier. It has been hypothesized, however, that the lower levels of prosodic structure are related to syntax in a more fixed way, in that there is a fixed correspondence between selected nodes of the syntactic tree and the various prosodic levels. This hypothesis was stated by Hale and Selkirk (1987) as the Designated Category Parameter, given in (6a):

6. Mapping from Σ to Σ': (Hale & Selkirk, 1987)
   a. *The Designated Category Parameter*: For each level P_i of the prosodic hierarchy there is a single designated category DC_i in the syntactic structure with respect to which phonological representation at level P_i is defined.
   b. *The End Parameter*: Only one end (Right or Left) of the designated category DC_i is relevant in the formation of a prosodic constituent P_i; a P_i extends from one instance of the appropriate end of DC_i to the next.

Thus, in some languages the relevant syntactic category for defining the phonological phrase may be the maximal projection of a category or set of categories X, henceforth called X^{max}; in others, it may be the head of X, X^{head}. A lexical category (e.g., a noun, N) is said to project a series of phrasal categories (in X-bar theory, N', N'', etc.) of which it is the head; the largest such category is its maximal projection (in the case of a noun, the maximal projection is the noun phrase N'' = NP). Further conditions have been proposed as being relevant: Whether or not the category is lexically governed, whether it is an argument or adjunct, or whether it is in focus.

There are a number of proposals as to how mapping from designated categories into prosodic categories should proceed. Selkirk (1986), building on proposals of Clements (1978) for Ewe and Chen (1987) for Xiamen, proposed that prosodic domains are demarcated by either the left or right ends of the syntactic constituents selected in (6a) - thus, each language requires setting what Hale and Selkirk call the End Parameter, given in (6b).

For example, consider how the syntactic structure in (7) is mapped into phrases in two different dialects of Chinese:

7. Parameter settings for P-phrases in Shanghai and Xiamen

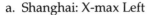

a. Shanghai: X-max Left

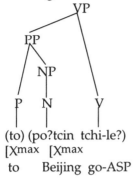

(to) (po?tcin tchi-le?)
[Xmax [Xmax

to   Beijing go-ASP

b. Xiamen: X-max Right

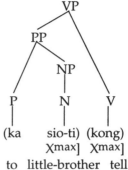

(ka   sio-ti) (kong)
         Xmax] Xmax]

to little-brother tell

In Shanghai (Selkirk & Shen, 1990), a phrase boundary is placed at the left end of a maximal projection, in this case, VP, PP, and NP. By contrast, Xiamen phonological phrases are delimited by the right ends of maximal projections (Chen, 1987).

Although these two Chinese dialects have similar syntax but opposite settings of the End Parameter, Nespor and Vogel (1986) suggested that P-phrase formation tends to follow the direction of syntactic branching in a language. They, as well as Hayes (1989), proposed that the mapping of syntax into prosodic structure proceeds by means of relation-based mappings (e.g., "form P-phrases by grouping a head with its specifiers on the left"). The results are often similar to that achieved by an end-based approach. Selkirk (1986) argued that the end-based approach allows for fewer possibilities, and so is more constrained, hence explanatorily more adequate. End-based mapping also has interesting implications for perception and acquisition, as it suggests a general strategy of "pay attention to ends"; however, the issue is currently the subject of some debate, and arguments for relation-based mapping have also been made (see Bickmore, 1990; Cho, 1990, for opposing views).

As with the formation of utterances and intonational phrases, the formation of the lower level prosodic categories is not rigidly tied to designated categories, but depends also on other factors. Geometric notions such as branchingness have been shown to play an important role in the mapping from syntactic to prosodic structure. Cowper and Rice (1987) argued that P-phrase formation in Mende is obligatorily sensitive to syntactic branching. They observe that Mende consonant mutation (a rule whereby the first consonant of a word is changed due to the influence of a preceding word) applies within a phonological phrase that is delimited by the left end of a branching X^{max}:

8. Mende: Left end of branching X^{max} (Cowper & Rice, 1987)

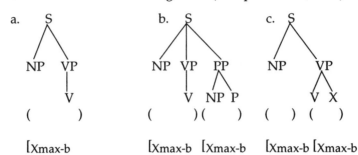

Thus, consonant mutation triggered by the subject affects the verb in structures (8a) and (8b). In (a), the only branching maximal projection is S itself; in (b), S and PP branch, but not NP and VP. But consonant mutation does not apply from the subject to the verb in (c), where the branching VP forms a P-phrase on its own. Cowper and Rice proposed, then, that branchingness be considered a parameter of P-phrase construction. Further evidence for the importance of this parameter has been adduced in the formation of phonological phrases in a number of diverse languages, including Mandarin (Cheng, 1987), Kinyambo (Bickmore, 1990), Korean (Cho, 1990), and Hausa (Zec & Inkelas, 1990).

Branchingness, together with the choice of designated category, both play a role in determining how big phonological phrases in a language are, what we could call the "grain" of a language's prosodic structure. Languages with small phrases are relatively fine-grained; those with large phrases are more coarse-grained. Grain appears to be highly variable from language to language. For example, Kenstowicz and Kisseberth (1990) observed that "the prosodic structure of Chizigula is considerably less articulated than that of Chimwiini" (p. 194), its sister Bantu language, despite having a similar syntax.

Variability of phrasing exists on a wide scale in Biblical Hebrew. A study of Biblical Hebrew phrasing, as indicated by the detailed annotations of the Biblical text, shows that grain depends on context: In prominent positions of the prosodic tree, phrases tend to be very small; in less prominent positions, they tend to be larger (Dresher, 1994b).

The Phonological Word

The next level down in the prosodic hierarchy is the phonological word, W. There are various kinds of mismatches between words as they are generated by the lexicon and the morphology (i.e., the grammatical words) and what count as words for the purposes of phonology. Some examples are given in (9), where two or three grammatical words join to form only one phonological word in each case:

9. Grammatical words and phonological words
   a. I'm (= I am)
   b. wanna (= want to)
   c. Mary's (= Mary is)
   d. djaleave (= did you leave)

Here, too, we require rules of correspondence mapping grammatical words into phonological words. The major mismatches have to do with clitics, formatives that are independent words as far as the grammar is concerned, but that must join to a host in the phonology. Hayes (1989) has proposed that the clitic group be considered as part of the prosodic hierarchy, between the phonological phrase and the word. In many respects, however, the clitic group can be considered simply to be the same as the phonological word.

With respect to mapping, an end-based approach would lead us to expect that clitics associate to a host, or content word, either always to their left or to their right; while true in some cases, there are also more complex situations. Nespor and Vogel (1986) observed that there are clitics that can attach only leftwards or rightwards; Hayes (1989) proposed that the direction of attachment of English clitics depends on syntactic closeness (see also Klavans, 1985).

The formation of phonological words is thus sensitive to lexical category membership and syntactic structure. Cheng (1987) showed that Mandarin word formation is sensitive also to considerations of branching. On the basis of tonal alternations, it can be shown that the subject pronoun *wo* in (10a) is cliticized to the verb *da*. In (10b), the subject pronoun fails to cliticize, because its potential host associates first with another clitic, the object pronoun *wo*.

10. Formation of words in Mandarin (Cheng, 1987)

	a. FW-CW1	CW2		b. FW1	CW-FW2
	2 2	3 2		3	2 3
	(Wo-da	Xiaoming)		(Ni	da-wo)
	'I hit	Xiaoming'		'You	hit me'

Cheng understands these facts in terms of constraints on branching at the level of the phonological word: A word may contain two daughters (i.e., grammatical words), but not more; a function word (FW) such as a pronoun may cliticize to an adjacent content word (CW), provided that CW is not already joined to a FW. Thus, Mandarin shows that word formation depends on geometric, as well as on substantive, aspects of the syntactic tree.

The Prosodic Hierarchy Below the Word

It is reasonable to suppose that the prosodic hierarchy extends below the level of the word. What the units are at these lower levels, however, is the subject of much controversy. At the lowest levels, it appears that subconstituents of the syllable, the rime and the nucleus, play a role, and perhaps the syllable itself. Other proposals recognize the mora as the only subsyllabic prosodic constituent. Less controversial is the existence of a unit that is larger than the syllable but smaller than the word: This is the foot. It is convenient here to assume that the foot is the next level down from the word on the prosodic hierarchy (but see Inkelas, 1989, for a contrary view). The foot is a part of metrical structure, usually but not exclusively associated with stress. Let us, then, turn to consider the nature of linguistic stress.

METRICAL THEORY

Stress merits special attention because of its unique properties and its effects on prosodic structure. Unlike other features, there is no absolute acoustic or articulatory property associated with stress; an element is stressed by contrast to another element. Second, stress is nonbinary: While a binary feature [±stress] can distinguish between stressed and stressless elements, we must also distinguish further among primary, secondary, and tertiary stresses. Third, stress has nonlocal effects: A change in the stress of one element can have cascading effects on the stress of many other elements in the string. These observations led Liberman (1975) and Liberman and Prince (1977) to propose the metrical theory of stress. The theory takes its name from the analysis of poetic meter, from which it borrows its central concepts.

The basic insight of metrical theory is that stress is not characterized by a feature, but is an expression of relative prominence. Prominence may be represented by a tree, as in (11), in which every branching node dominates one element that is strong (S), while others are weak (W) (R represents the Root of each tree):

11. Relational word trees (Liberman, 1975)

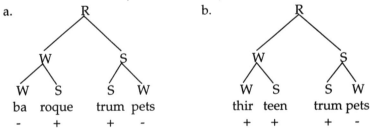

Alternatively, prominence can be represented by a grid, as in (12), where the height of a column of marks represents relative prominence:

12. Grids: Prosodic hierarchy, no constituency (Prince, 1983)

	a.					b.					
			*						*		Phrase
		*		*				*		*	Word
		*		*			*		*		Foot
	*	*	*	*		*	*	*	*		Rime
	ba	roque	trum	pets		thir	teen	trum	pets		

A brief review of the evolution of these two formalisms serves to illustrate some important developments in metrical theory.

Trees and Grids

In Liberman and Prince (1977), trees and grids represent different types of information. Trees indicate hierarchy and constituency, and indicate stress; grids indicate hierarchy without constituency, and are used to compute rhythm. But grids are not just reduced trees: Whereas trees embody the notion that stress is purely relational, grids also indicate substantive levels. In purely relational terms, the words *baróque* and *thirtéen* have the same tree: In each, the first syllable is weak relative to the second. The different stress levels of the first syllables of these words are indicated in Liberman and Prince (1977) outside of the tree by assigning [-stress] to the first syllable of *baroque*, and [+stress] to the first syllable of *thirteen*, as in (11). The associated grids in (12) must reflect this difference if they are to account for the fact that stress can shift from the second syllable of the word *thirtéen* to the first in a phrase like *thírteen trúmpets*; but no such shift occurs in *baróque trúmpets* (*bároque*). In (12b), the unrhythmical clash between the stresses on *teen* and *trum* can be alleviated by sliding the highest grid mark on *teen* to the left, changing *thirtéen* to *thírteen*. In (12a), this operation is not allowed, because *ba* has no grid mark on the second row to support the row 3 mark; therefore, the stress clash remains unresolved.

Selkirk (1978) proposed that the prosodic levels indicated in (12) be incorporated into metrical trees, obviating the need for the feature [stress]. With substantive levels added to trees, grids become reductions of trees, preserving hierarchy and prosodic levels, but without constituency.

The question then arises as to whether the extra information conveyed by trees is in fact necessary. Prince (1983) and Dell (1984) proposed grid-only theories, in which constituency plays no role. However, a number of arguments in favor of constituency have been advanced. First, it has been suggested that there is a natural cognitive tendency to group a series of elements into constituents, in which one is the head and the others are dependents (Halle & Vergnaud, 1987). Second, Hayes (1987) and McCarthy and Prince (1986) observed that there are interesting asymmetries between the trochee, which is a left-headed binary foot, and the iamb, a right-headed binary foot. These asymmetries play important roles in the prosodic structures of many languages. If this is correct, then we must recognize foot-sized constituents such as these. Third, some further arguments in favor of metrical constituency have been advanced on a language-particular basis. The amount of structure encoded in metrical trees, however, is not great, and can be as well displayed on a grid that incorporates constituent boundaries, as in the formalism used by Halle and Vergnaud (1987), shown in (13):

13. Grids with constituency (Halle & Vergnaud, 1987)

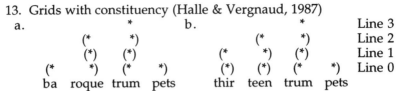

In (13b), there are three constituents on line 0. The heads of these constituents are found on line 1 (these constituents are for exemplification purposes only—actual English metrical structure involves some further complexities). This amounts to saying that the word *thirtéen* has two feet, where each foot contains one syllable, and the word *trúmpets* has one foot, whose head, or strong branch, is the first syllable. At line 1, the feet are grouped into word-sized constituents, whose heads are indicated on line 2. Thus, the second foot in *thirtéen* is stronger than the first. Finally, the whole phrase is grouped into a constituent at line 2, whose head is on line 3. This kind of grid is a notational variant of a tree that incorporates prosodic levels.

Some Parameters of Metrical Theory

Assignment of metrical structure can thus be viewed as involving the construction of a stress plane, controlled by a number of parameters. Some of these parameters are listed in (14); here we are concerned only with word stress, not phrasal stress:

14. Some metrical parameters for word stress
    a. Main stress: Assign a line 2 * to the [left/right]most line 1 *.
    b. Foot construction: Line 0 constituents are [bounded/unbounded].
    c. Bounded feet are constructed from the [left/right] end of a word.
    d. Headedness: Assign a line 1 * to the [left/right]most line 0 * of each foot.
    e. The [left/right]most * on line X [is not/is] marked extrametrical.
    f. Metrical structure [is not/is] sensitive to syllable quantity.

Although the main stress parameter allows only two options, main stress can occur anywhere in a word, depending on where the line 1 marks are. Parameter (b) determines the maximum constituent size on line 0. If bounded, then there is an upper limit to how big a constituent is: This limit is usually two. Otherwise, there is no fixed limit to size. If feet are bounded, parameter (c) comes into play. Parameter (d) requires feet to be uniformly left-headed or right-headed. If parameter (e) has a positive setting, then a peripheral element at the stipulated level may be ignored for purposes of the stress plane; such an element (a syllable, foot, word, etc.) is said to be extrametrical.

Parameter (f) deals with quantity sensitivity. In many languages, the rules of metrical structure are not concerned with the internal structure of syllables; in such languages, stress is said to be insensitive to quantity (QI). However, many languages have quantity-sensitive (QS) stress systems, which means that they distinguish light and heavy syllables. In such languages, a heavy syllable may not occupy a dependent position in a foot (i.e., they must be heads). The definition of what a heavy syllable is is itself subject to parametric variation: In some languages, syllables with long vowels as well as syllables with short vowels that are followed by a consonant (closed syllables) count as heavy, while in other languages only syllables with long vowels are heavy.

An example of a language with quantity-sensitive stress and unbounded feet is Koya:

15. Quantity sensitivity (QS): Koya stress
    Stress falls on the head of every closed or long syllable (H) as
        well as on the head of the initial syllable, whether heavy (H)
        or light (L). Main stress falls on the initial syllable.

The analytic question is how to ensure that heavy syllables in such languages receive stress. One way of doing this is shown in (16a); in quantity-sensitive languages, every heavy syllable projects a line 1 asterisk prior to the construction of metrical constituents:

16. QS 1: (Prince, 1983; Halle & Vergnaud, 1987)
    a. H projects line 1 *   b. Left-headed feet

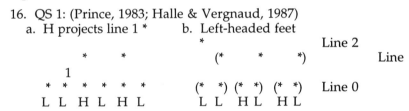

In Koya, we build unbounded line 0 constituents that are left-headed. Starting at the left end, we open a parenthesis, and proceed until we hit a heavy syllable (H). Hs have line 1 heads presupplied, so may not be in dependent positions in a constituent. We must therefore end the first constituent and begin a new one at the H. We continue until the next H, where we repeat the process. We thus derive three feet, and each H receives a secondary stress.

A different approach was proposed by Halle (1990). Rather than line 1 grid marks, he proposed that heavy syllables project line 0 brackets (17a):

17. QS 2: (Halle, 1990)
    a. H projects line 0 (b. Left-headed feet

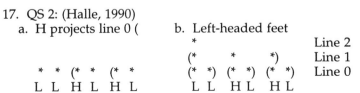

This bracket guarantees that heavy syllables must be at the left end of a constituent. In conjunction with the construction of left-headed constituents, in (17b), this ensures that each heavy syllable will be the head of its foot.

This approach has been extended by Idsardi (1992). Idsardi proposes that the only way that segmental or syllable information can interact with the metrical grid is at line 0, by the placement of brackets. He shows how a number of properties of metrical systems can be neatly accounted for by bracket placement, especially placement of brackets at ends. This sort of theory of metrical grid construction has obvious affinities with end-based mapping of prosodic structure, and serves to underscore the general importance of ends.

Parameters and Cues

The versions of metrical theory sketched earlier are in keeping with the Principles and Parameters conception of Chomsky (1981), where it is assumed that the basic principles governing all languages are universal and innate, though considerable variation is allowed for by a series of parameters that must be set on the basis of experience. With respect to acquisition, the problem for the learner is to correctly set each parameter to its proper value. Since the parameters are stated in terms of abstract structures that are not part of the input (e.g., heavy and light syllables, bounded and unbounded feet, heads, etc.), the main question for the learning theory is how the learner knows which parts of the input are relevant to each parameter.

One approach (Dresher & Kaye, 1990) is to associate each parameter with invariant triggers, or cues. When we try to construct an explicit learning algorithm of this kind, we quickly discover that the parameters interact in potentially destructive ways. For example, we have seen that the parameter for main stress involves placing a line 2 grid mark on the leftmost or rightmost line 1 mark: If the line 1 marks are not positioned properly, then the main stress parameter cannot be correctly set. It follows that parameters are intrinsically ordered, and define a learning path, as pointed out some years ago by Mackie (1981). The parameters must therefore be set in order, or in the equivalent of an order: A parameter cannot be correctly set until the parameters it depends on are.

Another somewhat surprising result is that cues are local: There is no global evaluation, or overall measure of goodness-of-fit (for a different view, see Clark, 1992). This means that if the cues fail, or if the learner makes a mistake that is not detected immediately, the learner has no direct way of locating the source of the error, and hence could not know how to fix it. These results have a number of further implications for issues in learnability, but we cannot pursue them here (see Dresher, 1994a).

CONCLUSION

I conclude this brief survey with some remarks about the relation of prosodic and metrical structure to models of bootstrapping from speech to grammar in early acquisition. Recall that Chomsky and Halle's explanation for the existence of Σ' had to do with perception: A stripped-down prosodic structure may be useful to a listener in real time who already knows the language. But a language learner is in a different situation: A structure that plays the hypothesized role in real-time perception may, for that very reason, not be ideal for purposes of bootstrapping to syntactic structure in the course of acquisition. Moreover, language is not only acquired and perceived, it is also produced, and some properties of prosodic structure may be best accounted for as aiding speech production. Therefore, it cannot be assumed that prosodic structure only facilitates the acquisition of syntax.

Finally, I emphasize that prosodic and metrical structures are not present in the data any more than is syntactic structure. Like every other level of linguistic representation, they must be constructed by the learner in the course of acquisition.

REFERENCES

Bickmore, L. (1990). Branching nodes and prosodic categories. In S. Inkelas & D. Zec (Eds.), *The phonology-syntax connection* (pp. 1-17). Chicago: University of Chicago Press.

Bierwisch, M. (1966). Regeln für die Intonation deutscher Sätze (Rules for the intonation of German sentences). In M. Bierwisch (Ed.), *Studia Grammatica 7: Untersuchungen über Akzent und Intonation im Deutschen* (pp. 99-201). Berlin: Akademie-Verlag.

Bing, J. (1979). *Aspects of English prosody*. Unpublished doctoral dissertation, University of Massachusetts, Amherst. Distributed by the Indiana University Linguistics Club, 1980.

Chen, M. (1987). The syntax of Xiamen tone sandhi. *Phonology Yearbook, 4*, 109-149.

Cheng, L. L. S. (1987). Derived domains and Mandarin third tone sandhi. *Chicago Linguistic Society*, 23/2, 16-29.

Cho, Y. Y. (1990). Syntax and phrasing in Korean. In S. Inkelas & D. Zec (Eds.), *The phonology-syntax connection* (pp. 47-62). Chicago: University of Chicago Press.

Chomsky, N. (1981). Principles and parameters in syntactic theory. In N. Hornstein & D. Lightfoot (Eds.), *Explanation in linguistics* (pp. 32-75). London: Longman.

Chomsky, N., & Halle, M. (1968). *The sound pattern of English*. New York: Harper & Row.

Clark, R. (1992). The selection of syntactic knowledge. *Language Acquisition, 2*, 83-149.

Clements, G. N. (1978). Tone and syntax in Ewe. In D. J. Napoli (Ed.), *Elements of stress, tone, and intonation* (pp. 21-99). Washington, DC: Georgetown University Press.

Cowper, E. A., & Rice, K. D. (1987). Are phonosyntactic rules necessary? *Phonology Yearbook, 4*, 185-194.

Dell, F. (1984). L'accentuation dans les phrases en français (The accentuation of sentences in French). In F. Dell, D. Hirst, & J.-R. Vergnaud (Eds.), *Forme sonore du langage* (pp. 65-122). Paris: Hermann.

Downing, B. (1970). *Syntactic structure and phonological phrasing in English*. Unpublished doctoral dissertation, University of Texas, Austin.

Dresher, B. E. (1994a). Acquiring stress systems. In E. S. Ristad (Ed.), *Language computations (DIMACS series in discrete mathematics and theoretical computer science, Vol. 17)* (pp. 71-92). Providence, RI: AMS.

Dresher, B. E. (1994b). The prosodic basis of the Tiberian Hebrew system of accents. *Language, 70*, 1-52.

Dresher, B. E., & Kaye, J. D. (1990). A computational learning model for metrical phonology. *Cognition, 34*, 137-195.

Hale, K., & Selkirk, E. (1987). Government and tonal phrasing in Papago. *Phonology Yearbook, 4*, 151-184.

Halle, M. (1990). Respecting metrical structure. *Natural Language and Linguistic Theory, 8*, 149-176.

Halle, M., & Vergnaud, J.-R. (1987). *An essay on stress*. Cambridge, MA: MIT Press.

Hayes, B. (1987). A revised parametric metrical theory. In J. McDonough & B. Plunkett (Eds.), *Proceedings of NELS 17 (Vol. 1*, pp. 274-289). UMass, Amherst: GLSA.

Hayes, B. (1989). The prosodic hierarchy in meter. In P. Kiparsky & G. Youmans (Eds.), *Rhythm and meter* (pp. 201-260). Orlando, FL: Academic Press.

Idsardi, W. J. (1992). *The computation of prosody*. Unpublished doctoral dissertation, MIT, Cambridge, MA.

Inkelas, S. (1989). *Prosodic constituency in the lexicon*. Unpublished doctoral dissertation, Stanford University, Palo Alto, CA.

Kahn, D. (1980). Syllable-structure specifications in phonological rules. In M. Aronoff & M.-L. Kean (Eds.), *Juncture* (pp. 91-106). Saratoga, CA: Anma Libri.

Kenstowicz, M., & Kisseberth, C. (1990). Chizigula tonology: The word and beyond. In S. Inkelas & D. Zec (Eds.), *The phonology-syntax connection* (pp. 163-194). Chicago: University of Chicago Press.

Klavans, J. L. (1985). The independence of syntax and phonology in cliticization. *Language, 61*, 95-120.

Liberman, M. (1975). *The intonational system of English*. Unpublished doctoral dissertation, MIT, Cambridge, MA.

Liberman, M., & Prince, A. (1977). On stress and linguistic rhythm. *Linguistic Inquiry, 8*, 249-336.

Mackie, A. (1981). A computer simulation of metrical stress theory. Unpublished manuscript, Brown University, Providence, RI.

McCarthy, J. J., & Prince, A. (1986). *Prosodic morphology*, Unpublished manuscript, University of Massachusetts, Amherst, and Brandeis University, Waltham, MA.

Miller, G. A., & Chomsky, N. (1963). Finitary models of language users. In R. D. Luce, R. R. Bush, & E. Galanter (Eds.), *Handbook of mathematical psychology (Vol. 2*, pp. 419-492). New York: Wiley.

Nespor, M., & Vogel, I. (1986). *Prosodic phonology*. Dordrecht: Foris.

Prince, A. (1983). Relating to the grid. *Linguistic Inquiry, 14*, 19-100.

Selkirk, E. O. (1972). *The phrase phonology of English and French*. Unpublished doctoral dissertation, MIT, Cambridge, MA.

Selkirk, E. O. (1978). On prosodic structure and its relation to syntactic structure. Distributed 1980 by the IULC. Also in T. Fretheim (Ed.), *Nordic prosody II* (pp. 111-140). Trondheim: TAPIR, 1981.

Selkirk, E. O. (1984). *Phonology and syntax: The relation between sound and structure*. Cambridge, MA: MIT Press.

Selkirk, E., & Shen, T. (1990). Prosodic domains in Shanghai Chinese. In S. Inkelas & D. Zec (Eds.), *The phonology-syntax connection* (pp. 313-337). Chicago: University of Chicago Press.

Zec, D., & Inkelas, S. (1990). Prosodically constrained syntax. In S. Inkelas & D. Zec (Eds.), *The phonology-syntax connection* (pp. 365-378). Chicago: University of Chicago Press.

4 Some Biological Constraints on the Analysis of Prosody

Philip Lieberman
Brown University

If we are to determine whether and how prosodic information may facilitate the acquisition of language by children, we must first take note of the particular characteristics of the prosodic signal, some of its central biological functions, and some of the factors that may constrain the analysis of prosody.

THE PHYSIOLOGY OF SPEECH PRODUCTION

Human speech results from the activity of three functionally distinct systems: (1) the lungs, (2) the larynx, and (3) the supralaryngeal airway—the supralaryngeal "vocal tract." The acoustic consequences of the physiology of these systems have been studied in detail since the time of Johannes Muller.

Muller (1848) explicitly formulated what has come to be known as the "source–filter" theory of speech production (Fant, 1960). He discovered that the outward flow of air from the lungs provides the power for speech production. During inspiration the lungs are distended. The lungs resemble two rubber balloons and energy is stored in them as they expand. Speech is usually produced during expiration when the elastic lung walls force air out of the lungs. Various muscles act to regulate the pressure of the airflow during speech, but the primary energy for speech production is that stored in the elastic recoil of the lungs. At this juncture, it is important to note that the primary function of respiratory activity is to extract oxygen to meet metabolic needs. Therefore, the rate at which a person breathes and the degree to which the lungs inflate and deflate vary. This will produce a different prosodic signal for a linguistically similar utterance when a person is vigorously exercising (Bouhuys, 1974). Respiratory activity also is affected by psychological stress that may be induced in an individual as a consequence of the difficulty of a task or because of emotion. This again may yield a different prosodic signal for a linguistically similar utterance (Scherer, 1986; Kagan, Reznick, & Snidman 1988).

If the human auditory system were capable of perceiving acoustic energy at extremely low frequencies, we would hear the expiratory airflow. However, the acoustic energy present in the outward flow of air is inaudible. Muller (1848) correctly noted that "sources" of audible acoustic energy are generated by modulating the outward, expiratory flow of

55

air. Two fundamentally different sources enter into the production of human speech; periodic *phonation* and turbulent *noise* sources provide the acoustic energy for speech.

Phonation is the result of the activity of the larynx. The vocal folds of the larynx, which are extremely complex structures, move inwards and outwards, converting the air steadily flowing outwards from the lungs into a series of "puffs" of air. Both the basic rate and the detailed airflow through the phonating larynx can be modulated by adjusting the tensions of various laryngeal muscles and the alveolar (lung) air pressure. The *fundamental frequency of phonation*, F_0, by definition, is the rate at which the vocal cords open and close. The perceptual response of human listeners to F_0 is the perceived *pitch* of a speaker's voice. Young children, for example, generally have high F_0s during phonation; their voices therefore are "high pitched." It is important to note that acoustic energy occurs during phonation at the F_0 and at the *harmonics* of the F_0. For example, if F_0 is 100 Hz, energy can occur at 200 Hz, 300 Hz, ... N (100) Hz where N = an integer ≥ 1. The amplitude of the harmonics typically decreases as frequency increases for the phonatory patterns typical of human speech.

Noise sources have very different waveforms and power spectrums. They are aperiodic and often have acoustic energy evenly distributed across a wide band of frequencies. Noise sources can be generated at *constrictions* along the airway leading out from the trachea when the airflow becomes turbulent. The noise source can be generated at the larynx by forcing air through the partly abducted vocal cords as, for example, at the start of the word *hat*. Noise can also be generated by forcing high airflows through constrictions in the *supralaryngeal* vocal tract, for example, at the constriction formed in the mouth when the tongue blade is raised close to the hard palate in the initial consonant of the word *shoe*. Momentary *bursts* of noise excitation typically occur on the release of *stop consonants* such as [t], as the tongue moves away from the hard palate at the start of the word *to*. The burst is momentary since the turbulent noise is a consequence of the constricted airway. Turbulent noise abruptly ceases as the airflow changes from turbulent to laminar. Slight differences in alveolar air pressure can determine whether turbulence will occur.

Although noise sources can be generated at constrictions along the supralaryngeal vocal tract, its primary function is that of an acoustic *filter*. Muller, in his pioneering experiments with excised larynges, correctly noted that the sound produced by the larynx did not resemble speech. When he placed a tube having the shape of the supralaryngeal vocal tract (SVT) above the phonating larynx, the resulting sound was speech-like. The SVT always filters the source or sources of acoustic energy. When the SVT is positioned between a source and the listener's ear it acts in a manner similar to the tube of a woodwind instrument. The transmission of acoustic energy is impeded (i.e., *attenuated*) as a function of frequency. At certain frequencies minimum attenuation occurs; these frequencies are termed *formant* frequencies. The formant frequencies are determined by the shape and length of the supralaryngeal vocal tract, which is continually modified during the course of speech production by the movements of the tongue, lips, and soft palate, and the position of the larynx. Research since the late 18th century consistently shows that formant frequency patterns are one of the primary determinants of phonetic quality. Vowels and consonants differ by virtue of their formant frequency patterns as well as because of distinctions in relative duration.

NEURAL REGULATION AND THE EXPRESSION OF AFFECT AND EMOTION

The neural regulation of these different physiologic components of speech production appears to involve different structures of the brain, connected by complex pathways into functional circuits (Stuss & Benson, 1986; Lieberman, 1991; Cummings, 1993). The voluntary control of the supralaryngeal vocal tract for linguistic ends appears to be a unique human characteristic. The neural structures that are implicated in the regulation of the human SVT essentially store and rapidly access *automatized* patterns of muscular activity that have a linguistic rather than an emotive function. Automatized muscular commands are, in essence, "overlearned" responses that are performed without conscious thought or effort. The automatized SVT patterns of human speech are largely independent of affect and psychological state. Humans, therefore, can produce sounds that have an arbitrary relationship to their emotional state. The sounds that make up the word *help*, for example, in themselves do not have any inherent emotional quality. The sound [h] can just as well be used in the word *hello*. In contrast, the vocal signals of other mammals appear to be tied to their affective state. A chimpanzee will produce a food-bark on seeing food. However, he cannot produce an arbitrary sequence of sounds to signal food.

In contrast, the neural structures that regulate the *prosodic* features of human speech—the modulations of F_0, amplitude, and the distribution of energy produced by the laryngeal source with respect to frequency, over the course of an utterance—appear, for the most part, to be similar to ones found in other animals. The cingulate gyrus (the "old motor cortex") and various midbrain structures appear to be implicated in the regulation of the subglottal and laryngeal components of human speech physiology that generate these prosodic features (Sutton & Jurgens, 1988; MacLean & Newman, 1988; Newman, 1985, in press). There is a substantial body of experimental evidence that shows that these brain mechanisms also initiate changes in heart rate, pupil dilation, and other physiologic variables mediated by affect and emotion (Newman, in press). Studies of pathologic conditions in human beings, particularly of neurodegenerative diseases that affect the midbrain regions regulating emotion, indicate that humans, like other mammals, transmit emotional information by means of prosodic signals regulated by subcortical structures and the cingulate gyrus. Lesions in these subcortical circuits and the cingulate gyrus can result in mutism (Cummings, 1993). Though neocortical structures such as the supplementary motor area are also implicated in human laryngeal control, the primary neural appears to be distinct from that involved in the regulation of the tongue, lips, and so forth (Lieberman & Tseng, 1994). It is clear that one of the primary communicative functions of prosody in human beings is the transmission of emotion and affect. This indeed is the central point of Lewis' (1936) classic study of child-directed and infant speech. Accordingly, the pattern of F_0 variation, amplitude modulation, and durational cues that comprise the prosodic signal inherently cannot be linked to linguistic phenomena alone.

MOTHER–INFANT ATTACHMENT

Assisting mother–infant attachment is yet another central biological function of prosody that must be considered if we are to evaluate the contribution of prosodic information to the acquisition of syntactic ability. Mammals differ from reptiles in that infants must remain in close contact with their mothers for a prolonged period. Accordingly, mammalian infants and their mothers maintain communication by means of the *isolation cry*. Although the basic form of the primate isolation cry is similar to the *breath-group* F_0 contour that often segments the flow of speech into sentence-length units (Lieberman, 1967, 1991), we retain this basic mammalian characteristic. Human infants utter stereotyped prosodic signals—cries, to which their mothers and other adult caretakers respond. The cry patterns of human infants fall into the general category of isolation cries; the neural circuits implicated in their regulation appear to include the anterior cingulate gyrus (MacLean & Newman, 1988). The anterior cingulate gyrus also forms part of the neural circuits that regulate the basic mother–infant interactions that are one of the defining characteristics of mammalian behavior; lesions in this area disrupt maternal care in rodents (Slotnick, 1967). The robust prosodic effects found by Fernald and her colleagues (Fernald, 1982; Fernald & Kuhl, 1987; Fernald, Taeschner, Dunn, Papousek, Boysson-Bardies, & Fukui, 1989) reflect this basic biological function of prosody; mothers increase the range of their F_0 excursions when they direct their speech to infants. These exaggerated F_0 excursions serve as "directing" signals; infants consistently direct their attention to speech signals that have wider F_0 excursions. The effect, again, clearly cannot be regarded as an exclusively "linguistic" facilitation mechanism; they serve to direct attention to information in many situations (e.g., to messages transmitted in aircraft disasters). Humans communicating with domesticated dogs and other animals tend to interact in much the same manner.

Human infants, like other mammals, likewise can identify their mothers' cries at birth. This aspect of mammalian behavior has been documented in many species, including aquatic mammals such as dolphins (Sayigh, Tyack, Wells, & Scott, 1990). The animals act preferentially to familiar vocalizations, ones that they have heard before. Accordingly, claims linking the identification of prosodic signals by human neonates to a *language-specific* capacity that enhances their ability to learn their native language are incorrect (Mehler et al., 1988). Dolphins demonstrably have the same capacity, which has the biological basis noted by Charles Darwin—enhancing the survival of the individual neonate by providing cues that direct them to appropriate adult caretakers (Lieberman, 1991).

SOME METHODOLOGICAL FLAWS IN STUDIES OF PROSODY

The data on which Mehler et al. (1988) based their inferences are of interest here insofar as they illustrate methodological problems that commonly occur. First, auditory impressions of pitch are not precise specifications of the fundamental frequency contours of utterances. Although auditory transcriptions can sometimes yield approximate specifications of F_0, it is impossible to determine the details of an F_0 contour by simply listening to the speech signal. Comparisons of the transcriptions of trained phoneticians with the actual F_0 contour show that they are unable to accurately transcribe these contours (Lieberman, 1965). Fundamental frequency contours differing by more than an octave were transcribed as though they were similar within the time frame of a single sentence. Fundamental frequencies that were transcribed with the same F_0 index could differ by an octave. The F_0 contours of the signals presented to infants by Mehler et al. (1988) were not determined by instrumental means. Therefore, the effects noted in these perceptual experiments may reflect the presence of exaggerated "motherese" F_0 excursions (Fernald, 1982; Fernald & Kuhl, 1987; Fernald et al., 1989), which may account for the infants directing their attention to particular speech samples. Resolution of these issues is possible, though finegrain analysis of F_0 contours is difficult and time-consuming; the overall characteristics of the F_0 contour can readily be determined using several computer-implemented procedures (Lieberman & Blumstein, 1988).

Second, the signals that the infants in the Mehler et al. (1988) experiments listened to contained acoustic cues that signal segmental as well as prosodic information. Many investigators have assumed that they can isolate the acoustic cues that convey prosodic information (e. g., intonation and stress) by simply low-pass filtering the speech signal. They reason that a filter that has a "cut-off" frequency of 400 Hz will not allow significant acoustic energy above 400 Hz to pass through it, yielding an acoustic signal that conveys only prosodic cues. This is not the case. The "cut-off" frequency of a low-pass filter is the frequency at which it is attenuated 3 dB; significant energy will still be present at 800, 1,200, and 1,600 Hz for a low-pass filter cut-off frequency of 400 Hz. Energy at these frequencies will specify most of the segmental speech-sounds of human language. Since the human auditory system can hear acoustic signals over a range that exceeds 90 dB, the acoustic cues for the segmental speech-sounds will, therefore, be present in the filtered speech (Lieberman & Blumstein, 1988).

Resolution of these issues is also straightforward. Signals that convey prosodic cues, eliminating all but the durational elements of segmental speech-sounds, can be created using analysis–synthesis techniques in which the F_0 of the speech signal is first determined on a period-by-period basis. Using this information, speech can then be synthesized using suitable equipment to produce a fixed vowel (Lieberman, 1965). The amplitude of the original signal can be used to modulate the synthesized signal, making it possible to determine the perceptual effects of amplitude and F_0, respectively (Lieberman & Michaels, 1962). These analysis–synthesis procedures were used by Fernald and Kuhl (1987) to demonstrate infants' preference for the F_0 excursions that typify motherese.

The determination of F_0 is a difficult endeavor. No satisfactory "pitch-extractor" presently exists. The outputs of commercially available devices that purport to derive the F_0 contour must be verified. Many F_0 tracking devices typically confound energy present at the first formant frequency with F_0 for speech sounds having low F_1s, such as the vowel [u]. Moreover, commercially available F_0 tracking devices typically fail to discern the F_0 contour at the end of an utterance, where the amplitude and high-frequency content of the periodic speech signal rapidly diminishes. Errors in F_0 tracking can be avoided by using interactive computer-implemented systems such as the BLISS system (Lieberman & Blumstein, 1988), in which the waveform of the speech system can be compared with the computed F_0 signal. Close observation of the computed F_0 signal and full speech signal will also reveal the interactions between the SVT and F_0 track that reflect coupling between the SVT and larynx (Fant, 1960). The perturbations of F_0 caused by these interactions (e.g., the fall in F_0 on the closure of the SVT for a voiced stop consonant) must be differentiated from any effects conveying affect, or from stress contrasts, or syntactic boundaries.

GENDER AND SPEAKER IDENTIFICATION

Another function of the prosodic signal is gender identification. The prosodic signal differentiates male from female speech (Klatt & Klatt, 1990). It also serves to convey the identity of individual speakers. An observation that commonly occurs in the course of research projects that study the prosodic signals of a set of human speakers is that the indi-

vidual subjects can be identified by looking at the idiosyncratic variations of their F_0 contours (Lieberman, 1967). The magnitude of the differences noted by Atkinson (1976) between the F_0 contours produced by
five different speakers reading a short English sentence (50 Hz variations were noted) far exceeds the hypothetical F_0 and durational cues to
syntactic structure postulated by Cooper and Sorenson (1977, 1981) or
Pierrehumbert (1979).

COGNITIVE AND LINGUISTIC PROCESSING

A complex interaction involving cognitive processing and the linguistic
output clearly occurs during normal speech.   During connected discourse, speakers typically plan ahead, "blocking out" the complex pattern of respiratory maneuvers that is necessary to reconcile the oxygen
demands of the body with the length of a sentence.   Sentences (or sen-
tence-like units) clearly have a "psychological reality." Human speakers
typically take more air into their lungs before they utter a long sentence
(Lieberman & Lieberman, 1973).   Their lungs, consequently, are inflated to a greater degree at the start of a long versus a short sentence.
In the absence of speech, this would generate a high alveolar (lung) air
pressure that would blow the vocal folds apart if the speaker attempted
to phonate, because the force generated by the elastic recoil of the lungs
is proportional to the inflated volume of the lungs (Bouhuys, 1974).
Therefore, during speech the muscles that are used to expand the lungs
are programmed to oppose the lungs' elastic recoil, generating a fairly
steady alveolar air pressure (about 10 cm H_2O; Lieberman, 1967;
Bouhuys, 1974).   Sentences and major constituent elements usually are
segmented by these breath-groups, which terminate with a sudden,
sharp inspiration.

This central linguistic role of intonation has been studied for many
years; the acoustic correlates of the breath-group consist of a sudden
terminal fall in F_0 in the last 150 msec of an utterance, a terminal decrease in amplitude, a decrease in high-frequency harmonics of the glot-
tal source (Armstrong & Ward, 1926; Trager & Smith, 1951; Lieberman,
1967), and an increase in the duration of the terminal segment (Klatt,
1976).   However, these articulatory maneuvers and acoustic events do
not consistently occur during normal discourse or when a written text is
read aloud.   As Armstrong and Ward (1926) first noted, people generally know which words constitute a sentence and they often do not
segment the flow of speech into breath-groups.   Although other intonational constructs such as "declination," a gradual fall in F_0 keyed to the
constituent structure, have been proposed, the data of Lieberman et al.
(1984) show that 35%–45% of the F_0 contours of a set of 19 sentences produced by 7 speakers fit neither breath-group nor declination models.
The breath-group model, which entails a F_0 fall restricted to the terminal part of the sentence, appears to be a better fit for spontaneous

speech. Although some speakers typically produce utterances in which F_0 gradually falls over the course of a sentence or major syntactic boundary, that is not the case for other speakers for whom declination appears to be an artifact of reading texts aloud.

Although pauses generally are a more robust cue for syntactic boundaries than the F_0 contour (Lieberman, 1967; Klatt, 1976), they do not invariably occur at syntactic boundaries. During connected discourse speakers pause; many of these pauses reflect "thinking time" (Goldman-Eisler, 1972). The pattern of pauses, moreover, differs from that of discourse when speech is read (Goldman-Eisler, 1972; Tseng, 1981). Since much of the present database on which claims concerning the relation of pauses to syntactic boundaries is based on read speech, a certain degree of caution must be exercised before one accepts the efficacy of pauses as a cue for syntax.

COMPETENCE–PERFORMANCE AND READ SPEECH

In this connection, if the goal of linguistic research is to discover the linguistic functions of prosody, the use of read text introduces artifacts. Read text can easily be differentiated from spontaneous speech; phonetically naive listeners reliably differentiate read speech samples from spontaneous speech (Remez, 1986). The standard deviation of F_0 of the spontaneous speech in the acoustic analysis of Lieberman, Katz, Jongman, Zimmerman, and Miller (1984) was 50 Hz/second; the standard deviation of F_0 was 24 Hz/second for the same speakers reading identical sentences that had been transcribed from their own discourse. (The 7 speakers in this experiment were first recorded during spontaneous conversations. Each speaker then read 19 of his or her own transcribed sentences aloud at least 3 days later.) The F_0 variations noted in this experiment would wash out the small 5-15 Hz F_0 variations that supposedly signal syntactic phenomena in studies that attempt to interpret the F_0 contour produced by a single speaker reading a single token of a sentence (e.g., Pierrehumbert, 1979). Therefore, it is necessary to present speech signals that preserve the range of variability typical of actual infant-directed speech in studies of the perceptual responses of infants to intonation.

Linguists tend to think of variation as a "performance" effect that masks a speaker's "competence." The procedures used to collect the samples of speech for linguistic studies of intonation often implicitly assume that the competence of a speaker will be manifested by the reduction of variation, and a number of techniques have been used to reduce variation by means of explicit control of the speakers' production. For example, in a number of studies, speakers have been "prepared" for their productions or have been asked to reread sentences until their productions meet the expectation of the experimenters (Cooper & Sorenson, 1977, 1981). Similarly a number of researchers have served as their own subjects (O'Shaugnessy & Allen, 1983) or have relied on a single subject's utterances (Maeda, 1976). These procedures, at best, obscure the truth. There is no motivated way in which the supposed effects of competence can be differentiated from performance—indeed the competence–performance distinction is not an acceptable construct in the domain of science (Bunge, 1984). In practice this distinction has been used to place arbitrary limits on the range of data that can test linguistic theories, excluding "inconvenient" results.

PERCEPTUAL CONSTRAINTS

Some further methodological considerations follow from perceptual constraints. Although many insights on the nature of language have been made by linguists and phoneticians who relied on their impressions of the phonetic content of the speech signal, phonetic transcriptions often reflect one's general knowledge of the lexicon, morphology, syntax, and so forth, of the specific language under study as well as the content of specific utterances. The theoretical expectations of scholars also enter into this process. The Trager and Smith (1951) analysis of English prosody postulated four levels of "phonemic" stress distinctions and four "pitch" or "accent" levels that hypothetically signaled the constituent structure of an utterance. Trager and Smith (1951) claimed that these prosodic cues showed "what goes with what," a claim that underlies Pinker's (1984) "prosodic bootstrapping" and other prosodic facilitation hypotheses. However, controlled perceptual experiments and acoustic analyses showed that the acoustic signal can at most convey a binary *stressed* versus *unstressed* distinction. Moreover, there was no acoustic basis for the four "pitch" distinctions of the Trager–Smith system. The multilevel stress and pitch distinctions of phoneticians using this system reflected their knowledge of the constituent structure of English and the conventions of the Trager–Smith system (Lieberman, 1965). Therefore, arguments to the effect that prosody facilitated the recovery of the detailed constituent structure of the utterance were circular.

Studies of stress and meter still commonly are based on perceptual impressions of a system of multilevel stress distinctions similar to those proposed by Trager and Smith. Though the stress-level distinctions of the Trager–Smith system were accepted at face value by Chomsky and Halle (1968) and are still part of current linguistic theory, no data exist that support these claims. Perceptually based transcriptions of prosodic signals are inherently suspect since they reflect the expectations of the listener as well as the acoustic signal. Theories that differentiate "stress" and "pitch-accents" are also suspect. It is impossible to differentiate the effects of duration, amplitude, and F_0 when listening to speech signals. The perceived "loudness" of a vowel, for example, is a function of the integral of amplitude with respect to time, a phenomenon first noted by Lifshitz (1933). The acoustic correlates of stress are the duration, amplitude, and F_0 of the speech signal (Lieberman, 1960). Therefore, it is impossible to perceptually resolve independent "pitch accents" and "stress levels." Prosodic theories positing independent linguistic roles for pitch accents and stress levels are inherently suspect.

To conclude, the speech signals directed to infants and young children may include prosodic cues that facilitate the acquisition of syntax. Mammals are capable of learning the relationships between subtle acoustic cues and events. My dog, for example, has learned to recognize the engine noise of UPS delivery trucks. He clearly associated the exciting arrival of a package with the particular acoustic characteristics of the Providence UPS fleet. Children undoubtedly have at least the same capability. However, unless we differentiate between the many nonlinguistic aspects of prosody and its presumed linguistic functions, and then identify appropriate acoustic parameters using objective procedures, we will never be able to ascertain whether or how prosody assists the acquisition of syntactic ability in human beings.

REFERENCES

Armstrong, L. E., & Ward, I. C. (1926). *Handbook of English intonation.* Leipzig and Berlin: Teubner.

Atkinson, J. R. (1976). Inter and intraspeaker variation in fundamental voice frequency. *Journal of the Acoustical Society of America, 60,* 440-446.

Bouhuys, A. (1974). *Breathing.* New York: Grune & Stratton.

Bunge, M. (1984). Philosophical problems in linguistics. *Erkenntnis, 21,* 107-173.

Chomsky, N., & Halle, M. (1968). *The sound pattern of English.* New York: Harper & Row.

Cooper, W. E., & Sorenson, J. M. (1977). Fundamental frequency contours at syntactic boundaries. *Journal of the Acoustical Society of America, 62,* 682-692.

Cooper, W. E., & Sorenson, J. M. (1981). *Fundamental frequency in sentence production.* New York: Springer.

Cummings, J. L. (1993). Frontal-subcortical circuits and human behavior. *Archives of Neurology, 50,* 873-880.

Fant, G. (1960). *Acoustic theory of speech production.* The Hague: Mouton.

Fernald, A. (1982). *Acoustic determinents of infant preference for "motherese."* Unpublished doctoral dissertation, University of Oregon, Eugene.

Fernald, A., & Kuhl, P. K. (1987). Acoustic determinants of infant preference for motherese speech. *Infant Behavior and Development, 10,* 279-293.

Fernald, A., Taeschner, T., Dunn, J., Papousek, M., Boysson-Bardies, B., & Fukui, I. (1989). A cross-language study of prosodic modifications in mothers' and fathers' speech to preverbal infants. *Journal of Child Language, 16,* 477-501.

Goldman-Eisler, F. (1972). Pauses, clauses, sentences. *Language and Speech, 15,* 103-113.

Kagan, J., Reznick, J. S., & Snidman, N. (1988). Biological bases of childhood shyness. *Science, 240,* 167-171.

Klatt, D. H. (1976). Linguistic uses of segmental duration in English. Acoustic and perceptual evidence. *Journal of the Acoustical Society of America, 59,* 1208-1221.

Klatt, D. H., & Klatt, L. (1990). Analysis, synthesis, and perception of voice quality variations among female and male talkers. *Journal of the Acoustical Society of America, 87,* 820-857.

Lewis, M. M. (1936). *Infant speech: A study of the beginnings of language.* New York: Harcourt Brace.

Lieberman, M. R., & Lieberman, P. (1973). Olson's "projective verse" and the use of breath-control as a structural element. *Language and Style, 5,* 287-298.

Lieberman, P. (1960). Some acoustic correlates of word stress in American English. *Journal of the Acoustical Society of America, 32,* 451-454.

Lieberman, P. (1965). On the acoustic basis of the perception of intonation and stress by linguists. *Word, 21,* 40-54.

Lieberman, P. (1967). *Intonation, perception and language.* Cambridge, MA: MIT Press.

Lieberman, P. (1984). *The biology and evolution of language.* Cambridge, MA: Harvard University Press.

Lieberman, P. (1991). *Uniquely human: The evolution of speech, thought, and selfless behavior.* Cambridge MA: Harvard University Press.

Lieberman, P., & Blumstein, S. E. (1988). *Speech physiology, speech perception, and acoustic phonetics.* Cambridge, England: Cambridge University Press.

Lieberman, P., & Michaels, S. B. (1962). Some aspects of fundamental frequency, envelope amplitude and the emotional content of speech. *Journal of the Acoustical Society of America, 34,* 922-927.

Lieberman, P., Katz, W., Jongman, A., Zimmerman, R., & Miller, M. (1984). Measures of the sentence intonation of read and spontaneous speech in American English. *Journal of the Acoustical Society of America, 77,* 649-657.

Lieberman, P., & Tseng, C.-Y. (1994). Subcortical pathways essential for speech, language, and cognition: Implications for hominid evolution. *American Journal of Physical Anthropology, 93* (Suppl. 16), 130.

Lifshitz, S. (1933). Two integral laws of sound perception relating loudness and apparent duration of sound impulses. *Journal of the Acoustical Society of America, 7,* 213-219.

MacLean, P. D., & Newman, J. D. (1988). Role of midline frontolimbic cortex in the production of the isolation call of squirrel monkeys. *Brain Research, 450,* 111-123.

Maeda, S. (1976). *A characterization of American English intonation.* Unpublished doctoral dissertation, MIT, Cambridge, Mass.

Mehler, J., Jusczyk, P., Lambertz, G., Halsted, N., Bertoncini, J., & Amiel-Tison, C. (1988). A precursor of language acquisition in young infants. *Cognition, 19,* 143-178.

Muller, J. (1848). *The physiology of the senses, voice and muscular motion with the mental faculties.* Translator W. Baly. London: Walton & Maberly.

Newman, J. D. (1985). The infant cry of primates: An evolutionary perspective. In B. M. Lester & C. F. Z. Boukydis (Eds.), *Infant crying* (pp. 307-323). New York: Plenum.

Newman, J. D. (in press). Forebrain mechanisms mediating crying and related vocalizations. In B. M. Lester, J. D. Newman & F. A. Pederson (Eds.), *Social and biological aspects of infant crying.* New York: Plenum

O'Shaughnessy, D., & Allen, J. (1983). Linguistic modality effects on fundamental frequency in speech. *Journal of the Acoustical Society of America, 74,* 1155-1171.

Pierrehumbert, J. (1979). The perception of fundamental frequency declination. *Journal of the Acoustical Society of America, 66,* 363-369.

Pinker, S. (1984). *Language learnability and language development.* Cambridge, MA: Harvard University Press.

Remez, R. E. (1986). On spontaneous speech and fluently spoken text: Production differences and perceptual distinctions. *Journal of the Acoustical Society of America, 79* (Suppl. 1).

Sayigh, L. S., Tyack, P. L., Wells, R. S., & Scott, M. D. (1990). Signature whistles of free-ranging bottlenose dolphins *Tursiops truncatus:* Stability and mother-offspring comparisons. *Behavioral Ecology and Sociobiology, 26,* 247-260.

Scherer, K. R. (1986). Vocal affect expression: A review and a model for future research. *Psychological Bulletin, 99,* 143-165.

Slotnick, B. M. (1967). Disturbances of maternal behavior in the rat following lesions of the cingulate cortex. *Behavior, 24,* 204-236.

Stuss, D. T., & Benson, D. F. (1986). *The frontal lobes.* New York: Raven.

Sutton, D., & Jurgens, U. (1988). Neural control of vocalization. In H. D. Steklis & J. Erwin (Eds.), *Comparative primate biology* (Vol. 4, pp. 625-647). New York: Arthur D. Liss.

Trager, G. L., & Smith, H. L. (1951). *Outline of English structure: Studies in linguistics, No. 3.* Norman, OK: Battenberg.

Tseng, C. Y. (1981). *An acoustic study of tones in Mandarin.* Unpublished doctoral dissertation, Brown University, Providence, RI.

5 Combining Linguistic With Statistical Methods in Modeling Prosody

Patti Price
SRI International

Mari Ostendorf
Boston University

In contrast to the other chapters in this volume that focus on human bootstrapping from signal to syntax, this chapter presents an overview of automatic methods of analyzing prosody. We outline advantages of statistical approaches in combination with speech and language knowledge, and illustrate these approaches with examples from computational models of prosody.

Why is this chapter on automatic processing of prosody included in a volume on human acquisition of prosody? Automatic algorithms may be viewed by psychologists and linguists as "uninteresting" collections of ad hoc methods for limited domains that are not at all aimed at solving "the real problem." In the automatic speech recognition community, on the other hand, it has been argued that cognitive models are not relevant by analogy with the flying of birds and of airplanes. Airplanes do not fly by flapping their wings; therefore, automatic speech recognition should not be modeled after human speech recognition. Further, while airplanes cannot land very well on a telephone wire, they can fly faster and carry larger loads than birds can. That is, the tasks and goals of the machines are very different from those of the biological entities, hence the methods are very different. Thus, in this view, cognitive models are not "interesting" because they are not aimed at solving "real problems."

Although airplanes do not flap their wings, they do share many aerodynamic properties with birds, and it might be argued that understanding flight, or at least lift, is common to both; hence understanding one can help understand the other. In this respect, human communication is at least an existence proof, and a fuller understanding of this process should help in human–machine communication. Spoken language, however, as linguists and psychologists will agree, is different from flight in that it is a SOCIAL mechanism evolved for communication among entities whose biological properties (sound production, perception, and cognition) constrain the possibilities. Thus, the mechanisms that are successful for machines are likely to share many properties with those successful for people, whether they are discovered independently or not. Further, in automatic spoken language applications (speech recognition, understanding, and synthesis), at least one human being is involved (whether speaking or listening). Thus, not only can the understanding of human communication assist in human–machine communication technologies, it may be essential if we are to develop generalizable methods robust to the variability manifested by humans.

Similarly, psychologists and linguists could view the automatic techniques as theories of human communication made explicit enough to test. Furthermore, studying where the techniques work and where they fail could shed light on the human communication process. Combining the knowledge and techniques from cognitive science and from speech recognition technology could yield approaches that neither community alone could achieve.

There is too little overlap between the two communities for much of this interaction to have yet occurred: The communities differ in techniques, approaches, goals, and culture. There is much to gain, however, on both sides, from the multidisciplinary approach. Many of the recent gains in automatic speech understanding have been due to multidisciplinary cooperation: Combining knowledge-based approaches with statistical methods. In the following sections, we motivate the use of statistical methods generally, survey examples from prosody modeling, and then summarize and discuss implications.

MOTIVATION FOR THE USE OF STATISTICAL MODELS

By statistical models, we mean models that use probability estimation and/or that treat the objects modeled (speech and language, in this case) as at least partly probabilistic processes. Examples include: Classification and regression trees, Markov models, hidden Markov models, and stochastic models generally. We do not include as "models" statistical techniques for estimating reliability, such as significance tests. We also do not cover artificial neural network models, which typically do not include a probabilistic component per se, but which share many of the desirable properties of statistical models.

In recent years, major gains have been achieved in spoken language processing through the use of corpus-based methods involving statistical models in particular. The classic example is the use of hidden Markov models (HMMs) in speech recognition (e.g., Bahl, Jelinek, & Mercer, 1983; Rabiner, 1989), and variations of Markov models for language modeling (e.g., Bahl, Brown, deSouza, & Mercer, 1989; Jelinek, Merialdo, Roukos, & Strauss, 1991; Lau, Rosenfeld, & Rousko, 1993; Meteer & Rohlicek, 1993). More recently, corpus-based techniques have been applied to text-to-speech synthesis (Sagisaka, Kaiki, Iwahashi, & Mimura, 1992; Sproat, Hirschberg, & Yarowsky, 1992), and even natural language processing (Kuhn & De Mori, 1993; Seneff, 1992) and translation (Brown, Cocke, Della Pietra, Della Pietra, Jelinek, Lafferty, Mercer, & Roossin, 1990). In addition, the range of statistical tools used for such applications has expanded to include, for example, decision trees as well as information theoretic measures of similarity (e.g., mutual information, information divergence) and mechanisms for parameter estimation (e.g., maximum entropy). These techniques, which have led to advances in many areas of speech processing, can also be useful for problems in prosody modeling.

Although statistical models are certainly not the only tool for investigating speech and language, they do provide several important features: They can be trained automatically, they can provide a systematic way to combine multiple knowledge sources, they can express the more continuous properties of speech and language, they make it easier to deal with large corpora, they provide a means for assessing incomplete knowledge, and they provide a means for acquiring knowledge about speech and language. Each of these areas is described briefly.

AUTOMATIC TRAINING is important because it allows for tuning to special cases, rather than starting from scratch. For example, generic models can be tuned to specific speakers or styles. This adaptation, for humans and for algorithms, generally improves performance. Further, automatic training methods are easier to maintain than complex sets of rules that could otherwise be used for this purpose. In addition, experts are not needed for the retraining, which makes the technology more portable.

COMBINING DIVERSE KNOWLEDGE SOURCES is important because it provides a mechanism to delay decisions. Robust biological (and social) mechanisms "know" that any one source of information may be degraded, distorted, unintelligible, or otherwise unreliable. By combining and weighting several different knowledge sources, ambiguity or inspecificity in one area can be compensated for by more information in other areas. For example, uncertainty at the acoustic level can be clarified by taking into account syntax and semantics. It is often useful to delay decisions or combine knowledge sources as late as possible to avoid errors associated with early hard decisions. Statistical modeling with Markov assumptions provides a practical mechanism for doing this.

The CONTINUOUS PROPERTIES OF SPEECH are those that cannot be well modeled by discrete models. All areas of language include some more continuous aspects. However, whether language is inherently discrete or not is a hypothesis difficult to prove or disprove. We argue only that some aspects of language are conveniently modeled continuously. Examples of more continuous aspects include language and sound changes as they propagate through a community and some aspects of prosody (e.g., relative prominence and pitch range).

LARGE CORPORA can be conveniently accessed and organized by means of statistical tools. One might argue that such large corpora would not be necessary if we did not have such data-hungry algorithms. However, large corpora are important to speech researchers for more than just training these algorithms. In particular, they offer another data point between the extremes currently observed in speech research. These are (1) the "ecological validity" proponents, who acknowledge that any change in conditions can affect the data, and therefore limit the data to speech and language occurring in conditions as natural as possible; and (2) the "speech science" proponents, who acknowledge that any change in conditions can affect the data, and therefore limit the data to speech and language occurring in strictly controlled environments (e.g., sound-proof booths, read speech, etc.). Both sides start with the same premise and choose opposite approaches. Because language is so rich and variable, there will continue to be a need for both approaches. However, large corpora offer a data point somewhat in between: If the variable of interest occurs frequently enough, large corpora can provide enough naturally occurring instances to "wash out" the effects of the various environments in which it occurs.

INCOMPLETE KNOWLEDGE can be assessed and modeled using statistical models because one need not wait until every source of variability is well understood. Instead, one can model explicitly aspects that are known, and model remaining sources of variability statistically. Given a statistical formalism, one can assess the value of new sources of knowledge or compare models by a variety of techniques, including analysis of variance and measurement of the likelihood of a dataset, as well as overall performance gains in the application of interest.

ACQUIRING KNOWLEDGE using statistics is, of course, possible, and in some sense has been common practice in speech research: Statistical validity tests and analyses of variance, for example, are well-used sources of psycholinguistic knowledge. Other statistical methods can be used to acquire knowledge, including the rather well-used principal components analyses and the increasingly popular classification and regression trees (see, e.g., Breiman, Friedman, Olshen, & Stone, 1984). Decision trees allow the speech researcher to input the types of information that are known to affect variability (of duration of a phone, for example). The resulting tree shows how much of the variability is accounted for by each source of information (for example, voicing of following consonant, compared to existence of following silence).

In addition to the motivations outlined previously, psychological reality may even dictate statistical models, though this is not our area of expertise. We only observe that statistical models and psychological models are starting to look much more alike than they did 10 or 15 years ago (see, for example, the chapters in this volume).

Of course, the biggest disadvantage of many of the existing statistical models is cultural discomfort. This can be new terrain, and it can feel uncomfortable and threatening. However, the advantages offered by multidisciplinary approaches are large, and it is worth trying to bridge the gap. The gap can be bridged by becoming fluent in the new techniques, but it can also be bridged by collaboration with others who are already fluent in the techniques, and by encouraging students to learn more about the techniques.

COMBINING STATISTICS AND LINGUISTICS IN THE MODELING OF PROSODY

In this section, we provide some background and definitions, discuss issues in prosody labeling, and then survey research in the integration of linguistic and statistical models of prosody.

Background

Prosody can be defined as the suprasegmental information in speech; that is, information that cannot be localized to a specific sound segment, or information that does not change the segmental identity of speech segments. For example, patterns of variation in fundamental frequency, duration, amplitude or intensity, pauses, and speaking rate have been shown to carry information about such prosodic elements as lexical stress, phrase breaks, and declarative or interrogative sentence form. Prosody consists of a phonological aspect (characterized by discrete, abstract units) and a phonetic aspect (characterized by continuously varying acoustic correlates).

Prosody, perceptually, can be thought of as the relative temporal groupings of words and the relative prominence of certain syllables within these groupings. Acoustic correlates of prosody include patterns of relative duration of segments and silences, fundamental frequency, amplitude, and "vowel color," although fundamental frequency and duration are the primary correlates and are the focus of most studies of prosody. Functionally, in languages of the world, prosody is used to indicate segmentation and saliency (e.g., Bolinger, 1978; Cutler, 1991). The segmentation (or grouping) function of prosody may be related more to syntax (with some relation to semantics), while the saliency or prominence function may play a larger role in semantics than in syntax.

An example of prosody's functional role in salience and in segmentation is the following sentence pair, in which prosody alone can be used to separate two syntactic and semantic structures:

1. (Marge would never DEAL) (in ANY guise)
2. (Marge would never (deal IN) (any GUYS))

In the sentences above, parentheses are used to indicate grouping/segmentation and capitalization to indicate saliency/prominence.

Labeling

We have described the prosodic functions of grouping and of prominence (segmentation and salience). Perceptual studies (e.g., Price, Ostendorf, Shattuck-Hufnagel, & Fong, 1991, among many others) have shown that people can disambiguate sentences even when prosody is the only cue to the distinction, and even when the speakers are not aware of the ambiguity in question. What are the units of segmentation and salience? If we can define units and label them reliably, we can test hypotheses about their respective roles, and we can use the labeled data to train statistical models to learn more about their acoustic correlates and about context dependencies involving higher linguistic levels.

In order to devise a notation system to describe the perception of segmentation and saliency, and to provide data for further research and modeling, several criteria apply: (1) The labeling definitions should be explicit enough that there is good consistency of labeling within and across labelers, (2) the units should be relatively concrete if we are to hope to detect them automatically, (3) the units should be abstract enough to provide relevant information to higher linguistic levels, and (4) the labeling should be based primarily on the percept, by the trained ear, of the functional role of the units. In general, definitions involving theories about what possibilities should occur can compromise the data, which should be a record of observation about what does occur, and acoustic detail should be avoided since machines are better than people at analyzing the acoustic detail, whereas people are better than machines at the perceptual level. For use in labeling a large corpus, a system that is relatively easy to learn and to put in practice is highly desirable.

If we can devise a labeling system that meets these criteria, we can use statistical methods to try to sort out the many acoustic ways in which words can be grouped or made prominent. It appears that different people tend to favor, for example, pitch or duration as a prosodic cue in their speech production, and that there is also variability across individuals in how these cues are used perceptually. Despite this variability, relatively reliable labeling results can be achieved (Price et al., 1991; Silverman et al., 1992, address some of these issues).

In the system developed in Price et al., and in the ToBI (TOnes and Break Indices) system described in Silverman et al., break indices are used to describe the perceptual separation between each pair of words. "0" represents the least degree of separation (cliticization), "1" represents the "default" word boundary, and higher numbers represent progressively higher degrees of separation. The ToBI system uses "4" as the highest level noted; it corresponds to a major intonational boundary. In correlating these perceptual labels with acoustic measures, Wightman et al. (1992) found four significantly different levels of break indices based on vowel duration normalized to factor out phone-dependent variation. Levels 0 and 1 were not distinguished by duration, although they may be distinguished by phonological rules across word boundaries. Recent work on a larger dataset (Fong, 1993) using the same normalized duration score observed significant differences at 5 levels for vowels and at 7 levels for consonants.

The ToBI system is a modified version of the break indices described in Price et al. and the tonal system described in the work of Pierrehumbert (e.g., Beckman & Pierrehumbert, 1986). In the Price et al. system, major prominences and minor prominences and unmarked syllables were distinguished. Most listeners were convinced that there was more than one level of prominence, but disagreed on which syllables had the minor prominences. In our experience, good agreement across labelers (more than 90% overlap between any pair) is achieved by labeling only presence vs. absence of phrasal prominences. Agreement across labelers on break indices is also good (more than 95% agreement within ±1 break).

A shared, standard transcription method that meets the needs of prosody researchers has many important advantages: Researchers can reproduce results on the same data, they can more easily understand results of other researchers, and researchers (as well as statistical methods) have access to far more labeled data than otherwise possible. The goal of the ToBI system is to provide a minimal transcription system that researchers can share. Since many researchers will want to add more details as part of their own research, there are also mechanisms for augmenting the transcription for particular needs.

OVERVIEW OF RESEARCH IN PROSODY MODELING

In conjunction with Shattuck-Hufnagel and colleagues at Boston University, the Massachusetts Institute of Technology, and SRI International, we are involved in an approach to modeling prosody that consists of: (1) automatic statistical and nonautomatic linguistic analyses of speech data, (2) integration of these analyses in a computational model of prosody for both synthesis and analysis, and (3) evaluation of the model in speech recognition, speech understanding, and speech synthesis. In our integration of linguistic knowledge with statistical modeling, linguistic theory provides the basic units and structure of the model and guides the signal processing algorithms for feature extraction, and statistical modeling captures some of the randomness in speech and provides a formalism for automatically training the models. In addition, using a statistical approach facilitates integration with existing spoken language systems, which have components that are also based on statistical models.

We focused on prosodic phrase boundaries (segmentation) and phrasal prominences (salience). We model a phonological, discrete level of abstract units (break indices, phrasal prominences, and boundary tones). We also model a phonetic, continuous level of the acoustic attributes of the more abstract level. Initially we focused on speech read by professional FM radio newscasters—a style that is particularly well suited for many synthesis applications and that is particularly consistent, which facilitates initial efforts at the statistical modeling. In synthesis, the starting point is text, and the models are used to predict the location of the abstract units (see the section titled "Prediction of Prosodic Abstract Units From Text"). The next step is to realize these abstract units acoustically ("Acoustic Modeling of Prosodic Units"). In analysis the steps are somewhat reversed: We first find the prosodic structure (or hypothesize several potential structures), given the acoustics ("Detecting Prosodic Units in Speech"), and then use this structure to help select the correct words, correct parse, or correct interpretation ("Using Prosodic Information in Speech Understanding").

Of course, modeling prosody is not quite as compartmentalized as the preceding outline suggests. For efficiency and elegance, and because people are both speakers and hearers, it is desirable to have models that can be used for synthesis or for analysis. For example, consider a model trained on all available information: acoustics, word transcriptions, phonetic transcriptions, syntactic structure, prosodic structure, and so on. (Where the information comes from and how it is modeled are important, but separate, issues.) When one or more of these knowledge sources are removed, the model can then be used to predict the missing values given the available sources. In synthesis the acoustics are missing, but the orthographic transcription is given. In recognition, the case is the reverse. For statistical models, this means maximizing the probability of X (the parameter to be predicted) given Y (the known parameters), or, if X is continuous, finding the estimated value of X given Y. Another common way to use the same models for synthesis and analysis is the "analysis-by-synthesis" approach, in which a synthesis model is used to generate utterances to be compared against the observed utterance. The structure of the synthesis model that yields the best acoustic match is chosen as the analysis model.

Prediction of Prosodic Abstract Units From Text

In synthesis, prediction of the prosodic structure can benefit from a variety of knowledge sources (e.g., part of speech [POS] information, syntax, semantics). In many traditional applications, POS by table lookup is almost the only source of additional information that can be computed efficiently enough, except for the types of syntactic information readily available from punctuation. More recently, as computers become more of a dialogue partner, the automatic generation of speech from concept is a real possibility (e.g., House & Youd, 1991). In this case, since the computer has generated the syntax and semantics, it presumably has ready access to this information for computing an acceptable prosodic structure. These concepts are also being used in speech-to-speech translation (e.g., Rayner, Bretan, Carter, Collins, Digalakis, Gamback, Kaja, Karlgren, Lyberg, Pulman, Price, & Samuelsson, 1993).

Some rule-based, nonstatistical techniques have been used in prosodic parsing (e.g., Bachenko & Fitzpatrick, 1990; O'Shaughnessy, 1989; Sorin, Larreur, & Llorca, 1987). Rule-based approaches can be modified so that the rules are not binary. That is, rather than having contexts that either trigger a rule or not, one can assign a probability to a rule and train the probabilities from labeled data. Decision trees have been used to combine a variety of cues, both categorical and numerical, for predicting prosodic salience (e.g., Hirschberg, 1993a) and segmentation (e.g., Wang & Hirschberg, 1991). In addition, decision trees can be embedded in probabilistic sequence models to form a joint model of the prosodic structure of an utterance (Ostendorf & Veilleux, 1994; Ross, 1995). Some of the types of information used in decision trees for predicting salience/prominence include lexical stress, part of speech, and segmentation (which may be either included by hand in order to test the other components, or included by automatic prediction in a previous stage of processing). Some of the types of information used for segmentation include part of speech, number of syllables or number of words since the previous break, and number of syllables or words until the end of the sentence.

Acoustic Modeling of Prosodic Units

The problem of predicting abstract prosodic units was addressed in the previous section. Given these abstract units (as predicted by an algorithm or as inserted by hand), the next synthesis problem is to determine an appropriate acoustic output. Of course, one presumably has more than just the abstract prosodic units; the orthographic transcription is usually available, and from it and a lexicon one can have access to a phonetic transcription, typical placement of lexical prominence, and part of speech information.

Pierrehumbert's (1981) pioneering work on intonation modeling is a good example of rule-based prediction of intonation contours based on the underlying prosodic structure. More recently, several researchers have looked into corpus-based techniques for predicting critical points and global characteristics of intonation contours (e.g., Sagisaka, 1990; Traber, 1992), segmental perturbations to intonation contours (e.g., Scordilis & Gowdy, 1989), and clustering to find intonation "templates" (e.g., Aubergé, 1993; Traber, 1992). Although these techniques do not typically use statistical models, analogous statistical approaches could easily be envisioned. Examples of explicitly statistical models for predicting fundamental frequency contours include work by Ljolje and Fallside (1986) and Chen, Chang, and Lee (1992).

Statistical modeling of duration has followed two very different approaches. One direction involves the use of regression trees, either to predict duration directly (e.g., Pitrelli, 1990; Pitrelli & Zue, 1989; Riley, 1992), or to determine the coefficients of a parametric duration model (Fong, 1993). For linguists and psychologists, an important aspect of the regression tree is that it can be used to automatically discover the relative contribution to duration variability of different factors without making explicit assumptions about the relationships among those factors. An alternative approach is to use statistical methods to determine the coefficients in an additive-multiplicative parametric model (e.g., Kaiki, Takeda, & Sagisaka, 1990; van Santen, 1993). In either case, duration models can be useful for recognition as well as synthesis, as demonstrated for the tree-based approach by Pitrelli (1990) with prediction error and by Fong (1993) with clustered Gamma distributions.

Automatically trained models, such as those outlined earlier, allow us to consider much more data than previously could be envisioned. In the modeling of duration, the work of Crystal and House (1988) has shown that much of what we "know" about duration is limited to the conditions of isolated utterances that were used in the experimental paradigms of most perceptual experiments. These results did not appear to generalize well to longer read passages. How much more of our "knowledge" will be compromised when we move from read to spontaneous speech? Large corpora and statistical techniques give us the tools to address many of these important issues.

Detecting Prosodic Units in Speech

In the previous section, the problem of predicting acoustics given the abstract prosodic unit was considered. The inverse of that problem is to predict those abstract units given the acoustics. This task is not so different from the standard speech recognition problem of predicting the segmental content, or the words, given the acoustics. Hidden Markov modeling, which has proved successful in standard speech recognition tasks, has been used in intonation recognition (e.g., Butzberger et al., 1990; Ljolje & Fallside, 1987). These studies focused on recognizing tune patterns in isolation. It is a more complex task to generalize these results to running speech (e.g., detecting which syllables are prominent, which have boundary tones of which type, etc.). In the case of boundary-tone detection, most of the syllables do not have boundary tones, and word-spotting techniques (e.g., Rohlicek, Russell, Roukos, & Gish, 1989) could be applied, in which there are a few models of the type of boundary tone to be detected, and a separate model for all other syllables. Such was the approach taken in Butzberger et al. (1990) for boundary tone detection, and by Chen and Withgott (1992) for detecting emphasized words.

These techniques are examples of what we call "pre-recognition" prosody detection algorithms, as opposed to "post-recognition" algorithms, which are based on the output of a speech recognition system. An advantage of post-recognition algorithms is the ability to use duration cues in addition to intonation cues for detecting phrase boundaries. These algorithms have access to segment identity, which may be useful for factoring out segment-related effects on duration and pitch and for capturing timing information. For example, a rise that starts late after vowel onset can mean something very different (e.g., incredulity) from one that starts at vowel onset. Of course, duration and other acoustic cues at the segment or syllable level are not well suited to standard hidden Markov modeling approaches that use frame-based homogeneous features. One alternative approach uses syllable- and word-level features with probabilistic decision trees embedded in a Markov sequence model (Wightman & Ostendorf, 1994), and has been successfully applied to both phrase break and prominence detection.

An important aspect of prosodic patterns that is not adequately addressed in current models is the suprasegmental nature of prosody above the syllable or word level (i.e., accounting locally for the prosodic contribution of phrase-level, discourse, and other more global effects). One step in this direction is the work of Wightman et al. (1992), which proposes a mechanism for adapting duration models according to an estimate of speaking rate. However, this is only a small step, and much more work is needed to account for more global influences on patterns of both duration and intonation.

Many studies have focused on either salience or segmentation, which is somewhat problematic since their acoustic manifestations can be similar. For example, the pitch and duration patterns correlated with boundary tones are often similar to those patterns observed in prominent syllables. If the two are not both modeled, each can be a likely false alarm for the other. Further, a syllable can be both prominent and carry a boundary tone. In Wightman and Ostendorf (1992), four categories of syllables were modeled: prominent, both prominent and marked with a boundary tone, marked with a boundary tone, and unmarked. Of course, one would prefer a detection algorithm that could make finer distinctions than these gross categories, since, for example, syllables can be prominent in many ways. However, such modeling techniques require a corpus of labeled data, and, as we have argued earlier, it is easier to obtain consistent labels within and across labelers on what counts as a prominent syllable than on exactly how they are prominent.

Many of the algorithms discussed earlier were developed first on isolated speech, and then generalized to read continuous speech (much as has been the structure of research in speech perception and production). However, the same acoustic attributes that indicate much of the prosodic structure (pitch and duration patterns) are also very common in aspects of spontaneous speech that seem to be more related to the speaker's speech planning process than to the structure of the utterance/sentence. For example, an extra long syllable followed by a pause can indicate either a large boundary that may be correlated with a syntactic boundary, or that the speaker is trying to figure out what the next word should be. Similarly, an extra prominent syllable may mean that the syllable is new information, or that it replaces something previously said in error. There is hope that these phenomena can be isolated, for example, by means of a posited "edit signal" (e.g., Hindle, 1983), by joint modeling of intonation and duration (as mentioned earlier), and by models that take into account syntactic patterns as well as acoustic patterns (e.g., Bear, Dowding, & Shriberg, 1992; Shriberg, Bear, & Dowding, 1992). However, for the moment these issues certainly complicate the story.

Using Prosodic Information in Speech Understanding

Once the prosodic units have been detected or hypothesized, as described in the previous section, they can assist in speech recognition, parsing, or understanding. The useful role prosody could play in these areas has long been alluded to (see e.g. Lea, 1980). However, it has only been since the emergence of spoken language understanding that there has been a focus on bridging the gap between speech and language. In the past, speech researchers tended to stop at the orthographic level, and therefore did not pursue parsing and prosody in depth, and language understanding researchers tended to start with orthographic input and did not consider the acoustics of prosody.

Bear and Price (1990) explored ways of passing to a parser segmentation information automatically extracted from the acoustics, namely prosodic break indices detected as described in Wightman and Ostendorf (1991). Price et al. (1991) found that listeners were able to reliably disambiguate utterances when these utterances had a relatively large prosodic "break" that coincided with the boundary between major syntactic constituents. In the Bear and Price work, the break information has been used in two different parsers in two different ways. In one parser, we introduced a new rule that blocked "local" attachment for prosodic breaks larger than a threshold. In a parser that makes hard decisions, the rules must be very conservative or the parser will rule out too many viable parses. In another parser, one that had a parse preference mechanism, we could use the prosodic information to reorder the parse preferences and obtain better performance. This is an example of improving robustness by postponing decision making until more knowledge sources have been considered.

Statistical modeling techniques can be used in comparing prosodic to syntactic structures and can allow more sources of information to be considered in making decisions. Wightman et al. (1991) and Ostendorf et al. (1993), based on an analysis–synthesis approach, developed methods to compare the recognized prosodic break sequence for an utterance with a synthesized break sequence and scored the match. Subsequent work on prosody–parse scoring (Veilleux & Ostendorf 1993) led to a reformulation to avoid explicit detection of prosodic patterns, which is a suboptimal intermediate decision. Specifically, the new score is the probability of observed acoustic features (i.e., fundamental frequency and duration cues) given a hypothesized word sequence and associated syntactic parse. In calculating this score, both an acoustic model and a prosody–syntax model are combined to represent the probability of the utterance using intermediate phonological units, which include prosodic breaks and prominences.

DISCUSSION

We argued in favor of the usefulness of statistical techniques for modeling prosody in speech processing applications, and we outlined our view on using such approaches in prosody modeling. In general, we believe in a cross-disciplinary approach to prosody modeling, combining linguistic knowledge with statistical techniques. In particular, we think that the use of a shared transcription system for representing salience and segmentation is critical for simplifying model structure, testing hypotheses about prosody, and integrating prosodic information in speech understanding and synthesis systems. In addition, we believe that models that can be used for both synthesis and recognition applications are important for advancing our general understanding of the sources of variability in speech communication. Finally, we have illustrated the use of statistical techniques in four speech processing problems: prediction of abstract prosodic labels, generation of acoustic parameters, detection of prosodic labels, and integration of prosody in speech understanding. Of course, prosody is much more complex than the process represented in our current simple models, so at this point we turn to a discussion of factors that complicate the modeling process.

Prosody research has shown that people can reliably use prosody to disambiguate utterances under some circumstances. The use of a prosodic notation system allows us to better elucidate the prosodic conditions under which listeners can separate distinct readings. Our work (Price et al., 1991) shows that disambiguation is facilitated when a major prosodic break coincides with the boundary of a relatively large syntactic constituent. On the other hand, speakers are not obliged to mark large syntactic boundaries with prosody. If they don't, however, listeners apparently do not assume that there is no syntactic boundary there, and the utterances are more ambiguous than if the structure were marked prosodically. Prosodic structure need not mirror syntactic structure, though when it does listeners appear to be able to use this information. Of course, the relation of syntactic to prosodic structure depends on the grammatical system used to represent syntax. Steedman, for example (this volume and elsewhere), argues that syntax and prosody are better aligned in categorial grammars than in other representations.

Prosody research has shown that duration and intonation both play roles in the prosodic indication of salience and of segmentation. It has been shown that relative normalized duration can be a reliable cue to the segmentation function of prosody: Relatively lengthened syllabic rhymes, even in the absence of a following silence, can indicate a major prosodic boundary that listeners try to associate with a major syntactic boundary. The work on Dutch by de Pijper (in press) shows that intonational patterns can also be used by speakers and detected by listeners reliably. Most perceptual studies have used read speech, and often they have used speech read by a professional or by an "expert." In these speech styles, the cues tend to be clear and consistent, and durational and intonational factors tend to be highly correlated. In spontaneous speech, however, the time extent of the cues and their consistency tend to vary as other factors (such as planning) can intervene.

Acoustic representations of utterances (pitch tracks and spectrograms) do not effectively represent prosody's auditory percept. In large part this is because it is relative differences in acoustic patterns that are important; these acoustic cues are a function of many different levels of linguistic information. For example, the role of duration is difficult to discern from the sequence of segment durations, as observed in a spectrogram, since the inherent duration of each segment, lexical context, and overall speaking rate all play a role in determining duration patterns. Similarly, intonation patterns are not interpretable in isolation. They are a function of contrasts with what could have been realized in other contexts (paradigmatic contrast) and with what has occurred in the local context (syntagmatic contrast). Semantic aspects of prosody, such as focus indication through prominence, are particularly sensitive to the contextual effects.

Though both intonation and duration are involved in segmentation and salience, and though both segmentation and salience are involved in pointing to syntactic and semantic distinctions, it is not always easy to separate these various functions. The particle-preposition contrast in English is a simple example. For example, a rise on the verb and a fall on the particle/preposition could indicate a particle reading, because the intonation has grouped together the two words into one unit. However, if the timing and extent of the rise are such that a prosodic boundary is perceived after the verb (and the rise can be interpreted as a continuation rise and not prominence), then the prepositional reading will be perceived. A grouping together of the verb and the following word combined with a prominence on the word following the verb will enhance the particle reading; a separation between the verb and following word (and perhaps a lack of prominence on the following word, though prepositions can have prominences) will enhance the preposition reading. The percept of grouping and prominence are the keys to the interpretation, even though many different combinations of rises and falls and durational patterns can give rise to these percepts.

These complications are only a few of the difficulties faced in prosody modeling. Discourse, for example, adds yet another dimension to the problem (see Hirschberg, 1993b, and the references therein). It is clear that our knowledge of prosody is far from complete, and further linguistic and psycholinguistic studies are needed. However, statistical modeling offers the possibility of making use of what knowledge we do have, by modeling this knowledge in a probabilistic context that allows for as yet unexplained variability.

Combining statistical with linguistic models of prosody has led to increased knowledge about the roles of prosody in speech understanding and to more powerful tools for acquiring further knowledge. These models have also provided important results for applications in speech synthesis and in speech understanding. Prosody is, however, complex in that it straddles the full range of language and speech. Achieving a fuller understanding will require knowledge that spans all these levels from acoustics through semantics and pragmatics/discourse. Few people are trained in all these areas; still fewer also have training in statistical methods. Therefore, for the near term, it appears that multidisciplinary collaborations will be essential for rapid progress.

ACKNOWLEDGMENTS

We gratefully acknowledge the support of ARPA/NSF funding through NSF grant number IRI-8905249. We are also grateful to Jared Bernstein, Katherine Demuth, and Jim Morgan for comments on earlier versions, and to Katherine Demuth and Jim Morgan for their efforts in the organization of the conference that brought the group represented in this volume together.

REFERENCES

Aubergé, V. (1993). Prosody modeling with a dynamic lexicon of intonative forms: Application for text-to-speech synthesis. *Proceedings of the ESCA Workshop on Prosody*, Working Papers 4, Dept. of Linguistics & Phonetics, Lund, Sweden.

Bachenko, J., & Fitzpatrick, E. (1990). A computational grammar of discourse-neutral prosodic phrasing in English. *Computational Linguistics, 16*, 155-170.

Bahl, L. R., Brown, P. F., deSouza, P. V., & Mercer, R. L. (1989). A tree-based statistical language model for natural language speech recognition. *IEEE Trans. Acoust., Speech, and Signal Proc., 37*, 1001-1008.

Bahl, L. R., Jelinek, F., & Mercer, R. L. (1983). A maximum likelihood approach to continuous speech recognition. *IEEE Trans. Pattern Analysis and Machine Intelligence*, PAMI-5, 179-190.

Bear, J., Dowding, J., & Shriberg, E. (1992). Integrating multiple knowledge sources for detection and correction of repairs in human-computer dialog. *Proceedings of the 30th Annual Meeting of the Association for Computational Linguistics*, 56-63. Also published as SRI Technical Note 518.

Bear, J., & Price, P. (1990). Prosody, syntax, and parsing. *Proceedings of the 28th Annual Meeting of the Association for Computational Linguistics*, 17-22.

Beckman, M. E., & Pierrehumbert, J. (1986). Intonational structure in Japanese and English. *Phonology Yearbook, 3*, 255-309.

Bolinger, D. (1978). Intonation across languages. In J. Greenberg (Ed.), *Universals of human language: Vol. 2. Phonology* (pp. 471-524). Stanford: Stanford University Press.

Breiman, L., Friedman, J. H., Olshen, R. A., & Stone, C. J. (1984). *Classification and regression trees*. Monterey: Wadsworth & Brooks/Cole.

Brown, P., Cocke, J., Della Pietra, S., Della Pietra, V., Jelinek, F., Lafferty, J., Mercer, R., & Roossin, P. (1990). A statistical approach to machine translation. *Computational Linguistics, 16*, 79-85.

Butzberger, J., Jr., Ostendorf, M., Price, P., & Shattuck-Hufnagel, S. (1990). Isolated word intonation recognition using hidden Markov models. *Proceedings, IEEE International Conference on Acoustics, Speech and Signal Processing, 2*, 773-776.

Chen, F., & Withgott, M. (1992). The use of emphasis to automatically summarize a spoken discourse. *Proceedings, IEEE International Conference on Acoustics, Speech and Signal Processing, I*, 229-232.

Chen, S.-H., Chang, S., & Lee, S.-M. (1992). A statistical model based fundamental frequency synthesizer for Mandarin speech. *Journal of the Acoustical Society of America, 92*, 114-120.

Crystal, T., & House, A. (1988). Segmental durations in connected-speech signals: Current results. *Journal of the Acoustical Society of America, 83*, 1553-1573.

Cutler, A. (1991). Prosody in situations of communication: Salience and segmentation. *Proceedings of the Twelfth International Congress of Phonetic Sciences* (Vol. 1), 264-270.

Fong, C. (1993). *Duration modeling for speech synthesis and recognition.* Unpublished Master's thesis, Boston University.

Hindle, D. (1983). Deterministic parsing of syntactic non-fluencies. *Proceedings of the 21st Annual Meeting of the Association for Computational Linguistics*, 123-128.

Hirschberg, J. (1993a). Pitch accent in context: Predicting prominence from text. *Artificial Intelligence, 63*, 305-340.

Hirschberg, J. (1993b). Studies of intonation and discourse. In D. House & P Touati (Eds.), *Proceedings of an ESCA Workshop on Prosody* (pp. 90-95). Working Papers 41, Department of Linguistics and Phonetics, Lund University, Sweden.

House, J., & Youd, N. (1991). Synthesizing intonation in a dialogue context. *Speech, Hearing and Language, 5*, 77-89.

Jelinek, F., Merialdo, B., Roukos, S., & Strauss, M. (1991). A dynamic language model for speech recognition. *Proceedings of the DARPA Workshop on Speech and Natural Language Understanding*, 293-295.

Kaiki, N., Takeda, K., & Sagisaka, Y. (1990). The control of segmental duration in speech synthesis using linguistic properties. *Proceedings of the Workshop on Speech Synthesis*, Autrans, France, 165-168.

Kuhn, R., & De Mori, R. (1993). Learning speech semantics with keyword classification trees. *Proceedings of the International Conference on Acoustics, Speech and Signal Processing, II*, 55-58.

Lau, R., Rosenfeld, R., & Roukos, S. (1993). Trigger-based language models: A maximum entropy approach. *Proceedings of the International Conference on Acoustics, Speech and Signal Processing, II*, 45-48.

Lea, W. (1980). Prosodic aids to speech recognition. In W. Lea (Ed.), *Trends in speech recognition* (pp. 166-205). New York: Prentice-Hall.

Ljolje, A., & Fallside, F. (1986). Synthesis of natural sounding pitch contours in isolated utterances using hidden Markov models. *IEEE Transactions on Acoustics, Speech, and Signal Processing, 34*, 1074-1080.

Ljolje, A., & Fallside, F. (1987). Recognition of isolated prosodic patterns using hidden Markov models. *Computer, Speech and Language, 2*, 27-33.

Meteer, M., & Rohlicek, J. R. (1993). Statistical language modeling combining n-gram and context-free grammars. *Proceedings of the International Conference on Acoustics, Speech and Signal Processing, II*, 37-40.

O'Shaughnessy, D. (1989). Parsing with a small dictionary for applications such as text-to-speech. *Computational Linguistics, 15*, 97-108.

Ostendorf, M., & Veilleux, N. (1994). A hierarchical stochastic model for automatic prediction of prosodic boundary location. *Computational Linguistics, 20*, 27-54.

Ostendorf, M., Wightman, C., & Veilleux, N. (1993). Parse scoring with prosodic information: An analysis/synthesis approach. *Computer Speech and Language, 4*, 193-210.

Pierrehumbert, J. (1981). Synthesizing intonation. *Journal of the Acoustical Society of America, 70*, 985-995.

Pijper, J. R. de, & Sanderman, A. A. (1994). On the perceptual strength of prosodic boundaries and its relation to suprasegmental cues. *Journal of the Acoustical Society of America, 94*, 2037-2047.

Pitrelli, J. (1990). *Hierarchical modeling of phoneme duration: Application to speech recognition.* Unpublished doctoral dissertation, MIT.

Pitrelli, J., & Zue, V. (1989). A hierarchical model for phoneme duration in American English. *Proceedings of the European Conference on Speech Communication and Technology, 2*, 324-327

Price, P., Ostendorf, M., Shattuck-Hufnagel, S., & Fong, C. (1991). The use of prosody in syntactic disambiguation. *Journal of the Acoustical Society of America, 90*, 2956-2970.

Rabiner, L. R. (1989). A tutorial on hidden Markov models and selected applications in speech recognition. *IEEE Proceedings, 77*, 257-286.

Rayner, M., Bretan, I., Carter, D., Collins, M., Digalakis, V., Gamback, B., Kaja, J., Karlgren, J., Lyberg, B., Pulman, S., Price, P., & Samuelsson, C. (1993). Spoken language translation with mid-90's technology: A case study. *Proceedings Eurospeech, Berlin, 2,* 1299-1302

Riley, M. (1992). Tree-based modeling of segmental durations. In G. Bailly, C. Benoit, & T. Sawallis (Eds.), *Talking machines* (pp. 265-273). New York: Elsevier.

Rohlicek, J. R., Russell, W., Roukos, S., & Gish, H. (1989). Continuous hidden Markov modeling for speaker-independent word spotting. *Proceedings, IEEE International Conference on Acoustics, Speech and Signal Processing, S1,* 627-630.

Ross, K. (1995) Modeling of intonation for speech synthesis. Unpublished doctoral dissertation, Boston University.

Sagisaka, Y. (1990). On the prediction of global F_0 shape for Japanese text-to-speech. *Proceedings of the International Conference on Acoustics, Speech and Signal Processing, 1,* 325-328.

Sagisaka, Y., Kaiki, N., Iwahashi, N., & Mimura, K. (1992). ATR nu-talk speech synthesis system. *Proceedings, International Conference on Spoken Language Processing, 1,* 483-486.

Scordilis, M., & Gowdy, J. (1989). Neural network based generation of fundamental frequency contours. *ICASSP, 89,* 219-222.

Seneff, S. (1992). TINA: A natural language system for spoken language applications. *Journal of the Association for Computational Linguistics, 18,* 61-86.

Shriberg, E., Bear, J., & Dowding, J. (1992). Automatic detection and correction of repairs in human-computer dialog. *Proceedings of the DARPA Speech and Natural Language Workshop,* 419-424.

Silverman, K., Beckman, M., Pitrelli, J., Ostendorf, M., Wightman, C., Price, P., Pierrehumbert, J., & Hirschberg, J. (1992). TOBI: A standard for labeling English prosody. *Proceedings of the International Conference on Spoken Language Processing, 2,* 867-870.

Sorin, C., Larreur, D., & Llorca, R. (1987). A rhythm-based prosodic parser for text-to-speech systems in French. *Proceedings of the International Congress of Phonetic Sciences, 1,* 125-128.

Sproat, R., Hirschberg, J., & Yarowsky, D. (1992). A corpus-based synthesizer. *Proceedings, International Conference on Spoken Language Processing, 1,* 563-566.

Traber, C. (1992). F_0 generation with a database of natural F_0 patterns and with a neural network. In G. Bailly, C. Benoit, & T. Sawallis (Eds.), *Talking machines* (pp. 287-304). New York: Elsevier.

van Santen, J. (1993). Quantitative modeling of segmental duration. *Proceedings of the ARPA Workshop on Human Language Technology,* 323-328.

Veilleux, N., & Ostendorf, M. (1993). Probabilistic parse scoring with prosodic information. *Proceedings of the International Conference on Acoustics, Speech and Signal Processing, II,* 51-55.

Wang, M., & Hirschberg, J. (1991). Predicting intonational boundaries automatically from text: The ATIS domain. *Proceedings of the Fourth DARPA Workshop on Speech and Natural Language,* 378-383.

Wightman, C., & Ostendorf, M. (1991). Automatic recognition of prosodic phrases. *Proceedings, IEEE International Conference on Acoustics, Speech and Signal Processing, 1,* 321-324.

Wightman, C., & Ostendorf, M. (1992). Automatic recognition of intonation features. *Proceedings, IEEE International Conference on Acoustics, Speech and Signal Processing, I,* 221-224.

Wightman, C., & Ostendorf, M. (1994) Automatic labeling of prosodic patterns. *IEEE Trans. Speech and Audio Processing, 2,* 469-481.

Wightman, C., Shattuck-Hufnagel, S., Ostendorf, M., & Price, P. (1992). Segmental durations in the vicinity of prosodic phrase boundaries. *Journal of the Acoustical Society of America, 91,* 1707-1717.

Wightman, C., Veilleux, N., & Ostendorf, M. (1991). Use of prosody in syntactic disambiguation: An analysis-by-synthesis approach. *Proceedings of the Fourth DARPA Workshop on Speech and Natural Language,* 384-389.

PART II

SPEECH AND THE ACQUISITION OF WORDS

6 Prosody and the Word Boundary Problem

Anne Cutler
MRC Applied Psychology Unit

THE WORD BOUNDARY PROBLEM

The problem with word boundaries lies in locating them. In most spoken language, few cues are available to signal reliably where one word ends and the next begins. However, understanding spoken language must be a process of understanding discrete words rather than utterances as indivisible wholes, because most complete utterances have never previously been experienced by the listeners to whom they are directed. To understand a spoken utterance, therefore, listeners must somehow, in the absence of explicit signals, locate the boundaries between the individual words (or more precisely, the lexically represented units, whatever these may be) of which the utterance is composed.

Models of spoken-word recognition have addressed the word boundary problem in several ways, but the proposed solutions fall into two principal classes: Those which incorporate some explicit mechanism for the location (or at least postulation) of word boundaries, versus those which avoid the need for explicit word boundary location, by proposing that boundary information simply falls out of the normal processes of word recognition. The former class, which we can term Explicit Segmentation models, is differentiated according to the principles that various models propose for guiding word boundary location. The latter class, Serendipitous Segmentation models, essentially contains two candidate solutions: one based on word recognition in strictly sequential order, and one based on competition between word candidates for recognition.

Explicit Segmentation models include the proposal that, in English, listeners apply a strategy of assuming that any strong syllable in the input is word-initial (Cutler & Norris, 1988; Cutler & Butterfield, 1992). This "Metrical Segmentation Strategy" (Cutler, 1990) is efficient in that most English lexical words do indeed begin with strong syllables, and most strong syllables in typical utterances are indeed word-initial (Cutler & Carter, 1987; see that article for more details on the proposal for English, including separation of the access of open- versus closed-class words). Similar prosodically based proposals for explicit segmentation exist for other languages, for example, the proposals that French listeners use a syllabic segmentation procedure (Mehler, Dommergues,

87

Frauenfelder, & Segui, 1981) or that Japanese listeners use a mora-based procedure (Otake, Hatano, Cutler, & Mehler, 1993).

Serendipitous Segmentation models see word boundary information as arising incidentally from the processing operations of recognition. Cole and Jakimik (1978) made a clear statement of such a model in the elaboration of their proposal that recognition of spoken utterances proceeds in strictly temporal order: "one word's recognition automatically directs segmentation of the immediately following word" (1978, p. 93). A similar sequential recognition proposal is embodied in Marslen-Wilson and Welsh's (1978) Cohort Model, which focused on the fact that some words become unique (distinct from all other words in the language) prior to their acoustic offsets; the claim here is that the recognizer can in such cases predict in advance where the current word will end and, by implication, where the next will begin. Competition among candidate words, as embodied in recent connectionist models such as TRACE (McClelland & Elman, 1986) and SHORTLIST (Norris, 1991, 1994), provides another mechanism by which segmentation emerges from independent processing operations. Given an input string, candidates matching any part of the string will be activated, and competition will occur among them. The competition will in general be won by any highly activated sequence of competing candidates that successfully accounts for the entire string without any leftover portions. This process permits no role for boundary detection processes, since words beginning *at any point* in the input can be activated.

A feature of the major classification into explicit versus serendipitous segmentation that is rarely acknowledged is that only the proposal that segmentation be explicit simultaneously addresses the word boundary problem from the point of view both of the adult language user and of the prelinguistic infant. As Mehler, Dupoux, and Segui (1990) spelled out in detail, the word boundary problem for an infant is substantially greater than that for an adult language user. For the prelinguistic infant, most speech input is continuous, just as it is for the adult listener; although caretakers will, in many communities, explicitly teach words, this caretaker behavior appears *after* the infant has begun to produce language (i.e., essentially after the initial segmentation problem has been solved; see Cutler, 1994, for a review). In solving the initial segmentation problem, though, the infant cannot rely on lexical knowledge at all; a lexicon must be constructed, and the construction process must be begun from the most minimal of bases. The most an infant can be born with in this respect might be, perhaps, the expectation that there will be words (i.e., that linguistic means will exist to express communicable knowledge in discrete memorizable chunks). Further than that there can be no specific expectations—for example, there can be no expectations regarding the *structure* of words, since this varies widely from language to language. Certainly the infant confronted with the first samples of speech input can have no preexisting stock of words or word templates on which to build. For this simple reason, any proposal involving serendipitous segmentation (i.e., the emergence of word boundary information from the normal process of recognizing known words in speech input) offers no aid to the prelinguistic infant attempting to decompose continuous speech input into its component words.

Explicit segmentation, on the other hand, does offer such aid. The infant has to start somewhere with the decomposition of continuous speech input, and an explicit segmentation proposal amounts to a claim that this *starting point* arises from an explicit procedure. Once a start has been made, and a small stock of known words exists, the way is of course open for serendipitous segmentation to begin operating; even then, however, serendipitous procedures will only work at the boundaries of those known items, so there will be limits on their effectiveness until a very much greater lexical stock has been built up. Thus explicit segmentation models offer advantages that may be overlooked if they are considered only in comparison with their rivals as accounts of the adult word recognition process.

EVIDENCE FROM ADULT PROCESSING

Adult word recognition evidence offers substantial support for the explicit segmentation position. As mentioned earlier, experiments in English have suggested that listeners segment speech at strong syllable onsets. For example, finding a real word in a spoken nonsense sequence is hard if the word is spread over two strong syllables (e.g., *mint* in [mɪntef]) but easier if the word is spread over a strong and a following weak syllable (e.g., *mint* in [mɪntəf]; Cutler & Norris, 1988). The proposed explanation for this is that listeners divide the former sequence at the onset of the second strong syllable, so that detecting the embedded word requires recombination of speech material across a segmentation point, while the latter sequence offers no such obstacles to embedded-word detection as the non-initial syllable is weak and so the sequence is simply not divided. Similarly, when English speakers make slips of the ear that involve mistakes in word boundary placement, they tend most often to insert boundaries before strong syllables (e.g., hearing *by loose analogy* as *by Luce and Allergy*) or delete boundaries before weak syllables (e.g., hearing *how big is it?* as *how bigoted?*; Cutler & Butterfield, 1992). These findings prompted the proposal of the Metrical Segmentation Strategy for English (Cutler & Norris, 1988; Cutler, 1990), whereby listeners are assumed to segment speech at strong syllable onsets because they operate on the assumption, justified by distributional patterns in the input, that strong syllables are highly likely to signal the onset of lexical words.

Moreover, there is strong reason to believe that one of the serendipitous segmentation proposals simply could not work for English; the efficiency of strictly sequential word-by-word recognition is dependent upon words not being mistaken for one another, but it is clear that in the case of the English vocabulary this criterion cannot be met. Words have other words embedded in them, and these are overwhelmingly at the beginning (McQueen & Cutler, 1992; McQueen, Cutler, Briscoe, & Norris, in press). Thus *fundamentalism* contains *fun*, *fund*, *fundament*, and *fundamental* (as well as *men*, *meant*, *mental*, and *mentalism*), *circumference* contains *succumb* (in British English), *chemotherapy* contains *key*, *battery* contains *bat* and *batter*, *startle* contains *star* and *start*, and so on. This problem is in fact not unique to English, since at least in Dutch the same pattern is found (Frauenfelder, 1991). The problem is not solved by relying, for instance, on syntactic disambiguation, since embedded words and the words in which they are embedded often match in syntactic class (McQueen, Cutler, Briscoe, & Norris, in press).

The effect of this embedding is that a sequential recognition model will often not be able to assume that an incoming string matching a lexical entry is indeed a token of that lexical entry until subsequent input has ruled out the possibility that the string is only part of a larger word; for example, *star* cannot be recognized as *star* until subsequent input has ruled out the possibility of *start*, *startle*, *starling*, and so forth. Indeed, Luce (1986) has computed that in typical speech contexts more than a third of all words are likely to be potentially continuable in this fashion. Thus listeners simply cannot capitalize on the apparent efficiency of strictly sequential word recognition, because the vocabulary itself does not meet the necessary uniqueness criterion.

Under these circumstances it is not surprising to discover that experimental evidence confirms that listeners indeed do not recognize words strictly sequentially. Using a gating task in which words were presented incrementally in fragments, Grosjean (1985) showed that many short words could not be recognized until some time after their offset. In a similar task, differing from Grosjean's in that the input was spontaneous speech and was presented whole word by whole word, Bard, Shillcock, and Altmann (1988) found that words were often recognized in groups—that is, a word was not recognized until the following word was itself recognized.

Sequential recognition was initially justified by the possibility of exploiting early uniqueness—that is, identifiability of a word prior to its offset. However, the statistical analyses described earlier have shown that true cases of early uniqueness are rare, and the experimental evidence has shown that, without early uniqueness, word recognition may not even be strictly sequential. Therefore sequential recognition models should probably be abandoned as a class.

Competition models do not, however, suffer from the same problems. At the present time competition is a serious contender in the word recognition field, and the competition-based version of serendipitous segmentation built into models such as TRACE (McClelland & Elman, 1986) and SHORTLIST (Norris, 1991, 1994) offers a potential alternative to explicit segmentation accounts. In a direct test of competition and explicit segmentation (the Metrical Segmentation Strategy version for English), McQueen, Norris, and Cutler (1994) demonstrated, however, that evidence can simultaneously be found for both. When listeners were presented with a word-spotting task in which some words were embedded in strings with a preceding weak syllable (e.g., *mess* in [nəmɛs], *sack* in [kləsæk]) while others were embedded in strings with a following weak syllable (e.g., *mess* in [mɛstəm], *sack* in [sækrək]), the former set proved easier to spot than the latter. This is exactly as predicted by the Metrical Segmentation Strategy: Segmentation at the onsets of strong syllables would place a boundary prior to *mess* in [nəmɛs], for example, while no boundary would be placed between the syllables of a strong-weak string such as [mɛstəm], so segmentation could not affect recognition in this case. However, it was also the case that words that were embedded in strings containing no potential competitor word (*mess* in [nəmɛs], *sack* in [sækrək]) were detected more easily than words embedded in potentially competing strings (e.g., *mess* in [dəmɛs], which is the onset of *domestic*, or *sack* in [sækrəf], which is the onset of *sacrifice*). This is exactly as predicted by competition models, and indeed, as McQueen et al. (1994) pointed out, it constitutes more direct evidence for competition than had previously been available in the literature. Abundant evidence had been available for simultaneous activation of potential word candidates consistent with a given input (e.g., Goldinger, Luce, & Pisoni, 1989; Zwitserlood, 1989; Shillcock, 1990; Cluff & Luce, 1990; Goldinger, Luce, Pisoni, & Marcario, 1992). But words may be simultaneously active without actively competing with one another. The inhibition of *mess* by *domestic* in the input [dəmɛs] (in comparison with [nəmɛs]) in the McQueen et al. study, though, seems to provide clear support for actual competition—*mess* was less easily recognized when *domestic* was actively contending for recognition.

Following the McQueen et al. finding, a subsequent study by Norris, McQueen, and Cutler (in press) confirmed the joint influence of metrical segmentation and competition in word recognition by demonstrating effects of the *number* of competitors for a given input string. In a word-spotting task, the disadvantage for detecting a word in a string of two strong syllables (e.g., *mint* in [mɪntɛf] in comparison with a strong-weak string (e.g., [mɪntəf]) was larger when there were many potential words in the vocabulary beginning with the final consonant of the target word (here, the /t/ of *mint*) and the following vowel in the stimulus string than when there were few potential competitor words. In a cross-modal priming task (in which activation of lexical candidates by spoken input is measured via facilitation of recognition of simultaneously presented visual input) an analogous effect of number of competitors was demonstrated for Dutch by Vroomen and de Gelder (1995).

LANGUAGE-SPECIFICITY OF ADULT SEGMENTATION PROCEDURES

The fact that English listeners showed BOTH explicit segmentation and competition effects in the same recognition situation further suggests that competition cannot "explain away" the evidence that supports models involving explicit segmentation. Competition exists, but it does not offer a complete account of human word recognition, because the serendipitous segmentation that it allows does not appear to be the whole solution to the word boundary problem. Listeners use explicit segmentation as well. Given the additional dimension that explicit segmentation offers in the form of a potential handle on the infant's initial word boundary problem, it is particularly interesting that it appears to be used by adult listeners for whom it might have been thought to be potentially dispensable. As was described previously, however, the Metrical Segmentation Strategy version of explicit segmentation for English is undoubtedly efficient; such efficiency may be all that is needed to maintain the use of a segmentation procedure in adult recognition.

On the other hand, efficiency has not necessarily been demonstrated for explicit segmentation in the processing of languages other than English. Yet there is experimental evidence that clearly supports explicit segmentation in other languages. Unsurprisingly, though, the form that explicit segmentation takes in other languages is not exactly the form it takes in English; the Metrical Segmentation Strategy for English is founded on the opposition between strong and weak syllables that is such an important feature of English phonology, but other languages may have quite different phonologies, in which no such opposition can be drawn.

In French, for example, a contrast between strong and weak syllables is not a salient feature of phonological structure. Evidence from a wide variety of experimental tasks in French favors explicit segmentation into syllable-sized units (Mehler, Dommergues, Frauenfelder, & Segui, 1981; Segui, Frauenfelder, & Mehler, 1981; Cutler, Mehler, Norris, & Segui, 1986; Kolinsky, 1992; Pallier, Sebastian-Gallés, Felguera, Christophe, & Mehler, 1993). Confirming evidence suggests that syllabic segmentation can be observed under certain conditions in other languages also—for instance, in Spanish (Sebastian-Gallés, Dupoux, Segui, & Mehler, 1992; Bradley, Sánchez-Casas, & García-Albea, 1993), in Catalan (Sebastian-Gallés et al., 1992) and in Dutch (Zwitserlood, Schriefers, Lahiri, & van Donselaar, 1993). Syllabic segmentation is by no means the same process as the stress-based segmentation proposed, in the form of the Metrical Segmentation Strategy, for English.

Yet in one sense the procedures that have been experimentally demonstrated for English and for French are closely parallel. Both stress in English and the syllable in French are the basis of rhythmic structure in their respective languages. This parallelism prompted the hypothesis (see e.g., Cutler, Mehler, Norris, & Segui, 1992) that listeners might in

fact adopt a universally applicable solution to the word boundary problem, in that to solve it they exploit whatever rhythmic structure happens to characterize their language. This universal rhythmic segmentation hypothesis in turn led to the proposal that where a language has a
rhythmic structure based on some phonological construct other than
stress or the syllable, it should be possible to find evidence for exploitation of this construct in speech segmentation.

Japanese is such a language; its rhythm is described in terms of a
subsyllabic unit, the mora. A mora can be a CV structure, or a single
vowel, or a syllabic coda (usually a nasal consonant); thus *Honda*, for example, has three moras: Ho-n-da. (This is not a completely exhaustive
list of mora structures, but it covers the vast majority.) Otake, Hatano,
Cutler, and Mehler (1993) undertook to test the hypothesis that Japanese
listeners should exhibit evidence of mora-based segmentation. They
presented listeners with spoken words and required them to detect CV
(consonant-vowel) or CVC targets within these words. For instance, detection responses were compared for TA- versus TAN- targets in *tanshi*
(mora structure ta-n-shi) and *tanishi* (mora structure ta-ni-shi). In *tanshi*
the TA- target corresponds to the first mora and the TAN- target to the
first two moras. Subjects had no difficulty detecting either target (though
they were faster detecting the one-mora than the two-mora target). In
tanishi, TA- corresponds to the first mora; subjects detected it readily,
and with the same speed that they detected the same target in *tanshi*.
TAN- in *tanishi*, however, constitutes all the first mora and part of the
second; that is, it does not correspond exactly to mora structure at all. In
fact, subjects simply did not respond in this case—TAN- targets were
overwhelmingly not detected in *tanishi*. Otake et al. interpreted this response pattern as evidence of mora-based segmentation by Japanese listeners.

Subsequent experiments extended this finding to other mora structures; detection of single-phoneme targets is faster and more accurate if
they constitute exactly a mora (e.g., O in *aoki*, a-o-ki, N in *kanko*, ka-n-
ko) than if they are part of a mora (e.g., O in *tokai*, to-ka-i, N in *kanoko*,
ka-no-ko; Cutler & Otake, 1994).

The universal rhythmic segmentation hypothesis was thus supported: Explicit segmentation procedures are language-specific but only
insofar as rhythmic structure is language-specific. Note that the presence
of a particular rhythmic structure in the input does not of itself produce
segmentation based on that structure. English listeners show no evidence of syllabic segmentation with French input, for example (Cutler
et al., 1986), and neither do Japanese listeners (Otake, 1992); English listeners likewise show no evidence of mora-based segmentation of Japanese input (Otake et al., 1993; Cutler & Otake, 1994), nor do French listeners (Otake et al., 1993). The segmentation procedures are, instead,
part of the processing repertoire of the listener rather than an input-
driven phenomenon. Indeed, given the opportunity, listeners will apply their native language-specific procedures to foreign language input,

even in cases where the procedures may not operate efficiently at all. Thus French listeners apply syllabic segmentation to English input (Cutler et al., 1986) and to Japanese input (Otake et al., 1993), and Japanese listeners apply moraic segmentation where possible to English input (Cutler & Otake, 1994).

EVIDENCE FROM LANGUAGE ACQUISITION

The pattern of results summarized earlier suggests that development of a rhythmically based segmentation procedure is part and parcel of development of one's native language. Exactly how such procedures arise cannot as yet be illuminated by direct experimental evidence. One hypothesis might be that they arise as a result of fairly extensive exposure to the input language and the consequent acquisition of accurate models of the statistical probabilities of input patterns. For instance, as Cutler and Carter (1987) showed, stress-based segmentation is an extremely efficient strategy for solving the word boundary problem in English. However, there is evidence that adjustment to statistical probability patterns as a result simply of exposure to the language is *not* the source of segmentation procedures. If it were, then language users who have experienced extensive exposure to two languages with differing rhythmic structures should develop the segmentation procedures appropriate to both. However, they do not. Cutler, Mehler, Norris and Segui (1992) studied a group of balanced English–French bilinguals (i.e., speakers who were equally in command of both languages to indistinguishable native levels); these speakers, they found, commanded only one such procedure—either syllabic segmentation (characteristic of French) or stress-based segmentation (characteristic of English). A measure of language preference determined which procedure was available—if on this measure a subject was classed as "English-dominant," he or she used stress-based segmentation with English but did not use syllabic segmentation with French. If a subject was "French-dominant," then syllabic segmentation was used with French but stress-based segmentation was not used with English.

The explanation that Cutler et al. proposed for this finding was one based in the earliest stages of language acquisition. They proposed that explicit segmentation really does link the infant and adult processing situations. The beginning language user needs only one starting point; and whichever one the bilingual infant happens to get, that is the one that remains available throughout life. (Of course, establishing the precise parameters that determine the infant's options at this point is necessary to complete this explanation.) In consequence, the explicit segmentation procedures used by any adult have their source in that early experience of beginning lexical acquisition.

The Cutler et al. proposal is supported by evidence that infants are indeed highly sensitive to language rhythm (see Cutler, 1994, for a review of this evidence). Already in the first days of life, infants can make durational discriminations between sets of bisyllables with versus without an internal word boundary (Christophe, Dupoux, Bertoncini & Mehler, 1994). Furthermore, there is also evidence that at the age at which infants are building up a receptive vocabulary without yet being in a position to use it, they are sensitive to the very prosodic characteristics of words that explicit segmentation procedures exploit. For instance, Jusczyk, Cutler, and Redanz (1993) showed that 9-month-olds in an English language environment prefer to listen to lists of words beginning with strong syllables than to lists of words beginning with weak syllables. These 9-month-old subjects were not yet producing any language; and the words in the input lists were largely low-frequency words to which they were unlikely ever to have been exposed. Accordingly their preferences seem likely to have been determined by development of a concept of what phonological form English words are most likely to take. Six-month-olds, Jusczyk et al. found, did not exhibit any preferences among the experimental word lists; so the 9-month-olds' performance seems likely to have been based on their recent experience with the initial stages of (as yet passive) vocabulary acquisition. That the 9-month-olds' preference was actually for a prosodic structure rather than for specific words was confirmed by the fact that the preference also emerged when the input was low-pass filtered to produce input with clear prosody but no discernible segmental structure.

Further supporting evidence appears in a series of studies by Morgan and his colleagues (Goodsitt, Morgan, & Kuhl, 1993; Morgan, 1994; Morgan & Saffran, in press). Infants show a preference for distributionally regular over irregular sequences, and in English-acquiring 9-month-olds, this preference extends to trochaic (e.g., strong-weak) over iambic (weak-strong) sequences. Moreover, the 9-month-olds showed evidence of integrating the prosodic and the segmental structure of the input, lending support to the Jusczyk et al. claim that infants at this age have acquired a concept of *word*-level prosody. (In contrast, 6-month-old infants in Morgan's studies showed no such evidence of integration.)

The Cutler et al. proposal remains as yet in need of direct test. One open question, for example, is the time span over which infants might develop the ability to segment speech input. Is the acquisition of a segmentation procedure a sudden, one-off experience? Or is it a process that takes place over a certain critical period? In the latter case, could statistical properties of the input *during that period* play a determining role (even though they may not be sufficient to induce segmentation procedures in the absence of critical-period sensitivity)? Cutler and Mehler (1993) referred to the infant's rhythmic sensitivity as an instance of a more general "periodicity bias"; their aim, the integration of the rhythmic segmentation proposals into a more general picture of the initial stages of language acquisition, depends upon empirically established answers to questions such as these.

THE WORD BOUNDARY SOLUTION

This chapter has attempted to give a summary overview of a range of research addressing the recognition of words in continuous speech. The central argument has been that the word boundary problem is a real one: For infants, it consists of dividing continuous speech input into lexically significant chunks to be stored, while for adults it consists of identifying known lexical items in the continuous input stream. Models of adult speech recognition exist that claim that there is no word boundary problem once one is in possession of a lexicon—segmentation occurs serendipitously, as a by-product of the normal recognition processes either of sequential processing or of competition. However, statistical analyses of vocabulary and speech corpora indicate that the distributional assumptions embodied in sequential models are unjustified; moreover, experimental evidence indicates that recognition is often not sequential. Although competition, on the other hand, is supported by experimental evidence from adult processing, the same findings also indicate that it co-exists with explicit segmentation, for which extensive evidence now exists across many languages.

Explicit segmentation has the strong theoretical advantage that it offers a solution to the word boundary problem both for the adult and for the infant listener. The second major argument presented here has been that the nature of this solution is in fact the same for adult and infant listeners, namely exploitation of prosodic structure. Summarized evidence from English, French, and Japanese suggests that the explicit segmentation procedures used by native speakers of these languages differ, but in a very systematic way. English listeners exploit stress patterns in speech segmentation, French listeners exploit the syllable as a unit, and Japanese listeners exploit mora structure; but underlying the language-specific realization of segmentation procedures is a universal similarity in that all three of these procedures can be interpreted as exploitation of the characteristic rhythm of the language. Prosodic structure, in the form of language rhythm, allows adult listeners to increase recognition efficiency via the application of explicit segmentation.

The claim that infant listeners use the same explicit segmentation procedures is based on less direct evidence, but is supported by a number of independent arguments. First, adult evidence from balanced bilinguals indicates that adult listeners can command only one rhythmically based segmentation procedure. This suggests that adult segmentation procedures are not developed simply as a result of extensive exposure to statistical properties of the native language, but may instead originate in a single learning experience. Second, evidence exists that infants are highly sensitive to rhythmic structure in language. And third, experimental studies have shown that at the stage that infants are developing a passive vocabulary (but before they show evidence of an active vocabulary), they are already sensitive to the prosodic probabilities of word structure in the language they are acquiring. Together these strands of evidence motivate the claim that the explicit segmentation procedures used by adult listeners may in fact have their origin in the infant's exploitation of rhythmic structure to solve the initial word boundary problem.

It is no accident that explicit segmentation is satisfying at a theoretical level in that it offers an integration of adult and infant models of recognition: Adults use explicit segmentation precisely because infants do. Prosody bootstraps lexical segmentation and offers a solution to the word boundary problem. The prosodic option is in fact all that the infant has to rely on; but it is still sufficiently practical that the adult listener retains it in the repertoire of recognition processes.

ACKNOWLEDGMENTS

Much of the research reported in this chapter was supported by grants from the Joint Councils' Initiative in Cognitive Science (UK) and from the Human Frontier Scientific Program. Thanks to all the colleagues with whom the work was jointly conducted, especially James McQueen, Dennis Norris, and Takashi Otake. Further thanks to James McQueen, Jacques Mehler, Jim Morgan, and Katherine Demuth for comments on an earlier version of the manuscript.

REFERENCES

Bard, E. G., Shillcock, R. C., & Altmann, G. T. M. (1988). The recognition of words after their acoustic offsets in spontaneous speech: Effects of subsequent context. *Perception & Psychophysics, 44*, 395-408.

Bradley, D. C., Sánchez-Casas, R. M., & García-Albea, J. E. (1993). The status of the syllable in the perception of Spanish and English. *Language & Cognitive Processes, 8*, 197-233.

Christophe, A., Dupoux, E., Bertoncini, J., & Mehler, J. (1994). Do infants perceive word boundaries? An empirical study of the bootstrapping of lexical acquisition. *Journal of the Acoustical Society of America, 95*, 1570-1580.

Cluff, M. S., & Luce, P. A. (1990). Similarity neighborhoods of spoken two-syllable words: Retroactive effects on multiple activation. *Journal of Experimental Psychology: Human Perception & Performance, 16*, 551-563.

Cole, R. A., & Jakimik, J. (1978). Understanding speech: How words are heard. In G. Underwood (Ed.), *Strategies of information processing* (pp. 67-116). London: Academic Press.

Cutler, A. (1990). Exploiting prosodic probabilities in speech segmentation. In G. Altmann (Ed.), *Cognitive models of speech processing: Psycholinguistic and computational perspectives* (pp. 105-121). Cambridge, MA: MIT Press.

Cutler, A. (1994). Segmentation problems, rhythmic solutions. *Lingua, 92*, 81-104.

Cutler, A., & Butterfield, S. (1992). Rhythmic cues to speech segmentation: Evidence from juncture misperception. *Journal of Memory & Language, 31*, 218-236.

Cutler, A., & Carter, D. M. (1987). The predominance of strong initial syllables in the English vocabulary. *Computer Speech & Language, 2*, 133-142.

Cutler, A., & Mehler, J. (1993). The periodicity bias. *Journal of Phonetics, 21*, 103-108.

Cutler, A., Mehler, J., Norris, D. G., & Segui, J. (1986). The syllable's differing role in the segmentation of French and English. *Journal of Memory & Language, 25*, 385-400.

Cutler, A., Mehler, J., Norris, D., & Segui, J. (1992). The monolingual nature of speech segmentation by bilinguals. *Cognitive Psychology, 24*, 381-410.

Cutler, A., & Norris, D. G. (1988). The role of strong syllables in segmentation for lexical access. *Journal of Experimental Psychology: Human Perception & Performance, 14*, 113-121.

Cutler, A., & Otake, T. (1994). Mora or phoneme? Further evidence for language-specific listening. *Journal of Memory & Language, 33*, 824-844.

Frauenfelder, U. H. (1991). Lexical alignment and activation in spoken word recognition. In J. Sundberg, L. Nord, & R. Carlson (Eds.) *Music, language, speech and brain* (pp. 294-303). London: Macmillan.

Goldinger, S. D., Luce, P. A., & Pisoni, D. B. (1989). Priming lexical neighbours of spoken words: Effects of competition and inhibition. *Journal of Memory & Language, 28,* 501-518.

Goldinger, S. D., Luce, P. A., Pisoni, D. B., & Marcario, J. K. (1992). Form-based priming in spoken word recognition: The roles of competition and bias. *Journal of Experimental Psychology: Learning, Memory & Cognition, 18,* 1211-1238.

Goodsitt, J. V., Morgan, J. L., & Kuhl, P. K. (1993). Perceptual strategies in prelingual speech segmentation. *Journal of Child Language, 20,* 229-252.

Grosjean, F. (1985). The recognition of words after their acoustic offset: Evidence and implications. *Perception & Psychophysics, 38,* 299-310.

Jusczyk, P., Cutler, A., & Redanz, N. (1993). Infants' preference for the predominant stress patterns of English words. *Child Development, 64,* 675-687.

Kolinsky, R. (1992). Conjunction errors as a tool for the study of perceptual processing. In J. Alegria, D. Holender, J. Morais & M. Radeau (Eds.), *Analytic approaches to human cognition* (pp. 133-149). Amsterdam: North Holland.

Luce, P. A. (1986). A computational analysis of uniqueness points in auditory word recognition. *Perception & Psychophysics, 39,* 155-158.

Marslen-Wilson, W. D., & Welsh, A. (1978). Processing interactions and lexical access during word recognition in continuous speech. *Cognitive Psychology, 10,* 29-63.

McClelland, J. L., & Elman, J. L. (1986). The TRACE model of speech perception. *Cognitive Psychology, 18,* 1-86.

McQueen, J. M., & Cutler, A. (1992). Words within words: Lexical statistics and lexical access. *Proceedings of the Second International Conference on Spoken Language Processing,* Banff, Canada; Vol. 1, 221-224.

McQueen, J. M., Cutler, A., Briscoe, E. J., & Norris, D. G. (in press). Models of continuous speech recognition and the structure of the vocabulary. *Language and Cognitive Processes.*

McQueen, J. M., Norris, D. G., & Cutler, A. (1994). Competition in spoken word recognition: Spotting words in other words. *Journal of Experimental Psychology: Learning, Memory & Cognition, 20,* 621-638.

Mehler, J., Dommergues, J.-Y., Frauenfelder, U., & Segui, J. (1981). The syllable's role in speech segmentation. *Journal of Verbal Learning & Verbal Behavior, 20,* 298-305.

Mehler, J., Dupoux, E., & Segui, J. (1990). Constraining models of lexical access: The onset of word recognition. In G. Altmann (Ed.) *Cognitive models of speech processing: Psycholinguistic and computational perspectives* (pp. 236-262). Cambridge, MA: MIT Press.

Morgan, J. L. (1994). Converging measures of speech segmentation in preverbal infants. *Infant Behavior and Development, 17,* 389-403.

Morgan, J. L., & Saffran, J. R. (in press). Emerging integration of sequential and suprasegmental information in preverbal speech segmentation. *Child Development.*

Norris, D. G. (1991). Rewiring lexical networks on the fly. *Proceedings of EUROSPEECH 91,* Genoa; Vol. 1, 117-120.

Norris, D. G. (1994). SHORTLIST: A connectionist model of continuous speech recognition. *Cognition, 52,* 189-234.

Norris, D. G., McQueen, J. M., & Cutler, A. (in press). Competition and segmentation in spoken word recognition. *Journal of Experimental Psychology: Learning, Memory & Cognition.*

Otake, T. (1992, July). *Morae and syllables in the segmentation of Japanese.* Paper presented at the XXV International Congress of Psychology, Brussels.

Otake, T., Hatano, G., Cutler, A., & Mehler, J. (1993). Mora or syllable? Speech segmentation in Japanese. *Journal of Memory & Language, 32,* 358-378.

Pallier, C., Sebastian-Gallés, N., Felguera, T., Christophe, A., & Mehler, J. (1993). Attentional allocation within the syllabic structure of spoken words. *Journal of Memory & Language, 32,* 373-389.

Sebastian-Gallés, N., Dupoux, E., Segui, J., & Mehler, J. (1992). Contrasting syllabic effects in Catalan and Spanish. *Journal of Memory & Language, 31*, 18-32.

Segui, J., Frauenfelder, U. H., & Mehler, J. (1981). Phoneme monitoring, syllable monitoring and lexical access. *British Journal of Psychology, 72*, 471-477.

Shillcock, R. C. (1990). Lexical hypotheses in continuous speech. In G. T. M. Altmann (Ed.), *Cognitive models of speech processing* (pp. 24-49). Cambridge, MA: MIT Press.

Vroomen, J., & de Gelder, B. (1995). Metrical segmentation and lexical inhibition in spoken word recognition. *Journal of Experimental Psychology: Human Perception and Performance, 21*, 98-108.

Zwitserlood, P. (1989). The locus of the effects of sentential-semantic context in spoken-word processing. *Cognition, 32*, 25-64.

Zwitserlood, P., Schriefers, H., Lahiri, A., & van Donselaar, W. (1993). The role of syllables in the perception of spoken Dutch. *Journal of Experimental Psychology: Learning, Memory & Cognition, 19*, 260-271.

7 Coping With Linguistic Diversity: The Infant's Viewpoint

Jacques Mehler, Emmanuel Dupoux, Thierry Nazzi, and Ghislaine Dehaene-Lambertz
CNRS-EHESS, Paris

Because multilingual environments are the norm rather than the exception, infants must have the capacity very early in life to distinguish one language from another. Without such a capacity, infants might acquire linguistic systems that amalgamate properties of different languages. The ensuing confusion would be overpowering. Fortunately, this never arises, despite the intuitive fears of monolingual parents. Infants raised in multilingual societies do not become dysphasic. Nor do children who learn more than one language at once pay a high price in terms of time or effort.

These informal observations constitute one of the central mysteries that psycholinguists are faced with. Although the striking efficiency of the Language Acquisition Device has been acknowledged, little attention has focused on how its phonological and prosodic components are implemented. In this chapter, we review some of the adult and infant work that has begun to explore this area of research. We present evidence gathered over the last fifteen years shifting from results observed in adults to those observed with infants. The research strategy that looks both at the initial and stable states of the mind is part of an approach that is ideally suited for psycholinguistics.

The potential problems for a child confronted with several languages become all the more apparent in the light of findings that suggest that the processes underlying speech recognition may vary from one language to another. For instance, it has been claimed that adult speakers of French, English, and Japanese use segmentation strategies relying on different pre-lexical units when processing speech signals. Mehler, Dommergues, Frauenfelder, and Segui (1981) discovered that speakers of French detect a segment (e.g., BA or BAL) faster when the segment coincides with the first syllable in the word (e.g., BALANCE or BALCON, respectively) than when it is either longer or shorter than this first syllable. This finding led the authors to propose that speakers of French rely on the syllable for pre-lexical segmentation. However, Cutler, Mehler, Norris, and Segui (1986) failed to replicate this effect with English subjects. Further research, by Cutler and Norris (1988) and by Cutler and Butterfield (1992), lent support to the idea that stress plays a very important role in English, especially in lexical access. *A posteriori*, these findings make sense. Indeed, the syllabic structure of French is transparent to native speakers of this language but this may not be the case with speakers of English. Widespread ambisyllabicity makes syllable boundaries far less clear in English than in French. Work by Treiman and her colleagues (Treiman & Breaux, 1982; Treiman & Danis, 1988; Treiman & Zukowski, 1990) suggested that English subjects have rather stable intuitions about syllables in English. Without denying the importance of these findings, it remains to be demonstrated whether such "intuitive" syllables play a role in the on-line perception of English, in the same way as they do in French (see Dupoux & Hammond, in preparation).

Further research done on Japanese has revealed another pattern of results with the segment detection task. Otake, Hatano, Cutler, and Mehler (1993) showed that the performance of Japanese speakers in this task is influenced by the moraic structure of this language.[1] Although the alternative explanation of an orthographic bias could not be totally discarded, the authors took this result as preliminary evidence that the segmentation strategy used by speakers of Japanese is based on the mora. Even if a full assessment of the role or indeed the absence of the role of syllables in processing remains to be made across languages, it is clear that when they are confronted with the same stimuli, speakers of different languages behave differently. This is shown by the fact that although Japanese subjects use a mora-based strategy in a segment detection task, French and English speaking subjects, listening to Japanese words, employ their habitual strategies (i.e., syllabic and non-syllabic strategies, respectively; Otake et al., 1993). This finding corroborates the observation made by Cutler et al. (1986) that English and French subjects tend to use whichever strategy they developed to cope with their first language even when listening to stimuli in a foreign language.

One reason that such contrasting results have been found could relate to the existence of classes of languages that differ fundamentally with respect to their rhythmic structure. Writers such as Lehiste (1977) argued that languages may have different perceptual units. Port, Dalby and O'Dell (1987) argued that natural languages have rhythmic structures that are related to "timing units." Traditionally, French is described as a syllable-timed, English as a stress-timed (stressed vowels being more or less isochronous), and Japanese as a mora-timed language (Abercrombie, 1967). There is, certainly, a compelling need for more data to render these statements about timing empirically reliable. However, let us, for the time being, assume that they are correct. Given

---

[1]In Japanese, syllables can have one of two kinds of mora structure. Open syllables with short vowels (like V or CV) are monomoraic, and closed syllables (like CVC) or syllables with long vowels (CVV) count as being bimoraic. Hence the word *tanka* has 2 syllables (*tan, ka*) and 3 moras (*ta, n, ka*). Japanese only allows nasal consonants (N) or geminate consonants (represented as Q) in the post-vocalic position of CVC syllables, and hence only these consonants can count as moras.

this assumption we propose that the reason why English, French, and Japanese speaking subjects behave in such a contrasting fashion when confronted with a straightforward task like fragment detection is that the timing properties of the maternal language determine the adult's behavior. Moreover, Mehler, Sebastian, Altmann, Dupoux, Christophe, and Pallier (1993), using adaptation to compressed speech, found that two languages with syllable timing (Spanish and Catalan) showed cross-linguistic adaptation (i.e., that listening to compressed sentences in one language enhanced comprehension of compressed sentences in the other). This was not the case with English and French.

Of course, language rhythm may not be the only parameter that accounts for the language differences reported earlier. Number and position of vowels, permissible syllabic structures, and existence of vowel reduction may also play a role in distinguishing languages. Moreover, we view the rhythmic space in which languages are distributed as a discrete one, with definite categories like syllable- or stress-timing. Some authors have proposed, in contrast, that timing is a continuous notion rather than a discrete one (Dauer, 1983). We are planning some experiments to investigate if the way adults discriminate languages can bring support to the claim that rhythmic categories do have a psychological reality.

In brief, no one would claim that speakers of different languages process speech in the same way. A large number of studies have established language-specific results, making a universal language processing system seem unlikely, at least for adults. Where disagreement exists is about the nature of language-specific processing strategies. At one extreme, there are indications that different languages rely on processing units of different sizes (say syllables in French, stress units in English, and moras in Japanese). At the other extreme, some models propose quite similar processing units, with only some type of tuning from one language to another (Dupoux & Hammond, in preparation; Klatt, 1980). Only further research will allow us to tease apart the two types of models. Later, we ask what the consequences of language specificity may be for the infant in the process of language acquisition and for bilinguals.

Cutler, Mehler, Norris, and Segui (1992), in a study with highly proficient French-English bilingual subjects, found that subjects were unable to switch from one processing strategy to the other depending on the language they were trying to process. The authors concluded in agreement with Grosjean (1989) that "the bilingual is not two monolinguals in one person." This claim is not incompatible with the existence of extremely proficient bilinguals in two or even more languages. Nevertheless, the task used in the Cutler et al. (1992) experiment possibly engaged behaviors that are intimately related to the way in which languages are represented. And it might be that one person cannot build more than one type of system to represent speech.

If natural languages rely on different types of representation, then, it is very important to understand how children select the one appropriate for their native language. We propose that the basic representation of speech is based on the prosodic structures of the language that is heard at the beginning of life. In the first section of this chapter, we present some evidence showing that infants from an early age on are able to distinguish languages, and we argue that they do so by focusing on the prosodic properties of the languages in question. In the second section, we present a set of experiments investigating infants' abilities to process rhythmic structures. These experiments suggest that vowels are highly salient parts of the speech signal for infants. In the last section, we propose a theoretical framework to understand how infants succeed in keeping languages apart. This framework is called the *Time and Intensity Grid REpresentation* (TIGRE), and has been drawn on the evidence that is presented in the two following sections.

KEEPING LANGUAGES APART

Bahrick and Pickens (1988) showed that 4-month-olds notice a language change when tested with the habituation-dishabituation paradigm. Infants habituated to an English sentence and tested with a novel English utterance dishabituated less than experimental subjects who were tested with a Spanish sentence. Mehler, Jusczyk, Lambertz, Halsted, Bertoncini, and Amiel-Tison (1988) studied the abilities of French-born four-day-olds and American-born 2-month-olds for noticing a change in language when presented with sets of varied sentences. They found that French newborns could discriminate Russian utterances from French ones, although only the infants who shifted from Russian to French displayed a significant increase in sucking when compared to their control. But the original analyses suggested that these newborns couldn't discriminate English from Italian utterances. It was also found that these newborns had a greater sucking rate when listening to French than when listening to Russian.[2] Although the procedure used wasn't designed specifically to test for a preference, this result was explained as a preference for the native language. We shall return to this issue later on. Regarding discrimination abilities, it was found that 2-month-old American infants behaved differently than did the French newborns: They did discriminate English from Italian sentences, but failed to discriminate Russian and French sentences. No preference for either English or Italian was found.

Two conclusions were drawn from these experiments. First, infants, regardless of whether they are neonates or a little older, can discriminate utterances that belong to their familiar language from others that do not. This assumption was reinforced by new results showing that

---

[2]A bilingual speaker uttered the sentences in both languages suggesting that potential differences in timbre are not likely to explain these results.

four-day-olds, under similar testing conditions, discriminate French from English sentences, extending the previously discovered discrimination to a new pair of languages. Note that in this study, the infants discriminated regardless of which language they had been habituated with. In addition, and in contrast to the French-Russian experiment, no preference for the familiar or native language was observed. Later, we propose an explanation for these conflicting results.

Second, Mehler et al. (1988) speculated that, regardless of age, infants fail to discriminate utterances taken from two unfamiliar languages. Nevertheless, a recent reanalysis of the above results has led us to reconsider the role of familiarity in the processing of speech by newborns. Looking back at the French-born newborns' ability to discriminate English from Italian, it appears that both experimental groups, that is, the one that was habituated to English and shifted to Italian, as well as the one that was habituated to Italian and then shifted to English, exhibited an increase in sucking rate during the post-shift phase. However, neither of these experimental groups differed significantly from their corresponding control. This led the authors to conclude that newborns don't discriminate Italian from English. However, given that the interaction between the groups is not significant, there is no valid reason to evaluate both groups separately. Merging the two groups into a single one is therefore more appropriate. When one assesses the results for both groups jointly it appears that four-day-old French infants do discriminate the two unfamiliar languages. In contrast, even when one combines the results of both experimental groups, 2-month-old American infants do not notice an equivalent change (e.g., between French and Russian).

In brief, at four days of age, infants are able to distinguish sentences drawn from two different languages, regardless of whether the two languages are familiar to them or not. Over and above this finding, there seems to be a pattern of preference for the native language but this proves to be rather difficult to replicate using the standard high-amplitude sucking paradigm. In contrast, the behavior of the 2-month-olds differs interestingly from that of neonates. By this age, infants' ability to notice a language change is observed only when one of the languages is the native language. This suggests that infants' capacity to segregate and categorize utterances according to the language from which they are drawn changes during the first two months: Although younger infants try to classify sentences according to the model they implement, older ones already classify utterances as either fitting the model that corresponds to their native language or as coming from a different language. If such models are built in terms of the prosodic properties of the sentences, then one would have to conclude that, by the age of 2 months, the infant has already set the first values that specify some of the structure of its native language. When sentences from two different unknown languages (even with different prosodic types) are presented, the infant treats both of them as not fitting a familiar model.

Mehler et al. (1988) investigated the role of prosody in the infants' ability to discriminate between two languages. They showed that when infants listen to speech that has been low-pass filtered with a cutoff frequency of 400Hz, they still react to a language change. This suggests that the properties infants attend to are carried primarily by the lower 400Hz of the spectrum. In contrast, they do not react when the utterances are played backwards. These observations support the conjecture that infants begin by mainly paying attention to the prosodic properties of speech (that is, overall properties of utterances such as intonation and rhythm). This strategy allows them to classify inputs according to the natural language from which they are drawn. Apparently, they are able to extract rapidly a representation that captures the prosodic properties characteristic of their native language.

To summarize, the empirical assessment of young infants' ability to discriminate languages seems clear. This is not the case for their preference for their native language. We would now like to present two more experiments that bear more specifically on this issue.

Recently, Moon, Panneton-Cooper, and Fifer (1993) used a different experimental sucking procedure to explore language preferences in the newborn. In this procedure, the infant determines which language he/she will hear. Two stimuli that infants can easily discriminate, A and B, are presented alternately, each one for 5 seconds. If the infants initiate sucking during stimulus A, they hear a sentence in English until sucking stops; in contrast, whenever sucking is initiated during stimulus B, the infants hear a sentence in Spanish. The rationale behind this paradigm is that if infants notice the association between stimuli A and B and the languages, and if they prefer one language to the other, they will tend to activate the preferred language more often than the non-preferred one. In the Moon et al. study, half of the infants had Spanish-speaking parents and half had English-speaking ones. These two-day-old infants showed a preference for the parental language, whether Spanish or English. These results suggest that during the very first days following birth, infants display a sensitivity for the distinctive structure of their native language. This finding is compatible with the preference for French over Russian that Mehler et al. (1988) found. However, we must keep in mind that Mehler and his colleagues failed to observe this preference in subsequent replications. These apparently conflicting results suggest that even if newborns have a preference for their native language, such a preference can only be observed when certain specific methods are used. As we noted earlier, the habituation-dishabituation sucking procedure was developed to study discrimination; it may not be very reliable for establishing preferences. The Moon et al. paradigm, on the other hand, is explicitly designed to test preference, and seems much better suited for this purpose as attested by the results obtained. In the future, we hope to see it used to investigate whether the neonates' preference emerges when many utterances from each language are used, rather than 25 seconds as was the case in the Moon et al. study (1993).

If one accepts the previous argument, namely that the classical habituation methods are not effective to test for preference, the question of whether 2-month-olds display a preference for their native language remains open and has to be reassessed. Dehaene-Lambertz (in preparation) has adapted a method previously used to study visual preference (Johnson, Posner, & Rothbart, 1991) to assess preference for auditory stimuli in 2-month-olds. The procedure is the following. The infant's gaze is attracted by a multicolor moving spiral pattern displayed on a screen. Once the infant's eyes are centered on the spiral, an auditory stimulus is presented 30 degrees to his/her right or to his/her left. The independent variable in this new paradigm is the time the infant needs to initiate a saccade towards the source of the sound. Dehaene-Lambertz used French and English utterances less than 3 seconds long. Utterances were presented either intact or low-pass filtered. The results, as illustrated in Fig 7.1., show that American-born infants initiate a saccade towards the side of the English utterances significantly faster than to that of the French ones. The result obtained is similar for both filtered and unfiltered utterances. These results show that 2-month-old American infants orient with greater speed towards English utterances, suggesting a preference for the native language similar to the one previ-

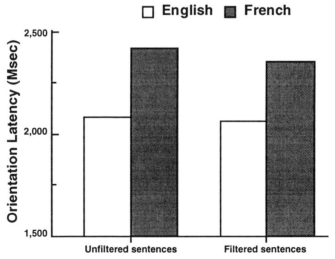

FIG. 7.1 Preference for the maternal language in American 2-month-olds (from Dehaene-Lambertz, in preparation).

ously reported with neonates.[3] Moreover, the fact that this "preference" holds both for filtered and unfiltered speech supports the view that infants rely on distinctive prosodic properties of the language to categorize the utterances.

To recapitulate, the picture that arises from these studies is that neonates are sensitive to the prosodic properties of utterances, and that they show a preference for their native language. Two months after birth, infants still show a preference for their native language, but they appear to have partially lost the ability to characterize the prosodic properties corresponding to utterances in a novel language. With these results in mind we can now return to our initial question, namely to try to understand how infants manage to avoid utter confusion when confronted with several languages in their surrounding environment. We have established the infants' ability to discriminate between languages. But how do they manage to classify utterances according to the language to which they belong? How do they manage to construct distinct files, let us say, for the English and French utterances?

A good candidate that has traditionally been invoked to explain how the child bootstraps into the sound pattern of a language is prosodic structure. In describing the prosodic properties of a language, rhythm appears to be an important parameter. We reviewed studies showing the influence of linguistic rhythmic units on the segmentation stage of adults' speech processing. Knowing whether infants are sensitive to the properties of rhythm thus appears to be a very interesting issue. In the next section, we present some experiments investigating the abilities of very young infants to process units of speech.

THE UNITS OF SPEECH

If natural languages determine different systems of representation, it becomes important to understand how the child converges on the appropriate representation for the language he or she is trying to learn. We argue that the basic representation of speech is based on the rhythmic structures (determined by their periodicity property) embodied in the utterances of a language. If this is correct, the rhythmic structures that are characteristic of a language must be acquired at a very early age.

In our review of the adult literature, we pointed out three speech unit candidates: the syllable, the stress unit, and the mora. As Dupoux and Mehler (1992) argued, it is difficult to investigate units of segmentation and representation in adults given the methods available to ex-

---

[3]It should nevertheless be asserted that this result is not due to some physical property of the stimuli used, unrelated to the properties of the English language. To prove this, French infants could be tested with the same procedure and stimuli. If a preference for the French utterances were found, the preference for the native language would be confirmed. If a preference for the English utterances were obtained, then the problem of the stimuli used should be raised.

perimental psycholinguists (adults making decisions involving complex calculations that rely on several codes, the lexicon and the alphabetic code being two examples among many others). Nevertheless, the way infants cope with rhythmic units has been studied. In the following, we discuss whether the experience with a particular language leads to the forming of the representational unit most pertinent to that language, out of some universal, unspecified unit, or whether this experience favors the selection of one such representational possibility already in place at birth. We now present experimental studies asking whether the properties of rhythm discovered as being used by speakers of Japanese, French, and English are already exploited by infants at the initial state. Unfortunately, at present, only a very rough and incomplete picture can be given.

We know from work by Starkey and Cooper (1980), Starkey, Spelke, and Gelman (1983), and Antell and Keating (1983) that infants are able to extract the number of items in a set when the number is small. Bijeljac-Babic, Bertoncini, and Mehler (1993) exploited this ability to assess whether infants represent the number of syllables in simple CV sequences. They habituated French-born infants to a list containing either varied bisyllabic or varied trisyllabic items. In the post-shift phase, the infants who had heard the list made up of bisyllabic items faced one of two situations: Either they still heard the bisyllabic items (control condition) or they heard the list of trisyllabic items (experimental condition). The infants who had been habituated to the trisyllabic items were treated in a similar way. The results showed that the infants discriminated between the bisyllabic and the trisyllabic stimuli. Moreover, using a speech compression/extension algorithm, it was shown that duration could not account for the infants' performance. Fig. 7.2 illustrates the results of these studies. These findings suggest that infants, habituated to either the list of bisyllabic or trisyllabic items, behaved as if they had represented the number of CVs per item. Bijeljac-Babic et al. concluded that the French infants must have counted the number of syllables in the items on the list.

However, it must be pointed out, as number of syllables and number of vowels are identical, that the result is also compatible with the notion that infants count the number of vowels in the items used. The importance of vowels in infant speech perception receives support from several other observations. Bertoncini, Bijeljac-Babic, Jusczyk, Kennedy, and Mehler (1988) habituated infants with a set of four syllables, presented in random order. In one experiment infants were habituated to a set of syllables sharing the same vowel (/bi/, /si/, /li/, and /mi/ were used) while in another they were habituated to a set of syllables sharing the same consonant (/ba/, /bae/, /bi/, and /bo/ were used). During the post-shift phase the infants were tested with a set of syllables containing the four syllables used during the habituation phase plus a new syllable. The new syllable shared either a consonant or a vowel with the habituation syllables, or differed from them in both consonant and

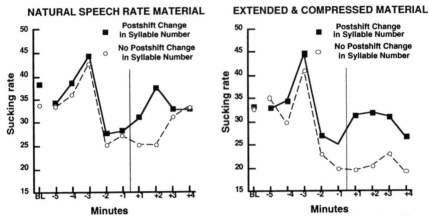

FIG. 7.2. Discrimination of 2- vs. 3-syllable utterances by 4-day-old French infants (from Bijeljac-Babic et al., 1993).

vowel. Two-month-olds noticed the addition of the new syllable regardless of how it differed from the four initial ones. In contrast, newborns noticed the addition of a new syllable only when it differed from the other syllables in vowel quality. In a situation like the one described, the newborns even failed to discriminate the presence of the syllable /is/ in the context of /bi/, /si/, /li/, and /mi/. This further strengthens the view that vowels are important in early infancy.

In a follow-up study of the Bijeljac-Babic et al. experiment, Bertoncini, Floccia, Nazzi, Miyagishima, and Mehler (in preparation) explored whether French-born three-day-old infants extract number of syllables, even when the pronunciation of the items does not correspond to the language to which they were exposed during the first hours after birth. The experiment used bisyllabic and trisyllabic Japanese words. The words presented were separated according to their intonational pattern (either ascending or descending). It was shown that French newborns react to a change in the number of syllables, generalizing the result obtained with French stimuli to words from another phonological system.[4]

These results support the view that syllables or some correlate thereof (e.g., number of vowels) are processed and represented by young infants. However, many questions are left open. Is the infants' performance determined by the number of syllables in the items, or alternatively do they pay attention to the vowels that constitute the stimuli? If the infants are presented with stimuli that are organized by

---

[4]However, a preliminary experiment, also reported in Bertoncini et al. (in preparation), showed that, when words were presented without separating them according to their intonational contours, infants failed to discriminate the two lists on the basis of syllable numerosity. Further research will be needed to determine the reason of the non-discrimination obtained when using varying intonational contours. This result suggests, however, that extracting syllable numerosity is not an easy operation.

rhythmical units other than the syllable, are they still able to count them? Studying newborns' capacities to discriminate two lists of Japanese bisyllabic items that differ in number of moras (2 versus 3, one of the syllable of the trimoraic items being made of two moras) seems one way of collecting information concerning the above questions.

Bertoncini et al. (in preparation) also showed that French-born three-day-old infants, habituated to a homogeneous list of bimoraic bisyllabic items (or to a list containing trimoraic bisyllabic items), failed to react to a change in the number of moras during the post-shift phase, even when infants were provided with similar lists except that the intonative contour was kept unchanged. This result shows that infants born to French parents in Paris do not notice a change in the number of moras in the context of an unchanging number of syllables. The authors proposed that the trimoraic bisyllables are represented like the bimoraic bisyllables, on the basis of their number of vowels, namely two in each case. These results support the view that newborns represent speech as a sequence of vowels. Of course, the infants' behavior may be guided by a more sophisticated representation. Possibly, the entire syllable is represented and the number of syllables counted. However, we argue later that infants may represent speech input in terms of a sequence of vowels including some information about their duration and energy. If this is true, then a metric grid might be all they need to tell languages apart.

So far, we have presented two seemingly unrelated series of experiments. The first explores infants' ability to discriminate between languages. We suggest that one reason why infants are not confused by multilingual environments may lie in their innate ability to place utterances from different languages in separate files. The second is concerned with the way in which newborns perceive rhythmic speech units. From this, it appears that newborns perceive different rhythmic units in different ways. We propose that the relation between rhythmic units and vowels may play a crucial role in this phenomenon. In the next section, we attempt to connect the previous lines of research.

THE TIGRE

In this conclusion, we provide a framework in which the abilities of young infants can profitably be discussed. We believe that the newborns' ability to extract and represent the prosodic structures of languages is a biological endowment that prevents them from becoming utterly confused when growing up in a multilingual environment. Multilingual environments are not as exceptional as monolinguals have a tendency to think. Therefore, it is reasonable to expect that the human baby has specific devices to overcome this potential problem.

The competence that allows newborns to distinguish utterances drawn from different languages may seem surprising given their severe processing limitations. First, the brain of the infant is not fully mature at birth. Yakovlev and Lecours (1967) showed that there are myelogenetic cycles that determine the maturation of the brain. Investigators have also shown that in very young infants the brain's activity is predominantly subcortical, and that cortical activity increases several months later (see Chugani & Phelps, 1986, for a positron emission tomography experiment). Therefore, it seems unlikely that infants engage in adultlike reasoning strategies in order to determine whether a given utterance belongs to one language or other. Second, infants are faced with the problem of multilingual surroundings long before they have established a lexicon, or even the repertoire of consonants and vowels in their native language (respectively, Werker & Tees, 1984; Kuhl, 1991). Hence, they cannot rely on such information in order to discriminate languages. Third, we know that young infants discriminate languages on the basis of little information (e.g., a few sentences). Thus the mechanism they use cannot be based on statistical computations over large samples of speech. We take all these observations to imply that the behavior of the infant must rest on a rather simple procedure based on robust acoustic cues in the signal.

What kind of acoustic information can correlate with different languages, and be extracted with ease, speed, and reasonable reliability? Mehler et al. (1988) showed that infants can distinguish languages when only low frequency information (i.e., less than 400Hz) is made available. This result lends support to the view that languages can be sorted into classes according to their prosodic/rhythmic characteristics. But how can prosodic characteristics be extracted and represented? In the following, we propose that vowels are the cornerstone of prosodic representation in very young infants. Indeed, vowels carry most of the energy in the speech signal, they last longer than most consonants, and they have greater stability. They also carry accent and signal whether a syllable is strong or weak. Hence relatively robust cues such as duration and intensity of vowels may inform infants about the rhythmic nature of a language. Moreover, we have provided evidence (Bertoncini et al., 1988) that very young infants pay more attention to vowels than to consonants. Newborns can also discriminate bi- versus trisyllabic words (Bijeljac-Babic et al., 1993; Bertoncini et al., in preparation) suggesting that they perceive and represent the number of vowels in the speech string.[5] Other studies suggest that the baby also represents accent in its sequential locus. With these fragments of empirical evidence we are in a position to propose a framework to pursue the study of speech processing in very young infants. Let us first explore the value of postulating

---

[5]The quality of vowels do not appear to be used at the age when utterances already provide good pointers as to the language of origin. Indeed, as we mentioned earlier, the vowels for one's native language emerge at around six months of age (Kuhl, 1991), which indicates that infants do not represent the quality of vowels to infer the language of an utterance.

an initial speech representation that rests on a *Time and Intensity Grid Representation*, henceforth, TIGRE.

The TIGRE is a gridlike representation of the vocalic nuclei in the speech signal. All the vowels are represented in it so that the sequential information is preserved. We assume that each vowel receives an index indicating its duration and amplitude.[6] Since the TIGRE is a representation of the vowels in the speech signal, the spacing between the vowels reflects the intervocalic distance in the signal. Could TIGRE capture the periodicity that characterizes the utterances of a given language? That is an empirical question that requires an empirical answer. Since languages differ in their typical periodicity, we expect that utterances from different languages will be represented in a contrasting way on the basis of some prelexical knowledge. How otherwise could the baby perform as he/she does?

In its simplest version the TIGRE only specifies the duration and intensity of vowels arranged isomorphically to the signal. If, however, it appears that this is insufficient to establish classes of languages, additional cues might also have to be represented in the grid. A worthwhile feature of TIGRE is its probable failure to distinguish utterances from any arbitrary pair of languages. Therefore, TIGRE fits our intuition that infants are unable to distinguish utterances drawn, say, from two moraic languages or from two stress marked languages. TIGRE also predicts the existence of at most a dozen metrical patterns, into which all languages can be classified. It further predicts that languages belonging to the same class will not be discriminated by young infants while languages belonging to different classes will. The initial sorting of utterances will thus be determined by language classes, rather than by individual languages. We encourage the reader to conceive of TIGRE as a first-order filtering device that sorts utterances into their adequate classes.

Our presentation of TIGRE as a first-order filtering device leads us to predict that, during the first months of life, infants group utterances into different linguistic files according to the class to which they belong. We assume that, for each class, an innately specified file stipulates the most relevant properties for this class. Specialized mechanisms lead the infant to shift its attention so as to privilege utterances that belong to the class of its native language. The metric properties of the native language class determine the perceptual mechanisms that will then be used when listening to any utterance. Thus, the specific language class strategies discovered through research with adults are bound to arise from this early innate specification. If so, TIGRE must be seen as having

---

[6]The durational information could be the duration of the vowels and/or the time between two adjacent vocalic nuclei (calculated from some particular acoustic point in the vowel, such as the onset or the perceptual center). We believe that recent work by Scott (1993) suggests that P-center distributions may provide an excellent cue as to the periodicity in languages. Indeed, she proposed a local model of P-centers that, if adapted to fluent speech, would allow the calculation of P-centers during on-line processing.

a dual function: as a device that sorts utterances from different language-classes into separate files, and as a device that can help to understand how the infant bootstraps into the appropriate language processing.

We must also consider how infants raised with two languages that belong to the same class avoid confusion. First let us acknowledge that TIGRE has not been developed to deal specifically with this issue. However, we owe TIGRE our awareness about the potential complications that this situation may bring about. If languages are arranged into classes, bilinguals who hear utterances of languages within the same class should have great difficulty in acquiring these languages, as all utterances should be sorted into the same file. At the beginning, they may even ignore that all utterances do not belong to the same language. We believe that the child will only become aware of the existence of different languages when growing older, maybe through the processing of the relevant information specified in the linguistic files. As a consequence, language acquisition in intra-class bilinguals may be slower than that of monolinguals or between-class bilinguals (which represent the two languages in entirely separate files from the onset of acquisition). However, the delay in acquisition may already have been overcome by the time infants begin to speak, in which case only perceptual experiments on younger infants could reveal it. But if such a delay exists, we expect that its importance depends crucially on when the intra-class bilinguals succeed in separating the two languages involved.

Following Cutler and Mehler (1993), we propose a more specific partitioning of the languages on which infants might rely. In this chapter, we have presented work showing that languages with different rhythmic properties (e.g., syllable-, stress-, and mora-timed languages) are processed in contrasting ways by adults. Our proposal is that very young infants also use these broad rhythmic classes while classifying speech inputs. Several predictions follow from this proposal. First, the pattern of language discrimination should follow the rhythmic classes described by phonologists. Hence, languages belonging to the same rhythmic class, such as syllable-timed French and Spanish, should not be distinguished by newborns, while mora-timed Japanese should be discriminated from both stress-timed English and syllable-timed French. Second, we predict that, in a categorization task, newborns will be able to build a category out of utterances belonging to languages from the same rhythmic class, but will not be able to do so with languages belonging to different rhythmic classes.

To recapitulate, we present two related hypotheses about early language acquisition. The first one affirms that young infants use a gridlike representation of vowels to distinguish between languages (the TIGRE). The second asserts that infants sort utterances into the classes according to how they pattern rhythmically. Although these two hypotheses are specific, we would like the reader to think of them as part of a framework to further our knowledge of the infants' linguistic behavior. Our general framework makes several claims. First, utterances drawn from different languages can be sorted by the infant into different linguistic files on the basis of robust and salient acoustic cues in the signal. Second, there is not a file for every language in the world; the files only define a first-order partitioning of languages. Third, the different linguistic classes trigger class-specific acquisition mechanisms, and lead to class-specific processing strategies in the adult.

We hope that our general framework will help us to refine our ways of thinking about early linguistic acquisition and prompt innovative research in this area. In particular, in the years to come, we would like to test some of the predictions made in this chapter. We would like to test the prediction that very young infants do not discriminate languages from the same rhythmic class until a certain age. We would like to establish whether infants put utterances from different languages in the same class when, and only when, these languages belong to the same rhythmic class. Furthermore, we would like to determine whether very young infants can discriminate Japanese (a mora-timed language) from both French and English, as predicted by the rhythmic hypothesis. Moreover, we hope that the reader will find many extensions of the views presented in this chapter to be worth exploring. The answers to these questions will have to be left to some later date.

ACKNOWLEDGMENTS

This research was supported by grants from the Human Frontier Scientific Program, the European Communities Human Capital Program, and CNET (Convention 837BD28 00790 9245 LAA/TSS/CMC). We would like to thank Josiane Bertoncini, Anne Christophe, Caroline Floccia, and Brit Van Ooyen for their help, comments, and fruitful discussion.

REFERENCES

Abercrombie, D. (1967). *Elements of general phonetics*. Edinburgh: Edinburgh University Press.

Antell, S. E., & Keating, D. P. (1983). Perception of numerical invariance in neonates. *Child Development, 54*, 695-706.

Bahrick, L. E., & Pickens, J. N. (1988). Classification of bimodal English and Spanish language passages by infants. *Infant Behavior and Development, 11*, 277-296.

Bertoncini, J., Bijeljac-Babic, R., Jusczyk, P. W., Kennedy, L., & Mehler, J. (1988). An investigation of young infants' perceptual representations of speech sounds. *Journal of Experimental Psychology: General, 117*, 21-33.

Bertoncini, J., Floccia, C., Nazzi, T., Miyagishima, K., & Mehler, J. (in preparation). *Morae and syllables: Rhythmical basis of speech representation in neonates*.

Bijeljac-Babic, R., Bertoncini, J., & Mehler, J. (1993). How do 4-day-old infants categorize multisyllabic utterances? *Developmental Psychology, 29*, 711-721.

Chugani, H. T., & Phelps, M. E. (1986). Maturational changes in cerebral function in infants determined by [18]FDG positron emission tomography. *Science, 231*, 840-843.

Cutler, A., & Butterfield, S. (1992). Rhythmic cues to speech segmentation: Evidence from juncture misperception. *Journal of Memory and Language, 31*, 218-236.

Cutler, A., & Mehler, J. (1993). The periodicity bias. *Journal of Phonetics, 21*, 103-108.

Cutler, A., Mehler, J., Norris, D., & Segui, J. (1986). The syllable's differing role in the segmentation of French and English. *Journal of Memory and Language, 25*, 385-400.

Cutler, A., Mehler, J., Norris, D., & Segui, J. (1992). The monolingual nature of speech segmentation by bilinguals. *Cognitive Psychology, 24*, 381-410.

Cutler, A., & Norris, D. G. (1988). The role of strong syllables in segmentation for lexical access. *Journal of Experimental Psychology: Human Perception and Performance, 14*, 113-121.

Dauer, R. M. (1983). Stress-timing and syllable-timing reanalysed. *Journal of Phonetics, 11*, 51-62.

Dehaene-Lambertz, G. (in preparation). *Language recognition in 2-month-olds.*

Dupoux, E., & Hammond, M. (in preparation). *Syllabic effects in English: The role of stress.*

Dupoux, E., & Mehler, J. (1992). Unifying awareness and on line studies of speech: A tentative framework, In J. Alegria, D. Holender, J. Morais, & M. Radeau (Eds.), *Analytic approaches to human cognition* (pp. 59-76). The Netherlands: Elsevier.

Grosjean, F. (1989). Neurolinguists, beware! The bilingual is not two monolinguals in one person. *Brain & Language, 36*, 3-15.

Johnson, M. H., Posner, M. I., & Rothbart, M. K. (1991). Components of visual orienting in early infancy: Contingency learning, anticipatory looking and disengaging. *Journal of Cognitive Neuroscience, 3*, 335-344.

Klatt, D. H. (1980). Speech perception: A model of acoustic-phonetic analysis and lexical access. In R. A. Cole (Ed.), *Perception and production of fluent speech* (pp. 243-288). Hillsdale, NJ: Lawrence Erlbaum Associates.

Kuhl, P. K. (1991). Human adults and human infants show a "perceptual magnet effect" for the prototypes of speech categories, monkeys do not. *Perception and Psychophysics, 50*, 93-107.

Lehiste, I. (1977). Isochrony reconsidered. *Journal of Phonetics, 5*, 253-263.

Mehler, J., Dommergues, J. Y., Frauenfelder, U., & Segui, J. (1981). The syllable's role in speech segmentation. *Journal of Verbal Learning and Verbal Behavior, 20*, 298-305.

Mehler, J., Jusczyk, P. W., Lambertz, G., Halsted, G., Bertoncini, J., & Amiel-Tison, C. (1988). A precursor of language acquisition in young infants. *Cognition, 29*, 143-178.

Mehler, J., Sebastian, N., Altmann, G., Dupoux, E., Christophe, A., & Pallier, C. (1993). Understanding compressed sentences: The role of rhythm and meaning. *Annals New York Academy of Sciences, 682*, 272-282.

Moon, C., Panneton-Cooper, R., & Fifer, W. P. (1993). Two-day-olds prefer their native language. *Infant Behavior and Development, 16*, 495-500.

Otake, T., Hatano, G., Cutler, A., & Mehler, J. (1993). Mora or syllable? Speech segmentation in Japanese. *Journal of Memory and Language, 32*, 258-278.

Port, R. F., Dalby, J., & O'Dell, M. (1987). Evidence for mora timing in Japanese. *Journal of the Acoustical Society of America, 81*, 1574-1585.

Scott, S. K. (1993). *Perceptual centres in speech - An acoustic analysis.* Unpublished doctoral dissertation, University College, London.

Starkey, P., & Cooper, R. G., Jr. (1980). Perception of numbers by human infants. *Science, 210*, 1033-1035.

Starkey, P., Spelke, E. S., & Gelman, R. (1983). Detection of intermodal numerical correspondences by human infants. *Science, 222*, 179-181.

Treiman, R., & Breaux, A. M. (1982). Common phoneme and overall similarity relations among spoken syllables: Their use by children and adults. *Journal of Psycholinguistic Research, 6*, 569-598.

Treiman, R., & Danis, C. (1988). Syllabification of intervocalic consonants. *Journal of Memory and Language, 27*, 87-104.

Treiman, R., & Zukowski, A. (1990). Toward an understanding of English syllabification. *Journal of Memory and Language, 29*, 66-85.

Werker, J. F., & Tees, R. C. (1984). Cross-language speech perception: Evidence for perceptual reorganization during the first year of life. *Infant Behavior and Development, 7*, 49-63.

Yakovlev, P. I., & Lecours, A. R. (1967). The myelogenetic cycles of regional maturation of the brain. In A. Minkowski (Ed.), *Regional development of the brain in early life* (pp. 3-70). Oxford: Blackwell.

8 Models of Word Segmentation in Fluent Maternal Speech to Infants

Richard N. Aslin, Julide Z. Woodward, Nicholas P. LaMendola, and Thomas G. Bever
University of Rochester

Since the pioneering study of infant speech perception by Eimas, Siqueland, Jusczyk, and Vigorito (1971), it has become widely acknowledged that infants have sophisticated perceptual abilities that enable them to discriminate subtle phonetic distinctions (Aslin, Pisoni, & Jusczyk, 1983), some of which are not easily discriminated by adults (Werker & Tees, 1984; Werker & Polka, 1993). Unfortunately, these sophisticated perceptual abilities have been demonstrated under listening conditions that are not typical of the infant's natural environment. For example, high-amplitude sucking, conditioned headturning, and habituation-of-looking techniques present the infant with brief speech tokens, separated by pauses, and repeated many times in a low-noise environment. These are not the conditions typical of natural language processing where words are generally presented once, in rapid succession, and often in noisy environments. What remains unclear, therefore, is the extent to which infants deploy their sophisticated perceptual abilities when confronted with fluent speech.

One of the most salient problems associated with fluent speech is the segmentation of an utterance into words. As native speakers of a natural language, we take it for granted that words function as separate and distinct entities. However, when confronted with an unfamiliar spoken language, we become aware of the fact that in fluent speech there are many word boundaries that are not marked by obvious acoustic cues, such as a brief pause in vocal output. In fluent spontaneous speech, Cole and Jakimik (1980) estimated that only 40% of word boundaries in English contain a stop consonant or fricative, and these same acoustic cues to word boundaries occur at syllable boundaries within many English words, such as "bottle."

Because the young infant has neither an elementary lexicon nor a knowledge of the rules by which sounds are sequenced to create words, these relations must be discovered from listening experience. There are two general types of constraints that could facilitate the acquisition of a lexicon from parental speech. First, there may be constraints on auditory processing that highlight for the infant certain portions of the speech input. For example, the general property of primacy and recency in memory abilities may focus the infant's attention on the first and last portions of an utterance. Second, there may be constraints on the input provided initially to the infant. For example, parental speech may be simplified in a variety of ways to reduce the difficulty of word segmentation. Both of these constraints have been investigated in older infants' production of words (Echols & Newport, 1992; Peters, 1983), but only recently has interest turned to constraints on language perception that may operate in pre-productive infants.

Two obvious forms of simplification that could facilitate infants' segmentation of words from fluent speech are (a) frequently presenting words in isolation and (b) highlighting words using emphatic stress. Unfortunately, little descriptive evidence is available on the relative frequency of isolated and embedded word usage in maternal speech to infants (but see Vihman, 1993). Moreover, if infants have memory limitations for complex acoustic input, then words presented at the beginnings and ends of utterances should be easier to segment because of the silence that precedes or follows the word.

The use of emphatic stress, which consists of a combination of rising or rise-fall pitch pattern, an increase in intensity, and/or a lengthening of the highlighted word, has also received little attention in the language acquisition literature, except in the domain of so-called "motherese" or infant-directed speech. Although a number of studies have shown that mothers employ the prosodic cues of emphatic stress when speaking to their infants (Cooper & Aslin, 1990; Fernald, 1984, 1985; Fernald & Kuhl, 1987; Fernald & Simon, 1984; Fernald, Taeschner, Dunn, Papousek, Boysson-Bardies, & Fukui, 1989; Werker & McLeod, 1989), only Fernald and Mazzie (1991) have shown that mothers use emphatic stress at the semantic topic of the sentence. Thus, use of emphatic stress may provide the infant with a means of attending to a highlighted portion of a multiword utterance.

It is important to note, however, that the acoustic properties of emphatic stress are not discrete. For example, in the sample sentence "Where were you a year ago," it is possible to add emphatic stress to the word "you" or to the word "year." In both cases, the pitch rise and intensity increase are blended with the preceding and following syllable. Thus, on the basis of acoustic information alone, other plausible segmentations include "ereyou," "youa," "ayear," and "yeara." Note also that in this sample sentence all five word boundaries are continuously voiced. The only pause in voicing occurs at a syllable boundary within the word "ago."

There are, of course, combinations of information that could facilitate infants' word segmentation from maternal speech. For example, infants may initially encode only high-frequency words that are presented in isolation. From these robust entries in the lexicon, they may bootstrap the segmentation process by isolating non-familiar acoustic strings of phonemes from familiar words, thereby adding candidate words to the lexicon. Further distributional analyses would then fine tune these lexical entries. An empirical determination of these forms of word segmentation and word learning in infants is a daunting research task because it requires experimental control of the language input. Thus, another research strategy for examining the relative merits of certain input constraints and processing biases is a computation model. A detailed description of our attempts at implementing a connectionist model of word segmentation will conclude the present chapter. Before considering that model, a summary of what we have learned about the inputs presented to infants is described.

MATERNAL SPEECH INPUT

Woodward and Aslin (1990, 1991, 1992) began a series of studies to determine which input strategies are used by mothers in their speech to 12-month-olds. We chose 12-month-olds because they are just beginning to produce single words and presumably have already learned at least some rudimentary word-segmentation skills. Several questions motivated our first study: (1) what is the relative (and absolute) frequency with which mothers use words in isolation (or separated by pauses in multiword utterances), (2) do mothers use a consistent strategy of placing a target word in utterance-initial or utterance-final position, and (3) do mothers consistently highlight a target word in a sentence using emphatic stress cues?

To address these questions, we had 19 mothers attempt to teach their 12-month-old infant three new words: "lips," "wrist," and "lobe." We chose these words because they were judged to be novel (but actual words in English) for a 12-month-old, they contained an onset phoneme (a liquid) that is typically continuously voiced in English, and each word referred to a body part that could be used as a pointing-referent by the mother during the teaching task. Use of target words with potentially difficult-to-segment onset phonemes also allowed us to determine if mothers avoid such word boundaries or add acoustic information to highlight these boundaries.

Mothers were tape-recorded using a lapel microphone to obtain high quality audio recordings. They were instructed to teach their infant two of the three target words using any strategies they felt appropriate, even though it was clear that they were unlikely to elicit word productions from their infant. Transcripts were prepared from each recording session, and detailed acoustic analyses were conducted using a Kay Digital Sonograph.

The results of this first study indicated that, although some mothers presented the target word in isolation quite often, other mothers never presented the target word in isolation (see Fig. 8.1). Thus, the maternal strategy of using the target word in isolation to solve the word-segmentation problem cannot be sufficient for all infants. Moreover, it should be pointed out that all mothers tested were highly motivated to teach their infant the target words. In a more naturalistic setting, it seems unlikely that mothers would go to such great lengths to repeat a specific word as many as 70 times in 5-10 minutes.

The results also indicated that when the target word was presented in a multiword utterance, mothers placed the target word in utterance-final position. This utterance-final placement occurred an average of 89% of the time (range: 76%-100%). Moreover, only 19% of these utterance-final target words were preceded by a pause in voicing. Mothers also used emphatic stress to highlight the target word, with 68% of the utterances characterized by a rising or rise-fall pitch contour on the target word.

A final feature of this first study was the ability to determine if mothers highlight or avoid difficult-to-segment word boundaries. For example, the word "his" preceding the target word "lips" would provide a lengthy pause in voicing that could mark the word boundary. The results indicated that although mothers did use many easy-to-segment word boundaries, they also failed to avoid difficult-to-segment ones. For example, one of the most frequent word combinations was "your wrist" in which two /r/s are blended at the word boundary.

These results suggest that no single cue to word segmentation is sufficient for all infants. Some mothers never used the target word in isolation, although all mothers used utterance-final position as their domi-

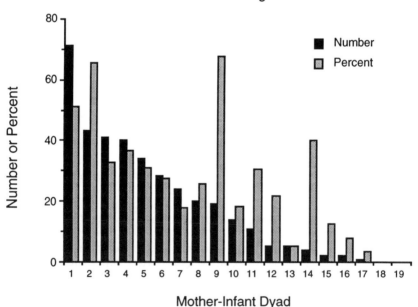

FIG. 8.1. The number of times (and percentage of utterances) that the target word was presented in isolation (i.e., not in a multiword utterance) by each mother to her 12-month-old infant.

nant locus for target-word placement and repeated the target word frequently under these test conditions. Pitch modulation was also used to highlight the target word, but this acoustic information does not provide a discrete segmentation from the surrounding words in an utterance.

It is important to point out that the placement of the target word in utterance-final position and the use of emphatic stress are common discourse strategies of any speaker who is attempting to communicate with an unsophisticated listener. Thus, the fact that mothers use these strategies when speaking to their infants does not imply that these strategies are unique to infant-directed speech.

One final type of information that may be important to word segmentation is the variability in the words preceding and following the target word. This could give rise to a form of perceptual contrast effect that various perceptual theorists (e.g., J. J. Gibson, 1966) have suggested is a critical cue to the extraction of an invariant property from a complex stimulus. Fig. 8.2 shows that the target word was preceded by a variety of words, ranging in different mothers from 3 to 11 (with a median of 6). Thus, in addition to pitch highlighting, utterance-final positioning, high frequency, and the possibility of some isolated presentations, the infant has available a number of distributional cues that may be beneficial to word segmentation.

A follow-up study was designed to examine in more detail the tentative conclusion that mothers do not enhance difficult-to-segment word

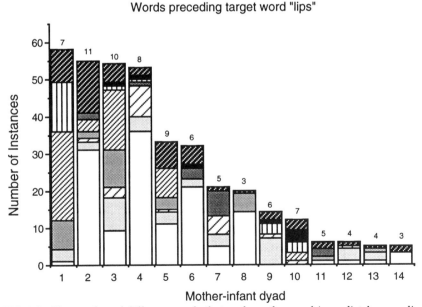

FIG. 8.2. The number of different words that each mother used immediately preceding the target word.

boundaries. This was accomplished by creating a storybook containing difficult-to-segment word pairs that the mothers were instructed to present to their 12-month-old infants. A sample of 20 mothers used the storybook to present the word pairs to their infants as well as to another adult. This allowed us to directly compare the acoustic properties of infant- and adult-directed speech by the same mothers. The word pairs contained identical word-final and word-initial phonemes (e.g., "four rocks," "some more," "this sock") and other continuously voiced word boundaries (e.g., "too old," "green eggs," "no more").

As expected, mothers used higher overall pitch, greater pitch excursion, and longer word durations in their infant-directed than in their adult-directed speech. However, there was no consistent evidence that mothers enhanced the segmental cues to word boundaries in infant-directed speech. They did not add or extend any pauses in voicing between words, and they did not enhance the burst intensity or frequency of occurrence of bursts for stop consonants. Moreover, some word pairs (e.g., "this shoe") contained the same acoustic information at the word boundary that was present within one of the control words ("tissue"). Thus, this second study confirmed the conclusion from the first study that mothers do not enhance the segmental information at word boundaries to facilitate word segmentation by their infants. The presence of heightened prosodic variation in infant-directed speech may focus infant attention on a limited portion of an extended utterance, but it does not provide a discrete cue to word boundaries.

The final study was an attempt to examine the potential importance of placing target words in utterance-final position. Our first study had shown that mothers use utterance-final position as the dominant location for target words in a word-teaching task. One hypothesis is that mothers have tacit knowledge that infants can better attend to and remember words placed in utterance-final position. Another hypothesis is that, because the target words used in our first study were nouns, and nouns naturally occur as the object of sentences in English, a language with a canonical subject-verb-object word order, mothers were simply speaking grammatically. To examine these hypotheses, we selected another language in which the target words were nouns but the canonical word order was verb-final: Turkish. We also tested another sample of English-speaking mothers using verbs as the target words to determine if these mothers would violate grammaticality in English by placing the verb in utterance-final position. Any evidence of sacrificing grammaticality would support at least some role for recency in mothers' strategies for providing optimal input to their infants.

The present study followed the protocol of our first study, except that the seven Turkish-speaking mothers attempted to teach their infants the words "yüz" (face), "lule" (lock of hair), and "yanak" (cheek) and the 20 English-speaking mothers taught their infants the words "lift," "wipe," and "ring." Note that all three of the English words were transitive verbs requiring a direct object.   Thus, placement of these verbs in utterance-final position was strictly ungrammatical.

As in the preceding two studies, mothers using either Turkish or English employed pitch excursion to highlight the target word.   As shown in Fig. 8.3, the use of a rising, a rise-fall, or a fall-rise pitch modulation occurred in 60% or more of the utterances. The most important aspect of the results, however, centered on grammaticality. There were several clear instances of grammatical sentences in both English and Turkish.

Turkish: "Cici yap annenin yüzüne cici yap."
            [Nice make (pat) to, your mother's face nice make (pat)]
English: "Can you wipe your mouth?"

And there were clear instances of ungrammatical sentences in English and Turkish.

*Turkish: "Göster kizim yüzünü."
             [Show my daughter your face]
             {grammatical: "Kizim yüzünü göster."}
*English: "David wanna wipe."

These results are shown in Fig. 8.4, along with comparisons from our first study using nouns in English. Note the dominant pattern of utterance-final position for nouns in English and the shift to a medial utterance position for verbs in English.   Subject-deletion was the most

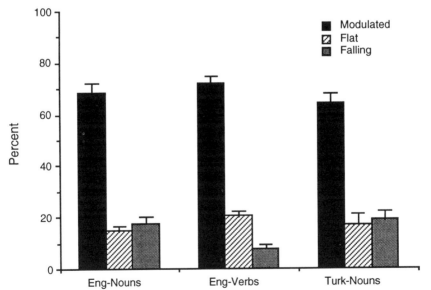

FIG. 8.3. The percentage of instances of three categories of pitch used by mothers when speaking the target word ("modulated" included rising, rise-fall, and fall-rise).

common form of ungrammaticality for English verbs (approximately one of every three utterances), although object-deletion occurred in approximately one of every six utterances. For the Turkish mothers, placement of the target noun was equally split between medial and final utterance position (medial or initial is grammatically correct). Across all utterances to infants, 36% were strictly ungrammatical (9% of the utterances were noun-final but could not be categorized as strictly ungrammatical because they were partial sentences). Although these results appear to offer strong support for a recency-over-grammaticality preference in Turkish, we know that in everyday conversation Turkish adults sometimes speak ungrammatically. Thus, to obtain a baseline we tape-recorded five native speakers of Turkish in adult-adult conversations and found that 15% of these utterances were ungrammatical. Thus, the speech to 12-month-olds in our sample of Turkish mothers was more than twice as likely to contain a target noun in utterance-final position, and to violate grammaticality, than in adult-adult speech.

One final aspect of the results from Turkish mothers' speech to their infants mirrored the results from our first study. Perceptual contrast was present in the utterances containing the target word, with between 5 and 18 different words preceding the target noun "yüz" across the seven mothers. The use of multiple surrounding contexts, which was also present for English verbs, appears to be a robust source of information for word segmentation in at least two quite different languages.

In summary, these studies of maternal speech input suggest that

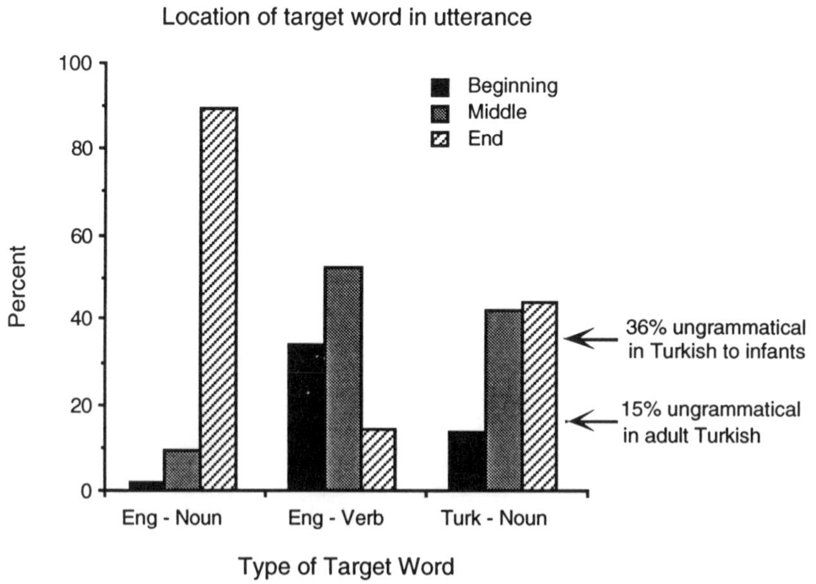

FIG. 8.4. The percentage of target words placed at the beginning, middle, or end of maternal utterances for English nouns, English transitive verbs, and Turkish nouns.

mothers have tacit knowledge of some global strategies that may facilitate word-learning in young infants. Presenting the target word in isolation, although not universally used by mothers, is effective in solving the segmentation problem, particularly if the word is repeated frequently. Placing the target word in utterance-final position may be advantageous, even if such placement violates strict grammaticality. Mothers' speech to 12-month-olds is by no means dominated by this recency strategy, but grammaticality is clearly sacrificed under certain circumstances when speaking to young infants. Since word segmentation is a prerequisite for the acquisition of grammar, the presence of even a substantial proportion of strictly ungrammatical sentences in early infancy may have little long-term effect, particularly since mothers may alter their strategy once infants begin producing a significant number of one- and two-word utterances. In general, mothers use heightened prosodic cues in infant-directed speech, but it is unclear whether these cues serve more than a global role in eliciting and maintaining the infant's attention, and perhaps focusing it on a portion of the utterance. The absence of a discrete signal in the prosody for the onset and offset of a word implies that such cues play a relatively minor role in word segmentation per se. Finally, the presence of multiple surrounding contexts may provide the infant, particularly after a word has been presented in isolation, with the opportunity to confirm that a candidate word is in fact a basic acoustic unit in fluent speech.

Until recently, the most serious problem facing researchers interested in word segmentation skills in early infancy was the absence of a technique to assess infants' ability to recognize a target word in fluent speech. Jusczyk and Aslin (in press; see also Jusczyk & Kemler Nelson, this volume) have provided the first evidence that infants can recognize words or portions of words in fluent speech. Thus, it may now be possible to examine which properties of fluent speech are essential or advantageous to the segmentation and extraction of words in the natural listening environment. However, given the difficulty of obtaining such data from infants, it is useful to consider a variety of computational models that can be used to explore, in a more systematic manner, constraints on word segmentation.

A CONNECTIONIST MODEL OF WORD SEGMENTATION

Connectionist models are particularly suitable for solving problems in which massive amounts of data are available to the learner and in which it is clear how feedback is given to the model so that it can learn appropriate responses to the input. There are, of course, an infinite number of learning models that one could use to attempt to "solve" the segmentation problem. Our research strategy has been to utilize a general purpose learning algorithm, the back-propagation architecture (Rumelhart & McClelland, 1986), without assuming that the actual "neural network" conforms to the details of this algorithm.

The difficulty associated with any neural network approach is to build in enough structure to allow the network to solve the task without building in so much of the solution that the network cannot fail, thereby making the task trivial. A critical issue in any learning model is how to code the input. To take a silly example, if we posited that the word was the input unit, then the task would be defined solely by this input coding. A more reasonable assumption is that the input is sublexical. This, of course, begs the question as to whether the input should be the syllable, the phoneme, or an acoustic representation of various speech gestures. Our strategy was to code the input as a set of articulatory features. This strategy was based on our working assumption that a phonemic input scheme would not allow the model to generalize to other phonemes that were not reinforced by the model. We could have used a phonetic feature encoding scheme, but we chose, for ease of transcription, the more limited output from an automated text-to-speech system.

A second critical aspect of the input coding scheme was to treat each iteration through the model as a sequence of phonemes. The length of this sequence determines how much of the utterance is used to predict when a word boundary will occur. Initially, we chose sequences of three phonemes, but this was a parameter that we then varied in the model. We could have chosen a recurrent network architecture (Elman, 1990), but we felt that the triplet input scheme used by Juliano and Bever (1990; see also Bever, 1992) was a simpler method of providing sequential inputs to the model.

Reinforcement, or feedback to the model when a word boundary has occurred, was limited to the simplest source of information available to the infant; namely, when the end of a sentence or the end of a major phrase was detected. That is, we assumed that the infant had the ability to recognize the end of a word if it was followed by a substantial (> 1 second) period of silence. Note that we did not reinforce the model with any other information that could serve as a cue to word boundaries. Although the pause prior to the initial phoneme in the utterance, like the pause after the final phoneme, could be treated as a word boundary, we felt that word-final information (due to recency) was a more plausible source of information. The hypothesis that syllable stress is an important source of information for word boundaries was proposed by Cutler and Carter (1987), who showed in a dictionary analysis of English that about 85% of everyday conversation contains words beginning with a stressed syllable. However, our goal was to provide the model with the most limited source of reinforcement to determine if this minimal level of information was sufficient for learning to take place. If it was not sufficient, then we could add more information to the model, such as the presence of syllable stress, in an attempt to enable the learning of word boundaries.

Our implementation of the model involved the following specific steps. First, we used two transcripts: one from our maternal speech study (with "wrist" and "lips" as the target words), and one from a spontaneous set of utterances obtained from a mother of a 12-month-old. We chose not to use other maternal transcripts from the existing child language literature because we suspected that speech to 12-month-olds, who are just learning their first words, is different in important respects from speech to 2- and 3-year-olds, who are producing multiword utterances.

Second, we transformed these two transcripts into feature notation by "playing" the ASCII text, stripped of all punctuation and stress markers, into a DECTalk™ text-to-speech synthesizer. This device has a decoding mode that provided us with a unique symbol for each phoneme in English. From this notation, we transformed each unique symbol into an 18-bit feature vector (see Table 8.1). This was done to allow the model to learn not just which specific phoneme ended an utterance, but also to generalize this end-of-utterance information to other phonemes in English that shared one or more features with this phoneme.

Third, each iteration through the model consisted of the simultaneous input of a sequence of three 18-bit feature vectors corresponding to three successive phonemes in the input utterance. For example, if the input was the sentence "Show mommy your wrist," then the first input triplet would consist of the three 18-bit feature vectors for the phonemes [sh]+[o]+[w], and the second input triplet would consist of the vectors for the phonemes [o]+[w]+[m]. The triplet input scheme, therefore, served as a "window" that passed over each maternal utterance. An additional input feature (the 55th bit after the three 18-bit feature vectors) was used to code the presence of a pause in the utterance. Thus, in all triplets for the sentence "Show mommy your wrist," this 55th feature was coded as "0" until the final three phonemes [i]+[s]+[t], when it was coded as "1." Thus, this 55th feature was used to code the presence of a word boundary at the end of the utterance.

Fourth, the input layer of the model was connected to a set of hidden units (of variable number). A standard Δ-rule learning algorithm (Rumelhart, Hinton, & Williams, 1986) was used to adjust the weights

TABLE 8.1.
18-bit Binary (0,1) Feature Vector For the Phoneme /l/.

Feature	Value	Feature	Value
flap	0	continuant	1
consonant	1	delayed release	0
sonorant	1	strident	0
nasal	0	voicing	1
anterior	1	syllabic	0
coronal	1	lateral	1
high	0	round	0
low	0	tense	0
back	0	reduced	0

between the input layer and the hidden unit layer, and a sigmoidal function was used to transfer the weighted sum of the inputs to each hidden unit. This sigmoidal transfer function is commonly used in back-propagation networks to compress the activations into the range from 0 to 1. The output layer consisted of a single unit that indicated the presence or absence of a phrase or utterance boundary. The learning algorithm for this output is also the standard Δ-rule, and the transfer function is a linear sum of the activation from the hidden units. The error in the model is calculated by finding the difference between the actual output and the desired output and then propagating this difference back through the network.

Fifth, the model was trained by passing the first two-thirds of the transcript from one mother into the model two or three times and then testing for generalization using the final one-third of the transcript. Table 8.2 summarizes the characteristics of the "wrist-lips" maternal input set. Notice that of the total words spoken (864), over 80% (710) were single-syllable words. Thus, the potential problem raised in the introduction—gaps in voicing can signal both between-word and within-word (syllable) boundaries—is largely irrelevant for maternal speech to 12-month-olds because the vast majority of words presented are single syllables. These data strongly suggest that if infants employed a strategy of "each syllable = a word," they would over-segment the input less than 20% of the time. Another important characteristic of the training set was the ratio of different words spoken to total words spoken. This type–token ratio was 0.096, indicating that there was a great deal of repetition in the maternal input. As expected, the most frequent words were the target words "wrist" and "lips" in this teaching task.

Sixth, after training the model, it was tested by fixing the weights assigned to each connection in the model and presenting as input the final third of the maternal transcript. One way to test the success of the model is to determine the mean output activation for various inputs. Fig. 8.5 shows that the model produced differential output activation to phrase/utterance, word, and within-word (i.e., no-boundary) inputs.

TABLE 8.2.
Characteristics of the Training Set For the First Connectionist Model.

Total number of words spoken		864
	Single-syllable	710
	Multisyllabic	154
Number of different words		83
	Single-syllable	67
	Multisyllabic	16
Most frequent words		
	wrist	68
	lips	68
	show	61
	his	57

The fact that the phrase/utterance boundary activation was highest is expected because that was the basis for reinforcement. The most important outcome, however, was the presence of significantly higher activation for word boundaries than for within-word phoneme triplets. This indicates that, in addition to learning phoneme triplets that preceded a phrase/utterance boundary, the model also learned phoneme triplets that preceded a word boundary. This learning of word boundaries occurred even though the model was never reinforced for a word boundary that occurred within an utterance.

Another way to look at the effectiveness of training in the generalization test is to examine the output activation for a sample input utterance. Fig. 8.6 illustrates a portion of several successive utterances and the activation that the model provided at each phoneme triplet. Notice that the model showed high activation after the word "wrist," which ended an utterance. The model also showed peaks in activation at several within-utterance word boundaries (e.g., "that's/his"), as well as an error when the phoneme triplet was similar to the reinforced "wrist" boundary ("hist/ongue"). As mentioned earlier, a phonetic input coding scheme might have eliminated or reduced these errors by enabling allophonic variations in a phoneme to be coded separately. Of course, to be relevant to our goal of understanding how a 12-month-old processes maternal input, such a phonetic coding scheme would have to assume that infants attend to these subtle allophonic variations (e.g., presence or absence of aspiration in the phoneme /b/).

Because we were concerned about the somewhat unusual characteristics of the maternal input set, we tested the model with another maternal sample that did not contain such highly redundant inputs. Table

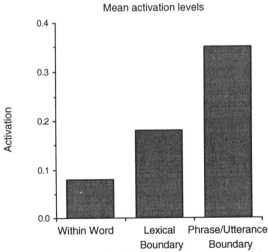

FIG. 8.5. Mean output activation levels, after training the connectionist model, for the test (generalization) sample at phrase/utterance, word, and within-word boundaries.

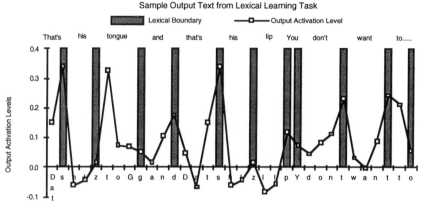

FIG. 8.6. Output activation levels for a sample test sequence of 33 phonemes.

8.3 summarizes the characteristics of this "spontaneous" maternal input set. Notice again that of the total words spoken (1146), over 80% (929) were single-syllable words. However, the type–token ratio was now 0.20 rather than 0.096 as in the "wrist-lips" sample.

To examine the effectiveness of the model, we computed the mean output activation across all the phoneme triplets in the generalization set (the final third of the maternal transcript) and then computed the percentage of output activations exceeding this mean, both at word boundaries and within words. Thus, an activation above the mean that occurred at a word boundary was a "hit" and an activation above the mean within a word was a "false alarm." Fig. 8.7 shows that hits exceeded false alarms, and that this evidence of learning and generalization was present for a wide range of numbers of hidden units. A concern that could be raised about any connectionist model, particularly one that is based on a relatively small input set, is whether the model is simply memorizing the input set. One way to examine this possibility is to increase the power of the model by varying the number of hidden units. If the model is memorizing, then increasing the number of hid-

TABLE 8.3.
Characteristics of the Training Set For the Second Connectionist Model.

Total number of words spoken		1146
	Single-syllable	929
	Multisyllabic	217
Number of different words		227
	Single-syllable	167
	Multisyllabic	60
Most frequent words		
	the	63
	ball	57
	see	51
	you	50

den units should increase performance and reduce generalization.   As shown in Fig. 8.7, this was clearly not the case in our model.

We also wanted to assure ourselves that the phoneme triplet input scheme was a reasonable one. Thus, we varied this input scheme to allow for three, two, or one 18-bit feature vectors. Fig. 8.8 shows that with both 30 and 70 hidden units, both 3 and 2 phoneme inputs allowed the model to perform well (i.e., hits exceeded false alarms). However, when only a single phoneme input was used, the model did not learn. Moreover, when we randomly reinforced the model during training (that is, once per utterance, but at some random location within the utterance rather than at the end of the utterance), the model did not learn. Thus, we have evidence that either 2 or 3 successive phonemes are required for the model to learn, and that consistent reinforcement at the end of each utterance is sufficient for learning to take place.

Finally, we asked whether the model would learn if we eliminated the phonetic feature coding scheme. That is, we changed the input from three 18-bit feature vectors to a unique code for each phoneme (e.g., [a] = 000, [b] = 001, [c] = 010, etc.). We found no evidence that this phoneme-triplet input scheme could be learned by the model, even with 100 hidden units. Thus, the use of a feature encoding scheme appears to be an essential aspect of the model if it is to learn within-utterance word boundaries from end-of-utterance pauses. The utilization of common sequential features (phonotactics) of one's native language appears to be a robust predictor of preferences for infant-directed speech by infants as young as 6 months of age (Friederici & Wessels, 1993; Jusczyk, Friederici, Wessels, Svenkerud, & Jusczyk, 1993).

One final point relevant to what the model learned concerns the

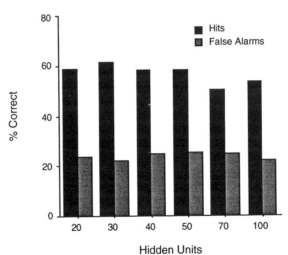

FIG. 8.7. Performance of the connectionist model as a function of the number of hidden units.

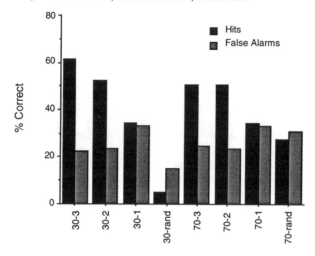

Hidden Units and Input Phonemes

FIG. 8.8. Performance of the connectionist model with inputs of 3, 2, 1, or randomly rein-forced phonemes for both 30 and 70 hidden units.

preponderance of single-syllable words in the input. It is possible that the model simply learned which phoneme triplets were syllables, resulting in some oversegmentation of the test set. Although there was some oversegmentation, the model actually performed better (activations were 2-3 times higher) at predicting word boundaries after 2-syllable words than after 1-syllable words. Thus, the addition of prosodic information, which spans multiple syllables, may enhance word segmentation, though it does not appear to be necessary, at least not in our model.

It is important to point out that even with the feature input scheme, the model did not succeed in learning when utterance length was significantly greater than typical infant-directed speech. That is, if the reinforcement received by the model occurred only after 25-30 phonemes (6-8 words), rather than after 10-15 phonemes (3-5 words), there was no evidence of learning or generalization. This suggests that a small input sequence may be essential to initiate the word-segmentation process, much like the "less is more" (Newport, 1984, 1988) and "starting small" (Elman, 1991) hypotheses proposed for learning other aspects of language.

SUMMARY

The results of three studies of maternal speech input to 12-month-olds provide the first comprehensive description of how native speakers of English and Turkish structure their spoken language to infants in a word-learning task. The highly intonated pitch contours of infant-directed speech were very prevalent, but detailed acoustic analyses revealed that word boundaries were not enhanced in infant-directed speech and difficult-to-segment words boundaries were not avoided. Moreover, the prosodic cues in infant-directed speech are not sufficiently discrete to mark precisely where word boundaries are located. Rather, these prosodic cues appear to direct infant attention to a general region of an utterance containing important segmental information. Mothers do present words in isolation, but not consistently or universally. Mothers did, however, present target words in utterance-final position, and the presence of ungrammatical sentences in both English and Turkish suggests that mothers have tacit knowledge that recency is more important for word-learning than grammaticality, at least for 12-month-olds.

The results from a series of connectionist models of word segmentation suggest that even the most minimal assumption about what an infant can recognize as a word boundary—namely, the pause after an utterance—is sufficient, in principle, for the learning of word boundaries within an utterance. Of course, it remains unclear whether these models of word segmentation are mirrored in the actual performance of infants learning a natural language. But the combination of computational models and the recent demonstration of a paradigm to assess infants' word recognition in fluent speech (Jusczyk & Aslin, in press) should provide powerful tools for exploring word segmentation in the future.

ACKNOWLEDGMENT

Portions of this research were supported by NIH grant HD 20286 to RNA.

REFERENCES

Aslin, R. N., Pisoni, D. B., & Jusczyk, P. W. (1983). Auditory development and speech perception in infancy. In M. M. Haith & J. J. Campos (Eds.), *Infancy and the biology of development* (pp. 573-686). New York: Academic Press.

Bever, T. G. (1992). The demons and the beast: Modular and nodular kinds of knowledge. In R. Reilly & N. Starkey (Eds.), *Connectionist approaches to natural language processing* (pp. 213-252). Hillsdale, NJ: Lawrence Erlbaum Associates.

Cole, R. A., & Jakimik, J. (1980). A model of speech perception. In R. A. Cole (Ed.), *Perception and production of fluent speech.* (pp. 133-163). Hillsdale, NJ: Lawrence Erlbaum Associates.

Cooper, R. P., & Aslin, R. N. (1990). Preference for infant directed speech in the first month after birth. *Child Development, 61,* 1584-1595.

Cutler, A., & Carter, D. M. (1987). The predominance of strong initial syllables in the English vocabulary. *Computer Speech and Language, 2,* 133-142.

Echols, C. H., & Newport, E. L. (1992). The role of stress and position in determining first words. *Language Acquisition, 2,* 189-220.

Eimas, P. D., Siqueland, E. R., Jusczyk, P. W., & Vigorito, J. (1971). Speech perception in early infancy. *Science, 171,* 304-306.

Elman, J. L. (1990). Finding structure in time. *Cognitive Science, 14,* 179-211.

Elman, J. L. (1991). *Incremental learning, or the importance of starting small.* Proceedings of the 13th annual conference of the Cognitive Science Society. Hillsdale, NJ: Lawrence Erlbaum Associates.

Fernald, A. (1984). The perceptual and affective salience of mothers' speech to infants. In L. Feagans, C. Garvey, & R. Golinkoff (Eds.), *The origins and growth of communication* (pp. 5-29). Norwood, NJ: Ablex.

Fernald, A. (1985). Four-month-old infants prefer to listen to motherese. *Infant Behavior and Development, 8*, 181-195.

Fernald, A., & Kuhl, P. (1987). Acoustic determinants of infant perception for motherese speech. *Infant Behavior and Development, 10*, 279-293.

Fernald, A., & Mazzie, C. (1991). Prosody and focus in speech to infants and adults. *Developmental Psychology, 27*, 209-221.

Fernald, A., & Simon, T. (1984). Expanded intonation contours in mothers' speech to newborns. *Developmental Psychology, 20*, 104-113.

Fernald, A., Taeschner, T., Dunn, J., Papousek, M., de Boysson-Bardies, B., & Fukui, I. (1989). A cross-language study of prosodic modification in mothers' and fathers' speech to preverbal infants. *Journal of Child Language, 16*, 477-501.

Friederici, A. D., & Wessels, J. M. I. (1993). Phonotactic knowledge of word boundaries and its use in infant speech perception. *Perception and Psychophysics, 54*, 287-295.

Gibson, J. J. (1966). *The senses considered as perceptual systems*. Boston: Houghton Mifflin.

Juliano, C., & Bever, T. G. (1990, March). *Clever moms: Regularities in motherese that prove useful in parsing*. Poster presented at the CUNY Sentence Processing Conference, New York.

Jusczyk, P. W., & Aslin, R. N. (in press). Infants' detection of the sound patterns of words in fluent speech. *Cognitive Psychology*.

Jusczyk, P. W., Friederici, A. D., Wessels, J. M. I., Svenkerud, V., & Jusczyk, A. M. (1993). Infants' sensitivity to the sound patterns of native language words. *Journal of Memory and Language, 32*, 402-420.

Newport, E. L. (1984). Constraints on learning: Studies in the acquisition of American Sign Language. *Papers and Reports on Child Language Development, 23*, 1-22.

Newport, E. L. (1988). Constraints on learning and their role in language acquisition: Studies of the acquisition of American Sign Language. *Language Sciences, 10*, 147-172.

Peters, A. M. (1983). *The units of language acquisition*. Cambridge, England: Cambridge University Press.

Rumelhart, D. E., Hinton, G. E., & Williams, R. J. (1986). Learning internal representations by error propagation. In D. E. Rumelhart & J. L. McClelland (Eds.), *Parallel distributed processing: Explorations in the microstructure of cognition: Volume 1. Foundations* (pp. 318-362). Cambridge, MA: Bradford/MIT Press.

Rumelhart, D. E., & McClelland, J. L. (1986). *Parallel distributed processing: Explorations in the microstructure of cognition: Volume 1. Foundations*. Cambridge, MA: Bradford/MIT Press.

Vihman, M. M. (1993). Variable paths to early word production. *Journal of Phonetics, 21*, 61-82.

Werker, J. F., & McLeod, P. J. (1989). Infant preference for both male and female infant-directed-talk: A developmental study of attentional and affective responsiveness. *Canadian Journal of Psychology, 43*, 230-246.

Werker, J. F., & Polka, L. (1993). The ontogeny and developmental significance of language-specific phonetic perception. In B. de Boysson-Bardies, S. de Schoen, P. Jusczyk, P. MacNeilage, & J. Morton (Eds.), *Developmental neurocognition: Speech and face processing in the first year of life* (pp. 275-288). Dordrecht: Kluwer.

Werker, J. F., & Tees, R. C. (1984). Cross-language speech perception: Evidence for perceptual reorganization during the first year of life. *Infant Behavior and Development, 7*, 49-63.

Woodward, J. Z., & Aslin, R. N. (1990, April). *Segmentation cues in maternal speech to infants*. International Conference on Infant Studies, Montreal.

Woodward, J. Z., & Aslin, R. N. (1991, April). *Word-segmentation strategies in maternal speech to infants*. Society for Research in Child Development, Seattle.

Woodward, J. Z., & Aslin, R. N. (1992, May). *Syntactic and prosodic cues to word segmentation in maternal speech to infants: Turkish and English*. International Society for Infant Studies, Miami.

9 From "Signal to Syntax": But What Is the Nature of the Signal?

Nan Bernstein Ratner
The University of Maryland at College Park

The human infant comes to the task of language learning with a number of advantages. First, as research over the past thirty years has indicated, infants possess strong abilities to discriminate a wide array of phonetic contrasts. Further, as separate lines of investigation over the same time period have discovered, the natural form of input directed to language learning children appears to be modified in ways that should logically facilitate children's attempts to construct initial mappings for language.

There are, however, a good many things yet to be learned about the child's task and its likely solutions. Infant speech discrimination ability, though impressive, has been tested for the most part using isolated and synthetic speech stimuli. Despite heated theoretical argumentation about the "poverty of the stimulus" and the limits it places on children's attempts to induce the grammar of their language, the nature of the actual signal to be decoded is still rather poorly understood. In particular, relatively little work has been done to specify the segmental properties of the child-directed speech register (CDS). This chapter reviews some of what is currently known about the structural properties of CDS, particularly its acoustical/perceptual properties, their possible consequences for child language acquisition, and directions for further explorations in this area.

As many chapters in this volume note, a major challenge facing the language learner is how to segment and parse the input language he or she hears (Peters, 1983). For a child to segment utterances into constituents such as words or morphemes, linguistically relevant segments need to be reasonably invariant in form and/or uniquely identifiable from surrounding stimuli. I suggest that segmental variability in CDS is much less than that seen in Adult-Directed Speech (ADS). Further, that level of variability that does exist seems to be "tuned" to the child's linguistic development and conversational responsiveness. It is also likely that some properties of CDS and infants' early lexicons limit the effects of normal segmental variability in spoken conversational speech on the parsing of the input signal. Finally, many of the structural properties of CDS support the child's efforts to perform initial segmentation of the input, which can then be used as a basis for further linguistic analysis.

SEGMENTAL VARIABILITY

As Pollack and Pickett (1963, 1964) discovered many years ago, single words excised from conversational speech among adults are of relatively poor intelligibility (to adult listeners, that is). Acoustical analysis suggests a number of reasons for such degraded perception. Segments in natural conversational speech are often short and underarticulated, thus falling outside canonical expected values. There is wide variability in the realization of vowel targets and voice-onset-time values. Finally, the concatenation of words in utterances encourages the expression of phonological rules that weaken, delete, and substitute segmental targets. Taken together, both perceptual and acoustic analyses suggest large variability in the conversational ADS signal (Reddy, 1976; Cole & Jakimik, 1980).

As has been repeatedly observed in discussion of machine speech recognition models as well as models of human speech perception, adult parsing ability is probably dependent, therefore, in many cases, upon higher-order phonological, lexical, grammatical, and conversational information, which assigns ambiguous slots in the input to likely phonetic targets (a sort of subconscious version of the *New York Times* crossword puzzle or *Wheel of Fortune*). Clearly, such higher-order information sources are lacking or wanting in infants, creating what might be described as a "Catch-22" situation: Segmentation of fluent speech into input usable for the purposes of language acquisition appears to depend upon lexical knowledge unavailable to the infant.

Some research has suggested that a certain proportion of the infant's burden is relieved by relatively clearer and less variable specification of phonemic targets in child-addressed speech. While up to 50% of voice-onset-time values for voiced and voiceless targets overlap in conversational A-A speech, Baran (1979) and Malsheen (1980) have noted a tendency for voice-onset-time to be somewhat more precisely delineated in speech to children between the one- and two-word stages of development. In Malsheen's data, overlap between observed VOT values for intended voiced and voiceless initial stops was almost 60% in speech between the mother and an adult addressee, and only about 11% when the same women spoke to their young children.

Additional segmental modifications have been noted in CDS: Ratner (1984a) found that vowels were quite clearly differentiated in speech to children at the one- and two-word stages of development. In particular, function word vowels, which are highly centralized and undifferentiated in A-A speech, are rather canonically produced in speech to children at the two-word stage of development, as shown in Fig. 9.1.

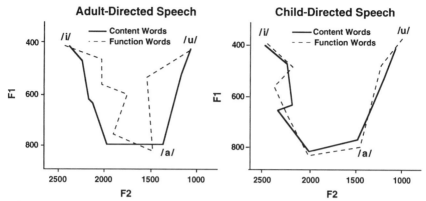

FIG. 9.1. Clarification of function word vowels to children at the two-word stage of language development. Figure adapted from Ratner (1984a).

Application of phonological rules, such as dental deletion (e.g., [want ɨt → wanɨt]) and initial [ð] deletion (e.g., [fold ðɛm] → [foldɛm]) in English conversational speech, has been observed to be somewhat less frequent in CDS than adult-adult speech (Ratner, 1984b; see Fig. 9.2). These data are not unequivocal; Shockey and Bond found a greater incidence of phonological rule usage in a sample of British mothers' conversations with children between two and four years of age, a somewhat older sample. Both studies, however, note that certain phonological rules, such as palatalization, are inherently frequent in within-clause sequences of dentals followed immediately by glides (e.g., [dɪd yu → dɪdžu]). Palatalization is actually less prevalent in ADS because it provides fewer candidate environments for its application than CDS. The frequency with which palatalization does occur in CDS can pose interesting problems for the language-learner, as I discuss in a later section of this chapter.

Even less information exists to describe the effects of clarifications in CDS on children's language development. It might be reasonable to associate more precisely articulated parental speech with a more rapid pace of child language acquisition. However, research to examine the phonetic characteristics of input speech has generally been cross-sectional, or has not followed a cohort longitudinally in order to appraise child language outcome. In a recent analysis of two children's acquisition of Danish, Plunkett (1993) found that one mother's use of "articulatorily imprecise" expressions was associated with her child's tendency to use a higher proportion of sublexical and formulaic forms than did the child whose mother exhibited a prosodically exaggerated style, suggesting that imprecise articulation can make accurate segmentation of the input by the child more difficult.

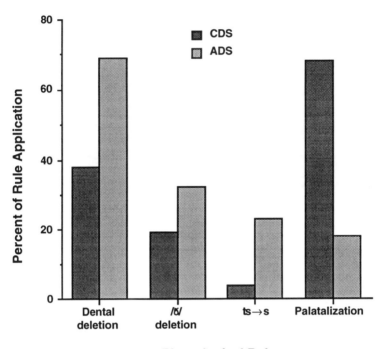

Phonological Rule

FIG. 9.2. Phonological rule usage in ADS and CDS. Figure adapted from Ratner (1984b).

SEGMENTAL VARIABILITY AND THE CONVERSATIONAL AGENDA

In ADS, context plays a strong role in determining the well formedness and/or intelligibility of word tokens in conversation. Items representing new information (first presentation within the conversational context or experiential frame) are likely to be produced with a higher degree of precision and resultingly higher intelligibility (Lieberman, 1963; Fowler & Housum, 1987; although Hunicutt, 1985 noted that the effect is neither strong nor predictable). If parental speech was governed by a strict and adult definition of "new," this tendency should theoretically adversely affect the wellformedness of CDS. Viewed most typically, the repetitive nature of CDS is likely to result in a high proportion of so-called "given" or previously uttered words. For example, in our own corpus of nine mothers and their young language-learning children, Type-Token Ratios (TTRs) calculated on all lexical types (across grammatical classes and including inflectional variants) were much smaller for adult-child speech than the same mothers' speech to an adult listener. In ADS, mothers used 2086 different items in a sample of 20,200 words (TTR = .103), while in CDS, mothers produced 1892 different words in a sample of over 35,000 words (TTR = .054).

Indeed, the one study that has investigated the actual *intelligibility* of CDS to adult listeners found it to be slightly less intelligible than ADS (Bard & Anderson, 1983), and attributed the findings in part to redundancy effects. But what is considered to be given or new in conversations among adults and between adults and extremely naive language users is probably not the same. For the adult listener, new information is usually the first mention of a known word within the targeted conversation. After you have said it once, it is considered given. It seems unlikely that similar rules operate when adults speak to very young language learners. Parents have both preconceived notions about their children's comprehension limitations, and actual feedback that often confirms them. In such adult-child interactions, a "new" lexical item is often either the very first introduction of the word into the receptive lexicon, or one of the first. Further, no assumption appears to be made that a single mention of either words or phrases suffices to make them old and redundant information. Table 9.1 illustrates a very typical interaction between a child at the one-word stage of language development and her mother. It would seem difficult to divide the interaction such that the first mention of *block* is considered "new" and all subsequent mentions "given." The first four mentions all appear to assume that the child may not be able to link [blak] with its referent in the interaction. After a hiatus of a few turns during which *block* does appear to be somewhat "given" ("Hit the blocks"), we return to a series of maternal utterances that appear rather blatantly directed toward either cementing the child's comprehension, or eliciting an attempt to replicate the input.

Review of the utterances in our database suggest that, either because of the child's attention to, or lack of attention to, aspects of the message, repetitions treat first and subsequent mentions of words and phrases in CDS very unevenly, at least when viewed phonetically (Ratner, 1984b). There also appears to be a very selective focus to the articulation of linguistic elements to children of varying levels of linguistic proficiency. Content words appear to receive most precise articulation during the period between one- and two-word utterance usage, while grammatical elements begin to be clarified as children move from the two-word stage onward (Ratner, 1984a). These are periods of what might be considered truly "new" encounters with the core lexicon and basic grammatical structure of the language.

Parental expectancies and children's feedback suggest that research on the acoustic characteristics of "motherese" cannot simply grab parents speaking to children of just any age or language proficiency. Stern, Spieker, Barnett, and MacKain (1983) are among those who documented large changes in the paralinguistic and linguistic characteristics of speech addressed to children between birth and the second year of life. Unfortunately, few studies of CDS have selected child addressees by linguistic stage, as opposed to chronological age, and documenting the "language maturity" of children prior to initial expressive lexical behavior is a particularly thorny problem. Further, many studies of input to children examine parental speech to either newborns or rather mature child listeners. Both of these problems complicate our understanding of the nature of the signal that feeds the earliest language mapping efforts of the child. From adult conversational behavior, we know that subtle speaker intuitions about the predictability of their lexical choices *to the listener* are a determinant of speaker intelligibility and articulatory accuracy (e.g., Lieberman, 1963).

Even on an impressionistic level, one can distinguish between parental utterances that appear to expose or reinforce new vocabulary, as opposed to language structure. It also appears, contrary to some conceptualizations of the relationships between input, feedback, and language acquisition, that the "rules" of the game can change markedly over time. Thus, a parent who (fervently) wishes to increase her child's single-word expressive vocabulary may be providing the appropriate signal to facilitate this acquisition by saying, "[zætə **dɔ:gi:?**]," lengthening and overarticulating the content words, whereas the parent seeking (and anticipating the possibility of) more advanced conversational output will use more carefully articulated syntax and less over-articulated lexicon ("[ɪz ðæt ə dɔgi?]"). Thus, segmental clarification in CDS is

TABLE 9.1

Sample Interaction From the Bernstein Corpus[a]

M: I'll go get your block! This's a block. Say ... mommy ... block! Here. OK. Now what?	C: &.
	M: Wha(t)'s ... you have to tell me ... block? You want the blocks?
C: gi ou:.	C: d&.
M: Alice ... ready? Is this a block? Oh ... What! OK. Hit the blocks! Oh! good! Ah. Wait a second ... lemme get this u ... Oh! You're a monkey! Okay. Now wait ... lemme get (th)em built up. Ah . Alice ... block.	M: Say block! Can you? Block? Oh f:oo.
	C: g&i.
	M: Yeah that! Daddy, this's a daddy? OK.
C: j&ji.	C: &g&?i.
M: Block. Get the block. Say mama ... get the block.	M: Daddy! OK. OK. Say block. S(ay) thank you for a block.
C: wa.	C: [laughs]
M: Oh, oh. Go wild, Alice. Okay.	
M: What's that, Alice?	[later]
C: ASjA.	
M: What's that, a block?	M: You like the blocks! Say blocks. W's this Alice?
C: D&.	C: blA lA lA j&.
M: That. That's a telephone. That's the phone. Huh! Say oh ... hello hello... You want to speak to Alice? Say hello?	M: A block, a block.

[a]Excerpts adapted from Alice1.Cha in CHILDES/Data/Eng/Bernstein. M = Mother, C = Child (13-month-old female). Child's utterances are transcribed in UNIBET.

probably highly dependent upon the distinctive conversational agenda of CDS, which incorporates parental expectations of what the child can understand (and perhaps attempt to replicate), what the adult plans to "teach" or "demonstrate," and what the parent wants the child to do (learn a new word, imitate, or repair a non-adultlike attempt). This agenda, as I argued, is not necessarily amenable to adult discourse definitions of redundancy, or the given–new distinction, and complicates acoustic analysis of CDS.

DOES VARIABILITY IN CDS POSE THE SAME PROBLEMS AS VARIABILITY IN ADS?

Most of the speech processing models that wrestle with the difficulties of variability in the acoustical realizations of words within utterances have a real problem to contend with: Adult speakers have almost limitless options in constructing utterances, and adult listeners must evaluate an equally large number of possible interpretations. While we can ask exactly how much variability characterizes CDS, the answer seems to be that CDS is relatively "clearer," rather than "clear," and we should also ask what level of precision in articulation is likely to be necessary for children at various stages of language acquisition to parse the input signal into its constituent parts and to assign meanings (or functions) to these parts (Ratner, 1987).

We should probably distinguish between intelligibility (the process of segmenting and assigning some identity to strings) and the level of phonetic representation sufficient to allow the child (given appropriate motor facility) to produce these target strings in adultlike form. The standard of intelligibility in this regard is somewhat less than that demanded for acquisition of adultlike productive capability.

Infants Probably Don't Entertain An Unlimited Number of Possibilities

For intelligibility, a number of factors serve to mitigate the only quasi-clarified nature of the input. The first is the limited cohort of meaningful possibilities available to any young child attempting to match input to previously stored information, as I noted elsewhere and Charles-Luce and Luce (1990) statistically analyzed. For five-year-old children, the youngest studied by Charles-Luce and Luce, over 70% of three-phoneme words had five or fewer possible phonetic neighbors (words differing from the target by only a single phoneme addition, deletion, or substitution), given typical words understood by children of that age group. Over 80% of their four-phoneme and 100% of their five-phoneme words have one or no neighbors at all. Phonetic neighbors are obviously less frequent for younger children with more limited lexicons. Further, depending upon the model of lexical access postulated for young infants, if lexical access cohorts are compiled by initial segments only as in models proposed by researchers such as Marslen-Wilson and Tyler (1980), the number of previously stored matches available to any input signal falls even further. It seems reasonable, given older children's parsing errors (e.g., *"I led the pigeons to the flag"*; Chaney, 1989; Safire, 1980), that language learners presume the input matches the most phonetically similar previously stored element. At early stages of the language acquisition process, this should lead to relatively good tolerance of variable realizations of words and rote phrases.

CDS is Short and Redundant

A second factor that theoretically offsets variability in the acoustical well formedness of CDS is the general length and structure of language addressed to the child. In my own corpus of twenty-seven 45-minute interactions between women and their language-learning infants (Bernstein corpus, CHILDES Archive, MacWhinney, 1991), 22% of almost 10,000 maternal utterances were only one word long, 16% were two words long, and 18% were three words long. The most frequent forms for maternal utterances were one- and two-word lengths. Taken together, a full 56% of CDS utterances were three or fewer words in length. At initial stages of expressive language acquisition, children are not forced to parse very long strings. They are not being asked to parse the contents of a linguistics book. Although we are researching this particular question further, one hypothesis is that words identified in single-word CDS utterances (a fairly trivial task by reasonable standards) can serve as input to the parsing of a larger number of slightly longer utterances. To test this hypothesis, we have recently conducted overlap analyses of the lexical items in maternal utterances of varying lengths (Ratner & Rooney, 1993) addressed to children just beginning to produce expressive one-word utterances. After collapsing inflected variants of common roots, we found an extremely high level of overlap between the words in maternal one- and two-word utterances to their young children, and two- and three-word utterances. Thirty-two percent of the lexical types in single- and two-word utterances overlapped, whereas 43% of types in two- and three-word utterances were common to both utterance lengths. Thus, children's segmentation efforts may be aided by a high frequency of isolated lexical presentation, and encounters with core lexical items in environments requiring few segmentation decisions.

Recent work by Goldfield (1993) suggested that nouns appear disproportionately more often than verbs in maternal one- and two-word utterances, a fact that is likely to encourage the relative predominance of nominals in early child language. Moreover, in Goldfield's study, there was a significant positive correlation between the proportion of nouns in children's first 50 words and the number of maternal noun tokens observed during play interactions. Plunkett (1993) observed a correlation between children's vocabulary spurts and a decline in their use of sublexical forms and formulaic expressions, which both can be hypothesized to stem from input segmentation difficulties. He remarked that, "a sufficient critical mass of target lexemes may provide the child with a set of lexical anchor points that constrain the generation of misleading non-standard segmentation, resulting in accelerated vocabulary growth" (p. 58).

Further, given the low Type-Token Ratio in maternal speech, these short CDS utterances are highly biased toward repetitive lexical items and syntactic frames. The same lexical items appear over and over again, though in contrasting frames (as in Table 9.1), while the repetitive carrier phrases frame a good proportion of the initial set of nouns children hear. This is not a new observation, but we are now more readily able to test its generality through computerized transcript analysis (MacWhinney, 1991). Finally, a phonetic cohort analysis of CDS has not been done, but would probably be quite similar in nature to that described for children by Charles-Luce and Luce. Lexical items in CDS probably do not show a high degree of phonetic similarity to one another. Thus, we should not presume that children seek to identify which of the thousands of entries in *Webster's Unabridged Dictionary* has been heard, nor that in fact they have been uttered.

A Methodological Note

It is interesting to note that in most studies that have compared the acoustic characteristics of CDS and ADS (including my own), word tokens from extremely short CDS utterances have been discarded from analysis, because they cannot be "matched" to the kinds of sentence environments in which words appear in ADS. This is a strong concern in establishing fair matches for acoustic analysis, since utterance length and segmental clarification are known to be inversely correlated. However, although it may be "fair" experimental design to exclude such items from analysis, the inescapable fact is that the infant hears these short utterances and the words embedded in them. And they constitute 50% of the input to them. In our lab, the recent (and welcome) resurgence of interest in the acoustic characteristics of CDS has prompted us to begin analysis of words embedded in CDS utterances of different lengths. It is very possible that the relative clarification that has been noted in CDS highly underestimates the actual clarity of the speech signal to which the language-learning infant is exposed.

Other Structural Cues to Segmentation in CDS

CDS in English, at least, does provide some "ancillary" cues to aid the parsing of the input signal. For example, my own work (1986) shows relatively exaggerated lengthening of vowel duration at clause boundaries when compared to CDS addressed to older children or ADS. Kemler Nelson, Hirsh-Pasek, Jusczyk, and Wright Cassidy (1989) showed infants to be sensitive to such natural boundary markers, preferring to listen to speech interrupted at boundaries, rather than randomly.

The duration of segments can mark off more than large constituents. My work, that of Morgan (1986), and recent work by Swanson, Leonard, and Gandour (1992) suggested that the relatively slower rate and perceived increases in segmental duration that characterize CDS are not evenly distributed. Content words are lengthened disproportionately to function words, regardless of position within utterance, potentially allowing the child to use vowel durations within words to identify form class membership.

Morgan suggested that additional aspects of the speech signal could be used by the infant to parse the signal into syntactic constituents. In English, for example, virtually all occurrences of initial [ð] are in function words, while final [ð] is basically nonexistent, thus allowing the possible hypothesis, "when you hear [ð], start a new grammatical constituent." An alternative hypothesis, however, supported by the relatively late acquisition of this sound in children's expressive repertoires, is that the relatively low stress, short durational properties of the functors themselves interfere with children even accurately mapping the initial phoneme at all. In the corpus of CDS I examined over the years, late-acquired phonemes, such as [ð], [s], [z], [l], and [r], cluster most frequently in grammatical environments (functors and grammatical affixes), and their first realizations in the child's productive repertoire are in these same environments. Either way, it is an empirical question whether the phonemes of languages distribute themselves in grammatically conditioned patterns that could be used by the child to establish rough form class hypotheses.

WE NEED TO UNDERSTAND THE NATURE OF THE SIGNAL TO UNDERSTAND HOW CHILDREN GET FROM THE SIGNAL TO SYNTAX

In this portion of the chapter, I argue that we have neglected to pay sufficient attention to the properties of CDS in understanding the role of parental input in language acquisition. In particular, I suggest that children occasionally appear to be more finely attuned to some of the more subtle properties of CDS than we might expect. Further, certain arguments about the "poverty of the stimulus" appear to be based on a characterization of CDS that overlooks some important features of the register (and of the speakers who use it).

The Nature of the Input Signal Is Not Irrelevant: Children Are Listening to It

Some data suggest that, occasionally, children pay closer attention to the input signal than we as adults do. Children's productive errors are an interesting source of evidence for segmentation errors, though they tend to occur relatively rarely and too late in the language acquisition process to inform the critical question of how the earliest segmentation decisions are made. In addition to the many productive segmentation errors that children make (Table 9.2), children also make errors that reveal very fine attention to phonetic detail. I offer a few examples.

Final consonant deletion in English (i.e., [bi] for *bead*) is a typical developmental process for children; typical explanations for the phenomenon appeal to the markedness of closed syllable sequences. It is not uncommon to find that children who omit final consonants use vowel duration to signal the intended voicing of deleted final elements (Velten, 1943). Ratner and Luberoff (1984) noted that in the Bernstein corpus, final consonant deletion was in fact very prevalent in maternal speech to the children (though less frequent than in ADS), whereas the vowel durational difference that typically cues final voicing status was extremely exaggerated in the input. This can yield very strange behaviors in children who, as Slobin suggested, "pay attention to the ends of words." What happens if the end is unrealized, while the medial element not only assumes final position, but is lengthened or shortened in what appears to be a contrastive fashion? We cannot be certain, but "strange" children who map vowel duration rather than specifying final consonants may simply be recreating the input.

Further, a typical response of parents to children who omit final consonants is to then exaggerate final consonant articulation. This may lead to the documented exhibition of final vowel epenthesis noted in a number of studies, including my own experience with my daughter. Thus, a child who hears [spu] for *spoon* produces [spu] (a match to the conversational example). The concerned parent, who knows the citation form of the word to be different, then begins to say [spuːn:ʰ], producing atypical aspiration of the final element. The child then responds by correcting the articulation to [spunə] and its inevitable plural form -

TABLE 9.2
Sample Segmentation Errors in Children's Spontaneous Speech

Mother: Once upon a time …
Child: What's a [sUpana]?
(M Shatz, 1984, personal communication)

Father: Who wants some mango for dessert?
Child: What's a [səmæŋo]?

Child: What did one strawberry say to the nother strawberry?

Children's attempts to say the "Pledge of Allegiance" (Chaney, 1989)
          … to the flag of the *nine of states* …
          … and to *three the pug lit* for …
          … and to the republic for *witches stands* …

[spunɨz] (Ratner, 1993).

Finally, although such instances may be rare (and they are definitely hard to perceive in children's speech), children may be sensitive to phonological rules in adult speech to such an extent that they create two lexical or grammatical mappings for what is simply conversational variability in pronunciation. The example I offer is palatalization, extremely common in CDS in phrases such as [dɨdžu], [wətšu], [gotčyou], and so on. Although my son (a late language learner) at age 4;0 had a large variety of well-formed and conversationally produced questions, such as, "What didžyou say," "Didžyou bring in my picture," and so on, he was also taped producing sentences such as, "Can džyou turn on the light?" In fact, all instances of *you* in questions were palatalized, whether or not the immediate phonetic environment made it appropriate in English. A possible hypothesis given the input is that *džyou* was a question-specific pronoun, something a little bizarre, but reasonable given its distribution in the spoken English addressed to him.

Such examples drive home an important point: If CDS plays a role in children's speech and language development, we may expect to see both "hits" and "misses" in its impacts on linguistic development. Not only can some aspects of the signal probably foster attempts to segment and identify constituents in the input, but aspects of CDS that either grossly deform typical ADS characteristics, or that do not differ markedly from the messier attributes of ADS can be expected to produce documented types of developmental errors in children's speech that relate rather directly to the acoustic characteristics of the speech they hear.

It would appear, then, that children are listening carefully—hardly a novel notion. But what are they listening to? Is CDS an abstract system of only marginally simpler, marginally clearer language than that shared between adults? I argue that it is not.

CDS Is Not a Static Signal, With Easily Generalizable Characteristics

How "impoverished" is CDS? Perhaps a better question is how impoverished, for what purpose, at what stage of language acquisition? The concept of bootstrapping implies that neither the child nor the input can accomplish everything at once, and shouldn't be expected to. My earliest work suggested that the properties of CDS change over time, as infants mature. This "fine tuning" at an acoustical level was consistent with other longitudinal changes in the structure of CDS that have been observed by large numbers of researchers. A question to ask is what such fine tuning can accomplish for the child. For English, there now seems to be mounting consensus that the structure and articulation of CDS to children who are just beginning to acquire their initial expressive lexicons heavily emphasizes a core set of nouns, through placement in short utterances, in stressed final position, and through extreme repetition (cf. Goldfield, 1993; Plunkett, 1993; Nelson, Hampson, & Shaw, 1993). This parental tendency does appear to be reasonably associated with a relative preference for nouns in early child speech. We should not presume that such a style of CDS is universal, and indeed it is almost certainly not, by virtue of differences in language typology and sociolinguistic variation (e.g., Rispoli, 1989; Pye, 1986; Schieffelin, 1979). The question to be asked is whether, within a given language, caregiver patterns of language input place a priority on particular aspects of the language that are in turn more likely to be among the child's earliest acquisitions, and used to bootstrap further analysis of the input.

During the conference, participants were quick to point out that not all cultures talk to children the way an American mother (such as the one in Table 9.1) does. To say that English "motherese" may profitably aid the child's attempts to reconstruct the syntax within the signal by virtue of its particular characteristics is not to say that all languages or cultures will do it in the same way. Rather, the suggestion is that CDS does exist in some form for all languages, even those that seem "atypical" by Western standards (Schieffelin, 1979; Pye, 1986; Ratner & Pye, 1984), and that these forms may impact the earliest efforts of the child to break the linguistic code, resulting in somewhat distinctive patterns of early language use.

Added to questions about universality, other participants added concerns about the relative frequency of the child's exposure to such a distinctive CDS register. How many of the utterances addressed to the child exhibit the canonical characteristics of CDS we have described? This is an interesting argument, especially inasmuch as it is typically advanced by researchers with strong doubts about the adequacy of the input to enable language acquisition. No serious observer of the CDS register would contend that parents use its more distinctive characteristics at all times. However, questions of frequency or quantity have never seriously hampered certain accounts of language acquisition, in which a robust innate component is assumed to render such issues uninteresting. Lightfoot (1991) made the reasonable assumption that, for parameter setting, for example, "the trigger is something less than the total linguistic experience. Neither the occasional degenerate data that a child hears nor idiosyncratic forms necessarily trigger some device in the emergent grammar that has the effect of generating those forms" (p. 14). While the relevant subset of data feeding the process of language acquisition should be defined structurally, (e.g., as Lightfoot and others have attempted to do), or by internal measures of the child's attention and processing (such as in Keith Nelson's [1987] Rare Event learning mechanism), or both, is a question for continued study, but should not seriously undermine the importance of research into CDS.

Hypotheses about the possible contributions of the CDS register to particular developments in children's evolving language capacity are empirically testable, though the endeavor appears unsatisfying to some, as indicated by a passage mailed to me during my tenure hearings by a colleague:

> ... the investigation of mother-child interaction is bound to have virtually no consequences, and in fact it has produced no significant results, predictably. The reason people do it is that it is easy to do. You can do it if you know nothing. You don't have to understand anything about language or children, you just sit there and get data about the mother-child interaction, analyze the data and publish books about it ... it is guaranteed to go nowhere. (Chomsky, 1984, p. 47)

Still, I persist in believing that we cannot abstract principles of language acquisition without regard to the particulars of the input used as grist for the system. The "signal" that feeds first language acquisition is, by definition, child-directed speech.

SOME FINAL THOUGHTS

Languages provide certain inherent parsing cues, such as prosodic contour, and relatively universal patterns of segmental lengthening at clause boundaries. CDS potentially further improves this mix, by presenting data at a slower rate, with relatively more accurate and invariant articulation of segments, and with repetitive presentations of content words in short, relatively unchanging grammatical frames. But it is not a clean signal. It slurs and elides elements, just as ADS does. Its segments are only relatively clarified. In this sense, the observed discrimination abilities of infants may be as much a hindrance as help, since, for example, ability to discriminate VOT along adultlike boundaries does not help to accurately label lexical items with inappropriate and noncanonical VOT values, a situation that occurs in CDS only somewhat less often than in ADS. In the end, the child must create order out of a signal that is still fairly untidy at times. We can better appreciate this process if we can begin to understand the determinants and pervasiveness of CDS modifications that may facilitate infants' attempts to decode input speech.

REFERENCES

Baran, J. (1979). *The mutual regulation of mother-child phonological behavior*. Unpublished doctoral dissertation, Purdue University.

Bard, E., & Anderson, A. (1983). The unintelligibility of speech to children. *Journal of Child Language, 10*, 265-292.

Chaney, C. (1989). I pledge a legiance tothe flag: Three studies in word segmentation. *Applied Psycholinguistics, 10*, 261-282.

Charles-Luce, J., & Luce, P. (1990). Similarity neighborhoods of words in young children's lexicons. *Journal of Child Language, 17*, 205-215.

Chomsky, N. (1984). *Modular approaches to the study of the mind*. San Diego: San Diego State University Press.

Cole, R., & Jakimik, J. (1980). A model of speech perception. In R. Cole (Ed.), *Perception and production of fluent speech* (pp. 134-164). Hillsdale, NJ: Lawrence Erlbaum Associates.

Fowler, C., & Housum, J. (1987). Talkers' signaling of 'new' and 'old' words in speech and listeners' perception and use of the distinction. *Journal of Memory and Language, 26*, 489-504.

Goldfield, B. (1993). Noun bias in maternal speech to one-year olds. *Journal of Child Language, 20*, 85-99.

Hunicutt, S. (1985). Intelligibility vs. redundancy - conditions of dependency. *Language and Speech, 28*, 47-56.

Kemler Nelson, D., Hirsh-Pasek, K., Jusczyk, P., & Wright Cassidy, K. (1989). How the prosodic cues in motherese might assist language learning. *Journal of Child Language, 16*, 55-68.

Lieberman, P. (1963). Some effects of semantic and grammatical context on the production and perception of speech. *Language and Speech, 6*, 172-175.

Lightfoot, D. (1991). *How to set parameters: Arguments from language change.* Cambridge, MA: MIT Press.

MacWhinney, B. (1991). *The CHILDES Project: Computational tools for analyzing talk.* Hillsdale, NJ: Lawrence Erlbaum Associates.

Malsheen, B. (1980). Two hypotheses for phonetic clarification in the speech of mothers to children. In G. Yeni-Komshian, J. Kavanagh, & C. Ferguson (Eds.), *Child phonology, Volume 2* (pp. 173-184.. New York: Academic Press.

Marslen-Wilson, W., & Tyler, L. (1980). The temporal structure of spoken language understanding. *Cognition, 8*, 1-71.

Morgan, J. (1986). *From simple input to complex grammar.* Cambridge, MA: MIT Press.

Nelson, K., Hampson, J., & Shaw, L. (1993). Nouns in early lexicons: Evidence, explanations and implications. *Journal of Child Language, 20*, 61-84.

Nelson, K. E. (1987). Some observations from the perspective of the Rare Event Cognitive Comparison Theory of language acquisition. In K. E. Nelson & A. van Kleeck (Eds.), *Children's language, Volume 6* (pp. 289-324). Hillsdale, NJ: Lawrence Erlbaum Associates.

Peters, A. (1983). *The units of language acquisition.* New York: Cambridge University Press.

Plunkett, K. (1993). Lexical segmentation and vocabulary growth in early language acquisition. *Journal of Child Language, 20*, 43-60.

Pollack, I., & Pickett, J. M. (1963). The intelligibility of excerpts from conversational speech. *Language and Speech, 6*, 165-171.

Pollack, I., & Pickett, J. M. (1964). The intelligibility of excerpts from conversational speech: Auditory vs. structural context. *Journal of Verbal Learning and Verbal Behavior, 3*, 79-84.

Pye, C. (1986). Quiche Mayan speech to children. *Journal of Child Language, 13*, 85-100.

Ratner, N. B. (1984a). Patterns of vowel modification in mother-child speech. *Journal of Child Language, 11*, 557-578.

Ratner, N. B. (1984b). Phonological rule usage in mother-child speech. *Journal of Phonetics, 12*, 245-254.

Ratner, N. B. (1986). Durational cues which mark clause boundaries in mother-child speech. *Journal of Phonetics, 14*, 303-309.

Ratner, N. B. (1987). The phonology of parent-child speech. In K. E. Nelson & A. van Kleeck (Eds.), *Children's language: Volume 6* (pp. 159-174). Hillsdale, NJ: Lawrence Erlbaum Associates.

Ratner, N. B. (1993). Interactive influences on phonological behaviour: A case study. *Journal of Child Language, 20*, 191-198.

Ratner, N. B., & Luberoff, A. (1984). Cues to post-vocalic voicing in mother-child speech. *Journal of Phonetics, 12*, 285-289.

Ratner, N.B., & Pye, C. (1984). Higher pitch in BT is *not* universal: Acoustic evidence from Quiche Mayan. *Journal of Child Language, 11*, 515-522.

Ratner, N.B., & Rooney, B. (1993). *Segmentation of the input signal: A problem with potential solutions.* American Speech, Language and Hearing Assn. annual convention, Anaheim.

Reddy, R. (1976). Speech recognition by machine: A review. *Proceedings of the IEEE, 64*, 501-531.

Rispoli, M. (1989). Encounters with Japanese verbs: Caregiver sentences and the categorization of transitive and intransitive action verbs. *First Language, 9*, 57-80.

Safire, W. (1980). *On language.* New York: Times Books.

Schieffelin, B. (1979). Getting it together: An ethnographic approach to the development of communicative competence. In E. Ochs & B. Schieffelin (Eds.), *Developmental pragmatics* (pp. 73-110). Orlando, FL: Academic Press.

Stern, D., Spieker, S., Barnett, R., & MacKain, K. (1983). The prosody of maternal speech: Infant age and context related changes. *Journal of Child Language, 10* , 1-16.

Swanson, L., Leonard, L., & Gandour, J. (1992). Vowel duration in mothers' speech to young children. *Journal of Speech and Hearing Research, 35,* 617-625.

Velten, H. (1943). The growth of phonemic and lexical patterns in language. *Language, 19,* 281-292. Also reprinted in Bar-Adon, A., & Leopold, W. (1971). *Child language: A book of readings.* Englewood Cliffs, NJ: Prentice-Hall.

10 A Role for Stress in Early Speech Segmentation

Catharine H. Echols
University of Texas at Austin

The child trying to figure out the structure of his or her native language will be faced with a segmentation problem on at least two levels. The child must identify word-level units in the stream of speech and must also identify the phrase-level units of the native language. Several other chapters in this volume describe potential roles for prosodic cues, including stress, in the identification of phrase-level units in language. In this chapter, I focus on the potential roles of stress in the initial identification of word-level units.

Recent research has suggested several ways in which stress may contribute to word-level segmentation. One position holds that the stressed syllable itself may provide the initial entry into word-level units in speech. Children may tend to extract perceptually salient syllables, such as stressed syllables, from the stream of speech and store those syllables as their initial representations for words (Gleitman & Wanner, 1982; Gleitman, Gleitman, Landau, & Wanner, 1988). This first segmentation strategy will be relatively universal. Although, as Gleitman and Wanner noted, the specific properties that enhance the salience of individual syllables will vary from language to language, most if not all languages will have some way of emphasizing particular syllables. A second proposal is that the patterning of stressed and unstressed syllables may provide cues to word-level units, that is, stress may play a role in segmentation by contributing to the rhythm of speech (e.g., Jusczyk, Cutler, & Redanz, 1993). For example, English-learning children may expect strong-weak disyllables, a common word-type in English, to correspond to a word. Because the specific stress patterns associated with words will vary from language to language, this second segmentation strategy will be language-specific; many languages will have some type of rhythmic cue useful for word identification, but the specific rhythmic cues will vary across languages. In this chapter, I discuss evidence favoring each of these possible influences of stress in the early phases of language acquisition, and I propose an account that may link them.

STRESS AND WORD EXTRACTION

A now sizable literature describes the role of prosodic cues, including stress, in word identification by adults (Cutler & Butterfield, 1992; Cutler & Foss, 1977; Cutler & Norris, 1988; Frazier, 1987; Grosjean & Gee, 1987; Nakatani & O'Connor-Dukes, 1979; Nakatani & Schaffer, 1978; Waibel, 1986). However, the problem faced by the child is somewhat different from that faced by the adult. The adult is seeking to identify boundaries between, for the most part, known words. In contrast, the child will, at least initially, need to determine the extents of words without knowledge of any of the words in a sentence. The solution proposed by Gleitman and Wanner (1982; see also Gleitman, et al. 1988) for this problem is that young children do not, in fact, start out seeking to identify all of the boundaries between words but, instead, may extract and store particular salient syllables, leaving behind the rest of the sentence as unanalyzed noise. In particular, Gleitman and Wanner argued that children may start out with the expectation that the unit "word" maps to a stressed syllable. Thus, young children may extract and store stressed syllables as their initial representations for words, thereby reducing the difficult problem of identifying boundaries between each of the words in a sequence of speech to the simpler problem of identifying the extents of stressed syllables (see also Peters, 1983, for a similar argument).

Observations consistent with this suggestion have been reported by a number of researchers: Young children tend to omit unstressed syllables, especially those that are not word-final, from their early productions (e.g., Allen & Hawkins, 1978; Ingram, 1978; Klein, 1981). Indeed, omissions of unstressed syllables have been reported for children learning languages as diverse as Hebrew (Berman, 1977), Mohawk (Feurer, 1980), Hungarian (MacWhinney, 1985), and K'iche' Mayan (Pye, 1983, 1992). Experimental support for these observations is provided by data from imitation studies: In studies using both real words (Oller & Rydland, 1974) and nonsense-word speech (Blasdell & Jensen, 1970; Frumhoff, Echols, & Newport, 1992) children are more likely to imitate syllables that are stressed or word-final than syllables that are both unstressed and nonfinal. Examples of early productions in English and in Italian, from which unstressed or nonfinal syllables have been omitted, are presented in Table 10.1.

In many of these studies, not only stressed but also word-final syllables seem to have an advantage. It may seem surprising that a perceptual salience account should apply to word-final as well as to stressed syllables. Stressed syllables are, after all, acoustically prominent: In English, they typically are higher pitched, louder, of longer duration, and have fuller vowel quality than do unstressed syllables (Lehiste, 1970). The rationale for including final position may seem less clear and, indeed, its potential utility for word-level segmentation may seem dubious: The listener should need to know where word boundaries are before final position can be identified. However, proposals concerning the perceptual salience of final syllables have been in the literature for some time (see e.g., Slobin, 1973, with respect to acquisition of morphology, and Peters, 1983, in relation to word-level segmentation). Moreover, a syllable that is word final does have the potential for being sentence-final, or at least clause- or phrase-final. In fact, infant-directed speech may be particularly useful in this regard: Fernald and Mazzie (1991) and Woodward and Aslin (1990) reported that parents tend to place novel nouns in sentence-final position. Even if a word is simply clause- or phrase-final, there appear to be more cues to boundaries at those locations than at word boundaries (Cooper, 1983; Paccia-Cooper & Cooper, 1981). Thus, for example, lengthening has been observed in clause-final syllables (Klatt, 1976) and in phrase-final syllables (Klatt, 1976; Lehiste, Olive & Streeter, 1976; Scott, 1982; Streeter, 1978). The lengthening per se may make these syllables more salient. Additionally, syllables at the end of a sentence or at a phrase boundary may benefit from a recency effect and may be easier to break off and store than a syllable elsewhere in a sentence. Thus, although the exact basis for the salience and extractability of stressed and final syllables will differ, both will tend to be more salient and extractable than syllables that are neither stressed nor word-final.

On the assumption that both stressed and word-final syllables are perceptually salient, the selective retention of stressed and final syllables in early productions would seem attributable to exactly the types of perceptual biases proposed by Gleitman and Wanner. However, production-based accounts have been proposed for these same phenomena (e.g., Allen & Hawkins, 1980; Gerken, Landau, & Remez, 1990; Pye, 1992). In the remainder of the chapter, I first provide additional evidence on children's selective omissions of stressed syllables. Then, I attempt to disentangle the perceptual and production-based accounts. Following that, I turn to a discussion of the possibility that stress may assist segmentation through its contribution to rhythmic or metrical structure in speech. The final portion of the chapter consists of a proposal for an integrated account of stress effects in word-level segmenta-

TABLE 10.1
Examples of Utterances With Omitted Syllables

	Adult Target	Child's Production
English		
Stressed Syllable Retained	/čakəlʌt/ (chocolate)	/čak/
Final Syllable Retained	/orańj / (orange)	/ańj/
	/bʌɾəflai/ (butterfly)	/lai/
Stressed & Final Retained	/iresɚ/ (eraser)	/raisə/
	/ɛləfənt/ (elephant)	/ɛlfʌn/
Italian		
Stressed & Final Retained	/formadʒo/ (formaggio) [cheese]	/mago/
	/makkina/ (macchina) [car]	/makka/

Note. English examples are from the data reported in Echols & Newport (1992). Italian examples are courtesy of Rosanna Carotti. Stressed syllables are boldfaced in the target word.

tion and in early productions.

Experimental Evidence on Selective Omissions of Stressed Syllables

In an analysis of a corpus of children's early productions, Newport and I provided evidence consistent with the suggestion that children may preferentially include in their early productions syllables of the target word that are stressed or word-final (Echols & Newport, 1992).   The analysis was based on corpora obtained from three children in the one-word speech period who ranged in age between 17 and 23 months during the period in which the data were collected.   (The mean MLU was 1.07 at the beginning of the study and at the end it was 1.42.)   Productions were recorded during naturalistic interactions in the child's home and were then phonetically transcribed and coded for omissions of syllables and for accuracy of segments in relation to stress and position of the syllable in the adult target word.

Analysis of children's omissions showed that syllables of the adult target word that were unstressed and nonfinal were far more vulnerable to omission in children's productions than were syllables that were either stressed or final.   Just over 50% of unstressed nonfinal syllables were omitted, compared to 6% of stressed nonfinal syllables and 11% of unstressed final syllables.   The analysis of children's omissions is thus consistent with the suggestion that young children may extract stressed and final syllables from the stream of speech, and may store them in their early representations for words, leaving behind unstressed nonfinal syllables.[1]

Although the proposed tendency to extract stressed and final syllables will account for many early words, children's first words do not always include only stressed syllables.   Evidence of the perceptual salience of stressed syllables may be present even when children's productions include some unstressed and nonfinal syllables.   In particular, children's errors may also provide evidence of effects of stress on early words. Accordingly, a second set of analyses compared the accuracy of stressed and final syllables with the accuracy of any unstressed and nonfinal syllables that children produced.   The notion here was that if stressed and final syllables are indeed particularly salient, then children should extract and represent those syllables more completely than any unstressed and nonfinal syllables that they do extract.   Whereas at least 66% of segments in syllables that were either stressed or final were correctly produced, only 36% of segments in syllables that were unstressed

---

[1]Although some phonologists have argued for distinct input and output representations (e.g., Menn, 1978, 1983), I use the term *representation* here and throughout this section to refer to a stored form of the word, which may serve as the basis for a production, but is not actually a representation of a production form. Thus, my usage would correspond most closely to representations in Menn's input lexicon.

and nonfinal were correctly produced. These data suggest that unstressed and nonfinal syllables are vulnerable not only to omissions, but also to errors. Those unstressed and nonfinal syllables that children produced were far less accurately produced than were syllables that were either stressed or final.

Additional evidence of the perceptual salience of stressed and final syllables can be found in several types of early utterances. One interesting class of early productions consists of utterances containing *reduplications* or *partial reduplications*, that is, utterances in which one or more segments of the target word are repeated in more than one syllable of the child's production (e.g., /bʌ-bʌ/ for *bunny*; an example of a partial reduplication is /nu-ni/ for *noisy*, in which the /n/ of the first syllable is repeated in the second). Also interesting from the perspective of perceptual salience effects are utterances containing *filler syllables*, in which at least one syllable is reduced to a schwa or other simple sound (e.g., /m-bɛ-dɛ/ for *all-better*, in which /ɔl/ of the target word is replaced by /m/ in the child's production). In utterances such as these, children must be doing something other than extracting only stressed and final syllables: In many cases they are producing some phonological material for each of the syllables of the target word, even if some of those syllables deviate quite substantially from the adult target. However, even if children are using cues other than the stressed syllable to identify these words, the productions may still provide evidence consistent with the perceptual salience perspective.[2] If syllables that are stressed or are final are more perceptually salient to young children than are unstressed, nonfinal syllables, then segments from those salient syllables should more frequently be included in children's representations. In reduplications, therefore, it should tend to be segments from stressed syllables of the adult target word, rather than segments from unstressed syllables, that should appear in more than one syllable of the child's production. On the other hand, filler syllables should tend to occur in the position of unstressed nonfinal syllables of the target, as it is those syllables that will most frequently be incompletely extracted.

In additional analyses of the corpus described earlier, I tested the predictions that segments that appear in more than one syllable in children's reduplications should tend to originate in stressed or final syllables of the adult target and that filler syllables should tend to occur in unstressed and nonfinal locations (these analyses are reported in more detail in Echols, 1993). Figure 10.1 shows the proportion of syllables serving as origins for reduplication as a function of stress and position of the target syllable. As can be seen in that figure, syllables that are

---

[2]Aside from attention to stressed syllables per se, other prosodic cues may assist in word identification (Cutler & Norris, 1988; Nakatani & Schaffer, 1978; Peters, 1981); one such cue, rhythm pattern, will be discussed shortly. Additional potential cues include segmental cues, such as allophonic variation (Nakatani & Dukes, 1977), as well as duration (Nakatani, O'Connor & Aston, 1981) and consistent morpho-syntactic frames (Peters, 1983).

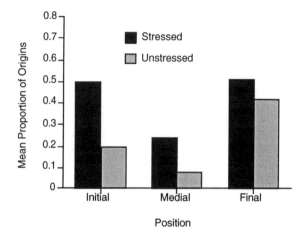

FIG. 10.1. Mean proportion of syllables serving as origins for reduplication at different stress levels and positions.

stressed or final are more likely than unstressed nonfinal syllables to serve as the source for reduplicated segments. A complementary set of results is observed for filler syllables: As can be seen in Fig. 10.2, schwa-like filler syllables are less likely to occur in the position of syllables that are stressed than in the position of unstressed syllables in utterances containing filler syllables.

These results are compatible with the possibility that unstressed, nonfinal syllables may be incompletely specified in children's early representations. In this view, these incompletely represented syllables may be filled in, at production, by segments spread or copied from adjacent syllables or by a default segment (e.g., a schwa). Thus, one interpretation of these influences of stress on the form of children's early productions is representational in nature, that is, stressed syllables are perceptually salient and, accordingly, are represented more frequently and more completely by children. Although the evidence from reduplications and filler syllables does not speak directly to a role for stress in segmentation, it is consistent with the view that stressed syllables are perceptually salient and more readily extracted and stored, a prerequisite for the claim that these salient syllables may correspond to the earliest notion of the unit "word." However, because the data for those studies were children's productions, the results do not distinguish the possibility that perceptual salience influences children's underlying representations from the possibility that it simply influences which elements are incorporated when production limitations restrict the length or complexity of children's utterances.

DISENTANGLING PERCEPTION AND PRODUCTION

Many of the very phenomena already described from the representational perspective have also been discussed from a production perspective. In an account of children's selective omissions of unstressed syllables, for example, Pye (1992) suggested that children may represent all of the syllables of the target words, but may be restricted by production limitations to producing only a few.   Perceptual salience is used to choose which syllables will be produced.   Allen and Hawkins' (1980) and Gerken's (1990, 1994a, 1994b) accounts for omissions specifically of syllables that are both unstressed and nonfinal are that children have a preference for trochaic (strong-weak) sequences in production and, as a result, will have difficulty producing syllables, such as unstressed syllables preceding a stressed syllable, which do not adhere to a trochaic pattern (see also Demuth, 1992a, 1992b, 1994; Fikkert, 1994, for similar arguments, including evidence for similar phenomena in Sesotho and Dutch, respectively).   Indeed, Gerken and her colleagues provided a substantial amount of evidence that young language learners perceive something about the segmental content of certain unstressed syllables (specifically, function words) even when they fail to produce them (Gerken et al., 1990; Gerken & McIntosh, 1993).   In essence, then, there are three sets of factors that need to be distinguished: (a) perceptual, (b) representational, and (c) production factors.   Representational factors refer to the representation for a word that is stored in memory; limitations at the representational level will imply a failure to accurately perceive or store phonological information and will result in a stored representation that is inaccurate or incomplete. Production factors refer to articulatory and processing factors that may constrain the physical production of

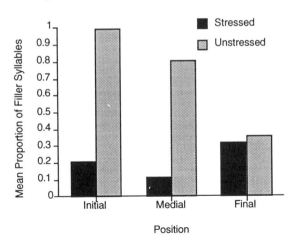

FIG. 10.2. Mean proportion of syllables produced as filler syllables at different stress levels and positions.

an utterance. Finally, perceptual factors may exert an influence either at the representational or at the production level. Perceptual salience can influence representations by increasing the likelihood that particular elements will be included in a stored representation; perceptual salience can influence productions by determining which elements are most likely to be incorporated into an utterance at the point of production.

Note, however, that even if stress does nothing more than influence the form of productions, the evidence described here makes it clear that children are sensitive to stress in the input. Thus, should it eventually prove to be the case that the phenomena described here as evidence for perceptual-representational phenomena are in fact accounted for by production factors, it could still be the case that children are using their sensitivity to stress earlier, or in different ways, for segmentation. I return to this issue shortly.

Experimental Evidence for Interactions Between Perception and Production.

In a recent experiment, Hura and I (Hura & Echols, in press) sought to disentangle certain influences of perceptual and production factors on the form of early productions. Thirty-two 26-month-old children participated in an imitation study in which stress and articulatory difficulty were independently varied: In a gamelike context, children were asked to imitate words containing target syllables that were either stressed or unstressed and articulatorily difficult or easy.[3] Examples of the stimuli are presented in Table 10. 2.

Our rationale was as follows: If production factors are the primary limitations on children's early productions, then clear effects of articulatory difficulty should be observed; effects of stress may or may not also be observed. If perceptual salience is a primary determinant of the form of early productions, then clear effects of stress should be observed. Moreover, the effects of these two factors may vary for the different dependent measures (probability of imitation of a target syllable, accuracy of the target syllable), which would permit some insight into the interaction of these two factors. Because the data are children's imitations, this study distinguishes only perceptual salience effects from

---

[3]Articulatory difficulty was defined, in part, with the use of a scale developed by Willerman and Lindblom (1991) in which penalty scores are assigned to consonants. The penalty scores are determined by the difficulty of articulatory features involved in the production of a consonant. The scale has been validated in an analysis of consonants used cross-linguistically in pronoun systems. A second factor contributing to articulatory difficulty was the amount of movement required in producing the consonant-vowel sequences making up a given syllable. Based on the work of MacNeilage and Davis (1990), it was assumed that syllables requiring different tongue configurations for consonants and vowels would be articulatorily more difficult.

TABLE 10. 2
Examples of Difficult and Easy Target Syllables in Different Stress and Position Contexts

	Easy Target Syllable: [pa]	Difficult Target Syllable: [ræ]
Stressed/Initial	**pa**natəm	**ræ**təno
Stressed/Medial	təm**pa**nə	nə**ræ**to
Unstressed/Initial	pənatəm	ræteno
Unstressed/Medial	tap**ə**nəm	neræto

Note. Stressed syllables are boldfaced. Stimuli adhere to standard English pronunciation in that unstressed vowels typically reduce to a schwa or other lax vowel. Accordingly, the target syllable differs slightly between stressed and unstressed contexts.

pure production effects; it does not determine whether any observed perceptual salience effects are representational in nature.

The results suggested that both stress and articulatory difficulty influenced the form of early productions, but in different ways. For present purposes, the results of interest concern the role of each of these factors on omissions of target syllables and accuracy of those target syllables that were imitated.

Based on the notion that children should tend to extract and store stressed syllables, we expected that the primary factor influencing omissions of target syllables would be stress. However, if, as has been suggested, one factor contributing to omissions of unstressed syllables is the difficulty of incorporating those syllables into utterances (e.g., Allen & Hawkins, 1980; MacNeilage & Davis, 1990), then it might be expected that other sources of articulatory difficulty would contribute to increased omissions of syllables. Our observations were consistent with the first prediction: Results suggested that children were far more likely to omit unstressed syllables (approximately 25%) than stressed syllables (approximately 2.5%). In this analysis, no significant effects of articulatory difficulty were observed.

A second set of observations concerned the accuracy of children's imitations. Based on previous results, we might expect both stress and articulatory difficulty to influence the accuracy of children's imitations: As was noted earlier, studies of both imitations and spontaneous productions have demonstrated effects of stress on accuracy of children's productions (Echols & Newport, 1992; Frumhoff et al., 1992). On the other hand, research focusing on phonological acquisition suggests that children will be slower to produce certain, more difficult, segments and segment combinations (e.g., Locke, 1983; Menn, 1983). Fig. 10.3 shows the effects of stress and articulatory difficulty on the proportion of accurate imitations of target syllables. As can be seen in this figure, children's imitations of articulatorily difficult syllables were less accurate than imitations of easy syllables. This time, no significant effect of stress was observed.

The failure to find the expected effects of stress is somewhat puzzling given the evidence of effects of stress on accuracy in other research (e.g., Echols & Newport, 1992; Frumhoff, et al., 1992). In fact, the one significant result involving stress was a significant stress X articulatory difficulty interaction, and that result was due to *poorer* performance on difficult stressed syllables. However, that interaction is most likely due to an artifact of the stimuli: In our stimuli, as in spoken English, vowels in unstressed syllables were reduced to a schwa or other lax vowel. Because one of the criteria of articulatory difficulty was the amount of movement required between the consonant and vowel within a syllable, unstressed syllables turned out to be articulatorily less difficult than stressed syllables. This interaction may therefore simply be another indication of the effect of articulatory difficulty on accuracy. Because of this artifact, it was not possible to evaluate potential effects of stress on accuracy in this study.

It is tempting to interpret these results as evidence of distinct perceptual-representational and production influences on early words. In this view, stress, a perceptual factor, would determine whether a syllable will be extracted from the stream of speech and subsequently produced whereas articulatory difficulty, a production factor, would influence the accuracy of target syllables that are included in the production. However, these results still do not distinguish representational from production factors. Certain production-based accounts could also explain the stress effects. In particular, our results are entirely consistent with the trochaic bias proposed by Gerken and her colleagues (e.g., Gerken, 1994a, 1994b; Gerken et al., 1990) and by Allen and Hawkins (1980). Children were far more likely to omit from their productions weak syllables in weak-strong sequences than in strong-weak sequences. This pattern can be seen clearly in Fig. 10.4, which shows children's omissions of target syllables as a function of stress and position. Thus, although we succeeded in demonstrating certain effects of production fac-

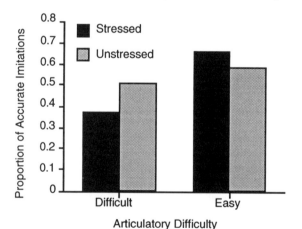

FIG. 10.3. Proportion of target syllables imitated accurately for different levels of stress and articulatory difficulty.

tors on children's imitations, and provided evidence for independent effects of articulatory difficulty and of stress on the form of early words, our results from this study did not succeed in demonstrating that unstressed syllables are less completely represented than stressed syllables. In fact, these results do not determine whether stress effects are due to the perceptual salience of stressed syllables or whether they are due to the role of stressed syllables in metrical rhythm.

It may be unnecessary to present the production and representational accounts for stress effects on early productions as entirely opposing accounts. In Echols and Newport (1992), we proposed an account for how the contributions of perceptual, representational, and production factors may change over the period of early language acquisition, and similar suggestions have been made by other researchers (e.g., Gleitman et al., 1988; Peters & Menn, 1990). The basic notion is that less salient elements, such as syllables that are unstressed and nonfinal in the target word, may initially either be omitted from children's stored representations or may be included but incompletely specified. As children acquire more experience with language and with a given word, they may begin to fill in the less salient elements. However, these elements will continue to be "fragile" and more vulnerable to omission in the presence of production limitations even after they are more completely represented.

Taking this proposed account one step further, it is possible that there is a perceptual-representational as well as a production component to the "trochaic bias." Jusczyk et al. (1993) recently suggested that young children may use typical stress patterns and, in particular, that English-learning infants may use the trochaic pattern that is dominant in English, to identify word-level units in the speech stream (see also Cutler & Butterfield, 1992; Cutler & Norris, 1988, for evidence of use of a similar strategy in adult speech processing). In partial support of that

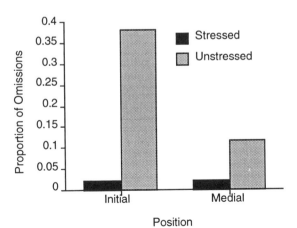

FIG. 10.4. Proportion of target syllable omissions for different stress levels and positions.

suggestion, they provide evidence that young English-hearing infants prefer trochaically accented disyllabic words over iambically accented words. Such an account may permit a perceptually based interpretation for the Hura and Echols results: If children expect words to adhere to a trochaic sequence then, particularly when storage demands are heavy, as when children are being called upon to recall and repeat a number of unfamiliar words, children may tend to focus on and store a strong-weak sequence. Thus, the greater vulnerability of prestress unstressed syllables in our imitation task may reflect a trochaic bias in perception and storage rather than a trochaic bias in production. Until additional research investigates more directly the question of whether children are representing the prestress unstressed syllables that they fail to imitate, the observed effects of position on children's imitations of unstressed syllables are consistent both with a perceptual and with a production-based account. Note, however, that in either event, the resulting account requires greater sophistication on the part of the young language learner than is implied by a pure perceptual biases account. Whether the trochaic sequence is used for perceptual segmentation, as a template for production, or for both, the child will have been required to identify this pattern as a typical pattern of English and then to make use of that knowledge in speech processing.

STRESS AS A CONTRIBUTOR TO METRICAL RHYTHM

The possibility that young children use the trochaic stress pattern to identify word-level units in speech leads us to another puzzle about early language learning. Attention to trochaic sequences will by no means be useful in all languages of the world. The young language learner must identify not only what particular stress patterns may be relevant in his or her native language but must also determine the size of any units that are indicated by stress pattern (e.g., word, clause, or phrase), as well as whether stress is even useful within that language. A substantial body of research suggests that, during the first year of life, infants are becoming attuned to the segmental distinctions of their native language (e.g., Best, 1994; Kuhl, Williams, Lacerda, Stevens, & Lindblom, 1992; Werker & Lalonde, 1988; Werker & Tees, 1984). There is also recent evidence suggesting that a similar tuning process may be occurring in relation to native prosody. Mehler, Jusczyk, Lambertz, Halsted, Bertoncini, and Amiel-Tison (1988), for example, provided evidence that infants between the ages of 4 days and 2 months can distinguish speech of their native language from non-native speech on the basis of prosody. Moreover, Jusczyk (1989) showed that infants may lose the ability to perceive certain cues to prosodic units in a nonnative language by as early as 6 months. The Jusczyk et al. (1993) results are also consistent with the notion that infants become attuned to the prosody of their native language in that 9-month-olds, but not 6-month-olds, showed a selective preference for trochaically accented words.

In a recent study, Crowhurst and I (Crowhurst & Echols, 1993) sought to extend these previous observations by investigating the extent to which infants recognize language-typical patterning of stress over sequences longer than two syllables. Our results provided some additional support for sensitivity to a trochaic–non-trochaic distinction (or, in this context, penultimately stressed versus final-stressed sequences). Because the multisyllabic stimulus sequences used in this study approximate English phrases or short sentences rather than English words, these results may speak to a developing ability to identify trochaic patterns that are embedded in (or at least are attached to) multiword phrases.

Experimental Evidence Concerning Sensitivity to Metrical Rhythm

In our experiment, 9-month-old English-hearing infants were presented with 5- to 6-syllable sequences in which two aspects of rhythm were varied. These aspects were metrical rhythm over the entire sequence and final versus penultimate stress. The variations in metrical rhythm included: (a) an alternating pattern in which stressed and unstressed syllables occurred in strict alternation, (b) a gap pattern in which two unstressed syllables occurred adjacently, and (c) a clashing pattern that contained two adjacent stresses. Rhythmic sequences were constructed from a set of consonant-vowel syllables that included stressed and unstressed versions of 9 different syllable types. Two variants of each of the three rhythmic sequences were created: one with a stressed penultimate syllable and unstressed final syllable, and one with an unstressed penultimate syllable and stressed final syllable. Examples of stimulus sequences are presented in Table 10. 3.

The metrical rhythms that children hear will be determined by the language to which they are exposed. Of the three metrical patterns, the gap sequences should be most typical of English. Examples of gap sequences in English include *Susan is eating her dinner* (penultimate stress) and *Matthew can run in the park* (final stress). Strictly alternating sequences should tend to occur less frequently. Examples of English sentences with alternating rhythm include *There's a pretty flower* (penultimate stress) and *Little children like to play* (final stress). The clashing pattern is least typical of English: In a sequence of two stressed syllables, the rightmost is usually de-emphasized (Hammond, 1988). Moreover, because multisyllabic words in English tend to be penulti-

TABLE 10. 3
Examples of Stimulus Sequences With Different Metrical Rhythms

	Penultimate Stress	Final Stress
Alternating	da**bi**bu**ga**diba	da**bi**bu**ga**di
Gap	da**bi**gadiba	da**bi**gadi**bagu**
Clash	da**bugа**diba	da**bugа**dibagu

Note. Stressed syllables are boldfaced.

mately stressed, we expected that the sequences bearing penultimate stress would be most native sounding to English-hearing infants. We predicted that if prelinguistic infants are sensitive to the metrical pattern typical of the ambient language, then they should attend differently to nativelike as opposed to non-native patterns. Thus, the English-hearing infant subjects should react differently to stimuli in the more common gap and alternating patterns than to stimuli in the less typical clashing patterns, and they should also respond differently to the penultimately than to the final stressed sequences.

The speech stimuli were constructed from syllable sequences recorded on a Macintosh computer by a native speaker of English. Syllable-sized units were extracted from these sequences and then spliced together to form several variants of each type of rhythmic sequence. The sequences could then be played in different random orders from the Macintosh through an amplifier and speakers. Infants' interest in the different sequences was assessed by pairing the auditory sequences with a visual stimulus (a slide of an abstract face), and measuring infants' attention to the visual stimulus when different types of rhythmic sequences were presented. Using this sequential preference procedure, infants' attention to the visual stimulus could be used as an index of their interest in the auditory stimuli.

Results suggested that infants were sensitive to the penultimate versus final distinction, but not the differences in rhythm over the entire sequence. Infants showed a preference for sequences carrying stress on the final syllable over sequences carrying stress on the penultimate syllable. The observed pattern is confirmed by a significant effect of final versus nonfinal stress, with $F(1,31) = 6.43$, $p < .02$. Differences between the different types of rhythmic sequences did not, however, reach significance.

The failure to find sensitivity to the differences in rhythmic sequence is puzzling given that very young infants are sensitive to nonlinguistic rhythm (e.g., Demany, McKenzie, & Vurpillot, 1977). It may be that the metrical rhythm was not sufficiently salient in this experiment. However, the finding of sensitivity to a penultimate–final distinction is consistent with the Jusczyk et al. (1993) results for disyllabic English words, and it extends those findings by providing evidence for a similar sensitivity with longer sentencelike sequences.

The results do, however, differ from those of Jusczyk et al. in that our results appear to imply a novelty preference; in other words, infants are looking longer for the stimuli that are less typical of their native language. In the Jusczyk et al. results the preference was for the more nativelike stimuli, that is, the trochaic sequences. Whereas a novelty preference is frequently obtained with nonlinguistic stimuli, familiarity preferences seem to be more common in research concerning infants' perceptions of linguistic stimuli. Thus, one possible interpretation for the discrepancy concerns our stimuli: It may be that our stimuli are not sufficiently languagelike for our infant subjects. In such a case, the infants may be treating the stimuli as nonlinguistic rhythmic stimuli, so are responding on the basis of novelty. A second possibility is that our expectation concerning which sequences are more Englishlike is incorrect. Although multisyllabic words in English do tend to be penultimately stressed, our stimuli more closely approximate phrases or short sentences of English. It is possible that phrases of parents' speech to infants may frequently end in a stressed syllable, a realistic possibility if the nouns that parents tend to place at ends of sentences (Fernald & Mazzie, 1991; Woodward & Aslin, 1990) are often monosyllabic. In that event, our results would indeed be evidence of a familiarity preference.[4] Assessing that possibility will, however, require analysis of the stress patterns in infant-directed speech.[5]

The evidence of sensitivity to a trochaic–iambic or a penultimate–final distinction leaves open the question of how children identify such sequences in speech. One possibility is that, in addition to being predisposed to attend to stressed and final syllables, infants are prepared to attend to stress pattern or rhythmic pattern. Such a possibility was proposed by Ann Peters (e.g., Peters, 1983) and has been discussed in previous work of mine (Echols, 1993). Within the first year of life then, children may begin to extract the typical stress or rhythmic patterns of the ambient language. This suggestion is supported by the evidence of very early sensitivity to nonlinguistic rhythm (e.g., Demany et al., 1977) as well as recent research of Morgan and Saffran (in press) that suggested that young infants recognize rhythmically defined sequences in speech. Stress pattern also appears to be highly salient to young preschool children; indeed, it may override segmental information in determining children's judgments of similarity between words (Echols, 1993). The notion that infants are prepared to attend to rhythm might imply that sensitivity to rhythm will be based on a relatively holistic representation, that is, that infants will identify and subsequently recognize rhythmic patterns over entire speech sequences. The problem with this proposal is that isolating the trochaic pattern will require frequent exposure to speech sequences consisting only of trochaically stressed disyllables. Given that infants will most likely be hearing multiword phrases far more often than single disyllabic words, it is unclear that such a pattern will be consistently available to them. Alternatively, infants would need to extract a disyllabic rhythm pattern from within a longer sequence (which is, in fact, what they appear to do in Morgan & Saffran, in press) but then an explanation is needed for why one type of disyllabic sequence is extracted over another.

---

[4]This explanation was proposed by Anne Cutler.
[5]Results of a recent study comparing characteristics of final syllables in infant- versus adult-directed speech suggests, in fact, that even when unstressed syllables do occur in final position, those syllables tend to carry some characteristics of stress (i.e., greater duration and amplitude than their counterparts elsewhere in adult speech; Albin & Echols, 1994).

An alternate approach is one in which sensitivity to language-specific sentence-level rhythm patterns is built up from sensitivity to the typical stress patterns of word-level units. One such account could further integrate the various processes proposed here: It was previously argued that stressed and final syllables are especially salient. For an English-hearing infant, a tendency to attend to stressed and to word-final syllables will frequently result in attention to a trochaic sequence.[6] Thus, the proposed account for the development of sensitivity to typical word-level stress patterns in English could be something like the following: Infants will tend to extract and store stressed and final syllables. They will also attend to stress pattern. As a result of the tendency to attend to and extract stressed and final syllables, and because stress is typically penultimate in English, children will frequently extract and store as their early representations for words sequences consisting of a stressed followed by an unstressed syllable. The tendency to attend to stress pattern will lead children to identify the trochaic stress pattern as a consistent characteristic of the extracted sequences. Children would then begin to use that stress pattern to identify word-level units, as suggested by Jusczyk et al. (1993). When children begin to form productions, they will also use that typical rhythmic pattern to structure their early productions, as described by Gerken (1994a, 1994b).

In this view, then, segmentation first involves the extraction of single salient syllables. The preferences underlying those syllable extractions are subsequently recruited into a more sophisticated (and language-specific) word extraction strategy, one based on metrical rhythm. The roles of stress and stress pattern will also change, over early language development, in relation to their importance for representational and production processes. Both will initially contribute to the segmentation of approximately word-level units from the stream of speech. Over time, as children become increasingly competent with language or have greater exposure to particular words, their representations for those words will become increasingly complete, and representational limitations will decrease in importance as influences on the forms of words. Although production limitations also will have influenced the form of children's productions throughout the earlier period, certain limitations will continue even after children's representations for words are more complete. Two such production limitations will be related to the early representational limitations. First, syllables that are unstressed in the target word will now be fully specified but will still be vulnerable to omission when the processing requirements of forming a production are heavy. Second, the trochaic "template" used in segmentation will, as

---

[6]Although infants may hear numerous monosyllabic words, the predominance of penultimate stress in high frequency multisyllabic words of English will mean that the vast majority of words of two or more syllables that infants are likely to hear will be penultimately stressed; indeed, the penultimate tendency of English is likely to be exaggerated by the frequent use of diminutives (e.g., *kitty, daddy*) in infant-directed speech.

described by Gerken, be used in constructing productions, thus contributing to the greater vulnerability of unstressed syllables that do not correspond to a weak syllable within a trochaic sequence (i.e., that do not follow a stressed syllable).

This account is undeniably speculative, and additional research will be needed if it is to be supported. Moreover, the complete story will undoubtedly be more complicated than that described here. However, this proposal is one possible way of constructing a coherent account for various effects of stress and stress pattern on the form of early words, and of explaining certain puzzles of early language learning.

ACKNOWLEDGMENTS

I thank Jim Morgan and Katherine Demuth for helpful comments on an earlier version of this chapter; Elissa Newport for valuable advice on all phases of the research; Anne Cutler, LouAnn Gerken, Peter Jusczyk, and Richard Meier for helpful discussion; Stephen Piché for programming assistance; and Jane Childers for assistance with the figures. I also extend my gratitude to a number of undergraduate students who assisted with this research and to the children and their parents. The research described herein was supported by a Cognitive Science/Artificial Intelligence Fellowship and a Graduate College Dissertation Research Grant from the University of Illinois, by NICHD Training Grant HD07205, by NIH grant DC00167, by INRSA HD07109 from NICHD, by a Summer Salary Award from the University Research Institute at the University of Texas, and by a grant from the Advanced Research Program of the Texas Higher Education Coordinating Board.

REFERENCES

Albin, D. D., & Echols, C. H. (1994, June). *The role of stress in speech to infants.* Poster session presented at the International Conference on Infant Studies, Paris.

Allen, G. D., & Hawkins, S. (1978). The development of phonological rhythm. In A. Bell & J. B. Hooper (Eds.), *Syllables and segments* (pp. 173-185). Amsterdam: North- Holland.

Allen, G. D., & Hawkins, S. (1980). Phonological rhythm: Definition and development. In G. Yeni-Komshian, J. F. Kavanagh, & C. A. Ferguson (Eds.), *Child phonology: Vol. 1. Production* (pp. 227-256). New York: Academic Press.

Berman, R. A. (1977). Natural phonological processes at the one-word stage. *Lingua, 43,* 1-21.

Best, C. T. (1994). The emergence of native-language phonological influences in infants: A perceptual assimilation model. In H. C. Nusbaum & J. Goodman (Eds.), *The development of speech perception: The transition from speech sounds to spoken words* (pp. 167-224). Cambridge, MA: MIT Press.

Blasdell, R., & Jensen, P. (1970). Stress and word position as determinants of imitation in first language learners. *Journal of Speech and Hearing Research, 13,* 193-202.

Cooper, W. E. (1983). The perception of fluent speech. *Annals of the New York Academy of Science, 405,* 48-63.

Crowhurst, M. J., & Echols, C. H. (1993, January). *Infants' perception of metrical rhythms.* Paper presented at the Annual Meeting of the Linguistic Society of America, Los Angeles.

Cutler, A., & Butterfield, S. (1992). Rhythmic cues to speech segmentation: Evidence from juncture misperception. *Journal of Memory and Language, 31,* 218-236.

Cutler, A., & Foss, D. J. (1977). On the role of sentence stress in sentence processing. *Language and Speech, 20,* 1-10.

Cutler, A., & Norris, D. (1988). The role of strong syllables in segmentation for lexical access. *Journal of Experimental Psychology: Human Perception and Performance, 14,* 113-121.

Demany, L., McKenzie, B., & Vurpillot, E. (1977). Rhythm perception in early infancy. *Nature, 266,* 718-719.

Demuth, K. (1992a, October). *What phonology shows about children's emerging syntax.* Paper presented at the Boston University Conference on Language Development, Boston, MA.

Demuth, K. (1992b). The acquisition of Sesotho. In D. I. Slobin (Ed.), *The cross-linguistic study of language acquisition: Vol. 3* (pp. 557-638). Hillsdale, NJ: Lawrence Erlbaum Associates.

Demuth, K. (1994). On the 'underspecification' of functional categories in early grammars. In B. Lust, M. Suñer, & J. Whitman (Eds.), *Syntactic theory and first language acquisition: Cross-linguistic perspectives.* (pp. 119-134). Hillsdale, NJ: Lawrence Erlbaum Associates.

Echols, C. H. (1993). A perceptually-based model of children's earliest productions. *Cognition, 46,* 245-296.

Echols, C. H., & Newport, E. L. (1992). The role of stress and position in determining first words. *Language Acquisition, 2,* 189-220.

Fernald, A., & Mazzie, C. (1991). Prosody and focus in speech to infants and adults. *Developmental Psychology, 27,* 209-221.

Feurer, H. (1980). Morphological development in Mohawk. *Papers and Reports in Child Language Development, 18,* 25-42.

Fikkert, P. (1994). *On the acquisition of prosodic structure.* Dordrecht: ICG Printing.

Frazier, L. (1987). Structure in auditory word recognition. *Cognition, 25,* 157-187.

Frumhoff, P., Echols, C. H., & Newport, E. L. (1992). *Perceptual salience and operating principles for language acquisition: The effects of stress and end of word.* Unpublished manuscript, University of Texas, Austin, TX.

Gerken, L. A. (1990). Performance constraints in early language: The case of subjectless sentences. *Papers and Reports on Child Language Development, 29,* 54-61.

Gerken, L. A. (1994a). A metrical template account of children's weak syllable omissions. *Journal of Child Language, 21,* 565-584

Gerken, L. A. (1994b). Young children's representation of prosodic structure: Evidence from English-speakers' weak syllable omissions. *Journal of Memory and Language, 33,* 19-38.

Gerken, L. A., Landau, B., & Remez, R. (1990). Function morphemes in young children's speech perception and production. *Developmental Psychology, 26,* 204-216.

Gerken, L. A., & McIntosh, B. J. (1993). The interplay of function morphemes and prosody in early language. *Developmental Psychology, 29,* 448-457.

Gleitman, L. R., Gleitman, H., Landau, B., & Wanner, E. (1988). Where learning begins: Initial representations for language learning. In F. J. Newmeyer (Ed.), *Linguistics: The Cambridge survey: Vol. 3. Language: Psychological and biological processes* (pp. 150-193). Cambridge, England: Cambridge University Press.

Gleitman, L. R., & Wanner, E. (1982). Language acquisition: The state of the state of the art. In E. Wanner & L. R. Gleitman (Eds.), *Language acquisition: The state of the art* (pp. 3-48). Cambridge, England: Cambridge University Press.

Grosjean, F., & Gee, J. P. (1987). Prosodic structure and spoken word recognition. *Cognition, 25,* 135-155.

Hammond, M. (1988). *Constraining metrical theory: A modular theory of rhythm and destressing.* New York: Garland.

Hura, S. L., & Echols, C. H. (in press). The role of stress and articulatory difficulty in children's early productions. *Developmental Psychology.*

Ingram, D. (1978). The role of the syllable in phonological development. In A. Bell & J. B. Hooper (Eds.), *Syllables and segments* (pp. 143-155). Amsterdam: North-Holland.

Jusczyk, P. W. (1989, April). *Perception of cues to clausal units in native and non-native languages.* Paper presented at the biennial meeting of the Society for Research in Child Development, Kansas City, MO.

Jusczyk, P. W., Cutler, A., & Redanz, N. J. (1993). Infants' preferences for the predominant stress patterns of English words. *Child Development, 64,* 675-687.

Klatt, D. H. (1976). Linguistic uses of segmental duration in English: Acoustic and perceptual evidence. *Journal of the Acoustical Society of America, 59,* 1208-1221.

Klein, H. B. (1981). Early perceptual strategies for the replication of consonants from poly-syllabic lexical models. *Journal of Speech and Hearing Research, 24*, 535-551.

Kuhl, P. K., Williams, K. A., Lacerda, F., Stevens, K. N., & Lindblom, B. (1992). Linguistic experience alters phonetic perception in infants by 6 months of age. *Science, 255*, 606-608.

Lehiste, I. (1970). *Suprasegmentals.* Cambridge, MA: MIT Press.

Lehiste, I., Olive, J. P., & Streeter, L. A. (1976). Role of duration in disambiguating syntacti-cally ambiguous sentences. *Journal of the Acoustical Society of America, 60*, 1199-1202.

Locke, J. J. (1983). *Phonological acquisition and change.* New York: Academic Press.

MacNeilage, P. F., & Davis, B. (1990). Acquisition of speech production: The achievement of segmental independence. In W. J. Hardcastle & A. Marchal (Eds.), *Speech production and speech modeling* (pp. 55-68). Dordrecht, Holland: Kluwer.

MacWhinney, B. (1985). Hungarian language acquisition as an exemplification of a general model of grammatical development. In D. I. Slobin (Ed.), *The cross-linguistic study of language acquisition: Vol. 2. Theoretical issues* (pp. 1069-1155). Hillsdale, NJ: Lawrence Erlbaum Associates.

Mehler, J., Jusczyk, P. W., Lambertz, G., Halsted, N., Bertoncini, J., & Amiel-Tison, C. (1988). A precursor of language acquisition in young infants. *Cognition, 29*, 143-178.

Menn, L. (1978). Phonological units in beginning speech. In A. Bell & J. B. Hooper (Eds.), *Syllables and segments* (pp. 157-171). Amsterdam: North-Holland.

Menn, L. (1983). Development of articulatory, phonetic and phonological capabilities. In B. Butterworth (Ed.), *Language production: Vol. 2. Development, writing and other language processes* (pp. 3-50). London: Academic Press.

Morgan, J. L., & Saffran, J. R. (in press). Emerging integration of sequential and supraseg-mental information in preverbal speech segmentation. *Child Development.*

Nakatani, L. H., & Dukes, K. D. (1977). Locus of segmental cues for word juncture. *Journal of the Acoustical Society of America, 62*, 714-719.

Nakatani, L. H., O'Connor, K. D., & Aston, C. H. (1981). Prosodic aspects of American Eng-lish speech rhythm. *Phonetica, 38*, 84-105.

Nakatani, L. H., & O'Connor-Dukes, K. D. (1979). *Phonetic parsing cues for word perception.* Unpublished manuscript, Bell Laboratories, Murray Hill, NJ.

Nakatani, L. H., & Schaffer, J. A. (1978). Hearing "words" without words: Prosodic cues for word perception. *Journal of the Acoustical Society of America, 63*, 234-245.

Oller, D. K., & Rydland, J. N. (1974). *Note on the stress preferences of young English-speaking children.* Unpublished manuscript, Mailman Center for Child Development, Miami, FL.

Paccia-Cooper, J., & Cooper, W. E. (1981). The processing of phrase structure in speech production. In P. E. Eimas & J. L. Miller (Eds.), *Perspectives on the study of speech* (pp. 331-336). Hillsdale, NJ: Lawrence Erlbaum Associates.

Peters, A. M. (1981). Language typology and the segmentation problem in early child lan-guage acquisition. *Proceedings of the Seventh Annual Meeting of the Berkeley Linguistics So-ciety, 7*, 236-248.

Peters, A. M. (1983). *The units of language acquisition.* Cambridge, England: Cambridge Uni-versity Press.

Peters, A. M., & Menn, L. (1990). *The microstructure of morphological development: Variation across children and across languages.* Unpublished manuscript, University of Colorado.

Pye, C. (1983). Mayan telegraphese: Intonational determinants of inflectional development in Quiche Mayan. *Language, 59*, 583-604.

Pye, C. (1992). The acquisition of K'iche' Maya. In D. I. Slobin (Ed.), *The cross-linguistic study of language acquisition: Vol. 3* (pp. 221-308). Hillsdale, NJ: Lawrence Erlbaum Associ-ates.

Scott, D. R. (1982). Duration as a cue to the perception of a phrase boundary. *Journal of the Acoustical Society of America, 71*, 996-1007.

Slobin, D. I. (1973). Cognitive prerequisites for the development of grammar. In C. A. Fer-guson & D. I. Slobin (Eds.), *Studies of child language development* (pp. 175-208). New York: Holt, Rinehart & Winston.

Streeter, L. A. (1978). Acoustic determinants of phrase boundary perception. *Journal of the Acoustical Society of America, 64,* 1582-1592.

Waibel, A. (1986). Suprasegmentals in very large vocabulary word recognition. In E. C. Schwab & H. C. Nusbaum (Eds.), *Pattern recognition by humans and machines: Vol. 1. Speech perception* (pp. 159-186). Orlando, FL: Academic Press.

Werker, J. F., & Lalonde, C. E. (1988). Cross-language speech perception: Initial capabilities and developmental change. *Developmental Psychology, 24,* 672-683.

Werker, J. F., & Tees, R. C. (1984). Cross-language speech perception: Evidence for perceptual reorganization within the first year of life. *Infant Behavior and Development, 7,* 49-63.

Willerman, R., & Lindblom, B. (1991). The phonetics of pronouns. *PERILUS XIII: Papers from the Fifth National Phonetics Conference, 13,* 19-23.

Woodward, J. Z., & Aslin, R. N. (1990, April). *Segmentation cues in maternal speech to infants.* Poster presented at the International Conference on Infant Studies, Montréal, Canada.

11 The Prosodic Structure of Early Words

Katherine Demuth
Brown University

Within the past few years researchers have begun to examine children's early word productions as a source of evidence regarding how and when linguistically meaningful prosodic representations are constructed (Demuth, 1992, 1994; Fee, 1992; Fikkert, 1992, 1994; Wijnen, Kirkhaar, & den Os, 1994). In this chapter I show that children's early productions, while often ill formed from a segmental, syllabic, or morphological point of view, are nonetheless prosodically well-formed minimal words. In so doing I draw on recent developments in phonological theory, specifically those dealing with the prosodic organization of words (e.g., Selkirk, 1984; Nespor & Vogel, 1986; Hayes, 1987; McCarthy & Prince, 1986, 1990). I conclude by showing that children exploit different levels of prosodic structure, using these to organize their early speech productions.

The chapter proceeds as follows: First I present some of the commonly found early word structure "errors" found in English, Dutch, Sesotho, a southern Bantu language, and K'iche' Maya. I then review some of the proposed perceptual and articulatory explanations regarding the "telegraphic" nature of early speech, and show that these cannot account for the crosslinguistic findings regarding the shape of early words. I then discuss recent work in prosodic phonology and morphology, and show that children's early word-formation "errors" conform to language-particular instantiations of what I call the Minimal Word Constraint. Finally, I sketch a Prosodic Model of Production to account for the shape of children's early words, and for the gradual move toward adultlike forms.

THE SHAPE OF EARLY WORDS

Language acquisition researchers have long noted that children tend to omit closed class grammatical function items in early speech (Bloom, 1970; Brown, 1973). More recently, however, it has been observed that children do not consistently omit all function items, but rather that some function items, as well as other "weak" (unstressed) syllables, only appear in certain contexts (Demuth, 1992, 1994; Gerken 1991; Gerken & McIntosh, 1993; Peters & Menn, 1993; Pye, 1983; Wijnen et al., 1994). Furthermore, this variability in the early production of certain "weak" syllables is found not only in English, but in languages as different as

Dutch, Sesotho, and K'iche'. I briefly review some of these findings in the following.

Echols and Newport (1992) noted that English-speaking children tend to include stressed syllables and final syllables in their early speech productions. Gerken (1991, 1994) provided a metrical explanation for these facts, showing that children's utterances tend to be organized into strong-weak disyllabic feet, and that this holds not only at the word level, but at the sentence level as well. Thus, although stressed syllables are undoubtedly important at a perceptual level, prosodic structure of a strong-(weak) trochaic foot appears to play a critical role in the organization of (at least) English-speaking children's early words and utterances. This prosodic perspective helps capture the fact that children at the early stages of language development frequently omit certain types of functional morphology (be they prefixes or suffixes) and other pretonic unstressed syllables. Typical examples of children's utterances at the one-word stage, where Echols and Newport (1992) reported that stressed and final syllables are generally preserved, are given in (1).

1. | Child | Adult Target |
    |-------|--------------|
    | [raisə] | eraser |
    | [ɛlfʌn] | elephant |

Fee and Ingram (1982) also reported that some English-speaking children's early words exhibit the use of a reduplication strategy to form disyllabic forms from monosyllabic words ($C_1V_2 \rightarrow C_1V_2C_1V_2$). Note that both the examples in (1) and the reduplication strategy result in disyllabic word forms.

Somewhat similar findings come from children at the same MLU learning Dutch, but the characterization of their early words is somewhat more complex. Given a word like *andere* "other," with a SWW (strong-weak-weak) stress pattern, children will produce a SW disyllabic form, but the weak syllable may be either the medial or the final, contrary to predictions by Echols and Newport (1992) that stressed and *final* syllables are the ones preserved. Consider the following Dutch examples from Wijnen et al. (1994):

2. | Child | Adult Target | |
    |-------|--------------|--|
    | ['sikhʌys] | ziekenhuis | "hospital" |
    | ['o:xant] | olifant | "elephant" |
    | ['ʌnRə] ~ ['ʌndə] | andere | "other" |

Furthermore, Dutch-speaking children have a tendency to transform monosyllabic words into a trochaic foot, either by inserting a vowel between two coda consonants (CVCC → CVCVC), or by adding a vowel to a closed syllable ((C)VC → CVCV). These epenthetic processes are shown in (3).

3. | Child | Adult Target | |
    |-------|--------------|--|
    | [ˈjoeRək] | jurk | "dress" |
    | [ˈmɛlək] | melk | "milk" |
    | [ˈomə] | oom | "uncle" |
    | [ˈbɑlə] | bal | "ball" |

Thus, Dutch-speaking children have both apocope (deletion) and epenthesis (addition) strategies for transforming early words into disyllabic,
trochaic feet (see Fikkert, 1994, for more detail).

Early words in Sesotho are also disyllabic, even though Sesotho has
no word-level stress. Connelly (1984) reported that early words in the
southern Bantu language Sesotho are typically disyllabic. Consider the
following examples, where syllable boundaries are marked by ".", and
morpheme boundaries between noun class prefixes and nominal stems
are marked by "-":

4. | Child | Adult Target | |
    |-------|--------------|--|
    | ta.te | n.ta.te | "father" |
    | tim.pa | ma.-sim.ba | "chips" |
    | tee.te | che.le.te | "money" |

Sesotho has no word level stress, only penultimate lengthening at
phrase boundaries (Doke & Mofokeng, 1957). However, penultimate
lengthening works somewhat like stress in that both assign *prominence*
to a syllable. Productions in the one-word stage in Sesotho can therefore
be represented by a strong-weak trochaic foot, just like that shown for
English and Dutch. Children's utterances at the two-word stage, however, where both words are part of the same noun phrase, show that
even words that are not phrase final nonetheless surface as disyllabic, as
seen in (5) (from Demuth, 1988).

5. | Child | Adult Target | |
    |-------|--------------|--|
    | ko.lo sa.-ne | se.-ko.lo sa.-ne | "school that" |
    | po.nko la.-ne | le.-pho.qo la.-ne | "green corn stalk that" |

The examples in (5) indicate that the disyllabic foot has an importance in Sesotho that is independent of syllabic prominence *per se*, and
that preservation of disyllabic feet is a more general word-level phenomenon.

The one-word stage in K'iche', however, looks very different from
equivalent stages of English, Dutch, and Sesotho. K'iche' has word final stress, and young children's first words are monosyllabic, as shown
in (6) (Pye, 1992).

6. | Child | Adult Target | |
    |-------|--------------|--|
    | lom | jolom | "head" |
    | met | lemet | "bottle" |
    | kop | chikop | "animal" |
    | 'ik | wa'ik | "eat" |

In sum, there is some variation across languages in the shape of early words. Specifically, it is not only stressed and final syllables that are retained (e.g., Dutch (2), Sesotho (5)), nor is a trochaic bias universal (e.g., K'iche' (6)). Rather, the shape of early words appears to vary across languages, but in a restricted fashion. I suggest that the shape of early words is constrained by principles of universal grammar, but also varies according to the prosodic characteristics of word structure in the language being learned. If this is true, then children's early words provide evidence for the early construction of prosodic representations. In the rest of this chapter I provide evidence for these proposals. First, however, I consider some of the traditional proposals that have been given for the shape of early words and show that these cannot account for the crosslinguistic data presented earlier.

PERCEPTUAL AND ARTICULATORY PROPOSALS FOR THE SHAPE OF EARLY WORDS

Several proposals have been offered to account for the omission of certain (unstressed) syllables/words and the presence of strong-weak trochaic foot structures observed in early child speech. Most appeal to perceptual or articulatory factors, though there have also been recent proposals regarding the syntactic impoverishment of early grammars (see Demuth, 1994, for a review). In the following section I consider some of the proposed explanations for the shape of early words, and show that they cannot account for data like those presented in (1) - (6).

Perceptual Constraints

Given the increased pitch, amplitude, and duration of English stressed syllables, plus the occurrence of vowel reduction in English unstressed syllables, it has been proposed that children's omission of unstressed syllables might be due to the low perceptual salience of such items (e.g., Gleitman & Wanner, 1982; Echols & Newport, 1992). However, several factors indicate that this is not the case. First, it has been shown that children understand connected discourse better when it includes stressless grammatical function items than when those items are omitted or replaced with nonsense elements (Petretic & Tweney, 1977; Shipley, Smith, & Gleitman, 1969). Furthermore, the variable appearance or omission of functional items in children's speech suggests that the problem is not perceptual: English-speaking children consistently select the grammatically appropriate form of the auxiliary in tag questions, even when the auxiliary in the main clause is omitted (e.g., *That making noise, isn't it?*; Radford, 1994), and Sesotho-speaking children consistently select the appropriate agreement form for demonstratives and possessives, even when they omit the class/gender prefix on the noun, as shown in (5) (Demuth, 1992, 1994). Furthermore, it is not always the case that children omit entire syllables: Rather, two syllables are often reduced to one, with parts of each syllable (onsets, nuclei, codas) remaining in the resulting syllable form. For example, in Sesotho the preverbal subject marker *ke-* and the future tense marker *-tla-* frequently surface as one syllable *ka-*, where the onset consonant from the first syllable is joined with the vowel nucleus from the second. Similar examples of syllabic "merger" have been reported in early Dutch (e.g., *microfoon* > [mi'kRon] "microphone"; Wijnen et al., 1994). Such cases indicate that children *perceive* the segments of the syllables they omit. In short, the data from children's early productions are compatible with the possibility that children already have adultlike segmental representations and use this knowledge in the construction of early words. If this is true, then an alternative explanation must be found for the omission of syllables in early speech.

Articulatory Constraints

Given English-speaking children's apparent bias for producing disyllabic trochaic feet, Allen and Hawkins (1980) proposed that the omission of syllables in early child speech has an articulatory explanation, where children's productions are limited to two (strong-weak) syllables. Such a proposal has at least two problems. First, it is inconsistent with the fact that prior to the onset of first words children generally babble in sequences of syllables, showing no disyllabic upper bound on the forms they produce (e.g., Menyuk, Menn, & Silber, 1986; Vihman, 1976). That is, there seems to be no principled articulatory prohibition on, say, trisyllabic forms at the babbling stage. Second, Allen and Hawkins (1980) proposed that the trochaic nature of early speech is universal— applicable to the early stages of development in all languages. This proposal obviously runs into problems with the early monosyllabic structures of stress-final languages like those of K'iche' shown in (6). Rather, it would appear that the prosodic structure of K'iche' itself may influence the monosyllabic nature of children's early words.

In short, neither perceptual nor articulatory explanations capture the crosslinguistic findings on the shape of children's early words. In the next sections I draw on recent developments in prosodic phonology to show that there is a unified, prosodic explanation for both the variable omission of grammatical function items and other weak syllables in early child speech, and the apparent constraint on maximally disyllabic forms. In other words, the shape of children's early words provides evidence of both access to universal grammar and a sophisticated prosodic awareness of the language being learned.

THE MINIMAL WORD

Research in the area of prosodic phonology has begun to identify hierarchical prosodic domains in language, both at the level of the word and at higher phrasal and utterance levels (e.g., Nespor & Vogel, 1986;

Selkirk, 1984). In the following discussion I restrict comments primarily to word-level phenomena. Consider the Prosodic Hierarchy in (7) (Selkirk, 1980a, 1980b).

7.   <u>Prosodic Hierarchy</u>

Pw   (Phonological Word)
|
Ft   (Foot)
|
σ   (Syllable)
|
μ   (Mora)

The Prosodic Hierarchy captures the fact that the *phonological word* is composed of at least one *foot*, that feet are composed of at least one *syllable,* and that syllables are composed on at least one *mora* or subsyllabic unit.

Recent work in prosodic phonology has demonstrated that there is abundant crosslinguistic evidence for a prosodic unit known as a "minimal word" (cf. Broselow, 1982; McCarthy & Prince, 1986, 1990, 1991; Prince, 1980; see McCarthy & Prince, 1995, for review). Critically, a minimal word must contain at least one binary foot, where a foot is composed of either two syllables (e.g., CVCV) or two moras (e.g., CVV, CVC). A long vowel (including tense vowels and diphthongs) or a vowel plus coda consonant counts as two moras and constitutes a foot, even though only one syllable is involved. Thus, monosyllabic English content words such as *buy, dog,* and *see* are all bimoraic forms that constitute a well-formed foot. This means that, crosslinguistically, open class items (nouns, verbs, adjectives, adverbs) must contain sufficient phonological information (i.e., at least a binary foot composed of two syllables or two moras) to be classified as a legitimate word. In Sesotho, evidence for the minimal word comes from both the verbal and nominal domains. This can be seen most readily by examining imperative verbs which generally take the bare stem form as in (8a). However, if the verb stem is monosyllabic, as in (8b), the imperative must affix an extra vowel to make the form disyllabic: This can be done either by prefixing an epenthetic "e-", or by lengthening the final vowel of the stem.

8.   *Infinitive*   *Imperative*
  a. ho-reka   "to buy"   reka   "buy!"
  b. ho-ja   "to eat"   eja ~ jaa   "eat!"

Given the crosslinguistic evidence for the minimal word, and given the fact that minimal words are binary feet, the crosslinguistic findings on children's early word structures take on new significance. Recall that the majority of words produced in early English, Dutch, and Sesotho were disyllabic forms. Children showed two types of "strategies" in producing such forms: Syllables were either deleted (processes of apocope; e.g., English (1), Dutch (2), and Sesotho (4, 5)), or syllables were added (processes of epenthesis; e.g., Dutch (3)). In both cases, children used adult input forms (i.e., full lexical representations) to create their own disyllabic output form. It would therefore appear that children's early words are sensitive to what I have called the Minimal Word Constraint (Demuth, 1992, 1994). A similar proposal has been independently advanced by Fee (1992) on the basis of evidence from the acquisition of English and Spanish.

The proposal that children's early words respect to the Minimal Word Constraint raises several questions. First, how does one explain the monosyllabic nature of early words in K'iche'? Second, how do Dutch-speaking children recover from "overgeneralizations" where an extra syllable is added to a monosyllabic target form, as in (3)? And finally, how does one account for the fact that children eventually come to produce adultlike target forms? In the following sections I show that the answer to the first question comes from the realization of possible foot structures, while the last two questions can be handled by appealing to a theory of learning that allows for the progressive relaxation of prosodic constraints.

THE REALIZATION OF FEET

Crosslinguistic research on metrical foot structure has shown that binary feet can be realized by any the surface forms shown in (9), where phonological weight is quantified as either heavy (H = 2 moras) or light (L = 1 mora; Hayes, 1987; McCarthy & Prince, 1986). Note that there are many moraic systems, where the "weight" of a syllable, or syllable quantity, plays a critical role in stress assignment. In contrast, languages where there is no word-level stress, and where quantity is irrelevant to the construction of feet, can be represented by two syllables only.

9. Surface Realization of Feet

    a. Iambic (quantity-sensitive)

H	LH	LL
σ	σ σ	σσ
/\	I /\	I I
μ μ	μ μ μ	μμ

    b. Trochaic (quantity-sensitive)

H	HL	LL
σ	σ σ	σσ
/\	/\ I	I I
μ μ	μ μ μ	μμ

    c. Trochaic (quantity-insensitive) σ σ

Note that both iambic and trochaic feet may be composed of just one heavy syllable (i.e., two moras), thereby still constituting a binary foot. Thus, the early CVC forms found in K'iche' constitute a binary foot, and conform to the Minimal Word Constraint. Note also that both iambic and trochaic feet can be composed of two light syllables. In the iambic case the right-most mora would be the head of the foot, while in the trochaic case the head would be the left-most. If a language is stress-sensitive, it would be these right-most and left-most heads that would receive stress, respectively (e.g., L'L = iambic, 'LL = trochaic).

Note further that it is only trochaic feet that can be oblivious to weight. That is, a form that is composed of two syllables, where the language does not consider weight in the construction of feet (i.e., is quantity-insensitive), will receive a trochaic interpretation by default. Such is the case for languages like Sesotho, where no lexical stress is assigned. In other words, the trochaic syllabic foot is the "default" form used for the construction of feet.

The metrical structures of English, Dutch, and Sesotho are trochaic (cf. Selkirk, 1984; van der Hulst, 1984; Kager, 1989; Doke & Mofokeng, 1957, respectively), whereas the structure of K'iche' is iambic, with final stress. Given the typology of feet in (9), one can now see why early words in English, Dutch, and Sesotho are disyllabic, but those in Maya K'iche' are not: The minimal word in early English and Dutch appears to be a stress-sensitive disyllabic foot. In Sesotho, stress is not a lexical phenomenon, nonetheless disyllabic feet are constructed by default. In contrast, the minimal word in K'iche' allows for one heavy, monosyllabic foot, resulting in the monosyllabic stressed syllables seen in (6). In other words, the shape of children's early words appears to be constrained by the prosodic realization of foot structure in the language being learned.

Given the high perceptual salience of stress, with increased duration, amplitude, and pitch excursions, one might predict that children learning languages with lexical stress would move directly to the stress-sensitive assignment of trochaic or iambic feet. But the correct realization of lexical stress in languages like English and Dutch is also sensitive to syllable weight, that is, they are "quantity-sensitive" languages. Furthermore, the characterization of heavy syllables is subject to language variation: Whereas open syllables (e.g., CV) are generally light, closed syllables (CVC), syllables with branching coda (CVCC), or syllables with long or tense vowels (CVV), may or may not be considered "heavy" in a given language. For example, in English only syllables with a branching coda (e.g., CVCC) are considered heavy enough to influence the placement of stress. Children must therefore learn what constitutes a heavy syllable for a given language and the role these syllables play in the construction of minimal words (see Fee, 1992). Fikkert (1994) and Wijnen et al. (1994) attributed changes in the structure of early words to children's developing awareness of what constitutes a heavy syllable in Dutch. Thus, children's early word structures may change as they learn more about how syllable weight is realized in a given language, all the while conforming to the minimal word constraint.

It is now possible to make predictions about the course of acquisition. First, trochaic syllabic structures may be used as a first pass at organizing prosodic words, a default possibility given by Universal Grammar. Second, for languages in which lexical stress is assigned, children will easily determine that stressed syllables are the heads of feet, and will organize their early words as either iambic or trochaic accordingly. Finally, for those languages where syllable weight plays a role, we expect to find some reorganization in the syllables that occur in children's early words. This is found not only in Dutch, but also in English, where disyllabic CVCV forms gradually give rise to bimoraic CVC forms (Fee, 1992). These three "stages" of development are outlined in the following.

10. The Early Development of Feet/Minimal Words

	Linguistic Awareness	Shape of Minimal Words
Stage 1.	Default (UG)	Trochaic syllabic feet
Stage 2.	Stress sensitivity	Iambic or Trochaic feet
Stage 3.	Weight sensitivity	Reorganization of syllables included in feet

Given the perceptual salience of stress, it may be that children learning languages where stress is relevant will pass the "default" Stage 1 and move directly to the stress-sensitive Stage 2. Stage 3 will only be reached once the language particular encoding of what constitutes a heavy syllable has been learned.

FROM MINIMAL WORDS TO PHONOLOGICAL WORDS

In the foregoing sections samples of early words from several different languages were presented. In each case the shape of the early words is consistent with the possibility that children have early access to the notion of a binary foot, or Minimal Word. Why should children's early words conform to a Minimal Word? There are at least two possibilities: First, there is emerging evidence from the perception literature that infants are aware of both prosodic structure at the phrasal level (Jusczyk, Kemler Nelson, Hirsh-Pasek, Kennedy, Woodward, & Piwoz, 1992) and rhythmic structures at the word level (Mehler, Dupoux, Nazzi, & Dehaene-Lambertz, this volume; Morgan, in press). In attempting their first words children may give priority to rhythmic well formedness, even at the cost of sacrificing semantic content. Second, Fee (1992), Fikkert (1994), and Wijnen et al. (1994) found that children using Minimal Words demonstrate a growing awareness of the language particular relationship between stress and syllable weight, and that this also influences the shape of early words. It might be that the Minimal Word stage provides a constrained learning space for children, where they can gradually resolve language particular instantiations of foot structure including head direction (iambic vs. trochaic), parsing direction (right > left, left < right), stress, and weight.[1]

But children eventually move beyond the Minimal Word stage to produce word structures that are more adultlike. Why and how does this take place? I suggest that the answer may lie with the notion of changing prosodic representations, where change would be triggered by children's growing awareness of prosodic structure at the level of the foot.

One possibility for the move from Minimal Words to phonological words is that children's prosodic hierarchy changes. It could be that children's early prosodic hierarchy may differ from that of the adult, being more like that in (11), where the Prosodic Word and the Foot are collapsed into one, undifferentiated level of structure.

11.   Ft/Pw   (Foot = Phonological Word)
        |
        σ   (Syllable)
        |
        μ   (Mora)

A fuller treatment of these issue might also posit the syllable and the mora as undifferentiated at the earliest levels of structure, as suggested by Fee (1992). Thus, a more constrained prosodic hierarchy for young children might look something like the following:

12.   Ft/Pw   (Foot = Phonological Word)
        |
        σ/μ   (Syllable = Mora)

If children's early representation of phonological words is identical to the foot, or Minimal Word, it is no surprise that the Minimal Word is also the *Maximal Word* that is prosodically licensed. Later, as children's prosodic awareness develops, the structure of the phonological word becomes more fully articulated, allowing inclusion of extrametrical syllables and the possibility of more than one foot. At this later stage of development children begin to produce words with more than two syllables and to include closed class grammatical function items into their phonological words. In other words, the phonological word is no longer constrained to being only a Minimal Word, or foot. Rather than constituting the *maximal upper bound* on the shape of phonological words, the Minimal Word Constraint now assumes its role as a truly *minimal constraint* on the shape of phonological words, as it does in adult grammars. The progressive development of representations within the Prosodic Hierarchy is presented in (13), where the foot at Time 1 is the maximal form a phonological word can take, whereas the foot at Time 2 is the minimal form a phonological word can take.

---

[1]See Dresher (this volume) for further discussion of these issues, and Dresher and Kaye (1990) for a parameterized computational model for learning stress systems.

13. Prosodic Model of Production

In sum, children begin with word structures that are well formed from a prosodic point of view given the nature of the Prosodic Hierarchy. As their linguistic awareness of the Prosodic Hierarchy increases, so do the possible word structures they employ. Children's early grammars therefore contain only a subset of the possible prosodic structures provided by Universal Grammar. Given that the Minimal Word is a universal unit found in all languages, it is not surprising that children's first words take this shape. Children must then learn, on a language by language basis, the higher level prosodic structure of words, and this takes place after issues of quantity sensitivity and stress assignment have been determined.

DISCUSSION

In this chapter I showed that children learning languages as different as English, Dutch, Sesotho, and K'iche' all have early sensitivity to the prosodic structure of words. I suggest that this sensitivity comes in part from Universal Grammar, which provides children with the linguistic notion of the Minimal Word as a binary foot. This accounts for the fact that minimal word structures are created in the early speech of children in all of the above languages, either through processes of epenthesis (syllable addition) or apocope (syllable deletion). However, I also showed that part of children's early sensitivity to prosodic structure is language particular, thereby accounting for the early trochaic structures in English, Dutch, and Sesotho, but the early iambic structures in K'iche'.

These findings are interesting in light of previous perception and production/articulation proposals regarding the nature of early words. Perception proposals cannot account for the variable inclusion of weak syllables in Dutch (3), the appearance of correct agreement forms on nominal modifiers in Sesotho (5), nor the case of syllable "merger" found in both languages. Similar arguments to this effect have been made for K'iche' (Pye, 1983) and English (Gerken, 1994). However, production/articulatory constraint proposals are also problematic in suggesting that the limit on a maximally binary structure is an articulatory one: Such a proposal is incapable of explaining why in K'iche' this limit is one syllable and not two, and it would predict that in Sesotho, with no lexical stress, any two syllables could satisfy the binarity constraint. Rather, the evidence presented here points strongly to the fact that children's early words are not randomly truncated forms, but well-organized Minimal Words. Early Minimal Words therefore provide evidence of children's construction of prosodic representations—representations that are sensitive both to the properties of Universal Grammar, and to language particular instantiations of feet.

In sum, the phonological approach developed in this chapter provides both a means for more accurately describing the shape of children's early words, as well as a theoretical framework for understanding why early words take the particular shapes they do. Given recent developments in Optimality Theory (Prince & Smolensky 1993), where languages are hypothesized to differ primarily in the ordering and ranking of phonological "constraints," we might see the acquisition of phonological words as a process in which constraints on the realization of prosodic structure are reorganized over time. These issues are pursued in Demuth (1995).

Specifically, it appears that children's early word productions are determined not by perceptual capacities, but rather by constellations of constraints on output forms. The fact that children's early words are well-formed linguistic units indicates that children have access to linguistic representations. However, the fact that some of the segments and syllables children hear do not consistently appear in the word-forms they produce indicates that processing and planning factors may interact with children's linguistic representations to yield minimal linguistic units such as Minimal Words. Analyses of children's early word productions therefore provide a critically important link in our understanding of the connections between children's developing perceptual abilities, their segmentation of the speech stream into grammatical categories, and their gradual use of larger syntactic structures.

ACKNOWLEDGMENTS

Earlier versions of this chapter were given at the 17th Boston University Conference on Language Development, Johns Hopkins University, and McGill University. I thank those audiences, Jane Fee, Paula Fikkert, and Jim Morgan for fruitful comments and discussion.

REFERENCES

Allen, G., & Hawkins, S. (1980). Phonological rhythm: Definition and development. In G. Yeni-Komshian, J. Kavanagh, & C. Ferguson (Eds.), *Child phonology* (Vol. 1, pp. 227-256). New York: Academic Press

Bloom, L. (1970). *Language development: Form and function in emerging grammars*. Cambridge, MA: MIT Press.

Broselow, E. (1982). On the interaction of stress and epenthesis. *Glossa, 16*, 115-132.

Brown, R. (1973). *A first language: The early stages*. Cambridge, MA: Harvard University Press.

Connelly, M. (1984). *Basotho children's acquisition of noun morphology*. Unpublished doctoral dissertation, University of Essex, Colchester.

Demuth, K. (1988). Noun classes and agreement in Sesotho acquisition. In M. Barlow & C. Ferguson (Eds.), *Agreement in natural languages: Approaches, theories and descriptions* (pp. 305-321). CSLI: University of Chicago Press.

Demuth, K. (1992). Accessing functional categories in Sesotho: Interactions at the morpho-syntax interface. In J. Meisel (Ed.), *The acquisition of verb placement: Functional categories and V2 phenomena in language development* (pp. 83-107). Dordrecht: Kluwer Academic Publishers.

Demuth, K. (1994). On the 'underspecification' of functional categories in early grammars. In B. Lust, M. Suñer, & J. Whitman (Eds.), *Syntactic theory and first language acquisition: Cross-linguistic perspectives.* (pp. 119-134). Hillsdale, NJ: Lawrence Erlbaum Associates.

Demuth, K. (1995). Markedness and the development of prosodic structure. *Proceedings of the NELS, 25.*

Doke, C. M., & Mofokeng, S. M. (1957). *Textbook of Southern Sotho grammar.* Cape Town: Longman.

Dresher, E., & Kaye, J. (1990). A computational learning model for metrical phonology. *Cognition, 34,* 137-195.

Echols, C., & Newport, E. (1922). The role of stress and position in determining first words. *Language Acquisition, 2,* 189-220.

Fee, E. J. (1992). *Exploring the minimal word in early phonological acquisition.* Proceedings of the 1992 Annual Conference of the Canadian Linguistics Association.

Fee, E. J., & Ingram, D. (1982). Reduplication as a strategy of phonological development. *Journal of Child Language ,9,* 41-54.

Fikkert, P. (1992, October). *The acquisition of Dutch stress.* Paper presented at the 17th Conference on Language Development, Boston University.

Fikkert, P. (1994). *On the acquisition of prosodic structure.* Unpublished doctoral dissertation, University of Leiden.

Gerken, L. A. (1991). The metrical basis of children's subjectless sentences. *Journal of Memory and Language, 30,* 431-451.

Gerken, L. A. (1994). Young children's representation of prosodic structure: Evidence from English-speakers' weak syllable omissions. *Journal of Memory and Language, 33,* 19-38.

Gerken, L. A., & McIntosh, B.(1993). The interplay of function morphemes and prosody in early language. *Developmental Psychology, 29,* 448-457.

Gleitman, L., & Wanner, E. (1982). Language acquisition: The state of the state of the art. In E. Wanner & L. Gleitman (Eds.), *Language acquisition: The state of the art* (pp. 3-48). Cambridge: Cambridge University Press.

Hayes, B. (1987). A revised parametric metrical theory. In J. McDonough & B. Plunkett (Eds.), *Proceedings of NELS 17* (pp. 274-289). Amherst, MA: Graduate Linguistic Student Association, University of Massachusetts.

Jusczyk, P., Kemler Nelson, D., Hirsh-Pasek, K., Kennedy, L., Woodward, A., & Piwoz, J. (1992). Perception of acoustic correlates of major phrasal units by young infants. *Cognitive Psychology, 24,* 252-293.

Kager, R. (1989). *A metrical theory of stressing and destressing in English and Dutch.* Dordrecht: Foris Publications.

McCarthy, J., & Prince, A. (1986). *Prosodic morphology.* Unpublished manuscript, University of Massachusetts and Brandeis University.

McCarthy, J., & Prince, A. (1990). Foot and word in prosodic morphology: The Arabic broken plural. *Natural Language and Linguistic Theory, 8,* 209-283.

McCarthy, J., & Prince, A. (1995). Prosodic morphology. In J. Goldsmith (Ed.), *Handbook of phonological theory* (pp. 318-366). Oxford, England: Blackwell.

Menyuk, P. Menn, L., & Silber, R. (1986). Early strategies for the perception and production of words and sounds. In P. Fletcher & M. Garman (Eds.), *Language acquisition* (pp. 198-222). Cambridge: Cambridge University Press.

Morgan, J. (in press). A rhythmic bias in preverbal speech segmentation. *Journal of Memory and Language.*

Nespor, M., & Vogel, I. (1986). *Prosodic phonology.* Dordrecht: Foris Publications.

Peters, A., & Menn, L. (1993). False starts and filler syllables: Ways to learn grammatical morphemes. *Language ,69,* 742-778.

Petretic, P., & Tweney, R. (1977). Does comprehension precede production? The development of children's responses to telegraphic sentences of varying grammatical adequacy. *Journal of Child Language, 4 ,* 201-209.

Prince, A. (1980). A metrical theory for Estonian quantity. *Linguistic Inquiry, 11*, 511-562.

Prince, A., & Smolensky, P. (1993). *Optimality theory: Constraint interaction in generative grammar.* Unpublished manuscript., Rutgers University, New Brunswick, NJ and University of Colorado, Boulder.

Pye, C. (1983). Mayan telegraphese: Intonational determinants of inflectional development in Quiche Mayan. *Language, 59*, 583-604.

Pye, C. (1992). The acquisition of K'iche' Maya. In D. Slobin (Ed.), *The cross-linguistic study of language acquisition,* (Vol. 3, pp. 221-308). Hillsdale, NJ: Lawrence Erlbaum Associates.

Radford, A. (1994). Tense and agreement variability in child grammars of English. In B. Lust, M. Suñer, & J. Whitman (Eds.), *Syntactic theory and first language acquisition: Cross-linguistic perspectives* (pp. 135-157). Hillsdale, NJ: Lawrence Erlbaum Associates.

Selkirk, E. (1980a). Prosodic domains in phonology: Sanskrit revisited. In M. Aranoff & M.-L. Kean (Eds.), *Juncture* (pp. 107-129). Saratoga, CA: Anma Libri.

Selkirk, E. (1980b). The role of prosodic categories in English word stress. *Linguistic Inquiry, 11*, 563-605.

Selkirk, E. (1984). *Phonology and syntax: The relation between sound and structure.* Cambridge, MA: MIT Press.

Shipley, E., Smith, C., & Gleitman, L. (1969). A study in the acquisition of language: Free responses to commands. *Language, 45*, 322-342.

van der Hulst, H. (1984). *Syllable structure and stress in Dutch.* Dordrecht: Foris Publications.

Vihman, M. (1976). From prespeech to speech: On early phonology. *Papers and Reports on Child Language Development, 12*, 230-244.

Wijnen, F., Kirkhaar, E., & den Os, E. (1994). The (non)realization of unstressed elements in children's utterances: Evidence for a rhythmic constraint. *Journal of Child Language , 21*, 59-83.

PART III

SPEECH AND THE ACQUISITION OF GRAMMATICAL MORPHOLOGY & FORM CLASSES

12 The Prosodic Structure of Function Words

Elisabeth Selkirk
University of Massachusetts, Amherst

It seems likely that all languages make a distinction between words belonging to *functional* categories and those belonging to *lexical* categories, a distinction that roughly coincides with the sets of open and closed class items. Nouns, verbs ,and adjectives constitute the class of lexical categories in English, while determiners, prepositions, auxiliaries, modals, complementizers, conjunctions, and other sorts of particles fall into the class of functional categories. The distinction between lexical and functional categories plays an important role in characterizing the syntactic properties of sentences (Abney, 1987; Chomsky, 1986; Fukui & Speas, 1986; Grimshaw, 1991; Jackendoff, 1977; Pollock, 1989).

Words belonging to functional categories display phonological properties significantly different from those of words belonging to lexical categories (Berendson, 1986; Inkelas, 1989; Kaisse, 1985; Kanerva, 1989, 1990; Nespor & Vogel, 1986; Selkirk, 1972, 1984, 1986; Zec, 1993). For example, in English, monosyllabic function words may appear in either a stressless "weak" form or a stressed "strong" form, depending on their position in the sentence, whereas a lexical category word always appears in a stressed unreduced form. In standard Serbo-Croatian, a lexical word always bears a high tone accent on one of its syllables, whereas a function word does not. In Tokyo Japanese, a function word loses its high tone accent if it is preceded by another accented word in the same phrase, but in the same circumstances a lexical word does not lose its accent. The mere fact of a systematic phonological difference between words belonging to lexical and functional categories raises the possibility that this distinction might be exploited by language learners in their acquisition of the syntactic distinction between lexical and functional categories, where what needs to be learned as the first order of business is which words are functional and which lexical. The aim of this chapter is to lay out the elements of a theory that provides some insight into the lexical–functional contrast in phonology. Such a theory can provide a framework for discussion of a possible relation between the learning of the phonology of the functional–lexical distinction in a language and the acquisition of syntax in this domain.

A phrase consisting of a sequence of lexical words (Lex)[1] in morpho-syntactic representation (S-structure) is characteristically prosodized as a sequence of prosodic words (PWd) in phonological representation (P-structure) (*lex* stands for the phonological content of Lex):

1. S-structure   [Lex Lex]
    P-structure $(\,(\,lex\,)_{PWd}\,(\,lex\,)_{PWd}\,)_{PPh}$

The PWd structure of phrases with function words, by contrast, is more various. In this chapter evidence will be presented that a function word (Fnc) may be prosodized either as a PWd, or as one of three different types of prosodic clitic. The term *prosodic clitic* will be taken to stand for a morphosyntactic word that is not itself a PWd. I argue that options in the surface prosodization of function words simply reflect the manner in which function words are organized into *prosodic words* in the sentence (see Berendsen, 1986; Inkelas, 1989; Kanerva, 1989, 1990; Selkirk, 1986; Zec, 1988, 1993; who also argue for this position). Corresponding to a syntactic phrase [Fnc Lex], for example, four different organizations into prosodic word are in principle available (*fnc* stand for the phonological content of Fnc).[2]

2. i.   Prosodic Word $(\,(\,fnc\,)_{PWd}\,(\,lex\,)_{PWd}\,)_{PPh}$
           Prosodic Clitics:
    ii.   *free clitic* $(\,fnc\,(\,lex\,)_{PWd}\,)_{PPh}$
    iii.   *internal clitic* $(\,(\,fnc\ lex\,)_{PWd}\,)_{PPh}$
    iv.   *affixal clitic* $(\,(\,fnc\,(\,lex\,)_{PWd}\,)_{PWd}\,)_{PPh}$

In (ii), the *free clitic* case, the function word is sister to PWd and daughter to phonological phrase (PPh). In (iii), where the function word is an *internal clitic*, it is dominated by the same PWd that dominates its sister lexical word. In the *affixal clitic* case, (iv), the function word is located in a nested PWd structure, both sister to PWd and dominated by PWd. The claim is that these and only these prosodic structures for function word are motivated by the facts of the two languages to be examined here—English and Serbo-Croatian.[3]

---

[1]The X-bar theory of phrase structure (Jackendoff, 1977) is assumed in this chapter. The theory distinguishes three levels of morphosyntactic category: *word*, designated by X , or simply X; *maximal projection*, designated by X^{max}; and intermediary projections, designated by X'. **Lex** designates a morphosyntactic word belonging to a lexical category, i.e., N, V, or A. **Fnc** designates a morphsyntactic word belonging to a functional category.
[2]Berendson (1986) sorts weak, clitic, function words into those incorporated into an adjacent prosodic word, type (iii) here, and those immediately dominated by a phonological phrase, type (ii) here. Neijt (1985) argues for the recursive PWd type in (iv) as a candidate structure. The Zec (1993) proposal for Serbo-Croatian presupposes all three possibilities, shown later.
[3]The claim implicit here is that accounting for the special phonological behavior of clitics does *not* require the postulation of a further prosodic constituent *clitic group* (contra Hayes, 1989; Nespor, 1993; Nespor & Vogel, 1986; Vogel, 1988). Rather the contention is that prosodic clitic is definable with respect to the category *prosodic word*, and, more specifically, that prosodic clitics fall into one of three configurations, namely the free, internal, or affixal

A goal of this chapter is to explain *why* it is that function words appear in this array of prosodic structures, and under what circumstances. I argue that whether a function word in a particular syntactic configuration in a particular language is a prosodic word or not, and if not, what type of prosodic clitic it is, depends crucially on the interaction of various well-attested types of constraints on prosodic structure. That diverse families of constraints—both morphosyntactic and phonological—contribute to defining the prosodic organization of function words lends support to the modular theory of prosodic structure expounded in work by Selkirk (1989, 1993), Selkirk and Tateishi (1988, 1991), Selkirk and Shen (1990), Prince and Smolensky (in press), and McCarthy and Prince (1993, in press). That an appeal to constraint interaction bears considerable fruit in this area lends support to optimality theory (McCarthy & Prince, 1993, in press; Prince & Smolensky, in press), which holds that the relative ranking of constraints constitutes a central aspect of grammatical description.

Constraints on Prosodic Structure

Prosodic structure theory holds that a sentence is endowed with a hierarchically organized prosodic structure that is distinct from the morphosyntactic structure of the sentence, and that phenomena of sentence phonology and phonetics are defined in terms of units of prosodic structure, not morphosyntactic structure (see Dresher, this volume, for an overview of prosodic theory). According to prosodic structure theory, in any language sentences are organized into a structure whose categories are drawn from the set defined in the Prosodic Hierarchy, as shown in (3). This hierarchy of prosodic categories forms the core of the theory of phonological constraints on prosodic structure. It is in terms of this hierarchy that certain fundamental constraints on prosodic structure are defined, as shown in (4). For ease of reference I call these *constraints on prosodic domination*. According to the Strict Layer Hypothesis (Nespor & Vogel, 1986; Selkirk, 1981, 1984) these constraints universally characterize prosodic structure. Expressed as a monolithic whole, the Strict Layer Hypothesis reads as a single constraint requiring that a prosodic constituent of level C^i immediately dominate only constituents of the next level down in the prosodic hierarchy, C^{i-1}. That the Strict Layer Hypothesis should instead be factored out into more primitive component constraints, each with an independent status in the grammar, is argued by Inkelas (1989) and Itô and Mester (1992). The set of constraints on prosodic domination given earlier constitutes just such a decomposition of the Strict Layering.

clitic structures, all distinguishable in terms of domination and sisterhood relations defined with respect to PWd. To defend the clitic group hypothesis it must be shown that there exist relevant phenomena that *cannot* be insightfully accounted for by assuming one of these three PWd-based structures for prosodic clitics.

3. *Prosodic Hierarchy*

Utt	Utterance
IP	intonational phrase
PPh	phonological phrase
PWd	prosodic word
Ft	foot
σ	syllable

4. *Constraints on Prosodic Domination*

(where C^n = some prosodic category)

Layeredness

No C^i dominates a C^j, $j > i$,
   e.g. "No σ dominates a Ft."

Headedness

Any C^i must dominate a C^{i-1} (except if $C^i = \sigma$),
   e.g. "A PWd must dominate a Ft."

Exhaustivity

No C^i immediately dominates a constituent C^j, $j < i-1$,
   e.g. "No PWd immediately dominates a σ."

Nonrecursivity

No C^i dominates C^j, $j = i$,
   e.g. "No Ft dominates a Ft."

Layeredness and Headedness, which together embody the essence of the Strict Layer Hypothesis, appear to be properties that hold universally, in all phonological representations. In optimality theoretic terms the inviolability of these constraints implies that they are undominated in the constraint ranking of every language. Exhaustivity and Nonrecursivity, on the other hand, turn out not to hold of all instances of P-structure. For example, it has been widely observed that there exist cases where a syllable is immediately dominated by a prosodic word, in violation of Exhaustivity (see, e.g., Hayes, 1995; Inkelas, 1989; Itô & Mester, 1994; Kager, 1989, 1993; Kanerva, 1989; McCarthy & Prince, 1991, 1993, in press; Mester, 1993; Prince & Smolensky in press). The inviolability of Nonrecursivity has been challenged as well (Inkelas, 1989; Ladd, 1986, 1992; McCarthy & Prince, 1993, in press). Later I present additional evidence in favor of viewing Nonrecursivity and Exhaustivity as constraints on prosodic structure that may be violated. In particular, free clitics (cf. (2-ii)) violate Exhaustivity-with-respect-to-Phonological Phrase (Exh$_{PPh}$) and affixal clitics (cf. (2-iv)) violate Nonrecursivity-with-respect-to-Prosodic Word (NonRec$_{PWd}$).

The class of constraints on prosodic domination constitute one central class of constraints on prosodic structure. Another significant class is constituted by *constraints on alignment* of edges of constituents (McCarthy & Prince, 1993, in press; Selkirk, 1986 et seq.). Selkirk (1986 et seq.) argued that the relation between syntactic structure and prosodic structure is to be captured by constraints on the alignment of the two structures, ones that require that, for any constituent of category α in syntactic structure, its R (or L) edge coincides with the edge of a constituent of category β in prosodic structure:

5. *Edge-based theory of the syntax-prosody interface*
   Right/Left edge of $\alpha \rightarrow$ edge of β,
   α is a syntactic category, β is a prosodic category

Edge-alignment constraints of this type have been shown to allow an insightful characterization of the influence of sentential phrase structure on prosodic structure in a wide array of languages and have been argued to play a role in characterizing the influence of word-internal structure on prosodic structure as well (see, e.g., Cohn, 1989; Kang, 1992a, 1992b; McCarthy & Prince, 1993, in press; Myers, 1987; Rice, 1991). In recent work, McCarthy and Prince (1993, in press) argued that the notion of edge alignment should be generalized; they showed that a remarkable range of phonological phenomena yield to analysis in terms not only of constraints on grammatical structure–prosodic structure alignment but also in terms of constraints on the alignment of edges of various sorts of prosodic entities within phonological representation. McCarthy and Prince (1993) enlarge the class of alignment constraints to include constraints of the following general types:

6. *Generalized alignment*
   Align (αCat, E; βCat, E)
   a. Align (GCat, E; PCat, E)
   b. Align (PCat, E; GCat, E)
   c. Align (PCat, E; PCat, E)
   (GCat ranges over morphological and syntactic categories;
   PCat ranges over the prosodic categories; E = Right or Left.)

These all state: "For any αCat in the representation, align its edge (R,L) with the edge (R,L) of some βCat." I show that alignment constraints of the various subclasses defined here arguably play a role in the characterization of the prosodic structure of function words.

A central concern in this chapter, then, is the alignment of words in morphosyntactic representation with the prosodic words of phonological representation. It is here that the morphosyntactic distinction between function words and lexical words comes into play. My proposal, one that echoes the position taken in Selkirk (1984, 1986) and Selkirk and Shen (1990), is that *the set of constraints governing the interface between morphosyntactic and prosodic structure makes no reference to functional categories at all*. Rather, it is only lexical categories and their phrasal projections that would figure in the statement of morphosyntactic constraints on prosodic structure; GCat would stand only for "LexCat" in any constraint of the Align (GCat;PCat) variety. The proposed form of the constraints that align grammatical words with prosodic words is accordingly as in (7); it is the restriction of word alignment constraints to lexical category words that is responsible for the availability of prosodic clitic analyses for function words.

7. *Word Alignment Constraints (WdCon)*
    i. Align (Lex, L; PWd, L)   (= WdConL)
    ii. Align (Lex, R; PWd, R)   (= WdConR)

The generalized alignment theory also sanctions word-level alignment constraints of the Align (PCat; GCat) type in (8), where the category types are reversed:

8. *Prosodic Word Alignment Constraints (PWdCon)*
    i. Align (PWd, L; Lex, L)   (= PWdConL)
    ii. Align (PWd, R; Lex, R)   (= PWdConR)

The PWdCon constraints say that, for any PWd in the representation, its L (or R) edge must coincide with the L (or R) edge of some Lex. A representation in which *both* were respected would contain no function word that itself had the status of a prosodic word. Thus, the PWdCon constraints form part of the explanation for the fact that function words typically do not have the status of PWd.

Summarizing briefly, the analysis of function word prosodization to be offered in what follows gives crucial roles to constraints on prosodic structure from two well-known families: constraints on prosodic domination such as Exhausitivity and Nonrecursivity, and constraints on the alignment of prosodic structure and morphosyntactic structure such as WdCon and PWdCon. The precise manner in which these constraints are ranked in the grammar of a particular language provides the basis for explaining which of the variety of function word prosodizations is realized in a particular morphosyntactic configuration in that language.

Constraint Ranking and Optimality Theory

Optimality theory (McCarthy & Prince, in press; Prince & Smolensky, in press) understands the phonological component of a language to consist of a set of constraints on surface phonological representation. The grammatical output representation corresponding to a particular underlying input representation is that representation (out of all the candidate representations generable on the basis of that input) that best satisfies the constraint system of the language. Constraints on representation are assumed to be *violable*. The violability of a constraint is hypothesized to be a function of the *ranking* of the constraint with respect to other constraints. The grammar of a language will stipulate a ranking of constraints. Thus a grammatical output representation is not necessarily well formed with respect to all the relevant constraints, rather it is the best-formed, or *optimal*, representation evaluated with respect to the other candidate representations that are generable on the basis of the input.

Optimality theory assumes the constraints at play in grammars to be universal (with certain limited parameterizations available). Differences between languages or dialects are claimed to be reducible to language-particular differences in the ranking of the constraints. The task of a language learner, then, is to learn the constraint hierarchy of a particular language, the substance of the constraints being universally given. Tesar and Smolensky (1993) demonstrated that the learning of a constraint hierarchy is in principle a tractable enterprise.

WEAK AND STRONG FORMS OF FUNCTION WORDS IN ENGLISH

In English, a large number of the monosyllabic function words— prepositions, determiners, complementizers, auxiliary verbs, personal pronouns— may appear in either a "weak" (i.e., stressless and reduced) or a "strong" (i.e., stressed and unreduced) form (Berendsen, 1986; Gimson, 1970; Jones, 1964; Kaisse, 1985; Selkirk, 1972, 1984; Sweet, 1891, 1908; Zwicky, 1970). This simple fact presents a challenge to any theory of syntax-phonology interaction: It needs to be explained why, in the same language, function words appear with different surface prosodizations. What I show is that these different surface prosodizations result from different underlying input structures, and that one and the same English-particular ranking of constraints is responsible for deriving the variety of surface prosodic structures attested.

Pronounced in isolation, function words appear in strong form and are indistinguishable stress-wise and vowel quality-wise from monosyllabic lexical category items:

9. for   [fɚr]   four
    can   [kæn]   (tin) can
    him   [hɪm]   hymn
    at   [æt]   hat

Strong forms also appear when the function word is focused (see "Focused Fnc"), and when it is phrase-final (see "Final Fnc"). Weak forms appear when the function word is nonfocused and not phrase-final (see "Nonfinal Fnc"), and also when phrase-final but object of a verb or preposition (see "Morphosyntactic Enclitic Fnc"). In their weak form(s), illustrated in (10), monosyllabic Fnc words display the properties of stressless syllables: Vowel reduction, appearance of syllabic sonorants, loss of onset *h*, etc.[4].

---

[4]Not all monosyllabic function words are able to appear in weak form (e.g., *up, too, off*). I assume that those that do alternate between weak and strong forms receive foot status as a result of constraints on surface representation. Invariably strong formed function words, I assume, are already footed in the input to the phonological component. This implies there is no defooting possible.

It is also true that not all weak forms are derivable through regular phonological phenomena like vowel reduction or *h* loss (cf. Kaisse, 1985; Zwicky, 1970, 1977). A certain

11. She spoke AT the microphone not WITH it.
    Bettina CAN speak, but refuses to.
    We need HER, not HIM.

10. fŏr	[fr̩]	for Timothy	(cf. fertility)
căn	[kən], [kn̩], [km̩]	can pile	(cf. compile)
hĭm	[ɪm], [m̩]	need him	(cf. Needham)
ăt	[ət]	at home	(cf. atone)

Prosodic theory analyzes stressed syllables as the prominent or only syllable of the prosodic constituent *foot*. Thus, the strong forms of monosyllabic function words in English have the status of a head of a foot and the weak forms do not. The foot-head status of strong forms is in most instances the consequence of the assignment of Prosodic Word status to the Fnc. Weak forms, by contrast, are prosodic clitics.

Focused Fnc

When focused, a function word always appears in strong form, as in (11). It is a fact that, whether a Fnc or a Lex, a focused word is assigned a pitch accent in the morphosyntactic structure of the sentence in English (cf. Pierrehumbert, 1980; Selkirk, 1984). The presence of that pitch accent is arguably responsible for the strong form of focused Fnc. It has been widely observed that pitch accents in English are associated only with stressed syllables (Hayes, 1995; Ladd, 1980; Liberman, 1975; Pierrehumbert, 1980, 1993; Selkirk, 1984).

12. *Association of Pitch Accent (AssocPA)*
    A pitch accent associates to (aligns with) a stressed syllable (i.e. the head of a foot).

Such a constraint guarantees that the pitch accent that is assigned to a word in morphosyntactic representation will never be realized on a stressless syllable in prosodic structure, and thus rules out *ASSign, *strucTURE, *PROsodic, *foCUS. Compare the grammatical forms as-SIGN, STRUCture, proSODic, FOcus, which respect this constraint. This same constraint explains why the morphosyntactic assignment of a pitch accent to a monosyllabic function word entails the strong form foot-head status of *fnc* in P-structure. For a syllable to carry stress it must be the head of a Foot. Thus the presence of pitch accent in the input structure in effect induces the presence of the prosodic structure required in order for the constraint AssocPA to be satisfied in English:

13. [can]$_{Mod}$ →   (*can*)$_{Ft}$
    | |
    H*   AssocPA   H*

---

amount of allomorphy may have to be appealed to, sensitive to the prosodic status of the function word as foot-head, PWd or stressless syllable.

The proposal, then, is that the strong form of a function word that is in focus is called for by an independently required constraint on the relation between tonal structure and prosodic structure. The surface form of a nonfocused function word, by contrast, arguably results from the interplay of constraints on prosodic domination and constraints on the alignment of morphosyntactic and prosodic structure.

Fnc in Isolation

A function word uttered in isolation appears in strong form, cf. (9). Its foot-head status falls out immediately from the basic prosodic structure principle of Headedness. An isolation pronunciation is an utterance; an utterance is analyzed at the highest level of prosodic structure, the prosodic category Utterance (Utt). Assuming the Prosodic Hierarchy in (3), by Headedness, Utt must dominate an Intonational Phrase (IP), IP must dominate a Phonological Phrase (PPh), a PPh must dominate a PWd, and a PWd a Ft, hence the strong form of the isolation pronunciation of a monosyllabic Fnc:

14. $((((((\text{fnc})_\sigma)_{\text{Ft}})_{\text{PWd}})_{\text{PPh}})_{\text{IP}})_{\text{Utt}}$

Note that this representation violates PWdCon, the pair of constraints that require that for every L/R edge of PWd in P-structure there is a L/R edge of some Lex in S-structure. Given an optimality-theoretic approach, the violation of PWdCon is ascribed to the higher ranking of Headedness in the constraint hierarchy. Indeed, since Headedness is a defining property of prosodic structure, it may be considered to be inviolable, more highly ranked than any other violable constraint.

15. Headedness >> ... >> PWdCon ...

Quite generally, the inviolability of Headedness makes the prediction that any word pronounced in isolation would have the prosodic properties of entities at all the levels of the Prosodic Hierarchy. This prediction appears to be borne out in English and elsewhere.

Nonfinal Fnc

It is a fact that, in the absence of pitch accent, the prosodic structure of a Fnc word correlates with the position in which that Fnc is embedded in the sentence. A Fnc followed by a Lex within the same syntactic phrase standardly appears in weak form:

16. Diane *căn* paint *hĕr* portrait *ŏf* Timothy *ăt* home.
    Bŭt shĕ found *thăt thĕ* weather *wăs* too hot *fŏr* painting.

I will assume that such Fnc-Lex sequences appear in the phrase structure configuration in (17a), one in which the function word heads a functional phrase FncP within which it is followed by a phrase LexP that is itself headed by Lex. The structures in (17b) and (17c) are representative examples.

17.   a. FncP   b. MP   c. DP

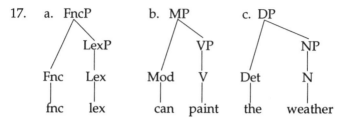

It is on the basis of such inputs, then, that the grammar of constraints on prosodic structure must derive the weak prosodic clitic form of the function word in the output.

As pointed out earlier, there are in principle a number of different prosodic structures in which a function word in structures like (17) may appear. So the first question to be addressed here is an empirical one. Which prosodic structure correctly represents the structure of English non-phrase-final weak function words like these?   The candidates in (18a–d) represent the four different possible organizations of function words into PWd given in (2). They have in common that the function word has the representation of a stressless syllable (one that does not head a foot).

18.   a.   PPh   b.   PPh   c.   PPh   d.   PPh

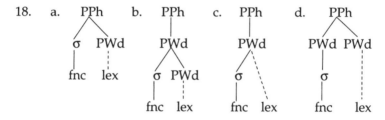

In (18a) *fnc* is a free clitic; in (18b) it is an affixal clitic; in (18c) it is an internal clitic; and in (18d) it is a prosodic word.

(18d) violates the inviolable constraint Headedness, which calls for every PWd to dominate at least one Ft, and therefore is excluded. Note that if *fnc* in (18d) were also to be a foot, in accordance with Headedness, then it would have the status of a stressed syllable, contrary to fact. So (18d) is not a possible prosodization for a weak form Fnc.

Neither is (18c) a possible representation of non-phrase-final stressless monosyllabic function words. In this representation, that of an internal clitic, *fnc* and *lex* are dominated by the same, single, PWd. This representation implies that a Fnc-Lex combination should display phonological behavior identical to that of PWd constituted of a single Lex alone, and this is arguably not correct. It is a well-known fact about patterns of English stress that at most one stressless syllable may occur at the left edge of a Lex:

19. mǎsságe   Màssǎchúsĕtts, *Mǎssǎchúsĕtts
    tĕnácity   Ténnĕssée, *Tĕnnĕssée
    tĕlĕpathy   tèlĕpáthic, *tĕlĕpáthic

McCarthy and Prince (1993) suggested that this fact argues for the existence of an alignment constraint of the Align (PCat; PCat) variety, whereby the left edge of any PWd is required to coincide with the left edge of a Foot:

20. Align (PWd, L; Ft, L)

Assuming on the basis of the evidence in (19) that this constraint goes unviolated as long as the initial syllable(s) of a PWd can indeed be organized into a well-formed foot, it follows that non-phrase-final function words do not have the structure of (18c). This is because sequences of stressless syllables made up wholly or in part by non-phrase-final function words are systematically possible, in violation of (20). Therefore, (18c) is not a possible representation for a non-phrase-final Fnc.

21. i. ǎ méssage   ǎ mǎsságe
        fŏr cónferences   fŏr cŏnvérsions
        hĕr áptitude   hĕr ǎbílities
        cǎn pérch   cǎn pĕrtúrb
    ii. fŏr ǎ méssage   fŏr ǎ mǎsságe
        ŏr fŏr cónferences   ŏr fŏr cŏnvérsions
        ǎt hĕr áptitude   ǎt hĕr ǎbílities
        yŏu cǎn pérch   yŏu cǎn pĕrtúrb

In contrast, either of the representations (18a) or (18b) would allow for sequences of stressless syllables such as those in (21) without incurring a violation of constraint (20). In (18a), the *fnc* is not PWd-initial, and hence would not be subject to the constraint Align (PWd, L; Ft, L) in the first place. In (18b), the *fnc* is PWd-initial, but so is any syllable that follows it (because of the recursive PWd structure there). In this case no Ft could dominate the two, because the resulting structure would not constitute a well-formed bracketing. This means that positing (18b) would not lead to the prediction that the *fnc* should be stressed if followed by a stressless syllable. What further empirical considerations, then, might decide between these two remaining structures?

Initial position in PWd is often associated with effects involving the phonetic realization of segments. In English, a word-initial voiceless stop is aspirated, even when the syllable to which it belongs is stressless.

22. grow t^homatoes, grow p^hetunias, grow c^halendula

Cooper (1991, 1994) showed that there is a distinct word-initial aspiration effect (one that cannot be reduced to a simple syllable-initial effect).
Prosodic structure theory takes such "word-initial" effects to be a PWd-
initial effects. It is significant, therefore, that aspiration does not appear
to be attested in initial position in weak non-phrase-final function
words, as shown among other things, by the appearance of the flapped
version of /t/ (impossible in word-initial position):

> 23. They grow *to* the sky. So *can* delphiniums. Take Grey *to* Lon-
> don.

It can therefore be concluded that function words in this position do not
initiate PWds, as (18b) would have it, and instead that they are immediately dominated by PPh, as in (18a), and illustrated here[5]:

24.

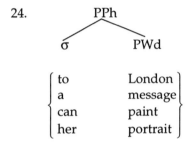

to	London
a	message
can	paint
her	portrait

The next question to ask, the analytical one, is *why* it is (18a) rather
than one of the set (18b-d), that is the optimal (grammatical) representation of non-phrase-final function words in English. It is here that optimality theory comes crucially into play. Note that *all* of the representations in (18a-d) violate *some* constraint. (25) lists the representations and
the constraints they violate:

25.   Output representation   Constraint violated

  i. PPh(fnc PWd(lex)PWd)PPh   *ExhPPh*
                                          [since PPh immediately domi-
                                          nates σ]

 ii. PPh(PWd(fnc PWd(lex)PWd)PWd)PPh *NonRecPWd*
                                          [since PWd dominates PWd]

---

[5]A small subset of English monosyllabic function words, the ones written as orthographic
'contractions', e.g. *Mary's coming, Nina's left, I'll leave too, I'd like to stay,* behave as if they
are enclitic to the preceding word (Inkelas, 1989; Kaisse, 1985; Klavans, 1985), rather than
proclitic to the Lex in the following PPh, as the account given here would predict. It is an
interesting fact that these contracted forms are only possible if they are *not* phrase-final
(see Selkirk, 1984). The atypical prosodic encliticization that they display must somehow
reflect this fact. For now, this remains a puzzle.

iii. $_{PPh}(_{PWd}($ fnc lex $)_{PWd})_{PPh}$ *WdCon, PWdCon*

[WdCon since L edge of Lex not
aligned with L edge of some PWd;
PWdCon since L edge of PWd not
aligned with L edge of some Lex]

iv. $_{PPh}(_{PWd}($ fnc $)_{PWd\ PWd}($ lex $)_{PWd})_{PPh}$ *PWdCon* (twice)

[since L and R edges of the
lefthand PWd not aligned with
L/R edges of some Lex]

I showed earlier that the optimal output representation is (18i/25i), which violates Exh_{PPh}. Optimality theory holds that constraints on phonological representation are violable. That is, the grammatical, optimal, prosodic output representation that the constraint hierarchy of a grammar defines based on a particular morphosyntactic input representation may violate some constraint. Such surface violations in an optimal output form are claimed to occur under two circumstances: (i) when the alternative, nonoptimal, output representations that could be constructed (based on the same input) violate a constraint that is higher ranked than the constraint violated in the optimal representation, or (ii) when the alternative candidates contain *more* violations of the same constraint, or of some other same-ranked constraint(s). Within the context of optimality theory, then, the fact that the free clitic candidate, which incurs a single violation of Exh_{PPh}, is the optimal one rather than the affixal clitic candidate, which incurs a single violation of $NonRec_{PWd}$, indicates that the $NonRec_{PWd}$ is higher ranked than Exh_{PPh}.

26. $NonRec_{PWd} \gg Exh_{PPh}$

(This in itself is an interesting result, further evidence for the decomposition of the Strict Layer Hypothesis into the different constraints on prosodic domination.) As for the ranking of Exh_{PPh} with respect to WdCon and PWdCon, it may be concluded at this point that it is *not* higher ranked than either of the two (if it were, an output violating Exh_{PPh} would not be the optimal one). However, whether Exh_{PPh} occupies the same rank as WdCon or PWdCon, or whether it is lower ranked than them cannot be ascertained at this point. This is because the other nonoptimal candidates—the internal clitic and the affixal clitic— each incurs multiple violations of constraints other than Exh_{PPh}. Additional cases will have to be scrutinized in order to determine the precise ranking of Exh_{PPh} with respect to WdCon and PWdCon. I turn to these now.

Final Fnc

Consider next the case of monosyllabic Fnc appearing in phrase-final position. The italicized function words in (27) appear in strong form, and cannot appear in the weak form they may adopt when not phrase-final.

27. I can eat more than Sara *cán*.   [kæn], *[kən], *[kn̩]
    If you think you *cán*, go ahead and do it.
    I don't know whether Ray *ís*.   [ɪz], *[z]
    Wherever Ray *ís*, he's having a good time.
    What did you look *át* yesterday?   [æt], *[ət]
    Who did you do it *fór* that time?   [fɔr], *[fr̩]

Given that they are stressed, these monosyllables have at least the status of a foot, i.e. $((fnc)_s)_{Ft}$. Further evidence suggests that phrase-final Fnc elements are final in a PWd. The evidence comes from the behavior of intrusive *r* in the Eastern Massachusetts dialect described by McCarthy (1991, 1993).

Intrusive *r* is inserted after a word-final low vowel when the following word begins with a vowel. Significantly, McCarthy shows, intrusive *r* appears in just two contexts: at the right edge of Lex, (28i-a), and at the right edge of a phrase-final Fnc, (28i-b). It never appears at the right edge of non-phrase-final Fnc, (28ii).[6]

28.
   i. *Presence of Intrusive r*
      a. After Lex
         The spa-r is broken.   saw-r-ing
         He put the tuna-r on the table.   rumba-r-ing
         The boat'll yaw-r a little.   guffaw-r-ing
      b. After phrase-final Fnc (compare to examples in (ii))
         I said I was gonna-r and I did.
         Did you-r, or didn't you.
  ii. *Lack of Intrusive r after non-phrase-final Fnc*
      a. Modal + reduced *have*
         should have, could have, might have
         He shoulda eaten already.   [šudə(*r) ij?ən]
      b. Fnc-like verbs + reduced *to*
         going to, ought to, have to, got to, used to, supposed to
         I'm gonna ask Adrian.   [gənə(*r) æsk]
      c. Auxiliary + reduced *you*
         did you, should you, would you, could you
         Did you answer him?   [dɪdžə(*r) ænsər ɪm]
      d. Reduced *to, do, of*
         To add to his troubles   [tə(*r) æd tə(*r) ɪz trəbəlz]
         Why do Albert and you   [waj də(*r) ælbət ən juw]
         A lotta apples   [ə latə(*r) æpəlz]

The McCarthy analysis is that PWd-final position defines the locus of intrusive *r* insertion. This analysis assumes, and at the same time gives crucial support for, the generalization that a phrase-final function word

---

[6]This table of facts is due to McCarthy (1991, 1993) and a 1994 lecture handout.

is PWd-final. An additional set of examples shows that a phrase-final Fnc is preceded by a PWd as well:

29. It's more scary than a subpoena-r is.
    What did they convict Wanda-r of?
    That's nothing to guffaw-r at!

The appearance of intrusive *r* at the end of the lexical word preceding the phrase-final fnc indicates that the *lex* is PWd final.

This evidence from intrusive *r* is consistent with two possible surface prosodic structures for phrase-final *fnc*: $(lex)_{PWd}$ $(fnc)_{PWd}$, in which the *fnc* is a PWd on its own, and $((lex)_{PWd} fnc)_{PWd}$, in which the *fnc* is located in a nested PWd structure. In both cases the phrase-final *fnc* is PWd-final, and so is the preceding *lex*. But only the analysis of the *fnc* as a PWd itself will explain why it is always stressed. By assuming that the fnc *is a* PWd (rather than just as the end of one), its stressedness simply falls out from Headedness, which entails its Foot-head status. Thus, I conclude that phrase-final Fnc has PWd status.

The question then is *why* phrase-final function words have the status of PWd, in violation of PWdCon. Why aren't they simply one of the variety of prosodic clitics that are in principle available? In particular, why aren't they free clitics, just like the non-phrase-final *fnc* are? This is what the grammar as currently constituted would predict. Explaining the asymmetry in the prosodic status of phrase-final and non-phrase-final Fnc will therefore require appeal to some constraint(s) that have not yet had a crucial role to play. I believe the relevant constraints concern prosodic structure at the level of the phonological phrase.

It has often been observed that phonological phrase breaks typically occur at the edges of morphosyntactic phrases. Investigation of the sentence phonology of a variety of languages has led to the conclusion that there are alignment constraints requiring that the Right, or Left, edge of a maximal phrasal projection coincide with the edge of a phonological phrase (PPh). More specifically, the phrasal alignment appears to be defined with respect to Lex^{max}, the maximal phrase projected from a Lex (Selkirk & Shen, 1990). These constraints are expressed in the generalized alignment format as (30):

30. a. Align (Lex^{max}, R; PPh, R)
    b. Align (Lex^{max}, L; PPh, L)

They state that the right (resp. left) edge of any Lex^{max} in morphosyntactic structure coincides with the right (resp. left) edge of some phonological phrase in prosodic structure. The two constraints, available universally, must be independently rankable, for it has been shown that languages may show either predominantly right edge or left edge effects. As for English, the PWd status of phrase-final Fnc suggests very strongly that the constraint (30a) calling for the alignment of a PPh edge with the right edge of a maximal projection is higher ranked than any of the other constraints under consideration.[7]

Assuming that Align (Lex^{max}; PPh) is for all intents and purposes an undominated constraint in English, this means any element that is final in a morphosyntactic phrase will also be final in a phonological phrase. The sentence in (31a), with its morphosyntactic phrase-final Fnc *át*, will be parsed into phonological phrases as in (31b) in all of the candidate output representations, putting *át* in PPh-final position.

31. a. [What did you $_{VP}$[look $_{PP}$[at___]$_{PP}$]$_{VP}$ last time]
    b. $_{PPh}$(What did you look át)$_{PPh}$ $_{PPh}$(last time)$_{PPh}$

Observe that the candidates for the output representation of *look at* that satisfy Align (Lex^{max}; PPh), as well as Headedness, include the structures shown in (32).

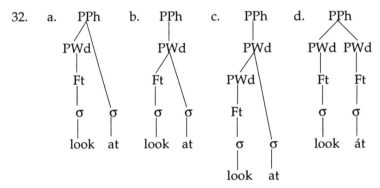

An explanation for the non-optimality of the free clitic case in (32a) now suggests itself, namely that there is a constraint that calls for the right edge of a PPh to be aligned with the right edge of a PWd, and that it is violated in candidate (a). This is just the sort of constraint that alignment theory claims will be typically seen to play a role in grammars, a constraint of the Align (PCat; PCat) family:

33. Align (PPh, R; PWd, R)

If unviolated, this constraint ensures that, given the presence of a PPh edge after *át* (itself called for by Align [Lex^{max}, R; PPh, R]), there must be also a PWd edge after *át*. It excludes the free clitic candidate (a), and provides the basis for an explanation for the asymmetry between

---

[7]Independent evidence for or against this right-edge alignment of phonological and syntactic phrases in English will most likely come from phenomena involving intonation or durational patterns, which are argued to be characterized in terms of phrase-sized units of prosodic structure (cf. Beckman & Pierrehumbert, 1986; Beckman & Edwards, 1990; Shattuck-Hufnagel, Ostendorf & Ross,1994).

phrase-final and non-phrase-final prosodizations in English. The ordering of Align (Lex^{max}; PPh) and Align (PPh;PWd) above Exh$_{PPh}$ is all that it takes to render the free clitic candidate non-optimal:

34. Align (Lex^{max}; PPh), Align (PPh;PWd) >> Exh$_{PPh}$

The assumption of these phrasal alignment constraints and the constraint hierarchy in (34) does not, however, provide an explanation for why the optimal candidate is (d), rather than the affixal or internal clitic candidates (b-c), since in them *at* is also PWd-final in PPh. But the explanation is readily available. In order that (d) be chosen instead of (b,c) one need only assume that WdCon and NonRec$_{PWd}$ are ranked higher than PWdCon:

35. WdCon, NonRec$_{PWd}$ >> PWdCon

(Recall that no ranking amongst these constraints was earlier established.) The optimality theoretic ranking of WdCon above PWdCon means that the candidate violating WdCon, (b), is "less well formed" than the candidate violating PWdCon, (d). ((b) violates WdCon since there is no PWd edge at the right edge of *look*.) And the ranking of NonRec$_{PWd}$ above PWdCon rules (c) "less well formed" than (d). (The nested PWd structure of (c) violates NonRec$_{PWd}$.) So despite the violations of PWdCon seen in it, (d) is the "best formed" candidate relative to the others, that is, the optimal one.

The assumptions about constraint rankings that have been posited thus far are consistent with each other, and give the amalgamated ranking in (36):

36. Align Lex^{max}, Align PPh >> WdCon, NonRec$_{PWd}$ >> PWdCon, Exh$_{PPh}$

(This ranking mentions only constraints that are assumed to be violable. A full ranking statement would include Headedness and Layeredness, universally undominated constraints, at the left extreme.)

Morphosyntactic Enclitic Fnc?

Object pronouns present a special case: They may appear either in strong form or in weak form (cf. Selkirk, 1972, 1984). There are pronunciations of verb plus object pronoun, for example, in which the phonetic realization of the pronoun and its rhythmic adherence to the verb is identical to that of a word-final stressless syllable.

37.   need him, them   ≅   Needham   [nid m̩]
       will it   ≅   billet   [bɪlɨt]
       gimme (give me)   ≅   Jimmy   [ʤɪmi]
       see you   ≅   Mia   [mijə]

Such a pronunciation is not necessary, however. Pronouns in the locu-
tions in (37a) may also be pronounced in strong form (e.g., *hím* [hɪm],
thém [ðɛm], *ít* [ɪt], *mé* [mij], *yóu* [juw]). The appearance of these phrase-
final pronouns in strong form is what is expected, given the constraint
hierarchy posited thus far, if it is assumed that in the input morphosyntactic representation the pronoun has the status of a phrasal object of the
verb, as in (38a).

38.   a.
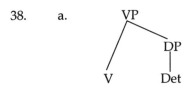

       b.   ((need)$_{PWd}$ (him)$_{PWd}$)$_{PPh}$
       c.   ((need)$_{PWd}$ 'm)$_{PWd}$

Given this input, the constraint hierarchy predicts the prosodic structure
in (38b), where the pronoun is a PWd on its own, hence a Foot, hence
stressed and in unreduced strong form, just like stranded *át* in *look át*.
However, the weak form option that the pronouns may display in (37)
indicates that in this case they do not, on their own, have the status of
PWd. Rather, the reduced object pronouns arguably have the status of
affixal clitics, situated in a nested PWd structure as in (38c).

Intrusive *r* facts show that a reduced object pronoun that is phrase-
final is indeed final in a PWd[8]:

39.   I saw ya-r and asked about it
       If I see ya-r, I'll ignore ya.
       I'll see ya-r if I get done on time.

Moreover, a low-vowel-final verb before a vowel-initial weak object
pronoun shows intrusive *r*, indicating that a PWd boundary follows it
and precedes the pronoun:

40.   saw-r us, withdraw-r it, subpoena-r him

The evidence thus points to a nested PWd structure for reduced object
pronouns.[9] The task, then, is to explain why it is that object pronouns

---

[8]These examples were provided by John McCarthy.
[9]The fact that in double pronoun object constructions one finds no intrusive *r* after reduced *you* (*give ya it* NOT **give ya-r it*) suggests that the two pronoun clitics are sisters in
prosodic structure: ((give)$_{PWd}$ ya it)$_{PWd}$.

have the option of appearing in either one of these two different prosodic structure configurations.   What is it that is special about object
pronouns that allows them these options?

Consider the hypothesis that what is special about object pronouns
in English is captured in the morphosyntactic component of the grammar.   In quite a variety of other languages, including the Romance languages and Arabic, object pronouns are taken to form a constituent with
the verb, that is, they are morphosyntactic clitics. Suppose now that this
morphosyntactic clitic analysis were *optionally* available for object pronouns in English:

41.

```
              V
            /   \
          V      Pro
          |       |
        need     him
```

It is easy to see why such an input structure, with its nesting of constituents of category type Lex, would give rise to a nested PWd structure in
the output of the phonology. Such an output would simply respect the
alignment constraint WdCon, which calls for a right (resp. left) PWd
edge at every right (resp. left) Lex edge in the morphosyntactic input
representation. A constraint ranking of WdCon higher than $NonRec_{Pwd}$
would therefore explain why the latter constraint is violated in the prosodic affixal clitic output. Note that in the constraint ranking (36) that I
arrived at on the basis of earlier evidence, WdCon and $NonRec_{PWd}$ occupy the same niche in the constraint hierarchy. This is because their
relative ordering was immaterial in accounting for the earlier data.   If
the constraint hierarchy were modified as in (42), so that WdCon now
dominates $NonRec_{PWd}$,

42. Align Lex^{max}, Align PPh >> WdCon >> $NonRec_{PWd}$ >> PWdCon, Exh_{PPh}

not only would the account of the earlier data be retained, but it would
also be possible to derive the nested PWd structure from the nested
verb structure in (41) as well.

The fact that the minimally modified grammar of constraints in (42)
can derive the variant forms of object pronouns simply by assuming
that the morphosyntax generates both structure (38) and (41) for object
pronouns makes this approach to the object pronoun options in English
quite appealing. Of course, confirmation of these assumptions about the
morphosyntactic input based on an independent morphosyntactic
analysis of English object pronoun constructions would be required before committing to this solution.[10]

---

[10]One important fact that a morphosyntactic clitic analysis of object pronouns would have
to confront is the apparent restriction to intrusive *r* after reduced *you* to VP-final positions:

An alternative approach to accounting for the specialness of object pronouns would assume a single morphosyntactic object pronoun structure in the input to the phonology, presumably the phrasal object structure, and ascribe the options in surface prosodization to the constraint system of the phonological component, suitably revised. A constraint would be required that ruled out strong form pronouns, say *(Pro)$_{PWd}$, and its ranking would have to be such that both options in prosodization would be ruled optimal (J. McCarthy, personal communication). It turns out that assigning *(Pro)$_{PWd}$ the same ranking as NonRec$_{PWd}$ in the constraint hierarchy given in the revised ranking (42) has precisely the consequence that phrase-final object pronouns would have the prosodic options they do: One option violates NonRec$_{PWd}$, the other violates *(Pro)$_{PWd}$, but they are both equally wellformed with respect to the other constraints.[11]

In any case, what is clear about phrase-final object pronouns is that they may appear with two different surface prosodizations: as a prosodic clitic of the affixal variety or, like other phrase-final function words, as a prosodic word. And it is clear that, in some way, the grammar must single out pronouns from other functional elements. Deciding between the two alternative approaches sketched here will have to await further research.

Summary

To sum up, I have adduced evidence for three different prosodic structures for function words in English, (43b). These different prosodizations may be ascribed to differences in the morphosyntactic inputs, (43a):

43.

a.

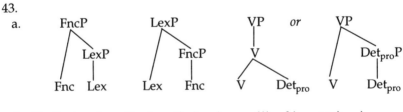

b. (fnc(lex)$_{PWd}$)$_{PPh}$ ((lex)$_{PWd}$(fnc)$_{PWd}$)$_{PPh}$ (((verb)$_{PWd}$pro)$_{PWd}$)$_{PPh}$
    free clitic   prosodic word   affixal clitic

Given the different inputs, the grammar of constraints, organized in the hierarchy of domination argued for previously, derives these outputs.

I'll get ya(*r) another one.
I'll call ya(*r) up.
We saw ya(*r) on TV.
[11]Note that adopting a solution based on a constraint like *(Pro)$_{PWd}$ would require a weakening of the claim put forward here that constraints on the alignment of morphosyntactic structure and prosodic structure do not refer to functional categories.

The optimality theoretic hypothesis is that the constraints are universal, but the hierarchical ordering of constraints is not. With modifications in the constraint hierarchy, different pairings of morphosyntactic input and prosodic output would be derivable.

ACCENT AND PROSODIC WORD IN SERBO-CROATIAN

Because languages may differ in constraint ordering, it is predicted that in different languages (or dialects) an identical morphosyntactic input structure may give rise to different optimal prosodic structure outputs. Illustration of this is provided by the three NeoŠtokavian (NŠ) dialects of Serbo-Croatian analyzed by Zec (1993), who argued that dialect differences in the realization of tonal word accents in the same morphosyntactic environment reflect systematic differences in the organization of function words into prosodic words.

The underlying representation of root or affixal morphemes in Serbo-Croatian may or may not contain a high tone accent. When a lexical category word does not contain any underlyingly accented morphemes, a default accent must be assigned. In all the NŠ dialects, an unaccented lexical word like *graad* will receive a default accent on its initial mora when preceded by another Lex word in the sentence, e.g., (44), where *vidiim* is underlying accented.[12]

44. vídiim   +   graad   →   vídiim gráad
    'I see'   'city'   'I see a city'

When an unaccented Lex is preceded by a function word within the same syntactic phrase, however, there are dialect differences in the treatment of default accent.

45. NŠ-1: ú graad   'to the city'
    NŠ-2: u gráad   'to the city'
    NŠ-3: ú glaavu
              or   'into (the) head'
          ú gláavu

In the NŠ-1 dialect (E. Herzegovina), the default accent is realized on the first mora of the function word; the lexical word bears no default accent. In the NŠ-2 (Belgrade, the standard), the default accent falls on the first mora of the lexical word (where it fails to spread to the preceding function word); the function word bears no accent. And in NŠ-3 (Šrem, Mačva) there are two options: The default accent may simply fall on the first mora of the function word, or it may fall on the first mora of the lexical word, in which case it also spreads onto the last mora of the pre-

---

[12] In the following examples,acute accents (´) designate high tone accents.

ceding function word.[13] The examples in (45) involve a preposition followed by a noun. Other Fnc Lex combinations are reported to behave in the same way.

Following Zec (1993), I assume (i) that in all dialects there is a constraint, call it Initial Accent, that is responsible for the presence of a default accent on the first mora of a word and (ii) that the differences in assignment of default accent in Fnc-Lex sequences reflect differences in PWd structure. More specifically, assuming the PWd structures in (46), then the position of the default accent will fall out:

46. NŠ-1: (u graad)$_{PWd}$ *internal clitic*
    NŠ-2: u (graad)$_{PWd}$ *free clitic*
    NŠ-3: (u (glaavu)$_{PWd}$)$_{PWd}$
                   or   *affixal clitic*
         (u (glaavu)$_{PWd}$)$_{PWd}$

Assuming an internal clitic analysis for NŠ-1, only the Fnc is PWd-initial and susceptible of receiving the default accent. If a free clitic analysis is assumed for NŠ-2, the Fnc is not PWd-initial and so cannot receive the accent, which instead must fall in the initial mora of the Lex. As for NŠ-3, the nested PWd structure of the affixal clitic analysis provides the basis for understanding the options in accent placement that are observed: Either on first mora of the PWd-initial Fnc, or on the first mora of the PWd-initial Lex (from which it spreads, to the immediately preceding mora, cf. footnote 13). In NŠ-3, and quite generally in Serbo-Croatian, two accents are never permitted within the same PWd, therefore the constraint calling for initial default accent can be satisfied only with respect to one of the two nested PWds. Both options in the realization of initial accent in NŠ-3 are therefore both equally "(non)well formed" with respect to the Initial Accent constraint, and hence both are optimal.[14] It would appear, then, that the three NeoŠtokavian dialects

---

[13]The spreading of an accent from its site of origin to the preceding mora is an absolutely general phenomenon within prosodic words in NS dialects (cf. Zec, 1993). In the NS-3 case cited here, evidence that the spreading onto the preceding function word is indeed an instance of this general phenomenon would be provided by polysyllabic function words, if it were the case that only the final mora of the polysyllabic Fnc were spread onto from an accent originating in initial position in the following Lex. Unfortunately the relevant data are not available.

[14]Since Serbo-Croatian never allows two accents within the same PWd, the fact that both the preposition and the initial mora of the noun bear H tone in the second option in NS-3 should be analyzed as a double-linking of a single H accent. Spreading of an underlying accent to immediately preceding mora, creating such a double-linking, is a general phenomenon (cf. note 13), and so this double-linking can be seen an instance of this spreading. The question remains why this spread configuration cannot be seen as satisfying the Initial Accent requirement with respect to *both* PWds at the same time. Evidence that it doesn't is the availability of the other option in default accent realization, which incurs one violation

exploit the three different types of prosodic clitic structure that the present theory makes available for assigning a surface prosodic structure to a Fnc-Lex sequence in the morphosyntactic input to the phonology.

Just how do the grammars of these dialects differ, then? Only in the ranking of the universal constraints that have already been shown to play a role in English—namely the alignment constraints WdCon and PWdCon and the prosodic domination constraints $NonRec_{PWd}$ and Exh_{PPh}:

47. a. NŠ-1: $NonRec_{PWd}$, Exh_{PPh} >> WdCon, PWdCon

   b. NŠ-2: WdCon, PWdCon, $NonRec_{PWd}$ >> Exh_{PPh}

   c. NŠ-3: WdCon, Exh_{PPh} >> $NonRec_{PWd}$, PWdCon

These rankings give rise to the different prosodic clitic structures attested, on the basis of a Fnc-Lex input sequence.

CONCLUSION

Functional category words are distinguished from lexical category words in that (i) they need not have the status of prosodic word in phonological representation, and (ii) they may appear in a variety of distinct prosodic clitic structures, both cross-linguistically and in the same language. It was proposed that the first property follows from the invisibility of function words (and functional projections) to constraints governing the interface of prosodic structure and morphosyntactic structure. Of central importance is the notion that the constraint WdCon requires only that the L/R edges of word-level Lex items align with PWd edges; words of the Fnc variety suffer no such requirement and hence are free to be otherwise organized. The second property, namely the variety in prosodization of function words, can come about in just two different ways, given an optimality theoretic perspective: through differences in the morphosyntactic input structure in which the Fnc is located and/or differences in the ranking of the relevant constraints. The constraints themselves are held to be universal. In English, the same ranking of constraints on prosodic structure will give rise to differences in the prosodic structure of function words when the morphosyntactic input structures differ in relevant ways. In the Serbo-Croatian dialects, function words located in identical morphosyntactic input structures differ in prosodization, and hence that it is differences in the ranking of the relevant constraints that must be given responsibility for this cross-linguistic surface variety in prosodic structure.

Given this understanding of function word prosodization one may ask in what ways the language learner could conceivably exploit

---

of the Initial Accent constraint. That other option should not be available if the doubly linked option contains no violation of the constraint. The answer probably lies in the characterization of the default accent phenomenon itself, and its relation to word stress (see Zec, 1994).

phonological knowledge in learning something about the syntax of the functional–lexical distinction. It does seem that phonology could potentially be of help in learning which words belong to the Fnc category and which to the Lex category. Consider the case of English monosyllabic words. Assuming that children have already learned that there is a prosodically relevant distinction between strong unreduced syllables and weak reduced syllables, they would be in a position to observe in the speech of adults that some words always appear in strong form, while others alternate between weak and strong realizations. Given children's innate knowledge of the universal constraints on prosodic structure, they could conceivably draw the inferences sketched in (48), and thereby make an assignment of monosyllabic words to either the Fnc or the Lex category:

48. *Inferring Lex–Fnc status from strong–weak status*
   a. Always strong(X) → Always Foot(X) → Always PWd(X) → Lex(X)
   b. ¬Always strong(X)→ ¬Always Foot(X)→ ¬Always PWd(X)→ Fnc(X)

Learners of English could also, in principle, gain access to information about the surface morphosyntactic phrase structure of the sentence in which a Fnc is embedded, given their knowledge of the universal prosodic constraints at play: Strong form status for an unaccented Fnc is ultimately attributable to its morphosyntactic phrase-final position.

All this is to say that a certain amount of information about the syntax is retrievable from the phonological contrasts between Lex and Fnc items and the alternations in form that Fnc words exhibit. But retrieving this information assumes the acquisition of sufficient knowledge of the workings of the phonology itself. Whether children's knowledge of phonology develops early enough to be of use to the acquisition of this aspect of syntax, and in case it does, whether it is indeed exploited, remain questions for future research.

ACKNOWLEDGMENTS

The research for this chapter was carried out in part with the support of NSF grant BNS-86-17827. Earlier versions of the chapter were presented in the fall 1992 Phonology Proseminar at UMass, at the conference *Signal to Syntax* held at Brown in February 1993, at talks the University of Tübingen and the University of Konstanz in summer 1993, and at the First Rutgers Optimality Workshop held in October 1993. I want to thank the participants for their comments. I also want to particularly thank Geert Booij, Pat Deevy, Elan Dresher, Caroline Féry, Junko Itô, Angelika Kratzer, Aditi Lahiri, John McCarthy, Armin Mester, Sharon Peperkamp, Draga Zec, and Katya Zubritskaya for further comments and discussion.

REFERENCES

Abney, S. (1987). *The English noun phrase in its sentential aspect.* Unpublished doctoral dissertation, MIT, Cambridge, MA.

Beckman, M., & Edwards, J. (1990). Lengthening and shortening and the nature of prosodic constituency. In J. Kingston & M. Beckman (Eds.), *Papers in laboratory phonology:
I. Between grammar and the physics of speech* (pp. 152-178). Cambridge, England: Cambridge University Press.

Beckman, M., & Pierrehumbert, J. (l986). Intonational structure in English and Japanese.
Phonology, 3, 255-309.

Berendson, E. (1986). *The phonology of cliticization.* Unpublished doctoral dissertation,
Utrecht.

Chomsky, N. (1986). *Barriers.* Linguistic Inquiry Monograph 13, MIT Press.

Cohn, A. (1989). Stress in Indonesian and bracketing paradoxes. *Natural Language and Linguistic Theory, 7,* 167-216.

Cooper, A. (1991). *An articulatory account of aspiration in English.* Unpublished doctoral dissertation, Yale University, New Haven, CT.

Cooper, A. (1994). *Aspiration in English: How should it be defined and where should it be described?.* Manuscript, University of Michigan.

Fukui, N., & Speas, M. (1986). Specifiers and projection. In N. Fukui, T. Rappaport, & E.
Gagey (Eds.), *MIT working papers in linguistics 8* (pp. 128-172). MIT.

Gimson, A. (1970). *An introduction to the pronunciation of English.* 2nd ed. London: Edward
Arnold.

Grimshaw, J. (1991). *Extended projection.* Unpublished manuscript, Brandeis University,
Rutgers University.

Hayes, B. (1989). The prosodic hierarchy in meter. In P. Kiparsky & G. Youmans (Eds.),
Rhythm and meter (pp. 201-260). Phonetics and Phonology, 1. Academic Press, New
York.

Hayes, B. (1995). *Metrical stress theory: Principles and case studies.* Chicago: University of Chicago Press.

Inkelas, S. (1989). *Prosodic constituency in the lexicon.* Unpublished doctoral dissertation,
Stanford University, Palo Alto, CA.

Inkelas, S., & Zec, D. (1988). Serbo-Croatian pitch accent. *Language, 64,* 227-248.

Itô, J., & Mester, A. (1992). Weak layering and word binarity. To appear in *Linguistic Inquiry.*

Jackendoff, R. (1977). *X-bar syntax.* Cambridge, MA: MIT Press.

Jones, D. (1964). *Outline of English phonetics.* 9th ed. Cambridge, England: Heffer.

Kager, R. W. J. (1989). *A metrical theory of stress and destressing in English and Dutch (Een
metrische theorie over klemtoon en klemtoonverlies in het Engels en het Nederlands).* Dordrecht: ICG.

Kager, R. W. J. (1993). Alternatives to the iambic-trochaic law. *Natural Language and Linguistic Theory, 11.*

Kaisse, E. (1985). *Connected speech.* New York: Academic Press.

Kanerva, J. (1989). *Focus and phrasing in Chichewa phonology.* Unpublished doctoral dissertation, Stanford University, Palo Alto, CA.

Kanerva, J. (1990). Focusing on phonological phrases in Chichewa, in S. Inkeles & D. Zec
(Eds.), *The syntax/phonology connection* (pp. 145-162). Chicago: CLSI/University of
Chicago Press..

Kang, O. (1992a). *Korean prosodic morphology.* Unpublished doctoral dissertation, University
of Washington, Seattle.

Kang, O. (1992b). Word internal prosodic words in Korean. *Proceedings of Northeast Linguistic
Society, 22.*

Klavans, J. (1985). The independence of syntax and phonology in cliticization. *Language 61,*
95-120.

Ladd, D. R. (1980). *The structure of intonational meaning.* Bloomington, Indiana: Indiana University Press.

Ladd, D. R. (1986). Intonational phrasing: The case for recursive prosodic structure. *Phonology 3,* 311-340.

Ladd, D. R. (1992). *Compound prosodic domains.* Occasional Paper, Linguistics Department,
University of Edinburgh.

Liberman, M. (1975). *The intonational system of English.* Unpublished doctoral dissertation,
MIT.

McCarthy, J. (1991). Synchronic rule inversion. In L. A. Sutton, C. Johnson, & R. Shields (Eds.), *Proceedings of the 17th Annual Meeting of the Berkeley Linguistics Society* (pp. 192-207). Berkeley: Berkeley Linguistics Society.

McCarthy, J. (1993). A case of surface constraint violation. *Canadian Journal of Linguistics/Revue canadienne de linguistique 38*, 169-195.

McCarthy, J., & Prince, A. (1991). *Prosodic minimality.* Lecture presented at University of Illinois conference The Organization of Phonology.

McCarthy, J., & Prince, A. (1993). Generalized alignment. In G. Booij & J. van Marle (Eds.), *Yearbook of Morphology 1993* (pp. 79-153). Dordrecht: Kluwer.

McCarthy, J., & Prince, A. (in press). *Prosodic morphology: I. Constraint interaction & satisfaction.* Cambridge, MA: MIT Press.

Mester, A. (1994). The quantitative trochee in Latin. *Natural Language and Linguistic Theory 12*, 1-61.

Myers, S. (1987). *Tone and the structure of words in Shona.* Unpublished doctoral dissertation, University of Massachusetts, Amherst.

Neijt, A. (1985). Clitics in arboreal phonology. In H. van der Hulst & N. Smith (Eds.), *Advances in nonlinear phonology* (pp. 179-192). Dordrecht: Foris.

Nespor, M. (1993). The phonology of clitic groups. In L. Hellan & H. van Riemsdijk (Eds.), *Clitic doubling and clitic groups* (pp. 67-90). Eurotyp Working Papers.

Nespor, M., & Vogel, I. (1986). *Prosodic phonology.* Dordrecht: Foris.

Pierrehumbert, J. (1980). *The phonetics and phonology of English intonation.* Doctoral dissertation, MIT; distributed by IULC.

Pierrehumbert, J. (1993). Alignment and prosodic heads. To appear in ESCOL proceedings.

Pierrehumbert, J., & Beckman, M. (1988). *Japanese tone structure.* Cambridge, MA: MIT Press.

Pollock, J.-Y. (1989). Verb movement, universal grammar, and the structure of IP. *Linguistic Inquiry, 20*, 365-424.

Prince, A., & Smolensky, P. (in press). *Optimality theory: Constraint interaction in generative grammar,* Cambridge, MA: MIT Press.

Rice, K. (1991). *Word-internal prosodic words in Slave.* Unpublished manuscript, University of Toronto.

Selkirk, E. O. (1972). *The phrasal phonology of English and French.* Unpublished doctoral dissertation, MIT.

Selkirk, E. O. (1978). On prosodic structure and its relation to syntactic structure. In T. Fretheim (Ed.), *Nordic Prosody II* (pp. 111-140). Trondheim: Tapir.

Selkirk, E. O. (1981). On the nature of phonological representation. In T. Myers, J. Laver, & J. Anderson (Eds.), *The cognitive representation of speech* (pp. 379-388). Amsterdam: North Holland.

Selkirk, E. O. (1984). *Phonology and syntax: The relation between sound and structure.* Cambridge, MA: MIT Press.

Selkirk, E. O. (1986). On derived domains in sentence phonology. *Phonology, 3,* 371-405.

Selkirk, E. O. (1989). *Parameterization in the syntax-phonology mapping: The case of Chinese dialects.* Paper presented at the 12th GLOW Colloquium, Utrecht.

Selkirk, E. O. (1993, September). *Constraints on prosodic structure—A modular approach.* Paper presented at ESCA Workshop on Prosody, Lund University.

Selkirk, E. O., & Tateishi, K. (1988). Minor phrase formation in Japanese. *CLS, 24,* 316-336.

Selkirk, E. O., & Shen, T. (1990). Prosodic domains in Shanghai Chinese. In S. Inkeles & D. Zec (Eds.), *The syntax/phonology connection* (pp. 313-338). Chicago: CLSI/University of Chicago Press.

Selkirk, E. O., & Tateishi, K. (1991). Syntax and downstep in Japanese. In C. Georgopoulos & R. Ishihara (Eds.), *Interdisciplinary approaches to language: Essays in honor of S.-Y. Kuroda* (pp. 519-544). Dordrecht: Kluwer.

Shattuck-Hufnagel, S., Ostendorf, M., & Ross, K. (1994). Stress shift and early pitch accent placement in American English words. To appear in *Journal of Phonetics.*

Sweet, H. (1891). *A handbook of phonetics.* Oxford: Henry Frowde.

Sweet, H. (1908). *The sounds of English—An Introduction to Phonetics.* Oxford: Clarendon Press.

Tesar, B., & Smolensky, P. (1993, October). *The learning of optimality theory: An algorithm and some basic complexity results.* CU-CS-678-93. Department of Computer Science, University of Colorado at Boulder.

Vogel, I. (1988, December*). The clitic group as a constituent in prosodic phonology.* Paper presented at LSA Meeting, New Orleans.

Zec, D. (1988). *Sonority constraints on prosodic structure.* Unpublished doctoral dissertation, Stanford University, Palo Alto, CA.

Zec, D. (1993). Rule domains and phonological change. In S. Hargus & E. Kaisse, (Eds.), *Studies in lexical phonology* (pp. 365-405). New York: Academic Press.

Zec, D. (1994). *Footed tones and tonal feet: Rhythmic constituency in a pitch accent language.* Unpublished manuscript, Cornell University.

Zwicky, A. (1970). Auxiliary reduction in English. *Linguistic Inquiry, 1,* 323-336.

Zwicky, A. (1977). *On clitics.* IULC, Bloomington, Indiana.

13 The Role of Prosody in the Acquisition of Grammatical Morphemes

Ann M. Peters
University of Hawai'i

Sven Strömqvist
University of Göteborg

The world's languages all employ pitch, duration, and some kind of rhythm in their individual prosodic systems. These tonal and temporal characteristics not only give shape to utterance contours, and perform discourse related functions, they also interact with grammar in ways that may have interesting consequences for both processing by adult speakers and learning by children. The specific kinds of interrelations between prosodic features on the one hand and aspects of lexical and grammatical structure on the other vary a good deal across languages, however.

In English, for instance, "open class" lexical items (nouns, verbs, adjectives, adverbs) are prosodically prominent, carrying at least one stress, whereas among the grammatical, or "closed-class," morphemes, even the non-affixed ones (articles, auxiliaries, pronouns, prepositions) tend to carry no stress. On the other hand, many of these latter morphemes are crucially located at the beginnings of grammatical phrases, with articles signaling the onsets of noun phrases, and modals or auxiliaries signaling the onsets of verb phrases. Moreover, English stress is associated with both the presence of full (i.e., unreduced) vowels (Cutler, this volume) and with pitch prominence. These observations raise the following questions: What role does the rhythmic alternation between stress and lack-of-stress play in an adult English speaker's ability to perceive and make syntactic use of closed-class morphemes? What about learners? Does lack of stress make these morphemes harder to discover, or does their participation in the rhythm of phrases confer its own kind of salience? What is the role of pitch in the perception of closed-class morphemes?

We are currently exploring the idea that the prosodic patterning characteristic of a particular language can indeed serve to draw the attention of language learners to the presence of certain elements of the linguistic system. Awareness of the *presence* of such a form may then help focus the learner's attention on its other attributes, including exactly what it sounds like and what functional role(s) it has.

Our interest in the role of prosody has grown out of both theoretical considerations and empirical observations. The written language bias in linguistics has left prosody underexplored, and this means a special challenge to the study of early child language, which is a preeminently spoken language.[1]

Further, in order to bridge the gap between studies of infant perception (focusing on the first year of life) and studies of early grammatical development (from 18 months and onwards), hypotheses need to be formulated, explored, and tested about how elements in prelinguistic development can be put to use for the eventual construction of linguistic structures.

An empirical observation suggesting the important role for prosody in the child's construction of certain aspects of grammar is that some (though not all) children learning a variety of languages initially indicate an early awareness of the presence of unstressed syllabic grammatical morphemes by approximating them with underspecified vowels or syllables (Peters & Menn, 1993). Moreover, the way these "fillers" fit into the rhythm of their utterances suggests that the *rhythm of the phrase* may be a salient attribute that these learners are trying to reproduce. Although we realize that prosodic patterns may not play the same role in acquisition as they do in adult perception or production, we feel there is a need to identify patterns that seem to be useful to learners, to map out how they are used in acquisition, and to specify how they eventually are reanalyzed to fit into an adultlike system. More specifically, we propose the following "Spotlight Hypothesis":

> Perceptually salient prosodic patterns, including pitch contours, rhythm, and increased duration, may serve as "spotlights" on any phonological forms that are regularly associated with these patterns; if such forms happen to be grammatical morphemes, learners will focus on them earlier than on morphemes not so spotlighted.

This Spotlight Hypothesis thus concerns children's perception of salient prosody that fortuitously coincides with grammatical inflections, with evidence to be drawn from what they *produce*.

To illustrate how such a spotlight might work, we present a developmental analysis from our ongoing research on the role of prosody in the acquisition of grammatical morphemes in Swedish. We then broaden our focus to raise questions about the role prosody might play in other languages. We conclude with suggestions for further research that utilize crosslinguistic variation as part of the design.

EVIDENCE FROM SWEDISH

As a preliminary testing ground for our hypothesis we have chosen to focus on Swedish because, although Swedish has a morphological system similar to German and English, it is unlike most other Indo-

---

[1] In particular, the practice of transcribing child speech tends to foster an ignorance of prosody, partly because our writing systems (both orthographic and phonetic) favor segments and leave prosodic features uncoded.

European languages in that it has two tonal word accents that interact in interesting ways with certain grammatical morphemes, particularly word-final inflections. These two accents are referred to as "acute" (or "accent 1") and "grave" (or "accent 2"). It is commonly held that the grave accent represents the marked member of the pair, both in terms of its phonetic salience and in terms of its function (shown later).

Before looking at the details of these accents and their development, let us first note four linked attributes that render them interesting in the context of the acquisition of grammatical morphemes. First, the phonetic shape of the accents is determined by an interaction of word level and utterance/sentence level prosody. Second, when the grave accent occurs on a word form in sentence focus, it assumes a two-peaked contour that is very salient from a perceptual point of view. Third, the linguistic distribution of the accents can be predicted from a combination of phonological and morphological information. And fourth, of most central interest from the standpoint of morphosyntax, several important inflections can occur in conjunction with the highly salient grave pitch-pattern. Thus, for example, *bil-ar* "car-PLUR" takes the grave accent, with a pitch peak on the second syllable containing the plural allomorph. These four properties of the Swedish grave accent—in particular the second and fourth—thus provide a testing ground for our Spotlight Hypothesis.

Elements of the Swedish Tonal Word Accent Distinction

From a phonetic point of view, since each of these accents involves a pitch contour (fall and/or rise), the essential elements of the acute–grave distinction can be described in terms of fundamental frequency (F_0) contours, with each basic contour containing one F_0-maximum and one F_0-minimum target (Bruce, 1977; Engstrand, 1989a; Engstrand, 1989b). According to Bruce, although each word accent is characterized by a fall (connecting the F_0-maximum and minimum), the timing of this fall is earlier for the acute accent than for the grave in relation to the stressed syllable of the word to which the accent applies. Thus, the acute accent is typically characterized by an F_0-maximum in the prestress syllable and an F_0-minimum in the stressed syllable, while for the grave accent the corresponding F_0-maximum occurs in the stressed syllable and the F_0-minimum in the poststress syllable. Furthermore, this fall tends to be steeper for the acute than for the grave accent.

These basic word accent contours interact with the sentence accent, that is, the F_0-contour associated with the information focus of the whole utterance. When sentence accent coincides with an acute word form, F_0 shows a one peaked contour. In contrast, when it interacts with a grave word form, F_0 shows a two peaked contour. Bruce (1977) showed how an acute word (e.g., *nûmmer* "number") and a grave word (e.g., *nùnnor* "nuns") are affected according to whether they are in focus position (see

(1), where focus is indicated by capital letters) or in positions after focus (in (2) one stress group after focus and in (3) two stress groups after focus).[2] The F_0 contours of *númmer* and *nùnnor* in these three positions are shown in Fig. 13.1.

1. *man vill lämna nåra långa NÚMMER/NÙNNOR*
   'one would like to deliver some long numbers/nuns'
2. *man vill lämna nåra LÅNGA númmer/nùnnor*
3. *man vill LÄMNA nåra långa númmer/nùnnor*

Engstrand (1989a, 1989b) argued (contra Bruce, 1977) that only the grave accent can be reliably identified by acoustic criteria, which reinforces its status as the marked member of the pair.[3] On the basis of data from spontaneous adult-directed speech (among other sources), Engstrand defines two positive criteria for the grave accent: a fall on the stressed syllable and a rise on the post-stress syllable within the same word, the rise being optional in that it is associated with utterance focus position. Engstrand finds the fall to be an extremely reliable criterion for the grave accent in adult speech. In this view, the acute accent can be operationalized as an *absence of grave* characteristics on a stressed syllable. In the present study we focus on the more marked (and also the more peculiarly "Swedish") grave tonal word accent, which also makes life easier for investigators by virtue of its greater acoustic reliability. Because the grave accent can only occur on a word that contains at least

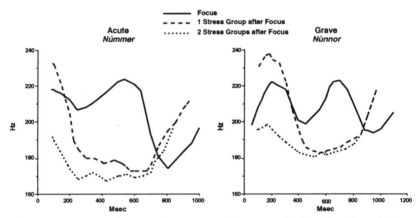

FIG. 13.1. F_0 contours of acute and grave accents in sentence final position (Bruce 1977, p. 45)

---

[2]We will denote the acute accent by ´ and the grave accent by ` on the stressed syllable. Thus, *númmer* contains the acute accent whilst *nùnnor* contains the grave accent.
[3]Bruce (personal communication) agrees that the acute characteristics are harder to identify by acoustic criteria because of their greater variability as compared to grave characteristics.

one post-stress syllable, from a processing point of view, the *Fall* on the stressed syllable carries the information that there is yet another syllable of this word to come, whereas the *Rise* indicates utterance focus. Following Engstrand (1989a, 1989b), we summarize the elements of the grave word accent in Fig, 13.2.

In standard Swedish, the rules for predicting the linguistic distribution of the two word accents make reference to both phonological and morphological information. The great majority of compound words receive the grave accent independently of whether the elements of the compound have the acute accent or the grave accent in isolation. For non-compound words, in contrast, the situation is very complex. Since the realization of the grave contour requires a post-stress syllable (whether unstressed or secondary stressed), word accent can only be distinctive in polysyllabic word forms with non-final stress. Such word forms often consist of a lexical stem and an inflectional or derivational suffix. In that context, word accent assignment is sensitive to grammatical categories. Thus, regularly inflected verbs always receive the grave accent in the infinitive (e.g., *lèt-a* "search-lNF" and *hèt-a* "be called-lNF") and in the preterite (e.g., *lèt-ade* "search-PRET" and *hèt-te* "be called-PRET"), whereas in the present tense some of the verbs receive the grave accent (e.g., *lèt-ar* "*search*-PRES") and others the acute (e.g., *hét-er* "be called-PRES"). Further, word forms with a syllabic suffix encoding definite singular receive, as a rule, the acute accent, for example, *bíl-en* "car- DEF:SG." In contrast, word forms with a syllabic suffix encoding plural (PLUR) receive, as a rule, the grave accent (e.g., *bìl-ar* "car-PLUR," *ràd-er* "line-PLUR"). Minimal pairs of words distinguished solely by their word accent properties are rather infrequent in Swedish.[4]

Elements of the Grave Accent in a Developmental Context

In order to study the fate and function of grave elements in a developmental context extending over pregrammatical and early grammatical development, data were drawn from a longitudinal case study of a monolingual Swedish boy, Markus, comprising 23 data points from 15;19 (15 months; 19 days) to 30;20. Each data point represents around

C V₁ C V₂

FIG. 13.2. Model of Swedish grave accent characteristics. *Fall* is operationalized as V_1 onset > V_1 offset; *Rise* is operationalized as V_2 offset > V_2 onset or V_2 offset > V_1 offset.

---

[4]Minimal pairs such as [pó:len] "Poland" versus [pò:len] "pole-DEF:SG" are more likely to be encountered in introductory texts on Swedish pronunciation than in authentic spoken interaction.

45 minutes of spoken interaction recorded during Markus's everyday activities (Plunkett and Strömqvist, 1992; Strömqvist, Richtoff, & Andersson, 1993).[5]

Figure 13.3 shows the profile of Markus's MLU-morphemes from 15;19-30;20. The shaded area indicates a region in development where there is evidence of several important developmental changes: Markus's vocabulary spurt starts around 20-21 months, the first inflectional morphemes show up in his production around the same period, and grammatical subject begins to be more consistently realized in contexts with finite verbs. The first inflectional morphemes emerging in Markus's early grammatical development are the definite singular, the indefinite plural, and the present tense. During the latter half of the total developmental period under study the supine (close to English past participle) and past tense also become productive. (Details are presented in Plunkett & Strömqvist, 1992, pp. 522-532.)

As can be seen from Fig. 13.3, these early lexical and grammatical developments just precede the beginning of a steep increase in MLU-morphemes. Moreover, since the great majority of Markus's early inflectional morphemes are syllabic (e.g., plural -ar, definite singular -en), his increase in inflectional morphemes beginning at 20-21 months entails a concomitant increase in word forms with a post-stress syllable. We might predict that one consequence of this increase in the production of

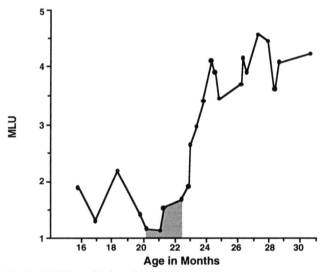

FIG. 13. 3. Markus's MLU-profile from 15;19 to 30;20

---

[5]The case study material, which relates to "Strömqvist's corpus," is accessible in CHILDES/CHAT-format through anonymous ftp at poppy.psy.cmu.edu, where it is located in the file "Swedish.tar" in the /noneng directory.

multisyllabic inflected words could be a corresponding increase in grave word accent contours, especially if the learner is assigning grave accent purely on the basis of the presence of a post-stress syllable. To test this prediction, two independent coders were given the task of making an exhaustive auditory identification of grave contours in the 23 recordings from 15;19 to 30;20. They were given two coding options: Clear case of grave versus Unclear case of grave. Forms that were judged to lack this contour—including adult forms that would normally receive the grave accent—were left uncoded.

In Fig. 13.4 the development of inflectional morphemes has been plotted against the developmental profile for the grave contour. Only instances coded as Clear cases of grave have been included.[6] As can be seen, Markus begins to produce recognizable grave contours at about 17 months, approximately 3 months before he begins producing inflected word forms. During this early period in his development he tends to produce disyllabic word forms having *initial stress* (and therefore a post-stress syllable) with *grave*-like contours (e.g., *nàlle* "teddy"), but disyllabic word forms with *final stress* with *acute* like characteristics (e.g., *giràff* "giraffe").

As inflectional morphology begins to emerge during the next period (20–23 months), Markus's production of grave contours continues to

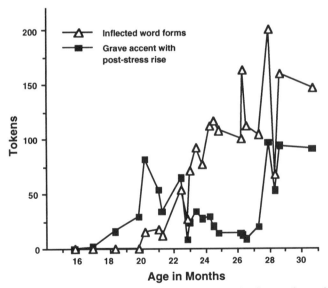

FIG. 13.4. The interaction between the grave word accent and inflectional morphology in Markus 15;19-30;20

---

[6]The grave-accent line represents the mean scores from the two coders.

increase to a point where they are overrepresented as compared to the adult norm. Overgeneralizations from this period include, for example, *hùnd-en* "dog-DEF:SG" (target is *húnd-en*), *sàng-en* "bed-DEF:SG" (target is *sång-en*), and *kòmm-er* "come-PRES" (target is *kómm-er*). At 23-24 months, however, although there is a dramatic increase in inflectional morphemes, there is just as dramatic a *decrease* in grave word accent characteristics, resulting in what is now a clear *under*representation of the grave accent as compared to the adult norm.   For example, Markus now says *títta-r* "look-PRES" (target is *tìtta-r*) and *båt-ar* "boat-PLUR" (target is *bàt-ar*). A possible interpretation of this decrease is that it represents an overgeneralization of the acute accent, the unmarked member of the accent pair. This may have come about in the following way: As Markus's attention to inflectional morphemes increases, his attention to word forms that have a post-stress syllable but no grave characteristics must also increase, perhaps to the point where he loses sight of which disyllables should actually be grave. The incidence of grave remains low during the 25-27 month period. From 28 months onwards, however, grave contours regain frequency in Markus's speech production. In this phase, however, not only is the grave contour more frequently instantiated, but, in contrast to the earlier phases of first over- and then undergeneralization, it attains a balanced, targetlike distribution.

Further information on the linguistic distribution of tonal word accent characteristics is given in Table 13.1 which shows how well Markus's production of grave and acute accents matches adult targets and in what ways it deviates. In the upper part of Table 13.1 we see the phase between 23;12 and 24;25 during which production of grave contours decreases drastically, while in the lower portion of the table we see the later phase of massive return of grave characteristics from 27;28 to 30;20.[7]

At 23;12 the grave accent contour is overgeneralized, being used 42% of the times in situations where acute is required. This is followed by a period of vacillation from 23;25 to 24;25 during which the acute contour begins to be overgeneralized. At 24;09, however, there is a major change in the distributional pattern: Now it is the acute accent that is overgeneralized with the grave one being undergeneralized. The use of the acute contour has two peaks, one at 24;09 when it is used 67% of the times in place of grave and the other at 24;25 (also 67%). Grave characteristics are still overproduced, but at a much lower level, at 24;16 (17%). By 27;28, however, a more targetlike balance between grave and acute accent has emerged; by 28;09 neither accent is being used erroneously on more than 6% of the coded tokens. This new dis-

---

[7]Only those instances of grave and acute accent that the two coders agreed upon have been included in the figures in Table 13.1.

TABLE 13.1
Percents of Productions Matching/Not Matching Target Contours (N=388)

Age	Grave		Acute	
	Target	Non-Target	Target	Non-Target
23;12	26	42	32	0
23;25	46	0	39	15
24;09	11	2	20	67
24;16	0	17	56	28
24;25	8	0	25	67
27;28	41	18	35	6
28;09	56	5	39	0
28;18	45	6	45	5
30;20	63	5	32	0

tributional pattern grows more and more pronounced as we approach the end of the developmental period under investigation at 30;20.

The results presented so far have been based solely on auditory analysis. In order to validate the auditory identifications and to get a more detailed picture of the acoustic properties of the grave candidates in Markus's development, a digitized acoustic data base of 510 disyllabic word forms was derived from recording sessions 18;10 through 26;10.[8] The word forms were fed into MacSpeechLab, an analysis package in PC environment, where the first and second vowels of each disyllable were delimited through spectrographic analysis. Each vowel was subjected to measurements of duration and pitch contours.[9] Each disyllabic word that entered the acoustic data base form was classified according to utterance position (one-word utterance, or initial, medial, or final position in a multiword utterance) and morphological make up (mono-morphemic or di-morphemic; among the di-morphemic disyllables were distinguished a subclass of lexical compounds and subclasses of different types of inflectional categories).

From this acoustic analysis we find that only 20% of the 510 sampled grave candidates meet the target criterion for a Fall (on the stressed first syllable of the word form), whereas 51% meet the criterion for a Rise (on the post-stress syllable). This tendency is most pronounced in the early phase from 18;l0 to 23;l2: 10% Fall versus 65% Rise. This finding is in accord with Engstrand, Williams, and Strömqvist (1991), who, in an experimental study of the spontaneous vocalizations in Swedish and American infants of approximately 17 months of age,

---

[8]In this process several disyllabic candidates were ruled out from analysis (did not enter the data base) for technical reasons. The aim, however, was to end up with approximately 30 word forms per recording session (15 mono-morphemic and 15 di-morphemic).

[9]For this analysis we operationalized the Fall and Rise parameters as follows: for Fall the pitch of the onset of the first vowel was required to be greater than its offset by at least 20Hz; for Rise the offset of the second vowel was required to be greater than either its own onset or the offset of the first vowel by at least 20Hz.

found the Swedish experiment group to differ significantly from the American controls in their production of the Rise but not the Fall parameter (Engstrand et al., 1991).

One conclusion that we can draw from these results is that the Swedish tonal word accent contrast is acquired, not as a "package deal" with all important aspects of the system immediately in place, but rather as a gradual integrative build-up process with dynamic developmental properties. The first element seized upon by Markus is the pitch rise associated with the grave accent, and this rise is established well before his MLU spurt and the emergence of his first inflectional morphemes. In a first phase of interaction between the grave rise and inflectional morphology, the rise is overgeneralized in relation to the adult norm. In a second phase, it is undergeneralized, suggesting that Markus is now concentrating on the distribution of acute characteristics. In a third phase, towards the end of the developmental period under study, the two aspects of the Swedish tonal word accent distinction—grave and acute—are integrated, and Markus's speech production is characterized by a balanced, targetlike distribution between the two.

Why is the post-stress Rise rather than the Fall on the stressed syllable the first element acquired? And what role is the Rise playing in that early phase of Markus's language development, which extends from the first appearance of grave Rise at 16;27 to the beginning of its decline around 23½ months? As we will try to show, these two questions are particularly relevant to our Spotlight Hypothesis.

We believe that one explanation for the fact that Markus first attends to and reproduces the Rise/High pitch (rather than the Fall) is its *perceptual salience*. Another parameter that may have explanatory value is *communicative functional load*. The rise is the outcome of the interaction between word accent and sentence accent, with the latter adding to the communicative functional load of the Rise because it is associated with the information focus of the utterance. The Fall, in contrast, is less functionally loaded since it merely signals that there is yet a syllable to come within the word form.

To explore the hypothesis that the Rise is attracting attention, we looked to see if there were systematic acoustic correlates of the judgments of our coders on the 510 disyllabic word forms in our computerized acoustic database.[10] We note that in the rating task the coders actually had three possible options: Clear instance of grave, Unclear instance of grave, and No instance of grave (with the last being left unmarked). Of the two raters, coder 2 made use of these three options in a more differentiated fashion than coder 1.[11] For this reason, we limited

---

[10]To be sure, the hypothesis is about the child's attention, but in the absence of data from perception experimental with the child in question, we explore data on the coders' attention as auxiliary evidence.

[11]By and large, coder 1 almost exclusively used the two extreme categories (Clear instance and No instance), whereas coder 2 used the intermediate category as well. The great ma-

our analysis to the decisions of coder 2. Among the 510 word forms in the sample, coder 2 judged that 123 were Clear instances of grave, 54 Unclear instances, and 333 No grave. We asked whether these three sets of word forms have distinct acoustic characteristics. The results of our analyses are summarized in Table 13.2.

Our results suggest that the combination of pitch and length can be used to predict the assignment of Markus's disyllabic word forms to the three categories. Words coded as Clear have a much *higher average pitch peak*; on the post-stress rise and a considerably *longer duration of their second vowel* than those coded as Unclear or No grave. Further, the words recognized as grave, whether Clear or Unclear, have, on average, a *longer second than first vowel*, whereas the reverse is true of the words not recognized as grave. There is also a strong positional effect: The great majority of the words recognized as grave (Clear or Unclear) were *utterance final*. This finding helps explain the increased duration of the second vowels—it is due to the phonetic effect known as final lengthening.[12]

The predominance of utterance-final position in our material is also

TABLE 13.2
Correlates of Judgments of Graveness (N Disyllabic Word Forms = 510)

Parameter	Judgment		
	Clear Grave N = 123	Unclear Grave N = 54	No Grave N = 333
Fall	16%	17%	22%
Rise	65%	79%	41%
Mean Pitch Peak[a]	433Hz	385Hz	363Hz
Neither	19%	4%	37%
V1 > V2	24%	44%	56%
Mean Duration	245 msec	192 msec	202 msec
V2 > V1	76%	56%	44%
Mean Duration	363 msec	208 msec	185 msec
Utterance Final	96%	89%	45%

[a]For technical reasons, all frequency values > 500 Hz were ruled out from the analysis.

jority of the word forms that were coded as Unclear by coder 2 were coded as Clear by coder 1.

[12]Utterance-final lengthening in the input is the kind of acoustic cue that we might expect would be both perceived and produced early by babies, and which could serve as a useful segmentation cue. Although there is clearly a cross-linguistic tendency towards utterance-final lengthening, it is not an absolute universal. Babies seem to be sensitive to its presence or absence, however, as early as 18 months Hallé et al. have found that four French-learning babies of this age reliably produced final length, while four Japanese learning babies just as reliably did not (Hallé et al., 1991).

probably intertwined with the high incidence of the grave post-stress Rise, since in adult Swedish not only is the Rise associated with the information focus of an utterance, but there is a syntactic preference to place focused information towards the end of a sentence (cf. e.g., Diderichsen's, 1946 "weight principle"). A study we have yet to do is an investigation of the occurrence of Rise and Fall in the input to Markus, looking at the interaction between focal accent, sentence-final position, and final syllable length for grave and acute disyllables.

This acoustic reanalysis of the codings of graveness supports our hypothesis that the grave Rise is likely to attract attention, particularly because of its high pitch.[13] Our results further indicate that utterance-final position is especially salient when final lengthening is combined with the grave Rise. Any morphological material located in this position will indeed be "spotlighted." What inflectional morphemes does Markus produce in this salient position in this phase of his language development? And how does this material change with development? Figure 13.5 shows how Markus's inflectional morphemes developed in terms of the utterance position of the word form containing the morpheme during the period 19;25-26;10. One-word utterances have been calculated separately and the shaded area in Fig. 13.5 represents the number of one-word utterances with a word-final syllable containing an

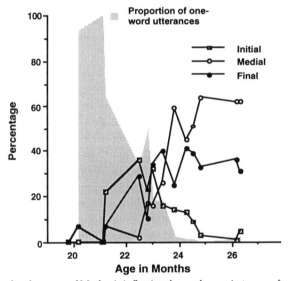

FIG. 13.5. The development of Markus's inflectional morphemes in terms of utterance position in Markus 19;25 26;10 (N=1084)

---

[13]We reiterate that these results are not as direct evidence for our hypotheses as would be perception experiments with infants.

inflectional morpheme. The total number of word forms analyzed is 1084.

As can be seen, almost all (90-100%) of the earliest instances of inflectional morphemes are located in one-word utterances. This means that the word forms constituting these one-word utterances will receive the prosodic prominence associated with the information focus of a whole utterance. Furthermore, if we describe the sequential structure in terms of syllables, rather than words, the syllable containing an inflectional morpheme will be in utterance-final position and subjected to final lengthening. In the next phase, from 23;12 to 23;25, there is a shift in the location of the majority of these inflections, from one-word utterances and utterance-final position to utterance-medial position.

We interpret this developmental evidence as further support for our argument that the spotlight of extra pitch and duration found in one-word utterances and utterance-finally in multiword utterances serves to focus Markus's initial awareness of inflectional morphology, an awareness that he is subsequently able to transfer to utterance-medial position.[14]

Faced with the task of learning a language with a fair amount of grammatical morphology located at the ends of words, Swedish-learning children do well to attend to prosodic salience, which spotlights what goes on in this position. Such a strategy has been well expressed by Slobin (1971), p. 335, in his Operating Principle "pay attention to the ends of words." Our findings suggest that utterance-final position in Swedish proves particularly felicitous for application of this principle because the final syllables of many inflected words are prosodically spotlighted through increased duration and high pitch. The increased duration is due to the cross-linguistically attested final lengthening effect, whereas the high pitch is due to the particularly Swedish grave post-stress rise. Figure 13.6 offers a schematic view of the spotlight effect of that post-stress rise.

We plan to continue to build the empirical basis for our hypothesis

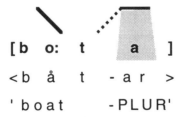

FIG. 13.6. The spotlight effect of the Swedish grave post-stress rise

---

[14]To the extent that Markus pays attention to his own speech, the kind of productions that we have been discussing here could serve as "input data" to reinforce his attention to utterance-final morphemes. Whether the same pattern of utterance-final salience is also present in the adult input to Markus during this period of development is a question we will seek to answer in our future research.

by looking at longitudinal development in at least one other Swedish child, for whom we are currently collecting data. We also plan to analyze the input to Markus, looking at salience of the inflections that Markus first produces: How often they occur utterance finally, and how often they are associated with sentence-accent and/or phrase-final lengthening. This will allow us more accurately to specify the relation between input and early production. A third prong of needed research involves perception experiments with Swedish infants, in order to test the degree to which our hypothesized spotlight really attracts infants' attention.

FUTURE DIRECTIONS

We now broaden our perspective on the relationship between prosody and grammatical morphemes (both affixed and free) by considering a wider range of languages and a wider range of prosodic phenomena. In our introduction we mentioned that, in a variety of languages, at least some learners are observed initially to approximate grammatical morphemes with underspecified vowels or syllables, and that these syllables often seem to be integrally involved with the rhythm of the utterance. Peters and Menn (1993) argued that such fillers may reflect a child's *partial* knowledge of several aspects of the target morphemes, including where they go, what they sound like, and their structural role. In stress-timed languages, such as Scandinavian, German, or English, stressless syllabic morphemes seem to be the ones that may be reproduced as fillers. Examples 4-11 illustrate children's productions of such fillers in Norwegian, German, and English. (Glossable fillers are given in square brackets, unglossable ones are glossed as "F".)

Norwegian (Simonsen, 1990), Nora 2;3.0 (stresses transcribed from tape by AP)

```
4. | ´    ` | ´     ` | ´      ` | ´    ` |
     hun e    2datt e    den   E  seng-en
     hun F    datt  av   den   F  seng-en
     she F    fell [out-of] that F bed-DEF

5. | ´    `  | ´    `     `  | ´   `    #   ´   ` |
     E  dEn  likhE    æ     2fa :Leð  #  1seŋ:ən
     F  den  ikke   [har/er] fall-e   #  seng-en
     F  it   not   [have/be] fall-PRET   bed-DEF
```

German (Stern & Stern, 1928) pp. 100-102, Günther 2;5 (stresses reconstructed from diary data)

```
6  |        `          ´  |    `      ´  | `    `    ´ |
          ä       hut?     ä    han  -da   ä    hut?
     [wo-ist-der] Hut? [auf-der] Veran- -da  der  Hut?
     [where-is-the] hat? [on-the] veran-  da  the  hat?
```

7. `  |  ´  ˘  `| ´ ˘   `  |  ´  ˘    ` | ´ ˘   `  |   ´  ` |
    E hosser E heller E   hünter   E heine   E   hilde
  eine grossen F Teller hat Günther, einen kleinen   F   Hilde
    a   big   F plate [has] Günther, a   little [one/has] Hilde

English (Peters, unpublished data) Seth (stresses transcribed from tape by AP)

8.   `   |  ´    `| ´ ` | 1;10.2
      m   pIk   ə fawis
    want? pick F flowers

9.   `  |  ´    `   ´ | ´ | 2;1.0
     ə   bez In   ə bEd
    I/you bounce in DET bed

English (Bloom, 1970, pp. 108-109), Eric at 1;8.2 (stresses reconstructed from published data)

10. ´ | ´   ´ | ´ ` |
     ə put   ə   baby
     I? put DET baby

11. ´ | ´   ` | ´ |
     də see the 'chine
     F   see the machine

In examples 4, 5, 6, 8, and 9 it is possible to identify with some confidence a small range of possible targets for most of the phonologically underspecified filler syllables. In examples 5 and 7, however, the fillers seem to have been motivated as much by rhythmic considerations as by morphological ones, illustrating the simultaneous development of these two strands of knowledge.

A rather different prosodic-grammatical configuration is found in a language like Mandarin in which each syllable of each open-class word is lexically assigned a tone. Each tone is either one of the four "full" tones or the shorter, less tonally distinctive "neutral tone."[15] Many grammatical morphemes, which are free/unaffixed, carry the neutral tone. This renders their single syllables both shorter and less tonally distinctive than those of open-class words and helps to impart a stress-timed sort of rhythm to Mandarin utterances (M. Beckman, personal communication). Moreover, many of these less-salient closed-class morphemes reliably occur phrase finally. We suspect that these changes in contrast from full to neutral tones help adult Mandarin speakers perceive and make syntactic use of these phrase delimiting closed-class morphemes. Examples from the adult language are shown in example

---

[15]Each open-class word has at least one full tone on its first syllable; final syllables may or may not carry neutral tone.

12 and 13.[16] An acquisition question that has not yet been answered is whether these attributes also help Mandarin learners parse the speech stream into phrases and discover that there is a separate class of words that play functional roles in the language. Although we do not yet have any reports of fillers in early Mandarin, we suspect that the conditions are right for their appearance.

12. .

hudieER	san-wu-cheng-qun	DI	fei guo shucong
butterfly	three-five-compose-group	ADV	fly over bush
Butterflies	in groups		fly over bushes

13.

shi-GE zhiTOU	zhang DI	bu yiyang chang DE
ten-CL finger	grow RESULT	not same long ADJ
(The) ten fingers	are of	different lengths

Yet another configuration exists in Japanese, an agglutinative language that has little stress as English speakers know it. It does have a pitch-accent system in which a single pitch change may occur within an open-class word. To the ears of English speakers, a Japanese sentence tends to sound like a staccato rat-a-tat-tat of relatively unhighlighted syllables concluded with a sentence-final particle on a clearly different tune. We do not yet know what kinds of clues Japanese learners are able to use to find the internal structure of such syllable sequences.

Minimal Pair Languages

Our investigation of the interaction of prosody with grammatical morphemes has made us aware of a host of as-yet-unanswered questions about language acquisition. These include the following:

1. Do (subsets of) the grammatical morphemes in some languages have distinctive phonological characteristics that might help learners perceive them as a separate class? For instance, English functors tend to have weak stress, a reduced set of (lax) vowels, and a somewhat distinctive set of consonants (especially /w/, /n/, /ð/, /t/, /z/); Mandarin functors tend to have neutral tone.
2. Does the availability of a distinguishable class of phrase bounding morphemes help first-language learners segment the speech stream into phrases? (The work of Morgan, Meier, & Newport, 1987, shows that it does help in the learning of Miniature Artificial Languages.)
3. What, if anything, serves the same function as stress and rhythm in languages with little stress (such as Finnish, Georgian, Turkish, West Greenlandic Eskimo)?

---

[16]Examples provided by Shu-Hui Chen. Mandarin tones are represented as follows: 1: ¯, 2: ´, 3: ˇ, 4: `, neutral: ˙; neutral-toned syllables are also capitalized; CL = classifier.

One way to expand our investigation of the influence of prosody on the acquisition of grammatical morphemes is to compare the process in "minimal pair" sets of languages: languages that are as closely related as possible in their morphosyntactic systems, but that differ interestingly in their prosody. Closest to our current project, the minimal internal variation within the typologically homogeneous group of Mainland Scandinavian languages offers a natural laboratory for testing our Spotlight Hypothesis. The "experiment languages" would be Norwegian and standard Swedish, both languages that have tonal word-accent distinctions that interact with lexicon and morphology. The "control language" would be Finnish Swedish, a regional variant of Swedish, of interest because it lacks tonal word-accents, even though its lexicon and morphology are extremely close to those of standard Swedish. If the grave word accent really spotlights certain word-final inflections such as plural or past tense, then we would expect standard Swedish learners to acquire these inflections earlier than Finnish Swedish learners

Going further afield, we suggest some other interesting pairs or sets of languages on which such contrastive studies could be carried out. For instance, Polish and Russian are morphologically very similar, but differ prosodically, with Polish having fixed stress and no vowel reduction and Russian having movable stress and considerable vowel reduction. It is notable that Polish children acquire the inflectional system considerably earlier than Russian children (Slobin, 1966; Smoczyńska, 1985; Johnston, 1991).

Another interesting pair of morphologically similar languages is Spanish and (Brazilian) Portuguese, where Spanish is more "syllable timed" with no vowel reduction and a more even rhythm, while Portuguese has three degrees of stress that engender considerable changes in vowel quality and drastically reduce the salience of word-final inflections (Major, 1985). French, a third Romance language with a closely related system of grammatical morphemes, has roughly even syllable lengths except for marked word-final lengthening (Gårding, 1981), thus setting up a "minimal triad" with Spanish and Portuguese. It is interesting that, as French word-final inflections have eroded away phonologically, they have been replaced by grammatical morphemes that now precede their heads. This raises the possibility that contrastive studies of the acquisition of morphosyntax in morphosyntactically similar but prosodically different languages could also shed new light on the psycholinguistic underpinnings of language change.

ACKNOWLEDGMENTS

This study was supported by The Swedish Research Council for the Humanities and Social Sciences (HSFR), grants no. F 783/91 and F 517/92. Thanks go to the members of the Gothenburg research group Anders-Börje Andersson, Lennart Andersson, and Ulla Richtoff for help with the coding work.

REFERENCES

Bloom, L. (1970). *Language development: Form and function in emerging grammars.* Cambridge, MA: MIT Press.

Bruce, G. (1977). *Swedish word accents in sentence perspective,* volume 12 of *Travaux de l'Institut de linguistique de Lund.* Lund: CWK Gleerup.

Diderichsen, P. (1946). *Elementær dansk grammatik.* Copenhagen: Gyldendal.

Engstrand, O. (1989a). F_0 correlates of tonal word accents in spontaneous speech. *PERILUS, 10,* 1-12.

Engstrand, O. (1989b). Phonetic features of the acute and grave word accents: Data from spontaneous speech. *PERILUS, 10,* 13-37.

Engstrand, O., Williams, K., & Strömqvist, S. (1991). Acquisition of the Swedish tonal word accent contrast. Actes du XIIème Congres International des Sciences Phonétiques, Aix-Marseille: Publications de l'Université de Provence, 324-327.

Gårding, E. (1981). Contrastive prosody: A model and its application. *Studia Linguistica, 35,* 146-165.

Hallé, P., Boysson-Bardies, B. de, & Vihman, M. (1991). Beginnings of prosodic organization: Intonation and duration patterns of disyllables produced by Japanese and French infants. *Language and Speech, 34,* 299-318.

Johnston, B. (1991). *The acquisition of morphology in Polish and Russian: A comparative study.* Unpublished manuscript, University of Hawaii, Honolulu.

Major, R. C. (1985). Stress and rhythm in Brazilian Portuguese. *Language, 61,* 259-282.

Morgan, J. L., Meier, R. P., & Newport, E. L. (1987). Structural packaging in the input to language learning: Contributions of prosodic and morphological marking of phrases to the acquisition of language. *Cognitive Psychology, 19,* 498-550.

Peters, A. M., & Menn, L. (1993) False starts and filler syllables: Ways to learn grammatical morphemes. *Language, 69,* 742-777

Plunkett, K., & Strömqvist, S. (1992). The acquisition of Scandinavian languages. In D. Slobin (Ed.), *The crosslinguistic study of language acquisition, Vol. 3* (pp. 457-556). Hillsdale, NJ: Lawrence Erlbaum Associates.

Simonsen, H. G. (1990). *Barns fonologi: System og variasjon hos tre norske og et samoisk barn* [Child phonology: system and variation in three Norwegian children and one Samoan child]. Unpublished doctoral dissertation, University of Oslo.

Slobin, D. I. (1966). The acquisition of Russian as a native language. In F. Smith & G. Miller (Eds.), *The genesis of language: A psycholinguistic approach* (pp. 129-148). Cambridge, MA: MIT Press.

Slobin, D. I. (1971). Developmental psycholinguistics. In W. Dingwall (Ed.), *A survey of linguistic science* (pp. 298-400). College Park, MD: University of Maryland Press.

Smoczyńska, M. (1985). The acquisition of Polish. In D. Slobin (Ed.), *The crosslinguistic study of language acquisition Vol. 3* (pp. 595-686). Hillsdale, NJ: Lawrence Erlbaum Associates.

Stern, C., & Stern, W. (1928). *Die kindersprache.* Leipzig: Barth.

Strömqvist, S., Richtoff, U., & Andersson, A.-H. (1993). Strömqvist's and Richtoff's corpora - A guide to longitudinal data from four Swedish children. *Gothenburg Papers in Theoretical Linguistics, 66.*

14

Deficits of Grammatical Morphology in Children with Specific Language Impairment and Their Implications for Notions of Bootstrapping

Laurence B. Leonard and Julia A. Eyer
Purdue University

One of the most widely studied groups of children with language learning difficulties is a group described as "specifically language-impaired." These are children with significant limitations in language ability who do not exhibit obvious problems in other areas of cognitive functioning. They display normal hearing, age-appropriate scores on nonverbal tests of intelligence, and show no signs of frank neurological impairment nor behaviors suggestive of autism. A common profile among specifically language-impaired children acquiring English is a mild to moderate deficit in a range of language areas, such as syntax and the lexicon, and a more serious problem with grammatical morphology.

It appears that these children might serve as an interesting test case for the role of grammatical morphology in bootstrapping from speech to syntax. As is often noted, grammatical morphemes frequently appear at the edges of major linguistic units whose boundaries must be identified. Furthermore, the appearance of particular grammatical morphemes in juxtaposition with unfamiliar words might assist children's identification of the grammatical category of these words (e.g., *the fiff* versus *fiffing*). Consequently, if children have difficulties processing grammatical morphology, they might be slower not only in forming initial grammatical representations of words but also in identifying the relevant linguistic boundaries before grammatical analysis can even begin. Such children, it would seem, should show protracted—or even unusual—development of language. This might be especially so in the case of specifically language-impaired (SLI) children because, as we will argue, the grammatical morphemes with which they have the greatest difficulty seem to be those whose acoustic characteristics pose problems for perception.

The purpose of this chapter is to examine the nature of SLI children's problems with grammatical morphology with an eye toward their potential effects on the bootstrapping process. We begin with a brief review of the grammatical morpheme deficits in SLI children acquiring English, as well as corroborating evidence suggesting that these children seem to have special difficulty with linguistic material of relatively brief duration. Evidence consistent with this view will then be presented from SLI children acquiring languages whose grammatical morphology is less dependent upon forms of short duration. In the final section, the implications of this type of weakness for the identification of linguistic boundaries and grammatical analysis will be discussed.

SLI CHILDREN ACQUIRING ENGLISH

Studies of English-speaking SLI children's use of grammatical morphology have appeared since the early 1970s. These investigations reveal that SLI children tend to use grammatical morphemes with lower percentages in obligatory contexts than younger normally developing children matched according to mean length of utterance (MLU) (see reviews in Johnston, 1988; Leonard, 1979, 1989). These grammatical morphemes include inflections such as plural -s, possessive 's, past -ed, and third person singular -s, as well as free-standing morphemes such as articles, copula forms, auxiliary forms of be, and the infinitival to. Less problematic are the progressive inflection -ing and the irregular past (e.g., threw), although in a few studies, the irregular past has also revealed group differences favoring the normally developing children (see reviews in Leonard, 1989; Leonard, McGregor, & Allen, 1992). To date, studies of SLI children's grammatical morphology have been limited primarily to production measures.

An example of the grammatical morpheme difficulties of SLI children can be seen in a study by Johnston and Schery (1976). These investigators examined the spontaneous speech of 287 SLI children ranging in age from 3 to 18 years. From these speech samples, Johnston and Schery computed the percentages of use in obligatory contexts of a variety of grammatical morphemes. For illustration, we present here the mean percentages reported for the 51 children in the sample whose MLUs in morphemes approximated 4.0, corresponding to Brown's (1973) Stage V: progressive -ing = 72, plural -s = 75, possessive 's = 24, past -ed = 23, third person singular -s = 20, articles = 57, uncontractible copula = 26. For sake of comparison, it can be noted that all of the normally developing children with comparable MLUs studied by deVilliers and deVilliers (1973) showed percentages above 80 for each of these morphemes.

As noted by a number of investigators of normal child language, the acoustic characteristics of many grammatical morphemes of English probably make the task of learning morphology relatively difficult for English-speaking children (e.g., Gleitman, Gleitman, Landau, & Wanner, 1988; Slobin, 1985). Although a variety of acoustic properties are probably responsible for this difficulty, the one that seems characteristic of most of these morphemes is short duration, at least relative to adjacent material. This is true not only for grammatical morphemes taking the form of single consonants, but also syllabic morphemes that are typically unstressed and shorter in duration than the words that follow or to which they are attached. However, this characterization is incomplete, in that intonational phrase-final syllables are significantly lengthened in English, even when they are not stressed (e.g., Beckman & Edwards, 1990). Thus, the assumption of short relative duration as a major player in the late acquisition of English grammatical morphology holds only to the extent that the syllabic morphemes do not occur frequently in positions that invite significant lengthening. The inflection -*ing*, for example, though unstressed, can often appear in utterance-final and other intonational phrase-final positions.

Leonard (1989) proposed that the short relative durations of English grammatical morphemes may also be partly responsible for SLI children's especially poor morphological abilities. There are two types of findings outside of the area of morphology that seem to support this view. First, phonological processes such as final consonant deletion and weak syllable deletion seem to be more frequent in the speech of SLI children than younger normally developing children matched according to size of consonant inventory (Ingram, 1981). Data from imitation tasks suggest that differences between SLI children and normally developing children widen when one shifts from strings of nonsense syllables with equal stress (e.g., [sɪgpɛbzol]) to strings containing unstressed as well as stressed syllables (e.g., [kəsæbən]) (Kamhi, Catts, Mauer, Apel, & Gentry, 1988).

Studies of speech perception in SLI and normally developing children also reveal differences that have parallels with those seen in morphology.[1] The perceptual contrasts that produce the clearest differences between the groups are those in which the contrastive portion of the stimulus (e.g., the formant transition in [ba] versus [da]) is shorter in duration than that of the remaining portions of the stimulus (e.g., Tallal & Stark, 1981). For example, Leonard, McGregor, and Allen (1992) compared SLI children and age-matched controls in their ability to distinguish several syllable contrasts using the target identification procedure of Tallal and her colleagues (e.g., Tallal & Stark, 1981). No differences were observed in the two groups' performance on [dab] versus [dæb] and [i] versus [u]. In the case of [dab] versus [dæb], the two syllables differed in the majority of the signal, principally, the steady state period of the vowel. In contrast, the SLI children performed significantly more poorly than the control children on the contrasts [das] versus [daʃ] and [dábibà] versus [dábubà].

These findings should certainly not be taken to mean that English-speaking SLI children's problems with grammatical morphology are at-

---

[1]Some of the most valuable data that could be obtained from SLI children would be perception data from the approximate ages of 6 months to 2 years. Unfortunately, such data are not available, largely because the language delay itself is the principal identifying factor in these children, and hence most of these children are not brought to the attention of professionals until shortly after 2 years of age.

tributable solely to the relatively short durations of these morphemes (see Leonard, McGregor, & Allen, 1992). For example, in English, plural -s and third person singular -s share the same phonetic form, but even though both are difficult for SLI children, the former is acquired more readily than the latter. In fact, Rice and Oetting (1993) argued that the gap between SLI children and MLU controls is larger for third singular -s than for noun plural -s. However, the findings do suggest that relative duration could be an important factor. One way of determining the feasibility of this view is to examine the use of grammatical morphemes by SLI children who are acquiring languages other than English.

SLI CHILDREN ACQUIRING OTHER LANGUAGES

It seemed that a first step in evaluating the role of relative duration in SLI children's grammatical morpheme difficulties would be to examine SLI children's use of grammatical morphology in languages where the bulk of grammatical morphemes are stressed and/or lengthened and thus of longer relative duration than those of English. For the past several years, we have pursued this question through the study of SLI children acquiring Italian and, more recently, Hebrew.

Italian

In Italian, noun, verb, and adjective inflections take the form of word-final vowels or word-final multisyllabic morphemes ending in vowels. Thus, singular and plural nouns can be distinguished on the basis of the final vowel (e.g., *libro - libri* "book - books"), as can adjectives that differ in their gender and number (e.g., *pettine giallo - nave gialla* "yellow (masculine) comb" - "yellow (feminine) ship"). Present tense verbs can be distinguished on the basis of the final vowel or the appearance of a multisyllabic inflection ending in a vowel (e.g., *dormo - dormi - dormiamo* "I sleep -you sleep - we sleep"). Most of these inflections do not receive primary stress. However, intonational phrase-final vowel lengthening does occur in Italian (e.g., Farnetani & Fori, 1982), and because the language has relatively flexible word order, all of these inflections can and do appear in final position. There are also several grammatical morphemes in Italian that are unstressed syllables that are not in a position to benefit from lengthening. Articles represent one such example (e.g., *il cane* "the dog," *la chiave* "the key").

A summary of some of these characteristics, as reflected in vowel durations, can be seen in Table 14.1. These are representative sentences of a larger set drawn from our own testing protocol and read by a native speaker of Italian. Although the speaker was asked to read the sentences with children as the intended audience, the productions were not, in fact, child-directed.

An example of utterance-final vowel lengthening can be seen in the longer durations noted for the final [a] of *lava* in Sentence 2 of Table 14.1 relative to the same vowel in *lava* in Sentence 4. Another example can be seen in a comparison of the [a] in *bella* in Sentence 5 versus Sentence 6.

Articles are unstressed monosyllables that do not receive lengthening. As can be seen in Table 14.1, the vowel of the article *la* in Sentence 2 is considerably shorter than both of the vowels in *lava* in the same sentence. (The first of the vowels in *lava* is stressed, the second appears in a position that receives lengthening.) Direct object clitics that precede finite verbs are also unstressed monosyllables. In this sentence position they do not receive lengthening. One example is the feminine singular clitic *la*, which is identical in form to the article *la*. As can be seen in Sentences 1 and 2 of Table 14.1, the [a] in this clitic form has shorter duration than the first [a] in *lava* and *lavano*, which is stressed, and the second [a] in *lava*, which is lengthened. The vowel durations of the clitic more closely approximate those seen in the articles (see Sentences 2 and 4).

Finally, there are grammatical morphemes composed of multiple syllables, one of which is problematic in terms of its surface characteristics. The prime example is the third person plural verb inflection. This inflection consists of two syllables (either *-ano* or *-ono*) but the primary stress of the word falls on the stem (e.g., *préndono*). Consequently, the

TABLE 14.1
Some Vowel Durations (in Milliseconds) in Representative Sentences Produced by an Italian Speaker

1. I ragázzi lávano la mácchina e poi la spíngono.
   183 128 67   66

   "The boys wash the car and then push it."

2. Il ragázzo spínge la mácchina e poi la láva.
                     61   81 175 150

   "The boy pushes the car and then washes it."

3. I bambíni mángiano la tórta e poi dórmono.
             128

   "The children eat the cake and then sleep."

4. Il ragázzo láva la mácchina e poi la spínge.
             114 56 69

   "The boy washes the car and then pushes it."

5. Baghdád è bélla.
             144

   "Baghdad is beautiful."

6. Iéri ho vísto una bélla bambína.
                     53

   "Yesterday I saw a beautiful little girl."

penultimate syllable—which is the first syllable of the inflection—is un-stressed and likely to be difficult to perceive.   Some indication of this potential difficulty can be seen in the relatively short duration of the second [a] in *lavano* in Sentence 1 of Table 1. It is true that the final syllable of the inflection can be lengthened in clause-final position, and therefore, this syllable, at least, should be reasonably salient. However, producing the word without the unstressed penultimate syllable is not a viable option for the child, as this would violate phonotactic constraints in the language (e.g., *prendno). For similar reasons, of course, the stem will not be produced without any inflection. Consequently, a child having difficulty with the unstressed syllable in such cases is likely to use a different, incorrect inflection with the verb.

If, as was assumed for English, SLI children have special difficulties with grammatical morphology when the morphemes are of relatively short duration, SLI children acquiring Italian should have extraordinary problems with only a few morphemes. The only inflection that should be especially difficult is the third person plural verb inflection. On the other hand, the free-standing unstressed monosyllabic morphemes that do not receive lengthening, such as articles and clitics, should be quite difficult for the SLI children.

These expectations were confirmed in a recent investigation by Leonard, Bortolini, Caselli, McGregor, and Sabbadini (1992) of 15 Italian-speaking SLI children (ages 4;0 to 6;0, MLU in words 1.9 to 4.3) and two groups of normally developing controls, one matched according to MLU, the other according to age.   The children described sets of pictures that, in conjunction with questions and sentence frames provided by the adult, obligated the use of the grammatical morphemes of interest. The percentages of use of these morphemes in the obligatory contexts were then computed. A summary of the results appears in Table 14.2.

As expected, the age controls showed the highest percentages of use in obligatory contexts for all of the grammatical morphemes of interest. The more informative comparisons concern those between the SLI children and their MLU controls, for it is here that one can determine if the SLI children's use of grammatical morphemes is more limited than one might expect for their mean utterance length.[2]

The two groups were similar in their percentages of use in obligatory contexts for noun plurals, third person singular verb inflections, and adjective inflections. In contrast, the SLI children showed significantly lower percentages than the MLU controls for third person plural verb inflections, articles, and clitics. The more difficult grammatical morphemes share the property of shorter duration relative to surrounding morphemes.

---

[2] In the interest of space, only the production data are discussed here. Comprehension data yielded comparable findings and are discussed in Leonard et al. (1992).

TABLE 14.2
Use of Grammatical Morphemes by Italian-Speaking Children Studied by Leonard,
Bortolini, Caselli, McGregor, and Sabbadini (1992)

Grammatical Morpheme	ISLI[a]	IND-MLU[b]	IND-A[c]
Inflections			
Plurals	87	89	98
Third Singular	93	93	93
Third Plural	50	82	91
Adjective	97	99	100
Function Words			
Articles	41	83	97
Clitics	26	66	92

Note. All values are mean percentages. [a]Italian-speaking children with specific language impairment. [b]Normally developing Italian-speaking children matched with the ISLI children according to mean length of utterance in words. [c]Normally developing Italian-speaking children matched according to age.

Hebrew

As in Italian, all nouns, verbs, and adjectives of Hebrew are inflected. However, Hebrew is quite different from Italian and other Indo-European languages in that words from these categories have a root composed of discontinuous consonants; permissible words are formed through the insertion of vowels between these consonants. Inflections of person, number, and gender are expressed through syllabic suffixes and/or changes in the intercalated vowels. For example, the root for the verb "ride" is the discontinuous form *r-x-v*. The present masculine singular is *roxev*, the present feminine singular is *roxevet*, and the (third person) masculine singular in the past is *raxav*. The great majority of these inflections involves a stressed syllable. In the remaining cases, they involve an unstressed word-final syllable. However, Hebrew shows significant syllable lengthening in intonational phrase-final position (e.g., Berkovits, 1993), and its flexibility in word order ensures that even the unstressed syllabic inflections appear frequently in this position. There are also grammatical morphemes in Hebrew taking the form of unstressed syllabic prefixes or free-standing monosyllables that do not appear in positions in which lengthening occurs (e.g., the definite prefix, as in *ha-kadur* "the ball," *ha-kelev* "the dog").

To illustrate some of these characteristics, vowel durations from seven sentences are provided in Table 14.3. These sentences were part of a larger set drawn from our testing protocol and read by a native speaker of Hebrew, following the same procedures used for the Italian sentences shown in Table 14.1.

An example of a stressed vowel serving a morphological role can be seen in the [e] of the masculine singular verb form *shote* in Sentence 1 of Table 14.3. An example of utterance-final lengthening can be seen by examining the same vowel in the same word in Sentence 6. Lengthen-

TABLE 14.3

Some Vowel Durations (in Milliseconds) in Representative Sentences Produced by a
Hebrew Speaker

1. ha-tinók shoté xaláv ve-ha-kélev lo'és étsem.
   50   103
   "the-baby drinks milk and-the-dog chews on (a) bone."

2. sába menashék et xána.
         41 102
   "grandfather kisses (def accus case marker) Hanna."

3. ha-sús oxél ésev ve-ha-xasidá oxélet dág.
   47   108   61
   "the-horse eats grass and-the-stork eats (a) fish."

4. tómi kotév et ha-mixtáv.
          36
   "Tommy writes (def accus case marker) the-letter."

5. ha-yéled yoshév al ha-éts ve-shlomít yoshévet be-óto.
                                  45
   "the-boy sits in the-tree and-Shlomit sits in-(a)-car."

6. ha-yaldá metsayéret al ha-lúax ve-ha-tinók shoté.
                                          131
   "the-girl draws on the-blackboard and-the-baby drinks."

7. ha-ísh menasér ve-shlomít yoshévet.
                              95
   "the-man sews and-Shlomit sits."

ing in an unstressed vowel can be seen in the second [e] of *yoshevet* in
Sentence 5 versus 7.   It can be seen that final lengthening is not dramatic, though nevertheless quite evident.

The definite accusative case marker *et* is an unstressed grammatical
morpheme that does not appear in intonational phrase-final position.
Examples of this morpheme can be seen in Sentences 2 and 4.   As can
be seen from a comparison of Sentences 4 and 7, [e] in *et* is shorter than
[e] in unstressed but lengthened inflections. Another frequent monosyllabic grammatical morpheme that is not in a position to be lengthened
is the definite prefix *ha-*. The duration of [a] in this morpheme (see Sentences 1 and 3) is relatively short and resembles that seen in an unstressed syllable in non-final position of a multisyllabic word, as in the
first [a] in *xasida* in Sentence 3.

According to the hypothesis that the grammatical morphemes caus-
ing special problems for SLI children are those of relatively short duration, we should expect that the definite accusative case marker and the
definite prefix would be used with lower percentages by Hebrew-
speaking SLI children than by MLU controls, but that the remaining
morphemes—the noun, verb, and adjective inflections (all of which are
stressed and/or frequently lengthened)—should not be any more difficult for the SLI children than for the MLU controls.

We explored this question in a study of 15 Hebrew-speaking SLI
children (ages 4;1 to 5;11, MLU in words 2.0 to 3.1) along with a group

of age controls and a group of MLU controls (Dromi, Leonard, & Shteiman, 1993). The procedure was similar to that used in the work on Italian. The children produced utterances containing obligatory contexts for the grammatical morphemes of interest, in response to pictures and accompanying questions and sentence frames produced by the adult. Percentages of use of the grammatical morphemes in the obligatory contexts were then computed. A summary of the data appears in Table 14.4.

The age controls showed the highest percentages of use of the grammatical morphemes in obligatory contexts, as expected. Again, the most illuminating comparisons concern the SLI children and their MLU controls.[3]

Consistent with expectations, the SLI children used all four of the inflection types with percentages as high as those shown by the MLU controls. Also expected was the finding that the definite accusative case marker *et* was used with significantly lower percentages by the SLI children than the MLU controls. Contrary to predictions, there were no differences between the SLI and MLU-matched children in the use of the definite prefix *ha-*.

It is not clear why the SLI children performed as well as the MLU controls in the use of the definite prefix. A preliminary study by Rom and Leonard (1990) using spontaneous speech samples of approximately 50 utterances revealed a difference between 7 Hebrew-speaking SLI children and their MLU controls (favoring the latter). However, given the small sample sizes and small number of subjects used in the Rom and Leonard study, we have no reason to be confident that the findings reported here constitute a Type II error.

TABLE 14.4
Use of Grammatical Morphemes by Hebrew-Speaking Children Studied by Dromi,
Leonard, and Shteiman (1993)

Grammatical Morpheme	HSLI[a]	HND-MLU[b]	HND-A[c]
Inflections			
Present Verb	76	79	96
Past Verb	56	29	85
Noun Plural	76	74	91
Adjective	70	78	93
Prefixes and Free-Standing Grammatical Morphemes			
Definite Prefix	78	65	97
Definite Accusative Case Marker	86	97	98

Note. All values are mean percentages. [a]Hebrew-speaking children with specific language impairment. [b]Normally developing Hebrew-speaking children matched with the HSLI children according to mean length of utterance in words. [c]Normally developing Hebrew-speaking children matched according to age.

[3]Findings for comprehension can be seen in Dromi et al. (1993).

It is highly possible that some facilitating factor was operative for *ha-*, enabling the SLI children to acquire this form without special difficulty, its brief duration notwithstanding. One such possibility is the fact that this form is affixed not only to nouns but to modifiers as well, including demonstratives. For example, "the little girl" is expressed as *ha-yalda ha-ktana*, literally, "the girl the little." "These little girls" is expressed as *ha-yeladot ha-ktanot ha-ele*, literally, "the girls the little the these." The multiple markings of the definite in phrases with modifiers might make *ha-* more salient in the input. This is essentially the complement of the work of Morgan, Meier, and Newport (1987) who found that concord morphology of this type helps the learner to identify phrases in the language. Here the concord morphology is assumed to assist the learning of the markers themselves.

Interpretation of the Data

Together the data from Italian- and Hebrew-speaking SLI children support the view that grammatical morphemes with relatively short durations pose particular problems for SLI children in general. When the language relies heavily on morphemes with this characteristic, as in English, grammatical morphology will stand out as an especially weak area in SLI children. When the grammatical morphology of the language makes less use of morphemes with this characteristic, as in Italian and Hebrew, extraordinary problems will be limited to those morphemes that possess this property.

As noted earlier, the argument is not that relative duration is the sole or even most important factor in SLI children's acquisition of grammatical morphology. Obviously, factors unrelated to speech acoustics are crucial, such as the degree to which the morpheme has semantic correlates, whether its features must agree with those of another element in the sentence, whether bare stems are even permissible in the language being learned, and so on.

Even within the area of speech acoustics it is likely that factors other than relative duration figure importantly in SLI children's difficulties. Once the absolute duration of some phonetic form reaches a certain point, its relative duration might be less important. In addition, amplitude and fundamental frequency clearly interact with duration in important ways. We have also been working thus far with the distinction between stressed and/or lengthened syllables on the one hand and unstressed syllables and final consonants on the other. Yet monosyllabic grammatical morphemes themselves differ in degree of stress (e.g., Altenberg, 1987; Coker, Umeda, & Browman, 1973). Finally, we have been disregarding the context in which grammatical morphemes in the form of final consonants occur. Yet, final consonants that follow stressed and lengthened vowels are longer than the same consonants in otherwise similar phonetic contexts (e.g., Coker et al., 1973).

Even with these qualifications in mind, it is difficult to avoid the conclusion that relative duration plays a role in SLI children's acquisition of grammatical morphology. We consider now the implications of this interpretation for SLI children acquiring English.

BOOTSTRAPPING IN THE CASE OF SLI CHILDREN ACQUIRING ENGLISH

There is reason to assume that the effects of SLI children's difficulty with relatively brief material will be that of late emergence and protracted development of many aspects of English rather than the formation of odd segmentations and bizarre rules. This is because, to the extent that intonational phrase boundaries co-occur with syntactic phrase and clause boundaries (see Beckman & Edwards, 1990), SLI children should not have special difficulties identifying the linguistic units within which grammatical and lexical analysis must take place. These boundaries are associated with significant syllable lengthening (Bernstein Ratner, 1986; Morgan, 1986; Swanson, Leonard, & Gandour, 1992), and SLI children provide evidence from their MLU-appropriate use of syllabic grammatical morphemes that are similarly lengthened that cues of this type are accessible to them.

On the other hand, once relevant phrase and clause boundaries are identified, the tasks of identifying words and grammatical patterns are likely to be hampered by these children's presumed difficulty with phonetic material of relatively short duration. Word-final syllables are lengthened to a small degree in phrase-medial position (e.g., Klatt, 1975), especially (at least in deliberately clear speech) when the next word begins with or consists entirely of an unstressed syllable (Cutler & Butterfield, 1990). However, for children whose perception of linguistic material with relatively short duration is rather poor (demonstrated in the perception studies reviewed earlier), such effects might be too subtle to assist parsing. Consequently, words of this type might have to be heard in a wider variety of phonetic contexts by SLI children before they are adequately identified. Presumably, this would require a longer exposure period.

It is often assumed that young children can form an initial grammatical representation of a new word on the basis of the linguistic context in which it appears. One part of this context is the grammatical morphology that surrounds the word. For example, upon hearing a new word preceded by an article, children assume the word is a noun; if the word is preceded by the infinitival *to*, they assume it is a verb, and so on (Golinkoff, Diznoff, Yasik, & Hirsh-Pasek, 1992). Because many of the grammatical morphemes of English are of relatively brief duration, it seems likely that SLI children learning the language will not detect some of the morphological cues to a new word's grammatical category. Thus, the word's entry into the child's grammar will be late, thereby delaying such things as the learning of a verb's argument structure.

Of course, grammatical morphemes are not only helpful in identifying the grammatical categories of adjacent words, they help form the syntax. For example, the unstressed morpheme *to* plays a critical role in distinguishing the prepositional dative structure (e.g., *Give the cup to Mommy*) from the double object dative structure (e.g., *Give Mommy the cup*). If this morpheme is not detected, the child might erroneously learn that, say, the order of nouns following certain verbs is variable, contrary to the rest of English. The passive, too, is a construction that could be problematic if the grammatical morphemes that contribute to this construction are not detected (e.g., *is, -ed, by* in *Chris is teased by the other children*).

Other syntactic constructions might not be expected to pose special problems for SLI children, at least to the extent that current learnability theories are correct. For example, in the theory of Pinker (1984), it is assumed that constituents can be ordered in the child's grammar without a final commitment as to how the constituents are attached in the phrase structure tree. This is accomplished by assigning a node, whose mother is not known, to an ancestor node. The node can be removed from temporary custody when and if the child discovers the evidence that there should be a node intervening between the node in question and the ancestor node. Temporary custody can become permanent custody if the child never encounters intervening nodes (e.g., if the language turns out to use case-marking affixes on nouns instead of prepositions).

Because SLI children will require a greater number of exposures to grammatical morphemes of relatively short duration, and hence more time to learn them, the provision of temporary custody will allow these children to acquire other elements of the syntax in the meantime, without creating peculiar, dead-end rules. When the grammatical morphemes are eventually learned, the intervening node can be created and the temporary custody configuration will be preempted.

In summary, then, given the assumption that SLI children have special difficulty with grammatical morphemes of relatively short duration, these children might be expected to identify major phrase and clause boundaries but be slower in their identification of words and syntactic structures. Syntactic constructions that depend heavily upon morphemes of relatively short duration for interpretation will be especially slow to develop. However, with these exceptions, the most remarkable characteristic of these children's speech will be its exaggerated telegraphic look, brought on by the children's ability to progress (albeit slowly) to utterances several words in length even when grammatical morphemes ordinarily associated with the same stage of development have not yet emerged.

How well do the available data accord with these expectations? The fact that SLI children have more difficulty with grammatical morphology than MLU controls has already been discussed. Comparisons between SLI children and MLU controls on lexical and syntactic measures show generally similar levels of development in the two groups (see reviews in Johnston, 1988; Leonard, 1988), though differences favoring MLU controls can be found. For example, SLI children and MLU controls are similar in the number and distribution of lexical types reflected in their speech (Leonard, Camarata, Rowan, & Chapman, 1982). However, on learning tasks (e.g., fast mapping tasks) in which SLI children and MLU controls receive equal exposure to a new word in story contexts, SLI children sometimes perform more poorly than the MLU controls (Rice, Buhr, & Nemeth, 1990). The findings for syntax suggest that SLI children and MLU controls are similar in the variety of syntactic constructions (Morehead & Ingram, 1973), and number of arguments reflected in their sentences (Johnston & Kamhi, 1984).   However, SLI children are more prone to grammatical errors, especially those involving the auxiliary system (Johnston & Kamhi, 1984). Although SLI children's MLUs increase at a relatively slow rate, utterances containing omissions of grammatical morphemes can sometimes reach surprising lengths (Weiner, 1974). Finally, SLI children seem to have particular problems with passive (Menyuk & Looney, 1972; van der Lely & Harris, 1990) and dative constructions (van der Lely & Harris, 1990).

It appears, then, that there is reasonably close correspondence between expectations based on current views of bootstrapping and SLI children's profiles of language, given the assumption made here that relative duration plays an important role in these children's processing of language. It is hoped that this observation serves as an impetus for additional, more finely tuned research on the possible consequences of morphological deficits in SLI children. By showing how under clearly specified learning conditions current assumptions about bootstrapping operations can accurately predict patterns of language behavior in language-disordered children, we also hope to have contributed substantively to the debate over whether bootstrapping operations actually work in the way they have been proposed.

REFERENCES

Altenberg, B. (1987). *Prosodic patterns in spoken English: Studies in the correlation between prosody and grammar or text-to-speech conversion.* Lund, Sweden: Lund University Press.

Beckman, M., & Edwards, J. (1990). Lengthening and shortening and the nature of prosodic constituency. In J. Kingston & M. Beckman (Eds.), *Papers in laboratory phonology: I. Between grammar and the physics of speech* (pp. 152-178). Cambridge, England: Cambridge University Press.

Berkovits, R. (1993). Progressive utterance-final lengthening in syllables with final fricatives. *Language and Speech, 36,* 89-98.

Bernstein Ratner, N. (1986). Durational cues which mark clause boundaries in mother-child speech. *Journal of Phonetics, 14,* 303-309.

Brown, R. (1973). *A first language.* Cambridge, MA: Harvard University Press.

Coker, C., Umeda, N., & Browman, P. (1973). Automatic synthesis from ordinary English text. *IEEE Transactions on Audio and Electroacoustics, AU-21,* 293-298.

Cutler, A., & Butterfield, S. (1990). Durational cues to word boundaries in clear speech. *Speech Communication, 9*, 485-495.

deVilliers, J., & deVilliers, P. (1973). A cross-sectional study of the acquisition of grammatical morphemes in child speech. *Journal of Psycholinguistic Research, 2*, 267-278.

Dromi, E., Leonard, L., & Shteiman, M. (1993). The grammatical morphology of Hebrew-speaking children with specific language impairment: Some competing hypotheses. *Journal of Speech and Hearing Research, 36*, 760-771.

Farnetani, E., & Fori, S. (1982). Lexical stress in spoken sentences: A study of duration and vowel formant pattern. *Quaderni del Centro di Studio per le Ricerche di Fonetica, 1*, 104-133.

Gleitman, L., Gleitman, H., Landau, B., & Wanner, E. (1988). Where language begins: Initial representations for language learning. In F. Newmeyer (Ed.), *Linguistics: The Cambridge survey. Volume III* (pp. 150-193). Cambridge, England: Cambridge University Press.

Golinkoff, R., Diznoff, J., Yasik, A., & Hirsh-Pasek, K. (1992, May). *How children identify nouns versus verbs.* Paper presented at International Conference on Infant Studies, Miami.

Ingram, D. (1981). *Procedures for the phonological analysis of children's language.* Baltimore, MD: University Park Press.

Johnston, J. (1988). Specific language disorders in the child. In N. Lass, L. McReynolds, J. Northern, & D. Yoder (Eds.), *Handbook of speech-language pathology and audiology* (pp. 685-715). Toronto: B. C. Decker.

Johnston, J., & Kamhi, A. (1984). Syntactic and semantic aspects of the utterances of language-impaired children: The same can be less. *Merrill-Palmer Quarterly, 30*, 65-85.

Johnston, J., & Schery, T. (1976). The use of grammatical morphemes by children with communicative disorders. In D. Morehead & A. Morehead (Eds.), *Normal and deficient child language* (pp. 239-258). Baltimore, MD: University Park Press.

Kamhi, A., Catts, H., Mauer, D., Apel, K., & Gentry, B. (1988). Phonological and spatial processing abilities in language- and reading-impaired children. *Journal of Speech and Hearing Disorders, 53*, 316-327.

Klatt, D. (1975). Vowel lengthening is syntactically determined in a connected discourse. *Journal of Phonetics, 3*, 129-140.

Leonard, L. (1979). Language impairment in children. *Merrill-Palmer Quarterly, 25*, 205-232.

Leonard, L. (1988). Lexical development and processing in specific language impairment. In R. Schiefelbusch & L. Lloyd (Eds.), *Language perspectives: Acquisition, retardation and intervention* (pp. 69-87, Second edition). Austin, TX: Pro-Ed.

Leonard, L. (1989). Language learnability and specific language impairment in children. *Applied Psycholinguistics, 10*, 179-202.

Leonard, L., Bortolini, U., Caselli, M. C., McGregor, K., & Sabbadini, L. (1992). Morphological deficits in children with specific language impairment: The status of features in the underlying grammar. *Language Acquisition, 2*, 151-179.

Leonard, L., Camarata, S., Rowan, L., & Chapman, K. (1982). The communicative functions of lexical usage by language impaired children. *Applied Psycholinguistics, 3*, 109-125.

Leonard, L., McGregor, K., & Allen, G. (1992). Grammatical morphology and speech perception in children with specific language impairment. *Journal of Speech and Hearing Research, 35*, 1076-1085.

Menyuk, P., & Looney, P. (1972). A problem of language disorder: Length versus structure. *Journal of Speech and Hearing Research, 15*, 264-279.

Morehead, D., & Ingram, D. (1973). The development of base syntax in normal and linguistically deviant children. *Journal of Speech and Hearing Research, 16*, 330-352.

Morgan, J. (1986). *From simple input to complex grammar.* Cambridge, MA: MIT Press.

Morgan, J., Meier, R., & Newport, E. (1987). Structural packaging in the input to language learning: Contributions of prosodic and morphological marking of phrases to the acquisition of language. *Cognitive Psychology, 19*, 498-550.

Pinker, S. (1984). *Language learnability and language development.* Cambridge, MA: Harvard University Press.

Rice, M., Buhr, J., & Nemeth, M. (1990). Fast mapping word- learning abilities of language-delayed preschoolers. *Journal of Speech and Hearing Research, 55,* 33-42.

Rice, M., & Oetting, J. (1993). Morphological deficits with SLI: Evaluation of number marking and agreement. *Journal of Speech and Hearing Research, 36,* 1249-1257.

Rom, A., & Leonard, L. (1990). Interpreting deficits in grammatical morphology in specifically language-impaired children: Preliminary evidence from Hebrew. *Clinical Linguistics and Phonetics, 4,* 93-105.

Slobin, D. (1985). Crosslinguistic evidence for the language-making capacity. In D. Slobin (Ed.), *The crosslinguistic study of language acquisition: Volume 2. Theoretical issues* (pp. 1157-1249). Hillsdale, NJ: Lawrence Erlbaum Associates.

Swanson, L., Leonard, L., & Gandour, J. (1992). Vowel duration in mothers' speech to young children. *Journal of Speech and Hearing Research, 35,* 617-625.

Tallal, P., & Stark, R. (1981). Speech acoustic-cue discrimination abilities of normally developing and language-impaired children. *Journal of the Acoustical Society of America, 69,* 568-574.

van der Lely, H., & Harris, M. (1990). Comprehension of reversible sentences in specifically language-impaired children. *Journal of Speech and Hearing Disorders, 55,* 101-117.

Weiner, P. (1974). A language-delayed child at adolescence. *Journal of Speech and Hearing Disorders, 39,* 202-212.

15 The Role of Phonology in Grammatical Category Assignments

Michael H. Kelly
University of Pennsylvania

The lexical entry for a word must contain information about its pronunciation, syntactic usage, such as grammatical class and argument structure, and semantics. If these variables are correlated with each other, then information about one variable could guide inferences about one or more of the others. In fact, both syntactic and semantic bootstrapping proposals claim that the syntax and semantics of verbs are not arbitrarily related. Given relationships between a verb's syntax and semantics, one could possibly infer something about a verb's semantics from its syntactic role in sentences and vice versa (Gleitman, 1990; Pinker, 1989).

Although a great deal of attention has been devoted to uncovering and characterizing syntax-semantic relationships, and how these relationships could be exploited in language acquisition and comprehension, potential relationships between phonology and other aspects of lexical structure have been relatively neglected. Consider, for example, discussions of how the grammatical class of a word might be identified. Such discussions often refer to semantic cues to grammatical class, such as the cross-linguistic tendency for nouns to denote concrete objects and verbs to denote actions (e.g., Bates & MacWhinney, 1982; Schlesinger, 1974, 1988). However, possible phonological predictors of grammatical class are hardly mentioned. For instance, in a recent edited work that focuses in large part on the development of grammatical classes (Levy, Schlesinger, & Braine, 1988), only a single page reference is listed under the heading "phonological," whereas semantic and syntactic headings receive over 50 page references each.

This neglect of phonological correlates to grammatical class can be attributed to a number of factors, only two of which will be mentioned here. First, whereas semantic correlates with grammatical class appear to be universal, any phonological cues are likely to be language-specific. Hence even if certain phonological variables are related to grammatical class, a child cannot predict in advance which variable or variables will be diagnostic. Phonology could therefore not be used by a naive learner to discover the grammatical categories of a language. Semantics, on the other hand, could provide a bootstrap given (a) universal mappings between semantics and grammatical class, and (b) children who enter language learning with the expectation that these

249

particular mappings exist. Second, one could argue that syntactic information is the ultimate determinant of grammatical class. Hence, such information is both necessary and sufficient to identify the grammatical class of a word. Phonological cues, on the other hand, are mere correlates with grammatical class. Hence the phonological features of a word are either superfluous when they agree with syntactic information or overridden when they conflict with that information.

Despite such doubts about the usefulness of phonological cues to grammatical class, it would be a mistake to dismiss such information prematurely. The existence and knowledge of such patterns could help to solve numerous problems that are confronted in language acquisition, comprehension, and production. I briefly touch upon a few such possibilities here. First, many proposals suggest that children make use of distributional evidence to identify the grammatical classes of various words in a sentence (e.g., Maratsos & Chalkley, 1980). However, this distributional evidence often consists of closed-class words such as "the" and "a" that are unstressed and so not perceptually salient. In fact, children do have difficulties with such unstressed material (Gleitman & Wanner, 1982). If phonological features of a word are related to its grammatical class, they could partially compensate for the incomplete perception and/or encoding of closed-class material. Second, children must not only assign words to grammatical classes in the course of parsing an utterance, but must also store in memory the grammatical classes of words so that they can use them appropriately in the future. Perhaps phonological features that are partly diagnostic of grammatical class increase the speed and accuracy of this memorization. Some evidence for this view can be found in investigations of artificial language learning. The grammatical classes of words in these artificial languages are learned more quickly when predicted by phonological properties (Brooks, Braine, Catalano, Brody, & Sudhalter, 1993). Third, listeners must make grammatical category assignments quickly, given that conversational speech rates typically reach 150 words per minute (Maclay & Osgood, 1959). By supplementing semantic and syntactic cues to grammatical class with phonological ones, listeners might be able to increase the speed and accuracy of these grammatical category assignments. This possibility is consistent with evidence from other areas of perception and cognition in which multiple information sources are used to solve various problems (e.g., depth perception, sound localization, categorization). Finally, sentences often contain local ambiguities in which the grammatical category of a word or words is temporarily unclear. For instance, the written version of "The group records. . ." could have an article-noun-verb or an article-adjective-noun structure. Although subsequent information will resolve the ambiguity, the reader might incur costs either by making an incorrect initial assignment or holding the possibilities in memory until the disambiguating material arrives (see Frazier & Rayner, 1987, for discussion). However, these costs might be reduced or eliminated in an auditory version of the sentence if phonological properties of the relevant words could be used to prevent or quickly resolve the ambiguity.

In order to be more than speculation, claims about the usefulness of phonological cues to grammatical class must be buttressed with evidence pertaining to several issues. First, are phonological correlates to grammatical class actually available, or is phonology truly unrelated to this domain? Second, can the child perceive and attend to the relevant phonological variables? Third, can human beings detect correlations between the phonological and syntactic domains? Finally, is this information actually exploited to solve various problems in language processing? These issues will be discussed briefly in the remainder of this chapter.

EXISTENCE OF PHONOLOGICAL CUES TO GRAMMATICAL CLASS

Linguists have noted a number of phonological correlates to grammatical class or subsets within a class. The tendency for disyllabic English nouns and verbs to differ in stress (e.g., the noun and verb pronunciations of "permit") is one oft-cited example. However, what is less emphasized is the strength of such phonological differences, and how many phonological variables are related to grammatical class. For example, analyses of the English noun-verb stress difference have revealed that not a single noun-verb homograph exists in which the verb has first syllable stress but the noun has second syllable stress. If the noun and verb versions of a word contrast in stress at all, the noun always has first syllable stress and the verb has second syllable stress. Furthermore, an examination of thousands of disyllabic nouns and verbs in English, which was not restricted to noun-verb homographs, has revealed that 90% of words with first syllable stress are nouns rather than verbs whereas 85% of words with second syllable stress are verbs rather than nouns (Kelly & Bock, 1988; Kelly, 1992). Finally, even noun-verb pairs that agree in stress, and so appear to be homonyms, nonetheless differ in their pronunciations. Sereno and Jongman (1995) asked subjects to read aloud sentences containing noun or verb versions of homographs like "practice." The noun and verb uses appeared in identical rhythmic contexts and serial positions within their respective sentences. However, acoustic analyses revealed that the noun-verb homographs differed in the ratios of first syllable duration and amplitude to second syllable duration and amplitude. These ratios were larger for the noun uses of the disyllabic words than for the verb uses, which is consistent with (a) the noun-verb stress asymmetry and (b) the correlations between syllable duration/amplitude and stress in English. It remains to be seen whether listeners can perceive the acoustic differences reported by Sereno and Jongman, but they at least raise the possibility that true cases of noun-verb homonyms might not exist. In sum, then, the noun-verb stress difference is both strong in magnitude and widespread throughout the English lexicon.

Stress is not an isolated case, as many variables have been shown to be related to grammatical class in English. These variables include syllable number, vowel type, consonant voicing, word duration, and the types of consonants contained in a word (see Kelly, 1992, for a review and Table 15.1 for a summary). Some of the variables, like stress and number of syllables, are strongly predictive of grammatical class, whereas others are less reliable. However, the assumption of an arbitrary relation between phonology and grammatical class is incorrect. Indeed, the default situation may be exactly the reverse.

PERCEPTUAL PREREQUISITES TO LEARNING CORRELATIONS BETWEEN PHONOLOGY AND GRAMMATICAL CLASS

Over the past two decades, extensive research has documented that infants have quite sophisticated speech perception abilities. For example, 2-month-old infants can perceive numerous phonetic contrasts, including those from languages that they have never heard before (see Jusczyk, in press, for a detailed review). In addition to segmental distinctions, infants can discriminate different prosodic structures, such as strong-weak versus weak-strong stress patterns (Spring & Dale, 1977; Jusczyk, Cutler, & Redanz, 1993), and consequently have met the most basic perceptual prerequisite for learning about the English noun-verb stress difference early in life.

Early use of phonological cues to grammatical class requires more than the ability to perceive the relevant variables, such as stress or different phoneme classes. Given that many of the cues are language-specific, children must learn the phonological structure of their native language and correlated patterns within that structure. Recent evidence has shown that infants are quite adept at these tasks. At just four days of age, babies can discriminate their parents' language from a foreign one (Mehler et al., 1988). Thus, newborn infants have learned at least gross characteristics of their language's sound structure, presumably

TABLE 15.1
Some Phonological Predictors of Grammatical Class in English

Variable	Description
Stress	Disyllabic nouns have trochaic stress, verbs have iambic stress
Syllables	Nouns contain more syllables than verbs
Duration	Controlling for syllable number, nouns are longer than verbs
Vowel quality	Nouns have more low vowels, verbs more high vowels
Consonant quality	Nouns are more likely than verbs to have nasal consonants
Phonemes	Controlling for syllable number, nouns contain more phonemes

through prenatal auditory experience. By 6 months of age, infants seem to have organized their vowel categories around prototypes appropriate to their native language (Grieser & Kuhl, 1989; Kuhl et al., 1992). In addition, they can discriminate the prosodic patterns of words in their native language from those in a foreign language (Jusczyk et al., 1993).

By 9 months of age, children can not only make native-foreign language discriminations, but are also sensitive to the relative frequencies of different subpatterns within their native language. For example, American infants of this age prefer listening to words with first syllable rather than second syllable stress, thus showing awareness of the dominant lexical stress pattern in English (Jusczyk, Cutler, & Redanz, 1993). Furthermore, 9-month-old children are sensitive not just to the phonetic units of their language, but also to correlations between those units. Jusczyk et al. (1993) presented American and Dutch infants with English and Dutch word lists. All of the words were composed of phonemes permissible in each language. However, some of the phoneme sequences in the two lists were not permitted in the other language. For instance, some of the Dutch words contained the sequence /kn/, which is not found in English. The subjects in the experiment preferred word lists drawn from their native language, suggesting that they had learned some of the distributional regularities governing phonemes in their languages (see also Friederici & Wessels, 1993).   Children's knowledge of these distributional regularities may be even more fine-grained   than   the   general   categories   of   "permissible"   and "impermissible." In particular, Jusczyk, Charles-Luce, and Luce (1994) presented 9-month-old American infants with lists of CVC nonsense words. All of the words contained phonemes and phoneme sequences that are permitted in English. However, one of the lists contained phoneme sequences that are relatively frequent in English, whereas the other contained sequences that are relatively infrequent. The infants preferred listening to the former list, suggesting that they are sensitive to distributional correlations between phonemes in their language.

In sum, children in the first year of life achieve a number of perceptual prerequisites to the use of phonological cues to grammatical class. First, they can perceive numerous phonological variables, including some, such as lexical stress, that are correlated with grammatical class. Second, they home in on the phonological structure of their native language very quickly, which is an important ability given that correlations between phonological variables and grammatical class are generally language specific. Third, they can perceive the relative frequencies of different linguistic events in their language. Finally, infants have the capability to detect correlations between linguistic events. None of these skills entails that young children can learn relationships between phonology and grammatical class early in life, but they are certainly necessary for such learning to proceed.

INFORMATION SENSITIVITY AND EXPLOITATION

Numerous experiments have been conducted to determine if English speakers have learned phonological cues to grammatical class. Some of this research will be described in this section. I focus primarily on the noun-verb stress difference, but some attention will be given to other cues to illustrate developmental and cross-linguistic themes. Although this research documents adult sensitivity to phonological cues to grammatical class, it remains to be seen whether that knowledge is actually exploited in solving problems in language processing or acquisition.

Pronouncing Novel Words

In Smith and Baker (1976) and Kelly and Bock (1988), native English speakers were asked to read sentences containing disyllabic pseudowords like "torvoot." The pseudowords acted as nouns or verbs in sentences, as in "The true torvoot arrived" and "The dukes torvoot conceit." In Kelly and Bock, the noun and verb versions appeared in the same rhythmic contexts and serial positions within the carrier sentences. As would be expected if the subjects had implicit knowledge of the noun-verb stress difference, they were more likely to pronounce the noun versions rather than the verb versions with first syllable stress.

Grammatical Category Extensions

One common form of lexical innovation in English involves the extension of a word from one grammatical class into another. For instance, "fumble" originated in English as a verb, but subsequently developed a noun use, whereas "police" originated as a noun, but now can also be used as a verb. Despite the high productivity of grammatical category extensions, words cannot be extended with equal ease. For example, although many vehicle nouns have attained verb status (e.g., "They biked/skated/taxied to the store"), "car" has not despite its very high frequency of use in general. Clark and Clark (1979) argued that "car" is blocked from becoming a verb because its most likely verb meaning is already expressed by an existing verb. In particular, vehicle verbs generally mean "To travel/convey by X," where X is the particular vehicle. "I dog-sledded to Nome" therefore means "to travel to Nome by way of dog sled." If "car" were used as a verb, its most obvious meaning would then be "to travel by car." However, English already has a verb to express this meaning, namely "drive." Given certain assumptions about pragmatic rules of conversation, Clark and Clark argue that the existence of "drive" preempts the extension of "car" to the verb class.

In addition to semantic/pragmatic considerations, Kelly (1988) examined the possibility that phonological factors could influence grammatical category extensions. The motivation for the research was the assumption that a word from grammatical class A would be more likely to develop a usage in class B if it possessed properties characteristic of class B. In terms of the phonological property of stress, this assumption leads to the prediction that nouns with second syllable stress would be more likely than nouns with first syllable stress to be used as verbs, and that verbs with first syllable stress would be more likely than verbs with second syllable stress to be used as nouns. In order to test these hypotheses, one group of subjects was presented with pairs of disyllabic nouns differing in stress, such as "gazelle" and "llama." None of the nouns had verb uses in current English according to a recent dictionary. In addition, the nouns in a pair were drawn from the same semantic category (e.g., animals, cities), and did not differ in prototypicality within that category or in their frequency of usage as nouns. Another group of subjects was presented with pairs of disyllabic verbs differing in stress, such as "beseech" and "grovel." None of the verbs had noun uses in current English, and did not differ in verb frequency. Subjects in the noun group were asked to select one member of each pair and use it as a verb in a sentence, whereas subjects in the verb group were asked to select one member of each pair and use it as a noun in a sentence. The subjects showed sensitivity to the noun-verb stress difference in their choices, as they were more likely to select nouns for verb use if they had the prototypical verb stress marking and verbs for noun use if they had the prototypical noun marking. A similar phenomenon was found in an analysis of noun-verb category extensions in the history of English. In the past, English nouns with second syllable stress have been more likely to develop verb uses than nouns with first syllable stress. On the other hand, verbs with first syllable stress have been more likely to develop noun uses (Kelly, 1988). Such findings indicate, first, that past speakers of English had knowledge of the noun-verb stress difference and, second, that knowledge of the stress difference is not just a laboratory curiosity, but can actually affect the course of language evolution.

Rapid Classification of Words as Noun or Verb

Although the prior experiments indicate that English speakers have learned the noun-verb stress difference, they do not demonstrate that lexical stress affects one's initial reaction to a word as noun or verb. For instance, the subjects in the grammatical category extension experiment might have recognized that "gazelle" was a noun as rapidly and accurately as they recognized "llama" as a noun, with effects of stress on their behavior occurring later. Kelly and Martin (1995) therefore examined whether stress affects the initial determination of a word's grammatical class. In addition, the experiment examined whether the presence of another cue to grammatical class, semantics, could reduce or eliminate effects of phonology.

TABLE 15.2
Examples of Stimuli Used in Noun-Verb Classification Study

Nouns		
	Trochaic concrete	Zebra, basket
	Trochaic abstract	Doctrine, tenure
	Iambic concrete	Giraffe, kazoo
	Iambic abstract	Taboo, career
Verbs		
	Trochaic concrete	Rotate, snuggle
	Trochaic abstract	Ponder, covet
	Iambic concrete	Revolve, explode
	Iambic abstract	Infer, adore

In the experiment, subjects heard a series of disyllabic words that they had to classify as nouns or verbs as rapidly as possible by pressing an appropriate button. Half of the nouns and verbs had first syllable stress and half had second syllable stress. In addition, half of the nouns and verbs had meanings that were prototypical of their class, whereas half did not. The prototypical nouns and verbs referred to concrete objects and actions, respectively, whereas the less prototypical items did not. The words were controlled statistically for a number of factors, such as word frequency (see Table 15.2 for examples of the stimuli).

Table 15.3 shows the mean times needed to classify the words as nouns or verbs as a function of their concreteness. In this and other tables, reaction time is measured from the end of the word. As expected, words with meanings typical of their class were categorized faster than words with less typical meanings. In addition, as Table 15.4 shows, stress affected the classification times in the predicted ways, with trochaic items classified faster if they were nouns rather than verbs and iambic items classified faster if they were verbs rather than nouns. Most importantly, however, the stress effects were not reduced or eliminated if a word already had a meaning characteristic of its grammatical class. Indeed, if anything, the presence of a semantic cue magnified the strength of the phonological cue. Hence, the superiority of iambic stress patterns was greater for concrete verbs than abstract verbs, whereas the superiority of trochaic stress patterns was greater for concrete nouns than abstract nouns. Indeed, in the case of abstract nouns, iambic items were classified slightly faster than trochaic items, though not significantly. The phonological variable appeared to reciprocate the reinforcing effects of semantics. Hence, the superiority of concrete words over abstract words was larger for trochaic nouns and iambic verbs than for iambic nouns and trochaic verbs. These patterns indicate that classification times are fastest when multiple cues converge to indicate that a word is a noun or a verb.

TABLE 15.3
Mean Reaction Times (Msec) to Classify Words as Nouns or Verbs as a Function of Their Concreteness

	Concrete	Abstract
Nouns	425	604
Verbs	485	542

Child Sensitivity

The prior experiments focused exclusively on adult sensitivity to correlations between phonology and grammatical class. Yet, if the existence of these correlations is to assist children in problems such as vocabulary learning, retrieval of words from memory, and sentence comprehension, then they must be capable of detecting and exploiting those correlations. Cassidy and Kelly (1991) examined whether three-to four-year-old children had learned the fact that English nouns tend to contain more syllables than English verbs. In this experiment, children were introduced to a puppet who liked to watch certain television shows. Each "show" contained a common object performing an action, such as an electric car driving in a circle or a door closing. During each show, the puppet would say a single pseudoword repeatedly, with each pseudoword consisting of one or three syllables (e.g., "gorp" or "gorpinlak"). The children were told that the puppet did not speak English, and that the words it spoke were from its own "puppetese" language. However, the child was asked to guess what the puppet meant by its word, and they were given a choice of two words, one denoting the object in the display and the other the action, with the order of object or action word presentation counterbalanced. For example, with the car-drive videotape, the child would be asked "Do you think 'gorp' means car or do you think it means drive?" Other children would receive "gorpinlak" instead of "gorp." The words given as choices were always monosyllabic because polysyllabic verbs that the children might know were too difficult to find (as would be expected by the correlation between syllable number and grammatical class in English). The children's choices were significantly affected by the syllable number of the pseudoword, as more object choices were made for trisyllabic words than for monosyllabic words.

Of course, future research needs to study younger children, which is important in determining the types of language acquisition problems

TABLE 15.4
Mean Reaction Times (Msec) to Categorize Words as Nouns or Verbs as a Function of Stress.

	Stress Pattern	
	Trochaic	Iambic
Nouns	503	526
Verbs	596	430

to which phonological cues to grammatical class might be relevant. Furthermore, the language-specificity of these cues should not be seen as an obvious problem for their acquisition and use given the evidence, discussed earlier, that young children are quite adept at learning certain phonological properties of their language very early in life. Given increasing documentation of the child's early learning and perceptual abilities in a variety of domains, we must be wary of the traditional assumption that infants and young children are not able to detect and learn regularities in their environment.

Other Languages

If phonological cues to grammatical class are to be generally useful, then relationships between the two domains need to exist in languages other than English. Little cross-linguistic evidence for such relationships is currently available. However, the same could have been said about English until recently since many of the cues in this language have been identified only in the last few years. Furthermore, new discoveries about well-known cues like stress continue to occur. For example, prior to Sereno and Jongman's (1995) research, few would have thought that analogues of the noun-verb stress difference could be found in so-called homonyms like the noun and verb uses of "practice" or "control."

Despite the general lack of attention to phonological cues to grammatical class, one domain has been examined cross-linguistically, and with positive results. This domain consists of nominal gender categories like those in German, French, and Russian. These categories are certainly not the first that are called to mind when we think of grammatical classes, but they are clearly involved in a number of grammatical phenomena, such as marking the number and/or case of their corresponding noun. As a consequence, they have received rather extensive attention in the literature on the acquisition of grammatical classes (e.g., Maratsos, 1983; Maratsos & Chalkley, 1980; the chapters in Levy et al., 1988).

Although these classes are denoted by the term "gender," they actually are not very predictable by this or other semantic criteria. Hence, we have cases like "la chemise" and "le chemisier" in French. The former denotes a man's shirt, and yet falls into the "feminine" gender class, whereas the latter denotes a woman's blouse, and yet falls into the "masculine" gender class. Perhaps because of their semantic arbitrariness, researchers have been more open to the possibility that phonological cues might predict membership in these classes. In fact, such cues have been identified in numerous languages, such as Hebrew, French, Russian, and German (see Kelly, 1992, for a summary). For example, masculine nouns in German are more likely to be monosyllabic than the nouns in the feminine and neuter categories. Furthermore, within monosyllabic nouns, those in the masculine class tend to contain more consonants than those in other classes (Zubin & Köpke, 1981).

In order to examine whether German speakers have learned the relation between consonant number and gender class in their language, Kelly and Martin (1995) presented native German speakers with a series of monosyllabic nouns that they had to classify as masculine or non-masculine as rapidly as possible. (The feminine and neuter categories were collapsed so that a simpler two-choice rather than three-choice task could be used.) Half of the nouns were masculine and half non-masculine, and, within the masculine and non-masculine categories, the words were evenly divided among those with CVC, CVCC, CCVC, and CCVCC structures. Word frequency did not differ across the four word types or the two gender classes. The items were recorded by a native German speaker. As would be predicted given knowledge of the relation between consonant number and gender in German, reaction time to the masculine nouns decreased as the number of consonants in the word increased, whereas the opposite pattern was found for the non-masculine nouns.

The experiment summarized here indicates that phonological cues to grammatical gender influence a listener's reactions to known words. Some developmental evidence supports the view that phonological properties can also affect the course of vocabulary learning. In particular, some studies have examined how children treat words whose semantic characteristics indicate that they should be in one class, but whose phonological characteristics suggest another class. For example, in Russian, feminine nouns tend to end in the vowel /a/, though exceptions exist. One interesting exception involves familiar words for father, grandfather, and uncle. These words all end in /a/, but denote males and are classified as masculine by grammatical gender. However, children early in the acquisition of these noun classes rely on the phonological cue, and hence treat these words as though they belonged to the feminine class (Popova, 1973). Similar phenomena have been reported in Hebrew (Levy, 1983) and Latvian (Ruke-Dravina, 1973). Finally, recent studies of artificial language learning have reported that the acquisition of nominal classes like gender categories is greatly facilitated if phonological cues to those classes exist (Brooks et al., 1993). In fact, within the time frame of the experiment, neither adult nor child subjects could successfully learn the categories in the absence of such cues. Note that such cues do not have to be perfect predictors of gender class, just significantly correlated with those classes.

Summary

Although this section has concentrated on only a few phonological cues to grammatical class, many other cues have also been studied, and results indicate that these have been learned as well (see Kelly, 1992, for review). In fact, no case has yet been found of a phonological cue to grammatical class that has NOT been learned, even in cases where the cue is only slightly predictive of grammatical class. Hence, human beings are very adept at detecting sometimes subtle, statistical regularities of their language. Of course, any such learning is done implicitly since most people do not have conscious knowledge of these cues, and are not given explicit instruction about their existence. However, such learning should not be seen as surprising or even indicative of some special sensitivity to linguistic patterns. Literally thousands of experiments have shown that human beings and other animals have the ability to learn numerous contingencies in their environments, and even show rather precise calibration to the quantitative strengths of these contingencies (Gallistel, 1990). This ability does not seem to be particularly domain-dependent, and indeed may reflect the fact that, across domains, environmental regularities tend to be statistical in nature, and hence animals who can detect and learn these patterns have advantages over animals who cannot (see Kelly & Martin, 1994, for further discussion).

Even in cases where sufficient information is present to solve a problem, additional redundant cues, though imperfect, are apparently used to increase speed while minimizing errors. For example, consider the following experimental task (Mordkoff & Yantis, 1991): Subjects are told to monitor for the appearance of a target, such as an X, on a computer screen. If the target appears, they are to press a button as rapidly as possible. On some trials, a non-target, such as an O, will appear, and the subjects are to do nothing. On other trials, both a target and non-target appear. In this case, the subject is to press the button, since the target appeared. The non-target that is also present is in principle irrelevant to the decision. However, unbeknownst to the subject, some non-targets are more likely than others to appear with the target. Subjects apparently learn these correlations, and hence respond faster to the target when it appears with the correlated patterns than when it appears alone. Note that the target is not visually distorted in any way. Sufficient information exists to identify it without the presence of an additional cue. However, subjects nonetheless take advantage of the additional cue to increase their speed while keeping errors to a minimum. By analogy, sufficient syntactic information exists in the phrases "A llama lives in the zoo" and "A gazelle lives in the zoo" to identify "llama" and "gazelle" as nouns. However, despite the sufficiency of this information, listeners might use the correlated stress cue to identify the grammatical class of "llama" faster than the class of "gazelle." As in the target detection example, exploitation of such correlations could increase the speed of language processing, while minimizing errors. We should keep in mind that language processing, like other human skills, is performed at high speed, and yet with relatively few errors. One way that human beings apparently blunt the effects of the inevitable speed–accuracy trade-off is to allow numerous cues to the solution of a problem to converge on an answer. In the case of grammatical category assignments, syntactic information, even when perfectly diagnostic, might yet act as only one of many contributors (see Kelly & Martin, 1994, for examples from other perceptual and cognitive domains).

CONCLUSION

Human beings and other animals confront many perceptual and cognitive problems that might be dealt with using multiple sources of information that are probabilistically related to a solution. One of those problems could be the assignment of words to grammatical categories, which is relevant to numerous aspects of language processing, including vocabulary learning, parsing, and word recognition. In order to determine how speakers solve this problem, we must identify the information sources available, which ones are used, and how they are weighed. Most discussions of grammatical categories have focused on syntactic and semantic determinants to the neglect of phonological factors. Numerous reasons could be cited for this neglect, but, as this chapter has argued, two of those reasons—that phonological cues are not available and people are not sensitive to them—do not have a "sound" basis in fact.

REFERENCES

Bates, E., & MacWhinney, B. (1982). A functionalist approach to grammar. In E. Wanner & L. Gleitman (Eds.), *Language acquisition: The state of the art* (pp. 173-218). Cambridge, England: Cambridge University Press.

Brooks, P. J., Braine, M. D. S., Catalano, L., Brody, R. E., & Sudhalter, V. (1993). Acquisition of gender-like noun subclasses in an artificial language: The contribution of phonological markers to learning. *Journal of Memory and Language, 32,* 96-114.

Cassidy, K. W., & Kelly, M. H. (1991). Phonological information for grammatical category assignments. *Journal of Memory and Language, 30,* 348-369.

Clark, E. V., & Clark, H. H. (1979). When nouns surface as verbs. *Language, 55,* 767-811.

Frazier, L., & Rayner, K. (1987). Resolution of syntactic category ambiguities: Eye movements in parsing lexically ambiguous sentences. *Journal of Memory and Language, 26,* 505-526.

Friederici, A. D., & Wessels, J. M. I. (1993). Phonotactic knowledge of word boundaries and its use in infant speech perception. *Perception and Psychophysics, 54,* 287-295.

Gallistel, C. R. (1990). *The organization of learning.* Cambridge, MA: MIT Press.

Gleitman, L. (1990). Structural sources of verb learning. *Language Acquisition, 1,* 1-63.

Gleitman, L., & Wanner, E. (1982). Language acquisition: The state of the state of the art. In E. Wanner & L. Gleitman (Eds.), *Language acquisition: The state of the art* (pp. 3-48). Cambridge, England: Cambridge University Press.

Grieser, D., & Kuhl, P. K. (1989). The categorization of speech by infants: Support for speech-sound prototypes. *Developmental Psychology, 25,* 577-588.

Jusczyk, P. W. (in press). Language acquisition: Speech sounds and the beginnings of phonology. In J. L. Miller & P. D. Eimas (Eds.), *Handbook of perception and cognition: Speech, language, and communication.* Orlando, FL: Academic Press.

Jusczyk, P. W., Cutler, A., & Redanz, N. J. (1993). Infants' preference for the predominant stress patterns of English words. *Child Development, 64,* 675-687.

Jusczyk, P. W., Friederici, A. D., Wessels, J. M. I., Svenkerud, V. Y., & Jusczyk, A. M. (1993). Infants' sensitivity to sound patterns of native language words. *Journal of Memory and Language, 32,* 402-420.

Jusczyk, P. W., Charles-Luce, J., & Luce, P. (1994). Infants' sensitivity to phonotactic patterns in the native language. *Journal of Memory and Language, 33,* 630-645

Kelly, M. H. (1988). Phonological biases in grammatical category shifts. *Journal of Memory and Language, 27,* 343-358.

Kelly, M. H. (1992). Using sound to solve syntactic problems: The role of phonology in grammatical category assignments. *Psychological Review, 99,* 349-364.

Kelly, M. H., & Bock, J. K. (1988). Stress in time. *Journal of Experimental Psychology: Human Perception and Performance, 14,* 389-403.

Kelly, M. H., & Martin, S. (1994). Domain-general abilities applied to domain-specific tasks: Sensitivity to probabilities in perception, cognition, and language. *Lingua, 92,* 105-140.

Kelly, M. H., & Martin, S. (1995). *Phonological cues to grammatical class.* Unpublished manuscript, University of Pennsylvania.

Kuhl, P. K., Williams, K. A., Lacerda, F., Stevens, K. N., & Lindblom, B. (1992). Linguistic experiences alter phonetic perception in infants by 6 months of age. *Science, 255,* 606-608.

Levy, Y. (1983). It's frogs all the way down. *Cognition, 15,* 75-93.

Levy, Y., Schlesinger, I., & Braine, M. (1988). *Categories and processes in language acquisition.* Hillsdale, NJ: Erlbaum.

Maclay, H., & Osgood, C. E. (1959). Hesitation phenomena in spontaneous English speech. *Word, 15,* 19-44.

Maratsos, M. (1983). Some current issues in the study of the acquisition of grammar. In P. Mussen (Series Ed.) & J. H. Flavell & E. M. Markman (Vol. Eds.), *Handbook of child psychology* (Vol. 3, pp. 709-777). New York: Wiley.

Maratsos, M., & Chalkley, M. A. (1980). The internal language of children's syntax: The ontogenesis and representation of syntactic categories. In K. Nelson (Ed.), *Children's language , Vol. 2* (pp. 127-214). New York: Gardner Press.

Mehler, J., Jusczyk, P., Lambertz, G., Halsted, N., Bertoncini, J., & Amiel-Tison, C. (1988). A precursor of language acquisition in young infants. *Cognition, 29,* 143-178.

Mordkoff, J. T., & Yantis, S. (1991). An interactive race model of divided attention. *Journal of Experimental Psychology: Human Perception and Performance, 17,* 520-538.

Pinker, S. (1989). *Learnability and cognition.* Cambridge, MA: MIT Press.

Popova, M. I. (1973). Grammatical elements of language in the speech of preschool children. In C. A. Ferguson & D. I. Slobin (Eds.), *Studies of child language development* (pp. 269-280). New York: Holt, Rinehart & Winston.

Ruke-Dravina, V. (1973). On the emergence of inflection in child language: A contribution based on Latvian speech data. In C. A. Ferguson & D. I. Slobin (Eds.), *Studies of child language development* (pp. 252-267). New York: Holt, Rinehart & Winston.

Schlesinger, I. M. (1974). Relational concepts underlying language. In R. I. Schiefelbusch & L. Lloyd (Eds.), *Language perspectives: Acquisition, retardation, intervention* (pp. 129-152). Baltimore, MD: University Park Press.

Schlesinger, I. M. (1988). The origin of relational categories. In Y. Levy, I. Schlesinger, & M. Braine (Eds.), *Categories and processes in language acquisition* (pp. 121-178). Hillsdale, NJ: Lawrence Erlbaum Associates.

Sereno, J. A., & Jongman, A. (1995). *Acoustic correlates of form class.* Unpublished manuscript, Cornell University.

Smith, P. T., & Baker, R. G. (1976). The influence of English spelling patterns on pronunciation. *Journal of Verbal Learning and Verbal Behavior, 15,* 267-285.

Spring, D. R., & Dale, P. S. (1977). Discrimination of linguistic stress in early infancy. *Journal of Speech and Hearing Research, 20,* 224-231.

Zubin, D. A., & Köpke, K. M. (1981). Gender: A less than arbitrary category. In R. Hendrick, C. Masek, & M. F. Miller (Eds.), *Papers from the seventh regional meeting of the Chicago Linguistic Society* (pp. 439-449). Chicago: Chicago Linguistic Society.

16 Perceptual Bases of Rudimentary Grammatical Categories: Toward a Broader Conceptualization of Bootstrapping

James L. Morgan, Rushen Shi, and Paul Allopenna
Brown University

Among the most fundamental components of syntactic systems are linguistic units, such as *phrase* or *clause*, and grammatical categories, such as *determiner*, *noun*, or *verb*. Arrangements of these elements constitute the basic phrase structure of such a system. In most contemporary grammatical theories, additional rules or constraints are formulated in terms of these elements and their configurations. Even theories that explicitly reject symbolic rules accept at least implicitly grammatical categories: Rumelhart and McClelland (1987) did not offer a theory of learning of past tenses of *words*, but rather a theory of learning of past tenses of *verbs*. Many of the chapters in this volume are concerned with whether the input speech stream might provide cues to syntactic units; in this chapter, we explore the feasibility of using aspects of the speech signal as means for bootstrapping rudimentary grammatical categories (see also chapters by Gerken, Kelly, Peters & Strömqvist, and Selkirk).

We have two major goals. The first is to advance the hypothesis that language input contains information sufficient to permit syntactically naive learners to assign words to two major categories, which closely correspond to *content* words and *function* words. We explicate the perceptual basis for this distinction and sketch some of the results of our analyses of English and Mandarin Chinese maternal speech to infants. Ultimately, this hypothesis must be confirmed or disconfirmed on the basis of more extensive cross-linguistic investigations of input speech (Shi, 1994, obtained comparable results from recent analyses of Turkish, a language that is typologically distinct from both English and Mandarin), but we present several arguments concerning why *universal* bootstrapping from speech to rudimentary categories is a likely possibility.

Our second goal is to argue that the bootstrapping information contained in input speech generally consists of *constellations* of overlapping, partially predictive cues. Indeed, each of the individual phonological or acoustic cues that we have measured has low validity with respect to distinguishing between the rudimentary categories we consider. Taken ensemble, however, the *set* of cues we measure can be shown to be sufficient in principle to allow a naive learner to assign words to categories with very high accuracy. Similarly, sets of cues in input speech may suffice to bootstrap additional aspects of syntax, such as phrase bracketing, even though individual cues may have low validity. Of course, recognition and use of correlated sets of cues require more sophisticated abilities than does use of individual cues. We note evidence, however, indicating that infants manifest abilities to use correlated cues during the second half of the first year—the period during which bootstraps from speech to rudiments of grammar can help propel the child toward successful acquisition of language.

THE ACQUISITION OF GRAMMATICAL CATEGORIES

Issues pertaining to the nature and acquisition of early grammatical categories have been a focus of many classical works in language acquisition (e.g., Bloom, 1970; Bowerman, 1973; Braine, 1963, 1976; Brown, 1973) and continue to be of central importance to the field (cf. Radford, 1990, and numerous other papers on the early status of functional categories). Of the several models proposed to account for acquisition of grammatical categories, the two most widely cited are those of Maratsos and Chalkley (1980) and Pinker (1984). Maratsos and Chalkley, noting that purely formal categories, such as genders, must be learned on the basis of distributional evidence, proposed that all categories might be learned as constellations of correlations among syntactic/semantic distributional features. Pinker (following Grimshaw, 1981) suggested that the canonical semantic properties of grammatical categories might provide a semantic bootstrap for acquisition of these categories.

Our interest here lies neither in defending nor critiquing either of these models. Each capitalizes on aspects of the available information that are likely to contribute to the eventual solution to the problem of category acquisition, but each has been abandoned or substantially revised by its principal proponent (Maratsos, 1988a; Pinker, 1987). Rather, we wish to draw attention to an assumption shared by these models: Analyses leading to grammatical categories must rely on input that has been segmented into words. Several chapters in this volume take up the problem of early word segmentation, and each makes clear that the solution to this problem requires sophisticated perceptual and/or computational capacities on the part of infant language learners. Since perceptual analyses of the input logically must (at least in part) succeed before syntactic or semantic analyses can proceed, we think it reasonable to ask whether such perceptual analyses might furnish additional linguistically useful information that, for example, could be used to separate words into classes that are forerunners of grammatical categories.

As noted previously, we focus here on distinction between function and content words.[1] We consider function words to include auxiliary verbs (or, more broadly, elements marking tense, aspect, or voice), case or gender markers, complementizers, conjunctions, determiners, prepositions, pro-forms, and sentence particles (e.g., question or imperative markers); content words include nouns, verbs, adjectives, and adverbs. Not all of these function word categories are used in every language, and some languages may contain categories we do not list here.   The inclusion of prepositions as function words is somewhat controversial, at least for English.   Those that serve as case markers (*of, by*) are clearly functional elements, whereas the classification of others (such as *out, up, over*) is less certain. However, our primary concern is not with learning, but rather with bootstrapping. That is, we are not concerned here with providing an account of the eventual accurate acquisition of form classes, but rather with suggesting how infants might be able to divide words into superordinate grammatical categories that are approximately correct.

A range of linguistic and psycholinguistic data supports this basic bifurcation of lexical categories. First, function words are members of closed classes, whereas content words are members of open classes. New nouns, verbs, and adjectives may be readily added to any language, but new auxiliaries, prepositions, and pronouns rarely appear. Second, these two classes have strikingly different word frequency profiles. Function words tend to occur very frequently (in Kucera & Francis, 1967, all of the 50 most frequent English words are function words), but many content words occur infrequently (in Kucera & Francis, 75% of tokens—virtually all content words—occurred 5 or fewer times, less than 0.01% as often as the most frequent function word). Third, function words and content words display different acquisition patterns (or at least different production patterns; Bloom, 1970; Brown, 1973; Radford, 1990).   Children's early productions have been characterized as "telegraphic" precisely because they tend to include content words, but exclude function words.   Fourth, function words and content words appear to be subject to different processing constraints in both normal (Bradley, 1978; Matthei & Kean, 1989; Shillcock & Bard, 1993) and impaired adults (Bradley, Garrett, & Zuriff, 1980; Rosenberg, Zuriff,

---

[1]We do not mean to imply that this is the only distinction that may be perceptually cued. Kelly (this volume) makes the case for the noun-verb distinction being similarly cued. His characterization of nouns (see his Table 1) is diametrically opposed to our characterization of function words. This raises the possibility that a tripartite, perceptually based distinction among form classes is possible—nouns, verbs, and function words. Such a three-way distinction appears to correspond to classes that are universally employed in languages—nouns, predicates, and functors (see Maratsos, 1988b, for further discussion of cross-linguistic form class regularities). We are skeptical about the possibility that finer distinctions may be made on perceptual grounds: Once these fundamental categories are in place, many basic word-order parameters can be set (see also Mazuka, this volume), and further syntactic and semantic analyses can yield a set of form classes appropriate for the language being learned.

Brownell, Garrett, & Bradley, 1985). For example, activation of function word homynyms is constrained by syntactic context, whereas activation of content word homonyms is not (Shillcock & Bard, 1993; Swinney, 1979); repeated function words are difficult to spot (the so-called "proofreader's error"), whereas repeated content words are easily detected (Rosenberg et al., 1985). Although certain findings on processing differences have not been readily replicable (e.g., Gordon & Caramazza, 1985), the weight of the evidence is consistent with a psycholinguistic distinction between these two overarching grammatical categories.

The notions that phonological correlates of the function word-content word distinction may exist and may be used in acquisition are hardly novel (cf. Selkirk, this volume). Kean (1979, 1980) suggested that the difficulties in processing of closed-class items characteristic of agrammatic aphasia might be attributable to the phonological characteristics of these items. Cutler (1993; Cutler & Carter, 1987) argued that in lexical access, function words and content words may be distinguished by the presence of *reduced vowels* in the initial syllables of the former. Gleitman and Wanner (1982; Gleitman, Gleitman, Landau, & Wanner, 1988) suggested that *stress* might be used as a basis for early acquisition of the distinction, with those words that fail to receive stress being identified as function words.

The hypotheses offered by Cutler and Gleitman et al. clearly capture some central native speaker intuitions and may provide first approximations of accounts of phonological influences on form class acquisition and processing. Nevertheless, for several reasons, neither hypothesis offers a definitive explanation. First, neither *reduced vowel* nor *stress* is completely well defined (these constructs are clearly not fully independent of one another). Reduced vowels are those vowels that are spectrally similar to schwas, or that have short durations, or some combination of these; other factors may also enter into speakers' judgments of vowel reduction. As Lieberman (1965) pointed out, even phoneticians' judgments of stress levels may be inconsistent, and levels of stress are not clearly correlated with any instrumental measures. These considerations are particularly important in the present context, for there is no basis for assuming that naive language learners will share adult speakers' intuitions. Second, as Selkirk (this volume) points out, function words sometimes carry stress and have unreduced vowels; conversely, under some circumstances, content words may be unstressed and have reduced vowels. Thus, neither of these will provide fully valid cues to the distinction between classes. Third, even if *reduced vowel* and *stress* were well defined, valid predictors of function word class membership in English, they would not be suitable universal predictors, inasmuch as vowel reduction and stress differences occupy much less prominent roles in the phonological systems of many languages than is the case for English.

THE ACOUSTIC-PHONOLOGICAL BASIS OF THE FUNCTION WORD-CONTENT WORD DISTINCTION

On our view, the typically reduced, unstressed character of English function words is but a single manifestation of a fundamental property of such words: Function words, in contrast to content words, tend to be productively and perceptually *minimal*. Evidence of minimality may be observed at several linguistic levels, as we shall describe later.

We presume that several factors universally impel function words toward minimality, at least historically. First, function words tend to occur with very high frequency. As noted earlier, all of the 50 most frequent words in Kucera and Francis' (1967) corpus of English text are function words (with the possible exception of *no*); collectively, these constitute only 0.1% of all word types, but 40.6% of all the word tokens included in the corpus. As Zipf (1949) noted, a negative correlation exists between word frequency and word length. Zipf imputed this to a principle of least effort: Behaviors that are frequently repeated are leading candidates to be streamlined.

Second, function words are often readily predictable from surrounding syntactic context. Context often constrains the possible categories of words that may occur in particular locations; because function word categories (as closed classes) have very small memberships, the likelihood of an individual function word occurring in a given location may be quite high. Conversely, although it may be possible to predict with high certainty that a particular type of open class content word, such as a noun, will occur in a given location, the likelihood of any individual noun occurring in that location is very low. Thus, function words with incomplete phonetic manifestations will generally be easier to identify than content words with incomplete phonetic manifestations. Speakers are at liberty to slur, swallow, elide, or otherwise garble function words without unduly disrupting discourse.

Third, function words carry light informational loads. Whereas the meanings that can be encoded in function words are highly constrained (Laudau & Jackendoff, 1993), the meanings that can be encoded in open-class content words are not. Hence, the semantics of function words are more predictable than are the semantics of content words. Under circumstances in which communication is costly (as, for example, in telegrams), function words may be truncated or omitted altogether, incurring only marginal increases in the ambiguity of the message.

Fourth, function words tend to be morphologically simple. Several word formation processes that apply productively to content words fail to apply, or apply in highly limited fashion, to function words (Aronoff, 1976; Golston, 1991). For example, function words do not take derivational affixes. Whereas verbs can be derived from nouns (e.g., *demon --> demonize*), nouns can be derived from verbs or adjectives (e.g., *damn --> damnation, good --> goodness*), and so forth, auxiliary verbs cannot be derived from prepositions (*of --> *ofoud*), nor can determiners be derived from conjunctions (*and* --> **thand*).   Content words can productively compound with other content words (*purple-people-eater, bottle-cap-opener*), but with the exception of a limited set of prepositions, function words do not enter into content word compounds.   Function words may compound with other function words but such compounding is not productive, and the results, at least in English, have a distinctly archaic ring (*hereinafter, whithersoever*).   Both content words and function words may be inflected, but irregularity is more likely to be found in function word paradigms, as in English, where suppletion dominates the inflectional paradigms of auxiliary verbs.

To the extent that these factors are characteristic of all languages, we would expect function words in language input to universally manifest properties flowing from minimality and, therefore, to be universally distinguishable from content words on an acoustic-phonological basis.[2] Relevant properties may be identified at a variety of linguistic levels.

At the *word* level, function words tend to have a minimal number of syllables or moras.   In many instances, such as unstressed *a* or *the* in English, function words comprise even fewer such units than are required for minimal content words in particular languages (see Demuth, this volume, for discussion).   Moreover, the status of function words as words is often precarious.   They may become cliticized, losing syllabicity, as when *he is* is contracted to *he's* (cf. Klavans, 1985).   Most bound function morphemes in English are now subsyllabic, although in many cases they were historically derived from free, syllabic function words.   In other languages, such as Turkish, bound morphemes may retain their syllabicity.

At the *syllable* level, function words tend to be simple, having minimal or null onsets, simple (non-dipthongized) nuclei, and minimal or null codas.   Note that one result of the suppletion often found in function word inflectional paradigms is that consonant clusters that might otherwise be produced as a byproduct of affixation are avoided.   In general, phonotactic constraints on syllable structure may be expected to apply more stringently to function words than to content words.   For example, in Mandarin, content word syllable codas are either null or contain a nasal, whereas function word syllable codas may only be null.

At the *segmental* level, function words tend to include unmarked or underlyingly underspecified phonemes.   Thus, function word segments are more likely to be subject to processes of assimilation or harmony than are content word segments; conversely, content word segments are more likely to govern such processes than are function word segments. The inventories of phonemes found in function words may be smaller

---

[2]Note also that syntax will enforce asymmetries on the distributions of function and content words relative to utterance boundaries. For languages that are specifier-initial, utterances will tend to begin with function words and to end with content word heads; the reverse will be true for specifier-final languages. Although such asymmetries are orthogonal to the notion of minimality we develop here, they may nevertheless provide perceptually available cues that can aid in distinguishing the two word classes.

than those found in content words; function word consonants are particularly likely to be coronal. In some languages, however, rather than being unmarked, certain function word segments may be phonotactically unique, as in English, where /ð/ occurs word-initially only in function words, such as *the, this, that, these, though*.   Although such unique segments do not appear to comport with our minimalist characterization of function words, they may nevertheless assist in distinguishing function words from content words.

At the *acoustic/phonetic* level, function words tend to be inconspicuous. The words of utterances with greatest duration, highest amplitude, and highest pitch are unlikely to be function words.   Rather, function words are likely to be short and have low amplitude.   Due to the minimal durations of function words, spectral changes across function words will also be minimal, so that F_0 contour will be flat and vowel quality will not shift. Function words excised from utterances are more likely to be unintelligible than are excised content words (Bard & Anderson, 1983).

One prediction that follows from our hypothesis is that the shift in grammatical category of a word from function word to content word (or vice versa) should have specific phonological restrictions or consequences. English contains several nominalized function words, such as *hereafter, insides, whereabouts*.   These are all atypical function words. Each is infrequent, morphologically complex, and multisyllabic. In contrast, typical, phonologically minimal function words do not appear to be candidates for nominalizations. Rapid category shifts from content to function word are quite rare in fully developed languages, but grammaticization of erstwhile content words is commonly found in creolization.   Sankoff and Laberge (1973) reported on one such instance, in which the Tok Pisin pidgin adverb /bəmbai/, "afterwards," evolved into the aspect marker "future." Concomitant with this shift in grammatical status were several phonological changes: shortening to a monosyllabic form, /bai/, acquisition of characteristic stresslessness, and, particularly among creole speakers (of which at the time of the report only a single generation existed), reduction of the diphthongized vowel to schwa, /bə/. These changes are fully consistent with our hypothesis.

Of course, not all function words will exhibit all of the characteristics noted here, and some content words will exhibit some of these characteristics. Exceptions are easy to find. *Underneath*, for example, contains three syllables, one of which receives full word stress, whereas *through* contains both a consonant cluster and a full, tense vowel. *Bee, can, eye, too, May,* and *wood*, among others, are content word homonyms of function words. Because the classification scheme we contemplate is multidimensional, words need not possess all of the prototypical properties of a category to be properly classified. Words lacking some of these properties may nevertheless be accurately classified, provided they manifest a sufficient subset of class-appropriate characteristics.

On the other hand, it is unlikely that words can be perfectly sorted into content and function word classes solely on perceptual bases. We wish to stress again that our concern is with bootstrapping, and bootstrapping is not tantamount to ultimate learning. Categories emerging from perceptual bootstrapping are subject to refinement and differentiation by syntactic and semantic analyses that may subsequently be brought to bear. However, so long as misclassifications are not too common, tend to be inconsistent across tokens of a given type, or primarily involve infrequent words, the bootstrapping value of perceptually based, rudimentary grammatical categories will not be diminished. Deciding whether suitable cues are available in early acquisition requires empirical investigation of relevant properties of input speech, a task to which we now turn.

CHARACTERISTICS OF FUNCTION WORDS AND CONTENT WORDS IN EARLY LANGUAGE INPUT

To investigate the properties of function words and content words in input—their statistical, distributional, phonological, and acoustic characteristics—we have recorded and analyzed maternal speech to 12-month-olds in American English and Mandarin Chinese. In this section, we will outline our methods and sketch some of our findings. The results we present here are based on analyses of 3 English-speaking dyads and 2 Mandarin-speaking dyads.

Mother-child dyads are recorded during free-play in a sound-treated laboratory, using a DAT recorder. Equal-sized random samples of function words and content words from the mother's speech are selected from tagged orthographic transcriptions for detailed analyses. For each word in the sample, measures on a series of variables are computed. One set of measures is based on analyses of the transcripts. These include *type frequency*[3], *rough utterance position* (initial, medial, or final; that is, following a pause, nonadjacent to a pause, or preceding a pause), and *number of syllables*. A second set of measures is based on closer phonetic transcriptions of the sampled words. These include *syllable complexity* (on a scale ordered from syllables with null onsets and codas to syllables with consonant clusters in both onsets and codas), *vowel diphthongization*, and, for Mandarin only, *predictability of tone* from the surrounding tonal context. A third set of measures is based on acoustic analyses. These include *vowel duration, syllable amplitude* (relative to the syllable with the highest amplitude in the utterance), F_0 *change*, and, for English only, *vowel quality*.

On our view, all of these measures reflect potential perceptually

---

[3]Relative frequencies of some content words—those referring to conversational topics—are often exaggerated in short samples. For example, the mother in one of our recordings used *alligator* more often than *and*, but this cannot reflect her overall word usage. To obtain less biased estimates of type frequencies, the transcript from each English-speaking dyad was combined with the transcripts from either Adam, Eve, or Sarah (Brown, 1973; MacWhinney & Snow, 1985), and frequencies were calculated over the combined transcript sets.

available cues to the function word-content word distinction. None of these cues requires the learner to engage in any syntactic or semantic analysis of input. Nor, with the possible exception of predictability of tone, do any of these cues require the learner to have completed any phonological analyses of the language being learned.

Four key points emerge from our analyses: (1) We found significant mean differences between function words and content words on virtually all of the measures for all of the mothers. This is not surprising, since we hand-picked those measures we thought most likely to yield such results. The one measure for which we failed to find consistent inter-class differences was F_0 change. Overall, content words do display greater F_0 change than do function words, but when change is normalized for time (i.e., F_u slope), the difference disappears. (2) For most measures, distributions of values were quite similar across individual speakers both within and between languages. (3) The distributions of these measures for the two classes displayed considerable overlap, so that none of the individual variables that we measured had high cue validity with respect to distinguishing between these classes. (4) Despite this last point, when included in multivariate classification analyses, the *sets* of measures were highly valid discriminators of the function word-content word distinction. We illustrate points (1)-(3) with respect to two of our individual acoustic measures and then discuss the results of our multivariate analyses.

The English vowel quality data shown in Fig. 16.1 are typical of our findings. Recall that it has been claimed (e.g., Cutler, 1993) that vowel quality provides a critical cue for the distinction between content and function words. According to this claim, content words characteristically have full vowels (particularly in stressed, initial syllables), whereas

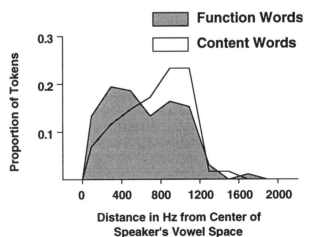

FIG 16.1. Vowel quality histograms for function words and content words in English speech to a 12-month-old.

function words have reduced (centralized) vowels. To obtain the measure of vowel quality illustrated here, we conducted LPC analyses at
vowel midpoint for the function word and content word syllables in our
samples, used the results of these analyses to calculate the center of F_1-
F_2 vowel space for each mother, and computed the Euclidean distance of
each token from the mother's center. Figure 1 shows the results of these
analyses for one mother. Significant mean differences between vowel
distance of function words and content words existed for all English-
speaking mothers (in this case, $p < .02$). Function words do tend to
have vowels that are closer to the center of the speaker's vowel space.

Despite this significant mean difference, vowel quality is not a very
powerful predictor of category membership. Note that the vowel quality distributions for function words and content words in Fig. 16.1
largely overlap.[4] Suppose that we were to establish a cutoff value so
that tokens with values smaller than the cutoff would be classified as
function words and tokens with values larger than the cutoff would be
classified as content words. Furthermore, we might wish to choose an
optimal value, so the proportion of correct classifications would be
maximized. For the data in Fig. 16.1, this optimal cutoff would be a
vowel distance of 640 Hz; the maximal proportion of correct classifications would be 63%. In other words, with an optimal cutoff value, one
set on the basis of prior knowledge of the category membership of all
measured tokens, vowel distance has a maximal cue validity of only
0.63. However, a learner lacking such prior knowledge would have no
means of independently discovering this optimal cutoff value. Hence, a
learner forced to rely solely on vowel quality as a basis for hypothesiz-
ing category membership would most likely do only slightly better
than a learner who categorized words at random.

Figure 16.2 provides another illustration of our findings, in this case
with respect to vowel duration. For both the English-speaking and
Mandarin-speaking mothers, mean vowel duration for content words is
significantly larger than mean duration for function words. Moreover,
note that the shapes and locations of these distributions are similar for
these two mothers. However, once again, the distributions of values for
function words and content words display substantial overlap. If we
were to set a cutoff value of duration that optimized category assignment in English, we would find that duration has a maximal cue validity of only 0.64 (with a cutoff of 95 msec, 71% of function words and 57%
of content words would be classified correctly). This is better than
chance, but not by much. Although bootstrapping cues need not be
completely accurate, a cue that leads to mistaken inferences at least a

---

[4]Consistent with the results we report here, Ratner (1984) provides some data from analyses of infant-directed speech suggesting that function word vowels are not always more
centralized than corresponding content word vowels. However, the degree to which
vowels from these word classes overlap in her data is not clear from the information she
presented.

third of the time may not be a great boon to learning. Moreover, we again set the cutoff value on the basis of prior knowledge of the category membership of the measured words. It is not clear how a learner lacking such knowledge could independently set an optimal cutoff

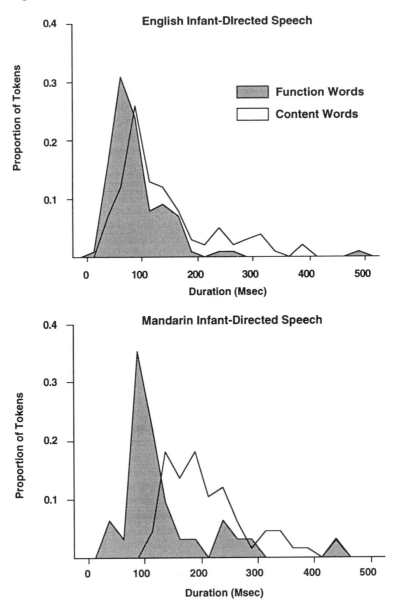

FIG 16.2. Vowel duration histograms for function words and content words in English and Mandarin speech to 12-month-olds.

value, since this value is not fixed across speakers (for the Mandarin data shown, for example, the optimal cutoff would be about 125 msec). Thus, cue validity for vowel duration with a cutoff value guessed by the learner would likely be substantially less than 0.64, and might well be no better than (and might even be worse than) chance.

Although single cues do not suffice to distinguish function words and content words, multiple cues do. This conclusion follows from our multivariate classification analyses. We began by conducting linear discriminant analyses that included the complete set of measures for each mother. Classification functions were computed, tokens were predictively assigned to classes on the basis of these functions, and concordances between actual and predicted category memberships were examined. Across all of the mothers, this multivariate procedure yielded classifications with accuracies ranging from 83 to 91 percent.

These results are certainly a substantial improvement over our findings for single cues. However, discriminant analysis suffers from a serious drawback as a model of learning. It computes only *post hoc* classification functions, requiring information concerning the correct classifications of at least some tokens as input. Such information is not plausibly available to naive language learners. To better simulate how language learners might use the set of perceptually available cues that we measured, we examined the development of classificatory "maps" in Kohonen-style neural networks.

Kohonen networks have three characterizing properties: self-organization, neighborhood structure, and dimensionality reduction. Self-organization refers to learning that is based only on the learner's relation to the relevant environment; no external "teacher" is presumed to play a role. Learning occurs not by minimizing error (no feedback is available), but rather by adjusting the response of the network over time to better approximate the distribution of the training inputs. Each training datum sparks a competition among units that has a winner that is consequently strengthened; units that can be computationally defined as neighbors of this winner are also incremented, according to their distance from the winner. Thus, the network's behavior can be generalized to novel instances in keeping with its neighborhood structure. One of the consequences of neighborhood-based learning is that of dimensionality reduction. Problems that exist in high dimensional input spaces are effectively projected onto a grid (usually of 2 dimensions) of network units. The resulting global organization of such a network is a non-linear projection of the input space onto a low-dimensional map of the input distribution. In classification problems such as ours, category memberships of test items may be determined by calculating their distances on the resulting map from the centers of clusters that have developed during training.

The results of our network simulations were quite similar to the results of our discriminant analyses. Accuracy of classification has ranged between 80% and 90% correct. These results are noteworthy for several reasons. First, these levels of accuracy are substantially higher than could be obtained on the basis of any individual measure and are likely to be sufficient for purposes of bootstrapping. Generally, tokens of particular types were not consistently misclassified, so inclusion of information concerning type membership would further boost accuracy. Second, with single cues, it is not possible to set optimal cutoffs without prior knowledge of category membership, which of course is precisely what learners lack. Naive learners provided with single cues can only guess where cutoffs may lie; such guesses will almost always be nonoptimal, often substantially so. However, when sets of correlated cues are analyzed, cue weightings can be optimized on the fly. The relation of any given cue to other available cues provides a frame of reference for the weighting of that cue. Third, these results were obtained with small numbers of tokens and without any feedback or explicit instruction about classifications being provided to the learner. Thus, these results demonstrate that it is computationally feasible for a naive learner to acquire categories approximating function and content word classes on the basis of perceptually available sets of cues.

CAN CHILDREN DISCOVER AND USE PERCEPTUAL CUES TO GRAMMATICAL CATEGORIES?

Analyses of the language learning environment, such as those we are engaged in, can provide evidence bearing on the plausibility or implausibility of particular types of learning. Obviously, evidence showing that the environment may furnish sufficient information for perceptual bootstrapping of rudimentary grammatical categories does not suffice to show that such bootstrapping actually occurs. Investigation of this latter issue will require testing of older infants or younger toddlers, perhaps using techniques similar to those used by Kuhl (1983), to determine whether children form phonologically based word categories similar to those we argue for here.

In the interim, however, we address two prerequisites for children's use of perceptual cues as a basis for inducing rudimentary categories. The first of these concerns how children might discover sets of cues appropriate for their native language. No universal set of cues exists (although a universal superordinate set from which cues are drawn may exist). First, not all cues are manifest in every language. For example, English function words tend to have centralized vowels, whereas vowel reduction is not a component process of Mandarin phonology. Conversely, Mandarin function words tend to have neutral (that is, underlyingly unspecified) tone, whereas tone does not figure prominently in English phonology. We speculate that functional and lexical elements are phonologically distinctive in sign languages as well as spoken languages, but if so, physical manifestations of cues must differ across gestural and articulatory modalities. Second, not all cues function contrastively in every language. For example, in Mandarin, function words tend to be monosyllabic, but so do content words.

A solution to this problem rests in the fact that cues to rudimentary categories in any language will be intercorrelated. By monitoring the cooccurrences of potential cues in input, a learner can detect which are functional in her native language and which are not. Note that although all of the cues to the function–content word distinction are not universal, a few cues are. One of these universal cues is word frequency, a second is asymmetry in utterance positions (see footnote 2); duration is perhaps a third. By attending to how other cues cooccur with these, the computational burdens involved in tabulating cooccurrences may be substantially reduced.

The second prerequisite for induction of rudimentary categories from perceptual cues is that young children be able to recognize and exploit appropriate correlations. At several points in our argument we have appealed to the notion of correlated cues to categories: as a means of discovering relevant cues in the native language, as a means of providing a frame of reference for establishing weightings for individual cues, and as a means of accurately assigning words to rudimentary form classes. Research by Younger and Cohen (1983, 1986) and Younger (1993) showed that by 9 or 10 months, infants can form visual categories based on correlated attributes. When the ability to form *linguistic* categories on the basis of correlated cues appears remains an open question. Recent evidence suggests, however, that this, too, emerges at some point late in the first year of life.

As an example of how correlations may figure in weightings and deployment of cues in speech perception, consider how infants might learn to use particular rhythmic patterns as a means of segmenting fluent speech into words. Across a series of papers, Anne Cutler has argued that speakers of English may efficiently use a "metrical segmentation strategy," under which strong syllables are presumed to be word-initial (see Cutler, this volume, for further discussion). With respect to bisyllabic words, this means that trochees should be more easily segmented than iambs. Jusczyk, Cutler, and Redanz (1993) showed that a preference for trochaic bisyllables in English-learning infants appears between 6 and 9 months; Morgan (in press) shows that novel trochees are perceived as more cohesive than novel iambs by 9-month-olds as well. However, analyses of input in Morgan (in press) demonstrate that this bias cannot result from simple statistical analyses of input. Bisyllabic *utterances* in input are more likely to be iambs than trochees, and utterances in general are more likely to begin with a weak syllable and end with a strong syllable than the reverse (due to the syntactic asymmetries between function and content words noted earlier). Rather, trochees come to be preferred because trochaic bisyllables are more likely to recur than are iambic bisyllables. In other words, distinctive weightings appear to be assigned to particular rhythmic patterns by virtue of correlations between those patterns and the distributional patterns of the input.

Correlations between rhythmic and distributional properties of bi-syllables also figure in infants' formation of representations of wordlike units, as a recent series of studies by Morgan and Saffran (in press) shows. In these studies, 10-month-olds required convergent rhythmic and distributional evidence to maintain representations of bisyllables as cohesive units; 6-month-olds required only consistent rhythmic evidence. The timing of this shift from reliance on single cues to reliance on correlated constellations of cues is consistent with Younger and Cohen's findings on infants' representations of visual categories (see Werker, Lloyd, Pegg, & Polka, this volume, for additional discussion of developmental synchronies between cognition and speech perception). The ability to detect and deploy correlational evidence thus appears at the same time that the ability to segment words from fluent speech emerges. As we have argued here, these abilities suffice to permit induction of rudimentary grammatical categories.

HOW BOOTSTRAPPING OF RUDIMENTARY CATEGORIES CAN CONTRIBUTE TO ACQUISITION

Precocious knowledge of rudimentary form classes can, in principle, assist in solving several basic problems in language learning. We will briefly discuss three of these problems here: The discovery of word-meaning mappings, the apprehension of sentence phrase structure, and the acquisition of a refined set of form classes. In none of these cases, to our knowledge, is knowledge of rudimentary form classes *necessary* for learning. Rather, in each instance, such knowledge may reduce the computational burden imposed, particularly in the early stages of acquisition, when children lack other types of knowledge that could be brought to bear on these problems.

Discovery of Word-Meaning Mappings

The child's task is to discover proper mappings between individual words and their meanings, given input of multiple-word sentences uttered in contexts that are consistent with large numbers of possible propositional representations. The problem of multiple possible meanings has been discussed extensively elsewhere (see Quine, 1960; Gleitman, 1990) and is not of central concern here. Rather, we are concerned with the uncertainty in mapping arising from multiple-word input. There can be no doubt that children face such uncertainty. Aslin, Woodward, LaMendola, & Bever, (this volume) report that even when mothers are engaged in a word-teaching task, 72% of the utterances they address to their young children are multiple-word utterances; in our analyses of more typical conversation between Adam and Eve and their mothers, over 90% of maternal utterances were multiple-word utterances.

By way of illustration, suppose the child has heard an utterance consisting of N words. Our data indicate that, on average, at least N/2 of these words will be function words. Suppose further that the child has succeeded in representing an appropriate propositional meaning that consists of N/2 potential lexical concepts (e.g., concepts relating to objects, actions, attributes, and so forth). With no constraints or prior knowledge, the number of possible mappings between the words and the concepts is:

1. (Mappings | no rudimentary categories) $\cong N!/(N/2)!$

These mappings (or some subset thereof) must be held in memory so that they can be compared to mappings derived from other utterances heard at later times.

However, if the child knows which words in the utterance are function words and which are content words, the number of possible mappings is reduced to:

2. (Mappings | rudimentary categories) $\cong (N/2)!$

The ratio between the formulae in (1) and (2) increases exponentially with utterance length. For utterances with only four words, knowledge of rudimentary form class membership reduces the number of possible mappings by a factor of at least 6; for utterances with six words, by a factor of at least 20; for utterances with eight words, by a factor of at least 70, and so forth. Thus, fewer mappings need to be retained in memory, and particular word-meaning mappings may be fixed more rapidly. Once the child has fixed certain mappings, these can be used to further reduce the number of possible remaining mappings, but at the beginning of word learning, such knowledge will not be available.

What we are proposing is precisely the opposite of the semantic bootstrapping hypothesis advanced by Grimshaw (1981) and Pinker (1984, 1987). We are suggesting that knowledge of which (rudimentary) form class a word belongs to may serve as a constraint on hypotheses about what that word may mean. Of course, form classes are few in number, whereas meanings are many, so the amount of constraint in the direction we are proposing is much less than that available under the semantic bootstrapping hypothesis. Nevertheless, any property that can reduce uncertainty at the beginning of learning makes an important contribution to acquisition.

Apprehension of Sentence Phrase Structure

Several chapters in this volume discuss the availability in input of, and young children's sensitivity to, prosodic cues to phrase boundaries, including pauses, vowel lengthening, and discontinuities in fundamental frequency contour. These are of course cues to the *ends* of phrases, and in right-branching languages like English such cues provide only limited information about the geometry of phrase structure trees. This is because, in many instances, several phrases beginning at different points may all terminate at the same point. For example, in (3), *ours* terminates at least 10 phrases.

3. My wife chatted with a neighbor who lives in a house near ours.

Knowledge of rudimentary form class membership may help the learner to infer additional information about sentence phrase structure. Generally, function words appear at phrase boundaries. In English, as discussed by Kimball (1973), Clark and Clark (1977), and Morgan, Meier, and Newport (1987), function words typically signal beginnings of phrases, so that the structural information supplied by function words complements that supplied by prosody. In (3), function words mark the beginnings of 7 of the 10 phrases terminated by *ours*. In tandem, function words and prosodic cues can supply nearly complete bracketings of many sentences.

Whether function words occur at the beginnings or ends of phrases in a given language is readily learnable by attending to whether function words typically occur at the beginnings or ends of utterances, inasmuch as utterance boundaries almost invariably coincide with phrase boundaries. For example, our analyses of parental input in the Adam, Eve, and Sarah corpora show that 64% of parental utterances began with a function word and 66% of parental utterances ended with a content word. Inferring that properties occurring at the boundaries of utterances may also signal boundaries of units within utterances is a common feature of many of the models presented in this volume.

Acquisition of a Refined Set of Form Classes

The rudimentary categories of function words and content words (which may perhaps be further divided into nouns and predicates on the basis of perceptual information, as discussed earlier) do not exhaust the set of form classes in any language. The fashion in which these superordinate categories may be subdivided varies considerably across languages (Maratsos, 1988b). Thus, the process by which children acquire sets of form classes fully appropriate for their languages remains to be explained. As we noted previously, both semantic bootstrapping (Pinker, 1984) and distribution-analytic (Maratsos & Chalkley, 1980) accounts have been advanced as explanations. Here, we discuss how early knowledge of rudimentary form classes can assist learning under either account.

Under the semantic bootstrapping account, children are hypothesized to use the meanings of words as a basis for inferring their form class membership. This account hinges on children's abilities to assign appropriate meanings to particular words. As we discussed earlier, knowledge of which rudimentary form class words belong to can aid in constraining the word-meaning mapping problem. On this view, perceptual analyses of linguistic input help to bootstrap semantic analyses, which in turn bootstrap syntactic analyses. The child passes through a series of stages marked by use of increasingly diverse and grammatically sophisticated forms of information.

Under the distribution-analytic account, children are hypothesized to use constellations of co-occurrences among words as a basis for inferring their form class membership. However, not all co-occurrences are equally relevant for determining form class membership. Co-occurrences among content words are typically uninformative with respect to assignment of content words to more fine-grained grammatical categories. Rather, classes of content words may be distinguished most efficiently by restricting attention to cooccurring function words, particularly those that appear as phrase-mates, as Gleitman et al. (1988) suggested.

Recent modeling work by Mintz, Newport, and Bever (in press) lends support to Gleitman et al.'s suggestions and further provides evidence for the usefulness of a rudimentary, phonologically based function word category. Mintz et al. investigated classification of words as nouns and verbs on the basis of distributional evidence under three conditions: Function words were eliminated from the input, function words were represented as individual types in the input, and function words were represented as undifferentiated exemplars of a superordinate category. Their results showed that nouns were least accurately categorized when function words were omitted and most accurately categorized when monosyllabic, open-syllable function words were reduced to a common symbol (i.e., *the*, *a*, *to*, *of*, etc. were all represented as *F*); verbs were most accurately categorized when all function words were represented as a single, undifferentiated category. Thus, preliminary establishment of rudimentary, perceptually based grammatical categories can assist in the later acquisition of a more refined set of categories.

CONCLUSION

The data we have reported here show that over typologically distinct languages, children's input may include sets of cues—statistical, phonological, and acoustic—available to perception that are sufficient to support induction of rudimentary grammatical categories closely corresponding to function words and content words. None of the individual cues we measured has particularly high validity with respect to this distinction; taken together, however, these cues suffice in principle to allow a naive learner lacking any feedback to assign words to these rudimentary categories with very high accuracy. We hypothesize more generally that input speech may contain constellations of cues encoding linguistic information and consequently believe it unwise to prematurely dismiss the input speech stream as a potential source of information relevant for the acquisition of grammar. Analyses that narrowly focus on one or two cues risk seriously underestimating the informativeness of input speech.

Early possession of knowledge of basic categories may serve as an important bootstrap for acquisition of grammar, helping to set the stage for subsequent syntactic and semantic analyses to operate with enhanced efficiency. As we discussed earlier, such knowledge can assist in the discovery of word meanings, the representation of phrase structure, and the acquisition of a more fine-grained system of grammatical categories.

It is important to keep in mind that regardless of how richly endowed children might be with preprogramming for language acquisition, they will have to represent linguistically relevant elements, categories, and configurations in input speech to discover how general grammatical patterns are manifest in their native languages. It is universally true, therefore, that language acquisition is funneled, in part, through infants' capacities for perceiving speech. From this, it follows that explanatory influences on language and language acquisition might reasonably be sought in the nature of input speech and pertinent early perceptual capacities. Perceptual analyses of input speech will certainly not carry acquisition of grammar to its end, but such analyses are a most logical point for learning to begin.

ACKNOWLEDGMENTS

This research was supported by NIH grant HD 29426 to JLM. We thank John Mertus for technical advice, Rachel Kessinger for assistance in acoustic measurements, and Katherine Demuth for comments on a draft of this chapter.

REFERENCES

Aronoff, M. (1976). *Word formation in generative grammar.* Cambridge, MA: MIT Press.
Bard, E., & Anderson, A. H. (1983). The unintelligibility of speech to children. *Journal of Child Language, 10,* 265-292.
Bloom, L. (1970). *Language development: Form and function in emerging grammars.* Cambridge, MA: MIT Press.
Bowerman, M. (1973). *Early syntactic development: A cross-linguistic study with special reference to Finnish.* Cambridge, England: Cambridge University Press.
Bradley, D. C. (1978). *Computational distinctions of vocabulary type.* Unpublished doctoral dissertation, Monash University, Melbourne, Australia.
Bradley, D. C., Garrett, M. F., & Zuriff, E. B. (1980). Syntactic deficits in Broca's aphasia. In D. Caplan (Ed.), *Biological studies of mental processes* (pp. 269-286). Cambridge, MA: MIT Press.
Braine, M. D. S. (1963). The ontogeny of English phrase structure: The first phase. *Language, 39,* 3-13.
Braine, M. D. S. (1976). Children's first word combinations. *Monographs of the Society for Research in Child Development, 41.*
Brown, R. (1973). *A first language: The early stages.* Cambridge, MA: Harvard University Press.
Clark, H. H., & Clark, E. V. (1977). *Psychology and language: An introduction to psycholinguistics.* New York: Harcourt Brace Jovanovitch.
Cutler, A. (1993). Phonological cues to open- and closed-class words in the processing of spoken sentences. *Journal of Psycholinguistic Research, 22,* 109-131.
Cutler, A., & Carter, D. M. (1987). The predominance of strong initial syllables in the English vocabulary. *Computer Speech and Language, 2,* 133-142.
Gleitman, L. (1990). The structural sources of verb meanings. *Language Acquisition, 1,* 3-55.

Gleitman, L., Gleitman, H., Landau, B., & Wanner, E. (1988). Where learning begins: Initial representations for language learning. In F. Newmeyer (Ed.), *The Cambridge linguistic survey: Vol. 3. Language: Psychological and biological aspects* (pp. 150-193). New York: Cambridge University Press.

Gleitman, L. R., & Wanner, E. (1982). Language acquisition: The state of the state of the art. In E. Wanner & L. R. Gleitman (Eds.), *Language acquisition: The state of the art* (pp. 3-48). Cambridge, England: Cambridge University Press.

Golston, C. (1991). *Two lexicons*. Unpublished doctoral dissertation, University of California, Los Angeles.

Gordon, B., & Caramazza, A. (1985). Lexical access and frequency sensitivity: Frequency saturation and open/closed class equivalence. *Cognition, 21*, 95-115.

Grimshaw, J. (1981). Form, function, and the language acquisition device. In C. L. Baker & J. McCarthy (Eds.), *The logical problem of language acquisition* (pp. 163-182). Cambridge, MA: MIT Press.

Jusczyk, P. W., Cutler, A., & Redanz, L. (1993). Infants' sensitivity to predominant stress patterns in English. *Child Development, 64*, 675-687.

Kean, M.-L. (1979). Agrammatism: A phonological deficit? *Cognition, 7*, 69-84.

Kean, M.-L. (1980). Grammatical representations and the description of language processing. In D. Caplan (Ed.), *Biological studies of mental processes* (pp. 239-268). Cambridge, MA: MIT Press.

Kimball, J. P. (1973). Seven principles of surface structure parsing in natural languages. *Cognition, 2*, 15-47.

Klavans, J. (1985). The independence of syntax and phonology in cliticization. *Language, 61*, 95-120.

Kucera, H., & Francis, N. (1967). *A computational analysis of present day English*. Providence, RI: Brown University Press.

Kuhl, P. K. (1983). Perception of auditory equivalence classes for speech in early infancy. *Infant Behavior and Development, 6*, 263-285.

Landau, B., & Jackendoff, R. (1993). "What" and "where" in spatial language and spatial cognition. *Brain and Behavioral Science, 16*, 217-265.

Lieberman, P. (1965). On the acoustic basis of the perception of intonation and stress by linguists. *Word, 21*, 40-54.

Maratsos, M. P. (1988a). The acquisition of formal word classes. In I. M. Schlesinger, Y. Levy, & M. D. S. Braine (Eds.), *Categories and processes in language acquisition* (pp. 31-44). Hillsdale, NJ: Lawrence Erlbaum Associates.

Maratsos, M. P. (1988b). Crosslinguistic analysis, universals, and language acquisition. In F. Kessel (Ed.), *The development of language and language researchers: Essays in honor of Roger Brown* (pp. 121-152). Hillsdale, NJ: Lawrence Erlbaum Associates.

Maratsos, M., & Chalkley, M. A. (1980). The internal language of children's syntax: The ontogenesis and representation of syntactic categories. In K. Nelson (Ed.), *Children's language , Vol. 2* (pp. 127-214). New York: Gardner Press.

Matthai, E. H., & Kean, M.-L. (1989). Postaccess processes in the open vs. closed class distinction. *Brain and Language, 36*, 163-180.

Mintz, T. H., Newport, E. L., & Bever, T. G. (in press). Distributional regularities of form class in speech to young children. *Proceedings of NELS 25*. Amherst, MA: GLSA.

Morgan, J. L. (in press). A rhythmic bias in preverbal speech segmentation. *Journal of Memory and Language*.

Morgan, J. L., Meier, R. P., & Newport, E. L. (1987). Structural packaging in the input to language learning: Contributions of prosodic and morphological marking of phrases to the acquisition of language. *Cognitive Psychology, 19*, 498-550.

Morgan, J. L., & Saffran, J. R. (in press). Emerging integration of sequential and suprasegmental information in preverbal speech segmentation. *Child Development*.

Pinker, S. (1984). *Language learnability and language development*. Cambridge, MA: Harvard University Press.

Pinker, S. (1987). The bootstrapping problem in language acquisition. In B. MacWhinney (Ed.), *Mechanisms of language acquisition* (pp. 399-441). Hillsdale, NJ: Lawrence Erlbaum Associates.

Quine, W. V. O. (1960). *Word and object*. Cambridge, MA: MIT Press.

Radford, A. (1990). *Syntactic theory and the acquisition of English syntax*. Oxford: Basil Blackwell.

Ratner, N. B. (1984). Patterns of vowel modification in mother-child speech. *Journal of Child Language, 11*, 557-578.

Rosenberg, B., Zuriff, E., Brownell, H., Garrett, M., & Bradley, D. (1985). Grammatical class effects in relation to normal and aphasic sentence processing. *Brain and Language, 26*, 287-303.

Rumelhart, D. E., & McClelland, J. L. (1987). Learning the past tenses of English verbs: Implicit rules or parallel distributed processing. In B. MacWhinney (Ed.), *Mechanisms of language acquisition* (pp. 195-248). Hillsdale, NJ: Lawrence Erlbaum Associates.

Sankoff, G., & Laberge, S. (1973). On the acquisition of native speakers by a language. *Kivung, 6*, 32-47.

Shi, R. (1994). *Perceptual correlates of content words and function words in early language input*. Unpublished Ph.D. Dissertation, Brown University, Providence, RI.

Shillcock, R. C., & Bard, E. G. (1993). Modularity and the processing of closed-class words. In G. Altman & R. Shillcock (Eds.), *Cognitive models of speech processing: The Sperlonga meeting II* (pp. 163-185). Cambridge, MA: MIT Press.

Swinney, D. (1979). Lexical access during sentence comprehension: (Re)consideration of context effects. *Journal of Verbal Learning and Verbal Behavior, 15*, 545-569.

Younger, B. A. (1993). Understanding category members as "the same sort of thing": Explicit categorization in ten-month infants. *Child Development, 64*, 309-320.

Younger, B. A., & Cohen, L. B. (1983). Infant perception of correlations among attributes. *Child Development, 54*, 858-867.

Younger, B. A., & Cohen, L. B. (1986). Developmental changes in infants' perception of correlations among attributes. *Child Development, 57*, 803-815.

Zipf, P. (1949). *Human behavior and the principle of least effort: An introduction to human ecology*. Cambridge, MA: Addison-Wesley.

PART IV

SPEECH AND THE ACQUISITION OF PHRASE STRUCTURE

17 Prosodic Cues to Syntactic and Other Linguistic Structures in Japanese, Korean, and English

Jennifer J. Venditti, Sun-Ah Jun, and Mary E. Beckman
Ohio State University

A salient argument motivating the idea that prosody is used as a bootstrapping mechanism for the first-language learner acquiring syntactic structure is the observation that prosodic groupings often seem to match syntactic ones. In this chapter, we examine this argument by comparing the prosodic systems and the relationship between prosody and syntax in three languages—Japanese, Korean, and English. We conclude that, although we have little specific evidence about their role in acquisition, the complexity of the mappings, and the arbitrary language-specific aspects of the mappings, in particular, make it seem unlikely that the child can have them innately to use as an aid in syntactic acquisition except in the most general sense that groupings and prominence are universal cognitive categories.

In the following sections we first sketch the prosodic system of each of the three languages, drawing parallels among them to suggest what phonological and phonetic categories correspond functionally. We then outline some of the ways that prosody is used in adult-directed speech to indicate grammatical organization at levels above the word. This section emphasizes the aspects of prosodic form that map easily onto syntactic form, but also tries to convey an appreciation for the ways and extent to which the three languages differ. The next section discusses some examples that suggest that linguistic categories and structures in addition to syntactic ones also play a strong role in determining the prosodic structure of any given utterance. Again, we draw parallels among the three languages to show that, although prosodic structures and their mappings to these other linguistic categories are often roughly similar, the specific details show cross-linguistic variability of a sort that makes these mappings somewhat arbitrary.

THE PROSODIC STRUCTURES

Theoretical Underpinnings

Our view of prosodic structure is that of Metrical Phonology as developed in such work as Selkirk (1980), Nespor and Vogel (1986), and Pierrehumbert and Beckman (1988), among many others. We assume, as a first approximation, that prosodic structure can be described phonologically as a hierarchical organization of constituents, with elements at one level grouped together into larger elements at the next higher level. In addition to the notion of grouping per se, the prosodic hierarchy allows for the notion of relationships of greater and lesser prominence among constituents at any given level. For example, in English, the lowest level of grouping in the prosodic hierarchy—the *stress foot*— is defined by having an initial strong element: a heavy (or "stressed") syllable. Thus, the two heavy syllables in *Marianna* or *kindergarten* define two stress feet, as shown by the tree representation of *kindergarten* in Fig. 17.1. Here the two notions of prominence relationship and constituent structure work together: The stressed syllable acts both as the head of the stress foot and as the marker for the left-hand edge of the constituent at this level of the prosodic tree.

Another fundamental assumption in our view of prosody is that there is an essential connection to the intonation pattern. That is, some types of prominence relationship or some units in the prosodic constituency are defined phonologically by such intonational phenomena as pitch accents and boundary tones, which we define as follows: A *pitch accent* is a pitch event (a tone or tone sequence) that is phonologically linked to a particular syllable and phonetically realized at or around that designated syllable in a stretch of speech; whereas a *boundary tone* is a pitch event associated to a larger unit, such as a prosodic word or phrase, and realized phonetically at the left or right edge of that larger unit.

In English (and other similar "stress-accent languages"), pitch accents play an essential role in the prominence system. The heads of stress feet can be associated to pitch accents, and this association to a pitch accent defines an extra level of prominence. In other words, a pitch-accented syllable is more stressed than a merely heavy one. So in the example shown in Fig. 17.1, the syllable *want* and the second syllable in *behave*, both of which are accented, are more stressed than the merely heavy unaccented syllables in *kindergarten*.

Now, here prominence relationships and constituent structure do not coincide in the phonological formalism. There is no phonological constituent that we can identify as the unit that an accented syllable heads, in the way that we identify the stress foot as the unit that a heavy syllable heads. On the other hand, pitch accents do seem to be connected to our intuitions about constituency, because of two facts.

First, a word typically will not have more than one accented syllable even if it has more than one heavy syllable, so that we can usually talk about the word being accented instead of (more precisely) about the syllable within it being accented. Second, in many discourse contexts, function words tend not to be accented, giving them the feeling of not being quite full words. These facts about how accent placement works surely are the source of such common misparsings by children as the one given in the sample dialogue in (1).

1. Parent: I want you to behave in kindergarten.
   Child: But I *am* being have.

That is, *behave* feels phonologically to be the same sort of informational unit as *be good*, which the child then identifies as the same syntactic constituent with accent on the predicate adjective and no accent on the verb *be*.

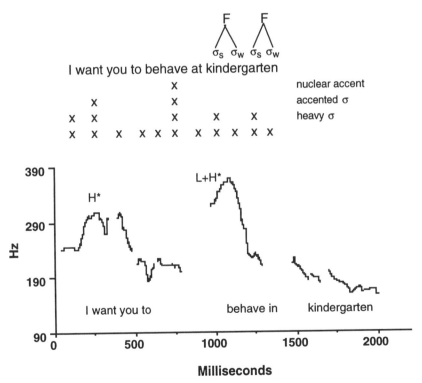

FIG. 17.1. Metrical representation and fundamental frequency (F$_0$) contour of an utterance of *I want you to behave in kindergarten.* with accents on *want* and *behave*. In the transcription that we adopt for English (see Pierrehumbert, 1980), "+" links the two tones of a complex accent and "*" denotes the tone associated to the stressed syllable.

Pitch Accents in Korean and Japanese

Korean and Japanese are very similar to each other and distinct from English in having no well-defined prosodic category like either of the two levels of stress that we have mentioned for English. Looking first at Korean, we see that it does not have anything like the distinction in English between light and heavy syllables. Some dialects do contrast short and long syllables, but this is a purely paradigmatic contrast rather than a syntagmatic one. That is, the long syllables are not inherently more stressed than the short, and they do not define a prosodic constituent like the stress foot in English. In addition, although most dialects of Korean have tonal events that can legitimately be described

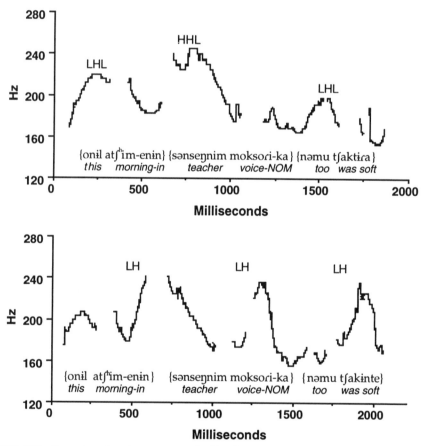

FIG. 17.2. F₀ contour for the utterance [onɨl atʃhim-enɨn sənseŋnim moksoɾi-ka nəmu tʃaktiɾa] "This morning the teacher's voice was too soft." in the (top) Chonnam and (bottom) Seoul dialects. Each pair of {...} in the transcription brackets a phrase at this level.

as "pitch accents," these also do not function as markers for prominent syllables. Instead, they are much more closely tied to the function of grouping that is only indirectly indicated by accent placement patterns in English. In Korean, a pitch accent defines the intonation contour that very clearly demarcates which words group together in forming the next larger phonological constituent, providing an explicitly marked phonological level where English has only the implicit informational grouping. Fig. 17.2, top panel, shows an example from the Chonnam dialect; each low-high-low (LHL) or high-high-low (HHL) sequence marks the beginning of a phrase (see Jun, 1989).

Fig. 17.2, bottom panel, shows an utterance of the same sentence produced in the standard (Seoul) dialect. Note that the edge that is phonologically marked by the accent is different (it is the end rather than the beginning), as is the shape of the phonological marker (it is a rising LH accent rather than a falling HL one). However, in both dialects, it is the same words that become grouped together at this level of prosodic phrasing. Also, note that the groupings here show a vague resemblance to the kinds of minimal syntactic phrases that we associate with the distribution of accents in English: For example, the deictic adjective is grouped together with the following noun into a single unit at this level.

Japanese is also different from English in the same ways. It does not have anything like the stress hierarchy of English, and instead makes the pitch accent an integral part of an intonationally defined phrasal constituent just above the word. The situation in Standard (Tokyo) Japanese is somewhat more complicated than the one in Korean because there is a lexical contrast between "unaccented" phrases (which are marked only by a delimitative LH pattern at the beginning edge) and "accented" phrases (which also have a distinctive HL fall on a designated mora somewhere within the constituent). Thus, in the sentences shown in Fig. 17.3, the place name *Me'jiro* is accented, whereas *Ueno* is not.

However, despite the complications introduced by the presence or absence of lexical accent, the tonally marked grouping at this level of phonological phrasing is functionally similar to that in Chonnam and Standard Korean. This level of tonally delimited prosodic phrasing that Japanese and Korean both have has been called many different things by different phonologists. Based on a common practice in Japanese dialectology, we will call it the *accentual phrase*, in order to emphasize the connection to the tonal pattern.

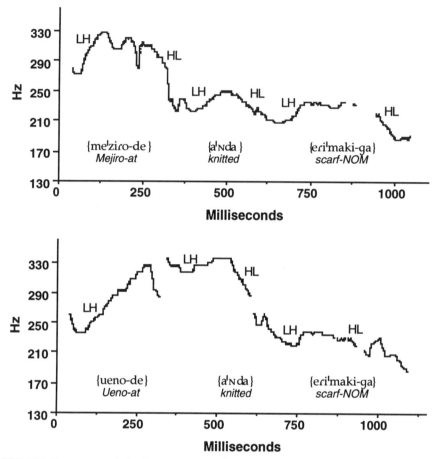

FIG. 17.3. F_0 contours of the Japanese noun phrases (top) [me'ziɾo-de a'Nda eɾi'maki-ga] and (bottom) [ueno-de a'Nda eɾi'maki-ga] "the scarf that I knitted at Mejiro/Ueno." Each ['] in the transcription marks the place for the HL fall of a pitch accent.

Boundary Tones and Intonational Phrases

Above this level, the three languages look rather more similar: Several accentual phrases, in Japanese and Korean, or several pitch-accented words, in English, can be grouped together into larger prosodic constituents characterized by tonal markings (boundary tones) at the larger constituent's edge. In all three languages, we can talk about a constituent that we will call the *intonation phrase* proper. This is a unit that is defined tonally by an H or L boundary tone aligned to its right edge. For example, each of the utterances shown in Fig. 17.4 has two intonation phrases, with the medial and final boundaries demarcated by H boundary tones.

In English, there is also an *intermediate phrase*, which is defined intonationally by an additional boundary tone that fills in the space between the last pitch accent and the phrase edge.   Adopting Pierrehumbert's (1980) terminology, we call this phrase boundary tone the "phrase accent," because it defines another level of prominence in English.   That is, the last accented syllable in the phrase—the one associated to the pitch accent just before the phrase accent—is the most prominent syllable in the phrase.   It has a level of stress that we call the *nuclear accent*, or the "sentence stress."   For example, in the utterance in Fig. 17.5, top panel, the nuclear-accented word *milk* is more stressed than *Marianna*.   As listeners, we are likely to interpret the nuclear-accented word as the attentional focus of the utterance.   If as speakers

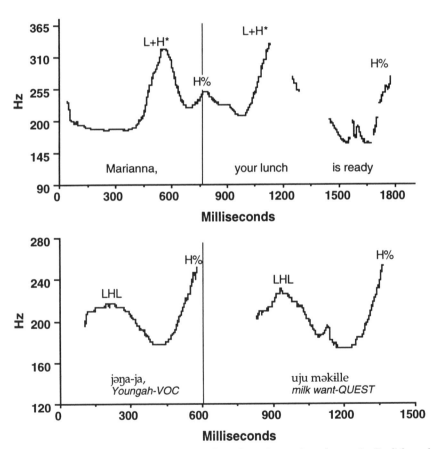

FIG. 17.4. F_0 contours of utterances consisting of two intonation phrases in English and Chonnam Korean. For both languages, we adopt the notation "%" introduced by Pierrehumbert (1980) for intonation phrase boundary tones. The cursor in each figure marks the medial intonation phrase boundary.

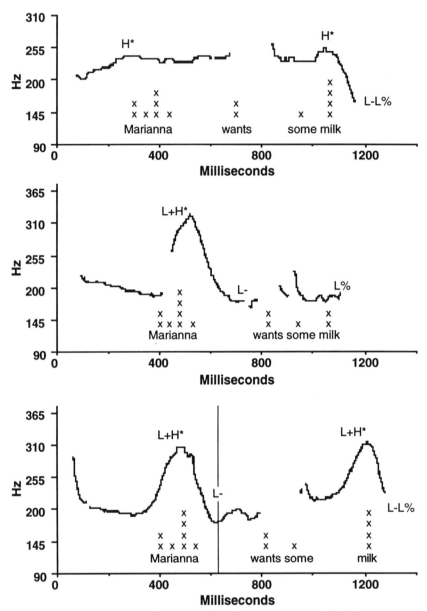

FIG. 17.5. F_0 contours and corresponding metrical grid representations of *Marianna wants some milk* (top) with nuclear accent on *milk*, (second) with nuclear accent on *Marianna*, and (third) with a phrase boundary after *Marianna* and nuclear accents on both *Marianna* and *milk*. The L-is an L phrase accent, and the cursor marks the medial intermediate phrase boundary.

we want to focus instead on the earlier word, we could make that pitch accent the nuclear accent, as in the utterance in Fig. 17.5, middle panel. Or if we wanted to focus equally on both words, we could divide the utterance into two intermediate phrases, so as to put a nuclear accent on both, as in Fig. 17.5, bottom panel. Thus, at this level of the prosodic hierarchy in English, prominence relationships and constituent structure coincide fairly closely in the phonology, as shown in the metrical grids in Fig. 17.5.

Since neither Korean nor Japanese has anything phonologically like the relationship between pitch accents and prominence in English, there is nothing like the nuclear accent either, although (as we will show later) there are well-defined prosodic means for indicating attentional focus. On the other hand, while it does not have phrase accents or the notion of nuclear accent, Standard Japanese, at least, does have something like the intermediate phrase in English, defined by the process of downstep, to which we now turn.

Downstep

Downstep is the process by which pitch range is reduced after some phonological trigger. In English, the trigger of downstep is any bitonal pitch accent. For example, in the utterance shown in Fig. 17.6, top panel, the bitonal accents on *Willy*, *Mary*, and *Anna* all trigger downsteps (redundantly marked here by "!" on the downstepped tones). Beckman and Pierrehumbert (1986) identify the intermediate phrase in English not just as the constituent headed by the nuclear accent, but also as the domain of downstep. Thus in the example shown in Fig. 17.6, bottom panel, the effect of the downstep triggered by the accent on *Willy* is undone and a new independent pitch range is chosen at the intermediate phrase boundary before *Youngah*.

A similar phenomenon occurs in many dialects of Japanese, including Tokyo Japanese, where the trigger is the HL lexical accent. In the contours shown in Fig. 17.3, the verb [aˈɴda] "knitted" is lower in Fig. 17.3, top panel, because it is in the reduced pitch range after the downstep triggered by the accent in [meˈdʒiɾo]. The figure also shows how the effects of downstep chain within the bounds of the intermediate phrase (here the whole noun phrase), resembling a descending staircase.

Standard Korean and Chonnam Korean also typically show pitch range patterns that resemble the staircasing chain of downstep in the other two languages, as seen in the Chonnam utterance shown in Fig. 17.7. However, since there is no contrast in either of these two dialects between having and not having some sort of phonological trigger, we cannot really support the notion of downstep here, and thus cannot use these pitch range relationships to formally define an intermediate phrase for Korean.

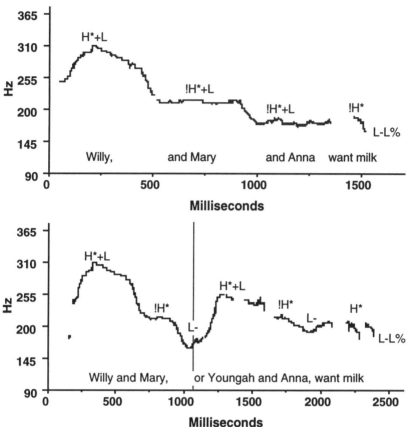

FIG. 17.6. F$_0$ contours for the utterances *Willy, and Mary and Anna want milk* (with down-stepping accents on *Willy, Mary,* and *Anna*) and *Willy and Mary, or Youngah and Anna, want milk* with the cursor marking the intermediate phrase boundary of interest.

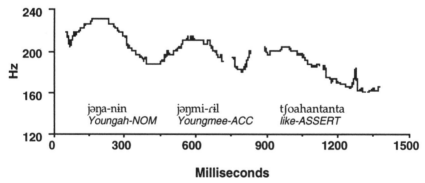

FIG. 17.7. F$_0$ contour depicting "downstep" in Chonnam Korean in the utterance [jəŋa-nin jəŋmi-ɾil tʃoahantanta] "Young-ah likes Young-mee."

THE SYNTAX-PROSODY MAPPING

Having sketched our picture of prosodic structure in the three languages, we turn now to the question "Can these patterns of prominence relationships or prosodic groupings give the child any clue to the syntactic organization of the utterance?" Let us start again at the lower levels of the hierarchy, at the levels where prosodic organization seems to be related somehow to the notion of what constitutes a minimal informational unit.

Accent and Accentual Phrasing for Compound Nouns

In English we have already said that although accents technically do not define any constituent in the prosodic hierarchy, they seem to function phrasally. That is, they often seem to organize the utterance into word- or phraselike informational units. Probably the most commonly cited example of this is the role of accent in differentiating compound words from syntactic phrases. For example, in citation form, the phrases in (2) might typically be distinguished from each other by having one versus two pitch accents.

2. syntactic phrase: a yéllow jácket
    compound word: a yéllowjacket (="hornet")

Of course, the more reliable clue to the difference here is the shift of the nuclear accent. When the syntactic phrase occurs in isolation, the tendency will be to place the nuclear accent on the second element unless there are reasons to place special focus on the first one. In the compound word, by contrast, the nuclear accent must be on the first element. That is, in English, we can talk about this syntactic difference between the two-word phrase and single compound word in terms of a difference in stress pattern, a different potential for pitch accent placement.

In Korean, there is nothing analogous to the accent manipulations that we find in English, since accent in Korean is strictly delimitative—marking the edge of the accentual phrase. However, even though we do not find the same function of accent in Korean, there is a similar differentiation between a syntactic phrase and a compound word, as shown in (3). (Here {...}$_{AP}$ brackets each accentual phrase.)

3. {tʃakin}$_{AP}$ {tʃip}$_{AP}$"small house"
      small   house
    {tʃakin tʃip}$_{AP}$ "younger brother's family"

As shown by the bracketing, when the adjective and noun form two separate accentual phrases, then the meaning is construed as a "small house." On the other hand, if they are pronounced together as one accentual phrase, as in the latter example, it is construed as a compound, and the meaning becomes "younger brother's family." Japanese can use accentual phrasing in the same way to differentiate syntactic phrases from compound words.

This relationship between accent placement and compounding, or between accentual-phrasing and compounding, is productive in all three languages, and particularly so in English, where the compound stress rule applies even to long compounds such as *gráde-school teacher*. Thus we might expect this to be the prime candidate for something prosodic that a child acquiring the language can use to learn about the syntactic organization. The little evidence that we know of, however, suggests that this is not the case. Atkinson-King (1973) showed that English-speaking children do not reliably command the accentual contrast between compound words and syntactic phrases until they are 10 or 11 years old. For example, in a test where the subjects were asked to point to pictures in response to audio stimuli, the children of kindergarten age performed at chance level, and it was not until grades 5 or 6 that they identified the stimuli as well as the adults. In contrast to this, the relationship between attentional focus and nuclear accent placement may be acquired earlier, as suggested by a small pilot study in Atkinson-King (1973).

Scope of Adjectival and Adverbial Modification

We mentioned that the relationship between compounding and accentuation is a very productive and quite regular aspect of the prosody-syntax mapping. However, this is not the only documented aspect. Research on a variety of languages has suggested that the prosodic structure can be used to disambiguate the syntactic structure for larger utterances as well. In English, for example, many researchers (e.g., Lehiste, 1973; Price et al., 1991) have suggested that some aspect of the prosody can help cue the adjective's scope of modification in phrases such as *old men and women*. There seem to be several factors involved in distinguishing the narrow-scope from the wide-scope interpretation, including the placement of pauses and pre-boundary lengthening. However, these two interpretations are perhaps most dramatically cued when there is a difference in intermediate phrasing or intonational phrasing, as shown in Fig. 17.8.

In Fig. 17.8, top panel, the adjective *old* modifies both *men* and *women*. Here, there is an intermediate phrase boundary intervening between the adjective and the nouns, marked by an L- phrase accent. In contrast, Fig. 17.8, bottom panel, shows the interpretation in which only the men are the ones who are old. In this interpretation, the adjective and the noun *men* are phrased together into one intermediate phrase, followed by a separate intermediate phrase for *women*. These figures show how a difference in syntactic structure can be cued by differing patterns of phrasing at a high level of the prosodic hierarchy— here the intermediate phrase.

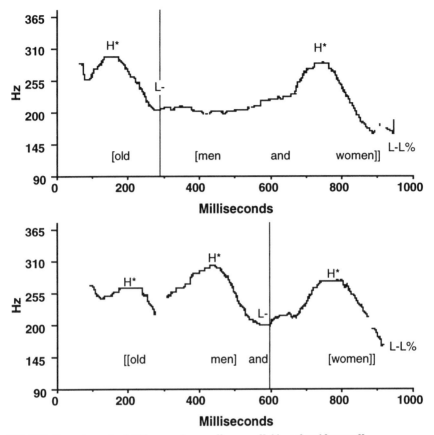

FIG. 17.8. F₀ contours for [old [men and women]] versus [[old men] and [women]].

In Japanese and Korean, syntactically ambiguous strings of words can be distinguished by means of the prosodic phrasing, just as in English. One such example involves constructions where the scope of an adverb is ambiguous, as in the Japanese string given in (4) and Fig. 17.9.

4. kjo'neN   a'Nda   eɾi'maki-ga   nusuma'ɾeta
    last year   knitted   scarf-NOM   was stolen

In this string, the initial adverb can be taken to modify the entire sentence, resulting in the structure in Fig. 17.9a ("The scarf that I knitted was stolen last year."). On the other hand, when the adverb is taken as part of the relative clause, it has the more narrow scope of modification shown in Fig. 17.9b ("The scarf that I knitted last year was stolen.").

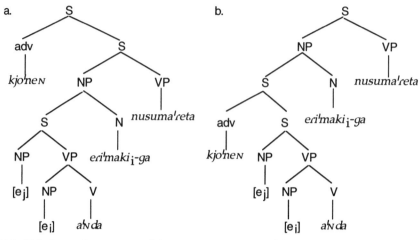

FIG. 17.9. Syntactic structures of the two interpretations of the sentence in (4).

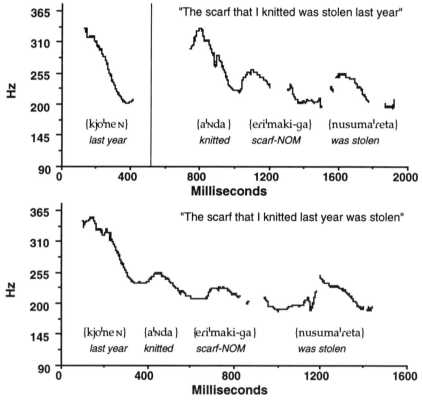

FIG. 17.10. F₀ contours of the Japanese sentences shown in Fig. 17.9. The cursor marks the intermediate phrase boundary in the top panel.

A study by Uyeno, Hayashibe, Imai, Imagawa, and Kiritani (1980) using a similar corpus suggested that these two interpretations can be distinguished prosodically by the relative height of the first two peaks, that is, by the choice of pitch range on the adverb and the following verb. In a recent experiment we have shown that this choice of pitch range is indeed a major cue. Fig. 17.10 shows typical contours from the utterances in this experiment of the sentences in Fig. 17.9. Close examination of the two fundamental frequency contours of this ambiguous sentence shows that at the level of the accentual phrase they are identical. There are as many accentual phrases in Fig. 17.10, top panel, as in Fig. 17.10, bottom panel. However, note that there is a clear difference at the level of the intermediate phrase. When the adverb modifies the whole sentence, as in Fig. 17.10, top panel, there is an intermediate phrase boundary intervening between the adverb and the rest of the sentence, manifested by a reset in the pitch range on the second peak. In contrast, when the initial adverb modifies the verb of the relative clause, as in Fig. 17.10, bottom panel, there is no reset in pitch range, but rather a pattern of downstep lowering each successive peak. Thus the syntax is influencing the prosody at the level of the intermediate phrase. Note that in these examples, there is a pause coinciding with the intermediate phrase boundary (Fig. 17.10, top panel). However, a pause is not necessary for this pitch pattern to occur, nor must there be an intermediate phrase boundary for a pause to occur. A study by Azuma and Tsukuma (1991) using similar sentences indicated that it is the fundamental frequency contour, rather than the presence or absence of a pause, which is the more salient cue to the syntactic structure.

Korean is syntactically very similar to Japanese, and there are sentences with exactly this same ambiguity. Fig. 17.11 shows fundamental frequency contours of Chonnam Korean for the contrasting interpretations of a similar ambiguous sentence. These also are prosodically distinct. The choice of a higher pitch range on the following verb when it is not modified by the adverb is similar to the pattern in Japanese (cf. Fig. 17.10, top panel). However, there is another prosodic difference here. Where the Japanese contrast was associated with a difference in intermediate phrasing, the Korean contrast is associated with a difference in intonational and accentual phrasing. In Fig. 17.11, top panel, there is an intonation phrase break between [tʃaŋnjən-ɛ] "last year" and [iɾəpəɾin] "lost" (marked by an HL% boundary tone sequence), corresponding to the intermediate phrase break in the analogous Japanese utterance. In contrast, the contour in Fig. 17.11, bottom panel, groups the initial adverb and the verb of the relative clause into one accentual phrase, followed by a separate accentual phrase for the head noun. In other words, where the Japanese examples mark the syntactic difference by a contrast between an intermediate phrase break versus an accentual phrase break, the Korean examples mark it by a contrast between an intonational phrase break and no phrase break. On the other hand,

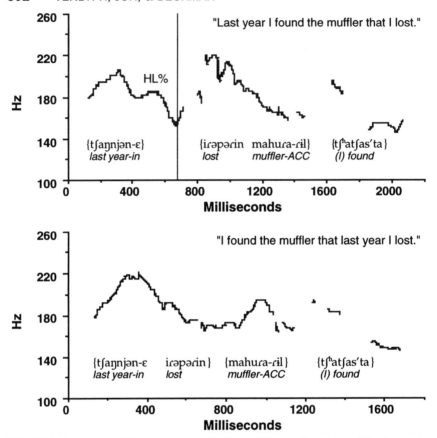

FIG. 17.11. F₀ contours of Korean utterances with contrasting adverbial modification. The two utterances correspond to different structures exactly like those shown in Fig. 17.9 (top) and (bottom) for the analogous Japanese sentences.

both languages manipulate the pitch range similarly to cue the syntactic structure.

Irregularities in the Mapping from Syntax to Prosody

From these examples of compound nouns versus syntactic phrases and of ambiguous adjectival and adverbial modification, it is clear that there is an intimate connection between syntax and prosody. However, to know whether the connection can help the child acquire the syntax from the prosody, we need to know how, exactly, the prosodic structure corresponds to the syntactic structure. Do the two structures coincide in any simple algorithmically determinable way? Early accounts in fact assumed a very simple isomorphism. For example, Hattori (1947) suggested that accentual phrasing is often isomorphic with the minimal syntactic phrase in Japanese, using the term *bunsetsu* to denote this unit, and defining it in terms of the tonal pattern for the level that we are calling the accentual phrase. For Hattori, the most typical *bunsetsu* is an NP consisting of a noun and following postposition. However, we have seen that larger sequences can combine into one accentual phrase. For example, when the NP and following verb are short, or the verb is relatively predictable from the noun, they are far more likely to phrase together, as shown in (5).

    5. {udon-o   ta'beta}$_{AP}$ "(someone) ate noodles"
       noodles-ACC   ate

In addition to the length of the words and the semantic relationship between them, the lexical accent patterns also influence the likelihood of different accentual phrasings in Japanese. Grouping the noun and verb together is especially likely when the noun is unaccented, as in (5). Also, it is not uncommon to have a sequence of unaccented syntactic phrases, such as adjectival nouns modifying other nouns, in which no accentual phrase breaks occur, as in (6).

    6.   {honto:-ni mazime-na eiga}$_{AP}$ "a really serious movie"
       really   serious   movie

Examples such as these, in which syntactic phrase boundaries and accentual phrase boundaries do not coincide, have prompted various more sophisticated notions about the syntax-prosody mapping. One of the most noteworthy of these is Selkirk's (1986) notion of prosodic constituents corresponding to the left or right edges of syntactic constituents at various levels of the syntactic representation. For example, she claims that boundaries at higher levels of phonological phrasing correspond to the left or right edges of maximal projections in the syntactic tree (with the edge being a language-specific parameter). Selkirk and Tateishi (1991) applied this notion to Japanese, positing the major phrase—our intermediate phrase—as the relevant level of the prosodic structure whose edge corresponds to the left edge of a maximal projection. Under this assumption, the edge-based theory of syntax-prosody mapping can account for the phrasings in (5) and (6), each of which comprise one intermediate phrase (as well as one accentual phrase). The corresponding syntactic structures of (5) and (6) are given in Fig. 17.12. The fact that intermediate phrase boundaries coincide with accentual phrase boundaries falls out from the nature of the prosodic hierarchy in Japanese, and of hierarchical structures in prosody in general under the theory that Selkirk and we assume (see, e.g., Nespor & Vogel, 1986; Pierrehumbert & Beckman, 1988; Selkirk, 1980).

However, although this edge-based theory can account for the patterns of prosodic phrasing observed for some syntactic structures, it cannot, without modification, explain the phrasing observed for utterances of the Japanese constructions with contrasting adverbial scope of modification. If we assume the syntactic structures given in Fig. 17.9, the left

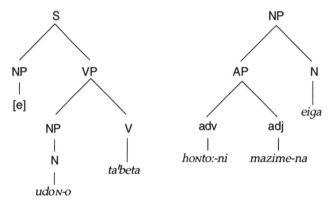

FIG. 17.12. Syntactic representations of the utterances in (5) and (6).

edges of several maximal projections intervene between the adverb [kjoʰneɴ] and the verb [aʰɴda] in the utterance where the adverb modifies the predicate of the root sentence (Fig. 17.9, top panel). However, there are also edges coming between [kjoʰneɴ] and [aʰɴda] in the utterance where the adverb modifies only the embedded sentence of the relative clause (Fig. 17.9, bottom panel). The edge-based theory would incorrectly predict that a major phrase boundary (and thus a pitch-range reset) occurs after the adverb [kjoʰneɴ] in both interpretations. We have already seen (cf. Fig. 17.10) that this is not the case. Other syntactic frameworks suggest different structures from those shown in Fig. 17.9. However, all of the syntactic analyses that we have seen for these sentences have the same problem as these Standard Theory analyses. Because in these sentences involving relative clause constructions the structure of the relative clause is nearly identical at the lower levels of the tree, a theory making reference to edges of maximal projections cannot account for the differences in prosodic grouping. The difference in phrasing here seems not to be sensitive to the edges of major syntactic phrases, but rather to a higher level difference of whether or not the adverb is a clausemate to the verb it is modifying. Similar problems arise when we look at the Korean examples with analogous syntactic structures.

A similar kind of problem for an edge-based theory of syntax-prosody mapping in Korean involves the phrasal attachment of adverbs in adjective phrases, such as the one illustrated in Fig. 17.13. As in Japanese, the relevant edge for Korean must be the left one. As shown in Fig. 17.13, top panel, therefore, the syntactic structure predicts a phrase edge only utterance initially and between the head of the subject NP [kiɾim] and the verb [isʹninte]. However, this sentence is much more likely to be prosodically phrased as in Fig. 17.13, bottom panel, with an accentual phrase boundary utterance initially and between the adverb [atʃu] and the adjective [tʃoin]. By contrast to the previous example in which the prosody only lacks breaks where the syntax might

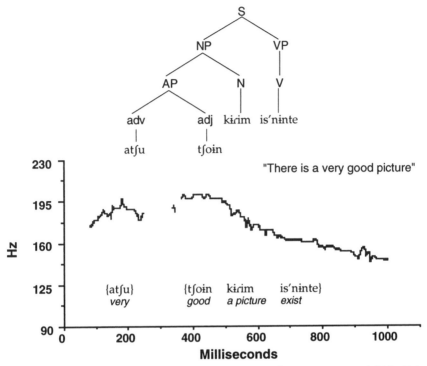

FIG. 17.13. (top) Syntactic tree and (bottom) F_0 contour for an utterance of [atʃu tʃoin kiɾim is'ninte] "There is a very good picture."

predict one, here the prosody puts a phrase boundary where one is not expected by Selkirk's theory. This kind of mismatch is arguably more problematic to the first-language learner who is trying to decipher the syntactic groupings from the prosodic ones.

Nespor and Vogel (1986) proposed an alternative theory of the syntax-prosody mapping, based on head-complement relationships. However, this also fails to predict the observed phrasing, and does so in both ways that Selkirk's theory does. It predicts prosodic breaks where none usually occur, and does not predict some breaks that can readily occur.

To recapitulate, then, syntactic structure certainly can influence prosodic structure. We know this because adult speakers and listeners often can use prosodic differences to disambiguate utterances of different syntactic structures resulting in the same surface string. While there must be some sort of mapping between these two components of the grammar, however, the exact nature of the mapping has yet to be defined well enough to predict whether the child acquiring the language can use the prosody to learn the syntax.

OTHER LINGUISTIC STRUCTURES

We would like to turn now to look at some ways in which linguistic categories and structures other than syntactic ones play a strong role in determining the prosodic structure of an utterance. We have already shown how attentional focus influences nuclear accent placement and intermediate phrasing in English. In Korean and Japanese, which do not have the notion of "nuclear accent," nuclear accent placement cannot be a clue to focus in the discourse. However, we see a similar tendency for attentional focus to affect the prosodic phrasing and pitch range patterns of an utterance in these two languages.

The three contours of Korean utterances in Fig. 17.14 show the same noun phrase with three different focus patterns. Notice that the prosodic phrasing varies according to the placement of focus. In the first contour, the utterance has no special focus on either of the words—that is, it has "neutral" focus. Here, each word in the noun phrase forms its own accentual phrase, with the second one being realized in a slightly lower pitch range than the first (resembling our familiar downstep relationship). In the second contour, there is narrow focus on the adjective, and the two words are phrased together into a single accentual phrase. In the third contour, there is narrow focus on the noun. Here again the two words form two separate accentual phrases, but notice that the second phrase in this utterance is realized in a wider pitch range than the analogous peak in the contour with neutral focus. The facts for Japanese are similar, except that there is a complicated interaction with the lexical accent specification, like that described earlier for the phrasing of a noun and following verb.

These facts about narrow focus make the discussion of the syntax-prosody mapping very complicated. For example, we have already said that in many discourse contexts in English, function words have the feeling of being not quite words because they are not accented. Thus, in many discourse contexts, a preposition typically will not be accented, so that a listener could parse it as belonging to the same informational unit as its complement noun. This intuition about informational organization is explicitly realized in the prosodic structure in Japanese and Korean, where the prototypical accentual phrase is a noun and its following postposition, as shown in Fig. 17.15, top panel, "I even saw a colt at the meeting yesterday." This is a typical neutral-focus production of the sentence in the Chonnam dialect. Each content word has its own accentual phrase, with the postpositions *at* and *even* grouping together with their preceding complement nouns.

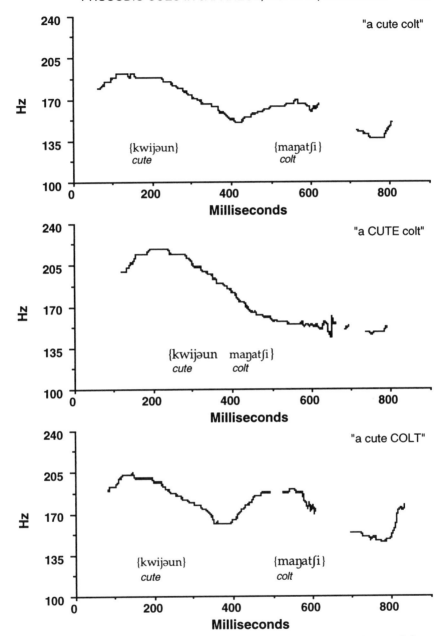

FIG. 17.14. F$_0$ contours for Korean [kwijəun maɲatʃi] "cute colt" with (top) neutral focus, (middle) focus on adjective, and (bottom) focus on noun.

However, in Chonnam Korean at least, it is possible to put special narrow focus on a postposition by starting a new accentual phrase there, as in Fig. 17.15, bottom panel. Here, a new accentual phrase starts at the postposition meaning *even* and the following verb is grouped together with that postposition. Note that it is the accentual phrasing that changes here, and not the intonational phrasing. Although the utterance is divided into two intonational phrases, so is the utterance in Fig. 17.15, top panel, at the same place. Note also that the accentual phrase break just before the focused word in Fig. 17.15, bottom panel, is accompanied by a local expansion of the pitch range, comparable to that seen on the focused word in Fig. 17.14, bottom panel. This phrasing (and the pitch range increase) corresponds functionally to the strategy of placing nuclear accent on the preposition in English. By putting the

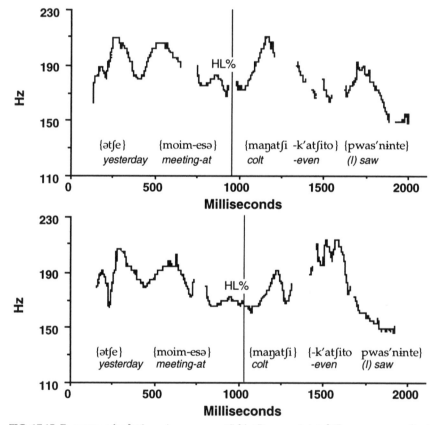

FIG. 17.15. F_0 contour for [ətʃe moim-esə maɲatʃi-k'atʃito pwas'ninte] "I even saw a colt at the meeting yesterday." produced (top) with neutral focus and (bottom) with narrow focus on [k'atʃito] "even." In each case, the cursors indicate a medial intonational phrase boundary, marked by an HL% boundary tone.

postposition first in the phrase, where the peak of the phrase's demarcative accent will fall on it, the phrasing (and local pitch range expansion) in effect puts the postposition in the most salient place in the informational unit.   But unlike the English strategy of manipulating accent placement, the Korean strategy of manipulating the accentual phrasing makes a prosodic grouping that violates the syntax; it creates an accentual phrase that cannot be a syntactic constituent.

(We have described these effects of focus as "special" or not "prototypical" phrasings.   However, linguists are only now beginning to gather the large databases of naturally occurring utterances that can tell us whether narrow focus really is special or atypical.   We suspect that it will be far more frequent than hitherto acknowledged and the "typical" citation form phrasings may be the actual special case.)

The kind of phrasing shown in Fig. 17.15, bottom panel, can easily occur in Japanese, too, when a postposition is focused. In addition, there is another kind of situation where Japanese—but not Korean—allows the postposition to be phrased separately from its preceding complement noun.   That situation occurred in a recent experiment where we tested whether speakers could disambiguate two interpretations of a noun phrase such as the one given in (7).

7. kimi'dorino   hima'wari-no   mojo:
   green   sunflower-GEN   pattern

The contrast involves the scope of modification of the first word [kimi'dorino].   The speakers said these phrases as descriptions of colored pictures in which either just the sunflowers were the things that were green (left-branching structure), or the whole pattern was green (right-branching structure).

Fig. 17.16 shows fundamental frequency contours for two different utterances of the left-branching phrase—the structure in which the adjective *green* modified just the *sunflower* and not the *pattern* as a whole. Notice first the phrasing of the genitive marker *-no*.   In both contours this postposition is phrased prosodically with the following noun, rather than with the previous one, making [no mojo:] one accentual phrase. This emphasizes the semantic grouping of *green* just with *sunflower* as distinct from the *pattern* as a whole. Note that this pattern of phrasing is independent of the insertion of the pause. In the first contour, the pause is inserted directly after *sunflower*, while in the second contour the pause occurs after the postposition. This variability in the location of insertion of a pause seems to be speaker dependent. More important, this prosodic attachment of the postposition with the following noun directly defies the syntactic constituency of the utterance, which would attach the postposition to the preceding noun phrase. Korean, in contrast, does not allow the postposition to be phrased separately from its complement noun in this case, suggesting that the mapping between prosody and discourse structure is language-specific.

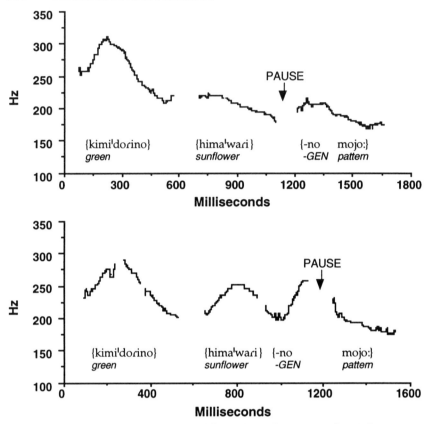

FIG. 17.16. F_0 contours for two utterances of [[kimi'doɾino hima'waɾi-no] mojo:] "a pattern of green sunflowers" with the postposition -*no* grouped prosodically with the following noun.

CONCLUSION

In summary, we discussed the following similarities and differences among the three languages. First, although Korean and Japanese differ from English in lacking such notions as nuclear accent and in having the category of accentual phrase not seen in English, many of the other categories of the prosodic hierarchy that are necessary to describe one language have counterparts in describing the systems of the other two languages. Second, the languages show similar tendencies in the mapping between syntax and prosody, although an algorithm that will predict this mapping has yet to be uncontroversially defined. Third, there are more or less similar ways to cue focus, which cause the prosodic structure to deviate considerably from the syntactic constituency, although the level of the prosodic hierarchy affected will not necessarily be the same. These similarities make it seem likely that prosodic organization may reflect fairly basic cognitive categories of informational grouping and attentional focus. However, the differences among the languages also show that the prosodic categories and their mappings to other linguistic structures are arbitrary enough that we cannot guess a priori that prosody will play a more important role in acquiring the syntactic structures than syntactic categories will play in acquiring the prosodic structures.

ACKNOWLEDGMENTS

The work reported in this chapter was supported in part by the Ohio State University Center for Cognitive Science through an Interdisciplinary Summer Fellowship to Jennifer J. Venditti, and by the National Science Foundation through grant number IRI-8858109 to Mary E. Beckman.

REFERENCES

Atkinson-King, K. (1973).   Children's acquisition of phonological stress contrasts. *UCLA Working Papers in Phonetics, 25.*

Azuma, J., & Tsukuma, Y. (1991). Role of F$_0$ and pause in disambiguating syntactically ambiguous Japanese sentences. *Proceedings of the XIIth International Congress of Phonetic Sciences* (Vol. 3, pp. 274-277). Aix-en-Provence: Université de Provence.

Beckman, M. E., & Pierrehumbert, J. (1986). Intonational structure in Japanese and English. *Phonology Yearbook, 3,* 255-309.

Hattori, S. (1947). *'Bunsetu' ni tuite—toku-ni nihongo oyobi eigo ni kansite. Festschrift for Dr. Ichikawa.* [Reprinted in Hattori (1960) *Gengogaku-no hoohoo* (pp. 415-427).   Tokyo: Iwanami-shoten.]

Jun, S.-A. (1989). The accentual pattern and prosody of the Chonnam dialect of Korean. In S. Kuno, I.-H. Lee, J. Whitman, S.-Y. Bak, Y.-S. Kang, & Y. Kim (Eds.), *Harvard studies in Korean linguistics III* (pp. 89-100). Cambridge, MA: Harvard University Press.

Lehiste, I. (1973). Phonetic disambiguation of syntactic ambiguity. *Glossa, 7,* 107-121.

Nespor, M., & Vogel, I. (1986). *Prosodic phonology.* Dordrecht: Foris Publications.

Pierrehumbert, J. (1980). *The phonology and phonetics of English intonation.* Unpublished doctoral dissertation, MIT, Cambridge, MA.

Pierrehumbert, J., & Beckman, M. E. (1988). *Japanese tone structure.* Cambridge, MA: MIT Press.

Price, P., Ostendorf, M., Shattuck-Hufnagel, S., & Fong, C. (1991). The use of prosody in syntactic disambiguation. *Journal of the Acoustical Society of America, 90,* 2956-2970.

Selkirk, E. (1980). The role of prosodic categories in English word stress. *Linguistic Inquiry, 11,* 563-605.

Selkirk, E. (1986). On derived domains in sentence phonology. *Phonology, 3,* 371-405.

Selkirk, E., & Tateishi, K. (1991). Syntax and downstep in Japanese. In C. Georgopoulous & R. Ishihara (Eds.), *Interdisciplinary approaches to language: Essays in honor of S.-Y. Kuroda* (pp. 519-543). Dordrecht: Kluwer Academic Publishers.

Uyeno, T., Hayashibe, H., Imai, K., Imagawa, H., & Kiritani, S. (1980). Comprehension of relative clause construction and pitch contours in Japanese. *Annual Bulletin, Research Institute of Logopedics and Phoniatrics* (University of Tokyo), *14,* 225-236.

18 Can a Grammatical Parameter Be Set Before the First Word? Prosodic Contributions to Early Setting of a Grammatical Parameter

Reiko Mazuka
Duke University

It has been argued that acquiring language is "doubtless the greatest intellectual feat any one of us is ever required to perform" (Bloomfield, 1933, p. 29). All normal children acquire a language with amazing efficiency and without apparent effort or overt instruction. However, the data that children are exposed to are too impoverished to inductively derive a sophisticated system of grammar. A grammatical parameter setting approach to language acquisition, articulated by Chomsky (1975, 1981, 1986), argues that this can be accounted for only if it is assumed that children are richly endowed with initial hypotheses about the nature of the language. The initial hypotheses the children are born with, called Universal Grammar, are assumed to include a "system of principles, conditions and rules that are elements or properties of all human languages" (Chomsky, 1975, p. 29).

This approach has provided a theoretical framework for numerous studies during the past few decades. A wide array of studies using this framework have shown that this approach is productive in explaining complex phenomena of language acquisition (cf. Lust, 1986, 1987, in press; Roeper & Williams, 1987; Wanner & Gleitman, 1982). However, how such a parameter can be set has not been satisfactorily explained. A quotation from Lightfoot summarizes this as follows:

> Generativists nowadays describe "parametric differences" between the grammars of, say, Japanese and Navaho, but they rarely mention how the parameters would be set for the particular grammars of these languages, or what the triggering experience would have to be for the Japanese or Navaho child. (1991, p. 8)

This chapter discusses how a basic configurational parameter such as Head Direction or Branching Direction may be set. It is argued that for language acquisition to succeed, it is not sufficient to have only a hypothesis about the nature of language. Children need to have a mechanism by which the linguistic input may be mapped onto this hypothesis. I argue that it is difficult to lay out a mechanism by which a

Head Direction parameter can be set in a timely manner such that it is useful in language acquisition. Alternatively, a child may be able to set a Branching Direction parameter during the first year of life using suprasegmental cues. Once this parameter is set, a child can use the deductive consequences of the parameter to facilitate further acquisition of the language.

THE GRAMMATICAL PARAMETER SETTING APPROACH

According to the general framework articulated by Chomsky (1975, 1981, 1986), Universal Grammar contains principles that characterize all natural languages, whereas grammatical parameters specify the dimensions along which languages may differ and what the possible variations may be. Children are biologically programmed to entertain only those hypotheses about natural languages that conform to the principles in Universal Grammar. They are also programmed to attend to specific types of possible language variation and to set the value of such parameters very early with only limited experience. Once a parameter is set, children should, theoretically, be able to deduce various aspects of the native language.

In theory, a parameter could specify language variation at various levels of generality. For example, parameters such as Head Direction and Branching Direction determine the basic configuration of a language, while other parameters may specify more specific variations among languages (e.g. a pro-drop parameter might specify whether a language allows an empty subject in a tensed clause).

Some have proposed specific ways in which children may set a particular parameter. Hyams' proposal for a pro-drop parameter (1986) is an example. She proposed that the parameter has a default value of [+ pro drop] for all languages in child grammar, making it thus look like Italian or Spanish, which would explain why young English-speaking children often drop subjects in their utterances. When English-speaking children notice the presence of expletives, such as pleonastic *it* or existential *there*, they change the value of this parameter to [-pro drop]. Similarly, in Wexler and Manzini's governing domain parameter (1987), children are assumed to use a subset principle to set the correct value of the parameter in their language.

Being able to set parameters such as pro-drop or governing domain entails that children be already relatively advanced in their language acquisition. For children to choose a possible value of governing domain such as root S, or local S, they must already understand the basic configuration of the language. Clearly, basic configurational parameters must be set before other, more specific parameters can be set. However, few attempts have been made to explicitly spell out how these parameters are set by very young children.

Configurational Parameters

At the most general level, the Head Direction parameter is defined in terms of the direction of heads and their complements in x-bar theory (Chomsky, 1986).

1a. [$_{VP}$ saw   [$_{NP}$ the man]]
1b. [$_{VP}$ [$_{NP}$ otokonoko-o]   mita]
    name-Acc   saw

Whether the head of a phrase (e.g., the verb of a verb phrase) precedes its complement, as in English in example (1a), or follows its complement, as in Japanese (1b), is a case of parametric variation. Languages such as English are head-initial, while languages such as Japanese are head-final.

The Branching Direction parameter (e.g., Lust & Chien, 1984) also determines the basic configuration of a language. It is defined in terms of the direction of recursive embedded clauses in relation to the main clause as follows:

"Principle Branching Direction" of a language evaluated with regard to major recursive structures of a language, e.g., relative clause and adverbial subordinate clause (Lust & Chien, p. 52).

Thus, a language that branches out to the right, such as English as in (2a), is a right-branching language, while a language such as Japanese that branches out leftward as in (2b) is a left-branching language.

2a. [I met the teacher [who called the student [who had an accident]]].
2b. [[[Ziko-ni atta]   gakusee-ni denwasita] sensee-ni   atta].
    had an accident student-Dat called   teacher-Dat met

The two parameters are related, but not identical. In most cases, a right-branching language is most likely a head-initial language, as in English, French, and Italian, and a left-branching language is most likely a head-final language, as in Japanese and Korean. However, there are exceptions. For example, German is a right-branching language where recursive embedded clauses occur to the right of the main clause, as in (3a). However, the verb follows its complement in subordinate clauses in German, i.e., the subordinate verbal phrase is a head-final construction as in (3a), even though most other phrases are head-initial (3b) (Comrie, 1981; Hawkins, 1990).

3a. [Ich weiß, [daß Heinrich die Frau liebt.]]
    I know that Henry the woman loves   (Hawkins, p. 130)
3b. [$_{NP}$ Die Frau, [$_{S}$ die ich liebe] Heinrich [$_{VP}$ liebt die Frau].
    the woman whom I love Henry loved the woman (Hawkins, p. 137)

An exception in the opposite direction is Chinese. Chinese is principally a left-branching language: Relative clauses and subordinate clauses position to the left of their head or matrix sentence in unmarked form as shown in (4a) and (4b). However, the basic word order of Chinese in a main clause is SVO. Thus, a VP has a head-initial structure.

4a. Zhën dú-le [[Mālì xië-de] shü]
    Jan read Asp. Mary wrote Rel. book
    "Jan read the book that Mary wrote." (Lust & Chien, p. 55)
4b. [Däng Mālì dāsāo fángzi-de shíhou], mäma huílái-le.
    While-Mary clean house-while, Mother came back Asp.
    "While Mary was cleaning the house, Mother came back."

In the general framework of Government and Binding theory (Chomsky, 1981), x-bar theory determines the basic configuration of a language. The Head Direction parameter, which specifies the cross-linguistic variation within x-bar theory, is considered to be one of the most fundamental parameters. Because this parameter specifies the very basic configuration of a language, language acquisition cannot proceed far unless this parameter is set.

Initial State

Suppose a child is born in Connecticut to a family that speaks English. Let us also assume that the child is born endowed with Universal Grammar. So, the child knows that human languages would be constrained by principles of Universal Grammar. For example, he or she knows that all linguistic operations will be structure dependent. The child also knows that her language will be either head-initial or head-final. This is the initial state from which the child starts the process of language acquisition.

The input available to this child who is at the initial state is a continuous flow of speech sounds. From this input, the child must somehow extract enough phrase structures to set the Head Direction parameter. The problem is that the information that must be extracted from the stimulus is not directly marked in the input. A child may be richly endowed with Universal Grammar, yet no matter how rich such an endowment may be, the child must still figure out a mapping between input tokens and linguistic structures (cf. Pinker, 1987). If a child is to set a parameter, such as a Head Direction parameter, she needs a mechanism by which she will be able to crack the code of the language such that she will be able to isolate phrases and identify heads and complements within such phrases. However, Universal Grammar itself does not spell out how such a process may take place.

A parameter such as Head Direction or Branching Direction determines the basic configuration of a language, and is a prerequisite for other linguistic operations. Therefore, setting a parameter such as a

Head Direction or a Branching Direction must be one of the first things a child must do in the process of language acquisition.

In the next section, I examine what a child needs to do to set a Head Direction parameter, and argue that children must be able to perform complex analyses of input stimuli, which is beyond the capability of children at the initial state. This means that a child must acquire a significant amount of language before she can set the Head Direction parameter. I argue that if children have to learn a significant amount of language in order to set the basic configurational parameter, this will void the value of having the parameter setting approach to language acquisition in the first place.

The Task of Setting the Head-Direction Parameter

In much of the literature on language acquisition, setting a Head Direction parameter is treated as a trivial task. For example, Radford (1990) stated that "once a child is able to parse an utterance such as 'Close the door!', he will be able to infer from the fact that the verb *close* in English precedes its complement *the door*, that all verbs in English precede their complements" (p. 61). Upon examination, however, this task is hardly simple.

As Radford noted, in order to determine the head–complement relation in this sentence, children must first parse the sentence. However, parsing a sentence in the usual sense of the term means to give a syntactic and semantic interpretation to the sentence according to the grammar of the language. Children who have not yet acquired the grammar cannot parse the sentence in order to acquire the grammar. Therefore, children must discover the head–complement relation of their language without referring to the grammar of the language they are trying to learn.

Consider more closely what children must do to set this parameter. First of all, we must assume that children understand the general state of affairs such a sentences refers to. Such mapping is not trivial, especially for children who know nothing about the language.

Second, the sentence must be segmented into phrases and words. Again, this is hardly a trivial task. Recent studies in infant speech perception have shown that young infants may be sensitive to suprasegmental cues that correlate to syntactic clauses (Fisher, 1991; Hirsh-Pasek, Kemler Nelson, Jusczyk, Wright Cassidy, Druss, & Kennedy, 1987; Morgan, Swingley, & Mitirai, 1993). However, Jusczyk, Kemler Nelson, Hirsh-Pasek, Kennedy, Woodward, and Piwoz (1992) found that infants' sensitivity to phrases that are internal to a clause do not appear until later in the first year of their life. Smaller units such as words are even harder than major phrases to segment.

There are some regularities in language that might be exploited to segment words and phrases. For example, in English, nouns tend to come at the end of an utterance. Such occurrences are particularly frequent in child-directed speech (Ratner, this volume). Once children recognize that a certain sequence of sounds repeatedly appears in a certain context, they may use such distributional analyses to segment words or phrases. Aslin et al. (this volume) demonstrated that a regular occurrence of sounds at the utterance-final position can be exploited by a connectionist machine to segment novel utterances. Other information such as occurrences of unstressed functional morphemes (Gerken & McIntosh, 1993) and language-specific rhythmic structure (e.g., stress-based timing in English, mora-based timing in Japanese and syllable-based timing in French; Cutler, this volume) may also be exploited to segment words and phrases from continuous speech.

However, these cues are language specific. For example, in a head-final language such as Japanese, it is not nouns, but verbs that appear at the sentence-final position. According to an informal tally of Japanese child-directed speech I have gathered, the utterance-final verbs do not seem to appear repeatedly in a short duration of time as English nouns are reported to do. The names of the object will appear both at sentence-initial as well as sentence-medial position, as Japanese allows empty arguments and the order of arguments is relatively free (Kuno, 1973; Shibatani, 1990). Furthermore, it has been reported that Japanese mothers do not label objects as often as American mothers do (Fernald & Morikawa, 1993). Therefore, before children can take advantage of these cues, they must have enough exposure to the language to find out what kind of regularities the language has.

Once children segment words and phrases, they must identify parts of speech. In Radford's example, they must learn that *close* is a verb, *the* is a determiner, and *door* is a noun. Again, this is a major task in language acquisition that has been investigated by many researchers. As a possible mechanism for learning grammatical categories such as verb and noun, it has sometimes been proposed that children use the meaning of the words to derive the grammatical categories, for example words that describe action are verbs, and names of objects are nouns – viz., semantic bootstrapping hypothesis (e.g., Pinker, 1987). However, for this hypothesis to work, children must somehow learn the meaning of words without referring to the grammar. In this example, it is not enough to understand the general state of affairs that the whole utterance refers to, but children also need to be able to isolate different words(i.e., *close*, *the*, and *door*) and identify which of these words refers to the action of closing, and the object *door*. In addition, they need to learn enough numbers of them to perform the type of distributional analysis necessary.

There are other types of information they may be able to use to learn the categories of word; the position of the word within an utterance, morphological/phonological properties, (e.g., the number of syllables, presence or absence of stress; see Morgan, Shi, & Allopenna, this volume). Again, this is language-specific information, and for children to exploit such information, they must first learn a significant amount about the regularity of the language.

Assuming that children somehow figured out that *Close the door* is an imperative sentence with an empty subject, they now have to find out that *close* is the head of the verb phrase and *the door* is the complement of the verb since the noun phrase *the door* is an object of the verb. From these analyses, they realize that in this language, the head should always precede its complements.

In summary, children must have learned to segment words and phrases, learned enough vocabulary to understand the meaning of the words, and identified parts of speech before they can determine the unmarked direction of heads and complements in her language. Each of these is a major task in the process of language acquisition and is certainly beyond the capability of an initial state child. Thus, setting a Head Direction parameter can hardly be the first thing children do in the process of language acquisition. However, as I discuss in the next section, children seem to have access to the basic configurations of languages almost from the very beginning of acquisition. Indeed, if one can assume that children begin the process of acquisition equipped with the knowledge about the basic configuration of their language, many of the puzzles of language acquisition can be explained.

How Soon Must a Configurational Parameter Be Set?

In the previous section, I showed that children must be able to perform sophisticated analyses of input stimuli before they can set a Head Direction parameter. Let us now turn to child acquisition data and examine how early children show evidence of having access to the basic configuration of their language.

Many researchers have noticed that word order errors are extremely rare when children start combining words. For example, a child may say "Lois read," "read book," or "Lois book" (Bloom, 1970) in the context of Lois reading a book. But she will rarely say "book read", "read Lois," or "book Lois" to mean the same thing. Brown (1973) reported that there were only 100 or so word order errors in his sample of many thousands of utterances collected for this stage of development.

More recently, evidence has become available to indicate that these early word combinations reflect a hierarchical phrase structure, rather than flat concatenation of words. For example, Bloom's (1990) study of young children's adjective-noun combinations indicates that from the very beginning of the two-word stage, children make a distinction between nouns and noun phrases (see also Radford, 1990).

In other words, there is no evidence in the literature that children make errors with regard to the basic configuration of their language by the time they start combining words. These data can be interpreted in two ways. First, one could argue that children have not figured out the basic configuration of their language yet. They will figure it out during or after the two-word stage. According to this scenario, one must first assume that children generate two-word strings with correct word orders, by rote imitation or some other non-configurational means. Then children will perform some sort of distributional analysis on their utterances and find the generalization (i.e., that the grammatical head always precedes its complements in this language).

The strength of the grammatical parameter setting approach is that children can set a grammatical parameter with minimal data. The role of a grammatical parameter is to facilitate language acquisition rather than to simply describe the language in terms of generalizations. If children must somehow learn to combine words correctly first, and set the Head Direction parameter by generalizing from the data, it will nullify the basic motivation of the parameter setting approach to language acquisition.

Alternatively, one could assume that children's two-word combinations do not violate the basic configuration of English because they have already available the value of this parameter by the time they start combining words. On this view, the Head Direction parameter must be set at the latest by the time children start combining words. If the value of the Head Direction parameter is available by the timechildren start to combine words, the actual setting of the parameter must take place before the end of the one-word stage.

The data do not exclude the possibility that the parameters may be set even earlier. Considering the fact that the word combination data are of children's spontaneous production and that comprehension usually precedes production, it is likely that the value of the parameter is available for their comprehension at an earlier stage. In fact, Hirsh-Pasek, Golinkoff, Fletcher, DeGaspe-Beaubien, and Cauley (1985) found that one-word stage children, when first presented with a potentially reversible sentence ("Cookie Monster is tickling Big Bird" versus "Big Bird is tickling Cookie Monster"), preferred to look at a movie that matched the sentence rather than a movie of the reverse. In this task, the syntax was the only cue to discriminate between the two movies. Gerken and McIntosh (1993) found that one-word stage children were able to distinguish grammatical articles and ungrammatical auxiliaries in a picture selection task. This shows that children already know the distinction between function words and content words and which function words should come where. These results suggest that children already have an understanding of the basic configuration of the language. If correct, this implies that the Head Direction parameter needs to be set even before the one-word stage.

AN ALTERNATIVE: BRANCHING DIRECTION PARAMETER

If I am correct in assuming that one-word stage children already know that English is a head-initial language, then it is necessary at the preverbal stage to perform an analysis of the input necessary to set the

Head Direction parameter. As discussed previously, the analysis necessary to set the Head Direction parameter is too sophisticated for preverbal infants.

Alternatively, in this section, I argue that if it is the Branching Direction parameter that infants set in order to determine the basic configuration of the language, it can be accomplished without delay.

Setting the Branching Direction Parameter

How, then, can the Branching Direction parameter be set? First of all,
children must be able to segment an input string into sentences and
recognize sentence internal clause boundaries. If they can find a sentence that has more than one clause, they then need to determine which
one of these units is the main clause, and on which side of the main
clause the rest of the material tends to come. However, as long as children can detect clause boundaries and identify the dominance relations
between them, they do not have to analyze the input string any further, nor is it necessary to understand the meaning of the sentence.

In general, one tends to think that smaller linguistic units are simpler than longer units for children acquiring language (e.g., words are
simpler than phrases and simple sentences are simpler than complex
sentences). This thinking may originate in the fact that children's productions proceed gradually from one-word utterances to longer utterances. However, the first task an initial state child must perform is to
learn to break the continuous flow of speech stream into discrete linguistic units, and from this perspective, larger, more global units such as
clauses may be simpler than smaller units such as phrases or words.

Infants Are Sensitive to Prosodic Cues in Speech

Recent studies in infant speech perception have demonstrated that prosody of speech may be one of the first things infants pay attention to.
For example, Mehler, Jusczyk, Lambertz, Halsted, Bertoncini, and
Amiel-Tison (1988) found that four days after birth, infants show a preference for their own language, and this preference is probably due to
the prosodic properties of the language. Studies such as DeCasper and
Spence (1986) indicate that such preferences are likely based on prenatal
exposure to maternal language.

Investigations of child-directed speech have found that exaggerated
prosody is one of the common characteristics of adults' speech to infants
(cf. Snow, 1977, for an early review; Fernald, Taeschner, Dunn,
Papousek, Boysson-Bardies, & Fukui, 1989, for cross-language data). It
has also been found that infants pay more attention to child-directed
speech that has exaggerated prosody (Fernald, 1985; Fernald & Kuhl,
1987).

Thus, if infants are sensitive to global, prosodic properties of speech,
and the input speech to infants tends to exaggerate such characteristics,

then large syntactic units such as clauses, the boundaries of which are one of the most reliably marked by prosody (see following section), are the primary target for infants to use to break into the code of language.

In fact, Hirsh-Pasek et al. (1987) demonstrated that infants as young as 4¹/₂ months old are capable of detecting prosodic clause boundaries in speech stimuli. Experiments using low-pass filtered material have indicated that it is the prosodic cues that the infants are using to detect the boundaries. However, young infants' sensitivity to clause-internal phrase boundaries, the realizations of which are more language specific, does not emerge until 9 months (Jusczyk et al., 1992). These results suggest that the clause may be one of the first syntactic units infants are sensitive to. If it is possible for infants to take advantage of this sensitivity to set a Branching Direction parameter, the problems of setting a Head Direction parameter discussed earlier may be avoided.

Cues for Branching Direction

If infants are to set a Branching Direction parameter, there ought to be reliable cues available in the input stimuli. Research has shown that clause boundaries are one of the best marked units prosodically. Pauses at clause boundaries tend to be longer (Cooper & Paccia-Cooper, 1980; Cruttenden, 1986), segments in the clause-final position tend to be lengthened (Cooper & Paccia-Cooper, 1980; Cruttenden, 1986; Fisher, 1991), and a rise or fall of the fundamental frequency tends to mark clause boundaries (Fisher, 1991; Garnica, 1977; Lea, 1975). These cues tend to be even more pronounced in child-directed speech (e.g., Broen, 1972; Fisher, 1991). Also, Fisher (1991) found that some of the cues that mark clause boundaries may be found across very different types of languages.

At present, there are few studies that have directly tested whether there are reliable prosodic cues that mark Branching Direction of clauses. However, there is some evidence indicating that the interclausal relations are also marked prosodically. Cooper and Sorensen (1977) showed that the magnitude of fall-rise at the clause boundaries between conjoined main-main clauses is somewhat more pronounced than at the boundaries between main and subordinate clauses of right-branching sentences. In smaller units, such as NPs, it has been reported that left-branching structures have prosodic characteristics distinct from right-branching structures (Kubozono, 1987; Selkirk & Tateishi, 1988). Since it is the general tendency that prosodic characteristics that correlate with syntactic structure become larger as the structure goes higher in a tree (Cooper & Paccia-Cooper, 1980; Selkirk, 1984), it is likely that left-branching and right-branching sentences will also have prosodic correlates.

In order to examine whether there is a prosodic correlate for branching direction, I have made several recordings of left-branching and right-branching sentences such as (5). A professional (American English) radio announcer read sentences such as these several times. Fig. 18.1 shows F_0 and power envelopes for one pair of sentences. The left-branching sentence (5a) had a longer pause at the clause boundary than the right-branching sentence (5b) (475 msec versus no pause). The data also showed that in a left-branching sentence, the rise of F_0 after the clause boundary was larger than that for the right branching sentence.[1] These data seem to indicate that the boundary of a left-branching sentence is more pronounced than that of a right-branching sentence.

　　5a. When Warren warmed the meal, Amy poured the mellow white wine into the narrow glass.
　　5b. Warren warmed the meal when Amy poured the mellow white wine into the narrow glass.

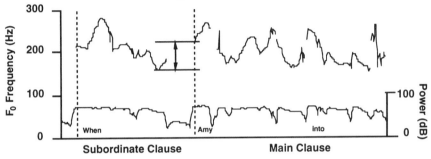

Left-Branching Sentence

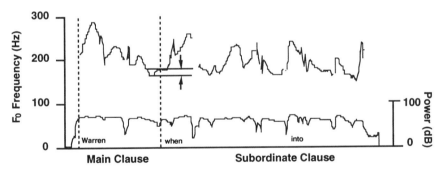

Right-Branching Sentence

FIG. 18.1 F_0 and power envelopes for sentences (5)a and (5)b. Onsets of main and subordinate clauses are marked by dotted vertical lines.

---

[1]The pitch pattern of an utterance is assumed to be determined by a combination of basic intonation pattern, which rises at the beginning of an intonation unit and declines gradually (downstep), and stress pattern for an individual lexical item (Fujisaki, 1992). The rise of the pitch after the clause boundary, thus, is calculated from the lowest F_0 of the first clause to the F_0 at the onset of the second clause.

It is not necessary for the cues that are used to determine the Branching Direction of a sentence to be universal. As discussed earlier, Mehler et al. (1988) demonstrated that even at four days after birth, neonates can discriminate the prosody of their own language from that of a foreign language. This means that infants have learned some overall property of the prosody of a language as a whole to be distinguished from that of another language. Thus, as long as there are reliable cues that can be used to determine the dominance relation between the clauses within that language, the cues that are used may differ somewhat from language to language.

For example, in English right-branching and left-branching sentences may have contrasting cues as discussed earlier. However, in a strict left-branching language such as Japanese, which does not allow a right-branching structure, children cannot compare left-branching and right-branching sentences directly. Instead, Japanese children may rely on the marked prosody of a right-dislocated construction to identify the branching direction of their language. In Japanese, a constituent that is dislocated to the right of the matrix verb receives a distinct prosodic marking. For example, expressions such as (6a) and(6b) are often found in the transcription of child-directed speech. In (6a), the end of the main clause is marked by a sentence final particle *yo*, lengthening of the final mora, and a pause. In (6b), the end of the main clause is marked by a rising pitch and a pause.

6a. Anpanman-ga tasuke-ni kita-yo, zoo-san-o.
Anpanman-Nom to help came-SFP, elephant-Acc
"Anpanman (Cartoon character) came to help the elephant."
6b. Dakko site goran, kuma-san
hold do try, teddy bear
"Try holding the teddy bear."

Note that it is not necessary that a complete two-clause sentence be marked as left-branching or right-branching for an unmarked branching direction to be identified. As in the case of Japanese right-dislocation, if the additional material other than the main clause is marked somehow when it is in the marked position, then it can signal the unmarked branching direction.

Are There Enough Sentences with More than One Clause in the Input?

There must be a sufficient number of occurrences of sentences with more than one clause in the input to infants if the Branching Direction is to be determined at an early age. Child-directed speech is generally known to have much fewer instances of embedding compared to adult-directed speech (Newport, Gleitman, & Gleitman, 1977; Ratner, this volume; Snow, 1977, for review).

Newport (1977) reported that the mean number of S nodes per utterance in child-directed speech was 1.16 in her sample. She found that of the grammatical sentences mothers uttered, 84% were simple sentences. This means that 16% of the sentences included embedding. Morgan (1986) analyzed the transcripts of Adam, Eve, and Sarah, and found that during stage I, 5.4% of all input utterances were degree-1 sentences (i.e., sentences with one level of embedding). These studies show that, compared to adult-directed speech, child-directed speech contains relatively few multi-clause sentences. Also, these analyses include embedded clauses whose boundaries are not likely to be marked prosodically (e.g., *I know you don't like carrots*). Thus, the percentage of degree-1 sentences with prosodically marked clause boundaries is likely to be even smaller. However, the studies show that children's linguistic environments do include a certain proportion of sentences with embedding. Obviously, there is no simple way to prove how much is enough for setting a particular parameter. However, sentences with prosodically marked embedded clauses are likely to be much more frequent than, say, pleonastic *it* or existential *there*, which have been proposed to provide triggering data for setting of the pro-drop parameter (Hyams, 1986).

Are Degree-1 Sentences Too Complex as a Triggering Experience?

As discussed previously, in order to set the Branching Direction parameter, the input to the child must contain sentences with one or more degrees of embedding. The fact that it requires data of at least degree-1 may be considered disadvantageous for language acquisition. For example, Lightfoot (1989, 1991) argued that for the parameter setting approach to work, the triggering experience must be "robust structures of minimal (degree-0) complexity" (1991, p. 321).[2] He proposed that all relevant parameters can be set with linguistic input with little or no embedding, implying that sentences with embedded clauses are too complex to function as a triggering experience for parameter setting. However, the complexity of input cannot be measured independent of what children have to do with it. The assumption underlying Lightfoot's claim is that input available to children are strings of words, and children who are attempting to set a grammatical parameter must analyze input sentences in complete detail. Determining the head-complement relation of a phrase will require a complex set of analyses as discussed previously, although the length of the input required for the analysis is even smaller than a simple sentence. On the other hand, I propose that while the length of input stimuli needs to be longer, the relatively superficial analysis required to determine branching direction could be performed by preverbal infants.

---

[2] Lightfoot's use of "degree" is not comparable to that of Wexler and Culicover (1980), inasmuch as Lightfoot's degree-0 data includes some embedded material.

In their degree-2 learnability theory, Wexler and Culicover (1980) argued that for a transformational grammar to be learnable, the input for language acquisition must contain sentences with two levels of embedding. Their assumption was that the input for language learner is pairs of surface and underlying strings. In other words, a language learner was presented with strings of words paired with the underlying representations of such surface strings, with no bracketing information. However, Morgan (1986) demonstrated that if it is assumed that the surface strings the language learner is presented with contain bracketing information (i.e., a skeletal phrase structure), the same transformational grammar is learnable with degree-1 stimuli. This result shows that depending on the type of analysis the learner must perform, the significance of the length of the stimuli will change.

DISCUSSION

In this chapter, I argued that children need to be able to set a basic configurational parameter prior to the onset of one-word stage if such a parameter is to be useful in the course of language acquisition. However, in order to set the Head Direction parameter, sophisticated analyses of input stimuli are necessary and children need to learn a significant amount about the language before setting this parameter.

In a way, setting the Head Direction parameter by analyzing the syntactic structure of the input involves a paradox. The Head Direction parameter is supposed to determine the order in which the head and its complement should appear in the language being acquired. But, for children to set this parameter, they must first find out which units are the heads and which are the complements in the sentences they hear. If their linguistic skills are sophisticated enough to know which are heads and complements, they will also know which order they came in. If they already know which order the head and complements come in sentences, there is no need to set the parameter.

Alternatively, I argued that it may be possible for preverbal infants to set the Branching Direction parameter using suprasegmental cues. Once they set the Branching Direction parameter, they can derive the value of the Head Direction parameter deductively. For exceptional cases, such as German and Chinese, children can use positive evidence to find out the exceptional head direction of their language.

Recent research has demonstrated that infants' sensitivity to fine-tuned, language-specific properties such as stress patterns or phonotactic rules does not emerge until late in the first year (Jusczyk et al., 1992; Jusczyk, Cutler, & Redanz, 1993). For the purpose of setting the Branching Direction parameter, young infants whose linguistic sophistication does not allow them to analyze more fine-tuned, language-specific properties of the input may have an added advantage. Newport (1990) proposed a "less is more" hypothesis that states that younger children may have an advantage over adults in acquiring language because of their limited information-processing ability. She argued that one of the advantages of limited processing ability is that it may perceptually highlight relevant units. In a similar manner, if young infants are tuning out the details of input at the beginning (e.g., the meaning of individual words, smaller phrasal units, language specific phonotactic constraints, or stress pattern etc.), this could enhance the salience of the prosodic cues relevant for the parameter setting.

Certainly, simply because there are acoustic cues that correlate with Branching Direction, it does not follow that infants are sensitive to these cues. Even if infants are shown to be sensitive to these cues, it does not mean that they use such cues to set a grammatical parameter. Neither of these issues are addressed in this chapter, and are open to further empirical tests. However, the current proposal shows that there exists a plausible mechanism by which children can set a basic configurational parameter in a timely manner such that the value of the parameter can be utilized in the early course of language acquisition. This was the original intent of the grammatical parameter setting approach to language acquisition. As discussed earlier, if the basic configurational parameter is available only to describe the generalization that exists in a language, it nullifies the strength of the grammatical parameter setting approach to language acquisition.

The current proposal is a kind of prosodic bootstrapping model where children use prosodic cues to break into syntax (e.g., Wanner & Gleitman, 1982). One of the major obstacles to using prosodic cues to bootstrap language acquisition is that syntax and prosody do not correspond one-to-one. Even though syntactic structure is one of the determinants of the prosody, there are many other factors that influence the prosody of an utterance (e.g., Cruttenden, 1986). Thus, it will be problematic if children have to rely solely on prosodic cues to acquire syntax (e.g., Pinker, 1987). However, if one assumes that young infants are predisposed to pay attention to particular acoustic cues (e.g., those that mark clause boundaries and branching direction), the difficulty will be significantly reduced. In fact, it is the poverty of stimulus of this sort that the parameter setting approach to language acquisition is supposed to account for. Thus, although prosodic cues may be too impoverished for a child to learn syntax from scratch, it may be just enough for a child to break the code of the language if she comes equipped with the specific parameter to pay selective attention to particular aspects of the stimuli.

As discussed previously, there are many regularities in language that could be exploited for such tasks as segmentation, learning the lexicon, and learning parts of speech—position of words (Ratner, this volume), presence of regular function words (Gerken & McIntosh, 1993), number of syllables (Kelly, this volume; Morgan, Shi, & Allopenna, this volume), regular stress pattern (Jusczyk et al., 1992), and language-specific rhythmic structures (Cutler, this volume). I argued that it is difficult for children to exploit these cues if they have to use these cues to find out the basic configuration of the language. However, if children have already set the Branching Direction and can attack the task of language acquisition equipped with the knowledge of the basic configuration of their language, these cues can be readily utilized. For example, if a child knows that the language he or she is acquiring is a head-initial language, the child can exploit this information to deduce that the frequently occurring sound units at the ends of utterances are likely to be nouns.

ACKNOWLEDGMENTS

I am indebted to Barbara Lust for the original idea of using Branching Direction to determine the basic configuration of a language. I have also benefited from additional comments from Katherine Demuth, Katherine Hirsh-Pasek, Peter Jusczyk, Kazuhiko Kakehi, Deborah Kemler Nelson, Haruo Kubozono, Barbara Lust, and James Morgan. Revision of this chapter was undertaken while I was staying as an invited researcher at NTT Basic Research Labs in Tokyo. I thank June Fox for reading left-branching and right-branching English sentences. Recording and analysis of sentences were done with the facilities at NTT Basic Research Labs; Tadahisa Kondoh and Kazuhiko Kakehi provided technical assistance.

REFERENCES

Bloom, L. (1970). *Language development: Form and function in emerging grammars.* Cambridge, MA: MIT Press.

Bloom, P. (1990). Syntactic distinctions in child language. *Journal of Child Language, 17,* 343-355.

Bloomfield, L. (1933). *Language.* New York: Holt, Rinehart & Winston.

Broen, P. A. (1972). The verbal environment of the language-learning child. *Monograph of American Speech and Hearing Association, 17.*

Brown, R. (1973). *A first language.* Cambridge, MA: Harvard University Press.

Chomsky, N. (1975). *Reflections on language.* New York: Pantheon Books.

Chomsky, N. (1981). *Lectures on government and binding.* Dordrecht: Foris.

Chomsky, N. (1986). *Knowledge of language: Its nature, origin, and use.* New York: Praeger.

Comrie, B. (1981). *Language universals and linguistic typology.* Oxford: Basil Blackwell.

Cooper, W., & Paccia-Cooper, J. (1980). *Syntax and speech.* Cambridge, MA: Harvard University Press.

Cooper, W. E., & Sorenson, J. M. (1977). Fundamental frequency contours at syntactic boundaries. *Journal of the Acoustic Society of America, 62,* 683-692.

Cruttenden, A. (1986). *Intonation.* Cambridge, England: Cambridge University Press.

DeCasper, A. J., & Spence, M. J. (1986). Prenatal maternal speech influences newborn's perception of speech sounds. *Infant Behavior and Development, 9,* 133-150.

Fernald, A. (1985). Four month old infants prefer to listen to motherese. *Infant Behavior and Development, 8,* 181-195.

Fernald, A., & Kuhl, P. K. (1987). Acoustic determinants of infant preference for motherese speech. *Infant Behavior and Development, 10,* 279-293.

Fernald, A., & Morikawa, H. (1993). Common themes and cultural variations in Japanese and American mothers' speech to infants. *Child Development, 64,* 637-656.

Fernald, A., Taeschner, T., Dunn, J., Papousek, M., Boysson-Bardies, B., & Fukui, I. (1989). A cross-language study of prosodic modifications in mothers' and fathers' speech to preverbal infants. *Journal of Child Language, 16,* 477-501.

Fisher, C. (1991, April). *Prosodic cues to phrase structure in infant directed speech.* Paper presented to the Stanford Child Language Research Forum, Stanford University.

Fujisaki, H. (1992). Modeling the process of fundamental frequency contour generation. In Y. Tohkura, E. Vatikiotis-Bateson, & Y. Sagisaka (Eds.), *Speech perception, production, and linguistic structure* (pp. 313-326). Ohmsha; Tokyo.

Garnica, O. (1977). Some prosodic and paralinguistic speech to young children. In C. E. Snow & C. A. Ferguson (Eds.), *Talking to children*, (pp. 63-88). Cambridge, England: Cambridge University Press.

Gerken, L. A., & McIntosh, B. J. (1993). Interplay of function morphemes and prosody in early language. *Developmental Psychology, 29*, 448-457.

Hawkins, J. (1990). German. In B. Comrie (Ed.), *The world's major languages* (pp. 111-138). Oxford: Oxford University Press.

Hirsh-Pasek, K., Golinkoff, R., Fletcher, P., DeGaspe-Beaubien, M., & Cauley, K. M. (1985, October). *In the beginning: One word speakers comprehend word order.* Paper presented at the Boston University Child Language conference, Boston, MA.

Hirsh-Pasek, K., Kemler-Nelson, D., Jusczyk, P., Wright Cassidy, K. L., Druss, B., & Kennedy, L. (1987). Clauses are perceptual units for young infants. *Cognition, 26*, 269-286.

Hyams, N. (1986). *Language acquisition and the theory of parameters.* Dordrecht: Reidel.

Jusczyk, P. W., Kemler Nelson, D. G., Hirsh-Pasek, K., Kennedy, L., Woodward, A., & Piwoz, J. (1992). Perception of acoustic correlates of major phrasal units by young infants. *Cognitive Psychology, 24*, 252-293.

Jusczyk, P. W., Cutler, A., & Redanz, N. J. (1993). Infants' preference for the predominant stress patterns of English words. *Child Development, 64*, 675-687.

Kubozono, H. (1987). *The organization of Japanese prosody.* Unpublished doctoral dissertation. University of Edinburgh.

Kuno, S. (1973). *The structure of Japanese language.* Cambridge, MA: MIT Press.

Lea, W. A. (1975). *Prosodic aids to speech recognition: Experiments on detecting and locating phrase boundaries.* Sperry Univac Report No. PX 11534.

Lightfoot, D. (1989). The child's trigger experience: Degree-0 learnability. *Behavioral and Brain Sciences, 12*, 321-375.

Lightfoot, D. (1991). *How to set parameters: Arguments from language change.* Cambridge, MA: MIT Press.

Lust, B. (Ed.). (1986). *Studies in the acquisition of anaphora.* Vol. 1. Dordrecht: Reidel.

Lust, B. (Ed.). (1987). *Studies in the acquisition of anaphora.* Vol. 2. Dordrecht: Reidel.

Lust, B. (in press). *Universal grammar and the initial state: Cross-linguistic study of their relations.* Cambridge, MA: MIT Press.

Lust, B., & Chien, Y. C. (1984). The structure of coordination in first language acquisition of Mandarin Chinese: Evidence for a universal. *Cognition, 17*, 49-83.

Mehler, J., Jusczyk, P., Lambertz, G., Halsted, N., Bertoncini, J., & Amiel-Tison, C. (1988). A precursor of language acquisition in young infants. *Cognition, 29*, 143-178.

Morgan, J. L. (1986). *From simple input to complex grammar.* Cambridge, MA: MIT Press.

Morgan, J. L., Swingley, D. C., & Mitirai, K. (1993, April). *Infants listen longer to speech with extraneous noises inserted at clause boundaries.* Presented at the Biennial Meeting of the Society for Research in Child Development, New Orleans.

Newport, E. L. (1977). Motherese: The speech of mothers to young children. In N. J. Castellan, D. B. Pisoni, & G. R. Potts (Eds.), *Cognitive theory* (Vol. 2, pp. 177-217). Hillsdale, NJ: Lawrence Erlbaum Associates.

Newport, E. L. (1990). Maturational constraints on language learning. *Cognitive Science, 14*, 11-28.

Newport, E. L., Gleitman, H., & Gleitman, L. R. (1977). Mother, I'd rather do it myself: Some effects and non-effect of maternal speech style. In C. Snow & C. Ferguson (Eds.), *Talking to children* (pp. 109-149). Cambridge, England: Cambridge University Press.

Pinker, S. (1987). The bootstrapping problem in language acquisition. In B. MacWhinney (Ed.), *Mechanisms of language acquisition* (pp. 399-441). Hillsdale, NJ: Lawrence Erlbaum Associates.

Radford, A. (1990). *Syntactic theory and the acquisition of English syntax.* Cambridge, England: Basil Blackwell.

Roeper, T., & Williams, E. (Eds.). (1987). *Parameter setting.* Dordrecht: Reidel

Selkirk, E. (1984). *Phonology and syntax.* Cambridge, MA: MIT Press.

Selkirk, E., & Tateishi, K. (1988). Constraints on manner phrase formation in Japanese. *CLS, 24,* 316-336.

Shibatani, M. (1990). *The languages of Japan.* Cambridge, England: Cambridge University Press.

Snow, C. E. (1977). Mother's speech research: From input to interaction. In C. E. Snow & C. A. Ferguson (Eds.), *Talking to children* (pp. 63-88). Cambridge, England: Cambridge University Press.

Wanner, E., & Gleitman, L. (Eds.). (1982). *Language acquisition: The state of the art.* Cambridge, England: Cambridge University Press.

Wexler, K., & Culicover, P. (1980). *Formal principles of language acquisition.* Cambridge, MA: MIT Press.

Wexler, K., & Manzini, L. (1987). Parameters and learnability in binding theory. In T. Roeper & E. Williams (Eds.), *Parameter setting* (pp. 41-76). Dordrecht: Reidel.

19 Phrasal Intonation and the Acquisition of Syntax

Mark Steedman
University of Pennsylvania

It is frequently suggested that prosodic information may be used by children as a cue to syntactic phrase boundaries and constituent categories during language acquisition. As in the case of word segmentation, to assume that there are properties of the speech stream that with some statistical reliability make these units perceptually salient certainly seems a reasonable working hypothesis, whatever else one thinks might be involved. However, the fact that fluent intonational phrasing may on occasion be completely orthogonal to traditional syntactic constituency, as in the following example, has appeared to present a problem for this proposal:

```
1. (YOU      want)     (a  BISCUIT!)
   L+H*       LH%         H*  LL%
```

The example uses Pierrehumbert's notation for the intonation contour. In this utterance, the subject and the verb constitute one intonational phrase with a pitch accent on the former and a "continuation rise" on the latter, while the object constitutes a separate intonational phrase.[1] (Readers who are unfamiliar with this notation should think of this as the intonation that conveys a meaning paraphrasable as "What you want is a biscuit.") The utterance gives rise to the perceptual structure suggested by the brackets (which are not part of Pierrehumbert's notation). This structure is orthogonal to the traditional syntactic surface structure for this sentence. Similar examples have led Selkirk (1984) and others to postulate a level of "Intonational Structure" orthogonal to syntactic structure. While intonational constituents are not entirely independent of syntactic constituency, they allow considerably freer bracketing of the string, and at the level of meaning convey distinctions of discourse focus and propositional attitude, rather than function-argument structure. Such a system therefore seems to present an obstacle for the child who relies on "prosodic bootstrapping" to identify syntactic constituency, since such prosodic groupings seem to be quite common in adult speech to infants (see Jusczyk & Kemler Nelson, this volume).

---

[1] Such intonational boundaries should be clearly distinguished from pauses engendered by prosodic disfluencies, such as hesitation pauses. Such interruptions are phonetically quite different from true intonational boundaries.

Combinatory Categorial Grammar (CCG) is a theory of syntax that was primarily developed to account for coordination and relative constructions without the use of movement, Wh-traces, or deletion. It has the property of allowing much freer constituent structure than traditional grammars, while still projecting semantic function-argument relations correctly. Under this novel view of syntactic constituency, the apparent disjuncture between syntactic and intonational constituency vanishes. These two "levels" of structure turn out to be simply the same.

This chapter begins with a brief review of the CCG account of intonation, before considering the implications for language acquisition. One implication is that the apparent complexity of the child's task in inferring syntactic boundaries from prosodic boundaries is somewhat simplified. According to this theory, whenever such a boundary is present, it can safely be assumed by the child to coincide with the boundary of a fully interpretable constituent.

Of course, this is not to suppose that phrasal intonation is the only source of information that the child has available, or that such information is sufficient for the child to acquire grammar. To identify constituent boundaries is not enough to identify the grammatical category of such constituents, or the rule by which they combine. It will also become clear that, at least at the level of the intonational phrase, the distinctive characteristics of the intonational tunes that appear on a given phrase specify something quite unrelated to syntactic category. The claim is that a complete or nearly complete semantic or conceptual representation of the meaning behind the utterance, commensurate with the child's limited understanding of the world, but held in common with the adult, and including limited information about the attitudes and focus of attention of participants in the discourse, remains an indispensable source of information for the child at even the earliest stages of acquiring the constructions of the language.

GRAMMAR AND INTONATION

CCG is fully described in Steedman (1991), to which the interested reader is referred for additional details. In such grammars, as in all categorial grammars, most of the work that in a phrase structure grammar is done by rules like (2) is done by lexical categories like (3):[2]

2. $S \rightarrow NP \; VP$
   $VP \rightarrow TV \; NP$
   $TV \rightarrow \{like, eat, want, ...\}$

3. want $:= (S \backslash NP)/NP$

---

[2] I pass over the details of number and person agreement, which are the same in both frameworks.

Such categories say that transitive verbs like *want* are entities that combine with an NP to the right to yield a predicate $S\backslash NP$—which is itself a category that combines with NPs to its left to yield sentences S.[3] Such a category defines the transitive verb as a *function*, and can also be viewed as defining the semantic type of the function in question. It is this semantics that further determines that the NP on the right takes the role of object, while that on the left takes the role of subject. That is to say that in CCG most of work in the grammar is done by the equivalent of subcategorization frames.

The combinations of such functions with arguments are effected by the following pair of "combinatory rules," which can be thought of as very general CFPS rule schemata:

4. FUNCTIONAL APPLICATION
  a. $X/Y \quad Y \quad \Rightarrow \quad X \quad$ (>)
  b. $\quad Y \quad X\backslash Y \quad \Rightarrow \quad X \quad$ (<)

I leave implicit all details of semantics here, merely noting that the combinatory rules effect semantic combination as well as syntactic combination, and have the character of *function* application. It is convenient to write derivations in such grammars as in (5a), with suitably annotated underlines corresponding to applications of the combinatory rules, a notation that is simply equivalent to the traditional tree diagram in (5b):

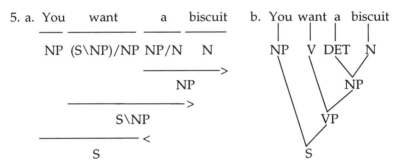

CCG extends this strictly context-free categorial base in two respects. First, I assume that all arguments, such as NPs, can freely *type-raise* to become functions over function categories. For example, subject NPs raise via the following rule:

6. SUBJECT TYPE RAISING (>T)
  $NP \Rightarrow \quad S/(S\backslash NP)$

The following derivation of the same simple transitive sentence is therefore possible (the details of the derivation of the object are omitted):

---

[3]Of course, such lexical items can have more than one category.

7. You   want   a biscuit
    ─────   ─────   ─────────
     NP   (S\NP)/NP   NP
    ────>T
    S/(S\NP)
                          ─────────────────>
                              S\NP
                 ──────────────────────────>
                            S

Although I do not discuss it here, the semantics of the rules of type-raising guarantees that this derivation yields the same interpretation as the previous one.

The combinatory rules are further extended by the inclusion of rules of *functional composition*, in addition to the earlier rules of application. The following rule is an important example:

8. FORWARD COMPOSITION (>B)
    X/Y   Y/Z $\Rightarrow_B$ X/Z

This rule, which can be thought of as "canceling" the term Y, as in fractional multiplication, allows a *second* non-standard syntactic derivation for the sentence "You want a biscuit," as follows. (Once again, although the details are passed over here, the semantics of the composition guarantees that the interpretation for the S that results is identical to those obtained in the earlier derivations.)

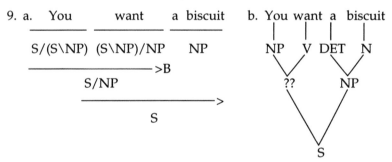

9. a.   You   want   a biscuit   b. You want a biscuit
        ─────   ─────   ─────────   │   │   │   │
       S/(S\NP)   (S\NP)/NP   NP   NP   V DET   N
       ──────────────────────>B   \ /   \ /
               S/NP   ??   NP
       ──────────────────────────>   \   /
                   S   \   /
                                                             \   /
                                                               S

The original reason for making this move was to provide the basis for a simple account of coordination and relativization. Most obviously, the theory accounts for the presence of similar non-constituent fragments in the following examples:

10. a. You want, and I need, a biscuit.
    b. The biscuit that you want.
    c. The biscuit that I want and you need.

(The last two examples require the assumption that the relative pronoun has the category $(N\backslash N)/(S/NP)$—that is, a category mapping fragments like *You want*$_{S/NP}$ onto noun modifiers, as its semantics would suggest.) Somewhat less obviously, the theory also covers unbounded extraction and various other non-constituent coordinations, such as the following (the interested reader is directed to Steedman, 1991, for details):

11. a. Harry seems to think that you want, and I certainly know
       that I need, a biscuit.
    b. The biscuit that Harry seems to think that you want.
    c. I gave you a biscuit and Harry a banana.

The last of these examples, which is of a type that presents considerable problems for other theories, provides very strong support for the claim that type-raising and composition constitute the correct set of elementary syntactic combinatory operations.

I pass over the further details here, together with all questions concerning the general class of rules from which the composition rule is drawn. The important point for present purposes is that the partition of the sentence in (9) into the object and a non-standard (but fully interpreted) constituent S/NP corresponding to the string *You want* makes this theory structurally and semantically suited to the demands of intonational phrasing.[4]

In other words, we can make CCG sensitive to the presence of intonational phrase boundaries, so that of the two preceding derivations (5) and (9) for the string *You want a biscuit*, only the latter will be allowed with the intonation shown in (1)—that is, the one meaning roughly "What you want is a biscuit," repeated here:

12. (YOU   want)   (a BISCUIT!)
    L+H*   LH%   H* LL%

By contrast, only the former derivation will be allowed with the following different intonation:

13. (YOU)   (want a BISCUIT!)
    H*L   L+H*LH%

(This is the intonation contour that conveys a meaning roughly paraphrasable as "It's you who wants a biscuit".) I pass over the formal details of how this is done, again referring the interested reader to Steedman (1991), apart from the following further remarks.

First, it should be intuitively clear, even in advance of the formal details, that the intonational "bracketings" exemplified earlier, together with the particular tunes that are involved, are associated with a very clear discourse semantics.   The "rise-fall-rise" tune that is written L+H*LH% appears to be associated with the "topic" or *theme* of the utterance—roughly, *what the speaker assumes the conversation to be about*. In the case of (12), the theme seems to be the one that would be estab-

---

[4]The interpretation in question can be written λx [want' x you'] using the standard notation of the λ-calculus (cf. Partee, ter Meulen, & Wall, 1990).

lished by the prior question "What do I want?" In (13), the theme is the one that would be established by the question "Who wants a biscuit?" Similarly, the part of both utterances that is marked by the "rise-fall" tune, written H*L or H*LL%, marks the "comment" or *rheme*—that is, the part of the utterance that conveys *what the speaker has to say* about the theme.[5]

The second point to note is that both the previous examples include regions of the sentence that have no tone marking in Pierrehumbert's system, and that in these examples are realized with low pitch and no stress or accent. Again, the discourse semantics seems intuitively clear. Pitch accents mark the parts of the theme and rheme that are "interesting," usually by reason of *contrast* with alternative concepts in the discourse model. The parts with no pitch accent are non-contrastive *background* information, as the reader can tell by comparing the following alternative with (12):[6]

14. (you   WANT)   (a BISCUIT!)
        L+H* LH%   H* LL%

It is important to note that the vast majority of utterances between adults consist mainly of such unmarked backgrounded content, with only a pitch accent and boundary tone at the end to indicate the contrastive rheme, as in (15):

15. you want a BISCUIT.
            H* LL%

According to the theory that has been sketched, such examples simply remain ambiguous between the two derivations permitted by the earlier more informative intonations. Although I continue to pass over the formal details, this is obviously a desirable result, considering the discourse semantics of such utterances. They are indeed ambiguous as to whether the topic is "You" or "What you want," as the reader can verify by observing that this utterance is an appropriate answer either to the question "What do I want?" or to the more open question "What about me?"

It should also be noted that in speech between adults, longer sentences with this sort of intonation, like (16), may be many-ways ambiguous as to syntactic derivation:

16. Harry seems to think that you want a BISCUIT.
                                                    H* LL%

Again this is correct: The interpretations associated with the major constituents of such derivations distinguish between occasions on which the

---

[5]The terms theme and rheme originate with Halliday (1970), although I have generalized his usage somewhat here.
[6]The contrast between contrast and background is comparable to Halliday's "new" and "given" information.

topic or theme of the discourse is "What Harry seems to think you want," "What Harry seems to think," "Harry" and so on, to all of which contexts it is appropriate.

Since such ambiguous intonation contours are actually more common in adult speech than the explicitly informative contours I examined earlier, it should be clear that there is no claim here that intonation disambiguates syntactic derivation. The claim is merely that when intonational boundaries *are* present, they will coincide with syntactic boundaries. Due to the fact that adult speech to children may well include a greater number of explicit boundaries, this seems to be encouraging news. However, there is reason to be cautious here. It is quite likely that the difference is one of degree rather than quality, and that children resemble adults in resolving ambiguities including this one by appeal to meaning and context.

There is every reason to have expected intonation to be congruent with syntax, because it makes for a simpler competence theory. But one should not be surprised to find that performance—including that of the child—has to cope with a great deal of ambiguity, since there is a great deal of ambiguity and nondeterminism in every other component of grammar. Nor is this particular type of ambiguity an artifact of CCG: The nondeterminism is a fact of English and every other language, and must be encountered by any theory that attempts to deal with the range of constructions covered by CCG. However, this observation prompts the further questions of what performance mechanism allows adult human sentence processors to cope with the nondeterminism of competence grammar in general, and whether it is reasonable to attribute a similar mechanism to the child.

PERFORMANCE

There is a growing consensus among psycholinguists that the principal resource that adult human parsers use to resolve grammatical nondeterminism calls on incremental interpretation of rival analyses, in order to "weed out" analyses that do not make sense in the context (see Altmann & Steedman, 1988; Clifton & Ferreira, 1989; Crain & Steedman, 1985; Frazier, 1989; Gibson, 1991; Marslen-Wilson, Tyler, & Seidenberg, 1978; Niv, 1993a; Pritchett, 1992; Steedman & Altmann, 1989; Tanenhaus, 1988; Trueswell, Tanenhaus, & Garnsey, 1994). Although these authors differ on the details of how exactly this might work, one extremely plausible alternative is the "semantically filtering beam-search" theory. According to this proposal, as each word of the sentence is processed, a partially specified interpretation of the sentence is produced for each alternative syntactic analysis compatible with that word, in parallel. These interpretations are immediately evaluated with respect to both semantic and contextual plausibility, the less plausible analyses being assigned low priority or weeded out entirely. On occasion of course, the context may resolve the ambiguity in a way that is incompatible with the syntactic continuation of the sentence. On such occasions, a "garden path" or other processing difficulty may be experienced.[7]

It seems likely that adults deal with the syntactic and information-structural ambiguity noted for examples like (15) in a similar way. The occasions on which it is appropriate to utter the informative and unambiguous contour in (12) are those in which there could be some doubt as to whether the topic or theme is what the hearer wants, or what some other person wants. If no part of the theme is in contrast to anything else, then the theme should be backgrounded and uttered with low pitch and no pitch accent, exactly as in (15).

What this means is that the ambiguity inherent in (15) arises only in *contexts that resolve the ambiguity*—that is, those contexts in which the theme is entirely given. It follows that this ambiguity is entirely comparable with the attachment ambiguities more commonly investigated by psycholinguists like those cited earlier, and can be resolved by the same semantically filtering beam-search.

ACQUIRING SYNTAX FROM SPOKEN LANGUAGE

It should not be surprising to find that adults treat children as less securely in control of the discourse context than themselves, and use informative intonations like that in (12) more frequently when speaking to them. And in fact there is a considerable amount of evidence that this is the case (cf. Ratner, this volume). Should one therefore conclude that CCG lends support to the "prosodic bootstrapping" hypothesis, according to which the child acquires syntactic structure from its explicit reflection in the prosody? Considerable caution may again be in order, for two reasons.

The first is the obvious reason that structure is not enough to determine syntactic categories and syntactic rules. This is a problem for all structural bootstrapping proposals, whether the source of information is prosodic, as in the work of Kelly (1992) and Lederer and Kelly (1991), syntactic, as in Gleitman (1990), or string-based and stochastic, as in the computational work of Brent (1991). The properties involved, which include prosodic characterizations of nouns versus verbs, and basic clause constituent order, are all language-specific. Although many of these studies establish that the relevant entities are perceptually available, something more is needed if the child is to decide which of these entities are nouns, which are verbs, and what order they can occur in. These proposals therefore presuppose the existence of some additional information identifying the basic categories and subcategorization frames for the language, as has been cogently pointed out by Braine

---

[7]The question of whether any *other* resource (such as parsing "strategies" or the exploitation of low-level stochastic properties of the language) is needed to explain human parsing in the face of nondeterminism is an open research question.

(1992). Of course, in the terms of categorial grammar, the categories and subcategorization frames of any given language simply *are* its grammar.

The second reason follows from the first. As soon as it is recognized that the very earliest stages in acquiring syntax require some language-independent source of information about grammatical categories and grammatical relations, the only plausible source that has ever been identified is the semantic interpretation that underlies the utterance.[8]

It is conceivable that if a language included a sufficiently reliable prosodic marker of, say, nouns, then the learning of the members of this class could begin in advance of the learning of the syntactic significance of that class or of the semantics of each member, much as if they were morphologically disambiguated with similar reliability. Although access to semantics for at least one member of the class would still be necessary to identify it as a noun, rather than some other category, all members of the class could promptly be categorized as nouns. Their interpretations could then be learned at leisure. Although such a process would allow some of the work of acquisition to be done "off line," perhaps at a stage when the conceptual apparatus necessary to support a semantics was still under development, it is hard to see any great payoff, especially if category markers are unreliable. It is striking in this connection that irregularity in form-class markers seems to be the rule rather than the exception across languages, particularly among the most frequent and earliest-acquired items. In any case, it is clear that access to semantics is crucial even here.

However, once one realizes that, sooner or later, the child needs access to semantic interpretations in order to acquire syntactic competence, it becomes even more plausible to think of the child's performance as being much like that of the adult language processor—that is, to think of both children and adults as processing utterances on the basis of an understanding of conceptual meaning and discourse context, both of which drastically limit the possible meanings for the utterance, and differing only in their degree of complexity and extent of world knowledge. Of course, conversation would be a dull business for all concerned if context were so completely informative as to render utterance completely redundant, and one cannot assume that the child invariably has a unique correct interpretation for every sentence that they encounter during learning. However, even for the child with no grammar at all, such a strong assumption is not needed, as the computational work of Siskind (1992, in press) makes clear. Siskind's learning program embodies the weaker assumption that the relevant conceptual structure is merely present with reasonably high probability among a fairly

---

[8]In the context of modern linguistics, the suggestion goes back at least to Chomsky (1965:56-59) and Miller (1967). But of course it is a much older idea. See Grimshaw (1981) for a more recent example, and Pinker (1979) for a review of some proposed mechanisms, including the computational work of Anderson (1977)

small set of candidate interpretations that are available to the program via its perceptual access to the situation, and provides an important existence proof for such a mechanism. It follows that Pinker's (1987) worry that, because "such inferences fall short of telepathy and hence are fallible," "incorrect conclusions [could] be made, and [further] learning based on them would spread the damage," may be too pessimistic.[9]

Of course, one should not assume that the conceptual structures in question are confined to those directly supported by instantaneous sense-data in any simple sense of the term. I have no reason to assume that the child lacks sufficient short-term memory and attention span to cope with reasonably immediate sequential relationships between utterances and the phenomena that they refer to. It would also probably be wise to assume that children have some grasp of the social context, including certain primitive concepts of attentional focus and intention on the part of the other participant(s) in the situation. This makes experimentation in this area very difficult indeed. However, it is significant that many of the discourse meanings that were associated earlier with intonational tunes are directly related to such attentional and intentional states. Work reported by Fernald (1993) suggests that intonational tunes and their discourse meanings are among the properties of language that are leaned earliest by infants.

To say this much is not to deny the relevance of the observation that prosodic cues to category and constituency are available, or to deny the reality of syntactic bootstrapping of the kind investigated by Gleitman (1990), who showed that children may on occasion learn subcategorization frames independent from semantics. On the contrary, some such process is probably crucial to human cognitive development for identifying concepts that are *not* prelinguistically salient. It seems highly likely that this is the primary mechanism underlying the explosive cognitive conceptual development that accompanies the onset of language in children, along the lines that Vygotsky (1962) suggested.[10] It is this process that affords the human child relatively effortless and immediate access to many concepts that are not simply and directly evident in the situation, and that represent the hard-won intellectual discoveries and cognitive bequest of generations that have gone before.

ACKNOWLEDGMENTS

Thanks to Katherine Demuth and Jim Morgan for helpful comments on the draft. The research was supported in part by NSF grant nos. IRI90-18513, IRI91-17110, and CISE IIP, CDA 88-22719, DARPA grant no. N00014-90-J-1863, and ARO grant no. DAAL03-89-C0031.

---

[9] I am grateful to Jim Morgan for drawing my attention to this passage.
[10] See Steedman (1993).

REFERENCES

Altmann, G., & Steedman, M. (1988). Interaction with context during human sentence processing. *Cognition, 30*, 191-238.

Anderson, J. (1977). Induction of augmented transition networks. *Cognitive Science, 1*, 125-157.

Braine, M. (1992). What sort of innate structure is needed to "bootstrap" into syntax? *Cognition, 45*, 77-100.

Brent, M. (1991). *Automatic acquisition of subcategorization frames from unrestricted English.* Unpublished doctoral dissertation, MIT, Cambridge, MA.

Chomsky, N. (1965). *Aspects of the theory of syntax.* Cambridge, MA: MIT Press.

Clifton, C., & Ferreira, F. (1989). Ambiguity in context. *Language and Cognitive Processes, 4*, 77-104.

Crain, S., & Steedman, M. (1985). On not being led up the garden path: The use of context by the psychological parser. In D. Dowty, L. Kartunnen, & A. Zwicky, (Eds.), *Natural language parsing: Psychological, computational and theoretical perspectives* (pp. 320-358), ACL Studies in Natural Language Processing. Cambridge, England: Cambridge University Press.

Fernald, A. (1993). Approval and disapproval: Infant responsiveness to vocal affect in familiar and unfamiliar languages. *Child Development, 64*, 657-674.

Frazier, L. (1989). Against lexical generation of syntax. In W. Marslen-Wilson (Ed.), *Lexical representation and process* (pp. 505-528). Cambridge, MA: MIT Press.

Gibson, E. (1991). *A computational theory of human linguistic processing.* Unpublished doctoral dissertation, Carnegie Mellon University, Pittsburgh, PA.

Gleitman, L. (1990). The structural source of verb meanings. *Language Acquisition, 1*, 3-55.

Grimshaw, J. (1981). Form, function, and the language acquisition device. In C. L. Baker & J. McCarthy (Eds.), *The logical problem of language acquisition* (pp. 163-182). Cambridge, MA: MIT Press.

Halliday, M. (1970). Language structure and language function. In J. Lyons (Ed.), *New horizons in linguistics* (pp. 140-165). New York: Penguin.

Kelly, M. (1992). Using sound to solve syntactic problems. *Psychological Review, 99*, 349-364.

Lederer, A., & Kelly, M. H. (1991). Prosodic correlates to the adjunct/complement distinction in motherese. *Papers & Reports on Child Language Development, 30*, 55-63.

Marslen-Wilson, W., Tyler, L. K., & Seidenberg, M. (1978). Sentence processing and the clause boundary. In W. J. M. Levelt & G. Flores d'Arcais (Eds.), *Studies in the perception of language* (pp. 219-246) New York: Wiley.

Miller, G. (1967). *The psychology of communication.* Harmondsworth: Penguin.

Niv, M. (1993a). *A computational model of syntactic processing: Ambiguity resolution from interpretation.* Unpublished doctoral dissertation, available as tech report MS-CIS-93-83, LINC LAB 257, University of Pennsylvania, Philadelphia, PA.

Niv, M. (1993b, June). *Resolution of syntactic ambiguity: The case of new subjects.* Proceedings of the 15th Annual Meeting of the Cognitive Science Society, Boulder CO.

Partee, B., ter Meulen, A., & Wall, R. (1990). *Mathematical models in linguistics.* Dordrecht: Kluwer.

Pinker, S. (1979). Formal models of language learning. *Cognition, 7*, 217-283.

Pinker, S. (1987). The bootstrapping problem in language acquisition. In B. MacWhinney (Ed.), *Mechanisms of language acquisition* (pp. 399-441). Hillsdale, NJ: Lawrence Erlbaum Associates.

Pinker, S. (1989). *Learnability and cognition.* Cambridge, MA: MIT Press.

Pritchett, B. (1992). *Grammatical competence and parsing performance.* Chicago: University of Chicago Press.

Selkirk, L. (1984). *Phonology and syntax.* Cambridge, MA: MIT Press.

Siskind, J. (1992). *Naive physics, event perception, lexical semantics, and language acquisition.* Unpublished doctoral dissertation, MIT, Cambridge, MA.

Siskind, J. (in press). A computational study of lexical acquisition. *Cognition.*

Steedman, M. (1991). Structure and intonation. *Language, 67*, 260-296.

Steedman, M. (1993). Acquisition of verb categories. *Lingua, 92*, 471-480.

Steedman, M., & Altmann, G. (1989). Ambiguity in context: A reply. *Language and Cognitive Processes, 4,* 105-122.

Tanenhaus, M. (1988). Psycholinguistics: An overview. In F. Newmeyer (Ed.), *Linguistics: The Cambridge survey* (Vol. 4, pp. 1-37). Cambridge, England: Cambridge University Press.

Trueswell, J. C., Tanenhaus, M. K., & Garnsey, S. M. (1994). Semantic influences on parsing: Use of thematic role information in syntactic ambiguity resolution. *Journal of Memory and Language., 33,* 285-318.

Vygotsky, L. (1962). *Thought and language.* Cambridge, MA: MIT Press.

20 Prosody in Speech to Infants: Direct and Indirect Acoustic Cues to Syntactic Structure

Cynthia Fisher and Hisayo Tokura
University of Illinois

THE ROLE OF SPEECH IN THEORIES OF SYNTAX ACQUISITION

In the first few years of life, every child discovers the mappings between sound and meaning that constitute a native language. Theories of language acquisition, however, have typically asked how a learner might begin with strings of words rather than sounds, building up phrase and clause structures from word-strings based on some combination of semantic and distributional cues (e.g., Bates & MacWhinney, 1982; Pinker, 1984). The adequacy of idealizing linguistic input as word-strings rests on the assumption that properties of the speech wave not represented in sequences of words have little to do with the acquisition of grammar.

This assumption is not an unreasonable one for the field to make: One must begin somewhere, and the word is a very natural candidate for a starting unit. Intriguing hints have emerged that this assumption is misleading, however—that physical properties of speech are not mere irrelevant noise to be ignored in models of language acquisition. On the contrary, it has been suggested that prosodic properties of speech, including rhythmic variations and pitch changes, might provide a natural bracketing of continuous speech into linguistically relevant units such as clauses and phrases (e.g., Gleitman, Gleitman, Landau, & Wanner, 1988; Morgan, 1986). By attending to the acoustic properties of speech, language learners might gain information about the locations of syntactic boundaries in the utterances they hear quite early in the learning process.

Acoustic Correlates of Syntactic Boundaries

What might these physical cues to phrase structure be? Phonological analyses of the intonational structure of speech have revealed a tendency for prosodic units to correspond to major syntactic units such as phrases and clauses (e.g., Hirschberg & Pierrehumbert, 1986; Selkirk, 1984). Phonetic studies of adult-directed speech have found three kinds of acoustic correlates of syntactic boundaries in English: (1) Syllables that end phrases or clauses tend to be lengthened relative to syllables elsewhere in constituents (e.g., Cooper & Paccia-Cooper, 1980; Crystal & House, 1988; Klatt, 1976; Lehiste, 1972; Scott, 1982; Streeter, 1978); (2) pauses are more likely to occur at major syntactic boundaries than arbitrarily within phrases (e.g., Goldman-Eisler, 1972; Scott, 1982), and pause length appears to reflect the hierarchical structure of phrases (e.g., Cooper & Paccia-Cooper, 1980; Gee & Grosjean, 1983); and (3) fundamental frequency (F_0) tends to decline at the end of a major syntactic constituent, and then rise at the start of the next syntactic unit (e.g., Cooper & Sorenson, 1977). So, for example, a speaker could insert prosodic breaks, characterized by final lengthening, pitch declination, or even pausing, at the locations in (1) marked with a Δ, but would be unlikely to introduce similar breaks at arbitrary locations in those utterances, as in (2).

1. A little girl Δ was eating bananas. Δ The rotten kid Δ dropped the banana skins Δ right on the floor. Δ
2. A little Δ girl was eating Δ bananas. The rotten kid dropped the Δ banana Δ skins right on the Δ floor.

Final lengthening and pitch changes can lead to the perception of a subjective pause or break in speech by adults (e.g., Duez, 1993; Wightman, Shattuck-Hufnagel, Ostendorf, & Price, 1992) even where there is no period of silence. These cues can be strong enough to disambiguate syntactically ambiguous sentences (e.g., Beach, 1991; Klatt, 1976; Scott, 1982; Streeter, 1978). Two recent studies found the same kinds of prosodic cues in stories read to toddlers: Phrase- and clause-final words were lengthened relative to phrase-medial words (Morgan, 1986) and traversed a greater distance in F_0 than words elsewhere in sentences (Lederer & Kelly, 1991).

The Prosodic Bootstrapping Hypothesis

If the input for language acquisition reliably consists of strings acoustically structured in this way, then perceptually natural groupings of words will tend to be the grammatically relevant ones. The learner could use acoustic evidence to rule out conjectures about grammatical structure inconsistent with the audible structure of input sentences. The notion that acoustic information could provide learners with a linguistically useful bottom-up segmentation of speech is known as the prosodic bootstrapping hypothesis (e.g., Gerken, Jusczyk & Mandel, 1994; Jusczyk et al., 1992; Kemler Nelson et al., 1989; Morgan, 1986).

It remains open to question, however, both how the learner could gain access to prosodic structure in the first place, and how useful prosodic structure could be in the acquisition of syntax (Fernald & McRoberts, this volume; Pinker, 1984). First, prosodic structure is not the same thing as acoustic structure. The central problem is one well stated by Klatt (1976, 1980): The acoustic patterns that lead to the perception of prosodic boundaries and stress patterns are subject to many other influences, including the inherent acoustic properties of individual vowels and consonants. This means that the acoustic shape of an utterance is ambiguous—it provides information about all of these levels of linguistic structure at once. Each influence must be considered, and compensated for, in order to see clearly the effects of any single factor. Klatt (1976, 1980) pointed out the resulting "chicken and egg" paradox for speech perception, and proposed an analysis-by-synthesis system in which the listener generates and tests many acoustic predictions based on phonetic, syntactic, and semantic information. How is the child to break into this circle?

Second, prosody constitutes an autonomous level of linguistic structure, with rules of its own that cannot be reduced to the rules of syntax. Prosodic structure defines domains within which phonological regularities hold, just as grammatical regularities hold within syntactic constituents. Alignment of prosodic and grammatical units is one of the constraints on prosody (e.g., Selkirk, 1984), but prosodic structure is generally hierarchically shallower than syntactic structure (e.g., Dresher, this volume), and reflects other factors including focal stress (e.g., Vogel & Kenesei, 1990) and the length of constituents (e.g., Gee & Grosjean, 1983). This guarantees that prosody will not transparently signal syntax.

In essence, the use of acoustic information to divide speech into linguistically relevant units depends on relations among three levels of structure—the acoustic pattern that reaches the listener's ear, the prosodic structure, and the syntactic structure of the utterance. In assessing the leap from sound to syntax, we need to explore both the detectability of prosodic boundary cues amid other influences on acoustic structure, and the correspondences between prosodic and syntactic boundaries. We present a beginning attempt at such an assessment, supported with evidence from acoustic analyses of infant-directed speech (IDS), and argue that, despite complications, acoustic groupings in speech can provide even a naive learner with both direct and indirect evidence for syntactic structure.

MULTIPLE CONSTRAINTS ON SOUND PATTERNS: INITIAL ACCESS TO PROSODIC STRUCTURE

The pitch and rhythm of syllables are influenced by information at every conceivable level of linguistic description, from phonetic content through syntactic and discourse structure to emotional valence. These complications raise serious questions about the status of acoustic properties as truly "bottom-up" cues to important linguistic boundaries (e.g., Fernald & McRoberts, this volume; Pinker, 1984).

For example, phonetic segments—particularly vowels (e.g., Klatt, 1976)—tend to be lengthened at utterance boundaries, or at smaller prosodic boundaries within utterances. However, the length of a vowel depends not only on its position in an utterance, but also on its inherent duration (e.g., the vowel in 'bad' is longer than the one in 'bed'; Klatt, 1976), its phonetic context (e.g., a vowel is lengthened when followed by a voiced consonant; Crystal & House, 1988), its position in a word (Klatt, 1976), and the status of the word in the discourse (e.g., Fisher & Tokura, in press; Fowler & Housum, 1987). The same observed duration will sound long, and therefore stressed or utterance-final, if it is identified as an inherently short vowel preceding an unvoiced consonant, but not if it is identified as an inherently long vowel preceding a voiced consonant.

Moreover, duration is itself one of the cues used to identify speech sounds. Listeners use the length of a vowel, among other cues, to determine what particular vowel they have heard, and whether the consonant that follows it is voiced (Klatt, 1976). This is an example of the paradox mentioned earlier: The listener seems to need to identify the speech segments in order to determine whether they are lengthened, but also to take lengthening into account in order to use duration to identify speech segments. Adult listeners, for example, can better discriminate voiced and unvoiced consonants if they can hear the surrounding sentential context (Gordon, 1989). This suggests that hearing a full sentence allows listeners to take final lengthening into account, and to interpret vowel duration as a cue to voicing with greater accuracy.

The same tangle of overlapping influences applies to pitch contours (e.g., Klatt, 1980; Fernald & McRoberts, this volume). The pitch contours of utterances can be drastically affected by the emotion expressed by the speaker. Fernald, Taeschner, Dunn, Papousek, Boysson-Bardies, and Fukui (1989) showed that parents in many cultures use the same intonational melodies to signal the same emotional content to their infants. For example, approving vocalizations will occur on an exaggerated, bell-shaped pitch curve, whereas vocal prohibitions are characterized by short, abruptly falling tones. Different consonants are also associated with brief changes in pitch (e.g., Klatt, 1980). Silverman (1986) showed that judgments of consonant voicing differed depending on the place of a consonant in an overall pitch contour. As was the case for duration, segmental pitch cues must be interpreted relative to information about the overall shape of the utterance.

In sum, changes in pitch or duration provide information about multiple levels of linguistic structure at once. Acoustic changes associated with prosody cannot be seen as isolated phenomena, that the infant might use to detect linguistic boundaries once the identification of segments has been accomplished. Rather, the identification of speech sounds and the perception of the intonation and rhythm of utterances are interdependent, with knowledge about each influence required for the accurate interpretation of the others (e.g., Klatt, 1976, 1980).

Adult listeners can draw on their knowledge of syntactic, semantic, and phonological properties of the language to interpret the sound patterns they hear, disentangling the acoustic values that indicate a prosodic boundary or an instance of focal stress from those which indicate a long vowel or an emotional statement. But what about the child? If learners also have independent information about the expected prosodic shape of utterances, then they could interpret observed durations and pitch changes relative to that basic template, much as adults do. This could come about if the influence of prosodic boundaries on the acoustics of syllables is very large relative to other influences. If so, then some information about the expected prosodic shape of utterances could be detected across a set of observed utterances even without a sophisticated algorithm for holding constant other effects. This knowledge could then provide the child with the beginnings of a solution for Klatt's "chicken and egg" problem: In general, provided the listener can anticipate one influence on acoustic structure, its effects could be teased apart from others in the process of interpretation.

It has been suggested that special characteristics of IDS may accentuate acoustic markers of utterance boundaries, increasing their salience. Final lengthening is more extreme (Bernstein Ratner, 1986; Morgan, 1986), and pitch excursions preceding pauses are larger (Stern, Spieker, Barnett & MacKain, 1983), in infant-directed than adult-directed English. However, previous studies of utterance-final lengthening and pitch changes have not been designed to assess the magnitude of acoustic correlates of prosodic boundaries relative to other sources of acoustic variation. Stern et al. (1983) compared prepausal pitch changes in IDS to those in adult-directed speech, but not to within-utterance pitch changes. Pitch changes not at the ends of utterances might tend to be exaggerated in IDS as well. Similarly, Bernstein Ratner (1986) and Morgan (1986) compared the same segments or words across sentence positions, thus controlling for many lower level influences on sound patterns. These, and similar acoustic studies of adult-directed speech (e.g., Cooper & Paccia-Cooper, 1980), therefore provide evidence that the prosodic boundaries often associated with the ends of phrases and sentences are one influence on the sound pattern of an utterance, but not necessarily that acoustic cues to these boundaries are readily available to the language learner without the simultaneous application of a great deal of knowledge about all the other influences (cf. Fernald & McRoberts, this volume; Pinker, 1984). Are acoustic correlates of prosodic structure large enough to be detected in spontaneous speech, without the ability to control for all the other sources of variation? That is, can they provide a source of initial information for the paradox in speech perception posed by Klatt (1976, 1980), and thus constitute bottom-up cues for the segmentation of speech?

Acoustic Analyses of Infant-Directed Speech

To address this question directly, we examined large samples of spontaneous speech addressed to infants (Fisher & Tokura, 1994). Three English-speaking and three Japanese-speaking mothers were recorded in spontaneous interactions with their 13- to 14-month-old infants, and connected multi-utterance samples were digitized for acoustic analysis. Measurements were made from the digitized waveforms of the duration and the range in pitch (peak F_0–valley F_0) of the vowel portion of each syllable, as well as the duration of any pause following each syllable. These acoustic measures were compared across positions in utterances, to examine whether the final syllables of phonological utterances differed from other syllables in their acoustic properties. Thus with these data we could begin to assess, for two quite different languages, the accessibility of acoustic markers of prosodic boundaries in ordinary talk to babies, relative to all the other sources of acoustic variability.

In order to make this assessment, we needed some independent means of identifying phonological utterances, without assuming a perfect correlation between prosodic units and sentences. The location of long pauses provides one obvious source of information. A pause does not necessarily represent an intended stop following a prosodic unit: Within-sentence hesitations can account for up to half of the observed pauses in adult-directed speech (e.g., Butterworth, 1980; Fernald & McRoberts, this volume; Goldman-Eisler, 1972). However, the short and fluent utterances of IDS effectively solve this problem: Long pauses in speech to infants and young children are nearly always at the ends of sentences or phrases used in isolation (Broen, 1972; Fernald & Simon, 1984). Given the very high correspondence between pauses and the boundaries of grammatical units in speech to children, we can be confident that where there is a pause there is a major prosodic boundary, and can look for preceding changes in the timing and pitch of syllables.

Acoustic Cues to Utterance Boundaries

The unconstrained conversations we recorded were subject to all of the influences on sound patterns discussed previously, from segmental content and context to emotional valence. Despite all these sources of variability, however, the characteristic prosodic shape of utterances in both English and Japanese was clearly revealed in the utterances of spontaneous IDS.

As previously found by Broen (1972) for English, and by Fernald and Simon (1984) for German, nearly all (96%) of the long pauses (≥ 260 msec) in both the English and Japanese samples occurred at the boundaries of grammatically distinct utterances. The majority of the grammatically distinct utterances in these samples—59% for English and 69% for Japanese—were followed by a long pause. The syllables preceding these prosodic boundaries were acoustically extremely distinctive: In both languages, long pauses were preceded by very long vowels and large pitch changes. Prepausal vowels were about twice as long[1], and covered pitch excursions twice as great, as vowels not preceding pauses. Despite the noise contributed by other sources of acoustic variability, syllables preceding pauses formed a quite distinct class from syllables not preceding pauses.

Thus, at least for utterance boundaries we can answer our first question affirmatively: Looking directly at spontaneous talk to infants, we find that acoustic changes marking major prosodic boundaries are very robust, detectable in two phonologically distinct languages amid all the quirks and variability of casual, spontaneous speech. These cues could be revealed by a bracketing algorithm, like our statistical analyses, that does not control for any of these other factors. At least in principle learners could detect these patterns in observed utterances, generating expectations for the sound patterns of utterances in the languages they hear.

Acoustic Cues to Within-Utterance Prosodic Boundaries

What about prosodic units within utterances? Again, to look for acoustic changes at prosodic boundaries, we need a way to predict where prosodic boundaries are likely to be found. Given findings from adult-directed speech, we might expect these to be at the major syntactic division of the sentence, between the subject and the predicate (e.g., Cooper & Paccia-Cooper, 1980). However, unlike utterance-final syllables, the final syllables of subject phrases within utterances in our samples of infant-directed English and Japanese were not grossly different from non-final syllables. As a class, syllables ending subject phrases were not longer than other syllables, and did not undergo more pitch movement.

However, the lack of obvious acoustic evidence of phrase boundaries in these samples is not necessarily evidence that acoustic markers of within-sentence prosodic boundaries, where they occur, are lost amid the variability of uncontrolled spontaneous speech. This could also be a case of mismatch between prosodic and syntactic structure. Of primary relevance here is the most striking property of speech to infants—that it consists largely of short sentences (e.g., Newport, Gleitman, & Gleitman, 1977). The kinds of long, multiword phrases found in the acoustic studies cited previously are rarely found in speech directed to young children. As mentioned, when longer sentences do appear in speech to

---

[1]The proportion of vowel lengthening was significantly larger in English than in Japanese, for these six mothers (see Fisher & Tokura, 1994). This difference is consistent with findings in the adult-directed speech literature on the two languages: English is generally said to have extreme final lengthening (e.g., Cruttenden, 1986), while there has been some controversy over whether Japanese has final lengthening at all (e.g., Campbell, 1992). Fisher and Tokura also report differences in amplitude patterns in English and Japanese, which are not discussed here. These differences in prosodic patterns across languages implicate a role for learning in generating a prosodic template for a particular language, as suggested here.

children, they provide reliable prosodic markings of phrase boundaries (e.g., Jusczyk et al., 1992; Lederer & Kelly, 1991; Morgan, 1986). However, the length and complexity of sentences strongly affect the likelihood and magnitude of acoustically marked prosodic breaks (Ferreira, 1993; Grosjean, 1983). Thus the short sentences characteristic of talk to babies should be less likely than longer and more complex sentences to contain major prosodic breaks associated with exaggerated lengthening or pitch changes.

Furthermore, an examination of the transcripts of our English speech samples revealed that the vast majority—84% across speakers—of the subject noun phrases were pronouns, as in (3). Pronoun subjects have been implicated in other work as a locus of systematic mismatch between prosodic and syntactic structure. A pronoun is extremely unlikely to form a separate intonational unit within an utterance. Instead, if the sentence has an audible prosodic break at all, it will tend to separate the postverbal NP from the main verb, as in (4) (see, e.g., Gee & Grosjean, 1983). In such cases, the prosodic structure of the utterance does not correspond to its major syntactic division.

3. That looks like a doggy.
4. You like Δ the doggy.

There is also evidence from perceptual studies that pronoun subjects do not constitute acoustic units for listeners. School children can learn a game in which they repeat the subject of a sentence; they have trouble with this task, however, when the subjects are pronouns (Read & Schrieber, 1982). Gerken et al. (1994) found that 9-month-old infants do not perceive a boundary between a pronoun subject and main verb—In a selective listening paradigm, infants show no preference for speech with pauses added between a pronoun subject and its main verb over pauses inserted elsewhere in the clause. Thus the frequency of pronoun subjects should also reduce the likelihood of within-utterance prosodic breaks at the subject/predicate boundary.

Local acoustic changes at phrase boundaries.   Taking these considerations into account, there appear to be some sentence environments in which acoustic evidence of a prosodic division within utterances can be found: Gerken et al. (1994) found that infants tended to perceive a boundary following a lexical noun phrase subject, as in (5), or following a subject pronoun in an inverted question, as in (6). Gerken et al. reported consistent local changes in the duration and pitch of syllables preceding the subject/verb boundary, but not preceding the verb/complement boundary, in both the lexical-subject and yes/no question samples.   As Read and Schrieber suggested, long subject phrases should be more likely to constitute separate prosodic units, and therefore provide an opportunity to look for acoustic changes preceding utterance-internal prosodic boundaries.

5. Sammy likes to play baseball.
6. Do you like to play baseball?

Our samples of spontaneous English and Japanese speech to infants included some sentences that, like those in (5) and (6), contained at least two syllables preceding a major internal phrase boundary. In these sentences, we found local acoustic regularities similar to those found by Gerken et al.: In English, phrase-final syllables were reliably longer than the immediately preceding syllable within the same utterance, whereas non-final syllables in other locations did not tend to be longer than the preceding syllable. In Japanese there was no tendency for subject-final syllables to be longer than the previous syllables; however, phrase-final syllables were reliably lower in pitch than preceding non-final syllables, whereas non-final syllables decreased less in pitch relative to the preceding syllable.

The different findings for Japanese and English are consistent with known differences between Japanese and English phonology. First, variations in vowel duration are generally smaller in Japanese than in English (e.g., Beckman, 1982); thus phrase-final lengthening, found in some contexts in adult-directed Japanese (e.g., Kaiki & Sagisaka, 1993), might not be readily detected without controlling for other sources of variation. Second, although acoustic analyses of read speech (Gerken et al., 1994) revealed pitch changes preceding phrase boundaries in English just as were found in this study for Japanese, variations due to emotional uses of prosody might interfere with the marking of utterance-internal prosodic boundaries in spontaneous IDS. This might be particularly true for the exaggerated speech addressed to infants by American English mothers (Fernald et al., 1989).

Two conclusions from these findings seem warranted. First, the variability of spontaneous speech to infants does not entirely overwhelm even the smaller within-sentence acoustic regularities found in the short sentences of speech to infants. These patterns, when they occur, might serve to create a perceptible discontinuity within utterances, suggesting to the naive listener that an utterance contains distinct parts (e.g., Gerken et al., 1994). Thus, in examining the acoustics of spontaneous speech addressed to babies, we uncovered powerful acoustic correlates of prosodic structure. In both English and Japanese, the acoustic changes associated with both the boundaries of phonological utterances and, in some environments, prosodic boundaries within utterances, are large and consistent enough to be detected even in the uncontrolled context of spontaneous IDS. This suggests that the learner's initial access to prosodic structure can be accomplished without the aid of a sophisticated procedure for subtracting out the effects of other influences on the sound patterns of utterances. The sheer size and regularity of acoustic changes associated with prosodic boundaries could provide the child with an initial source of information to help solve the conundrum posed by Klatt (1976, 1980) for the perception of speech.

Second, however, it must be noted that the majority of the short sentences characterizing both the English and Japanese samples did not constitute likely environments in which to find prosodic boundaries between subjects and predicates. In Japanese, most utterances did not contain an internal subject/predicate boundary at all, given the frequency of phrase deletion (e.g., Clancy, 1985). In the English samples, most subjects were pronouns. Thus the contexts in which acoustically marked prosodic boundaries inside utterances are likely to be found are rare, due to well known distributional factors of IDS.

PROSODIC STRUCTURE AS A LIMITED CUE TO SYNTAX

We reviewed evidence suggesting that prosodic boundaries in speech to children are associated with very robust acoustic markers, detectable amid the noise and variability of acoustic changes due to other linguistic factors. This suggests that a naive learner could detect these changes, and therefore that they could serve as bottom-up cues to aid the child in the interpretation of acoustic patterns in speech. Thus we have evidence for a positive answer to our first question, concerning the detectability of prosodic structures.

At this point, however, we have already seen evidence of limitations in the correspondence between prosodic and syntactic structures. In particular, although the majority of grammatically distinct utterances are separated by pauses, with associated prepausal lengthening and pitch changes, we found only intermittent evidence of within-utterance prosodic boundaries that coincide with grammatical boundaries. These limitations suggest that the answer to our second question—how useful will prosodic structure be in signaling syntactic structure?—will be more complex.

It is worth emphasizing that the dearth of direct prosodic evidence for hierarchical structure in the linguistic input is not unique to motherese. Very short sentences addressed to adults are no more likely than infant-directed utterances to be broken up into multiple intonational units (e.g., Ferreira, 1993). Detailed prosodic evidence of clause-internal hierarchical structure is probably fairly rare in everyday speech even to adults. Perhaps for this reason, the effects of prosodic structure on comprehension by adult listeners, although detectable in some cases, are not very powerful (see, e.g., Beach, 1991; Wales & Toner, 1976). In the next sections, we try to suggest some ways in which a limited prosodic bracketing, when combined with analyses of the distribution of recognizable items, can provide a perceptual basis for positing clause-internal structure.

The Acoustic Reduction of Pronoun Subjects: Indirect Cues to Phrase Boundaries

What can we say about the majority of cases in English, in which pronoun subjects do not tend to form separable prosodic units defined by lengthening, pausing, or pitch lowering? Notice that English pronouns are already perceptual units in the sense of being single syllables. Further, they are drawn from a closed class of items, and therefore have two relevant properties common to closed-class words: Pronouns, like other closed-class words, are extremely frequent, and are physically reduced relative to open-class words[2].

Both the physical diminution and the high frequency of pronoun subjects could provide children with indirect perceptual evidence for the verb phrase: Many of the sentences they hear will have one of these physically unassuming and highly familiar words in subject position. Such sentences might give the verb phrase some perceptual reality as a figure against a less attention-grabbing ground. Morgan (1986) has proposed a similar bracketing cue based on the juxtaposition of stressed and unstressed elements. The high frequency of pronouns may also facilitate their detection by learners as recurring units within the acoustically bounded utterances of IDS. The rest of the utterance, once one of these familiar items is stripped away, constitutes the verb phrase.

Ellipsis

A second relevant feature of our transcripts, also often noticed in motherese-style speech (e.g., Newport et al., 1977), is the prevalence of elliptical utterances, consisting of well formed parts of full clauses, as in (7),

> 7. Who's that? You saw one of these today. It's a doggy. Dog. Little puppy dog. Goes woof woof.

Ellipsis is generally more prevalent in Japanese than it is in English. The utterances in (8), for example, although quite analogous to the English ones in (7), cannot meaningfully be called sentence fragments, since the deletion of major constituents is so commonplace in Japanese (e.g., Clancy, 1985). Such utterances frequently occur even in adult-directed English, although they require more discourse set-up. For example, an isolated noun phrase or adjective phrase sounds odd as an opening gambit, but can occur alone when it adds descriptive informa-

---

[2]We present no description of the use of pronouns in Japanese IDS here, since a) the deletion of entire phrases is so common in our samples that pronoun use is quite rare, and b) Japanese pronouns are in a sense less pronoun-like than English ones (cf. Sugamoto, 1989): They occur with noun modifiers and inflections (as in the equivalent of "gentle shes," ungrammatical in English), and therefore need not stand in for a whole NP. The learning procedures sketched in this section could only work for a language, like English, that has true pronouns.

tion to a foregoing utterance, as in (9), or when responding to non-comprehension, as in (10).

8. Un, Chika-chan, suki-na-no atta ka na?
    "Yeah, Chika-chan, was there something you like, hmm?"
    Chunchun iru, yo. Chunchun. Chunchun, ne. Un, chunchun.
    "There is a birdie, hmm. Birdie. Birdie, yeah. Yeah, birdie."
9. I've finally bought a car. A Honda Civic. Bright red!
10. Can you lend me your camera? (My what?) Your camera!

Such fragments should indeed be more common in IDS than in talk to adults, both to keep utterances short and to respond to assumed non-comprehension on the part of the infant. Repetitive strings of utterances such as those in (7) and (8) sound fine when padded out with implicit clarification questions from the baby ("A what?" "A doggy!").

Approximately 18% of the utterances in our English samples, and 37% of those in our Japanese samples, were fragments of this type. An additional 9% of the English and 12% of the Japanese utterances in our samples were imperatives. Given the frequency with which well formed phrase fragments stand alone as utterances in speech to children (e.g., Broen, 1972; Newport et al., 1977), the correlation between the phonological utterance and the clause is not very high (Fernald & McRoberts, this volume). Therefore a learner who assumed that prosodic utterances must be fully specified clauses would make many errors. The presence of fragments in the input is not troublesome, however, on the hypothesis that learners might use utterance prosody to group syllables together in memory, and seek linguistic regularities within these groups (e.g., Morgan, 1986). Both phrases and clauses have internal structure defined by the rules of grammar, and can either stand alone or form part of a larger grammatical unit. Thus distributional analyses conducted over material grouped within phonological utterances will be revealing of the phrase structure rules of the language even if those utterances are often not full clauses.

The prevalence of ellipsis in speech to infants has interesting consequences for the perception of subclausal units. Well formed fragments of clauses can have the physical properties of full sentences—prosodic units defined by pausing, lengthening, and final pitch movement. Effectively, subclausal units such as noun phrases, verb phrases, and even adjectival phrases (e.g., "Very pretty!") are frequently marked as acoustically bounded units in the speech stream. Thus, there is direct prosodic evidence for the existence of linguistic units smaller than a clause. There is not, however, direct prosodic evidence to discriminate such grammatical fragments from entire clauses. Rather, the place of elliptically isolated phrases in a syntactic hierarchy must be inferred indirectly, from their distribution across acoustically marked utterances. Utterance sequences like the ones shown in (7–8) could cue children to the internal structure of clauses, provided they can recognize repeated phrases in differing acoustic contexts. There is some evidence that this feat of perceptual analysis is not beyond the capabilities of quite young infants: For example, Fernald (1994) has found that 15-month-olds can recognize familiar words in connected speech, particularly if the words are either stressed or utterance-final.

Direct and Indirect Acoustic Cues to Phrase Structure.

In examining the acoustic correlates of prosody in spontaneous speech addressed to babies, we uncovered both direct and indirect cues to phrase structure. First, the speech stream is quite robustly segmented into grammatically distinct utterances—clauses or phrases used in isolation—for the child. Thus, the input speech will naturally fall into parts consisting of linguistically analyzable units. Second, although the short sentences characteristic of IDS may be responsible for making utterance-internal prosodic breaks less likely than in adult-directed speech, both English and Japanese samples revealed evidence of acoustic regularities within the clause.

In addition, two properties of IDS—pronoun subjects and ellipsis—suggest ways in which a limited distributional analysis, combined with the robust acoustic correlates of utterance boundaries, could provide the child with indirect perceptual evidence for syntactic structure within utterances. The sketches of learning procedures presented are similar to a proposal by Gerken et al. (1994) that comparisons across sentences might compensate for the lack of acoustic cues to clause-internal structure in many of the utterances of IDS.

PROSODY AS A COMPLEX CUE TO SYNTAX: THE GIVEN–NEW DISTINCTION

In adult-directed speech, prosodic contours can express information not only about the syntactic structure of an utterance, but also about its intended interpretation relative to a larger discourse. To fully assess the utility of the prosodic structure of speech as a cue to syntactic structure, it will be necessary to construct a model of the uses of prosody, very broadly defined, that incorporates multiple constraints on the prosodic structure of utterances.

What discourse effects on prosody might be relevant to IDS? A common area of intersection between prosody and discourse is the marking of information as given versus new in the conversational context (see, e.g., Chafe, 1976; Clark & Haviland, 1977; Halliday, 1967). The acoustic correlates of stress, used to emphasize new at the expense of given information, include some of the same acoustic properties that signal prosodic boundaries—duration and F_0. The effect of given–new status on these acoustic measures is not negligible: Repeated words can be reduced enough to damage their intelligibility when not supported by discourse context (Fowler & Housum, 1987). The assignment of focal

stress is considered to be a part of prosodic structure, influencing the location of prosodic boundaries independently of syntactic structure (e.g.,
Vogel & Kenesei, 1990).

Given and New in Speech to Infants: Acoustic Analyses

The production and comprehension functions of distinguishing given
and new words suggest two possibilities for the appearance of this distinction in IDS. On one hand, speech to infants, as presumed incompe-
tent listeners, might be characterized by heightened word-level intelligibility. Speakers might assume that less is foregrounded for the infant
listener, and therefore be unwilling to demote words to given status by
physically reducing them. On the other hand, speakers addressing
novice listeners should want to avoid ambiguity by clearly marking intended reference. Since a clear distinction between given and new
items serves as an aid to comprehension (cf. Clark & Haviland 1977;
Fowler & Housum, 1987), one might even expect the distinction to be
broadened or exaggerated in speech to infants (cf. Fernald & Mazzie,
1991).

We began to examine simple discourses addressed to infants and
adults (Fisher & Tokura, in press) to determine whether and how the
distinction between given and new elements is marked in speech to infants. Our procedure was adapted from one used by Fernald and Mazzie (1991), designed to elicit spontaneous repeated use of a common set
of target words by a number of speakers. English-speaking mothers
watched a puppet show enacted for them twice, and were instructed to
tell the story of the sequence of events as they occurred, once to their 14-
month-old infants, and once to an adult experimenter. Each event had
two animal puppets as participants: One was common to all scenes, and
the other was unique to each scene. The name of the newly introduced
puppet in each scene was the target word (e.g., *tiger, elephant*). The target animal was always the patient of some action directed toward it, and
as such was nearly always named in sentence-final position. This
placement allowed us to abstract away from the effects of that position
on the acoustic form of words.

In describing these events, mothers routinely produced a first and
second use of a number of target words in each listener context, infant-
and adult-directed. Examples of speech from these two contexts are
shown in (11) and (12). Crucially, the content of the adult- and infant-
directed versions, limited by the events to be described, is virtually
identical. The utterances containing the first two uses of each target
word in each listener context were transcribed and digitized for analysis. Acoustic measures of each target word included the duration of its
stressed vowel, its average amplitude, and its maximum and minimum
fundamental frequency. Judgments of the most stressed word in each

target-containing utterance were collected[3]; each target word was also coded for whether it was on the pitch peak of the utterance containing it. These measures were compared across repetition (first and second use) and listener context (infant and adult), to examine the marking of given and new elements in these two styles of speech.

11. *Adult-directed context*: And there's the turtle. The pig's pulling 'n' pushing the turtle around.
12. *Infant-directed context*: Oh boy, a turtle. Ha, the pig's got the turtle. Taking him for a walk. Pushing the turtle all over.

The results of this study revealed that the given–new contract is upheld between mothers and their infants, and is expressed in much the same ways as in speech to adults. All acoustic measurements were reliably affected by repetition: The first uses of target words were significantly longer, reached a higher F_0, traversed a larger range in F_0, and were louder than the second-mentioned versions of the same words. First-mentioned words were also significantly more likely than second-mentioned words to be judged the most stressed word in the utterances containing them, and to appear on an F_0 peak. Two syntactic focusing devices were apparent: First-mentioned words were more likely than second-mentioned words to be marked with the indefinite article, and first uses of target words also occurred in significantly shorter utterances. In all of these ways, mothers drew a clear acoustic and grammatical distinction between their uses of new and old words in a simple discourse.

All of these effects were found in both the infant- and adult-directed contexts, despite differences between the speech styles themselves. As found elsewhere (e.g., Fernald & Simon, 1984), speech to infants was significantly slower, higher and more variable in pitch, and made up of shorter utterances than speech to adults, even in this constrained context. These differences may serve to increase the impact of various focusing devices in IDS, and allow mothers to distinguish given and new words acoustically without sacrificing intelligibility. For example, we saw that speakers shorten words that have already been introduced into the conversation. In speech to adults, this can result in decreased intelligibility of words removed from their supporting context (Fowler & Housum, 1987). Mothers talking to babies, however, are speaking much more slowly in general; this may help preserve the intelligibility of repeated words. In our data, repeated words in the infant-directed context were on average actually longer than even new words in adult-directed utterances. Similarly, in both listener contexts our subjects positioned new words on utterance pitch peaks more often than old words.

---

[3]These judgments were made by three graduate students in linguistics who were given transcripts and tapes of the target-containing utterances and asked to circle the word given the most emphasis in each utterance. For any word to be considered "most stressed," it had to be marked so by at least two of the three judges.

These pitch peaks are significantly higher in IDS, making them potentially more attention-eliciting for the infant (cf. Fernald & Kuhl, 1987). The short sentences characteristic of speech to young infants may also have a focusing effect: Shorter utterances provide simpler, less distracting carrier phrases for target words. In both speech registers mothers reserved the shortest sentences for new words; however, in IDS, all of the sentences tended to be short, and therefore presumably to provide less distracting settings for even repeated words.

Interpreting Overlapping Influences on Prosodic Structure

Direct Evidence for Utterance Boundaries

The foregoing description reveals strong discourse effects on the prosodic form of utterances. Words used for a second time are acoustically diminished to a significant degree. The prosodic form of a particular utterance will thus depend on its place in a discourse as well as its syntactic structure. Furthermore, the complexity of the mapping between prosodic and linguistic structure is not counteracted by special simplifications in speech to infants. The overlapping functions of prosody, however, need not mean that information about the syntactic structure of an utterance or the discourse status of a word cannot be extracted from a representation of its physical form. The examinations of speech/syntax correspondences in IDS described in the first sections of this chapter revealed a very good correspondence between grammatically coherent sequences and prosodic utterances even without controlling for the given–new status of words: Long pauses in IDS virtually always separate sentences or well formed phrases used in isolation (Broen, 1972; Fernald & Simon, 1984; Fisher & Tokura, 1994). These pauses were preceded by quite extreme final lengthening and pitch changes, readily detectable without controlling for discourse effects.

Indirect Evidence for Phrase Boundaries

The acoustic reduction of given items in speech might also provide indirect evidence for subclausal grammatical units in speech, much as we earlier suggested pronoun subjects could aid learners in the identification of the verb phrase. Given elements will tend to occur in subject position in sentences (e.g., Bates & MacWhinney, 1982). This is true across languages, and is a detectable tendency even in English, despite other strong constraints on word order. This trend, in combination with the attenuation of given elements in speech, provides another limit on the likelihood of an audible prosodic break between subject and verb phrase. That is, even those few sentences of casual IDS that have full noun phrase subjects will tend to have physically reduced, given words in subject position.

How could this pattern affect the infant's perception of sentence structure? The physical reduction of repeated words naturally serves the discourse function of de-emphasizing given elements relative to new ones, and makes the second-mentioned reduced form "sound like" an old word to adult listeners (Fowler & Housum, 1987). As a result, the reduced form of the subject noun phrase could function like a pronoun to provide evidence for the subject/verb-phrase boundary. First, like pronouns, old words in subject position will be less attention-getting. Thus, they could help the remaining material in the utterance—the verb phrase—to stand out as figure against ground. Second, we suggested that recognition of a pronoun as a frequently occurring item could establish it as a unit within the clause. The detection of the pronoun subject again leaves the verb phrase in isolation. In the case of an open-class word presented as given in a discourse, the listener will have recently heard the same word in its new, focused form. Whenever listeners recognize the repeated word in its differing phonetic context they receive evidence that it is a separable unit of speech within the audible boundaries of the utterance. This again results in indirect evidence for the division of sentences into subjects and predicates.

CONCLUSIONS: DIRECT AND INDIRECT ACOUSTIC CUES TO SYNTAX

Our goal in this chapter was to explore how readily information about the syntactic structure of utterances could be gained by attending to their acoustic structure, taking into account both the relation between acoustic and prosodic structure, and between prosodic boundaries and syntactic ones. To address these issues we reviewed evidence from acoustic analyses of spontaneous speech addressed to infants by their mothers. These studies reveal robust correspondences between the sounds of utterances and their syntax, but also raise some difficulties for a simple version of the prosodic bootstrapping hypothesis. Despite these limitations, however, we argued that spontaneous speech to infants provides both direct and indirect acoustic support for syntactic structure.

First, we asked how infants could interpret patterns of rhythm and pitch changes as cues to any level of linguistic structure without being able to simultaneously predict the likely influences of segmental content and context, lexical and focal stress, discourse structure and emotional valence, as well as the location of phonological boundaries (e.g., Fernald & McRoberts, this volume; Klatt, 1976, 1980; Pinker, 1984). The current evidence suggests that the sheer size of acoustic changes at prosodic boundaries could provide the child with an initial source of information. The final syllables of phonological utterances are grossly different from other syllables. Furthermore, in some environments in both English and Japanese, more modest acoustic changes associated with within-utterance prosodic boundaries were also detectable, again without controlling for the myriad other influences on the sound patterns of speech. This suggests that the learner could generate at least a rough prosodic template for a language, and thus use knowledge of prosody in much the same way adults do—to anticipate utterance boundaries and to interpret acoustic patterns with less error, through knowledge of one of the influences on sound patterns.

Second, we asked how close the correspondence between prosodic and syntactic boundaries might be in spontaneous IDS. In the majority of cases, utterances arrive at the learner's ear separated into clause- or phrase-sized units, separated by pauses and marked by exaggerated final lengthening and pitch change. With these crucial boundaries marked ahead of time, false hypotheses that build grammatical structure across grammatically distinct utterances can be ruled out on perceptual grounds. However, direct prosodic evidence for the existence of grammatical units within utterances is not frequently available in spontaneous IDS. In the preceding pages we uncovered two ways in which the prosodic structure of sentences tends to systematically deviate from their syntactic structure. First, the short sentences of motherese, and the prevalence of ellipsis in Japanese and pronoun subjects in English, left few opportunities for clear prosodic markings of the boundary between subjects and predicates within utterances. This has the effect of making prosody a limited cue to syntax, lacking the depth, or hierarchical detail, of syntactic structure. Second, speakers do not use prosody only for syntactic purposes: For example, mothers provide intonational cues to given and new status that children will eventually use to track reference unambiguously through a discourse. Overlapping uses of the same communicative channel make it impossible for the prosodic shape of an utterance, even in very simple discourses, to reflect its syntax transparently.

We tried to suggest ways in which the learner could escape from these two factors limiting the availability of direct prosodic reflections of phrase structure, by combining prosodic and distributional information to construct indirect evidence for subclausal units. Distributional properties of speech to infants—the prevalence of pronoun subjects and ellipsis—could provide indirect cues to phrase structure when combined with prosodic bracketing at the utterance level. Similarly, the acoustic reduction of repeated elements, combined with their tendency to appear in subject position in sentences, could aid the learner in identifying structure within the sentence.

The picture that is beginning to emerge from this is not as simple as we might originally have hoped. Sentences in everyday speech, perhaps particularly the speech addressed to young infants, often do not immodestly display their internal hierarchical details. In order to profit from mappings between the audible form of utterances and their more covert structure, children must come to subtract the many and various influences on the physical properties of speech from one another. By allowing acoustic and distributional analyses of the linguistic input to interact, we can begin to construct a realistic picture of how young children might bootstrap their way from speech to grammar.

ACKNOWLEDGMENTS

Some of the research reported in this chapter was supported by NSF grant DBC 9113580 to the first author. We wish to thank Renee Baillargeon, Judy DeLoache, LouAnn Gerken, Kevin Miller, James Morgan and Letitia Naigles for reading and making comments on a previous draft.

REFERENCES

Bates, E., & MacWhinney, B. (1982). Functionalist approaches to grammar. In E. Wanner & L. R. Gleitman (Eds.), *Language acquisition: The state of the art* (pp. 173-218). New York: Cambridge University Press.

Beach, C. M. (1991). The interpretation of prosodic patterns at points of syntactic structure ambiguity: Evidence for cue trading relations. *Journal of Memory and Language, 30,* 644-663.

Beckman, M. (1982). Segment duration and the 'mora' in Japanese. *Phonetica, 39,* 113-135.

Bernstein Ratner, N. (1986). Durational cues which mark clause boundaries in mother-child speech. *Journal of Phonetics, 14,* 1303-1309.

Bolinger, D. (1978). Intonation across languages. In J. H. Greenberg (Ed.), *Universals of human language, Volume 2: Phonology,* (pp. 471-524). Stanford, CA: Stanford University Press.

Broen, P. (1972). *The verbal environment of the language-learning child.* ASHA Monographs, Number 17. American Speech and Hearing Society: Washington, D.C.

Butterworth, B. (1980). Evidence from pauses in speech. In B. Butterworth (Ed.), *Language production* (pp. 155-176). New York: Academic Press.

Campbell, N. (1992). Segmental elasticity and timing in Japanese speech. In Y. Tokhura, E. Vatikiotis-Bateson, & Y. Sagisaka (Eds.), *Speech perception, production, and linguistic structure* (pp. 403-418). IOS Press.

Chafe, W. L. (1976). Givenness, contrastiveness, definiteness, subjects, topics, and points of view. In C. N. Li (Ed.), *Subject and topic* (pp. 25-56). New York: Academic Press.

Clancy, P. (1985) The acquisition of Japanese. In D. I. Slobin (Ed.), *The cross-linguistic study of language acquisition: Volume 1. The data* (pp. 373-524). Hillsdale, NJ: Lawrence Erlbaum Associates,.

Clark, H. H., & Haviland, S. E. (1977). Comprehension and the given-new contract. In R. O. Freedle (Ed.), *Discourse production and comprehension.* (pp. 1-40). Norwood, NJ: Ablex.

Cooper, W., & Paccia-Cooper, J. (1980). *Syntax and speech.* Cambridge, MA: Harvard University Press.

Cooper, W., & Sorenson, J. M. (1977). Fundamental frequency contours at syntactic boundaries. *Journal of the Acoustical Society of America, 62,* 683-692.

Cruttenden, A. (1986). *Intonation.* New York: Cambridge University Press.

Crystal, T. H., & House, A. S. (1988). Segmental durations in connected-speech signals: Current results. *Journal of the Acoustical Society of America, 83,* 1553-1573.

Duez, D. (1993). Acoustic correlates of subjective pauses. *Journal of Psycholinguistic Research, 22,* 21-39.

Fernald, A. (1993). Approval and disapproval: Infant responsiveness to vocal affect in familiar and unfamiliar languages. *Child Development, 64,* 657-674.

Fernald, A. (1994). *Infants' sensitivity to word order.* Paper presented at the Linguistic Society of America, Boston, MA.

Fernald, A., & Kuhl, P. (1987). Acoustic determinants of infant preference for motherese speech. *Infant Behavior and Development, 10,* 279-293.

Fernald, A., & Mazzie, C. (1991). Prosody and focus in speech to infants and adults. *Developmental Psychology, 27,* 290-221.

Fernald, A., & Simon, T. (1984). Expanded intonation contours in mothers' speech to newborns. *Developmental Psychology, 20,* 104-113.

Fernald, A., Taeschner, T., Dunn, J., Papousek, M., Boysson-Bardies, B. de, & Fukui, I. (1989). A cross-language study of prosodic modifications in mothers' and fathers' speech to preverbal infants. *Journal of Child Language, 16,* 477-501.

Ferreira, F. (1993). Creation of prosody during sentence production. *Psychological Review, 100,* 233-253.

Fisher, C. & Tokura, H. (1994). *Acoustic cues to clause boundaries in speech to infants: Crosslinguistic evidence.* Unpublished manuscript, University of Illinois.

Fisher, C. & Tokura, H. (in press). The given-new contract in speech to infants. *Journal of Memory and Language*

Fowler, C. A., & Housum, J. (1987). Talkers' signaling of "new" and "old" words in speech and listeners' perception and use of the distinction. *Journal of Memory and Language, 26,* 489-504.

Gee, J. P., & Grosjean, F. (1983). Performance structures: A psycholinguistic and linguistic appraisal. *Cognitive Psychology, 15,* 411-458.

Gerken, L., Jusczyk, P. W., & Mandel, D. R. (1994). When prosody fails to cue syntactic structure: Nine-month-olds' sensitivity to phonological vs. syntactic phrases. *Cognition, 51,* 237-265.

Gleitman, L., Gleitman, H., Landau, B., & Wanner, E. (1988). Where learning begins: Initial representations for language learning. In F. J. Newmeyer (Ed.), *Language: Psychological and biological aspects: Volume III. Linguistics: The Cambridge Survey* (pp. 150-193). New York: Cambridge University Press.

Goldman-Eisler, F. (1972). Pauses, clauses, and sentences. *Language and Speech, 15,* 103-113.

Gordon, P. C. (1989). Context effects in recognizing syllable-final /z/ and /s/ in different phrasal positions. *Journal of the Acoustical Society of America, 86,* 1698-1707.

Grosjean, F. (1983). How long is the sentence? Prediction and prosody in the on-line processing of language. *Linguistics, 21,* 501-529.

Halliday, M. A. K. (1967). Notes on transitivity and theme in English, Part 2. *Journal of Linguistics, 3,* 199-244.

Hirschberg, J., & Pierrehumbert, J. (1986). The intonational structure of discourse. In *Proceedings of the 24th Annual Meeting of the Association for Computational Linguistics,* (pp. 136-144).

Jusczyk, P. W., Hirsh-Pasek, K., Kemler Nelson, D. G., Kennedy, L. J., Woodward, A., & Piwoz, J. (1992). Perception of acoustic correlates of major phrasal units by young infants. *Cognitive Psychology, 24,* 252-293.

Kaiki, N., & Sagisaka, Y. (1993). Prosodic characteristics of Japanese conversational speech. *IEICE Transaction Fundamentals, E76-A,* 1927-1933.

Kemler Nelson, D., Hirsh-Pasek, K., Jusczyk, P. W., & Wright Cassidy, K. (1989). How the prosodic cues in motherese might assist language learning. *Journal of Child Language, 16,* 55-68.

Klatt, D. H. (1976). Linguistic uses of segmental durations in English: Acoustic and perceptual evidence. *Journal of the Acoustical Society of America, 59,* 1208-1221.

Klatt, D. H. (1980). Speech perception: A model of acoustic-phonetic analysis and lexical access. In R.A. Cole (Ed.), *Perception and Production of Fluent Speech* (pp. 243-288). Hillsdale, NJ: Lawrence Erlbaum Associates.

Lederer, A., & Kelly, M. H. (1991). Prosodic correlates to the adjunct/complement distinction in motherese. *Papers & Reports on Child Language Development, 30,* 55-63.

Lehiste, I. (1972). The timing of utterances and linguistic boundaries. *Journal of the Acoustical Society of America, 51,* 2018-2024.

Morgan, J. (1986). *From simple input to complex grammar.* Cambridge, MA: MIT Press.

Newport, E., Gleitman, H., & Gleitman, L. R. (1977). Mother, I'd rather do it myself: Some effects and non-effects of maternal speech style. In C. E. Snow & C. A. Ferguson (Eds.), *Talking to children: Language input and acquisition* (pp. 109-149). Cambridge, England: Cambridge University Press.

Pinker, S. (1984). *Language learnability and language development*. Cambridge, MA: Harvard University Press.

Read, C., & Schreiber, P. (1982). Why short subjects are harder to find than long ones. In E. Wanner & L. R. Gleitman (Eds.), *Language acquisition: The state of the art* (pp. 78-101). New York: Cambridge University Press.

Scott, D. (1982). Duration as a cue to the perception of a phrase boundary. *Journal of the Acoustical Society of America, 71*, 996-1007.

Selkirk, E. O. (1984). *Phonology and syntax: The relation between sound and structure*. Cambridge, MA: MIT Press.

Silverman, K. (1986). F_0 segmental cues depend on intonation: The case of the rise after voiced stops. *Phonetica, 43*, 76-91.

Stern, D. N., Spieker, S., Barnett, R. K., & MacKain, K. (1983). The prosody of maternal speech: Infant age- and context-related changes. *Child Language, 10*, 1-15.

Streeter, L. (1978). Acoustic determinants of phrase boundary perception. *Journal of the Acoustical Society of America, 64*, 1582-1592.

Sugamoto, N. (1989). Pronominality: A noun-pronoun continuum. In R. Corrigan, F. Eckman, & M. Noonan (Eds.), *Current issues in linguistic theory: Volume 61. Linguistic categorization* (pp. 267-291). Philadelphia: John Benjamins Publishing Company.

Vogel, I. & Kenesei, I. (1990). Syntax and semantics in phonology. In S. Inkelas & D. Zec (Eds.), *The phonology-syntax connection*. (pp. 339-364). Chicago: University of Chicago Press.

Wales, R., & Toner, H. (1976). Intonation and ambiguity. In W. E. Cooper & E. C. T. Walker (Eds.), *Sentence processing*. (pp. 136-158). Hillsdale, NJ: Lawrence Erlbaum Associates.

Wightman, C., Shattuck-Hufnagel, S., Ostendorf, M., & Price, P. (1992). Segmental durations in the vicinity of prosodic phrase boundaries. *Journal of the Acoustical Society of America, 91*, 1707-1717.

21 Prosodic Bootstrapping: A Critical Analysis of the Argument and the Evidence

Anne Fernald and Gerald McRoberts
Stanford University

The hypothesis that young infants rely on prosodic cues in speech to bootstrap their way into syntax has received considerable attention in recent discussions of early language development (e.g., Gleitman, Gleitman, Landau, & Wanner, 1988; Hirsh-Pasek, Kemler Nelson, Jusczyk, Cassidy, Druss, & Kennedy, 1987). The appeal of the prosodic bootstrapping hypothesis is easy to understand. If the boundaries between syntactic constituents in speech were indeed reliably marked by constellations of prosodic features such as pauses, pitch contours, and vowel lengthening, this acoustic punctuation could potentially be useful to the child beginning to learn language. And if this syntax-to-prosody mapping were more distinctive and reliable in infant-directed speech (IDS) than in adult-directed speech (ADS), the prosodic structure of IDS could provide even greater support for the infant's initial efforts at parsing the speech stream. The prosodic bootstrapping hypothesis has captured the imagination of many researchers in the field on the strength of its apparent plausibility and explanatory promise.

We argue here, however, that the popularity of the prosodic bootstrapping notion has proceeded far in advance of the data necessary to support it. Although a few critical voices have been raised (e.g., Pinker, 1987), there has been insufficient attention either to the logic of the argument or to the limitations of the data. Support for the prosodic bootstrapping hypothesis rests on a selective use of indirect evidence, and some of the central findings cited in its favor need further replication. Because this hypothesis is about how the child uses prosodic cues to induce grammatical rules, it can be *directly* tested only by manipulating the relation of syntactic and prosodic units in speech to the child and assessing the effects of these manipulations on language acquisition. In the absence of direct evidence, prosodic bootstrapping advocates rely on indirect evidence to argue that prosodic features in language input are operative in the child's induction of language structure. The force of the argument lies not in any particular finding, but in the broad sweep of what appears to be convergent evidence from diverse sources. Four major categories of indirect evidence are typically cited:

Descriptive studies suggesting that characteristic prosodic features are consistently associated with syntactic boundaries in ADS (e.g., Cooper & Sorensen, 1981);

Experimental studies showing that prosodic cues influence adults' perception of syntactic boundaries (e.g., Morgan, Meier, & Newport, 1987; Streeter, 1978);

Descriptive studies indicating that prosodic cues to utterance boundaries are more exaggerated in IDS than ADS (e.g., Fernald & Mazzie, 1991; Morgan, 1986);

Developmental research suggesting that young infants are sensitive to syntax–prosody relations, even in unfamiliar languages (e.g., Hirsh-Pasek et al., 1987; Jusczyk, Hirsh-Pasek, Kemler Nelson, Kennedy, Woodward, & Piwoz, 1992).

Our goal is to look closely at each of these frequently cited sources of evidence. We begin with a discussion of cue reliability, a central notion in the prosodic bootstrapping argument that is frequently misconstrued. Our review of the literature on syntax–prosody mappings in ADS leads us to conclude that the reliability of prosodic cues to syntax has been overestimated. We come to a comparably cautious conclusion for IDS, arguing that the cue reliability of prosodic features in speech to infants has not been properly assessed and is relatively low. Finally, we review results of recent experiments attempting to replicate and extend the widely cited finding that young infants prefer to listen to speech segmented at clause boundaries (Hirsh-Pasek et al., 1987; Kemler Nelson, Hirsh-Pasek, Jusczyk, & Cassidy, 1989). These results also suggest that the prosodic bootstrapping hypothesis does not have strong *prima facie* plausibility.

CUE RELIABILITY

The issue of cue reliability is critical to the prosodic bootstrapping story because of the central claim that linguistic novices exploit low-level prosodic cues, discernible to even very young infants, to gain access to higher order linguistic structures that are not at first discernible. Cue reliability is a measure of the extent to which a cue is consistently associated with a particular structure or function and not with others, expressed numerically as "the ratio of the cases in which a cue leads to the correct conclusion, over the number of cases in which it is available" (Bates & MacWhinney, 1987, p. 164). That is, if C = the number of times when a particular cue is present and leads to the correct conclusion, and I = the number of times when that same cue is present but leads to an incorrect conclusion, then the reliability of the cue is reflected in the ratio $C/(C+I)$. In the context of interest here, cue reliability is equivalent to the conditional probability that a particular linguistic structure is present given the occurrence of a particular prosodic cue, p(structure | cue). In the debate on prosodic bootstrapping this relation has frequently been confused with a second conditional probability, p(cue I structure), which is not an appropriate measure of cue reliability.

An analogy may help to make this distinction clear. Imagine a novice electrician confronted with a cable from which 100 identical wires emerge. Forty of these wires are "hot" because they are connected to switches at the other end of the cable, while the remaining 60 are unconnected and "cold." The task of the apprentice is to identify the hot wires and connect them to a panel controlling 40 lights. Since the apprentice cannot see the other end of the cable, she initially has no idea where to begin. To help her, a supervisor takes 30 red "cue" labels and tapes each to a different hot wire. Thus the probability that a hot wire is marked with a cue label, p(cue I hot wire), is 0.75. Although 25% of the hot wires are not marked, the labels still serve as highly informative cues to structure because they occur *only* in association with hot wires and never with cold wires. The structural information these labels provide may be incomplete, but it is never misleading. Because p(hot wire I cue) is 1.0, every time the apprentice selects a wire with a red cue flag, she makes a correct choice. Now imagine a similar situation, except that the supervisor, out of perversity or ineptitude, places 30 red labels on hot wires and another 30 labels on cold wires. In this case, p(hot wire I cue) drops from 1.0 to 0.50. When the apprentice searches for the hot wires and chooses those wires marked with cue labels, she will be wrong on average half the time. However, p(cue I hot wire) remains high at 0.75, because the proportion of hot wires marked with cue labels is unchanged. What has changed is that there are now misleading cues as well, resulting in frequent false alarms. Although the probability of a red label given a hot wire is as strong as before, the cue reliability of the labels has been reduced by half. Of course, whether or not cues with a reliability of 0.50 are still useful to the learner depends on how well the learner would do with no cues at all. In this case, choosing wires randomly would yield a hot wire on average only 40% of the time. Thus it would still be marginally more effective to use the cue labels than to ignore them, although the error rate would be high in either case.

The important point here is that from the perspective of a novice who has no initial knowledge of the structure and must rely entirely on cue markers to identify the structure, it is p(structure I cue) that is the relevant conditional probability, not p(cue I structure). However, proponents of prosodic bootstrapping have relied on the second of these conditional probabilities rather than the first to build their case. As we discuss in the following sections, p(cue I structure) can be reassuringly high while p(structure I cue), the appropriate measure of cue reliability, is often quite low.

PROSODIC CUES TO SYNTACTIC UNITS IN ADULT-DIRECTED SPEECH

One line of reasoning in the prosodic bootstrapping argument is that in ADS, clause and phrase boundaries are consistently marked by pauses, pitch movement, and vowel elongation. The same few studies are typically cited to support this claim (e.g., Cooper & Paccia-Cooper, 1980), although there is an extensive literature on prosody-syntax mappings in which the findings are far from consistent. In this section, we briefly review research on linguistic and non-linguistic factors that influence the distribution of the three prosodic features associated with syntactic boundaries: pauses, fundamental frequency (F_0), and duration.

Pause Structure as a Cue to Syntax

Systematic empirical research on pauses in fluent speech began in earnest in the 1950s (e.g., Goldman-Eisler, 1951). Reviewing early research on non-linguistic determinants, Rochester (1973) cited 23 studies published from 1956 to 1970 on the effects of cognitive, affective, and social variables on pause production. Factors such as task difficulty (Levin, Silverman, & Ford, 1967), anxiety level (Pope, Blass, Siegman, & Raher, 1970), personality (Ramsey, 1968), and audience (Lay & Paivio, 1969) all affect how often hesitations occur in speech. Psycholinguists also began to explore how pause structure relates to linguistic structure. Maclay and Osgood (1959) found that pauses in spontaneous speech occurred as often within phrases as between phrase or clause boundaries, and that speakers showed striking individual differences in the distribution of pauses in their speech.

   As described earlier, the relation between pauses and syntactic constituents in speech can be viewed from two angles. One approach is to consider the probability that a syntactic boundary will be marked by a pause, p(pause | boundary). In an analysis of formal academic speech, Goldman-Eisler (1972) reported that 90% of all sentences and 52% of all clauses within sentences were bounded by pauses >250 msec. The combined probability that a pause >250 msec occurred given a clause or a sentence boundary can be estimated at 0.60 from Goldman-Eisler's data. This finding that clauses are frequently *not* marked by pauses in fluent speech is echoed in other studies as well. Garro and Parker (1982) found that restrictive relative clauses were typically preceded by little or no pause ($M = 1$ msec) and followed by very short pauses ($M = 19$ msec). Grosjean, Grosjean, and Lane (1979) also observed that NP/VP boundaries are rarely marked by pauses when the NP is short.

   In Goldman-Eisler's (1972) data, 40% of the clause boundaries were not marked by pauses. This is not in itself a problem for the prosodic bootstrapping argument, since pauses could still be reliable cues to clause structure if they occurred only at boundaries and never at other locations in the sentence. To see if this condition holds, we need to examine the cue reliability of pauses in this sample, p(clause boundary | pause). If p(clause boundary | pause) were close to 1.0, a listener with no knowledge of syntax could infer with high accuracy that a stretch of speech bounded by pauses was in fact a clause. If so, even though pauses were present only 60% of the time they were "needed," they would rarely give *wrong* information when they were present. In reality, however, pauses were as likely to occur within clauses as at clause boundaries in Goldman-Eisler's data. Looking at the number of pauses 1000 msec or longer, she noted that 119 occurred between words within clauses, while 83 occurred at within-sentence clause boundaries and 116 occurred at sentence boundaries. Even when all pauses >250 msec are taken into account, p(clause boundary | pause) is well below 0.50. This estimate is consistent with the earlier findings of Maclay and Osgood (1959) and later studies using instrumental measures that confirmed that only about 50% of pauses occur at sentence, clause, and phrase boundaries (Boomer & Dittmann, 1962; Hawkins, 1971; Henderson, Goldman-Eisler, & Skarbek, 1966). What this means is that the linguistically naive listener who relied on pauses as cues to the beginnings and endings of syntactic constituents would make incorrect inferences about half the time.

As in the hot wire scenario, the conditional probability relevant to the prosodic bootstrapping argument is p(boundary | prosodic cue), although most arguments for the plausibility of prosodic bootstrapping have been formulated the other way around, in terms of p(prosodic cue | boundary). Gleitman et al. (1988), for example, support their claim that infants could potentially rely on prosody to identify clausal units with the statement that "recent evidence suggests that there are reliable acoustic cues to clause boundaries in speech, including longer pauses, segmental lengthening, declination of fundamental frequency, and stress marking" (p. 163). However, the one study of pauses cited as evidence was by Cooper and Paccia-Cooper (1980), who showed that when speakers read ambiguous sentences to convey alternative interpretations, pause durations vary with the interpretation. Cooper and Paccia-Cooper started with theoretical linguistic units and measured associated pauses, reporting that p(pause | boundary) was high. It was not their goal to determine whether equivalent pauses occurred elsewhere in the speech stream, although from the infant's point of view, this is crucial information. Because the infant must proceed from cue-to-structure rather than from structure-to-cue, these findings tell only part of the story and not the part most relevant to the infant's task. It is interesting that clauses of different types are bounded by pauses of different durations; however, for the novice with no knowledge of what constitutes a clause, it is more important to know how often pauses serve as reliable cues to clause boundaries and how often they are misleading.

No estimate of actual cue reliability can be derived from the Cooper and Paccia-Cooper (1980) data because unreliable pauses were not assessed. Moreover, the number of unreliable pauses in that study would undoubtedly underestimate the number of unreliable pauses in a more natural speech sample. Because the sentences analyzed by Cooper and Paccia-Cooper were constructed to be ambiguous and were read in lists, they were hardly representative of spontaneous conversation. Sentences when read typically have fewer pauses than when spontaneously spoken, and the distribution of pauses differs in read and spontaneous speech (Goldman-Eisler, 1972; Howell & Kadi-Hanifi, 1991), two reasons for caution when using data from artificial laboratory studies to make generalizations about spontaneous speech. In natural conversation, pauses unrelated to syntax occur often, and numerous factors other than syntactic structure influence the frequency, duration, and location of pauses.

To summarize, Cooper and Paccia-Cooper (1980) and related studies, frequently cited in support of the prosodic bootstrapping hypothesis, do not provide convincing evidence for the potential value of pauses as cues to syntax for the infant. These studies examined only reliable pauses—those that occur at constituent boundaries. Because they were not concerned with the distribution of boundary types given a pause, they did not address the issue of cue reliability. Going back to Maclay and Osgood (1959), numerous studies show that pauses in spontaneous speech are determined by multiple factors, both non-linguistic and linguistic, and are as likely to occur within as between syntactic constituents. What this means is that the reliability of pauses as cues to clause structure is relatively low, and that the infant relying on pauses to detect clause boundaries would frequently be in error.

F_0 as a Cue to Syntax

F_0 has been proposed as another cue infants might exploit to gain access to syntactic structure. Cooper and Sorensen (1981) claimed that rise–fall F_0 patterns are associated with certain types of clause boundaries, and that F_0 tends to fall over the course of declarative sentences. However, because these claims are based on analyses of isolated sentences read in lists, their generality has been questioned. Umeda (1982) and Lieberman, Katz, Jongman, Zimmerman, and Miller (1985) found F_0 declination to be much less common in spontaneous speech than in read speech, which often consists of sentences lacking a focus of attention and produced in a mechanical fashion. When an English sentence has a clear focus, the emphasized word is typically accented using F_0 prominence (e.g., Eady, Cooper, Klouda, Mueller, & Lotts, 1986), which can disrupt the pattern of linear decline in F_0 over the contour. Non-syntactic linguistic factors such as phonological (e.g., O'Shaughnessy, 1979) and discourse structure (e.g., Eady & Cooper, 1986) also affect F_0 patterns in English speech, as well as non-linguistic factors such as social interaction variables (e.g., Apple, Streeter, & Krause, 1979) and affective state (e.g., Scherer, 1986). Given these diverse and robust sources of F_0 variability, there is little to suggest that F_0 on its own could serve as a reliable cue to syntactic structure. Although under some conditions sentences read aloud show F_0 fall–rise patterns at certain types of clause boundary (Garro & Parker, 1982), such evidence fails to address the crucial question of cue reliability. In order to demonstrate high cue reliability, it must be shown that F_0 fall–rise occurs primarily at syntactic boundaries and *not* elsewhere in the sentence, and there is no evidence indicating that this is the case.

Duration as a Cue to Syntax

Several studies show that speech segments are lengthened in phrase- and clause-final positions (e.g., Cooper, Paccia, & Lapointe, 1978; Sorensen, Cooper, W. E., & Paccia, 1978), and thus that $p(\text{cue} \mid \text{boundary})$ is relatively high. For the linguistically naive listener, however, what is most important is how often lengthening occurs at syntactic boundaries as compared to other locations. Klatt (1976) provided detailed data on segmental durations that allow us to calculate $p(\text{boundary} \mid \text{cue})$ and assess cue reliability. In an acoustic analysis of 13 sentences of connected discourse, Klatt compared the durations of segments occurring between and within syntactic constituents. To normalize for differences in intrinsic duration associated with phonetic category, the durations of vowels and consonants located at phrase and clause boundaries were compared to the median duration of the same segments averaged across all positions in the sentence. In Klatt's sample, 61 words contained vowels or consonants greater than 1.2 times their median. Of these words with lengthened segments, 42 occurred at phrase or clause boundaries, and 19 occurred elsewhere within phrasal constituents; thus the cue reliability of segmental lengthening in this sample was 0.65.

That duration is only moderately reliable as a cue to syntactic structure should not be surprising, since many of the non-linguistic factors that influence pause structure and F_0 contour in fluent speech also influence segmental duration. Duration is affected by the speaker's mood (e.g., Williams & Stevens, 1972), speech rate (e.g., Crystal & House, 1982, 1990), and degree of emphasis (e.g., Cooper, Eady, & Mueller, 1985), as well as by non-syntactic linguistic factors (e.g., House & Fairbanks, 1953). One major source of variability in vowel duration is whether or not the syllable is stressed. Crystal and House (1988) found that stressed vowels in connected discourse were twice as long on average as unstressed vowels. However, the primary source of variability in segmental duration is the phonetic category of the segment. For example, the mean duration for stressed /e/ in Klatt's (1976) corpus was 155 msec, while the mean duration for stressed /I/ was 70 msec. In a factor analysis, Klatt found that 56% of the variance in stressed vowel duration was accounted for by differences in inherent duration among vowel categories. Although vowels in phrase-final syllables were on average 40 msec longer than the median for that vowel type, this syntactic factor accounted for only 16.2% of the variance.

There is another reason to be skeptical about the claim that duration is a cue to syntax accessible to very young infants. The problem is that segmental lengthening is a *relative* measure. Given substantial differences in intrinsic duration associated with different vowel categories, lengthening can only be appreciated in relation to the inherent duration of the vowel in question. For example, a lengthened /i/ is 30 msec *shorter* in duration than a non-lengthened /e/ (Klatt, 1976). As Klatt pointed out, in order to perceive lengthening as a cue to the end of a syntactic constituent, the listener needs to know the phonetic identity of the lengthened segment. The listener must also be able to take other factors simultaneously into account to compensate for lengthening or shortening effects due to speech rate, stress, emphasis, and phonetic context. It is not clear how adult listeners manage to use durational cues without first working out various other aspects of the sentence, and it is certainly not obvious that young infants should be able to do so.

THE ROLE OF PROSODY IN ADULT SPEECH PROCESSING

So far we have reviewed research on the availability of prosodic features as *potential* cues to syntactic structure. Next we consider research on whether adults actually make use of these prosodic features in speech processing. Numerous studies have examined how prosody influences listeners' perceptions of non-linguistic dimensions of speech such as affective state (e.g., Scherer, 1986), personality (e.g., Apple et al., 1979), and intention (e.g., Pierrehumbert & Hirshberg, 1990), as well as perceptions of linguistic organization at levels other than syntax, such as phonology (e.g., Nakatani & Schaffer, 1978) and discourse structure (e.g., Fowler & Housum, 1987; Nooteboom & Kruyt, 1987). These studies are not directly relevant to prosodic bootstrapping, except as a reminder that prosody is multiply determined and serves many kinds of communicative functions. We focus here on research on perceptual effects of particular prosodic features, the interaction of prosodic and syntactic cues, and grouping cues in artificial language learning, often cited in discussions of prosodic bootstrapping.

Prosodic Cues and Boundary Perception in ADS

When syntactically ambiguous sentences differing in prosodic structure are naturally spoken, listeners can usually identify the intended interpretation (Lehiste, 1973; Price et al., 1991). To discover which prosodic cues are important in resolving ambiguities, one approach has been to manipulate particular prosodic features while holding others constant. Henderson and Nelms (1980) studied the effects of pauses on segmentation, concluding that pauses were not a salient segmentation cue. However, Scott (1982) found that pauses were sufficient as a cue to word boundaries in ambiguous sentences, although a combination of pause plus lengthening was equally effective. The limited data on F_0 contour as a cue to boundary perception are also inconsistent. de Rooij (1976) found that F_0 fall alone was not effective as a boundary cue, and that duration alone was as powerful as duration plus F_0 fall in combination. In contrast, Streeter (1978) claimed that the effects of duration and F_0 contour were additive, while Beach (1991) found evidence that pitch and durational cues are perceived as an integrated percept. Although these few parametric studies do not provide a clear picture of the relative influence of different prosodic cues on segmentation, they suggest that duration may be the most consistently effective cue, and that prosodic cues in combination are probably more powerful than in isolation.

Syntactic Boundary Perception Without Syntactic Cues

Another approach to the question of how adults use prosody to parse the speech stream has been to use natural speech in which syntactic information is lacking or inaccessible, such as nonsense strings, filtered speech, or speech in an unfamiliar language. Here the question is whether listeners can identify constituent boundaries at all using only prosodic cues, in the absence of syntactic information. Since infants are also initially in the position of having no access to syntactic cues, studies using these methods seem particularly relevant to the prosodic bootstrapping hypothesis.

Wakefield, Doughtie, and Yom (1974) and Pilon (1981) investigated sensitivity to constituent boundaries in an unfamiliar language, using Korean sentences with pauses inserted either between or within phrases. When asked which sounded more natural, American subjects tended to choose the sentence in which the pause coincided with the phrase boundary. Performance was far from perfect, however, with means varying from 43% to 80% across groups. Although cited as evidence in favor of the prosodic bootstrapping notion, these results are equivocal. First, the stimuli lacked the prosodic variability typical of natural conversation. Also, although the subjects were unfamiliar with Korean, it was not the case that syntactic cues were completely inaccessible to them. In Korean, particles used as topic markers frequently occur at the end of noun phrases, for example, and these repeated elements could have served as a reliable non-prosodic cue to the NP/VP boundary.

A more convincing approach would be to show that listeners can identify constituent boundaries in conversational speech from which all segmental information has been eliminated. However, adults find it very difficult to identify constituent boundaries using only prosodic information, even in their native language. Lehiste asked listeners to locate sentence boundaries in normal speech and speech that was either spectrally inverted (Lehiste & Wang, 1977) or low-pass filtered (Lehiste, 1979) to remove segmental content. In both studies there was substantial disagreement between listeners' judgments of boundary locations in natural and content-filtered speech. Lehiste found that 50% of the sentences identified in the content-filtered condition were not heard as sentences in the normal speech condition. These included utterances such as *Sanskrit at least as a possible* and *core of courses now of course* that were preceded and followed by pauses >250 msec and other prosodic boundary cues. When only prosodic cues were available, listeners identified these fragments as sentences; in the natural speech condition, however, syntactic cues overrode prosody and dominated listeners' judgments. In a similar study using higher quality stimuli, Kreiman (1982) also found that subjects did not hear sentence boundaries in the same locations in normal and content-filtered speech. Because there was a 30% false alarm rate with filtered speech, and 35% of the normal speech sentences were not recognized when filtered, the overall rate of disagreement was high.

These findings illustrate several points relevant to the prosodic bootstrapping debate and the cue reliability issue. Adult listeners *do* use pauses and other prosodic cues to make decisions about the locations of syntactic boundaries. But to the extent that these prosodic features are uncorrelated with syntactic units (i.e., low in cue reliability), and that no syntactic information is available, listeners make mistakes. Moreover, when syntactic information is available, listeners rely on syntactic cues to override unreliable prosodic cues in identifying constituent boundaries.

Prosodic Cues to Syntactic Structure in Artificial Languages

A third approach to the question of how prosody affects syntactic processing focuses on conditions that facilitate rule induction in artificial linguistic systems. Morgan and Newport (1981) found that subjects learned the syntax of an artificial language much more effectively when information was available about constituent structure. When words in the input sentences were grouped visually into phrasal units, subjects were able to master the constituent structure; when words were not grouped at all, or were grouped arbitrarily with respect to syntactic boundaries, subjects failed to master the grammar of the language. Morgan et al. (1987) extended these findings in studies that included three different kinds of grouping cues: prosody, function words, and concord morphology. Here too they found that when cues to the phrase structure were present in the input, subjects learned the grammar of the artificial language; however, when cues were absent or arbitrarily located, subjects failed to learn the grammar.

These findings are frequently cited in discussions of prosodic bootstrapping because they suggest that phrase structure markers such as prosodic cues are crucial for language learning. As Morgan et al. (1987) acknowledged, however, a question of concern is whether research on artificial language learning can be generalized to the acquisition of natural languages. A major problem is that in these two studies, grouping cues were either absent altogether or present but uncorrelated with syntactic structure, or they were *perfectly* correlated with syntactic structure. That is, in the two conditions in which prosodic cues were available, cue reliability was either 0 (in the Arbitrary Prosody condition) or 1.0 (in the Phrase Prosody condition). When cue reliability was 1.0, subjects were successful at figuring out the rules of the grammar; when cue reliability was 0, subjects failed to learn the grammar, just as when no cues were present at all. In real conversational speech, as we have seen, prosodic cues are often missing at constituent boundaries, and when prosodic cues do occur, they are often misleading. So what can we conclude from these results about learning under more natural conditions in which cue reliability is somewhere midway between 0 and 1.0? Because Morgan et al. did not test subjects in a "noisy cue" condition with less than perfect cue reliability, it is unknown whether listeners would master the syntax in an artificial language more analogous to real speech.

To summarize, in discussions of prosodic bootstrapping, the same few studies of prosodic cues in adult speech production and perception are cited to support broad generalizations about how prosody marks syntactic boundaries and how listeners depend on prosodic cues in decoding speech. A closer reading of the extensive literature in these areas reveals that these generalizations are misleading. In spontaneous ADS, prosodic features are only moderately reliable as cues to syntax. While listeners benefit dramatically from prosodic cues perfectly correlated with syntax, performance is poor under more natural conditions, when listeners attempt to identify syntactic boundaries using only the imperfectly correlated prosodic cues typical of conversational speech.

PROSODY AND SYNTAX IN SPEECH TO CHILDREN

Even if prosody does not map reliably onto syntactic constituents in ADS, bootstrapping may still be an important mechanism during language acquisition. It is crucial to this argument, however, that prosodic and syntactic units should be highly correlated in IDS across languages.

Prosodic Cues in IDS

Although not directly related to the cue reliability issue, several studies show that prosodic features are exaggerated in IDS. Pauses are longer in IDS than in ADS in English and other languages; in fact, the pauses between ID utterances are on average longer than the utterances themselves (e.g., Fernald, Taeschner, Dunn, Papousek, Boysson-Bardies, B., & Fukui, 1989). Lengthening in clause- and phrase-final syllables is also exaggerated in English IDS (e.g., Bernstein Ratner, 1986; Morgan, 1986), although lengthening is not a prominent boundary marker in Japanese IDS (Fisher & Tokura, this volume). Finally, F_0 modulation is greater overall in IDS than in ADS across languages (e.g., Fernald et al., 1989). These exaggerated pitch patterns serve affective and attentional functions (e.g., Fernald, 1993) and may also serve linguistic ends. Because focused nouns typically occur on final pitch peaks in English IDS (Fernald & Mazzie, 1991), utterance boundaries are often marked by dramatic F_0 movement. However, rising terminal pitch is much more common in IDS than in ADS in English, given the frequent use of questions and attentionals with infants. Ryan (1991) found that 39% of English ID utterances and 45% of Japanese ID utterances ended with rising pitch. Thus falling pitch is not the only F_0 cue to utterance boundaries in IDS.

Very few studies have examined the reliability of prosodic cues in relation to syntax in IDS. However, two of the earliest systematic studies of language input were explicitly motivated by a version of the prosodic bootstrapping hypothesis. Broen (1972) and Dale (1974) were both aware of the findings of Maclay and Osgood (1959) and others that pauses occurred at grammatical boundaries in ADS only about 50% of the time. It was these findings that prompted them to investigate pause location in relation to sentence structure in IDS. In an analysis of pauses >260 msec, Broen found that 93% of sentence boundaries were followed by a pause in IDS, as compared to 29% in ADS. In addition to reporting p(pause | boundary), Broen also provided data on cue reliability, or p(boundary | pause), which was 0.99 in IDS and 0.54 in ADS. Based on similar methods, the data in Dale's study reveal that cue reliability of pauses was 0.96 in speech to 2- to 4-year-olds. In a later study of German mothers' speech to newborns, Fernald and Simon (1984) reported that the reliability of pauses as cues to sentence boundaries was 0.98.

In addition to these studies of isolated prosodic features, Fisher and Tokura (1993, this volume) examined constellations of cues associated with syllables at word, phrase, and utterance boundaries in American and Japanese IDS. In a discriminant function analysis, 43% to 64% of what Fisher and Tokura refer to as "clausal" boundaries were correctly categorized using a combination of pause, segmental lengthening, and pitch movement as predictor variables, although there was no evidence that phrasal boundaries were prosodically marked. In terms of cue reliability, the probability that these correlated cues resulted in the correct classification of "clausal" boundaries was high, averaging 0.88 across the English and Japanese samples. Thus, although approximately 44% of the "clausal" boundaries in IDS were not identified correctly, the constellation of cues most consistently associated with such boundaries led to classification errors only 12% of the time. In other words, very few initial and medial syllables were incorrectly classified as marking "clausal" boundaries.

It is tempting to conclude from these studies that prosodic cues to syntactic structure are much more reliable in IDS than in ADS. However, there is a serious problem with this interpretation: In none of these studies were "sentences" or "clauses" rigorously defined using a linguistic criterion, as clauses are in studies of ADS. Broen (1972) and Fernald and Simon (1984) classified vocatives and exclamations as complete sentences; Fisher and Tokura (1993) categorized exclamations and elliptical utterances such as *Oh* and *Very pretty* as complete clauses, and Japanese sentence-final particles such as *ne* were also classified as "one syllable clauses." Although there is linguistic debate as to what exactly constitutes a clause—whether *He wants to go* consists of one clause or two, for example—*Oh* and *ne* would not qualify as complete clauses by any reasonable syntactic criterion. It would have been more appropriate to refer to these units of IDS as "utterances," and then to distinguish between clausal and non-clausal utterances, as defined by linguistic criteria. Using such an analysis, these investigators would probably have found that prosodic markers were no more reliably associated with clausal than with non-clausal utterance boundaries in their samples. Such data are needed to address an empirical question of central relevance to the prosodic bootstrapping argument: Are prosodic features indeed uniquely diagnostic of particular syntactic constituents in IDS? As we discuss in the next section, declaring all ID utterances to be "sentences" or "clauses" by fiat begs this important question.

The Syntactic Structure of ID Utterances

If early language input came prepackaged in clausal units, each syntactically complete and acoustically demarcated from the next, then the prosodic bootstrapping hypothesis would seem quite reasonable. The problem with this optimistic premise is that although prosody does provide robust cues to *utterance* boundaries in IDS, many of these utterances are not in fact clauses, as Fisher and Tokura (this volume) point out. In Newport's (1977) sample of maternal speech, 40% of the utterances consisted of sub-clausal fragments or stock expressions. We found a comparable distribution in an analysis of 100 American English ID utterances from each of five mothers in the Fernald et al. (1989) sample, in which fewer than half the utterances were complete single clauses. More than 40% of the utterances were sub-clausal, consisting of single or multiword fragments (*Doggy. Big black nose*), attentionals (*Hey there!*), stock expressions (*Thanks very much*), and the like. Although a small proportion of these sub-clausal utterances consisted of complete noun or verb phrases, most were sub-phrasal as well.

The fact that a substantial proportion of ID utterances are sub-clausal fragments is problematic for the prosodic bootstrapping argument. A cornerstone of this argument is the claim that if infants can exploit bottom-up cues to identify utterance boundaries, they have access to a rudimentary phrase structure description of the sentence. As Gleitman et al. put it: "if we are correct in our reading of the evidence, bracketed (and partially labeled) clausal representations are available at the initial stage of language learning, and serve as the primary linguistic data to be paired with meanings" (1988, p. 154). Using prosody to identify clausal and phrasal units, even without knowing the words, could help infants discover the rules governing the distributional patterns of the ambient language. After all, fundamental rules of English syntax such as those governing subject-verb agreement prevail within the domain of the clause, and other rules such as those specifying the distribution of determiners relative to nouns hold up only to the phrase boundary. If through prosody the infant has access to a phrase structure parsing of heard sentences, the job of discovering these constraints should be easier, since the units within which the constraints prevail would be delimited in advance. However, to the extent that the "units" demarcated by prosodic cues are highly variable in constituent structure, it is less clear how this form of prosodic prepackaging would facilitate the discovery of syntax. In the Fernald et al. (1989) sample, for example, a prosodically bounded multiword utterance might be a complete clause, or it might be a noun phrase, a verb phrase, or something else (*Up and over! Hey good job!*). An infant biased to assume that each of these prosodically isolated utterances had clausal structure would obviously run into frequent analytical difficulties.

The assumption that IDS makes syntax transparent for the infant has another problem: Even when clauses are complete, they are frequently not in canonical form. Fewer than 20% of the clausal utterances in our sample were simple declaratives, whereas the great majority were imperatives and interrogatives, a distribution similar to that reported by Newport, Gleitman, and Gleitman (1977). Newport et al. have eloquently argued that although ID utterances are typically short and focused on the here and now, it is a mistake to equate these features with syntactic "simplicity." In fact, imperatives with their missing subjects, and yes/no questions with their fronted auxiliary verbs, are in some sense syntactically more complex than the longer declarative sentences predominant in ADS. Thus even when prosodically bounded utterances in IDS do contain complete clauses, the task of discovering the phrase structure of the utterance is hardly straightforward for the infant.

How Useful Are Prosodic Cues That Are Low in Cue Reliability?

In the Fernald et al. (1989) study, utterances were defined using an acoustic criterion—as stretches of speech bounded by pauses >300 msec. The mean pause duration in American English IDS was 1312 msec. Since the mean utterance duration was only 1345 msec, such substantial pauses provided prominent boundary markers often accompanied by other prosodic cues as well. But what kinds of linguistic units were these acoustic cues actually marking? When the infant heard a pause, the probability that the pause marked a single complete clause was on average less than 0.50, and the probability that the pause marked a clause in canonical form was less than 0.10. We can conclude that prosody buys the infant *utterance* boundaries in IDS, but only sometimes clause boundaries. Since utterances as units are neutral with respect to syntax, the claim that prosodic cues give infants highly reliable access to phrase structure is not consistent with the evidence.

This does not mean that prosody provides no information to the infant. Even when prosodic cues are often misleading, it may still be better to use them than to ignore them. Low reliability cues could still be beneficial if alternative strategies for discovering clause boundaries were even less effective. For example, if the infant ignored prosodic cues and assumed that every fifth syllable marked a clause boundary, the hit rate for identifying clauses might be only 0.20. By comparison, relying on prosodic markers, even when cue reliability is only 0.50, would be much more informative, at least in principle. However, the argument that even low reliability cues are useful to the learner rests on the assumption that when the learner makes incorrect inferences based on misleading cues, there is no cost incurred. In this respect, the hot wire scenario is more straightforward than the infant's task. When using a cue label to connect a wire, the apprentice gets immediate feedback as to whether the wire is hot or cold. The infant, in contrast, initially has no way of knowing whether a prosodically bounded utterance is a clause, a phrase, or a fragment. It is not clear how the learning process would be affected by recurrent erroneous inferences, although such errors could lead to frequent incorrect generalizations, interfering with the induction of correct syntactic rules. The point here is not that prosodic features in IDS are uninformative, but rather that their reliability as cues to syntax has been overestimated in discussions of prosodic bootstrapping.

INFANTS' SENSITIVITY TO PROSODIC STRUCTURE

The fourth source of indirect evidence for the prosodic bootstrapping argument is recent developmental research purporting to demonstrate an early, possibly innate, sensitivity to prosodic structure. In these auditory preference studies, infants are presented with speech in which pauses are either coincident with syntactic units, inserted at constituent boundaries, or non-coincident, inserted within constituent units, with stimulus presentation contingent upon a sustained head turn to the appropriate side of the test booth. "Preference" is operationalized as a significantly longer mean looking/listening time during coincident trials than during non-coincident trials.

In the first of these studies, Hirsh-Pasek et al. (1987) found that 7- to 10-month-old infants listened significantly longer to coincident than to non-coincident speech. In a follow-up study, Kemler Nelson et al. (1989) found a similar listening preference with IDS but not ADS stimuli. Jusczyk (1989) then tested 4- and 6-month-old infants with coincident and non-coincident speech in both English and Polish, a language unfamiliar to the English-learning infants. They found that the younger infants preferred the more natural stimuli in both English and Polish, but that the 6-month-old American infants showed a preference only in English, no longer discriminating between the coincident and non-coincident stimuli in Polish. Finally, in a series of studies by the same research group, infants were presented with English speech stimuli edited so that pauses were coincident or non-coincident with phrase boundaries rather than clause boundaries (Jusczyk et al., 1992). Nine-month-old but not 6-month-old infants preferred the coincident stimuli, even when the speech was filtered to remove all segmental content.

These results have been interpreted as evidence that "clauses are perceptual units" for preverbal infants (e.g., Hirsh-Pasek et al., 1987). If even very young infants listen longer to natural prosody in an unfamiliar language, they must need little or no experience to establish this bias. The implication is that infants are born sensitive to clause-typical prosodic patterns, and that these clause-typical contours are universal across languages. However, exposure to a particular language begins to show its effects midway through the first year. Infants' preference for coincident over non-coincident stimuli in Polish disappears by 6 months, although the preference for coincident stimuli in the ambient language is maintained. The story for sensitivity to phrasal units is different, since a preference for stimuli with appropriately segmented phrases, even in filtered speech, is shown by 9-month-old but not by 6-month-old infants. The explanation offered is that the larger clausal units are detected first, presumably by means of a language-independent awareness of the sound shape of clausal prosody, while sensitivity to the smaller subunits develops gradually with exposure to a particular language. Jusczyk et al. (1992) were careful to point out that infant listening preferences for speech with natural syntax–prosody mappings tell us nothing about whether infants actually use prosody in segmenting speech and figuring out syntax. However, these findings are often cited as if they pointed firmly in that direction. After all, if months before speaking a word, infants can recognize where clauses and phrases begin and end using only prosodic cues, this capability could potentially be powerful in enabling infants to induce the syntactic rules of their language.

There are several reasons to resist this interpretative leap. First, the research reviewed in previous sections indicates that neither in ADS nor in IDS are clauses consistently marked by prosodic cues. Thus even if infants can discriminate between natural and interrupted prosodic contours, this finding would not justify the inference that "clauses are perceptual units" for infants. Second, because the non-coincident speech stimuli used in these experiments consisted of artificially truncated utterances, they were "unnatural" in two quite different respects. The unnatural feature that was intentionally manipulated was the disruption of the normal relation of prosodic cues to utterance boundaries, since pauses were inserted midway through utterances without the correlated cues of falling pitch and final lengthening. However, since these truncated stimuli were created by splicing into continuous speech wave-forms, they were also unnatural in the sense that human vocal tracts cannot produce such sounds. Even if carefully prepared using a wave-form editor, the non-coincident stimuli stopped abruptly at points in the utterance where the vocal tract had not closed down. Thus the offset and onset characteristics of the non-coincident stimuli were different from those of naturally produced vocalizations. Because of this con-found between prosodic and physiological unnaturalness, an alternative explanation for the findings is not ruled out: If infants indeed listen less to the non-coincident stimuli, it could be because they recognize what kinds of sounds human vocal tracts can and cannot produce and prefer physiologically possible vocalizations. This finding would also be in-teresting, but it would not provide evidence that infants are sensitive to the relation of prosodic and syntactic units in speech.

In addition to concerns about how an infant listening preference for continuous as compared to truncated utterances should be interpreted, the developmental findings need further replication. Jusczyk (1989) claimed that English-learning infants as young as 4 months show this listening preference, even in an unfamiliar language such as Polish, but that by 6 months the preference for coincident stimuli is limited to Eng-lish. It is these results that are cited most often to support the inference that infants' sensitivity to clause-typical prosody is perhaps innate and is initially language-independent, and that exposure to the ambient language in the early months reduces sensitivity to clause-typical pros-ody in languages to which the infant is not exposed. Because these findings have broad implications for theories of language development, it is essential that their replicability and generality be confirmed by other researchers working independently.

With the goal of extending these findings to other languages, we first undertook a replication of the Hirsh-Pasek et al. (1987) experiment in which 7- 10-month-old infants were presented with coincident and non-coincident stimuli in English. Our speech stimuli were based on a simple children's story called *Bye Bye Baby* (Ahlberg & Ahlberg, 1989) spoken with ID intonation. As in the original study, 1000 msec pauses were inserted either at clause boundaries or within clauses. Extreme care was taken to interrupt the waveform only at zero crossings, to avoid splicing artifacts. As in the original study, infants were tested us-ing a modified version of the auditory preference procedure developed by Fernald (1985) in which stimuli were presented laterally, contingent on a criterion headturn. The only significant procedural difference was that in the Hirsh-Pasek et al. study the observer who controlled trial on-sets and offsets stood directly behind the test booth listening to music or speech over headphones, while the observer in our study was located in a soundproof control room and viewed the infant's eyes on a video monitor. This precaution was necessary in order to eliminate any pos-sibility of observer bias, since we have found that even when music and speech maskers are presented at very high intensities, they are not completely effective at masking acoustic stimuli if the observer is located close to the loudspeakers (Fernald, Pinto, Cole, & McRoberts, in preparation). In this first study we found no significant difference between infants' mean looking/listening times to stimuli with coincident (M = 4.8 sec) and non-coincident (M = 4.2 sec) pauses.

We decided to try again with subjects at 4, 7, and 10 months of age, using a potentially more sensitive auditory preference procedure. Developed by Cooper and Aslin (1990) for use with newborns, this procedure is also effective with older infants (Asgari, Pinto, & Fernald, 1993). Because sound presentation is contingent on the infant's fixation of a central checkerboard display, headturns are not required and task demands are reduced compared to the Fernald (1985) procedure. This study included German as well as English stimuli, a comparison language chosen because of the strong similarities between German and English prosodic structure. Moreover, because the German stimuli were based on a direct translation of the *Bye Bye Baby* story, as told to an infant by a native speaker of German, we could make the coincident and non-coincident stimulus sets structurally parallel across languages. Subjects were 144 English-learning infants, 48 in each age group; half heard English, and half heard German. We found that English-learning infants did not discriminate at any age between coincident and non-coincident speech stimuli in German. Nor did 4-month-old infants discriminate between coincident and non-coincident stimuli in English. However, 7- and 10-month-old infants did respond differentially to the two stimulus types: 7-month-olds looked significantly longer during non-coincident speech trials, while 10-month-olds looked significantly longer during coincident speech trials.

The results of these studies provide only partial support for the claim that infants prefer to listen to speech in which pauses coincide with utterance boundaries, even in an unfamiliar language. Four-month-old infants failed to discriminate coincident and non-coincident stimuli in either English or German, contrary to the results of Jusczyk (1989). Only when 10-month-old infants were presented with English did we find the significant listening preference for coincident speech reported by Hirsh-Pasek et al. (1987) and Kemler Nelson et al. (1989). When 7-month-old infants listened to English, they showed a significant preference for non-coincident speech. Although this preference was in the opposite direction from that reported in previous studies, it nevertheless indicates that 7-month-old infants were able to discriminate the two types of speech stimuli.

Given these inconsistent findings across studies, what general conclusions can be drawn about infants' sensitivity to "clause-typical" prosodic units? First, the notion that very young infants show a listening preference even in unfamiliar languages is not supported by the evidence. We were unable to replicate either the finding that 4-month-old English-learning infants prefer coincident speech in English, or that they show a preference in a foreign language prosodically similar to English. Since Jusczyk, Mazuka, Mandel, Kiritani, and Hayashi (1993) also recently reported that 4½-month-old English-learning infants fail to discriminate coincident and non-coincident speech in Japanese, the evidence overall seems to suggest that a listening preference for coincident speech does not emerge until later in the first year, and may be limited to speech in the ambient language.

Second, regardless of when this listening preference emerges, it is a misinterpretation of the evidence to claim that such a preference reveals infants' sensitivity to "clausal units." Although the stimuli in all these experiments were chosen because they contained complete clauses, in this respect they were not representative of spontaneous IDS, in which almost half the utterances are not clausal units. A more limited and appropriate interpretation of the findings of Hirsh-Pasek et al. (1987) and Kemler Nelson et al. (1989), as well as the findings presented here, is that by 7 months infants have learned to discriminate *continuous vocalizations* in their own language from those that are artificially interrupted. The premise that continuous vocalizations in IDS are isomorphic with clausal constituents is false (except in experiments). Thus the broad conclusion that clauses are perceptual units for infants does not follow from these findings.

CONCLUSIONS

In the 1970s, the first systematic studies of early language input agreed that ID utterances are generally short, often fragmentary, and often non-canonical in sentence form. When Snow (1972) and others suggested that IDS might provide an ideal language lesson for the infant, Newport et al. (1977) objected strenuously and convincingly that, even though short, these often fragmentary, often non-canonical utterances are not syntactically simple, and that we could not look to the structure of the input for easy answers to the question of how children induce syntax. This argument was so convincing, in fact, that the view that simplified speech is crucial for language learning was soon eclipsed by the view that clever infants rather than accommodating mothers are the "prime movers of the acquisition process" (Gleitman, Newport, & Gleitman, 1984, p. 70).

This more nativist position assumes that infants come equipped with perceptual filters and attentional biases that enable them to exploit acoustic correlates of linguistic units in speech. However, this new vision of processing biases as critical to language acquisition does not shift the burden entirely from the input to the infant, for the following reason: Processing biases require appropriately structured input to be useful. The frog's specialized sensitivity to moving dark spots is functional only because, in the frog's world, moving dark spots correspond to prey; if moving dark spots instead mapped randomly onto objects irrelevant to frogs, such a perceptual bias would have no utility. The prosodic bootstrapping argument also requires that speech input be structured to accommodate the hypothesized processing biases of the human infant. If infants are predisposed to attend selectively to a prosodic feature such as pauses in speech, this bias would be useful in language acquisition only to the extent that pauses are actually linguistically informative. That is, implicit in the new view of the perceptually prepared infant are complementary assumptions about the nature of the input that these infant processing biases require to operate effectively.

Unfortunately, the idealized input assumed in the prosodic bootstrapping argument is at odds with the empirical evidence. More recent descriptions of early language input have characterized ID utterances in terms of prosodic boundary markers. But have these detailed acoustic analyses actually increased our understanding of key features of IDS that might facilitate syntax acquisition? Not really. If individual clauses within multiclause utterances were prosodically segmented, this would be revealing—but multiclause utterances are extremely rare in spontaneous IDS. If phrasal boundaries within single clauses were prosodically segmented, this would also be revealing, but research on ADS and IDS has shown that NP/VP boundaries are not reliably marked by prosodic cues. Thus we have not learned much new about the prosodic fine structure of ID utterances that is relevant to the discovery of syntax. Moreover, declaring all ID utterances to be "clauses" or "sentences" regardless of their actual syntactic structure does not change the fact that almost half are sub-clausal fragments. So we are essentially back where we started: When ID utterances are respecified in terms of prosodic boundary markers, they still consist of the short, often fragmentary, often non-canonical sentences described in the 1970s. And the central argument of Newport et al. (1977) is as relevant today as it was then: Whatever their pragmatic merits, the modifications in maternal speech do not provide easy access to phrase structure trees.

This is not to say that prosody is unimportant in revealing language structure—only that its potential role has been oversimplified in the prosodic bootstrapping debate as we see it. We need to get beyond the notion that prosodic cues are sufficient to give direct access to constituent structure. What we really want to know is how infants learn to make sense of their language through listening to short utterances separated by long pauses, however fragmentary and syntactically heterogeneous these utterances may be, and how prosody helps infants to exploit semantic and distributional regularities in the input that in combination and over time enable the induction of syntactic rules.

REFERENCES

Ahlberg, J., & Ahlberg, A. (1989). *Bye bye baby*. Boston, MA: Little, Brown.
Apple, W., Streeter, L. A., & Krause, R. M. (1979). Effects of pitch and speech rate on personal attributions. *Journal of Personality and Social Psychology, 37*, 715-727.

Asgari, M., Pinto, J., & Fernald, A. (1993, March). *Infants' sensitivity to musical phrase structure*. Presented at the meeting of the Society for Research on Child Development, New Orleans, LA.

Bates, E. & MacWhinney, B. (1987). Competition, variation and language learning. In B. MacWhinney (Ed.), *Mechanisms of language acquisition* (pp. 173-218). Hillsdale, NJ: Lawrence Erlbaum Associates.

Beach, C. M. (1991). The interpretation of prosodic patterns at points of syntactic structure ambiguity: Evidence for cue trading relations. *Journal of Memory and Language, 30*, 644-663.

Bernstein Ratner, N. (1986). Durational cues which mark clause boundaries in mother-child speech. *Journal of Phonetics, 14*, 1303-1309.

Boomer, D. S., & Dittmann, A. T. (1962). Hesitation pauses and juncture pauses in speech. *Language and Speech, 5*, 215-220.

Broen, P. (1972). *The verbal environment of the language-learning child*. ASHA Monographs, Number 17. Washington, DC: American Speech and Hearing Society.

Cooper, R. P., & Aslin, R. N. (1990). Preference for infant-directed speech in the first month after birth. *Child Development, 61*, 1584-1595.

Cooper, W. E., Eady, S. J., & Mueller, P. R. (1985). Acoustical aspects of contrastive stress in question-answer contexts. *Journal of the Acoustical Society of America, 77*, 2142-2156.

Cooper, W. E., Paccia, J. M., & Lapointe, S. G. (1978). Hierarchical coding in speech timing. *Cognitive Psychology, 10*, 154-177.

Cooper, W. E., & Paccia-Cooper, J. (1980). *Syntax and speech*. Cambridge, MA: Harvard University Press.

Cooper, W. E., & Sorensen, J. M. (1981). *Fundamental frequency in sentence production*. New York: Springer-Verlag.

Crystal, T. H., & House, A. S. (1982). Segmental durations in connected speech signals: Preliminary results. *Journal of the Acoustical Society of America, 72*, 705-716.

Crystal, T. H., & House, A. S. (1988). Segmental durations in connected-speech signals: Syllabic stress. *Journal of the Acoustical Society of America, 83*, 1574-1585.

Crystal, T. H., & House, A. S. (1990). Articulation rate and the duration of syllables and stress groups in connected speech. *Journal of the Acoustical Society of America, 88*, 101-112.

Dale, P. S. (1974). Hesitations in maternal speech. *Language & Speech, 17*, 174-181.

de Rooij, J. J. (1976). Perception of prosodic boundaries. *IPO Annual Progress Report, 11*, 20-24.

Eady, S. J., & Cooper, W. E. (1986). Speech intonation and focus location in matched statements and questions. *Journal of the Acoustical Society of America, 80*, 402-415.

Eady, S. J., Cooper, W. E., Klouda, G. V., Mueller, P. R., & Lotts, D. W. (1986). Acoustical characteristics of sentential focus: Narrow vs. broad and single vs. dual focus environments. *Language and Speech, 29*, 233-251.

Fernald, A. (1985). Four-month-old infants prefer to listen to motherese. *Infant Behavior and Development, 8*, 181-195.

Fernald, A. (1993). Approval and disapproval: Infant responsiveness to vocal affect in familiar and unfamiliar languages. *Child Development, 64*, 657-674.

Fernald, A., & Mazzie, C. (1991). Prosody and focus in speech to infants and adults. *Developmental Psychology, 27*, 209-221.

Fernald, A., Pinto, J. P., Cole, S., & McRoberts, G. W. (in preparation). Problems of validity and reliability in research on infant auditory preferences.

Fernald, A., & Simon, T. (1984). Expanded intonation contours in mothers' speech to newborns. *Developmental Psychology, 20*, 104-113.

Fernald, A., Taeschner, T., Dunn, J., Papousek, M., Boysson-Bardies, B., & Fukui, I. (1989). A cross-language study of prosodic modifications in mothers' and fathers' speech to preverbal infants. *Journal of Child Language, 16*, 477-501.

Fisher, C., & Tokura, H. (1993). *Acoustic clues to clause boundaries in speech to infants: Cross-linguistic evidence*. Unpublished manuscript, University of Illinois.

Fowler, C. A., & Housum, J. (1987). Talkers' signaling of "new" and "old" words in speech and listeners' perception and use of the distinction. *Journal of Memory and Language, 26*, 489-504.

Garro, L., & Parker, F. (1982). Some suprasegmental characteristics of relative clauses in English. *Journal of Phonetics, 10*, 149-161.

Gleitman, L. R., Gleitman, H., Landau, B., & Wanner, E. (1988). Where learning begins: Initial representations for language learning. In F. J. Newmeyer (Ed.), *Language: Psychological and biological aspects* (pp. 150-193). Cambridge, England: Cambridge University Press.

Gleitman, L. R., Newport, E., & Gleitman, H. (1984). The current status of the motherese hypothesis. *Journal of Child Language, 11*, 43-39.

Goldman-Eisler, F. (1951). The measurement of time sequences in conversational speech. *British Journal of Psychology, 42*, 355-362.

Goldman-Eisler, F. (1972). Pauses, clauses, sentences. *Language and Speech, 15*, 103-113.

Grosjean, F., Grosjean, L., & Lane, H. (1979). The patterns of silence: Performance structures in sentence production. *Cognitive Psychology, 11*, 58-81.

Hawkins, P. R. (1971). The syntactic location of hesitation pauses. *Language and Speech, 14*, 277-288.

Henderson, A., Goldman-Eisler, F., & Skarbek, A. (1966). Sequential temporal patterns in spontaneous speech. *Language and Speech, 9*, 207-216.

Henderson, A. I., & Nelms, S. (1980). Relative salience of intonation fall and pause as cues to the perceptual segmentation of speech in an unfamiliar language. *Journal of Psycholinguistic Research, 9*, 147-159.

Hirsh-Pasek, K., Kemler Nelson, D. G., Jusczyk, P. W., Cassidy, K. W., Druss, B., & Kennedy, L. (1987). Clauses are perceptual units for young infants. *Cognition, 26*, 269-285.

House, A. S., & Fairbanks, G. (1953). The influence of consonant environment upon the secondary acoustical characteristics of words. *Journal of the Acoustical Society of America, 25*, 105-113.

Howell, P., & Kadi-Hanifi, K. (1991). Comparison of prosodic properties between read and spontaneous speech material. *Speech Communication, 10*, 163-169.

Jusczyk, P. W. (1989, April). *Perception of cues to clausal units in native and non-native languages*. Presented at the biennial meeting of the Society for Research in Child Development, Kansas City.

Jusczyk, P. W., Hirsh-Pasek, K., Kemler Nelson, D. G., Kennedy, L. J., Woodward, A., & Piwoz, J. (1992). Perception of acoustic correlates of major phrasal units by young infants. *Cognitive Psychology, 24*, 252-293.

Jusczyk, P. W., Mazuka, R., Mandel, D., Kiritani, S., & Hayashi, A. (1993, March). *A crosslinguistic study of American and Japanese infants' perception of acoustic correlates to clausal units*. Presented at the meeting of the Society for Research on Child Development, New Orleans.

Kemler Nelson, D. G., Hirsh-Pasek, K., Jusczyk, P. W., & Cassidy, K. W. (1989). How the prosodic cues in motherese might assist language learning. *Journal of Child Language, 16*, 55-68.

Klatt, D. H. (1976). Linguistic uses of segmental duration in English: Acoustic and perceptual evidence. *Journal of the Acoustical Society of America, 59*, 1208-1221.

Kreiman, J. (1982). Perception of sentence and paragraph boundaries in natural conversation. *Journal of Phonetics, 10*, 163-175.

Lay, C. H., & Paivio, A. (1969). The effects of task difficulty and anxiety on hesitations in speech. *Canadian Journal of Behavioral Science, 1*, 25-37.

Lehiste, I. (1973). Phonetic disambiguation of syntactic ambiguity. *Glossa, 7*, 107-122.

Lehiste, I. (1979). Perception of sentence and paragraph boundaries. In B. Lindblom & S. Ohman (Eds.), *Frontiers of speech communication research.* (pp. 91-101). New York, NY: Academic Press.

Lehiste, I., & Wang, W. S.-Y. (1977). Perception of sentence and paragraph boundaries with and without semantic information. In W. U. Dressler, & O. E. Pfeiffer (Eds.), *Phonologica 1977* (pp. 277-283). Innsbruck: Institut fur Sprachwissenchaft der Universitat Innsbruck.

Levin, H., Silverman, I., & Ford, B. L. (1967). Hesitations in children's speech during explanation and description. *Journal of Verbal Behavior and Verbal Learning, 6,* 560-564.

Lieberman, P., Katz, W., Jongman, A., Zimmerman, R., & Miller, M. (1985). Measures of the sentence intonation of read and spontaneous speech in American English. *Journal of the Acoustical Society of America, 77,* 649-657.

Maclay, H., & Osgood, C. E. (1959). Hesitation phenomena in spontaneous English speech. *Word, 15,* 19-44.

Morgan, J. L. (1986). *From simple input to complex grammar.* Cambridge, MA: MIT Press.

Morgan, J. L., Meier, R. P., & Newport, E. L. (1987). Structural packaging in the input to language learning: Contributions of prosodic and morphological marking of phrases to the acquisition of language. *Cognitive Psychology, 19,* 498-550.

Morgan, J. L., & Newport, E. L. (1981). The role of constituent structure in the induction of an artificial language. *Journal of Verbal Learning and Verbal Behavior, 20,* 67-85.

Nakatani, L. H., & Schaffer, J. A. (1978). Hearing "words" without words: Prosodic cues for word perception. *Journal of the Acoustical Society of America, 63,* 234-245.

Newport, E. L. (1977). Motherese: The speech of mothers to young children. In N. Castellan, D. B. Pisoni & G. Potts (Eds.), *Cognitive theory* (Vol. 2, pp. 177-217). Hillsdale, NJ: Lawrence Erlbaum Associates.

Newport, E. L., Gleitman, H., & Gleitman, L. R. (1977). Mother, I'd rather do it myself; Some effects and non-effects of maternal speech style. In C. E. Snow & C. A. Ferguson (Eds.), *Talking to children: Language input and acquisition* (pp. 109-149). Cambridge, England: Cambridge University Press.

Nooteboom, S. G., & Kruyt, J. G. (1987). Accents, focus distribution, and the perceived distribution of given and new information: An experiment. *Journal of the Acoustical Society of America, 82,* 1512-1524.

O'Shaughnessy, D. O. (1979). Linguistic features in fundamental frequency patterns. *Journal of Phonetics, 7,* 119-145.

Pierrehumbert, J., & Hirschberg, J. (1990). The meaning of intonational contours in the interpretation of discourse. In P. R. Cohen, J. Morgan, & M. L. Pollack (Eds.), *Intentions in communication* (pp. 271-311). Cambridge, MA: MIT Press.

Pilon, R. (1981). Segmentation of speech in a foreign language. *Journal of Psycholinguistic Research, 10,* 113-122.

Pinker, S. (1987). The bootstrapping problem in language acquisition. In B. MacWhinney (Ed.), *Mechanisms of language acquisition* (pp. 399-441). Hillsdale, NJ: Lawrence Erlbaum Associates.

Pope, B., Blass, T., Siegman, A. W., & Raher, J. (1970). Anxiety and depression in speech. *Journal of Consulting and Clinical Psychology, 35,* 128-133.

Price, P. J., Ostendorf, M., Shattuck-Hufnagel, S., & Fong, C. (1991). The use of prosody in syntactic disambiguation. *Journal of the Acoustical Society of America, 90,* 2956-2970.

Ramsey, R. W. (1968). Speech patterns and personality. *Language and Speech, 11,* 54-63.

Rochester, S. R. (1973). The significance of pauses in spontaneous speech. *Journal of Psycholinguistic Research, 2,* 51-81.

Ryan, S. (1991). *Pitch contours in Japanese mothers' speech to infants.* Unpublished manuscript, Stanford University.

Scherer, K. R. (1986). Vocal affect expression: A review and a model for future research. *Psychological Bulletin, 99,* 143-165.

Scott, D. R. (1982). Duration as a cue to the perception of a phrase boundary. *Journal of the Acoustical Society of America, 71,* 996-1007.

Snow, C. E. (1972). Mothers' speech to children learning language. *Child Development, 43,* 549-565.

Sorensen, J. M., Cooper, W. E., & Paccia, J. M. (1978). Speech timing of grammatical categories. *Cognition, 6,* 135-153.

Streeter, L. A. (1978). Acoustic determinants of phrase boundary perception. *Journal of the Acoustical Society of America, 64,* 1582-1592.

Umeda, N. (1982). "F_0 declination" is situation dependent. *Journal of Phonetics, 10,* 279-290.

Wakefield, J. A. J., Doughtie, E. B., & Yom, B.-H. L. (1974). The identification of structural components of an unknown language. *Journal of Psycholinguistic Research, 3,* 261-269.

Williams, C. E., & Stevens, K. N. (1972). Emotions and speech: Some acoustical correlates. *Journal of the Acoustical Society of America, 52*, 1238-1250.

22 Syntactic Units, Prosody, and Psychological Reality During Infancy

Peter W. Jusczyk
State University of New York at Buffalo

Deborah G. Kemler Nelson
Swarthmore College

For many years, the issue of how the infant extracts the relevant syntactic units from the speech signal was not seriously addressed in language acquisition research. Instead, most studies of language acquisition assumed that the input was already segmented into discrete words and proceeded from that point to investigate how the infant arrived at the syntactic organization that characterizes the native language. However, as investigators struggled with how the infant eventually discovers the organization that works for his or her native language, it became apparent that one should no longer overlook the possibility that the speech signal might actually provide some cues to the underlying syntactic organization.

The notion that there are potential cues to syntactic organization in the acoustic signal has a fairly long history in language acquisition research. Indeed, the notion was first raised when language acquisition research began in earnest in the 1960s. McNeill (1966) considered, and then dismissed, the possibility that the infant could derive information about syntactic structures from the acoustic signal. Drawing on Lieberman's (1965) work, he pointed to the fact that units derived from the acoustic signal do not necessarily correspond to the critical units in the linguistic analysis of the utterances. In fact, he believed that information from the acoustic signal would prove useful to the child only if the child already had access to the underlying grammatical units.

McNeill's arguments were actually directed at whether there was *sufficient* information in the speech signal to pull out the syntactic structure. He never did claim that there was no useful information about syntactic organization to be derived from the acoustic signal. Nevertheless, more than a decade passed before investigators such as Peters (1983) and Gleitman and Wanner (1982) once again seriously considered the possibility that the prosody of speech directed to children could provide cues to important grammatical units. The basic notion was that aspects of the hierarchical arrangement of grammatical categories within a sentence might be reflected in its prosodic organization. Thus, attention to prosodic groupings could provide the child with a starting point for extracting the syntactic organization of utterances in the native language (e.g., Gleitman, Gleitman, Landau, & Wanner, 1988; Morgan, 1986). One change in this view from the earlier position is that prosody is considered to be only one of the kinds of properties of the input that could be used to reveal the underlying syntactic organization of the native language. For instance, in their investigation of the kinds of local cues that could help in illuminating syntactic organization, Morgan, Meier, and Newport (1987) found that learning was facilitated not only by prosody but also by the presence of concord morphology and function words.

What conditions must hold in order to take seriously the possibility of prosodic bootstrapping? First, there must be some indication that there are acoustic correlates of syntactic organization present in speech. Second, the potential prosodic correlates must be ones that infants are able to detect in speech. Third, there must be some indication that infants actually rely on these correlates in organizing the input. With respect to the first of these conditions, there is now ample evidence of at least some prosodic marking of syntactic units in speech directed to both adults (Lehiste, 1973; Nakatani & Dukes, 1977; Price, Ostendorf, Shattuck-Hufnagel, & Fong, 1991; Scott, 1982) and to children (Bernstein-Ratner, 1985; Fisher, 1991; Lederer & Kelly, 1991) For instance, across a wide range of different languages, clause boundaries are often marked in prosody by pauses, changes in syllable durations, and in pitch contours (Cruttenden, 1986). The remainder of the chapter examines the available evidence concerning the latter two conditions.

SENSITIVITY TO PROSODIC MARKERS IN THE INPUT

Any potential prosodic correlates to syntactic structure must be ones that infants are able to detect in listening to fluent speech. Much of the early research that we conducted (in collaboration with Hirsh-Pasek) was directed at this issue. Our approach to this problem was to investigate how infants react to different ways of partitioning a particular utterance. We reasoned that if infants detect some perceptual organization to fluent speech, they may prefer to listen to speech that, when artificially segmented, is partitioned to coincide with the syntactic units that are represented in the utterance. For example, if clauses are perceptual units for infants, then infants might prefer listening to speech samples in which pauses are inserted at clause boundaries as opposed to in the middle of clauses. In our first investigation (Hirsh-Pasek, Kemler Nelson, Jusczyk, Wright Cassidy, Druss, & Kennedy, 1987), we recorded speech from a mother talking to her 18-month-old child. We selected a number of 15–25 sec passages from this recording and made two modified versions of each sample. The two versions of a particular sample were made by inserting artificial 1 sec pauses either at clause boundaries (coincident versions) or in the middle of clauses (non-coincident versions).

A headturn preference paradigm was used to test 9-month-old American infants on these samples.[1] The infant was seated on the parent's lap in the center of a three-sided enclosure. On the surface directly facing the infant was a green light, mounted at eye level, that could be flashed to attract attention to the center. A red light was mounted on each of the two side-panels and behind each of these was a small loudspeaker. An experimenter, seated behind the center panel, observed the infant through a small hole. She initiated and terminated trials, and recorded looking times by controlling a response box that was linked to a PDP 11/73 computer. At the start of an experimental trial, the green light on the center panel began to flash. When the experimenter was satisfied that the infant was facing straight ahead, she pressed a button on the response box that turned off the green light and caused the two red side-panel lights to flash. Coincident versions of the samples were initiated by looks to one side of the enclosure and non-coincident versions to the other. When the infant oriented in the direction of one of the side lights, the experimenter pressed another button that initiated the speech sample and began timing the infant's looking time. Whenever the infant looked away, the experimenter pressed another button that stopped the timer and, if the infant looked away for more than 2 sec, terminated the trial.[2] (For a fuller description of the original procedure the reader should consult Hirsh-Pasek et al., 1987, and for more recent versions of the procedure see Jusczyk, Kemler Nelson, Hirsh-Pasek, Kennedy, Woodward, & Piwoz, 1992.)

In their original study, Hirsh-Pasek et al. recorded both the direction and duration of looking on a given trial. However, only the durational measure proved effective in differentiating the infants' responses to the two types of samples (i.e., coincident vs. non-coincident). The results indicated that the 9-month-olds listened significantly longer to the coincident than to the non-coincident versions of the samples. This finding was verified and extended in subsequent studies that revealed longer listening times for speech segmented at clause boundaries, even for infants as young as 4½ months of age (Jusczyk, 1989).

How certain can we be that infants were responding to the prosodic organization, rather than some other information available in these ut-

---

[1]It has been suggested to us that a more descriptive name for this procedure might be something like "visually indexed listening preference procedure." This would avoid confusion with the "conditioned headturning procedure" that has been used by other laboratories (e.g., see Werker et al., this volume). Although we are sympathetic to the suggestion about the name for our procedure, the label "headturn preference procedure" is the one that has been used most often previously. Renaming it now might only cause more confusion.

[2]Beginning with the investigation by Jusczyk et al. (1992) the procedure was changed so that when the center light is turned off, only one of the two red side-panel lights flashes on a given trial. Timing of the trial begins once the infant orients to the light. This change was made because the earlier investigations had proven the duration measure to be much more sensitive than was the directional measure. The procedural change also eliminates the possibility that infants might develop a response bias to one particular side.

terances? To investigate this issue, we examined whether the prosodic information alone was sufficient to produce the longer listening times to the coincident samples (Jusczyk, 1989). For this purpose, we low-pass filtered the coincident and non-coincident samples at 400 Hz to eliminate most of the available phonetic information in the samples. Six-month-old infants exposed to these low-pass filtered samples displayed the same listening preferences for the coincident versions. These results suggest that infants are sensitive to information in prosodic patterns that might serve to segment the speech stream into linguistically relevant units such as clauses.

What is the basis of infants' sensitivity to prosodic marking of clausal units? Have they developed this sensitivity as a result of their experience with native language patterns, or is there a more general basis for the way in which they respond? There are indications that the kinds of prosodic changes that occur at clause boundaries in English also occur for many other languages (Cruttenden, 1986). Hence, it may be that infants are responding preferentially to the coincident versions of the samples, not because they have picked up something specific to English prosodic structure. Rather, their responsiveness to these types of changes may reflect a more general bias for processing auditory input. Some support for the latter view comes from other studies that we have conducted. First, $4^{1}/_{2}$-month-old American infants also listened significantly longer to coincident versions of samples in an unfamiliar language (Polish) than they did to non-coincident versions (Jusczyk, 1989). Second, studies with musical stimuli (Mozart minuets) indicate that $4^{1}/_{2}$-month-olds listen significantly longer to samples with pauses inserted at musical phrase boundaries than they do to samples with pauses inserted in the middle of musical phrases (Jusczyk & Krumhansl, 1993; Krumhansl & Jusczyk, 1990). Interestingly enough, the cues that appear to signal musical phrase boundaries for infants are a decline in pitch and a lengthening of the final note at the musical phrase boundary. These cues parallel ones associated with clause boundaries (i.e., decline in pitch and clause-final syllable lengthening). Consequently, young infants' sensitivity to prosodic markers of clausal units may be an aspect of a more general tendency associated with auditory event perception.

Although sensitivity to prosodic markers of clausal units is certainly of use to infants in segmenting fluent speech, it would not take them very far towards discovering the syntactic organization of utterances in the native language. This is because acquiring the syntax of a language requires learning about the organization of units inside clauses. Consequently, we were interested in the extent to which infants are sensitive to potential prosodic cues about sub-clausal units such as subject or predicate phrases (Jusczyk et al., 1992). Using materials drawn from either child-directed spontaneous speech or from stories read to a child, we inserted pauses either at boundaries between subject and predicate phrases (coincident versions) or at locations in the middle of phrases (non-coincident versions). Nine-month-olds, but not 6-month-olds, proved to be sensitive to the location of these artificial pauses. Specifically, only at 9 months of age was there an indication that infants listened significantly longer to coincident versions than they did to the non-coincident versions.

The failure of 6-month-olds to respond to potential prosodic markers of phrasal units is interesting in view of the fact that infants this age do respond to prosodic marking of clausal units. One possible reason for the discrepancy has to do with the fact that there may be considerably more cross-linguistic variability in prosodic marking of phrasal units than of clausal units. Consider that some languages (e.g., English) use word order constraints to signal important syntactic relations, whereas other languages allow great freedom in word order (e.g., Polish) and use extensive case-marking systems to convey syntactic relations. Because case marking languages have considerable flexibility in ordering words that appear together in the same clause, it seems reasonable to expect that they would differ from word order languages in degree or type of prosodic marking for phrasal units. Consequently, language learners may well have to become more attuned to the sound patterns characteristic of the native language before they can detect any potential prosodic marking of sub-clausal units. In any case, it looks as though, by 9 months of age, American infants have developed some sensitivity to possible prosodic markers of major phrasal units (i.e., Subject and Predicate phrases) in English.

Although the prosodic organization of the language appears to provide the learner with a start toward working out the syntactic organization of the native language, it seems likely that it will only carry the learner so far. Even if the infant is able to detect the prosodic organization of child-directed speech, it will not always be possible to read the syntactic organization from the prosody. Many other factors (e.g., pragmatic intent, emotional tone, contrastive stress, etc.) can also affect the prosodic organization of sentences (Fairbanks & Pronovost, 1939; Williams & Stevens, 1972). Moreover, as has been noted in many contemporary accounts of prosodic phonology, prosodic boundaries do not always map directly onto syntactic ones (Hayes, 1989; Nespor & Vogel, 1986; Selkirk, 1981). Indeed, there are mismatches in the prosodic and syntactic organizations of even the simple kinds of sentences directed to children just beginning to acquire language. Consider the difference between the following two sentences.

1. Ellen threw the ball.
2. She threw the ball.

In (1), the talker is likely to produce prosodic boundary cues after the subject NP, "Ellen." However, in (2), even 2-year-old talkers (Gerken, 1991, 1994) are likely to either produce no prosodic boundary cues or to produce them between the verb, "threw," and the object NP, "the ball." This is because a weakly stressed pronoun subject tends to be phonologically joined (or "cliticized") to a following stressed verb. In other words, in cases like (2), in contrast to (1), the subject and verb tend to form a prosodic unit. Consequently, there is no prosodic marking of the syntactic boundary between the subject and the predicate phrases in cases of this sort.

These considerations bring up the interesting question of how infants might respond to utterances in which there is a mismatch between prosodic and syntactic boundaries. Remarkably, only a small percentage of the spontaneous speech samples (about 15%) used by Jusczyk et al. contained potential mismatches of the sort found in (2) and these tended to be interspersed with cases such as (1) throughout the different passages.[3] For this reason, it is probably not surprising that infants in this study listened longer to passages with pauses inserted between the Subject and Predicate Phrases.

To examine how infants respond to prosody–syntax mismatches, Gerken, Jusczyk, and Mandel (1994) constructed new stimulus materials that allowed for a systematic comparison between infants' responses to sentences with pronoun subjects, as in (2), and sentences with lexical NP subjects, as in (1). Half of the infants heard pairs of passages that only contained sentences with lexical noun phrase subjects like the following.

> 3. This is a story about a little boy named Sammy. Sammy is a baseball player. Sammy can run fast. And Sammy never misses a ball. Every Saturday, Sammy plays baseball in the park.

The other half of the infants heard passages in which, after a lead-in sentence, all remaining sentences had a pronoun subject such as the following.

> 4. This is a story about a little boy named Sammy. He is a baseball player. He can run fast. And he never misses a ball. Every Saturday, he plays baseball in the park.

Coincident versions of both types of passages were prepared by inserting a 1 sec pause in all sentences (after the lead-in sentence) between the subject and predicate phrases. Non-coincident versions had the same number of pauses inserted but between the verb and its complement. Nine-month-olds who heard the sentences with lexical NP subjects behaved exactly like the infants in the Jusczyk et al. study (viz., they listened significantly longer to samples in which pauses were inserted between the subject and verb phrases than to ones in which pauses were inserted between the verb and object NP phrases). However, the 9-month-olds who heard the sentences with pronoun subjects did not show a significant preference for either type of segmentation of the input. The latter results were consistent with the speech patterns of the talker who had recorded the passages. She typically produced no sen-

---

[3]The storybook samples that were used in other experiments from this study were actually constructed so as to contain long subject noun phrases. None of these sentences had pronoun subjects. Thus, these materials maximized the likelihood that the syntactic break between the subject and predicate phrases would correspond to a prosodic boundary.

tence-internal prosodic boundary cues for the sentences with pronoun subjects.

Of course, English-learning children eventually have to be able to extract information about the internal organization of sentences with pronoun subjects. How could they begin to do this given the apparent absence of prosodic marking of the subjects-predicate boundary in such sentences? One possibility is that they use other (nonprosodic) cues to work out the syntactic relations of such sentences (for suggestions of other potential cues, see Morgan et al., 1987). Another possibility is that learners may be able to benefit by contrasting cases in which pronouns and verbs belong to the same prosodic group with those in which they belong to different groups. Resolving the conflict in prosodic organization across these situations could actually lead the learner towards the discovery of the syntactic organization. Naturally, such a solution assumes that the learner has access to such contrasting cases in the input and is able to recognize the similarities that exist across these (e.g., the presence of familiar words or word sequences).

In fact, there are indications that the necessary contrasting cases are readily available in the input that the learner receives. In sentences that involve yes–no questions, there is a tendency for the pronoun and auxiliary to form a prosodic group that may be separate from the verb. For example, a talker tends to impose a prosodic boundary just before the verb in an utterance like "Did she / throw the ball?" In these cases, the prosodic input favors a marking of the boundary between the pronoun and the main verb. But are infants sensitive to these markers? In a follow-up experiment, Gerken, Jusczyk, and Mandel (1994) constructed passages with sentences involving inversions between a pronoun and an auxiliary (i.e., yes–no questions). Pauses were inserted either before or after the main verb in these sentences to create the coincident and non-coincident versions. Nine-month-olds listened significantly longer to versions in which the pauses occurred between the subject and verb phrases (i.e., the coincident versions). The implication of these findings is that 9-month-olds are sensitive to the prosodic break between the pronoun and main verb in such sentences. So, in some situations, they may be able to assign a phrase with a pronoun subject to a separate prosodic group other than the one that includes the predicate phrase. This suggests that they are, at least, positioned to notice contrasting cases in which pronouns and verbs belong sometimes to the same and other times to different prosodic groups.

To summarize to this point, it appears that there is some prosodic marking of syntactic units in speech directed to children, and that infants are sensitive to these potential markers. However, the correlation between prosodic and syntactic units is less than perfect. In cases in which the two diverge, prosodic cues may provide the infant with no, or even misleading, information about the syntactic constituents of the sentence. Resolution of any mismatches between prosody and syntax may lead to further discoveries about the underlying syntactic organization of the input.

DOES PROSODY HELP INFANTS IN ORGANIZING THE INPUT?

Given that infants demonstrate some sensitivity to potential prosodic markers of syntactic units, we can ask when they might actually begin using this information in segmenting speech. With respect to the way that prosodic bootstrapping unfolds, it could be that sensitivity to prosodic markers actually develops before the groupings available in the prosody are used to organize the information provided in fluent speech. Alternatively, it may be that infants are able to make immediate use of their sensitivity to prosodic markers as a means for organizing the input.

How can we determine when the organization that is potentially available in the prosody begins to play a significant role in speech processing? That is, how are we to know that infants are truly organizing the incoming speech signal into units such as clauses or phrases? The problem here is akin to one that early psycholinguistic researchers faced when trying to convince skeptical behaviorists that certain units of linguistic analysis corresponded to psychologically real processing units for listeners. A tack for proponents of prosodic bootstrapping is to take the approach that the early psycholinguists used to convince the rest of the field that clauses and phrases do correspond to units of psychological processing. One means by which the early psycholinguists were able to make their case was to show that linguistic units tend to be natural units for encoding and remembering information conveyed in speech.

A method used successfully with adults to demonstrate that linguistic units are actually used in on-line speech processing was to show that the organization provided by the linguistic structures had an impact on what information was remembered. Specifically, it was shown that adults could better remember information from stimuli with a linguistic, as opposed to arbitrary, organization (e.g., Epstein, 1961). Analogously, one can ask whether, for the language learner, a sensitivity to prosodic information also affords an organizational structure for encoding and remembering speech information.

Mandel, Jusczyk, and Kemler Nelson (1994) investigated whether the availability of prosodic organization actually enhances infants' memory for what they hear. Two-month-olds were tested using the high amplitude sucking procedure. This method had been used effectively in the past to investigate infants' memory for speech sounds (Jusczyk, 1985; Jusczyk, Pisoni, & Mullennix, 1992). To determine the role that sentential prosody might play in organizing infants' memory for speech, Mandel et al. contrasted conditions in which prosodic information was available to conditions in which it was not. In particular, they examined whether the sound properties of words that are prosodically linked within a single clause are better remembered by infants than are the sound properties of the same words when they were produced as individual items from a list. If prosody really helps in perceptual organization during on-line speech processing, then memory for words should be better in the sentential context. Alternatively, one could actually make a case on certain perceptual grounds for predicting the opposite pattern of results (i.e., better performance in the list conditions than in the sentence conditions). This is because the words in the list condition were all produced in citation form, whereas the phonetic characteristics of those words produced in sentential contexts are more apt to be influenced by the phonetic characteristics of surrounding words. It is well known that words produced in fluent speech contexts are often less clearly articulated and more difficult to perceive when excised from context than the same words produced in citation form (Lieberman, 1963; Pollack & Pickett, 1964).

The sentential materials for the experiment were 3 sentences that had been recorded and selected from a larger group of unrelated sentences. The list materials were selected from a longer list of unrelated words. The words from the list were excised and rearranged to form 3 different word sequences that were ordered identically to the 3 sentences. The overall durations of the list sequences were equated to the comparable sentences. Half of the infants in the study heard the sentences; the other half heard the lists. During the preshift phase of the experiment, each criterion sucking response resulted in the presentation of either a single sentence or list sequence (e.g., "The rat chased white mice"). For a given infant, the same sentence or list sequence was played throughout the preshift phase. When the infant's sucking response habituated to this stimulus, the preshift phase ended and was followed by a two-minute silent interval in which a series of colorful slides was presented. Then the postshift phase began. The infants heard either the same stimulus as in the preshift phase (control), one that differed by a single word (1 phonetic change, e.g., "The cat chased white mice"), or one that differed by two words (2 phonetic changes, e.g., "The cat raced white mice"). The results indicated that infants were more likely to increase their sucking in response to changes involving two words rather than one, but, most importantly, that performance was significantly better for the sentential materials than for the lists. Thus, even 2-month-olds are apparently able to benefit from the organization offered by sentential prosody in remembering speech information. This suggests not only that infants are sensitive to prosodic markers in the speech stream, but that sensitivity to prosodic units may play a role in how infants, even very young infants, remember speech.

The full extent of infants' abilities to use prosodic information in organizing the input is still to be determined. One further set of questions is whether infants can use prosodic information that corresponds to sub-clausal units to serve the memory-enhancing function that sentential prosody has been shown to serve in 2-month-olds. However, because our earlier work indicates that sensitivity to sub-clausal markings does not develop until around 9 months of age, we would not expect to see sub-clausal prosody play this kind of role until at least that time. Relevant investigation of 9-month-olds will have to use new procedures because the HAS procedure cannot be used with infants this old. An additional set of further questions pertains to the possible functional role of prosodic units not only in enhancing the memorability of speech, but also in determining exactly how the speech stream is segmented. Once again, new methodologies applicable to older infants need to be developed to answer such questions.

We have made some progress on a somewhat different kind of question about the psychological reality of the prosodic and syntactic structure of sentences in 9-month-olds' processing of speech. In collaboration with LouAnn Gerken, we asked how infants' attention to a set of sentences is affected by the kinds of variablity—including structural variability—within the set. Consider the following set of sentences.

5. The farmer's wife heard the devout man in church.
6. The bus driver saw the big truck on the curb.
7. The farmer's wife heard that the brown cow escaped.

Sentences (5) and (6) have the same syntactic and prosodic structures, but sentence (7), which has a sentential complementizer, does not. One of the questions that we posed was whether infants would prefer to listen to a set of sentences with variable structure as opposed to a set in which the structure is held constant. Thus, in a modification of the headturn preference procedure, one group of 9-month-olds was familiarized with the same-structure sentence pair, (5) and (6), and another group with the different-structure pair, (6) and (7). At the time of test, both groups heard both the familiar pair and a pair of new sentences that was created by simply exchanging the subject noun phrases of the two familiar sentences.[4] For example in the different-structure condition, infants heard

8. The farmer's wife saw the big truck on the curb.
9. The bus driver heard that the brown cow escaped.

Our results indicated that infants listened longer to sentences within the set that had structural variability (i.e., the different-structure set) than they did to the ones without it (i.e., the same-structure set). In other words, on the sentences that the two groups of infants heard in common (the best point of comparison), infants in the different-structure condition listened longer than did infants in the same-structure condition.

Further comparisons suggest that what is attention-getting about the different-structure sentences is not simply their overall variability, but

---

[4]Note that in order to avoid any discontinuities or other unnaturalness in the prosody, these new sentences were not prepared by cross-splicing the original sentences. Rather, the same talker who recorded the original sentences also recorded versions of the new sentences in the context of other filler sentences.

the fact that their variability has to do with sentence structure. That is, the sentences contain the same words within different prosodic (and syntactic) structures. Support for this conclusion comes from other conditions tested in the study. In these conditions, the new sentences that the infants heard in the test phase were composed of entirely different words from the ones heard during the familiarization phase (e.g., "Five little boys ate oatmeal for their breakfast" and "The zoo keeper fed the elephants at the zoo"). Infants in these conditions who experienced variability at the word level (either alone or in combination with structural variability) listened significantly less than did infants who had heard the different-structure condition in which familiar words were exchanged.

Overall, this pattern of differential attention is suggestive of an interesting and arguably very useful listening bias on the part of 9-month-olds: *Pay particular attention to sets of sentences in which the same words get re-used in different prosodic and (syntactic) structures.* It is exactly this type of attention to cross-sentential cues to phrase structure that Morgan, Meier, and Newport (1989) found was useful to adult subjects in learning the complex aspects of syntax of artificial grammars. Moreover, recasts and repetitions of these sorts have been found to occur frequently in the input to language learning children (e.g., Newport, 1977; Snow, 1972; and see also Ratner, this volume). Thus, the fact that infants are apparently prone to attend to such structural variations lends credence to the view that these sorts of structural variations may serve as an important source of information about phrasal organization in the native language. If evidence for such a bias continues to hold up in follow-up work that we are conducting with Gerken, we will have established a novel kind of evidence for the psychological reality of prosodic cues correlated with syntactic structures in infants' processing of speech.

In summary, there are some indications that infants' processing of speech information is affected by some aspects of the underlying structural organization of sentences. The organization provided by sentential prosody appears to enhance memory for speech information even in 2-month-olds. Moreover, 9-month-olds' listening behavior provides some indication that they may be sensitive to differences in the structural organization of sentences. Much more information about the impact of prosodic organization on infants' speech processing is required to adequately assess the validity of the prosodic bootstrapping hypothesis. Nevertheless, the available evidence is certainly consistent with the view that infants may be able to use prosodic organization to help in recovering aspects of the syntactic organization of native language input.

BEYOND PROSODY

Although the prosodic organization of speech may be an obvious place to look for cues about syntactic units and their structural relations, there may be other aspects of the signal that can be exploited for the same purposes. For example, as Morgan et al. (1987) noted, re-occurring syllabic patterns could provide indications about case relations or even cues to syntactic categories (as in the case of function words). Moreover, the presence of other regularly occurring features in native language sound patterns might reveal something about the presence of word boundaries in the speech signal. In fact, Morgan (1994) found evidence that 8-month-olds benefit from the presence of regular rhythmic and distributional properties in processing strings of syllables. In addition, there have been suggestions that listeners could draw on information about typical native language word stress patterns (see Cutler, this volume) to help with the task of segmenting fluent speech into words.

Similarly, some have suggested that knowledge of native language phonotactic constraints could also play a role in segmenting words from fluent speech (Church, 1987). For example, in English, the acoustic characteristics of /t/ differ according to its context in syllables. In the initial positions of syllables /t/ is aspirated and realized as the phonetic segment [tʰ]. However, /t/ is unaspirated (i.e., [t]) when it occurs in syllable-final position. Thus, the listener, who is able to detect the difference between [tʰ] and [t], could conceivably use this information about these positional constraints as a help in determining boundaries between successive words.

Might these sorts of segmental differences be useful to infants in partitioning the speech stream? Two recent investigations have examined whether infants possess the necessary prerequisite capacities to benefit from any systematic segmental cues to word boundaries. Christophe, Dupoux, Bertoncini, and Mehler (submitted) examined whether French newborns could distinguish two types of bisyllables—one of which spanned a word boundary (e.g., "mati" in "panorama typique") and the other of which did not (e.g., "mati" in "mathematician"). Newborns were able to distinguish bisyllables with the word boundary from those without it. Hohne and Jusczyk (1994) conducted a similar investigation with American 2-month-olds listening to English stimuli. Specifically, they presented infants with pairs such as "nitrate" and "night rate." The allophones of /t/ and /r/ differ across these two utterances. In particular, whereas the allophone of /t/ in "nitrate" is aspirated, retroflexed, and released, in "night rate" the allophone of /t/ is unaspirated, not retroflexed, and unreleased. Similarly, the /r/ in "nitrate" is devoiced, but in "night rate" the /r/ is voiced. These allophonic differences are a potential source of information about the locus of word boundaries in English. Hohne and Jusczyk found that 2-month-olds were able to distinguish these kinds of allophonic differences even when other potentially distinguishing features such as prosody and vowel length were held constant. Thus, both of these studies indicate that infants possess the necessary discriminative capacities to make use of the kinds of segmental cues that could signal word boundaries. Whether and when they might begin to apply these capacities to segmenting fluent speech remains to be determined.

In any case, for these properties to be useful in the task of language acquisition, the learner must also be sensitive to the way that sounds pattern in the input. There is increasing evidence that even in the first year of life, infants are developing sensitivity to regularities in native language sound patterns. For example, Jusczyk, Cutler and Redanz (1993a) found that by 9 months, American infants listen longer to words that follow the predominant strong–weak stress pattern of English words. At the same age, infants also show some sensitivity to the constraints that the native language imposes on the possible orders of phonetic segments that can appear in its words. So when presented with the opportunity to listen to lists of isolated unfamiliar words, either in their own language or in a foreign language, both Dutch and American 9-month-olds listen longer to the lists from their own native language (Jusczyk, Friederici, Wessels, Svenkerud, & Jusczyk, 1993b). Moreover, even when listening to phonetic sequences that are permissible in their target language, 9-month-olds listen longer to ones that appear with high frequency in native language words than they do to ones that appear with low frequency (Jusczyk, Charles-Luce, & Luce, 1994). Such findings indicate that infants are engaged in learning about native language sound patterns long before they reach their first birthdays. Could infants' sensitivity to regularities in native language sound patterns also be an indication that they are beginning to segment fluent speech, and perhaps, learning to recognize familiar words in such contexts? If so, then this might provide another important foothold for working out the syntactic organization of the native language.

There are reports that infants begin comprehending at least some words at around 9 months of age (Benedict, 1979; Huttenlocher, 1974). However, there is very little information available on how infants this age might come to recognize and learn words from the speech stream. One possibility is that they first learn to identify words heard in isolation and then match their representations of these words to patterns heard in fluent speech (Suomi, 1993). However, there are some serious hurdles for this approach to overcome. First, the acoustic characteristics of a word spoken in sentential context may differ considerably from one spoken in isolation (Klatt, 1980). For example, a word spoken in a sentential context is apt to differ considerably in its overall duration than the same word spoken in isolation. Second, the acoustic characteristics of words spoken in sentential contexts may blend with those of surrounding words. Third, certain sound patterns associated with monosyllabic words (e.g., "can") may occur as parts of larger words (e.g., "cancer," "toucan," "uncanny," "candidate," etc.). Thus, the listener who matches "can" to any of these words ends up misparsing the signal. Fourth, some words in the language, such as function words, are unlikely ever to be heard in isolation, so these will have to be learned in some other manner. Consequently, even if some word learning does occur by first recognizing the sound pattern of a word in isolation, there must also be other routes to learning words. One such alternative is that when children are taught new words in sentential contexts, these items are placed in prominent positions in the utterance—such as at the ends of sentences (Woodward & Aslin, 1990). Christophe, Dupoux, and Mehler (1992) also suggested that segmental duration cues could provide a source of information about the location of word boundaries.

To begin to explore how and when infants begin to recognize words in fluent speech, Jusczyk and Aslin (in press) adapted the headturn preference procedure. They asked whether infants who were familiarized with a particular word, heard in isolation, would be more likely to listen to sentences containing that word. Four different monosyllabic words were chosen for the study: "feet," "bike," "cup," and "dog." These words were chosen for their sound qualities. They all have reasonably clear onsets and offsets, and they also contrast in their vowel qualities. Words were used instead of nonwords to ensure that they were not unduly emphasized when they appeared in sentential contexts. Fifteen repetitions of each word were recorded by the same talker. In addition, she also recorded four different passages, each one containing 6 different sentences. For a given passage, the same test word (e.g., "cup") appeared in all 6 sentences. The position of the test word within the sentences was varied so that it occurred twice at the beginning, middle, and end of the sentences. An example of one of the passages, the one designed around the word "cup," is the following:

10. "The cup was bright and shiny. A clown drank from the red cup. The other one picked up the big cup. His cup was filled with milk. Meg put her cup back on the table. Some milk from your cup spilled on the rug."

At the start of each experimental session, $7^1/_2$-month-old infants were familiarized with two of the words on alternating trials until they accumulated at least 30 sec of listening time to each word. Half of the infants were familiarized with "cup" and "dog" and the other half were familiarized with "bike" and "feet." Then the test phase began. During this phase, each of the four passages was played. The passages were randomly ordered within a block of four passages. There were 4 such blocks during the test phase. Listening times to each of the passages were recorded to determine whether infants listened longer to the passages containing the familiarized target words. The results indicated that the passages with the familiarized target words had significantly longer listening times than the ones with the unfamiliar target words.

Can we be certain that the infants' listening times to the passages were really the result of being familiarized with the words? After all, at least 3 of the words (i.e., "feet," "cup," and "dog") are ones that one might reasonably expect infants to hear with some frequency. Is it possible that prior experience with these words influenced the way that they listened to the passages during the test phase? Jusczyk and Aslin examined this possibility in two ways. At each test session, the infants' parents completed a questionnaire. The questionnaire asked about the words that they thought their infant "knew," and asked the parents to rate the likelihood that the infants knew the familiar or unfamiliar targets. There was no indication that the infants' prior knowledge of the words played any significant role in the listening times recorded in the experiment. Nor was there any indication, irrespective of the initial familiarization period, that infants found one of the passages simply more interesting to listen to. On the basis of these results, Jusczyk and Aslin concluded that exposure to the target words in isolation made them more likely to attend to passages containing these words. Thus, $7^{1}/_{2}$-month-olds demonstrate some capacity to recognize a word in sentential contexts after first hearing it in isolation.

A subsequent experiment was conducted with 6-month-olds to ascertain whether even younger infants would listen longer to the passages with the familiarized target words. In contrast to the $7^{1}/_{2}$-month-olds, 6-month-olds who were first familiarized with monosyllabic words, heard in isolation, did not display any significant tendency to listen longer to the passages with the familiarized target words. Thus, the ability to recognize the occurrence of a particular word in a fluent speech context may begin to develop some time between 6 and $7^{1}/_{2}$ months of age.

Although the capacity that $7^{1}/_{2}$-month-olds displayed in going from isolated words to words in sentential contexts is impressive, one could argue that it is a lot easier to learn words this way than the other way around. That is, the task for learners would seem to be considerably more difficult if they had to learn the word first from sentential contexts. This is because the acoustic characteristics of different tokens of the same word are apt to be influenced by surrounding items in fluent speech (Liberman & Studdert-Kennedy, 1978; Mills, 1980a, 1980b). For this reason, Jusczyk and Aslin decided to familiarize the infants with two of the passages first and then see whether the infants would listen longer to the target words that appeared in these. Infants were exposed to words in sentential contexts and then tested for their attention to words in isolation. During the familiarization phase, on alternate trials, the infants heard two of the passages until they accumulated 45 sec of listening time to each. In the test phase, the stimuli were the repetitions of the four target words produced in isolation (e.g., "dog," "dog," "dog," ... , "dog"). Evidently the infants had some capacity to recognize the repeated word from the passages because they listened significantly longer to the target words from these passages.

Could it have been that the infants were successful because the target words were more strongly emphasized in the sentences than the surrounding words? Acoustic analyses conducted on the passages indicated that this was not the case. The target words were seldom the first or even second most strongly stressed words in the sentences. In fact, in terms of their relative amplitudes, sometimes the target words were even the fourth most stressed items in the sentences.

To this point, Jusczyk and Aslin's study left unresolved the question of just how precisely detailed the infants' representations of the words are in this situation. For example, were the infants really responding to the presence of a particular word, or only a familiar sound from the word, such as its vowel or syllable rhyme? To address this issue, an additional experiment was conducted in which $7\frac{1}{2}$-month-olds were first familiarized with nonwords such as "tup" and "zeet" that were phonetically and acoustically highly similar to target words in the passages (i. e., "cup" and "feet"). If the infants in the previous experiments were responding not to the whole word, but only to a portion of it, then infants in this new experiment should also have listened longer to the passages containing words phonetically similar to the nonwords heard during the familiarization period (e.g., passages with "cup" after hearing "tup"). In fact, the infants did not display any significant tendency to listen longer to the passages with words that were highly similar to the nonwords heard during the familiarization period. These findings suggest that infants listening to the passages are doing more than responding to the presence of a salient vowel or syllable rhyme. Rather, it appears that they have fairly detailed representations of items from the familiarization period and recognize the occurrence of these items in the sentential contexts. Of course, there are many issues yet to be resolved concerning the circumstances under which infants are able to recognize words in fluent speech contexts. Nevertheless, it does appear that, by $7\frac{1}{2}$ months, infants have at least some rudimentary capacity to detect the occurrence of a particular word in sentential contexts. That word recognition processes may begin to develop at this time seems consistent with the earlier conclusion that, at this same age, infants are learning about fine-grained properties of native language sound patterns (Jusczyk et al., 1993b; Jusczyk et al., 1994).

PUTTING THINGS TOGETHER: A FIRST PASS

Let us review what we now know about infants' sensitivity to native language sound patterns. There is evidence that infants as young as $4\frac{1}{2}$ months of age are sensitive to prosodic markers of clausal units in the input. Sensitivity to potential units within clauses appears some time between 6 and 9 months of age. However, it is apparent that even in the kinds of input likely to be directed to infants learning language, prosodic boundaries do not always line up consistently with major phrasal boundaries. This suggests that infants cannot rely solely on prosodic markers as indicators of important syntactic units in the input. Nevertheless, at the same time that sensitivity to the prosodic organization of speech in the native language is developing, infants seem to be picking up information about the distribution of more fine-grained properties in the input. Learning something about the possible orderings of sounds within native language words and about predominant stress and rhythmic patterns of these words may not only be helpful in acquiring a vocabulary, but could also assist in segmenting fluent speech. Ultimately, infants' success at recovering the underlying syntactic categories and their organization depends on their ability to segment utterances into the correct sequences of words.

Suppose that attention to prosodic organization allows the 9-month-old to make a rough categorization of the input into a set of phrase-sized units. Assume that as a first pass, it would be useful for the infant to divide the clause into a subject and predicate phrase. In some cases (e.g., with lexical noun subjects), the prosodic units will be in accord with the major syntactic constituents of the sentence. However, in other cases (e.g., with pronoun subjects), the infant may receive either no information about the location of the subject and predicate phrases or information about another potential syntactic boundary (e.g., the one between a verb and its complement). In the latter instance, the infant has found information about a boundary, but may be misled about the hierarchical arrangement of the syntactic constituents.

How might infants learn to discern when prosodic organization provides an accurate guide to the underlying syntactic organization? One possibility is that they draw on other sources of information that are available in the speech signal. For instance, as they learn words, and begin to recognize words in fluent speech, they may be able to use information about the distributional properties of these words in utterances. Recognition that an item like "she" is, at least, sometimes found in a slot before the predicate may help in analyzing the input in those situations in which the subject and predicate occur within the same prosodic group. Of course, in order for this to work the infant not only needs to have some capacity for recognizing words, but also must be attentive to those situations when the right sort of contrastive information is available. In other words, they need to extract cross-sentential cues, as well as those that occur locally within a sentence (Morgan et al., 1989). The fact that infants in our ongoing study (in collaboration with Gerken) listen significantly longer to materials that involved familiar words arranged into different sentence structures is encouraging in this regard.

In the end, it seems unlikely that attention to prosodic organization alone will be able to take the infant much beyond a simple bracketing of the input. It is hard to see how labeled brackets (i.e., a detailed hierarchical arrangement of syntactic categories) could fall out of the prosody alone. Nevertheless, even a relatively simple unlabeled bracketing could help narrow the range of possibilities in any distributional analysis relating to the possible positions of words in the input. Furthermore, the fact that 9-month-olds display some sensitivity to the distributional properties of fine-grained features of native language sound patterns (Jusczyk et al., 1994) suggests that infants may be capable of performing similar analyses with respect to words. Consequently, an explanation that combines prosodic bootstrapping with sensitivity to other recurring patterns in the input has appeal as an account of how infants get started in learning about the syntactic organization of their native language. To go the full route, though, they will need additional help from other sources in deriving the appropriate syntactic categories and their organization (for suggestions about some of these possible sources, see Gleitman et al., 1988; Gleitman, 1990; Morgan, 1986; Morgan et al., 1987; Pinker, 1989).

CONCLUSIONS

Perceptual studies with infants have an important role to play in establishing the validity of prosodic bootstrapping models. Such studies provide critical information about the psychological reality of prosodic information for infants by demonstrating their sensitivity and attentiveness to the prosodic organization of speech input. The initial studies in this area indicate that infants are indeed sensitive to at least some aspects of prosodic organization. Furthermore, there is some evidence to suggest that the prosodic structures may have psychological reality in helping the infant encode and remember information in the speech signal. At the same time, there are indications that infants' preferences for segmentations of the input that preserve syntactic phrasal units may only hold for situations in which the prosodic and syntactic organizations coincide. However, prosodic packaging may provide the type of perceptual precategorization that allows the infant to segment the input in a way that makes the discovery of syntactic constituents more likely. It appears that prosodic markers are only one of a number of possible probabilistic sources of information that infants may rely on to recover the constituent structure of utterances.

ACKNOWLEDGMENTS

Preparation of this chapter was facilitated by a research grant from NICHD (#15795) to PWJ. The authors wish to thank Jim Morgan, Ann Marie Jusczyk, Denise Mandel, and Alice Turk for helpful comments they made on an earlier version.

REFERENCES

Benedict, H. (1979). Early lexical development: Comprehension and production. *Journal of Child Language, 6*, 183-201.
Bernstein-Ratner, N. (1985, November). Cues which mark clause-boundaries in mother-child speech. Paper presented at *ASHA Convention,*
Christophe, A., Dupoux, E., Bertoncini, J., & Mehler, J. (submitted). *Do infants perceive word boundaries? An empirical approach to the bootstrapping problem for lexical acquisition.*
Christophe, A., Dupoux, E., & Mehler, J. (1992). How do infants extract words from the speech stream? *Papers and Reports on Child Language Development, 31.*
Church, K. (1987). Phonological parsing and lexical retrieval. *Cognition, 25,* 53-69.
Cruttenden, A. (1986). *Intonation.* Cambridge, England: Cambridge University Press.
Epstein, W. (1961). The influence of syntactical structure on learning. *American Journal of Psychology, 74,* 80-85.
Fairbanks, G., & Pronovost, W. (1939). An experimental study of the pitch characteristics of the voice during the expression of emotion. *Speech Monographs, 6,* 87-104.
Fisher, C. L. (1991, April). *Prosodic cues to phrase structure in infant directed speech.* Paper presented at Stanford Child Language Research Forum, Stanford, CA.
Gerken, L. A. (1991). The metrical basis for children's subjectless sentences. *Journal of Memory and Language, 30,* 431-451.

Gerken, L. A. (1994). Young children's representation of prosodic phonology: Evidence from English-speakers' weak syllable omissions. *Journal of Memory and Language, 33,* 19-38.

Gerken, L. A., Jusczyk, P. W., & Mandel, D. R. (1994). When prosody fails to cue syntactic structure: Nine-month-olds' sensitivity to phonological *vs.* syntactic phrases. *Cognition, 51,* 237-265.

Gleitman, L., Gleitman, H., Landau, B., & Wanner, E. (1988). Where the learning begins: Initial representations for language learning. In F. Newmeyer (Ed.), *The Cambridge Linguistic Survey* (pp. 150-193). Cambridge, MA: Harvard University Press.

Gleitman, L., & Wanner, E. (1982). Language acquisition: The state of the state of the art. In E. Wanner & L. Gleitman (Eds.), *Language acquisition: The state of the art* (pp. 3-48). Cambridge, England: Cambridge University Press.

Gleitman, L. R. (1990). The structural sources of verb meanings. *Language Acquisition, 1,* 1-55.

Hayes, B. (1989). The prosodic hierarchy in meter. In P. Kiparsky & G. Youmans (Eds.) *Phonetics and phonology: Rhythm and meter* (pp. 201-260). San Diego, CA: Academic Press.

Hirsh-Pasek, K., Kemler Nelson, D. G., Jusczyk, P. W., Wright Cassidy, K., Druss, B., & Kennedy, L. (1987). Clauses are perceptual units for young infants. *Cognition, 26,* 269-286.

Hohne, E. A., & Jusczyk, P. W. (1994). Two-month-old infants' sensitivity to allophonic differences. *Perception & Psychophysics, 56,* 613-623.

Huttenlocher, J. (1974). The origins of language comprehension. In R. L. Solso (Ed.), *Theories in cognitive psychology* (pp. 331-368). New York: Wiley.

Jusczyk, P. W. (1985). The high amplitude sucking procedure as a methodological tool in speech perception research. In G. Gottlieb & N. A. Krasnegor (Eds.), *Measurement of audition and vision in the first year of postnatal life: A methodological overview* (pp. 195-222). Norwood, NJ: Ablex.

Jusczyk, P. W. (1989, April). *Perception of cues to clausal units in native and non-native languages.* Paper presented at the biennial meeting of the Society for Research in Child Development, Kansas City, Missouri.

Jusczyk, P. W., & Aslin, R. N. (in press). Recognition of familiar patterns in fluent speech by 7 1/2-month-old infants. *Cognitive Psychology.*

Jusczyk, P. W., Charles-Luce, J., & Luce, P. (1994). Infants' sensitivity to phonotactic patterns in the native language. *Journal of Memory and Language, 33,* 630-645

Jusczyk, P. W., Cutler, A., & Redanz, N. (1993a). Preference for the predominant stress patterns of English words. *Child Development.*

Jusczyk, P. W., Friederici, A. D., Wessels, J., Svenkerud, V. Y., & Jusczyk, A. M. (1993b). Infants' sensitivity to the sound patterns of native language words. *Journal of Memory and Language.*

Jusczyk, P. W., Kemler Nelson, D. G., Hirsh-Pasek, K., Kennedy, L., Woodward, A., & Piwoz, J. (1992). Perception of acoustic correlates of major phrasal units by young infants. *Cognitive Psychology, 24,* 252-293.

Jusczyk, P. W., & Krumhansl, C. (1993). Pitch and rhythmic patterns affecting infants' sensitivity to musical phrase structure. *Journal of Experimental Psychology: Human Perception and Performance, 19,* 1-14.

Jusczyk, P. W., Pisoni, D. B., & Mullennix, J. (1992). Some consequences of stimulus variability on speech processing by 2-month old infants. *Cognition, 43,* 253-291.

Klatt, D. H. (1980). Speech perception: A model of acoustic-phonetic analysis and lexical access. In R. A. Cole (Ed.), *Perception and production of fluent speech* (pp. 243-288). Hillsdale, NJ: Lawrence Erlbaum Associates.

Krumhansl, C. L., & Jusczyk, P. W. (1990). Infants' perception of phrase structure in music. *Psychological Science, 1,* 70-73.

Lederer, A., & Kelly, M. H. (1991). Prosodic correlates to the adjunct/complement distinction in motherese. *Papers & Reports on Child Language Development, 30,* 55-63.

Lehiste, I. (1973). Phonetic disambiguation of syntactic ambiguity. *Glossa, 7,* 107-122.

Liberman, A. M., & Studdert-Kennedy, M. (1978). Phonetic perception. In R. Held, H. W. Leibowicz, & H. L. Teuber (Eds.), *Handbook of sensory physiology* (pp. 143-178). Berlin: Springer-Verlag.

Lieberman, P. (1963). Some effects of semantic and grammatical context on the production and perception of speech. *Language and Speech, 6*, 172-179.

Lieberman, P. (1965). On the acoustic basis of the perception of intonation by linguists. *Word, 21*, 40-54.

Mandel, D. R., Jusczyk, P. W., & Kemler Nelson, D. G. (1994). Does sentential prosody help infants organize and remember speech information? *Cognition, 53*, 155-180.

McNeill, D. (1966). Developmental psycholinguistics. In F. Smith & G. A. Miller (Eds.), *The genesis of language* (pp. 15-84). Cambridge, MA: MIT Press.

Mills, C. B. (1980a). Effects of context on reaction time to phonemes. *Journal of Verbal Learning and Verbal Behavior, 19*, 75-83.

Mills, C. B. (1980b). Effects of the match between listener expectancies and coarticulatory cues on the perception of speech. *Journal of Experimental Psychology: Human Perception and Performance, 6*, 528-535.

Morgan, J. L. (1986). *From simple input to complex grammar.* Cambridge, MA: MIT Press.

Morgan, J. L. (1994). Converging measures of preverbal speech segmentation. *Infant Behavior and Development. 17*, 389-403.

Morgan, J. L., Meier, R. P., & Newport, E. L. (1987). Structural packaging in the input to language learning: Contributions of prosodic and morphological marking of phrases to the acquisition of language? *Cognitive Psychology, 19*, 498-550.

Morgan, J. L., Meier, R. P., & Newport, E. L. (1989). Facilitating the acquisition of syntax with cross-sentential cues to phrase structure. *Journal of Memory and Language, 28*, 360-374.

Nakatani, L., & Dukes, K. (1977). Locus of segmental cues for word juncture. *Journal of the Acoustical Society of America, 62*, 714-719.

Nespor, M., & Vogel, I. (1986). *Prosodic phonology.* Dordrecht: Foris.

Newport, E. L. (1977). Motherese: The speech of mothers to young children. In N. Castellan, D. B. Pisoni, & G. Potts (Eds.), *Cognitive theory* (Vol. 2, pp. 177-217). Hillsdale, NJ: Lawrence Erlbaum Associates.

Peters, A. (1983). *The units of language acquisition.* Cambridge, England: Cambridge University Press.

Pinker, S. (1989). *Learnability and cognition.* Cambridge, MA: MIT Press.

Pollack, I., & Pickett, J. M. (1964). The intelligibility of excerpts from conversation. *Language and Speech, 6*, 161-171.

Price, P. J., Ostendorf, M., Shattuck-Hufnagel, S., & Fong, C. (1991). The use of prosody in syntactic disambiguation. *Journal of the Acoustical Society of America, 90*, 2956-2970.

Scott, D. R. (1982). Duration as a cue to the perception of a phrase boundary. *Journal of the Acoustical Society of America, 71*, 996-1007.

Selkirk, E. (1981). On the nature of phonological representation. In T. Myers, J. Laver, & J. Anderson (Eds.), *The cognitive representation of speech* (pp. 379-388). Amsterdam: North Holland.

Snow, C. E. (1972). Mothers' speech to children learning language. *Child Development, 43*, 549-565.

Suomi, K. (1993). An outline of a developmental model of adult phonological organization and behavior. *Journal of Phonetics, 21*, 29-60.

Williams, C. E., & Stevens, K. N. (1972). Emotions and speech: Some acoustic correlates. *Journal of the Acoustical Society of America, 52*, 233-248.

Woodward, J. Z., & Aslin, R. N. (1990, April). *Segmentation cues in maternal speech to infants.* Poster presented at the International Conference on Infant Studies, Montreal.

PART V

SPEECH AND THE ACQUISITION OF LANGUAGE

23 Phonological and Distributional Information in Syntax Acquisition

LouAnn Gerken
State University of New York at Buffalo

Syntax can be characterized as a system of rules that apply to a hierarchical arrangement of distributionally defined lexical and phrasal categories. Given this characterization, children must solve at least three potentially distinct problems in order to acquire the syntactic structure of their language. First, they must be able to locate words and phrases in the continuous stream of speech, a problem sometimes called *segmentation* (e.g., Gerken, Landau, & Remez, 1990; Gleitman & Wanner, 1982; Gleitman, Gleitman, Landau, & Wanner, 1988; Morgan, Meier, & Newport, 1987). Second, they must be able to distinguish among words and phrases of different types (e.g., noun, noun phrase, etc.), a problem sometimes called *labeling* (Gerken & McIntosh, 1993; Gerken et al., 1990). And third, children must discover the hierarchical arrangement of words and phrases; I refer to this as the *structure* problem.

In this chapter, I discuss how infants and children might use a combination of phonological and distributional information to solve these problems. In particular, I suggest that learners employ prosody (intonation and rhythm), function morphemes (e.g., articles and verb inflections), and cross-sentence comparisons to solve the segmentation, labeling, and structure problems, respectively. In support of this proposal, I present perception and production data from 9- to 12-month-old infants and 21- to 30-month-old children showing that they are sensitive to the requisite phonological and distributional information. Where possible, I also attempt to draw parallels between infant perceptual abilities and young children's language perception and production.

Before examining the developmental data, let us consider two important issues that figure in the discussion. First, the phonological information that learners might employ in the service of syntax acquisition is carried in the acoustic signal. Therefore it is possible that learners are universally predisposed to perceive or attend to some salient *acoustic* features of the speech stream, and this universal perceptual bias might aid them in syntax acquisition (e.g., Echols & Newport, 1992; Gleitman & Wanner, 1982). However, as I illustrate in the subsequent sections, the acquisition data suggest that learners develop a sensitivity to those acoustic properties that are important for meaning in the particular language they are learning and that they employ this *phonological* knowledge in service of syntax acquisition. Thus, my proposal assumes that learners already have some representation of language-specific phonology before they can use this information in syntax acquisition.

The second point that figures heavily in the subsequent sections concerns language learners' use of distributional information in syntax acquisition. It has long been noted that an unconstrained distributional analysis of a language cannot result in the correct grammar (e.g., Chomsky, 1965; Morgan et al., 1987). In order to be potentially successful, any proposal that involves distributional analysis must be concerned with restricting the domain over which the analysis is performed. Therefore, in my discussion of function morphemes and cross-sentence comparisons, I speculate on how the learner might restrict the domain of distributional analysis.

PROSODY AND THE SEGMENTATION PROBLEM

Prosodic changes, such as pausing, syllable lengthening, and pitch resetting, tend to occur at clause and phrase boundaries (e.g., Cooper, 1975; Cooper & Paccia-Cooper, 1980; Klatt, 1975). Several researchers have proposed that young listeners might use salient prosodic changes to cue the locations of syntactic units in the speech stream (Gleitman et al., 1988; Gleitman & Wanner, 1982; Hirsh-Pasek et al., 1987; Jusczyk et al., 1992; Kemler Nelson et al., 1989; Morgan, 1986; Morgan & Newport, 1981; Morgan et al., 1987; Peters, 1983, 1985, in press). In support of this hypothesis, research by Jusczyk and his colleagues demonstrated that 9-month-olds, but not 6-month-olds, listened longer to passages in which pauses were inserted at major syntactic boundaries than when pauses were inserted at non-boundary positions (Jusczyk et al., 1992). Infants continued to demonstrate this listening preference even when the passages were low-pass filtered to leave intact only prosodic information.

One interpretation of these data concerns a tendency for two or more prosodic changes to co-occur at syntactic boundaries. For example, pausing might tend to be accompanied by pitch change in English sentences (Jusczyk et al., 1992). Thus, pauses inserted at boundary positions preserved normal co-occurrence patterns, while pauses inserted at non-boundary positions did not. On this interpretation, 9-month-olds' listening preference reflects their sensitivity to configurations of prosodic cues. The fact that 6-month-olds did not show a reliable listening preference suggests that learners must discover the particular configurations of prosodic cues in the target language and that this discovery takes place some time between 6 and 9 months of age. The notion that infants discover language-specific prosodic patterns during the second half of the first year is consistent with research showing that they also lose their sensitivity to non-native segmental contrasts during this period (e.g., Werker & Tees, 1984; Werker, Lloyd, Pegg, & Polka, this volume; but see Best, McRoberts, & Sithole, 1988). Perhaps infants can use their growing sensitivity to language-specific prosodic patterns to begin to solve the segmentation problem.

Evidence that prosody continues to be important for segmentation in early childhood comes from a study by Gerken and McIntosh (1993) on children's sensitivity to function morphemes (also see next section). Twenty-one- to 28-month-old children heard sentences asking them to point to a picture of a named target noun, which was preceded by either a grammatical article (1a) or an ungrammatical auxiliary (1b).[1] All sentences were generated on DECtalk text-to-speech synthesizer. Some of the children heard the standard female voice (Beautiful Betty), and others heard the standard male voice (Perfect Paul). Children with MLUs over 1.50 morphemes per utterance were better able to identify the correct picture in grammatical than ungrammatical sentences, regardless of the voice in which sentences were presented. But children with MLUs under 1.50 morphemes, who produced no articles in their spontaneous speech, showed better comprehension of sentences containing grammatical function morphemes only when these sentences were presented in the female voice. One difference between the male and female synthesized voices used in the experiment was prosodic in nature. In particular, the female voice exhibited a higher pitch and wider pitch excursions than the male voice, and it is possible that these properties allowed children to better segment the sentences into linguistically relevant units. Perhaps it is only when a first pass segmentation was achieved that the lower MLU children were able to distinguish between grammatical and ungrammatical sentences.

1a. Find the dog for me.
1b. Find was dog for me.

In addition to phrases and clauses, learners must also be able to locate individual words in the speech stream. A potential prosodic cue for word segmentation is the canonical patterns of strong and weak syllables exhibited by the words of many languages. For example, the vast majority of English words begin with a strong syllable (Cutler & Carter, 1987; also see Cutler, this volume) and tend to exhibit an alternating pattern of strong and weak syllables (e.g., Hayes, 1982). Several studies by Cutler and her colleagues have demonstrated that English-speaking adults exploit the correlation between strong and word-initial syllables to identify the beginnings of words in the speech stream (Cutler, 1990; Cutler & Butterfield, 1992; Cutler & Norris, 1988). When does sensitivity to canonical metrical patterns first emerge? To answer this question, Jusczyk, Cutler, and Redanz (1993) presented American 6- and 9-month-olds with word lists exhibiting either a strong–weak or weak–strong stress pattern. They found that 9-month-olds, but not 6-month-olds, listened longer to lists exhibiting the canonical English strong–weak pattern. These data are consistent with the notion that in-

---

[1]Other sentence types were also employed. See Gerken and McIntosh (1993) for details.

fants discover the phonological organization of the target language some time during the second half of the first year of life. Sensitivity to the canonical stress patterns of words in their language might allow learners to readily identify new words in the speech stream.

Canonical metrical patterns may also play an important role in organizing early utterances, as evidenced by children's weak syllable omission patterns in English and other languages (Demuth, 1992, 1994; Gerken, 1991, 1994b, 1994c; Gerken et al., 1990; Pye, 1983; Wijnen, Krikhaar, & den Os, 1994). For example, young English speakers omit weak syllables from weak–strong words like "giraffe" much more frequently than from strong–weak words like "zebra" (Allen & Hawkins, 1980). One account of this omission pattern is that children have observed the tendency for English words to exhibit a strong initial syllable and alternating stress, and they have incorporated this observation into their speech production system as a metrical template for strong syllable followed by an optional weak syllable (Gerken, 1991, 1994b, 1994c; Gerken et al., 1990; also see Wijnen et al., 1994). In contrast with the *strong–(weak)* template hypothesis, other researchers have suggested that children are biased to fully encode stressed and final syllables, based on perceptually salient acoustic properties (Echols, this volume, 1993; Echols & Newport, 1992; Slobin, 1973). To compare these two approaches, Gerken (in press) introduced 23- to 31-month-old children to novel four-syllable words like those in 2a-b (capital letters indicate stressed syllables).

2a. ZAM pa ka SIS
     S -- w *   S-(w)
2b. pa ZAM   ka SIS
  *   S — w S-(w)

The view that children encode stressed and final syllables predicts that children should omit the two weak syllables of both words equally frequently, because none of these weak syllables is word-final. In contrast, when *strong–(weak)* metrical templates are applied in 2a-b, as shown underneath the words, children should omit the second weak syllable in 2a but omit the first weak syllable in 2b. This was the pattern of omissions actually found. These data, taken together with the infant data described previously, suggest a consistent developmental sequence. Learners begin to discover the metrical pattern of their language during the second half of the first year and later employ this pattern to organize their own utterances when they begin to speak. It is interesting to note that a similar developmental sequence emerges with respect to the prosody of larger linguistic units. This is illustrated in the section on solving the structure problem.

FUNCTION MORPHEMES AND THE LABELING PROBLEM

Once children have segmented the speech stream into linguistically relevant units, they must distinguish among units of different types. One potential solution to the labeling problem is the set of the frequently occurring function morphemes, including articles, auxiliary verbs, and verb inflections. Particular morphemes occur in particular phrase types; for example, articles co-occur with nouns in noun phrases (NPs), and auxiliary verbs and verb inflections co-occur with verbs in verb phrases (VPs). Therefore, if children discovered these co-occurrence patterns, they could use function morphemes to distinguish among syntactic units. For example, a learner might infer that "cat" and "idea" are members of the same class, because both can immediately follow the function morpheme "the" (e.g., Bloomfield, 1933; Maratsos & Chalkley, 1980).

Most theories of syntactic category formation acknowledge the importance of function morphemes in this process (e.g., Grimshaw, 1981; Maratsos & Chalkley, 1980; Pinker, 1982, 1984; Schlesinger, 1971, 1981). However, the point in development at which children are able to use function morphemes to solve the labeling problem has been in dispute, largely because children in the early stages of language production fail to consistently produce function morphemes in their speech (e.g., Brown, 1973). Many researchers have noted that English function morphemes are either non-syllabic or weakly stressed and have suggested that such properties put function morphemes at a perceptual disadvantage (Brown, 1973; Gleitman et al., 1988; Gleitman & Wanner, 1982; also see Leonard & Eyer, this volume). Others have suggested that children begin labeling the syntactic or semantic categories of words and phrases based on the objects, actions, and properties in the world to which a word or phrase refers (e.g., Bowerman, 1973; Grimshaw, 1981; Pinker, 1982; Schlesinger, 1971, 1981). Later, it is proposed, when children begin to notice function morphemes, they change the basis of categorization from referential to distributional.

In contrast to the view that children's early linguistic representations do not include function morphemes, several studies suggest that children who fail to produce function morphemes are nevertheless sensitive to these elements (Gelman & Taylor, 1984; Gerken et al., 1990; Gerken & McIntosh, 1993; Katz, Baker, & MacNamara, 1974; Petretic & Tweney, 1977; Shipley, Smith, & Gleitman, 1969). The majority of these studies demonstrate that young children can distinguish between sentences with and without function morphemes, or between sentences with English and non-English morphemes. Although such research casts strong doubt on the notion that children fail to perceive or represent function morphemes, it does not allow us to determine if children are aware of the co-occurrence patterns in which particular morphemes are found. Only if children are aware of such patterns can they use function morphemes to solve the labeling problem (Gerken, 1994a; Gerken & McIntosh, 1993).

The study by Gerken and McIntosh (1993) discussed in the previous section suggests that children are sufficiently aware of morpheme co-occurrence patterns to distinguish between two English functors, one used grammatically (1a) and one used ungrammatically (1b). Recall that even children with MLUs under 1.50 morphemes per utterance, who produced no articles in their own spontaneous speech, were nevertheless better able to comprehend sentences containing a grammatical function morpheme than an ungrammatical one.[2] These data suggest that children who do not yet produce function morphemes have a sufficient representation of canonical function morpheme co-occurrence patterns to be disrupted if this pattern is violated. Their representation of morphological co-occurrence patterns might allow children to use function morphemes to solve the labeling problem from the very early stages of syntax acquisition.

In order to use function morphemes to distinguish among linguistic units, learners must perform a distributional analysis of the lexical patterns in the sentences they hear. As noted in the introduction, large scale distributional analyses are computationally costly; therefore, such a proposal has a greater chance of success if the scope of analysis is limited in some way. One potential delimiter is prosody. If learners can use prosody to segment the speech stream into phrase-sized units, they might restrict their search for co-occurrence patterns within these units (Morgan, 1986; Morgan et al., 1987). Another way that learners could limit the scope of their distributional analyses is to divide the lexical space into content words and function morphemes and look for co-occurrences only between elements of these two classes. How might learners come to identify the class of function morphemes in their language?

One possibility is that they can identify function morphemes as a *phonological* class based on the fact that the function morphemes in a particular language usually share several phonological properties (e.g., Jakobson & Waugh, 1987). For example, English function morphemes typically contain fricative and nasal consonants, are produced with the reduced vowel schwa (which only occurs in unstressed syllables), and are an integral part of the alternating stress pattern of the language (Gerken et al., 1990; Gerken, 1994a; Morgan, Shi, & Allopenna, this volume). Such properties might allow learners to discover function morphemes as an undifferentiated class before discovering the distributional regularities of particular morphemes (Gerken, 1994a; Peters, 1989, in press). In light of this proposal, it is interesting to note that children have difficulty learning a language in which the phonological properties of function morphemes are not distinct from those of content words (i.e., Signed English; Newport, personal communication).

The study by Gerken and McIntosh (1993) presented earlier suggests that, by the age of approximately 2 years, children have a representation of some specific function morphemes and the contexts in which

---

[2]This was true only for the subset of low MLU children who heard the female voice (see previous section).

they appear.   Therefore, if there is a stage at which learners represent function morphemes as an undifferentiated phonological class, it must occur earlier than this.   Perhaps such a phonological representation of function morphemes forms during the second half of the first year when infants appear to discover a variety of prosodic and segmental properties of the target language (e.g., Jusczyk et al., 1992, 1993; Morgan et al., this volume; Werker et al., this volume; see discussion in previous section).

To examine this issue, Shafer, Gerken, Shucard, and Shucard (1992, 1995) used the Averaged Evoked Potential procedure with 10- to 11-month-olds to assess their sensitivity to the phonological properties of function morphemes.   In this study, infants heard two versions of a story: a normal version that contained normal English function morphemes, and a modified version in which the phonological properties of a subset of function morphemes were modified.   In the modified version, all function morphemes containing a schwa alone (i.e., "a") or a schwa and a fricative consonant (e.g., "of," "was") were replaced by consonant–vowel nonsense syllables containing a stop consonant and a full vowel (e.g., /gu/). Note that these modifications increased the ratio of stops to fricatives over the normal version (a segmental property) and increased the ratio of stressed syllables (those with full vowels) to unstressed syllables (those with schwa vowels; a suprasegmental property).   During the presentation of each version of the story, a series of two tones was played at random points, and infants' cortical responses to the tones were recorded.   We found that infants exhibited significantly smaller responses to the tones in the modified version than in the normal version.   On the basis of previous research using the tone probe technique (e.g., Shucard & Shucard, 1990), we interpret an attenuated response to the tones to indicate greater attention to the ongoing stimulus (i.e., the story).   Thus, we believe that infants attended more closely to the modified version than the normal version of the story, perhaps because the modified version sounded much like normal English but with detectable segmental and/or suprasegmental differences.   More generally, the results admit the possibility that, by the age of 11 months, infants are sensitive to enough of the canonical phonological properties of their language to begin to identify function morphemes as a phonological class.

On the proposal offered here, it is not clear how learners might progress from a representation in which function morphemes are treated as an undifferentiated phonological class to one in which particular function morphemes and their patterns of occurrence can be used to solve the labeling problem. Perhaps computer models of distributional analysis will allow us to consider possible mechanisms for representational change over language development. One such model developed by Mintz (personal communication) uses a corpus of child-directed sentences to train an algorithm to categorize words based on the immediately preceding and following word.   The model successfully divides the corpus into categories resembling nouns and verbs. Furthermore, its success appears to be based on co-occurrences involving frequent function morphemes, as evidenced by a marked decline in performance when function morpheme cues are removed. Interestingly, combining the most frequent function morphemes into a single undifferentiated item does not substantially change the model's ability to classify nouns vs. verbs for the particular corpus examined. This suggests that learners who divide the lexical space into phonologically defined content words and function morphemes might begin to distinguish among linguistic units even before particular function morphemes are identified.

CROSS-SENTENCE COMPARISONS AND THE STRUCTURE PROBLEM

In most syntactic theories, sentences do not comprise a linear string of words and phrases of different types, but rather words and phrases are organized into a hierarchical structure. Therefore, in order to acquire the syntax of their language, learners must discover this hierarchical organization. For example, learners must determine that sentences are composed of an NP and a VP, the latter potentially containing an object NP.[3] Although it has been suggested that prosodic changes at syntactic boundaries can aid in the assignment of syntactic structure as well as in segmentation (e.g., Cooper & Paccia-Cooper, 1980; Lederer & Kelly, 1991), this suggestion has been questioned based on observations of the imperfect relation between prosodic cues and syntactic structure. Consider for example, the sentences in 3a-b (slashes indicate places where a speaker is likely to pause or produce other prosodic changes).

3a. Max / kissed the dog.
3b. He kissed (/) the dog.

In sentence 3a, prosodic changes divide the sentence into the main syntactic constituents—the subject NP and VP. However, the syntactic constituency is not accurately reflected by the prosodic changes in sentence 3b. The parentheses around the slash in this sentence indicate that a talker will either produce no prosodic changes or produce changes that serve to segment the object NP from the subject and verb (if focal stress is given to the verb; see Gerken et al., 1994; Vogel & Kenesei, 1990, for further discussion). Thus, although the talker might produce salient prosodic changes at a phrase boundary (i.e., the one between the verb and object NP), these changes do not reflect the main syntactic constituency of the sentence. Such examples in which prosody fails to mark syntactic structure have caused several researchers to posit

---

[3]The notion that a sentence is composed of a subject NP and VP is not consistent with some recent accounts of syntactic structure (e.g., Radford, 1990). However, the issues raised in this section are probably valid regardless of the particular syntactic theory that we adopt.

an independent prosodic structure, which is influenced by, but not identical to, syntactic structure (Gee & Grosjean, 1983; Hayes, 1989; Nespor & Vogel, 1986; Read & Schreiber, 1982; Selkirk, this volume). On this view, it is prosodic units such as *phonological phrases*, and not syntactic phrases, that are the domain of prosodic processes including pausing and metrical phenomena.   Thus, the slashes in 3a-b reflect phonological phrase boundaries.

Two studies, one with young children and the other with 9-month-old infants, suggest that learners might be sensitive to prosodic changes that mark prosodic, not necessarily syntactic, units (Gerken, 1994b; Gerken, Jusczyk, & Mandel, 1994). The first study employed children's weak syllable omissions from sentences to examine the organization of their intended utterances prior to production (Gerken, 1994b).   Recall from the previous section that young children's weak syllable omissions from multisyllabic words appear to reflect the application of a *strong–(weak)* metrical template.   Children's weak syllable omissions from sentences also suggest the application of a *strong–(weak)* template (Demuth, 1992, 1994; Gerken, 1991; Gerken et al. 1990; Wijnen et al., 1994).   For example, children are more likely to omit the second weak syllable than the first in phrases like 4, just as they did in comparably stressed words like 2a.

4.   PUSHes the DOG
       S – w *   S-(w)

On several recent linguistic proposals, the phonological phrase is the domain of metrical processes (e.g., Hayes, 1989); therefore, we might expect children to apply their metrical templates within phonological phrases. To test this hypothesis, 24- to 28-month-old children were asked to imitate sentences like 5a-c (Gerken, 1991, 1994b). (The slashes indicate   phonological phrase boundaries.   The verb in 5c was given focal stress.)

5a. MAX / KISSED the DOG.
     S-(w)   S ——w S-(w)
5b. the BEAR / KISSED the DOG.
     *   S-(w)   S ——w S-(w)
5c. he KISSED / the DOG
     *   S-(w) * S-(w)

As predicted by the view that children apply their *strong–(weak)* metrical templates within phonological phrases, children omitted the object article in 5c significantly more frequently than the object articles in either 5a or 5b (Gerken, 1991, 1994b). Furthermore, they omitted the subject pronoun and subject article at nearly the same rate as they omitted the object article in 5c, suggesting that the same production mechanism is responsible for all weak syllable omissions. These data suggest that children are sensitive to prosodic structure and use it to organize their own intended utterances.

A study with 9-month-old infants used the preferential listening technique to determine if infants are sensitive to configurations of prosodic cues occurring at prosodic boundaries. Recall that a previous experiment by Jusczyk and his colleagues demonstrated that infants listened longer to passages in which pauses were inserted at major syntactic boundaries than passages in which pauses were inserted at nonboundary positions (Jusczyk et al., 1992). However, this experiment did not contrast cases in which syntactic structure and prosodic structure matched (as in 5a-b) vs. those in which they failed to match (as in 5c). To do this, Gerken, Jusczyk, and Mandel (1994) presented one group of 9-month-olds with passages containing lexical NP subjects like 5a-b and another group with passages containing pronoun subject like 5c. In each group, half of the passages had a pause inserted after the subject and half had a pause inserted after the verb. The prediction was that infants in the lexical NP condition would listen longer to passages with the pause after the subject, just as they had in the previous experiment (Jusczyk et al., 1992). The question was how infants would respond in the pronoun subject condition. If infants are sensitive to configurations of prosodic cues after syntactic constituents (a possibility left open by the previous experiment), then they should listen longer to passages with pauses after the subject pronoun. In contrast, if configurations of prosodic cues are governed by prosodic structure, then infants might listen longer to passages with pauses after the verb if the talker produced other prosodic changes at this boundary. Or, they might show no significant preference for either pause location if the talker failed to produce reliable changes at any boundary in these sentences.

The results showed that infants in the lexical NP condition listened longer to passages containing pauses after the subject NP, while infants in the pronoun subject condition showed no preference for either pause location. These data, as well as subsequent acoustic analyses of the stimuli, suggest that the talker did not produce reliable prosodic changes marking linguistic boundaries in declarative sentences with pronoun subjects. Within the prosodic phonology framework, this is because talkers have an option to incorporate short object NPs into the phonological phrase containing the verb as long as the verb does not receive focal stress. Taken together, the infant and child research presented in this section suggests infants are sensitive to configurations of prosodic cues that occur at prosodic boundaries, not syntactic boundaries. The research also suggests that, later in development, children use the prosodic structure that they discovered in infancy to organize their own utterances. Recall that we saw a similar developmental relationship between infant perception and child production with respect to canonical word stress patterns.

The observation that prosodic information potentially cues learners to prosodic structure, not *syntactic* structure, is not problematic for the use of prosody in segmentation, because every prosodic boundary is also a syntactic boundary. Therefore, attending to prosodic changes will allow learners to locate linguistically relevant units in the speech stream. However, the observation that prosody is governed by an independent prosodic structure raises the question of how learners are able to discover syntactic structure. One possible solution to the structure problem is that learners might use prosodic changes such as pausing to infer prosodic structure and then infer syntactic structure from cross-sentence comparisons of prosodic structure. For example, one way that learners might discover that pronoun subjects are syntactic constituents on par with lexical NP subjects is by comparing declarative sentences like the one in 5c with other sentence types in which pronoun subjects are prosodically separated from verbs. In particular, yes/no questions like the one in 6 can provide prosodic information that pronoun subjects are distinct constituents from VPs, because such sentences are often produced with focal stress on the pronoun subject, resulting in a phonological phrase boundary between the subject and verb.

    6. Did he (/) kiss the dog?

To test whether 9-month-old infants are sensitive to configurations of prosodic cues occurring between the pronoun subject and verb of yes/no sentences, Gerken, Jusczyk, and Mandel (1994) presented infants with passages containing yes/no questions in which pauses had been inserted either after the subject or after the verb. The data showed that infants listened longer to passages with pauses after the subject. Thus, learners might infer from such sentences that pronoun subjects are separate constituents from verbs.[4] If learners are able to compare across sentence types, they might use prosody to infer that subjects and VPs are the main syntactic constituents of sentences and that pronoun subjects have the same syntactic constituent status as lexical NP subjects.

How can cross-sentence comparisons be constrained to prevent such a proposal from being computationally unrealistic? One possibility is that learners only attempt to compare the prosodic structures of temporally contiguous utterances that share lexical items. This notion is supported by a recent study in which 7-month-old infants were able to identify words across sentence contexts (see Aslin, Woodward, LaMendola, & Bever, this volume). Other preliminary research shows that 9-month-old infants prefer to listen to lists of sentences that are structurally different but that share several words vs. lists of sentences that are either structurally the same or that do not share words (see Jusczyk & Kemler Nelson, this volume). To determine the viability of temporally and lexically constrained cross-sentence analyses as a mechanism for inferring syntactic structure, it might be revealing to model distributional analyses that are constrained in this way vs. those that are not. It might also be useful to examine the frequency in caregiver input of tempo-

---

[4]For proposals about additional structure revealing properties of yes-no questions, see Newport, Gleitman and Gleitman (1977).

rally contiguous sentences in which the lexical content remains stable and the structural relations among lexical items vary (see Ratner, this volume).

SUMMARY AND CONCLUSION

I proposed a model of syntax acquisition in which learners use a combination of phonological and distributional information to acquire the syntactic structure of their native language. In particular, I proposed that learners use prosody, function morphemes, and cross-sentence comparisons to solve the segmentation, labeling, and structure problems, respectively. I also presented evidence suggesting that infants and children have access to the phonological and distributional information necessary to make such a proposal worth considering.

In order to determine if the current proposal is on the right track, future research must focus on three issues. First, because it appears that infants and children use phonological information in the service of syntax acquisition, it is important to understand how learners come to discover which acoustic properties of the speech signal are relevant in the target language. Although I assumed that the learner has a phonological organization in place before beginning the process of syntax acquisition, it is possible, indeed likely, that the acquisition of phonology and syntax interact to some degree. Thus, we must consider the nature of this interaction and how it might affect the current proposal. A second issue to consider is whether the constraints I have proposed on the domain of distributional analyses are sufficient to make such analyses computationally realistic. And finally, we must consider the kind of representation of syntax that learners have at different points in development. For example, it seems likely that the representation that allows an infant to perceptually discriminate phonological properties of two stimuli could be quite different from the representation that guides the utterances of 24-month-olds. I tried to demonstrate that these representations are related, but exactly how they are related remains an open question. Perhaps further studies that address parallel linguistic issues in infants and young children might reveal how syntactic representations develop over time.

ACKNOWLEDGMENTS

Research and chapter preparation were supported by National Science Foundation grant #BNS9120952.

REFERENCES

Allen, G. D., & Hawkins, S. (1980). Phonological rhythm: Definition and development. In G. Yeni-Komshian, J. F. Kavanagh, & C. A. Ferguson (Eds.), *Child phonology: Vol. 1. Production* (pp. 227-256). New York: Academic Press.

Best, C. T., McRoberts, G. W., & Sithole, N. M. (1988). Examination of the perceptual reorganization for contrasts: Zulu click discrimination by English-speaking adults and infants. *Journal of Experimental Psychology: Human Perception and Performance, 14,* 245-360.

Bloomfield, L. (1933). *Language.* New York: Henry Holt (reprinted 1961).

Bowerman, M. (1973). *Early syntactic development: A cross-linguistic study with special reference to Finnish.* Cambridge, England: Cambridge University Press.

Brown, R. (1973). *A first language.* Cambridge, MA: Harvard University Press

Chomsky, N. (1965). *Aspects of a theory of syntax.* Cambridge, MA: MIT Press.

Cooper, W. (1975). *Syntactic control of speech timing.* Unpublished doctoral dissertation, MIT.

Cooper, W., & Paccia-Cooper, J. (1980). *Syntax and speech.* Cambridge, MA: Harvard University Press.

Cutler, A. (1990). Exploiting prosodic probabilities in speech segmentation. In G. Altmann (Ed.), *Cognitive models of speech processing: Psycholinguistic and computational perspectives* (pp. 105-121). Cambridge, MA: MIT Press.

Cutler, A., & Butterfield, S. (1992). Rhythmic cues to speech segmentation: Evidence from juncture misperception. *Journal of Memory and Language, 3,* 218-236.

Cutler, A., & Carter, D. M. (1987). The predominance of strong initial syllables in the English vocabulary. *Computer Speech and Language, 2,* 133-142.

Cutler, A., & Norris, D. (1988). The role of strong syllables in segmentation for lexical access. *Journal of Experimental Psychology: Human Perception and Performance, 14,* 113-121.

Demuth, K. (1992, October). *Competence or performance? What phonology shows about children's emerging syntax.* Paper presented at the Boston University Conference on Language Development.

Demuth, K. (1994). On the 'underspecification' of functional categories in early grammars. In B. Lust, M. Suñer, & J. Whitman (Eds.), *Syntactic theory and first language acquisition: Cross-linguistic perspectives.* (pp. 119-134). Hillsdale, NJ: Lawrence Erlbaum Associates.

Echols, C. H. (1993). A perceptually-based model of children's earliest productions. *Cognition, 46,* 245-296.

Echols, C. H., & Newport, E. L. (1992). The role of stress and position in determining first words. *Language Acquisition, 2,* 189-220.

Gee, J., & Grosjean, F. (1983). Performance structures: A psycholinguistic and linguistic appraisal. *Cognitive Psychology, 15,* 411-458.

Gelman, S. A., & Taylor, M. (1984). How two-year-old children interpret proper and common names for unfamiliar objects. *Child Development, 55,* 1535-1540.

Gerken, L. A. (1991). The metrical basis for children's subjectless sentences. *Journal of Memory and Language, 30,* 431-451.

Gerken, L. A. (1994a). Sentential processes in early child language: Evidence from the perception and production of function morphemes. In H. C Nusbaum & J. C. Goodman (Eds.), *The transition from speech sounds to spoken words* (pp. 271-298). Cambridge, MA: MIT Press.

Gerken, L. A. (1994b). Young children's representation of prosodic phonology: Evidence from English-speakers' weak syllable omissions. *Journal of Memory and Language, 33,* 19-38.

Gerken, L. A. (1994c). A metrical template account of children's weak syllable omissions. *Journal of Child Language., 21,* 565-584

Gerken, L. A., Jusczyk, P. W., & Mandel, D. R. (1994). When prosody fails to cue syntactic structure: Nine-month-olds' sensitivity to phonological *vs.* syntactic phrases. *Cognition, 51,* 237-265.

Gerken, L. A., Landau, B., & Remez, R. E. (1990). Function morphemes in young children's speech perception and production. *Developmental Psychology, 27,* 204-216.

Gerken, L. A., & McIntosh, B. J. (1993). The interplay of function morphemes and prosody in early language. *Developmental Psychology, 29,* 448-457.

Gleitman, L., Gleitman, H., Landau, B., & Wanner, E. (1988). Where learning begins, initial representations for language learning. In F. Newmeyer (Ed.), *The Cambridge linguistic survey* (pp. 150-193). New York, Cambridge University Press.

Gleitman, L., & Wanner, E. (1982). Language acquisition: The state of the state of the art. In E. Wanner & L. Gleitman (Eds.), *Language acquisition: The state of the art* (pp. 3-48). Cambridge, England: Cambridge University Press.

Grimshaw, J. (1981). Form, function, and the language acquisition device. In C. L. Baker & J. McCarthy (Eds.), *The logical problem of language acquisition* (pp. 163-182). Cambridge, MA: MIT Press.

Hayes, B. (1982). Extrametricality and English stress. *Linguistic Inquiry, 13*, 227-276.

Hayes, B. (1989). The prosodic hierarchy in meter. In P. Kiparsky & G. Youmans (Eds.), *Rhythm and meter* (pp. 201-260). Orlando, FL: Academic Press.

Hirsh-Pasek, K., Kemler Nelson, D. G., Jusczyk, P. K., Wright, K., & Druss, B. (1987). Clauses are perceptual units for prelinguistic infants. *Cognition, 26*, 269-286.

Jakobson, R., & Waugh, L. R. (1987). *The sound shape of language*. Berlin: Mouton de Gruyter.

Jusczyk, P. W., Cutler, A., & Redanz, L. (1993). Infants' sensitivity to predominant word stress patterns in English. *Child Development, 64*, 675-687.

Jusczyk, P. W., Hirsh-Pasek, K., Kemler Nelson, D., Kennedy, L., Woodward, A., & Piwoz, J. (1992). Perception of acoustic correlates of major phrasal units by young infants. *Cognitive Psychology, 24*, 252-293.

Katz, B., Baker, G., & MacNamara, J. (1974). What's in a name? On the child's acquisition of proper and common nouns. *Child Development, 45*, 269-273.

Kemler Nelson, D., Hirsh-Pasek, K., Jusczyk, P. W., & Wright Cassidy, K. (1989). How prosodic cues in motherese might assist language learning. *Journal of Child Language, 16*, 53-68.

Klatt, D. (1975). Vowel lengthening is syntactically determined in connected discourse. *Journal of Phonetics, 3*, 129-140.

Lederer, A., & Kelly, M. H. (1991). Prosodic correlates to the adjunct/complement distinction in motherese. *Papers & Reports on Child Language Development, 30*, 55-63.

Maratsos, M., & Chalkley, M. A. (1980). The internal language of children's syntax: The ontogenesis and representation of syntactic categories. In K. Nelson (Ed.), *Children's language*, Vol. 2 (pp. 127-214). New York: Gardner Press.

Morgan, J. (1986). *From simple input to complex grammar*. Cambridge, MA: MIT Press.

Morgan, J. L., Meier, R. P., & Newport, E. L. (1987). Structural packaging in the input to language learning. *Cognitive Psychology, 22*, 498-550.

Morgan, J., & Newport, E. (1981). The role of constituent structure in the induction of an artificial language. *Journal of Verbal Learning and Verbal Behavior, 20*, 67-85.

Nespor, M., & Vogel, I. (1986). *Prosodic phonology*. Dordrecht: Foris.

Newport, E., Gleitman, H., & Gleitman, L. (1977). Mother, I'd rather do it myself. In C. Snow & C. Ferguson (Eds.), *Talking to children* (pp. 109-147). Cambridge, England: Cambridge University Press.

Peters, A. M. (1983). *The units of language acquisition*. Cambridge, England: Cambridge University Press.

Peters, A. M. (1985). Language segmentation: Operating principles for the perception and analysis of language. In D. I. Slobin (Ed.), *The crosslinguistic study of language acquisition: Vol. 2. Theoretical issues* (pp. 1029-1067). Hillsdale, NJ: Lawrence Erlbaum Associates.

Peters, A. M. (1989, October). *From schwa to grammar: The emergence of function morphemes*. Paper presented at the Boston University Conference on Language Development.

Peters, A. M. (in press). Language typology, prosody, and the acquisition of grammatical morphemes. In D. I. Slobin (Ed.), *The crosslinguistic study of language acquisition, Vol. 4.* Hillsdale, NJ: Lawrence Erlbaum Associates.

Petretic, P. A., & Tweney, R. D. (1977). Does comprehension precede production? The development of children's responses to telegraphic sentences of varying grammatical adequacy. *Journal of Child Language, 4*, 201-209.

Pinker, S. (1982). A theory of the acquisition of lexical interpretive grammars. In J. Bresnan (Ed.), *The mental representation of grammatical relations* (pp. 53-63). Cambridge, MA: MIT Press.

Pinker, S. (1984). *Language learnability and language development*. Cambridge, MA: Harvard University Press.

Pye, C. (1983). Mayan telegraphese. *Language, 59*, 583-604.

Radford, A. (1990). *Syntactic theory and the acquisition of English syntax*. Oxford: Basil Blackwell.

Read, C., & Schreiber, P. (1982). Why short subjects are hard to find. In E. Wanner & L. Gleitman (Eds.), *Language acquisition: The state of the art* (pp. 78-101). Cambridge, England: Cambridge University Press.

Schlesinger, I. M. (1971). Production of utterances in language acquisition. In D. I. Slobin (Ed.), *The ontogenesis of grammar* (pp. 63-101). New York: Academic Press.

Schlesinger, I. M. (1981). Semantic assimilation in the development of relational categories. In W. Deutsch (Ed.), *The child's construction of language* (pp. 223-243). London: Academic Press.

Shafer, V. L., Gerken, L. A., Shucard, J. L., & Shucard, D. W. (1992, October). *"The" and the brain: An electrophysiological study of infants' sensitivity of English function morphemes*. Paper presented at the Boston University Conference on Language Development.

Shafer, V. L., Gerken, L. A., Shucard, J. L., & Shucard, D. W. (1995). *An electrophysiological study of infants' sensitivity to the sound structure of English function morphemes*. Unpublished manuscript, State University of New York, Buffalo.

Shipley, E., Smith, C., & Gleitman, L. (1969). A study in the acquisition of language: Free responses to commands. *Language, 45,* 322-342.

Shucard, J., & Shucard, D. (1990). Auditory evoked potentials and hand preference in 6-month-old infants: Possible gender-related differences in cerebral organization. *Developmental Psychology, 26,* 923-930.

Slobin, D. I, (1973). Cognitive prerequisites for the acquisition of grammar. In C. A. Ferguson & D. I. Slobin (Eds.), *Studies of child language development* (pp. 175-208). New York: Holt, Rinehart & Winston.

Vogel, I., & Kenesei, I (1990). Syntax and semantics in phonology. In S. Inkelas & D. Zec, (Eds.), *The phonology-syntax connection* (pp. 339-363). Stanford, CA: Chicago University Press.

Werker, J. F., & Tees, R. C. (1984). Cross-language speech perception: Evidence for perceptual reorganization during the first year of life. *Infant Behavior and Development, 7,* 49-63.

Wijnen, F., Krikhaar, E., & den Os, E. (1994). The (non)realization of unstressed elements in children's utterances: Evidence for a rhythmic constraint. *Journal of Child Language, 21,* 59-83.

24

Putting the Baby in the Bootstraps: Toward a More Complete Understanding of the Role of the Input in Infant Speech Processing

Janet F. Werker, Valerie L. Lloyd, and Judith E. Pegg
University of British Columbia

Linda Polka
McGill University

This volume was designed to advance understanding of the bootstrapping problem by bringing together research from several different areas. We are pleased to participate in such an exciting and timely interdisciplinary endeavor. To this end, we discuss our research in infant speech perception within a general framework for considering the role of the input in developmental changes in language processing. Briefly, we are convinced that the role of the linguistic input may be best understood by considering not only the changing characteristics of the speech directed to and used in the vicinity of infants, but also the changing perceptual biases and cognitive capabilities that infants brings to the speech processing task. In this chapter we present some of the reasons we have come to hold so firmly to such a view. The chapter is divided into three general sections. First, we present a brief account of the characteristics of the linguistic input infants experience and infants' responses to that input. Second, we present a selective review of infant speech perception research, highlighting the descriptive data showing language-specific influences on infant speech perception. Third, we describe how linguistic, perceptual, and cognitive abilities change across infancy, and develop the argument that in order to fully understand the role of the input in infant speech processing and child language acquisition, it is imperative to consider not only the characteristics of the input, but also the changing perceptual biases and domain-general cognitive capabilities infants bring to the language acquisition process.

INFANT-DIRECTED SPEECH

There is considerable evidence that speech directed to infants is different in many respects than that directed to adults, or even to young children (e.g., Ferguson, 1964). The prosodic modifications in speech directed to young infants include elevated pitch, elongated vowels, expanded pitch contours, and increased rhythmicity (Fernald, 1984; Fernald & Kuhl, 1987; Papousek, Papousek, & Bornstein, 1985). In addition, it has been noted that infant-directed speech (IDS) is characterized
by shorter mean length of utterance (MLU), increased repetition of
words and phrases, and simpler words than adult-directed speech
(ADS) (Ferguson, 1964; Stern, Speiker, Barnett, and MacKain, 1983;
Snow, 1977). Furthermore there seem to be prosodic regularities in IDS
that could provide clues to syntactic and semantic class. For example, it
has been shown that in English, object labels occupy the prosodic peak
when mothers are attempting to teach their infants new words (Fernald
& Mazzie, 1991). Indeed, object labels not only occur on prosodic peaks,
but they are reported to be presented in isolation around 20% of the
time, occur in sentence-final position over 95% of the time, and are often
preceded by less clear speech (Aslin, 1993; Aslin, Woodward, LaMendola, & Bever, this volume). In English a high proportion of the words
directed to young children are short in duration (many are monosyllabic), and content words differ from function words in syllable type
(CVC vs. CV), amplitude, and pitch variation (Morgan, Shi, & Allopenna, this volume).

Although there is controversy concerning the question of whether
IDS occurs in all languages and all cultures (e.g., Ratner & Pye, 1984;
Schieffelin, 1979), there is strong evidence that the use of IDS is by no
means restricted to English-speaking mothers. IDS with similar F_0 characteristics has been noted in such diverse languages as French, German, Italian, Japanese, and Mandarin (Fernald, Taeschner, Dunn,
Papousek, Boysson-Bardies, & Fukui, 1989; Papousek, Papousek, &
Symmes, 1991). Of increasing interest is whether IDS in languages
other than English also contains phonological cues to syntactic class, and
if these cues are similar or different to those that have been described in
English IDS (Aslin, 1993; Aslin et al., this volume; Fisher & Tokhura,
this volume; Morgan et al., this volume).

Several studies have been conducted to determine whether infants
respond differentially to IDS. In a now classic study, Fernald (1985)
showed that 4-month-old infants will select to listen to IDS over ADS
when tested in a two choice headturn procedure. In our research, we
have extended this finding by showing that infants of 2 months (Pegg,
Werker, & McLeod, 1992), 4 to $5\frac{1}{2}$, and $7\frac{1}{2}$ to 9 months of age look
longer to both female and male IDS over ADS, and the two older
groups of infants also show greater affective responsiveness to female
IDS (Werker & McLeod, 1989). Cooper and Aslin (1990) showed that

even younger English-learning infants (1-month-old and neonates) look longer to English female IDS over ADS. We have recently found that the preference for IDS is evident in Cantonese infants listening to their native language and in English infants listening to an unfamiliar language such as Cantonese (Werker, Pegg, & McLeod, 1994; Pegg, Werker, & McLeod, in preparation). This latter research shows that infants not only pay attention to native, but also non-native IDS.

These studies confirm that IDS characterized by high and variable pitch is effective in attracting and maintaining infant attention. Given that infants choose to listen more to IDS than ADS,[1] it has been tacitly assumed by many that IDS may thus facilitate speech processing and subsequent language acquisition.[2] However, there have been only a few studies directly assessing this question.

In one study, Karzon (1985) compared 4-month-old infants on their ability to discriminate the multisyllabic utterances "marana" versus "malana" in several different prosodic conditions: flat, AD, or ID prosody. The results revealed that the infants were only able to discriminate these multisyllabic utterances when the contrastive medial syllable was highlighted by ID prosody (intonation and amplitude peak). This evidence elegantly demonstrates that the characteristics of IDS facilitate discrimination of these medial position phonemes.

In another study, Hirsh-Pasek and colleagues (Hirsh-Pasek et al., 1987) tested infants aged 6 months of age on their preference for utterances with pauses inserted either at clause boundaries or within the clause. The infants showed a preference for the sentences with pauses inserted at natural boundaries, but only showed this preference for pairs of utterances presented in IDS. When given the same test using ADS, the preference was not evident (Kemler Nelson et al., 1989). These results show that IDS may facilitate infants' processing of language, in this case by facilitating segmentation.

Fernald, McRoberts, and Herrera (1993) assessed the extent to which IDS facilitates word comprehension. In this series of studies, 15- and 19-month-old infants were shown a video display of an object accompanied by a word repeated using either ID or AD prosody. Although the precise magnitude of the effect varied somewhat from study to study, there was evidence that 15-month-old infants show better comprehension when familiar words are presented in IDS than in ADS. By 19 months of age infants perform equally well irrespective of whether the words are produced in IDS or ADS. These findings thus suggest that IDS

---

[1]It should be noted that it is not the case that infants completely avoid AD speech, they simply indicate a preference for listening to ID speech. As shown by Oshima-Takane (1988) at some point infants and children have to listen to speech that is not directed to them if they are to learn aspects of the language such as the personal pronoun system.
[2]There is considerable controversy as to the validity of the "motherese hypothesis" for explaining child language acquisition (e.g., Gleitman, Newport, & Gleitman, 1984). The issues reviewed in this chapter ask not whether simplified syntax facilitates acquisition of language per se, but whether prosodic and phonologic modifications in ID speech facilitate speech perception, segmentation, and word learning.

might facilitate single word comprehension, but only when infants are first starting to learn language.

Finally, Echols and Newport (1992; see also Echols, this volume) reported that children at the one- and two-word stage are less likely to omit and/or mispronounce words that are either sentence-final or stressed in the adult input. These results provide direct evidence that the often reported phonological emphasis of stress and final position given to content words actually influences children's correct use of such items.

The previous studies provide support for the possibility that the prosodic modifications in IDS do indeed facilitate speech processing, and in this way could ease children's entry into language. However, to complicate the story further, there is some evidence that the characteristics of IDS may change as a function of infant age and/or level of language development. As one example, Stern and colleagues compared the characteristics of IDS directed to infants of four ages: newborn infants, 4-, 12-, and 24-month-old infants. Their study revealed differences in MLU, tempo, and pitch in speech directed to infants of different ages (Stern et al., 1983). Others have shown that the speech directed to English-learning infants at the one-word stage contains a reduced number of function words and an increased number of content words in comparison to speech directed to older children and adults (Newport, 1976; Snow, 1977). The most detailed work, however, has focused on the question of whether there are age/stage-specific differences in the amount and type of phonetic and phonological clarification provided in IDS. This work, presented in detail in the chapter by Ratner (this volume), raises the possibility that the input may, in some way, be sculpted to the child's developmental level.

In summary, there is increasing evidence that adults modify their speech in many different ways when addressing infants and that infants attend more, respond with more affect to, and perhaps are better able to process speech with special ID prosodic modifications. It also appears that the characteristics of IDS change with infant age/development. Thus investigators concerned with the process of language acquisition are justified in asking whether the characteristics of the input help bootstrap infants into language. Similarly, those of us interested in the transition from speech perception to language comprehension are justified in attempting to formally describe the characteristics of the input that might help in this process. We argue, however, that the input cannot be studied in isolation from the changing characteristics infants bring to the task of speech processing. In this endeavor, in the next section we first describe the changing perceptual and linguistic biases infants bring to the speech perception process, and then consider other changing capabilities that may impact on speech and language processing.

CHANGES IN INFANTS' SPEECH PERCEPTION SKILLS

Experiential Influences on Consonant Discrimination

In a number of papers published during the 1970s and 1980s, it was revealed that infants can discriminate nearly every phonetic contrast on which they are tested, including phonetic contrasts that are not used in their language-learning environment. On the other hand, adults were shown to have difficulty discriminating at least some non-native phonetic contrasts (for reviews see Jusczyk, 1985; Kuhl, 1987). To attempt to demarcate when this change from language-general to language-specific discrimination occurs, we compared English-learning infants and English-speaking adults on their ability to discriminate two non-native (Hindi) consonant contrasts using a conditioned headturn procedure. First we verified the general finding by showing that even when tested with a similar procedure on the same contrasts, infants aged 6 to 8 months can discriminate non-native consonant contrasts that adults find difficult (Werker, Gilbert, Humphrey, & Tees, 1981). Furthermore, children aged 4, 8, and 12 years are all poor at discriminating these two Hindi (non-English) consonant contrasts (Werker & Tees, 1983).

We then began testing even younger children, and discovered important changes within the first year of life in cross-language speech perception. Specifically, we used as stimuli a retroflex vs. dental (/ʈa/–/t̪a/) place contrast from Hindi and a glottalized velar vs. glottalized uvular (/k'i/–/q'i/) place contrast from Nthlakampx, an Interior Salish language. We showed that although 6- to 8-month-old English-learning infants can discriminate these non-native contrasts with ease, 10- to 12-month-old English-learning infants, like English-speaking adults, have difficulty discriminating these non-native consonant contrasts (Werker & Tees, 1984).

In the last several years, this finding has been replicated both in our lab and in Catherine Best's lab with the same and new consonant contrasts. In our lab, this finding was replicated with a set of synthetic voiced retroflex /ɖa/ vs. dental /d̪a/ stimuli (Werker & Lalonde, 1988). Best and colleagues also replicated this finding using the Nthlakampx /k'i/–/q'i/ contrast in a habituation/dishabituation procedure (Best & McRoberts, 1989; Best, 1993). More recently, Best (1989, 1993) has revealed this pattern with three additional contrasts. Thus there is robust and replicable evidence of an effect from the language input between 6 and 12 months of age on infants' ability to discriminate non-native consonant contrasts.

In additional studies, we and others clarified many aspects of this age-related change in non-native speech perception. First, the change in performance between 6 and 12 months of age is not irreversible. Research with adults has shown that with enough training, with enough experience acquiring a second language, or when tested in a sensitive enough procedure, the ability to discriminate these difficult non-native contrasts is still evident (for a review, see Werker, 1993). Thus we tend to think of this change as a reorganization in processing biases rather than a "loss" of sensitivity.

Second, the age related change does not occur for all non-native consonant contrasts. For example, in a study published in 1988, Best, McRoberts, and Sithole showed that subjects of all ages—young infants, older infants (up to 14 months of age) and adult English speakers—can all easily discriminate the apical versus lateral (<ca>–<xa>) Zulu click contrast. These authors suggested that discrimination remains high for this contrast because it does not map onto the native language phonology, and hence there is no pressure on the speech perception system to reorganize. They suggest that the retroflex vs. dental contrast becomes less discriminable because the Hindi retroflex /ḍa/ and dental /ḍa/ phones may both be assimilated to the English alveolar /da/ phone. Similarly, the glottalized velar and uvular stimuli /kʼi/ and /qʼi/ may be perceived as atypical velar k's. Because there are no phones in English that even remotely resemble the apical and lateral Zulu clicks, these clicks fail to be assimilated to English phonology, and remain discriminable.

Experiential Influences on Vowel Perception

Kuhl and colleagues presented data showing that there are language-specific influences on the internal structure of vocalic categories by 6 months of age. Specifically, they have shown there to be a native-language "perceptual magnet" effect by this age. When tested using a peripheral member of a vowel category as the background stimulus, and then presented with the central member of that vowel category (e.g., a "poor" /i/ vs. a "good" /i/) listeners discriminate better than when tested in the reverse order. Kuhl explains this by suggesting that the center of the category acts as a magnet, pulling the other members toward it and rendering them less discriminable (Grieser & Kuhl, 1989; Kuhl, 1991). Kuhl showed this perceptual magnet effect to be language specific by 6 months of age (Kuhl et al., 1992). When tested on good and poor exemplars of Swedish vowels, Swedish-learning 6-month-old infants show the magnet effect, but do not show it for the English vowels, whereas English 6-month-old infants show the magnet effect for English but not Swedish vowels. Thus these data suggest that experience with the native language affects the internal structure of vowel categories by 6 months of age.

Two of us (Polka & Werker, 1994; Werker & Polka, 1993a, 1993b) recently completed a series of studies assessing age changes in between-category vowel discrimination. We wanted to know whether the pattern would be similar to that which has been reported for between-category consonant discrimination—a decline in performance discriminating non-native contrasts at around 10–12 months of age—or whether it would be similar to that which has been reported for within-category vowel generalization—a language-specific magnet effect by 6 months. We compared 6- to 8- and 10- to 12-month-old English-learning infants on their ability to discriminate two non-English, German vowel contrasts, with the vowels presented in a /dVt/ context. Both contrasts comprised high front rounded vs. high back rounded German vowels. One pair contrasted the tense vowels /ü/–/u/ and the other the lax vowels /ö/ –/ʊ/. These vowels were of interest because, although this contrast does not occur in English, English-speaking adults can nevertheless discriminate both of these non-English contrasts with ease (see Polka, 1995).

The results revealed that the 6- to 8-month-old infants performed significantly better than the 10- to 12-month-olds, but not as well as 6- to 8-month-olds typically perform on non-native consonant contrasts. Of the 14 English-learning infants aged 10 to 12 months, two discriminated the front–back tense vowel contrast, and one discriminated the front–back lax vowel contrast. Of the twenty 6- to 8-month-old English-learning infants, slightly less than half discriminated each German vowel contrast, whereas in previous consonant discrimination experiments virtually all of the 6- to 8-month-olds discriminate non-native contrasts.

In an attempt to understand why only about half of the 6- to 8-month-old infants discriminated the non-native vowel contrasts, we examined the data for evidence of a possible perceptual magnet effect in differential discrimination of "good" vs. "poor" exemplars. This was possible because, in a keyword identification task, Polka (1995) found a "goodness" difference for these stimuli. Specifically, English adults mapped all four German vowels onto the same English vowels (/u/ and /ʊ/), with no significant difference between front and back vowels for either contrast. However, the adults rated the high back rounded vowel in each pair (/u/ or /ʊ/) as a very good match to an English vowel, and the high front rounded vowels in each pair (/ü/ or /ö/) as a significantly poorer match (Polka, 1995). This enabled us to designate the back vowel in each contrast as more "typical" of the English vowel category than the front vowel, and to use this designation to test for a perceptual magnet effect in infant perception. In the headturn task, half the infants are tested using the back vowel as the background and the front as the change, and half in the reverse order. Hence a magnet effect would be revealed if infants performed better when the less typical (front rounded vowels; /ö/ or /ü/) served as the background in the headturn task, than when the more prototypical (back rounded vowels: /ʊ/ or /u/) served as the background.

As shown in Fig. 24.1, the results were consistent with the prediction of a perceptual magnet effect. Virtually all the 6- to 8-month-olds who discriminated the German vowel contrasts did so when the non-typical, high front rounded vowel was the background, and almost none of them discriminated when tested in the opposite direction.[3]

By providing evidence of an asymmetry in discrimination, these results replicate the finding of language-specific influences on speech perception by 6 to 8 months of age. More importantly, these result show that there is further change between 6 to 8 and 10 to 12 months of age, such that by 10 to 12 months, English-learning infants are unable to discriminate non-native vowel contrasts irrespective of the vowel that serves as the background. The 10- to 12-month-old English infants have difficulty discriminating these German vowel contrasts even though these contrasts are easy for adult English speakers to discriminate.

More research is required before we know whether something like a magnet effect occurs for all vowels, whether it occurs at all for consonants, and what its precise role in speech perception might be. On the basis of the data that are available so far, however, there is evidence of a language-specific influence on vowel perception (as shown by the magnet effect) at an earlier age than has been reported for consonants. Even so, there appears to be concordance between vowels and consonants in the age at which the full decline in the ability to discriminate non-native phonetic contrasts is found.

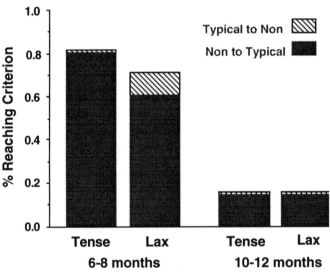

FIG. 24.1. The percent of subjects per group reaching criterion on the German vowel contrasts as a function of direction of change.

---

[3]A final study was done to ascertain whether even younger infants could discriminate the non-native contrasts. This study revealed that 4-month-old English-learning infants perform even better than 6-month-old infants on the German vowel contrasts (see Polka & Werker, 1994, for more details).

Experiential Influences on Other Aspects of Speech Perception

In addition to native language influences on consonant and vowel perception, it has become clear during the last several years that the ambient language also exerts profound influences on other aspects of speech processing during the first year of life. Some of these effects occur at close to the same time as was identified for consonant perception, and others occur at different points during development. Table 24.1 lists some of the experiential influences on speech processing seen at different points during infancy.

The discrimination abilities and perceptual preferences shown by newborn infants demonstrate that some tuning has taken place either prenatally or rapidly within the first several hours after birth. Newborn infants show a preference for their mothers' voices (DeCasper & Fifer, 1980) and for a story (DeCasper & Spence, 1986) and song (Panneton, 1985) heard prenatally. By 4 days of age infants show a processing advantage for their native language by consistently discriminating their native language from an unfamiliar language but sometimes failing to discriminate two unfamiliar languages (Mehler, Jusczyk, Lambertz, Halstead, Bertoncini, & Amiel-Tison, 1988). Moreover, this processing advantage remains when the speech is low-pass filtered, suggesting it is familiarity with the prosody, not the segmental structure, that facilitates processing of the native language. More recently, it has been shown that newborn infants also show a preference for listening to continuous speech samples in their native language (Moon, Cooper, & Fifer, 1993). Thus, by the time infants are days or even hours old, their speech processing preferences and capabilities re-

TABLE 24.1.
Experiential Influences

Newborn to 4 months

Ability to discriminate own from non-native language (Mehler et al., 1988)

Preference for native language (Moon, Cooper, & Fifer, 1993)

Preference for mother's voice (DeCasper & Fifer, 1980)

Preference for story and song heard prenatally (DeCasper & Spence, 1986)

6 months

Structure of native language vocalic categories changing (Kuhl et al., 1992)

Some decline in discrimination of non-native vowels (Polka & Werker, 1994)

Prefer pauses at clause boundaries in native language only (Jusczyk et al., 1992)

Prefer word lists reflecting native language prosody (Jusczyk et al., 1993)

10 months

No longer discriminate non-native consonant contrasts (Werker & Tees, 1984)

No longer discriminate non-native vocalic contrasts (Polka & Werker, 1994)

Prefer words that correspond to native phonotactic rules (Jusczyk et al, 1993)

Prefer words with common native stress (Jusczyk, Cutler, & Redanz, 1993)

veal experiential influences.[4]

The extensive work reviewed by Jusczyk and Kemler Nelson (this volume) shows that infant perceptual preferences are influenced by many aspects of the phonology of the linguistic input during the next several months of life. Language-specific sensitivity to clausal and phrasal information and to some prosodic differences in the way single words are pronounced is evident by as early as 6 months of age, whereas language-specific sensitivity to phonetic and phonotactic regularities is not evident until 9 or 10 months of age. Indeed, by 11–12 months of age (Hallé & Boysson Bardies, 1994) and possibly before (Jusczyk & Aslin, in press), infants show a preference for listening to familiar words. These findings have led to the suggestion that infants become sensitive to those aspects of the native phonology that are cued by more global prosodic cues at an earlier age than they do for strictly phonetic aspects of the native phonology (Jusczyk, 1992; Cutler & Mehler, 1993).

The research reviewed earlier suggests that infants become sensitive to the more global prosodic characteristics of their native language prior to showing a sensitivity to the finer details. This in turn suggests that there may be a sequence to becoming sensitized to the characteristics of the native language. We argue that this sequence is a necessary product of the joint influence between the characteristics of the input and the changing perceptual sensitivities of infants. To an inexperienced (infant) listener, global prosody may be the most salient and readily available characteristic of the input. Thus, in some ways, it is no surprise that infants first show language specificity in processing this kind of information in speech. As infants become familiar with the global prosody of their native language, other kinds of information in the input may become more salient. That is, familiarity with the global prosodic structure of the native language might provide a frame for allowing infants to access some of the finer information internal to that larger prosodic grouping, for example individual words or syllables. Familiarity with the next level of detail might in turn allow access to finer detail, such as unit internal phonetic detail. Thus as infants' perceptual sensitivities change as a function of increasing familiarity with the native language, different kinds of information in the speech stream become more readily perceptible. In other words, although the characteristics of the input might remain "constant" in some absolute sense, as the infants' perceptual sensitivities change, different sources of information come to the foreground. This could yield a pattern of regular, se-

---

[4]In a recent article, one of us has speculated that similar experiential influences, in combination with species-specific perceptual biases, might explain the "language-general" phonetic processing biases displayed by the very young infant. That is, perhaps prenatal and early postnatal experiences impact in "expectable" ways on early brain development, and thus help set perceptual sensitivity to those kinds of sounds that can be produced by a human vocal tract (Werker & Tees, 1992).

quential events in "perceptual tuning" to the characteristics of the native language.[5]

AN INTEGRATIVE FRAMEWORK FOR CONSIDERING THE ROLE OF THE INPUT

The changing relation between infants' perceptual sensitivities and "available" characteristics of the input is represented graphically in Fig. 24.2.

In this figure, the input and infants' capabilities are represented as different but integral dimensions of a single form. The speech perception capabilities of infants that can be measured at any single point in time will be the outcome of previous perceptual analysis, and will also lead to new kinds of information uptake.

The model represented in Fig. 24.2 accounts well for the regularity in the sequence of changes in perceptual sensitivity to the native language that occur across infancy. The model cannot, however, adequately account for the striking regularity in timing at which some of these changes in perceptual sensitivity are seen. Indeed, a model such as that shown in Figure 24.2 would predict that infants who are exposed to a greater "quantity" of input would advance more rapidly through the sequence of "tuning" to the various properties of the native phonol-

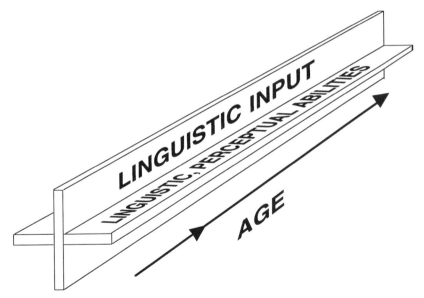

FIG. 24.2. A schematic representation of infants' speech processing performance as the joint product of both the changing characteristics of the input and the changing perceptual and linguistic abilities of infants.

[5]This is similar in many respects to the WRAPSA model proposed by Jusczyk (1992).

ogy than would infants who receive less input. Thus the model shown in Fig. 24.2 would allow for considerable interindividual variability around the age at which different language-specific milestones in perception are achieved.

The empirical data, however, yield quite a different story. In our research, almost all of the infants tested at 8 months of age discriminated both the native and the non-native consonant contrasts with equal ease, whereas almost none of the infants aged 10 months discriminated the non-native consonant contrasts (Werker & Tees, 1984; Werker & Lalonde, 1988). Similarly, in research recently reported by Jusczyk, Cutler, and Redanz (1993) 21 of 24 infants aged 9 months showed a preference for listening to lists of words following a common English, strong–weak stress pattern, whereas only 13 of 24 (virtually chance level in a 2-choice task) infants aged 6 months showed such a preference. Similar results were obtained for preference for native language phonotactic patterns (Jusczyk, Friederici, Wessels, Svenkerud, & Jusczyk, 1993). Although Jusczyk's work does not reveal how infants between 6 and 9 months of age might perform, the high level of consistency in performance within each age group is striking. We suggest that, in order to explain this regularity in performance across infants of the same age, some control factor other than the two factors represented in Fig. 24.2 needs to be posited.

At least two kinds of control factors can be proposed to account for the age regularity in changes in perceptual performance. One factor is biological maturation. For example, it could be that the module (or modules) used in speech processing becomes open to specific types of influence at specific points in development, with the timing of openness controlled by biological maturation (Christophe, Dupoux, & Mehler, 1993; and see Mazuka, this volume, for a discussion of sequential parameter setting). A second kind of factor is domain-general cognitive influences. For example, the regularity in age at which specific changes in perceptual performance occur could be explained by age-related changes outside of the linguistic/phonetic domain making possible new kinds of processing, in this case, speech processing. In the remainder of this chapter, we discuss the viability of this second kind of factor, and present some preliminary supportive evidence.

Before delving into the specifics of our (admittedly embryonic) model of how domain-general abilities might influence infants' ability to utilize information in the input, a few points of clarification are in order. First, we are *not* addressing the "speech is special" question (Liberman & Mattingly, 1985). We are simply asking whether, at some point in the information-processing stream, performance on speech perception tasks is influenced by domain-general capabilities. Domain-general capabilities could hypothetically influence the actual analysis of the input, and, in such cases, the notion that speech is special would be compromised. However, it is equally possible that domain-general influences could act on the outputs of a "speech-specific" perceptual analysis. In other words, domain-general capabilities could exert their influence in post-perceptual processing (see Fodor, 1985). If this turns out to be the case, the notion that "speech is special" (or that at least some aspects of speech perception rely on special-purpose computational devices) is intact. Although we have no evidence that would allow us to distinguish those two possibilities, our current preference is that domain-general influences are probably important in post- rather than pre-perceptual processing (see Lalonde & Werker, in press, for further argumentation). In either case, if domain-general influences are shown to influence performance in speech perception tasks, then it is important that they be considered in attempting to understand the role of the input on language processing.

Second, we are not necessarily suggesting that every identifiable manifestation of increasing sensitivity to the phonological structure of the native language necessarily relies on some advance in domain-general cognitive capabilities. Indeed, it is our thinking at the current time that many of the advances seen can be fully accounted for by the joint forces represented in Fig. 24.2. For example, we predict that some of the changes in sensitivity to the native language, such as tuning to global prosody and even language-specific magnet effects, might be adequately accounted for by a model such as that represented in Fig. 24.2. However, other advances in language-specific processing may rely on the emergence of new (or more advanced) domain-general capabilities. As a prime example, many of the chapters in this volume report there to be regularities in the input such as content words occurring in final position, occurring on the pitch peak, or having longer vowels. The tacit assumption made in reporting these regularities is that infants can remember and make use of this regularity and predictability. Research on cognitive development in infancy, however, tells us quite another story. There are age-related changes in infants' ability to detect and anticipate predictable sequences (Canfield & Haith, 1991), and there are age-related changes in both the kind of information infants can remember, and the delay across which they can remember it (Rovee-Collier & Schecter, 1992; see also Bertoncini, Bijeljac-Babic, Kennedy, Jusczyk, & Mehler, 1988, for speech perception data relevant to this issue). Thus at the very least, the ability to detect regular position and to remember something about the characteristics of the speech in that position is required for infants to take advantage of this characteristic of the input. Thus we would argue that in addition to considering infants' current perceptual status, it is also critically important to ascertain whether infants have the requisite domain-general cognitive skills to take advantage of whatever regularity there is in the input.

As another example (and one that will be addressed in considerably more detail), we would like to predict that the reorganization in the ability to discriminate non-native phonetic contrasts at around 10 months of age may be one of the class of changes that can only occur in concert with advances in domain-general cognitive abilities. As an initial step in addressing this possibility, Lalonde and Werker (in press) tested whether there is synchrony in the emergence of a more advanced level of performance on a speech perception task as well as on two non-linguistic tasks that have been shown to change at around the same age. Thirty infants aged 8 to 9 months of age were tested on tasks that approximately half the infants should pass and approximately half should fail. It was reasoned that if performance on the speech perception task is unrelated to performance on the two non-speech tasks, then different infants should pass and fail each task. If, however, successful performance on one (or both) of the non-speech tasks predicted performance on the speech task, support would be obtained for the possibility that successful performance on the tasks relies on the emergence of some more general common ability.

The speech perception task involved testing English-learning infants on their ability to discriminate the Hindi retroflex–dental contrast used in our earlier work (Werker & Tees, 1984; Werker & Lalonde, 1988). The two non-speech tasks were a visual categorization task and an object search task. The visual categorization task, taken from Younger and Cohen (1983), requires that infants detect category structure on the basis of the correlation among three visual features. The AB object search task (Piaget, 1954; present implementation similar to Diamond, 1990) requires that the infants search correctly in a 2-choice hiding task following a brief delay.

These two non-linguistic tasks were chosen using three criteria: They had to show replicable changes at the same age across several different experiments and/or several different labs; they had to be non-linguistic tasks; and they had to assess two different kinds of domain-general cognitive abilities to provide information about what the common domain-general ability might be if a relation were found. The visual categorization task was chosen to assess the possibility that the change in sensitivity to non-native phonetic distinctions relies on the ability to detect the criterial properties of a class of stimuli. The object search task, although no longer universally accepted as a measure of infants' understanding of object permanence (e.g., Baillergeon, 1992), is still thought to be a measure of means-ends understanding. As well, it is often used as a measure of more global cognitive change, and has been shown to be correlated with changes in functioning in the prefrontal cortex (Diamond, 1990). Thus the object search task was chosen to assess the possibility that the change in sensitivity to non-native phonetic distinctions reflects a more general change in cognition at around this age.

The results from this study revealed that the ability to detect categories on the basis of their (arbitrary) correlational structure, and the ability to search correctly in a 2-choice hiding task following a delay, emerge synchronously with the decline in the ability to discriminate non-native consonant contrasts. Importantly, this synchrony maintains even when age is partialed out.

The synchrony noted previously is consistent with the possibility that changes in speech perception are related to developmental events outside of the linguistic domain. Although considerably more research is required to verify this relation and to specify empirically what the common ability might be that underlies these synchronous changes, grounds for speculation exist. Some mileage can be gained by a consideration of the specific skills tapped by the two cognitive tasks together with a consideration of other advances infants make at around 10 months of age. At around this time infants are not only able to detect category structure as shown in our replication of Younger and Cohen's (1983) work, but are able to ignore counterexamples in a stimulus set and seek out the systematic correlations of visual features that specifies the category (Younger, 1993). Thus infants seem to be able to detect category structure on the basis of the most consistent correlation of attributes. Given the probabilistic nature of linguistic input, this is a domain-general skill that could help infants tremendously in detecting language-specific category structure.

In attempting to understand the meaning of the advance in performance on the AB task, it is useful to remember that this advance is thought to rely on an advance in infants' understanding of means-ends relations. In support, by this age infants are not only able to search correctly in a 2-choice object search task as shown in our work, but are simultaneously able to coordinate other indirect actions with an understanding of the location of information (for example, infants can "resist" attempting to put their hand through a clear acrylic barrier, and instead reach around the barrier; Diamond, 1990). This ability to remember and coordinate separate sources of information would allow infants to not simply show a preference for some familiar patterns over others, but to *make use* of some of the regularities in the input in their specific language. A critical component of successful means-ends behavior and successful detection of category structure is the ability to remember relational information across a delay. Recent evidence shows this to be firmly in place by 10 months. Infants at this age seem to be able to not only remember, but to reproduce complex sequences of actions, even over a 1-week delay (Meltzoff, 1988). Thus, it may be this very set of skills—the ability to detect, remember, and coordinate separate sources of information—that allows infants to coordinate their memory for phonetic detail with the specific contexts in which they have heard that detail. This would allow infants to discover which phonetic variation is criterial and which only arbitrary in their language-learning environment. Thus, with the advance in domain-general cognitive skills that seems to occur at around 10 months of age, infants may be poised to process the outputs from the analysis of speech information in new ways—in this case new ways that allow a restructuring of perceptual categories to reflect which variability is functional (will have phonemic status) in the infants' language-learning environment.[6]

We are not the only researchers to propose that domain-general abilities may influence special-purpose processing at critical points in development. A study reported by Hermer (1993) suggested that a modular spatial-orientation capacity becomes open to domain-general (or possibly other modular) processes at a critical point in development. Within the realm of speech perception, a recent study reported by Morgan and Saffran (in press) was designed to specifically test the age at which infants can coordinate disparate sources of information in a speech processing task. In the Morgan and Saffran study, infants of 6 and 9 months of age were tested on their ability to discriminate a change in a sequence of syllables when the syllables occurred in a random or predictable prosodic grouping. It was reported that infants of 9 but not 6 months of age were able to integrate the prosodic grouping (stress pattern) with the distributional (syllabic sequences) information. Infants of 6 months of age were able to discriminate changes in both stress pattern and syllabic sequence, but were not able to coordinate the two sources of information. Infants of 9 months, on the other hand, were able to integrate both sources of information. They could use the prosodic structure to search for regularities in the distributional information. Morgan and Saffran suggest that this ability to use one source of information (rhythm) as a frame or context for another source of information (syllabic sequence) relies on the emergence of means-ends understanding. Their research thus provides the first direct evidence that infants are able to make advances in speech processing when they apply a more general ability to coordinate two sources of information to the information in the speech stream.

We propose that in order to fully understand the role of the input, the model represented in Fig. 24.2 be expanded to include the influence of domain-general advances in cognitive functioning on infant speech processing. As a general model, we suggest that at certain points in development new cognitive capabilities emerge that allow infants to deal with information in the input in qualitatively new ways. These new found skills add a third dimension, then, to the set of influences we have been considering. As discussed before, as infants' perceptual sensitivities change, they are able to extract different kinds of information from the input. In addition, we would suggest that with the emergence of new domain-general cognitive skills infants can use the information they can extract from the input in different ways.

---

[6]We are not suggesting that the child necessarily has a system of phonemes at this point in development, rather we are suggesting that perhaps the perceptual categories become restructured in a way that reflects the phonetic variation that is functional in the native language. This would, of course, allow the child to have perceptual representations in place that would facilitate movement onto the next task, the task of word learning (see also, Werker & Pegg, 1992).

This expanded model is represented graphically in Fig. 24.3. The geometric shapes encircling the developmental trajectory represent the emergence of new found abilities. The processing that occurs after the addition of each geometric shape is thought to be different than that which preceded it. That is, the emergence of new found cognitive capabilities could make possible important advances in speech processing and language use. In this case, with perceptual representations that reflect the criterial variation in the native language, infants are poised to move on to the task of word learning.[7]

In closing, we point out that although this model is only embryonic at this time, its basic assumptions are testable. It makes the clear prediction that children who are delayed in cognitive development should be delayed in the achievement of some (but not all) milestones in speech processing and language use. The predictions that come from this chapter are that those skills that rely on the emergence of domain-general abilities—the skills that can only be explained by Fig. 24.3—will be delayed in children with cognitive delays. If our prediction is correct that the reorganization in cross-language consonant perception seen by 10-12 months is an advance that relies on new domain-general skills, then this particular milestone should be affected by cognitive development. Similarly, the ability to pull specific and regularly occurring forms out of the speech stream (i.e., to begin to learn words) should be affected by cognitive development, whereas changes that appear more continuous in nature, such as the advent of language-specific perceptual magnet effects, should not be related to cognitive delay.

SUMMARY

In summary, we argued that in order to fully understand the role of the input on infant speech processing it is necessary to describe not only the changing characteristics of the input, the language processing biases infants bring to the input at any point in time, and the joint influence of these two, but also any emergent skills in perceptual and cognitive analysis that infants may bring to the speech processing task. We anticipate that this approach to understanding age-related changes in speech processing will help bridge the gap between research in infant speech perception and research in child language acquisition. We suggest that because even the simplified speech directed to infants conveys multiple levels of information in a simultaneous fashion, it is essential to fully describe the changing capabilities of infants in order to fully understand the phenomenon of bootstrapping. Otherwise, we have no way of knowing just what information in the speech stream infants are perceiving, and we have no way of knowing just what functional linguistic task that information is serving. Thus, only with some guiding notions concerning the linguistic and perceptual biases of infants at dif-

---

[7]See Lloyd, Werker, and Cohen, 1993, for a new procedure for testing word learning in young infants.

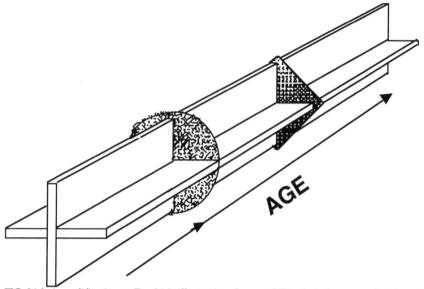

FIG. 24.3. A modification to Fig. 24.2, illustrating the possibility that there may be discrete points in development that reflect the coalescence of previous experiential and developmental processes, and enable the emergence of qualitatively new speech processing capabilities.

ferent ages and the domain-general abilities infants have available to apply to the perceptual/linguistic information they detect, can we make continuing progress in understanding the bootstrapping question. In other words, until we put the baby into the bootstraps, we will be unable to fully understand the role the input plays in language processing.

REFERENCES

Aslin, R. N. (1993). Segmentation of fluent speech into words: Learning models and the role of maternal input. In B. de Boysson-Bardies, S. de Schonen, P. Jusczyk, P. McNeilage, & J. Morton (Eds.), *Developmental neurocognition: Speech and face processing in the first year of life* (pp. 305-316). The Netherlands:Kluwer Academic Publishers.

Baillergeon, R. (1992). The object concept revisited: New directions in the investigation of infants' physical knowledge. In C. E Granrud (Ed.), *Visual perception and cognition in infancy* (pp. 265-315). Hillsdale, NJ: Lawrence Erlbaum Associates .

Bertoncini, J., Bijeljac-Babic, R., Kennedy, L., Jusczyk, P. W., & Mehler, J. (1988). An investigation of young infants' perceptual representations of speech sounds. *Journal of Experimental Psychology: General, 117*, 21-33.

Best, C. T., McRoberts, G. W., & Sithole, N. N. (1988). The phonological basis of perceptual loss for non-native contrasts: Maintenance of discrimination among Zulu clicks by English-speaking adults and infants. *Journal of Experimental Psychology: Human Perception and Performance, 14*, 345-360.

Best, C. T., & McRoberts, G. W. (1989, April). *Phonological influences in infants' discrimination of two nonnative speech contrasts*. Paper read at the Society for Research in Child Development, Kansas City, MO.

Best, C. T. (1989, July). *Phonologic and phonetic factors in the influence of the language environment on speech perception.* Paper read at the International Conference on Event Perception and Action, Miami University, Miami, OH.

Best, C. T. (1993). Emergence of language-specific constraints in perception of non-native speech: A window on early phonological development. In B. de Boysson-Bardies, S. de Schonen, P. Jusczyk, P. McNeilage, & J. Morton (Eds.), *Developmental neurocognition: Speech and face processing in the first year of life* (pp. 289-304). The Netherlands: Kluwer Academic Publishers.

Canfield, R. L., & Haith, M. M. (1991). Young infants' visual expectations for symmetric and asymmetric stimulus sequences. *Developmental Psychology, 27,* 198-208.

Christophe, A., Dupoux, E., & Mehler, J. (1993). How do infants extract words from the speech stream? A discussion of the bootstrapping problem for lexical acquisition. In E. V. Clark (Ed.), *Proceedings of the 24th Annual Child Language Research Forum* (pp. 209-224). Stanford: CSLI.

Cooper, R. P., & Aslin, R. N. (1990). Preference for infant-directed speech in the first month after birth. *Child Development, 61,* 1584-1595.

Cutler, A., & Mehler, J. (1993). The periodicity bias. *Journal of Phonetics, 21,* 103-108.

DeCasper, A. J., & Fifer, W. P. (1980). Of human bonding: Newborns prefer their mother's voice. *Science, 208,* 174-176.

DeCasper, A. J., & Spence, M. J. (1986). Prenatal maternal speech influences newborns' perception of speech sounds. *Infant Behavior and Development, 9,* 133-150.

Diamond, A. (1990). The development and neural bases of memory functions as indexed by the AB and delayed response tasks in human infants and infant monkeys. *Annals of the New York Academy of Sciences, 608,* 276-318.

Echols, C. H., & Newport, E. L. (1992). The role of stress and position in determining first words. *Language Acquisition, 2,* 189-220.

Ferguson, C. A. (1964). Baby-talk in six languages. *American Anthropologist, 66,* 103-114.

Fernald, A. (1984). The perceptual and affective salience of mothers' speech to infants. In L. Feagans, C. Garvey, & R. Golinkoff (Eds.), *The origins and growth of communication* (pp. 5-29). Norwood, NJ: Ablex.

Fernald, A. (1985). Four-month-old infants prefer to listen to "motherese." *Infant Behavior and Development, 8,* 181-195.

Fernald, A., & Kuhl, P. (1987). Acoustic determinants of infant preference for motherese speech. *Infant Behavior and Development, 10,* 279-293..

Fernald, A., & Mazzie, C. (1991). Prosody and focus in speech to infants and adults. *Developmental Psychology, 27,* 209-221.

Fernald, A., McRoberts, G. W., & Herrera, C. (1993). *The effects of prosody and word position on lexical comprehension in infants.* Unpublished manuscript, Stanford University.

Fernald, A., Taeschner, T., Dunn, J., Papousek, M., Boysson-Bardies, B., & Fukui, I. (1989). A cross-language study of prosodic modifications in mothers' and fathers' speech to preverbal infants. *Journal of Child Language, 16,* 477-501.

Fodor, J. A. (1985). Precis of "The modularity of mind." *Behavioral and Brain Sciences, 8,* 1-42.

Gleitman, L., Newport, E., & Gleitman, H. (1984). The current status of the motherese hypothesis. *Journal of Child Language, 11,* 43-79.

Grieser, D., & Kuhl, P. K. (1989). Categorization of speech by infants: Support for speech-sound prototypes. *Developmental Psychology, 25,* 577-588.

Hallé, P. & Boysson-Bardies, B. de (1994). Emergence of an early receptive lexicon: Infants' recognition of words. *Infant Behavior and Development, 17,* 119-129.

Hermer, L. (1993). Increases in cognitive flexibility over development and evolution: Candidate mechanisms. *Proceedings of the Cognitive Science Society, 15,* 545-549.

Hirsh-Pasek, K., Kemler Nelson, D. G., Jusczyk, P. W., Wright Cassidy, K., Druss, B., & Kennedy, L. (1987). Clauses are perceptual units for young infants. *Cognition, 26,* 268-286.

Jusczyk, P. W. (1985). On characterizing the development of speech perception. In J. Mehler & R. Fox (Eds.), *Neonate cognition: Beyond the blooming buzzing confusion* (pp. 199-229). Hillsdale, NJ: Lawrence Erlbaum Associates.

Jusczyk, P. W. (1992). Developing phonological categories from the speech signal. In C. Ferguson, L. Menn, & C. Stoel-Gammon (Eds.), *Phonological development: Models, research, and implications* (pp. 17-64). Timonium, MD: York Press.

Jusczyk, P. W., & Aslin, R. N. (in press). Infants' detection of the sound patterns of words in fluent speech. *Cognitive Psychology.*

Jusczyk, P. W., Cutler, A., & Redanz, L. (1993). Infants' sensitivity to predominant stress patterns in English. *Child Development, 64,* 675- 687.

Jusczyk, P. W., Friederici, A. D., Wessels, J. M., Svenkerud, V. Y., & Jusczyk, A. M. (1993). Infants' sensitivity to the sound patterns of native language words. *Journal of Memory and Language, 32,* 402- 420.

Karzon, R. (1985). Discrimination of polysyllabic sequences by one- to four-month old infants. *Journal of Experimental Child Psychology, 39,* 326-342.

Kemler Nelson, D. G., Hirsh-Pasek, K., Jusczyk, P. W., & Wright-Cassidy, K. (1989). How the prosodic cues in motherese might assist language learning. *Journal of Child Language, 16,* 55-68.

Kuhl, P. J. (1987). Perception of speech and sound in early infancy. In P. Salapatek & L. Cohen (Eds.), *Handbook of infant perception: Volume 2* (pp. 275-381). New York: Academic Press.

Kuhl, P. J. (1991). Human adults and human infants exhibit a prototype effect for phoneme categories: Monkeys do not. *Perception & Psychophysics, 50,* 93-107.

Kuhl, P. K., Williams, K. A., Lacerda, F., Stevens, K. N., & Lindblom, B. (1992). Linguistic experience alters phonetic perception in infants by 6 months of age. *Science, 255,* 606-608.

Lalonde, C. E., & Werker, J. F. (in press). Cognitive influences on cross-language speech perception in infancy. *Infant Behavior and Development.*

Liberman, A. M., & Mattingly, I. G. (1985). The motor theory of speech perception revised. *Cognition, 21,* 1-36.

Lloyd, V. L., Werker, J. F., & Cohen, L. B. (1993, March). *Age changes in infants' ability to associate words with objects.* Poster presented at Society for Research in Child Development, New Orleans, LA.

Mehler, J., Jusczyk, P. W., Lambertz, G., Halstead, N., Bertoncini, J., & Amiel-Tison, C. (1988). A precursor of language acquisition in young infants. *Cognition, 29,* 143-178.

Meltzoff, A. N. (1988). Infant imitation after a 1-week delay: Long-term memory for novel acts and multiple stimuli. *Developmental Psychology, 24,* 470-476.

Moon, C., Cooper, R. P., & Fifer, W. (1993). Two-day olds prefer their native language. *Infant Behavior and Development, 16,* 495-500.

Morgan, J. L., & Saffran, J. R. (in press). Emerging integration of segmental and suprasegmental information in preverbal speech segmentation. *Child Development.*

Newport, E. L. (1976). Motherese: The speech of mothers to young children. In N. J. Castellan, D. B. Pisoni, & G. R. Potts (Eds.), *Cognitive theory* (Vol. 2, pp. 177-217). Hillsdale, NJ: Lawrence Erlbaum Associates.

Oshima-Takane, Y. (1988). Children learn from the speech not addressed to them: The case of personal pronouns. *Journal of Child Language, 15,* 95-108.

Panneton, R. K. (1985). *Prenatal experience with melodies: Effect on postnatal auditory preference in human newborns.* Unpublished doctoral dissertation. University of North Carolina at Greensboro.

Papousek, M., Papousek, H., & Bornstein, M. (1985). The naturalistic vocal environment of young infants: On the significance of homogeneity and variability in parental speech. In T. M. Field & N. Fox (Eds.), *Social perception in infants* (pp. 269-297). Norwood, NJ: Ablex.

Papousek, M. Papousek, H., & Symmes, D. (1991). The meanings of melodies in motherese in tone and stress languages. *Infant Behavior and Development, 14,* 415-440.

Pegg, J. E., Werker, J. F., & McLeod, P. J. (1992). Preference for infant-directed over adult-directed speech: Evidence from 7-week-old infants. *Infant Behavior and Development, 15,* 325-345.

Pegg, J. E., Werker, J. F., & McLeod, P. (in preparation). *A cross-language investigation of infant preference for infant-directed interactions: Evidence from 7-week old infants.*

Piaget, J. (1954). *The child's construction of reality.* New York: Basic Books.

Polka, L. (1995). Linguistic influences on vowel perception in adults. *Journal of the Acoustical Society of America, 97,* 1286-1296.

Polka, L., & Werker, J. F. (1994). Developmental changes in perception of non-native vowel contrasts. *Journal of Experimental Psychology: Human Perception and Performance, 20,* 421-435.

Ratner, N. B., & Pye, C. (1984). Higher pitch in BT is not universal: Acoustic evidence from Quiche Mayan. *Journal of Child Language, 11,* 512-522.

Rovee-Collier, C., & Schechter, A. (1992). Perceptual identification of contextual attributes and infant memory retrieval. *Developmental Psychology, 28,* 307-318.

Schieffelin, B. (1979). Getting it together: An ethnographic approach to the study of the development of communicative competence. In E. Ochs & B. Schieffelin (Eds.), *Developmental pragmatics* (pp. 73-108). New York: Academic Press.

Snow, C. E. (1977). The development of conversation between mothers and babies. *Journal of Child Language, 4,* 1-22.

Stern, D. N., Speiker, S., Barnett, R. K., & MacKain, K. (1983). The prosody of maternal speech: Infant age and context related changes. *Journal of Child Language, 10,* 1-15.

Werker, J. F. (1993). Developmental changes in cross-language speech perception do not involve loss. In J. Goodman & H. Nusbaum (Eds.), *The transition from speech sounds to spoken words: The development of speech perception* (pp. 93-120). Cambridge, MA: MIT Press.

Werker, J. F., Gilbert, J. H. V., Humphrey, K., & Tees, R. C. (1981). Developmental aspects of cross-language speech perception. *Child Development, 52,* 349-353.

Werker, J. F., & Lalonde, C. E. (1988). Cross-language speech perception: Initial capabilities and developmental change. *Developmental Psychology, 24,* 672-683.

Werker, J. F., & McLeod, P. (1989). Development changes in attentional and affective responsiveness to "parentese." *Canadian Journal of Psychology, 43,* 230-246.

Werker, J. F., & Pegg, J. E. (1992). Infant speech perception and phonological acquisition. In C. Ferguson, L. Menn, & C. Stoel-Gammon (Eds.), *Phonological development: Models, research, and implications* (pp. 285-312). Parkton MD: York.

Werker, J. F., Pegg, J. E., & McLeod, P. F. (1994). A cross-language investigation of infant preference for infant-directed interactions. *Infant Behavior and Development, 17,* 323-333.

Werker, J. F., & Polka, L. (1993a). Developmental changes in cross-language speech perception: New challenges and new directions. *Journal of Phonetics, 21,* 83-101.

Werker, J. F., & Polka, L. (1993b). The ontogeny and developmental significance of language-specific phonetic perception. In B. de Boysson-Bardies, S. de Schonen, P. Jusczyk, P. McNeilage, & J. Morton (Eds.), *Developmental neurocognition: Speech and face processing in the first year of life* (pp. 275-288). The Netherlands: Kluwer Academic Publishers.

Werker, J. F., & Tees, R. C. (1983). Developmental change across childhood in the perception of non-native speech sounds. *Canadian Journal of Psychology, 37,* 278-286.

Werker, J. F., & Tees, R. C. (1984). Cross-language speech perception: Evidence for perceptual reorganization during the first year of life. *Infant Behavior and Development, 7,* 49-63.

Werker, J. F., & Tees, R. C. (1992). The organization and reorganization of human speech perception. *Annual Review of Neuroscience, 15,* 377-402.

Younger, B. A. (1993). Understanding category members as "the same sort of thing": Explicit categorization in ten-month infants. *Child Development, 64,* 309-320.

Younger, B. A., & Cohen, L. (1983). Infant perception of correlations among attributes. *Child Development, 54,* 858-867.

25 Dynamic Systems Theory: Reinterpreting "Prosodic Bootstrapping" and Its Role in Language Acquisition

Kathy Hirsh-Pasek and Michael Tucker
Temple University

Roberta Michnick Golinkoff
University of Delaware

Evidence from psychology, linguistics, and computational linguistics all points to the same conclusion: Prosody does not map transparently onto syntax (see Dresher, this volume; Fisher & Tokura, this volume; Venditti, Jun, & Beckman, this volume). It follows, therefore, that analyses of prosody cannot provide total access to linguistic structure. Children will have to integrate information from a number of input sources to induce the grammar of their native language.

The strong position that prosody could reveal complete phrase structure trees was never really endorsed by the framers of the "prosodic bootstrapping hypothesis" (Gleitman & Wanner, 1982; Morgan & Newport, 1981). Rather, they suggested that prosodic information might provide useful and important cues to form class, major constituents, open class versus closed class units, and so forth. This volume is testimony to the fact that there are a number of informative cues in the prosodic input; cues that may take the learner a long way towards discovering the units of language. The chapters in this volume, however, also highlight the need for ways to examine how children use prosody in conjunction with syntactic, semantic, social, and morphological cues to solve the "logical problem of language acquisition" (Baker & McCarthy, 1981). This chapter presents one way to think about how children might use multiple input sources to solve this complex acquisition problem. By introducing the metaphor of dynamic systems theory (see Thelen & Smith, 1994), we offer a new way of thinking about the problem space and offer concrete suggestions on how to empirically investigate the role of multiple inputs on the child's developing grammatical system.

To this end, the chapter has three main goals. The first is to evaluate the current status of the prosodic bootstrapping hypothesis as it was conceptualized and introduced by various authors in the early 1980s. The second is to introduce the theory of dynamic systems and to propose that this theory offers new ways of thinking about speech perception data. The third and final goal is to reconceptualize the role that prosodic analysis might play in language acquisition. A working model of language comprehension will be presented that springs from systems theory and that posits a strong initial role for prosodic analysis. This brief introduction to the model is then used to demonstrate how systems theory can be used to provide a framework for a set of empirical approaches.

THE CURRENT STATUS OF THE PROSODIC BOOTSTRAPPING HYPOTHESIS

What is meant by prosodic bootstrapping, and how has research progressed since the prosodic bootstrapping hypothesis was introduced? Gleitman and Wanner helped to initiate research on prosodic bootstrapping when they presented the following hypothesis:

> ...an infant who is innately biased to treat intonationally circumscribed utterance segments as potential syntactic constituents would be at a considerable advantage in learning the syntactic rules of his language. (1982, p. 26)

Five years later, Pinker articulated some reservations about this position:

> According to the prosodic bootstrapping hypothesis, the child uses [acoustic] regularities to infer the phrase structure tree from the sentence. Such a tree carves the sentence into roughly the correct units of analysis, and the child can couch generalizations about order and agreement in terms of these units. There has been no explicit model of how the child would actually accomplish these analyses, so it is hard to evaluate this hypothesis. (1987, p. 404)

Since these passages were written, much research has been directed towards evaluating the status of this hypothesis.

The prosodic bootstrapping hypothesis makes three fundamental claims: 1) that there are reliable cues to syntactic structure in the sound system of language; 2) that infants are sensitive to these cues and can exploit them in on-line speech processing; and 3) that the units thus extracted will assist children in the detection of the units and relations in their native language. Ample evidence exists to show that the first claim is mostly true. For example, research has documented that major syntactic boundaries are marked by changes in pausing, syllable lengthening, and intonation (Cooper & Paccia-Cooper, 1980; Kelly, 1992); that strong word-initial stress is present in the majority of content words in English (Cutler & Carter, 1987); and that word or syllable stress, syllable number, word duration relative to other words in an utterance, and voicing are all partially correlated with syntactic information about grammatical class (Kelly, 1992; Morgan, Shi, & Allopenna, this volume). Thus, cues are available to give the learner some hints about linguistic structure (clauses and phrases), class of word (open versus closed), and form classes (nouns and verbs).

As for the second claim, much research has now demonstrated that infants and young children can access these cues in on-line processing. Kelly (1992), for example, provided experimental evidence that both adults and 3-year-olds are sensitive to the phonological correlates of grammatical categories. That is, they are sensitive to the fact that nouns typically contain more syllables than do verbs and are pronounced with different stress patterns. Working with a selective listening paradigm, Hirsh-Pasek, Kemler Nelson, Jusczyk, Wright, Druss, and Kennedy (1987) showed that infants orient longer to speech samples that *preserve* prosodic cues to linguistic units than to samples that *fractionate* such indicators. Specifically, infants have been found to be sensitive to the acoustic correlates of linguistic units like clauses (i.e., sentences and embedded sentences; Hirsh-Pasek, et al., 1987), phrases (i.e., noun phrases and verb phrases; Jusczyk, Hirsh-Pasek, Kemler Nelson, Kennedy, Woodward, & Piwoz, 1992), and words (Woodward, 1989). At a segmental level, Jusczyk (see Jusczyk & Kemler Nelson, this volume) showed infant sensitivity to phonotactic cues for native (in this case, English) versus non-native (in this case, Dutch) languages, and for frequent phonological patterns and stress patterns within the native language. These discriminations are achieved between 6 and 9 months of age since infants of 6 months seem to show little sensitivity to the cues that 9-month-olds readily detect.

Finally, Jusczyk and Kemler Nelson (this volume) demonstrated that infants are not only sensitive to these cues, but that they use them in on-line processing. Using a high amplitude sucking technique, these investigators found that infants were more likely to detect changed phonemes within words if the words were delivered in the context of a clause (with clausal intonation) than if they were delivered in isolation.

In general, then, research from the last decade validates the first two claims made by the prosodic bootstrapping hypothesis. Indeed, much of the developmental data on infants' perception of prosody can be characterized in terms of three perceptual shifts.[1]

First, throughout the first year of life, infants seem to shift from sensitivity to psychoacoustic categories to phonological ones (see Jusczyk, 1986). Second, children move from being relatively adept at perceiving phonetic contrasts from many different languages to perceiving only those in the native language (e.g., Werker & Tees, 1984; Best, McRoberts, & Sithole, 1988). And finally, children move from perceiving suprasegmental properties of prosody to segmental properties. Support for this last shift comes from two sources. Research has demonstrated reliable developmental shifts from reliance on suprasegmental cues to clause structure at the earliest ages, to a reliance on the segmen-

---

[1]By shift, we do not want to imply that earlier information or processing is lost. Rather, the infant shifts to a new strategy—still able to return to the old if the situation requires.

tal cues to words (see Hirsh-Pasek & Golinkoff, 1993). Further, Echols (1987) demonstrated that preschool children are more likely to respond on the basis of intonational cues than are adults, who attend to phonemic cues. In all of these cases, the shifts are matters of relative weighing and probability. These data do not suggest that other information is *not* available to children, simply that children tend to put more weight on certain cues over others at various points in development. For example, Echols' (1987) children can attend to phonemic information, they just do so less reliably than do adults.

Researchers should be encouraged by this sizable body of research (see also Fernald, 1991), because it documents how children process the sound system of language. The way in which children process speech can also have enormous implications for how they learn language; in particular, for the role that speech segmentation could potentially play in grammatical learning. The question still to be answered, however,— and the question this volume is directed to—is one of degree: *How far can prosodic bootstrapping take us in accounting for the phenomenon of language acquisition?* That is, although there are now data on what Peter's (1985) termed unit "extraction," we have yet to address Pinker's (1987) doubts about whether children can "couch generalizations about order and agreement in terms of these units." Given that the correlation between prosody and syntax is imperfect, we must also ask whether prosodic information (or similar surface cues for deaf individuals) serves as a *foundation* for language learning, or merely as a *toehold* that helps infants uncover surface analogues to a more abstract system. That is, does prosody provide a base upon which language and grammar will be *constructed*, or does it provide an access route through which the grammar will be *discovered*? In sum, although data exist on the presence of prosodic cues in the speech stream and on infants' ability to use these cues, little is known regarding the third claim generated from the prosodic bootstrapping hypothesis: How prosodic analysis is actually used —if it is—in the service of grammatical development.

BASIC CONCEPTS IN DYNAMIC SYSTEMS THEORY.

We next introduce an old theory that has recently been imported into psychology—dynamic systems theory. Space limitations allow us to provide only a sketch of this theory. The interested reader can examine the theory in greater detail in two books by Thelen and Smith (1994) and Smith and Thelen (1993). Although we do not endorse all of the tenets of the theory, we will use the theory metaphorically to help explain selected developments in infant prosodic perception as well as in language acquisition in general.[2]

---

[2]Thelen and Smith offer a biologically-driven constructivist view of development that is decidedly anti-nativist and anti-maturational. The portrait of development that they paint is one embued with no a priori structure. While their extreme view may turn out to be correct, one need not adopt such a view to benefit from the insights of dynamic sys-

The force of the theory can be illustrated by an example from findings that infants have increasing sensitivity to acoustic cues that correlate with clausal, phrasal, and word units in the input stream (see Hirsh-Pasek & Golinkoff, 1993). Given the newness of these data, the emphasis has been on documenting the infant's perception of prosodic cues for these language units; little theoretical explanation for the mechanisms underlying these perceptual shifts has been offered. Systems theory, however, provides a framework in which to examine the mechanisms underlying these shifts (Thelen, 1989; Thelen & Ulrich, 1991; Thelen & Smith, 1994; Tucker & Hirsh-Pasek, 1993). It also, as we will discuss later, provides some tools for investigating these shifting sensitivities.

Our laboratory at Temple University utilizes a "selective listening paradigm" (see Hirsh-Pasek & Golinkoff, 1993), in which speech is "doctored" to either disrupt natural prosody (placing uniform pauses randomly within clauses) or to preserve prosody (placing pauses between clauses where they are normally found). Infants' preference for natural versus disrupted stimuli is measured by recording the duration of looking towards the speaker from which each sample type emanates (see Jusczyk & Kemler Nelson, this volume, for a fuller description of the method).

Results of this research program have yielded strong support for infant sensitivity to prosodic cues to linguistic structure. For example, infants who are $4^{1}/_{2}$ months of age are sensitive to cues for clause structure in both foreign (Polish) and native languages (Hirsh-Pasek et al., 1987). At 6 months, this sensitivity is only to those cues for the native tongue. By 9 months, our subjects are sensitive to cues like syllable lengthening and fundamental frequency shifts that are coincident with phrasal units (Jusczyk et al., 1992). Finally, by 11 months, infants demonstrate a sensitivity to the segmental information that signals word units in the language (see Hirsh-Pasek & Golinkoff, 1993, for a review). Ongoing research with Tucker and Kemler Nelson is replicating these findings in a paradigm that does not require the insertion of pauses. Rather, slides are used that either change at points in time coincident or non-coincident with accompanying language. So far, 10-month-old subjects prefer to look at the slides that change in a coincident manner rather than to those that do not.[3]

This brief example enables an illustration of a number of key systems theory concepts. Throughout this chapter, reference is made to the prosodic "system." From a dynamic perspective, a system is defined as

---

tems theory. Many of the processes that they outline could be helpful to both the "rationalist constructivist" (Gelman, 1990) who posits some initial structure that then gets embellished, or even to the nativist who posits a strong structural component that must be triggered through exposure to input cues (Wexler & Manzini, 1987).
[3]Morgan, Swingley and Mitirai (1993) have also obtained evidence for clausal discrimination by 10-month-olds by inserting noise instead of pauses at coincident vs. non-coincident spots.

any highly organized, interrelated collection of components dedicated to a particular task or function, e.g., the task of parsing the incoming language. Thus, the prosodic system is an organization of percepts, representations, and rules for parsing incoming speech. Ordinarily, systems remain in a state of dynamic or relative stability, also known as the *dynamic steady state*. For example, a consistent set of behavioral responses, such as those that are evidenced through the selective listening task, reveal that the infant is reliably using the same set of cues like lengthening, or change in fundamental frequency that coincide with the edges of linguistic units, to discriminate between "real" and fractionated linguistic units.

The dynamic character of the system can be appreciated only when focusing on the ways in which the steady state can be disrupted. Two changes—one from the "outside," the context, and one from the "inside," the child's perception—can throw the system into imbalance. First, when the context is altered, the system must adapt too. For example, infants who have had reliable and consistent exposure to one language and who are exposed to another must develop prosodic systems sufficiently adapted to both input languages. Thus, it is important to always characterize systems with respect to a given context (here, the input speech), one that has a fairly consistent or predictable pattern of acoustic information. The behavioral response can thus be altered—the system disrupted—with shifts in contextual input.

The second way in which the relatively steady system can be disrupted is when the child becomes more familiar with the input. Changes in the weights that certain prosodic cues have for the child can alter the system's organization. The cues that might receive differential weighing in the system, like syllable lengthening, fundamental frequency, or pausing, would be termed *control parameters* in systems language. They are called this because changes in the way the infant perceives these control parameters govern the way in which the system will respond. Thus, these control parameters are afforded special consideration in the theory. Indeed, changes in the weights assigned to control parameters can lead to system-wide changes, cascading organizational changes that could force the system into a new dynamic steady state.

The main point here is that there might be acoustic control parameters that drive the perceptual system towards more detailed, language-relevant analyses. Although this hypothesis is intriguing, the state of speech perception research does not allow us to *specify* what these control parameters are. Instead, educated guesses must be made (as in the earlier examples) about the potential of syllable lengthening, fundamental frequency shifts, and pausing to serve as control parameters.

Before demonstrating how these control parameters might work within acoustics, it is important to understand the concept more fully. Two examples from the domain of motor development (Thelen & Smith,

1994) serve the purpose. The first is the example of the horse's gait; the second, infants' early stepping and walking. As is well known, horses have several gaits, e.g., walking and trotting. What is interesting about these gaits is that they are qualitatively different—that is, galloping is not just a faster version of walking. What causes this shift in the entire pattern of movement? Thelen and Smith argued that one of the control parameters is "speed."

> As the horse continuously increases its speed, its gait shifts discontinuously from a walk to a trot to a gallop with no stable intermediate pattern... How does the horse shift gaits? Conventionally one might postulate a neural network or a code that switches from one output pattern to another at certain predetermined speed thresholds... A synergetic view, in contrast, would view the gait as a stable collective variable compressing the possible combinations of the structural components in an energetic and task context which would include not only the intentionality of the horse, but the qualities of the support surface, visual information guiding the horse and so on... The lesson from chemistry and physics is that self-organization is not mystical; patterns can be generated by a system seeking cooperative stability. (Thelen & Smith, 1994, pp. 119-120)

For both horses and humans, the preferred dynamic steady state is walking. Adjustments in the way in which the system operates must be made if the system is altered. By increasing speed the subsystems are thrown into a state of imbalance. Fig. 25.1 attempts to capture a graphic representation of the shifts from one steady state to another as the control parameter of the horse's speed is altered. Notice that there is a dip

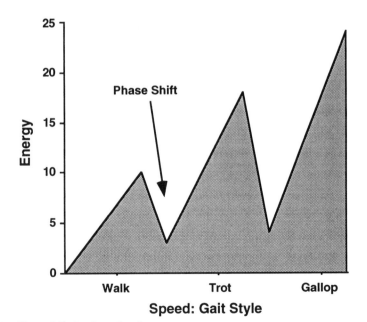

FIG. 25.1 Phase shifts in a horse's gait

in the horse's performance just at the point where the shift takes place. Then with increased speed, a new stability or steady state is achieved.

The second example comes from the case of stepping and walking in infants. Walking has always been thought to be the purest case of a maturational development. Although infants do not walk until 13 or 14 months, they do show stepping behavior as neonates. This stepping behavior appears to vanish only to reappear when the infant matures and is ready to walk. Yet, Thelen (1989) has data that call this into question. Working under the systems theory model, she assumes that one of the control parameters here is *weight* on the legs. When the infant gains body fat, the motor system can no longer support stepping. The system reorganizes and does not display stepping behavior until the weight is redistributed at about 8 to 10 months.

What Thelen did to make her point was to "tweak" the system by altering the weight on the legs. When an infant is immersed in water or supported on a moving treadmill, the effects of extra body weight are nullified. Stepping behavior is evidenced in both conditions. In fact, even in cases where the treadmill is constructed such that each leg could be driven at a different speed, infants maintained sophisticated stepping behavior with alternating steps. As we alter the control parameter (here weight on the legs) we force a reorganization in the system.

With these examples in mind, what might be hypothesized as control parameters for acoustic perception? One clear case from the segmental level seems to be the control parameter of voicing that, when varied, gives adults and infants different categorical percepts for consonants like "p" and "b" (see Venditti, Jun, & Beckman, this volume). The question to be raised given findings on the perception of linguistic units (Hirsh-Pasek & Golinkoff, 1993) is, what enables infants to move from perceiving the acoustic correlates of clauses to perceiving the acoustic correlates of phrases? It is at least possible that either vowel lengthening, pausing, or fundamental frequency shifts operate in similar ways to voicing, serving as control parameters at the suprasegmental level. A more likely control parameter, however, is some *coalition of cues* whose weights change relative to one another in the context of different unit boundaries. It is as if there were a recipe for the perception of acoustic cues to clausal units. The ingredients of this recipe for English, might be: one pause, one vowel lengthening, and two parts fundamental frequency declination. The recipe for acoustic correlates to phrasal units might contain the *same ingredients* but perhaps in different proportions. The result is a qualitative shift in the infant's perception. Although all of this is speculative, it does raise the illustrative point that shifts in the *weights* of cues can alter the way in which the system is mobilized. Just as the horse's movement shifts from a trot to a gallop with the control parameter of speed, so too will the infant's attention move from clauses to phrases with the child's attention to the appropriate control parameters from acoustics.

In sum, the control parameter is that cue or set of cues that drives a reorganization of the system. These reorganizations are called *"phase shifts"* and have been described by Thelen and Smith (1994) and Smith and Thelen (1993) as "soft assemblies" of the available system behaviors that mobilize to meet a certain function within a particular context. Each phase shift results in a new dynamic steady state—like trots and gallops or attention to cues signaling clauses or phrases. If the context remains fairly stable, then the system will become more and more adapted to a constrained environment. Thus, with consistent input in English, the child becomes more and more of an English specialist and the system becomes more detailed and refined. If, however, the child is exposed to new contexts (say, a foreign language), the new system will be more likely to adapt yet again to its context.

Thus far, what has been described is the notion of a dynamic system that rests at certain steady states. These states can be disrupted by control parameters with varying weights. As the control parameters exert their influence on the system, the system reorganizes and a phase shift occurs. Before moving from a definition of the concepts to some predictions about the ways in which these concepts might work in development, one further point must be made. The very fact that a cue or coalition of cues serves as a control parameter at a given stage of development does not guarantee that this variable will have the same status at other points in development. Phonotactic information that signals word boundaries is only available to the infant after much development has already occurred—at about 9 months. Before this time, manipulating these cues should have no discernible effects on the behavior of infant subjects—it is, in a sense, developmentally irrelevant to the child. Givon (1985) captured this point eloquently when he wrote,

> The adult input, so it seems, cannot be characterized once and for all, in a uniform, stable fashion. Rather, at any given point one must discover: a) what the child is ACTUALLY LEARNING, b) what the child has ALREADY LEARNED, and c) what the child is yet INCAPABLE OF LEARNING, for whatever reason. It is only (a) [that is, what the child is actually learning], and the input pertaining to it, that is actually relevant for the purpose of studying the relation between input and output in the acquisition of language. (p. 1008)

(See Werker, Lloyd, Pegg, & Polka, this volume and Ratner, this volume, for other examples of this point).

Dynamic systems theory not only introduces new ways of conceptualizing the data, but also makes specific theoretical predictions about the course of development. That is, the theory makes constrained global predictions about the ways in which systems develop and the ways in which systems interact with other systems. First, all systems begin developmentally in a relatively undifferentiated state. As development progresses and the system undergoes phase shifts, this globality gives way to organizations that are successively more complex, more integrated and differentiated, and increasingly dedicated to a constrained task domain. There is ample evidence of just this kind of developmental sequence in the cross-linguistic perceptual literature. Children begin life with a relatively undifferentiated perceptual system. That is, they are quite adept at perceiving a wide variety of prosodic cues to syntactic structure, even from those languages with which they have had little or no exposure. However, as development proceeds, their perceptual systems become increasingly sensitive to the cues most relevant to the native language, and sensitivity to cross-language cues diminishes (see Werker et al., this volume). Notice that this organizational change is a trade-off: While children become *less* sensitive to cues that do *not* appear in the parent language, they become *increasingly* sensitive to additional prosodic information in the parent language, information that was not accessible to them at earlier points in development.

Thus, the development of native-language perception is exemplary of systemic change. The system, undergoing developmental phase shifts in the service of adaptation to an average expectable context (the language input), becomes increasingly sensitive to just that context. The plasticity of the system is lost but what is gained is increased behavioral complexity. In fact, the theory also predicts that those infants who have had bilingual exposure should lose the ability to attend to non-native contrasts later than those exposed to only one language. This should manifest itself in a continuing sensitivity to cross-linguistic cues, even for those cues that are not represented in the bilingual environment. At least one study (Eilers, Gavin, & Oller, 1982) supports this prediction. In this study, 6- to 8-month-old English/Spanish exposed infants were adept at perceiving contrasts in Czech, while different infants at the same age exposed only to English did not discriminate the same Czech contrasts. Thus, the first prediction is that the system becomes more dedicated to its context over time.

Second, a global prediction of the theory centers around system behavior at the point of phase shift. Although the phase shifts are discrete and discontinuous, behavior while the shift takes place may often appear increasingly variable or inconsistent. Notice here that the period of variability exists at the level of the individual child, not as a between-group difference. Note also that both the developmentally prior and the developmentally later phases will last much longer than does the period of variability. The variable state is not a phase per se, but a transition between discrete phases. A phase shift can be signaled by increasingly variable performance. Those who reliably perform on one task may suddenly give erratic responses, only to perform well again at a later point. This is the U-shaped curve that we find so often in development. Such cases would be indicative of a phase shift wherein old rules or strategies are becoming reorganized to best fit newly realized aspects of the input. Evidence for phase shifts of this kind requires longitudinal research rarely conducted in this area, a new research area that has concentrated thus far on group differences.

What data would be necessary to validate the hypothesis that a phase shift has occurred? In English, an SVO language, nouns are often found at the ends of sentences (Aslin et al., this volume; Goldfield, 1993). Multisyllabic words are more often nouns than other parts of speech (Kelly, 1992). Nouns have word initial stress and greater pitch excursions than other parts of speech. As Morgan (1986) argued, these constellations of prosodic cues make sentence-final nouns very prominent and learnable in English. Yet we know that children must come to recognize nouns in other sentence positions. How do they do this? It is at least possible that after a preliminary analysis of early noun units through prosodic and positional cues, infants learn the syntactic or semantic distribution associated with these units (i.e., that these units are often proceeded by "the"). If this guess is correct, then prosody would be more heavily weighted for form class assignment *early* in development only to be later surpassed by assignment based on syntactic cues. The way to analyze whether a phase shift has occurred would be to pit prosodic cues against syntactic cues (using novel words) to see which set of cues wins out. On this hypothesis, early on, any word with noun-like prosody anywhere in the sentence should be judged a noun. Later even words with verb-like prosody would be judged to be nouns if embedded in noun syntax. To use Peter's (1985) terms, syntactic information from the surrounding "frames" or "slots" in which word classes occur may come to be weighted more heavily than the prosodic cues to form class.

Adoption of the systems theory metaphor highlights areas in the extant literature that deserve further research attention. While it is *a priori* difficult to make explicit predictions about the ages at which certain reorganizations will occur, the between-group data that have been generated license reasonable hypotheses that must obviously be verified with controlled, longitudinal study.

To complete this very brief review of the systems theory account, then, systems theory offers a way of looking at how children "marshal their available resources to solve a functional problem" (Thelen & Smith, 1994, p. 34). This research program must begin with the dedication to discover what counts as control parameters for children within particular contexts, and with a commitment to watching how the control parameters drive change (see Eimas, this volume, for a program of research that is investigating some of the so-called control parameters for infant language perception). To borrow from Thelen and Smith (1994), this strategy for research will "open up new operational strategies for truly understanding the motors of change, rather than providing only descriptions of the products of change" (p. 34). It can also be useful in documenting how "multiple interacting subsystems with a synchronous developmental pathway (be they multiple cues at the prosodic level or system wide interactions between syntax and semantics and prosody at a more macro level) cooperate to engender qualitative developmental shifts" (Thelen & Smith, 1994, p. 24; our parentheses).

REINTERPRETING PROSODIC BOOTSTRAPPING THROUGH SYSTEMS THEORY

Does systems theory just offer a new interpretation to some old and familiar data, or can it offer more to researchers and theorists? We propose that these concepts allow us to point our empirical microscope in new directions. We begin by moving from a narrow to a wide-angle lens on the bootstrapping issue. With the narrow lens, the role of prosodic bootstrapping is to help children abstract linguistic units by using particular correlations between acoustic properties and syntactic properties. Widening the lens a little and drawing on evidence supplied by Morgan (1986) and Morgan, Meier, and Newport (1987) it becomes apparent that unit abstraction at a later point in development comes from morphology plus acoustics, from what they termed "bracketed input." With an even wider lens (a level implied by Pinker, 1987, wherein he characterized numerous bootstrapping systems at work in development), the concepts of systems theory can be applied to evaluate the role of prosody in language acquisition in the broadest sense.

A number of points emerge from this perspective. First, multiple inputs including input from syntax, semantics, and prosody are all at work, are all available, and are all mutually informing during language development. It is not that these inputs *become* available at different developmental times. Rather, the relative weights of these systems in the overall acquisition process are subject to developmental shift. Second, as an offshoot of the multiple input hypothesis, there is no one-way information flow from primary (prosodic) to secondary (syntax) levels, from surface bootstrap systems to foundational levels. Indeed, this latter point leads one to question whether the term "bootstrapping" with its unidirectional flavor is the best metaphor to use if we are trying to capture the complexities inherent in the acquisition process. Metaphors from systems theory may be more appropriate.

The systems theory metaphor allows for the reformulation of the role of prosody within the broader context of language development. It allows one to look, not at unidirectional support for language learning—be it through prosodic, semantic, or syntactic bootstrapping—but rather at the interaction of each of these systems across time. Inspired by systems theory, Golinkoff and Hirsh-Pasek (1995), for example, are using some of the systems theory principles to guide research on early language comprehension. Their theory of comprehension is based on findings that infants appear to know considerably more about grammar than is reflected in their language production. Why do infants show such precocity in syntactic comprehension? Their response to this question rests on the premise (as others before them have emphasized, e.g., Morgan et al., 1987) that the grammar of language is found not just in the syntax (from the child's perspective) but in a richly correlated set of cues available in the social context, the prosody, semantics, and morphology. The child *mines* these correlations, different ones at different points in development, to crack the linguistic code and to demonstrate increasingly sophisticated language comprehension. Prosody plays a key role in language comprehension at the outset (when the child is in the first year and a half of life) although its importance diminishes with development. Further, in this theory, language comprehension can occur at first *only* when the cues coming from the semantic, prosodic, syntactic, and social systems are redundantly correlated. In other words, for early comprehension to occur, all the planets, as it were, must be in alignment. On this story, children tend to show precocious syntactic comprehension when comprehension is assessed in a way that provides redundant cues from all the supporting systems (see Hirsh-Pasek & Golinkoff, 1993; Golinkoff & Hirsh-Pasek, 1995, for reviews). With enough redundant support from the input, children can reveal even fragile syntactic knowledge. They are not forced to choose between systems (i.e., semantic systems that are in opposition to syntactic ones, as in, "The boy bit the dog."). In sum, without presenting the details of an evolving model of language comprehension, it is clear that thinking along the lines of systems theory can open up new ways of exploring old problems.

How can one go on to test this model or any of the issues suggested by a systems theory account? The power of the dynamic systems metaphor rests on its theoretical predictions and on its empirical validation. As noted in Table 25.1, five empirical approaches fall out from a systems theory perspective.

First, a systems perspective demands the collection of *longitudinal* data. Only through analysis over time can one detect a reorganization of the system in phase shifts, manifested as a temporary increase in intra-individual behavioral variability. Behaviors that were once reliably present seem to be performed only inconsistently as the system reorganizes. For example, early in development, there is reason to believe that children rely on syllable stress to determine word boundaries, at least in languages like English where this reliance has a high probability of being correct. The realization that other cues signal the same units may result in a phase shift as children come to rely on even more reliable cues like syntax. This phase shift would produce behavioral variability, and quite possibly an apparent developmental regression. Children who had previously been quite accurate in parsing words from speech might become less so. Once children come to understand the relation between the sets of cues, however, their success at parsing these units from speech should again become more reliable. Data of this sort could also show us how children, in their desire to understand and to be understood, shift to grammatical cues for reliable sentence interpretation. These kinds of powerful data can only be obtained by looking at data longitudinally. Both Jusczyk and Kemler Nelson (this volume) and Peters and Strömqvist (this volume) have provided examples of longitudinal research of this kind.

TABLE 25.1
Five Empirical Approaches Emerging from a Systems Theory Perspective

Longitudinal studies
Studies to discover control parameters
Additive studies
Subtractive studies
Conflict studies

Second, a systems theory perspective suggests that research be directed towards the *discovery of control parameters*. Within the prosodic system, we must discover which cue or cues have special status for the infant as control parameters. It could be that some acoustic parameters are merely "piggy-backing" on others and not really contributing to the infant's perception of various constituents. For example, Jusczyk et al. (1992) noted that syllable lengthening and changes in fundamental frequency tended to co-occur at the boundaries judged as coincident with linguistic boundaries. Whether one of these cues is more informative than the other for parsing at the clause versus the phrase level or whether one cue or the interaction of both cues is responsible for our findings is as yet unknown. By "tweaking" the system through cue manipulation, it is possible to find out which cue or cues serve as control parameters.

Third, systems theory with its emphasis on interactions among systems suggests emphasis on *additive studies*. In additive experiments various cues are systematically added to determine the point at which discrimination or categorization is achieved. One might ask, for example, do pauses *alone* signal clauses or must pauses be combined with final vowel lengthening? Perhaps discrimination will only be found when yet a third cue is added such as fundamental frequency declination at the end of clauses. This example is at the micro-system level, within the prosodic system, but one could perform additive experiments at the macro-level, combining across different systems. For example, what cues does a child use to analyze when a new word is a noun? For multisyllabic words, is it just relative syllable stress that gives away noun-hood or must there be determiners present as well? Must there also be support from the environment in terms of the presence of a concrete object? This example, then, begins with a cue from the prosodic system to which is added a syntactic/morphological cue, and then a cue from the semantic system. By beginning with just one set of input cues from one subsystem and systematically adding other cues, thresholds for the identification of units and rules in the language can be determined. Note that Morgan and Newport (1981) and Morgan et al. (1987) engaged in a number of these kinds of manipulations in their experiments on the learning of miniature, artificial languages in adults. Thus, additive studies are designed to find out which variables in combination, preferably added one at a time, make a change in the dependent variable.

Subtractive studies could obtain convergence with the findings from additive studies by taking just the opposite tack—systematically removing cues. This is the fourth direction in which systems theory would send research efforts. The basic question addressed by subtractive studies is, when does performance break down? The removal of which cue or cues causes the infant's performance to decline to chance? Fernald, McRoberts, and Herrera (in press) conducted the first study of which we are aware that has used this tactic. They tested infants' comprehension of familiar words. The study was conducted in a version of the preferential looking paradigm (Golinkoff, Hirsh-Pasek, Cauley, & Gordon, 1987). When the words were presented in the prosody of adult-directed speech, 15-month-old infants' comprehension of known words declined to chance. Using *novel* words, Golinkoff, Alioto, Hirsh-Pasek, & Kaufman (1992) showed that the prosodic aspects of motherese have powerful effects on word learning. Twenty-two and 34-month-olds were exposed to novel objects, labeled with words in the preferential looking paradigm. In a between-subjects design, children heard sentences naming the object delivered in either infant-directed or adult-directed speech. Two key effects emerged: First, many more subjects at the younger age level were lost due to fussiness in the adult-directed (17) condition than in the infant-directed (6) condition. This is important because it suggests that young children may "tune out" of word-learning opportunities without the added support of infant-directed prosody. Interestingly, subject loss was much smaller in *both* the adult-directed and infant-directed condition at the older age level (one each), suggesting that by the time a child is almost 3 years old, prosodic support for word learning is less crucial. Second, while it appeared that both the adult-directed and infant-directed groups learned the novel words, only the group that heard infant-directed speech showed this effect reliably in visual fixation. Thus, the prosody of infant-directed speech may serve to maintain the infant's attention longer in word-learning situations. As Fernald (1991) suggested, word learning may be very fragile at first, initially requiring the support of prosodic, semantic, and syntactic cues. Gradually, children have more stable systems that can support word learning in the absence of a prosodic scaffold. Thus, additive and subtractive studies can converge to give information about how children weight different systems at different points in language learning.

Fifth, and finally, dynamic systems theory suggests new research in *conflict studies*. Conflict studies are those that pit one prosodic variable against another, or one system against another, leading to a more complete understanding of the relative weights children attach to different systems components during development. Echols (1987) provides one such study in which this approach has been fruitful. Two- and 3-year-olds engaged in a word-learning task in which they were taught distinct names for two discriminable objects and then presented with a third name that was intonationally identical to one name and phonologically identical to the other. Children were asked to choose the object that corresponded to the new name. Echols' child subjects were more likely to base their judgments of similarity on intonation, whereas adults were more likely to rely on phonology as the critically similar feature.

In sum, systems theory can provide a way of rethinking the role that prosody might play in language acquisition. The crux of the story is this: Rather than characterizing the different language inputs as always being in some hierarchical relation to each other, it is much more useful to think of these inputs as systems of developing knowledge that are mutually informing and always available, but with differing weights along the developmental trajectory. Such a vision provides a non-linear framework for development. Further, the predictions outlined earlier are testable within the systems framework through at least five methods of study. Although a number of these methods have been used in the literature, the systems framework *unites* them and demonstrates ways to obtain convergence on how infants approach language processing at various points in development.

To fully understand the role of prosody in language acquisition, one must look at it as one of many contributing systems that coordinately enable the induction of grammar. Many of us have given lip service to this claim, but few (save Morgan, 1986; Morgan et al., 1987) have tried to examine it. Systems theory offers one way to look at the changing role of prosody in the acquisition of language across time. It also offers a set of empirical tools for testing our predictions.

ACKNOWLEDGMENTS

We thank Irene Vogel of the University of Delaware for her extremely helpful comments and Vickie Porch for her able secretarial assistance.

REFERENCES

Baker, C. L., & McCarthy, J. (1981). *The logical problem of language acquisition.* Cambridge, MA: MIT Press.

Best, C. T., McRoberts, G. W., & Sithole, N. M. (1988). The phonological basis of perceptual loss for non-native contrasts: Maintenance of discrimination among Zulu clicks by English-speaking adults and infants. *Journal of Experimental Psychology: Human Perception and Performance, 14,* 345-360.

Cooper, W. E., & Paccia-Cooper, J. (1980). *Syntax and speech.* Cambridge, MA: Harvard University Press.

Cutler, A., & Carter, D. M. (1987). The predominance of strong initial syllables in the English vocabulary. *Computer Speech and Language, 2,* 133-142.

Echols, C. (1987). *A perceptually-based model of children's first words.* Unpublished doctoral dissertation, University of Illinois at Urbana-Champaign.

Eilers, R. E., Gavin, W. J., & Oller, D. K. (1982). Cross-linguistic perception in infancy: The role of linguistic experience. *Journal of Child Language, 9,* 289-302.

Fernald, A. (1991). Prosody in speech to children: Prelinguistic and linguistic functions. *Annals of Child Development, 8,* 43-80.

Fernald, A., McRoberts, G., & Herrera, C. (in press). Effects of prosody and word position on lexical comprehension in infants. *Journal of Experimental Psychology.*

Gelman, R. (1990). Structural constraints on cognitive development: Introduction to a special issue of *Cognitive Science*. *Cognitive Science, 14*, 3-9.

Givon, T. (1985). Function, structure, and language acquisition. In D. I. Slobin (Ed.), *The crosslinguistic study of language acquisition* (Vol. 2, pp. 1005-1029). Hillsdale, NJ: Lawrence Erlbaum Associates.

Gleitman, L. R., & Wanner, E. (1982). Language acquisition: The state of the state of the art. In E. Wanner & L. R. Gleitman (Eds.), *Language acquisition: The state of the art* (pp. 3-48). Cambridge, MA: Cambridge University Press.

Goldfield, B. (1993). Noun bias in maternal speech to one-year-olds. *Journal of Child Language, 20*, 85-99.

Golinkoff, R. M., Alioto, A., Hirsh-Pasek, K., & Kaufman, D. (1992, October). *Infants learn lexical items better in infant-directed than in adult-directed speech.* Boston Child Language Conference.

Golinkoff, R. M., & Hirsh-Pasek, K. (1995). Insights into grammatical development: Children's comprehension of sentences. In P. Fletcher & B. MacWhinney (Eds.), *Handbook of language acquisition* (pp. 430-462). London: Basil Blackwell.

Golinkoff, R. M., Hirsh-Pasek, K., Cauley, K. M., & Gordon, L. (1987). The eyes have it: Lexical and syntactic comprehension in a new paradigm. *Journal of Child Language, 14*, 23-46.

Hirsh-Pasek, K., & Golinkoff, R. M. (1993). Skeletal supports for grammatical learning: What infants bring to the language learning task. In C. Rovee-Collier & L. P. Lipsitt (Eds.), *Advances in infancy research, Volume 8* (pp. 299-338). Norwood, NJ: Ablex.

Hirsh-Pasek, K., Kemler Nelson, D. G., Jusczyk, P. W., Wright, K., Druss, B., & Kennedy, L. J. (1987). Clauses are perceptual units for young infants. *Cognition, 26*, 269-286.

Jusczyk, P. W. (1986). Speech perception. In K. R. Boff, L. Kaufman, & J. P. Thomas (Eds.), *Handbook of perception and human performance* (pp. 1-57). New York: Wiley.

Jusczyk, P. W., Hirsh-Pasek, K., Kemler Nelson, D. G., Kennedy, L J., Woodward, A., & Piwoz, J. (1992). Perception of acoustic correlates of major phrasal units by young infants. *Cognitive Psychology, 24*, 252-293.

Kelly, M. (1992). Using sound to solve syntactic problems. *Psychological Review, 99*, 349-364.

Morgan, J. L. (1986). *From simple input to complex grammar.* Cambridge, MA: MIT Press.

Morgan, J. L., Meier, R. P., & Newport, E. L. (1987). Structural packaging in the input to language learning: Contributions of intonational and morphological marking of phrases to the acquisition of language. *Cognitive Psychology, 19*, 498-550.

Morgan, J. L., & Newport, E. L. (1981). The role of constituent structure in the induction of an artificial language. *Journal of Verbal Learning and Verbal Behavior, 20*, 67-85.

Morgan, J., Swingley, D., & Mitirai, K. (1993, March). *Infants listen longer to speech with extraneous noises inserted at clause boundaries.* Paper presented at the Society for Research on Child Development, New Orleans.

Peters, A. M. (1985). Language segmentation: Operating principles for the perception and analysis of language. In D. I. Slobin (Ed.), *The crosslinguistic study of language acquisition: vol. 2. Theoretical issues* (pp. 1029-1067). Hillsdale, NJ: Lawrence Erlbaum Associates.

Pinker, S. (1987). The bootstrapping problem in language acquisition. In B. MacWhinney (Ed.), *Mechanisms of language acquisition* (pp. 399-441). Hillsdale, NJ: Lawrence Erlbaum Associates.

Smith, L., & Thelen, E. (Eds.), (1993). *A dynamic systems approach to development: Applications.* Cambridge, MA: MIT Press.

Thelen, E. (1989). Self-organization in developmental processes: Can systems approaches work? In M. Gunnar & E. Thelen (Eds.), *The Minnesota Symposium in Child Psychology: Vol. 22. Systems and development* (pp 77-117). Hillsdale, NJ: Lawrence Erlbaum Associates.

Thelen, E., & Smith, L. (1994). *A dynamic systems approach to the development of cognition and action.* Cambridge, MA: MIT Press.

Thelen, E., & Ulrich, B. D. (1991). Hidden skills: A dynamic systems analysis of treadmill stepping during the first year. *Monographs of the Society for Research in Child Development, 56* (1, Serial No. 233).

Tucker, M. L., & Hirsh-Pasek, K. (1993). Systems and language: Implications for acquisition. In L. Smith & E. Thelen (Eds.), *A dynamic systems approach to development: Applications* (pp. 359-384). Cambridge, MA: MIT Press.

Werker, J. F., & Tees, R. C. (1984). Cross-language speech perception: Evidence for perceptual reorganization during the first year of life. *Infant Behavior and Development, 7,* 49-63.

Wexler, K., & Manzini, M. R. (1987). Parameters and learnability. In R. Roeper & E. Williams (Eds.), *Parameter setting* (pp. 41-76). Dordrecht: Reidel.

Woodward, A. (1989). *In the beginning was the word: Infants' early perception of word-units in the speech stream.* Unpublished honors thesis, Swarthmore College.

Author Index

Johnson, M. H., 107, *116*
Johnston, B., 231, *232, 246*
Johnston, J., 234, 245, *246*
Jones, D., 193, *211*
Jongman, A., 62, *65,* 251, 258, *262,* 370, *386*
Juliano, C., 126, *134*
Jun, S.-A., 16, 291, *311,* 449, 456
Jurgens, U., 57, *65*
Jusczyk, A. M., *38, 134, 261, 407, 446*
Jusczyk, P. W., 2, 4, 7, 9, 16, 17, *21,* 22, 26, 27, 29, 31, 33, 34, 35, *37, 38, 39, 65,* 95, *98,* 104, 109, *115, 116,* 117, 125, 131, 133, *134,* 143, *149,* 151, 161, 162, 164, 166, *168, 169,* 179, *183,* 252, 253, *261, 262,* 276, *282,* 317, 321, 322, 326, 327, *329,* 331, 344, 349, *362,* 365, 366, 379, 380, 381, 382, *386,* 390, 391, 392, 394, 395, 396, 400, 401, 402, 403, 405, *407, 408,* 412, 413, 417, 419, 420, 421, *423, 424,* 431, 435, 436, 437n, 438, 439, *444, 445, 446,* 451, 453, 461, 462, *465*

K

Kadi-Hanifi, K., 370, *386*
Kagan, J., 55, *64*
Kager, R., 178, *183,* 190, *211*
Kahn, D., 43, *54*
Kaiki, N., 68, 75, *82, 83,* 351, *362*
Kaisse, E., 187, 193, 198, *211*
Kaja, J., 74, *83*
Kamhi, A., 235, 245, *246*
Kanerva, J., 187, 188, 190, *211*
Kang, O., 191, *211*
Karlgren, J., 74, *83*
Karzon, R., 429, *446*
Katz, B., 415, *424*
Katz, W., 62, *65,* 370, *386*
Kaufman, D., 463, *465*
Kaye, J. D., 52, *54,* 180, *183*
Kean, M.-L., 265, 266, *282*
Keating, D. P., 109, *115*
Kelly, M. H., 11, 14, 19, *21,* 251, 252, 254, 255, 257, 258, 259, 261, *262,* 263, 265n, 327, 338, *341,* 344, 349, *362,* 390, *407,* 418, *424,* 450, 451, 459, *465*
Kemler Nelson, D. G., 2, 4, 9, 16, 17, *21,* 26, 33, 34, 35, *38,* 125, 143, *149,* 179, *183,* 317, *329,* 331, 344, *362,* 365, 366, 379, 382, 383, *386,* 390, 391, 396, *407, 408,* 412, 421, *424,* 429, 435, *445, 446,* 451, 453, 461, *465*
Kenesei, I, 345, 355, *363,* 418, *425*
Kennedy, L. J., 2, 16, *21,* 33, 34, 35, *37, 38,* 109, *115,* 179, *183,* 317, *329, 362,* 365, 366, *386,* 390, 391, *407, 424,* 439, *444, 445,* 451, *465*

Kenstowicz, M., 46, *54*
Killeen, P. R., 28, *38*
Kimball, J. P., 279, *282*
Kiritani, S., 301, *311,* 382, *386*
Kisseberth, C., 46, *54*
Klatt, D. H., 60, 61, 62, *64,* 103, *116,* 153, *168,* 243, *246,* 344, 345, 346, 347, 351, 359, *362,* 371, 372, *386,* 401, *407,* 412, *424*
Klatt, L., 60, *64*
Klavans, J. L., 47, *54,* 198, *211,* 268, *282*
Klein, H. B., 152, *168*
Klouda, G. V., 370, *385*
Kluender, K. R., 28, *38*
Kolinsky, R., 92, *98*
Köpke, K. M., 259, *262*
Krause, R. M., 370, *384*
Kreiman, J., 374, *386*
Krikhaar, E., 414, *425*
Krumhansl, C. L., 392, *407*
Kruyt, J. G., 372, *387*
Kubozono, H., 322, *329*
Kucera, H., 265, 267, *282*
Kuhl, P. K., 28, 31, 32, 33, *37, 38,* 58, 59, 60, *64,* 95, *98,* 112, *116,* 118, *134,* 162, *168,* 253, *261, 262,* 275, *282,* 321, *328,* 357, *361,* 428, 431, 432, 436, *445, 446*
Kuhn, R., 68, *82*
Kuno, S., 318, *329*

L

Laberge, S., 269, *283*
Lacerda, F., 31, *38,* 162, *168, 262, 446*
Ladd, D. R., 190, 194, *211*
Lafferty, J., 68, *81*
Lahiri, A., 92, *99*
Lalonde, C. E., 162, *170,* 431, 438, 439, 440, *446, 447*
LaMendola, N. P., 9, 277, 421, 428
Landau, B., 151, 153, *168,* 234, *246,* 266, *282,* 343, *362,* 365, *386,* 390, *407,* 411, *423*
Lane, H., 368, *386*
Lapointe, S. G., 371, *385*
Larreur, D., 74, *83*
Lau, R., 68, *82*
Lay, C. H., 190, 203, 368, *386*
Lea, W. A., 78, *82,* 322, *329*
Lecanuet, J.-P., 33, *38*
Lecours, A. R., 111, *116*
Lederer, A., 338, *341,* 344, 349, *362,* 390, *407,* 418, *424*
Lee, S.-M., 75, *81*
Lehiste, I., 102, *116,* 152, *169,* 298, *311,* 344, *362,* 372, 373, *386,* 390, *407*
Leonard, L., 14, 144, *150,* 234, 235, 236, 238, 239, 241, 243, 245, *246, 247,* 415
Levin, H., 368, *386*

Language Index

Subject Index